A Realistic Theory of Science

A Realistic Theory of Science

C.A. Hooker

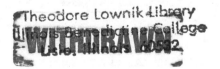
State University of New York Press

Published by
State University of New York Press, Albany

© 1987   State University of New York

For information, address State University of New York
Press, State University Plaza, Albany, N.Y., 12246

Library of Congress Cataloging in Publication Data
Hooker, C.A. (Clifford Alan), 1942-
  A realistic theory of science.

  Bibliography: p.
  Includes index.
  1. Science—Philosophy.   2. Realism.   I. Title.
Q175.H787   1986   501   86-19169
ISBN 0-88706-315-2
ISBN 0-88706-316-0 (pbk.)

10 9 8 7 6 5 4 3 2 1

Contents

Permissions

Acknowledgments

Where to begin? If I have been able to see even as far as some others it is because I have been tottering about on the chests of giants . . . (Apologies to Swift and Newton.) My debts are enormous. Some of the larger intellectual ones are acknowledged in "Statement". The reader may judge my debts to others by their occurrence in Notes. (I am particularly indebted to those I criticise.)

I have a wonderful family (mother-in-law included) whom I love very much. They accept the egocentric disruption of book manuscript deadlines as part of my job and compensate accordingly. This is a major personal contribution. (Thanks to daughter Claire and son Giles for hours of editing.) Particular thanks to Patrick Heelan for his encouragement of this publishing project. My largest specific personal debt is to my secretary, Mrs. Dorrit Nesmith. Her unfailing calm and graciousness smoothed the thorny path to production. Her intelligent and slightly bemused distance from my myopic flurries straightened the uneven path to production. And her capacity to force a recalcitrant computer to disgorge clean manuscript just hours after I submitted scrambled scribble can only be described as miraculous (well . . . marvellous, anyway). She specifically denies responsibility for barbarisms and other idiosyncracies of style, but the speling is all hirs.

To **all** *those referred to in the Acknowledgment.*
And to Canada for 12 good years.

Preface

To scientists, lay-persons and philosophers-of-other-stripes: The essay "Understanding and Control" gives the widest review of my views and is largely nontechnical; I recommend you read Chapter 7 first. Parts 8.2 and 8.3 of "Evolutionary Naturalist Realism" offer a broad overview of my version of realism in particular and I suggest reading this next. Thereafter you will be in a good position to pursue issues of interest into the remaining text.

To philosophers-of-science: The essays appear in their chronological order, with minimal retrospective editing. One approach is to follow the temporal development of ideas. For those who have other preferences I offer the following remarks. The structural work (the "archetectonic") is focused at "Philosophy and Meta-Philosophy of Science" and "Evolutionary Naturalist Realism," Section 8.2. The remaining essay material is largely concerned with developing specific doctrines. However defense is found throughout, see especially "Systematic Realism," Section 2.4, "Surface Dazzle, Ghostly Depths," Sections 6.4 to 6.6 and "Evolutionary Naturalist Realism," Section 8.4.

To all and sundry (especially students): I employ (or perhaps deploy) end notes, properly speaking, not footnotes. These are often substantial and are in pursuit of twin aims: (1) to move out from the text into the wider tapestry of issues, often attacking and qualifying as I go, while keeping the text relatively more straightforward and (2) to provide a reading background so that various themes, side issues and debates can be followed up if desired. "Systematic Philosophy and Meta-Philosophy of Science," "Understanding and Control" and "Evolutionary Naturalist Realism" particularly aim to provide connecting tissue and background.

1

Statement

The reader will find no definitive claims herein, no finished doctrines, only a set of open conjectures. Contributions and refutations are welcome.

In writing these essays I have had three purposes or goals in mind: (1) To capture something of the real complexity and counterintuitiveness of science/technology as it actually is. Here truth is often stranger than philosophical fiction. (2) To contribute to understanding the historical transformation of science/technology and provide a framework within which the complex science/society interrelations may be approached. (3) To state and defend a doctrine of scientific realism adequate to (1) and (2).

There is no sense to a strict priority ordering among the three goals just stated, for work toward any one of them interacts with that toward the others. I regard each as valuable. That is why, though the bulk of the words in this book perhaps directly concern goal (3), Chapter 4 and Chapter 7 are two of the most important essays in the book.

My earliest education was in physics. Here I was taught a respect for the empirical complexity and counterintuitiveness of the world. However currently satisfactory, however analytically elegant current theory might be, I was taught never to allow it to become a substitute for independent empirical investigation, to always look carefully and open-mindedly at what the real phenomena actually are. This was not because only the evidence mattered, to the contrary, but precisely because theories were about the real world and that real world has proved to be complex and mysterious.

Later, when I became a philosopher of science, I tried to apply this advice in the new field as well. Despite being surrounded by small, artificial examples on which whole philosophies of science were propped, I tried to keep an eye open for how real science was done, and how it was changing. What I think I have seen has often led me (sometimes protesting) away from the positions I was taught to revere in my philosophical training. When I speak of taking science seriously, as I do, for example, in Section 2.1, it is in this sense that I intend it. I intend to draw attention to the complexity and counterintuitiveness (*vis-à-vis* conventional philosophy of science) that science actually displays.[1]

Later I was trained as a philosopher in what might be described as the mid-century British analytic tradition. I was taught the primacy of logical argument and criticism. Philosopher's opinions notwithstanding, the priority in physics has always been on getting even *one* plausible theory off the ground. Speciously plausible theories were evidently commonplace in philosophy; the problem was to deduce the correct one by seeing which survived criticism. (None did.) Philosophy added a real feeling for the perennial nature of the deeper underlying problems in physics (the continuum, one versus many, etc.), and a sense of history. Overall, the philosophical education complemented the physics training nicely (and vice versa)—I strongly recommend dual degrees as an antidote to the inbred quality of much thinking on both sides.

Both my physics and philosophical education had other, subtler features. I was taught to respect certain crucial hierarchcial distinctions such as that between fact and value (between what is the case and what ought to be the case). So it was that I was taught to distinguish between psychology and rationality (between what happened to be persons' states of mind and what were rational states of mind), and so between philosophy of science as normative and science as descriptive, between philosophy as a critical theory of how science ought to be pursued and a description of science as a historical fact. Indeed, though I was raised in what was at the time (1960s) a tradition increasingly critical of empiricism—Popper was in ascendency, Kuhn and Feyerabend had just burst upon the scene—I was in fact taught all of the traditional distinctions which lie at the foundation of empiricism(!), namely

Normative	Descriptive
Logic	Psychology
Fact	Value
Cognitive	Pragmatic
Reason	Emotion
Objective	Subjective
Pure Science	Applied Science
Scientific Method	Public Policy

In this way the deeper underlying structure of what I was taught was empiricist while the immediate content often denounced empiricism. Worse, the deeper structure was often not announced, being rather 'shown' in the form of the content (which concepts were used and not, which arguments were even formulated, let alone criticized and so on). It took me some time to work my way out of this 'knot'. The essay in Chapter 3 was the public declaration not of release (I am still uncovering the layers of philosophy), but of the determination to work toward release. "Philosophy and Meta-Philosophy of Science" sets much of the framework for the later essays. During the course of these essays the reader will find specific arguments for rejecting each of these empiricist-inspired dichotomies.

The essays are published in a roughly logical order, but in fact this happens also to be roughly their temporal order since I 'think my position out' during their course. Temporally, the essays fall into two groups. The first group—Chapters 2, 3, 4, and 5—were all written in 1974 to 1975 and represent an earlier formulation of the basic issues for, and dimensions of, an evolutionary naturalistic realism. The second group—Chapters 6, 7, and 8—were written in the period 1980 to 1985 and represent the consolidation and enrichment of the earlier ideas and their extension to a wider set of issues.[2]

During the decade covered by this development I was busy thinking and writing about several other subjects, apparently quite diverse (see bibliography), and have had plenty of opportunity to change my mind. The underlying themes of these essays are remarkably constant. I have genuinely found the evolutionary naturalist perspective a challenge to develop and richly satisfying in its characteristics. The reader will find most of the continuing themes picked out in Chapter 8. I am not aiming here to show how they are to be defended against particular challenges (though several criticisms are in fact dealt with along the way), nor am I aiming to show how they deal in detail with particular slabs of science or the history of science (although several examples are met along the way). These are tasks for other occasions, and though I have written the occasional piece about them (see bibliography), I concede that many of them lie ahead.[3]

It is now common practice in English-speaking philosophy to ignore either or both of (1) those from whom one learnt and borrowed and (2) one's predecessors and contemporaries defending related views. Many philosophers write as if their positions sprang full blown from themselves like Minerva from the head of Zeus.[4] From time to time in this essay I have noted where arguments and ideas are reinventions, but not consistently (the task would be too great!). Many of these will be found set out in Urban's study (1949), which I found helpful.[5] To counteract in myself these tendencies let me candidly admit first of all the general intellectual debt I owe to Armstrong, Feyerabend, Piaget, Popper, Quine, Sellars and Smart. I have spent a happy young adulthood 'murdering' these fathers (see 1970b, 1971a, 1972a, 1973a, d, 1977a, 1981b). In fact, though, they were fundamental to the formation of my present views and approach and, midlife crisis over, it is time to reacknowledge origins.

Secondly, I confess to at least partially reinventing philosophical wheels. I have discovered that the realist views I espouse have important relations to those of the early U. S. Critical Realist movement, especially the doctrines of the unity of science and the primacy of metaphysics and science to epistemology expressed e.g., by Marvin, Perry and Pitkin of that movement.[6] By the later Critical Realist movement attention had shifted so strongly to epistemological issues, perception in particular, that I often no longer share much in common, though at least Pratt and R. W. Sellars are exceptions.[7] The more recent English realist tradition has likewise been dominated by theory of perception[8] and/or various brands of 'commonsense' realism[9] with which I have no great affinity. However I find commonality with the unjustly neglected realist Thomas Case (1888, 1906). A century ago Case argued the relevance of science to philosophy. Indeed, Case reversed the basic issue in the philosophy of perception to ask: Since the theoretical world of physics is real, how must perception be, to be consistent with it? Case concludes that perception is a causal, representational process. If I disagree with the details, the approach is right; Case comes as a reminder to realists how quickly the lessons of past battles are forgotten. (Those who do not know their history . . . but as van Fraassen so delightfully shows, this principle is a sharp *two*-edged sword.) Beyond this the realist theme fans out too widely and interconnects too complexly to follow here, but these interconnections are often worth pursuing.[10]

CHAPTER 2

Systematic Realism

2.1 INTRODUCTION: THREE REVOLUTIONS IN THE PHILOSOPHY OF SCIENCE

To be a Scientific Realist is not easy—it requires that science be taken realistically, hence seriously.

Formally, Scientific Realism is a semantical thesis, it is the view that the intended and proper sense of the theories of science is as literal descriptions of the physical world, as saying what there is and how it behaves. It is the view that if a scientific theory is in fact true then there is in the world exactly those entities which the theory says there is, having exactly those characteristics which the terms of the theory describe them as having.[1]

By Systematic Realism I mean Realism embedded in the repertoire of supporting philosophical doctrines which together provide a systematic view of man's activities, in particular of his scientific activities. For Scientific Realism, like any other significant philosophical doctrine, does not stand alone but is linked in an intimate fashion into a variety of other philosophical and scientific doctrines which are mutually compatible and mutually supportive (or which, if wrongly chosen, would prove mutually incompatible and disruptive).

The point of defending Scientific Realism is not simply to insist on a 'right' conception of the semantics of theory. The point of defending it is because it is part of a coherent account of the entire human animal and the world in which he lives. According to our best contemporary theories, humankind evolved slowly from more 'primitive' origins. This evolution was, for us, most importantly a conceptual evolution in the broadest sense—man emerged into consciousness of his world. But the evolution is fundamentally a neurophysiological one, an evolution radiating from the primitive perceptual centre—and its physiological origins lie even deeper in the skill of survival. Philosophers

7

and scientists aim at giving a reasonable account of this evolution, which must therefore include the physical evolution of the living world, in particular humankind, the evolution of language and thought, of consciousness, of science, of values and the general culture. Furthermore it must be a *reflective* account, it must explain why the account is reasonable. But knowledge and reason have themselves evolved, both in dynamic interaction with science and the general culture. Because of the evolution of the former our understanding of what reasonableness consists in has itself evolved. So Scientific Realism then is to play an integral part in the construction of a naturalistic, evolutionary epistemology, evolving in dynamic interaction with science itself, and in the construction of a naturalistic, evolutionary account of mind, of the use of concepts, of language and thought, both linking smoothly into the scientific picture to form the unbroken web of our worldview. Of course this goal is utopian, our ignorance is too great and epistemological evolution too rapid to hope to complete the task, but nothing less than this goal provides the proper perspective in which to view the defense of Scientific Realism. Its defense as an isolated thesis can only be hopelessly truncated because the stature of the issues is so reduced—in this form it belongs to boring academia rather than to the exciting evolution of the planet.

Let us be quite clear about the implications of what I have just said for the exposition of philosophies of science. According to this view, alternatives to Realism, e.g., Empiricism, Conventionalisms, themselves constitute world views, in the sense of containing (albeit sometimes only implicitly) all of the components mentioned above. And when the Realism/opponents issue is argued, it is the *entire* world views of the opposed alternatives that are brought to the attack. *Indeed, if we agree (counterfactually) to construe Realism strictly as just the semantical thesis outlined in the second paragraph and to restrict argument to strictly the semantical level than I do not know of a single argument against (or distinctively for) Realism that has ever been advanced (or for or decisively against any other purely semantical view for that matter).* The reason is simple enough—each view, even those which (unlike Realism) wish to tamper with theoretical terms, can surely set down a consistent syntax and semantics for their version of science (i.e., specify a language structure and define reference, denotation, satisfaction, truth in the usual model theoretic fashion), and in the cases where the semantics prevents exact reconstruction of the customary language of science simply deny that the residue belongs to science proper. I do not see how to refute any such *normative* position in itself, since nothing is argued and consistency is granted. No, *what occurs in the*

literature are proposals for semantics, and arguments against proposed se-
mantics, based upon other considerations, e.g., upon epistemological desi-
derata. Realism as such has never been argued against directly, only
indirectly through the world view in which it is embedded (and so
long as the alternatives to Realism remain normatively hard-nosed
about the definition of science, the same is true for them). Moreover,
this procedure has been fair enough, in my view, because of the
intimate way in which semantical theses are in fact linked to the
remainder of a world view.

This then is my first revolution in philosophy of science (it is a 'little'
one): to recognize explicitly the larger context in which Realism is
evaluated. I shall hope thus to escape from the misleading and confusing nature of much writing on the subject which leaves these
connections only tacit. I shall be aiming to explore a Realist world
view both to see which combinations of doctrine are possible and
which is the most plausible among them. But one can only offer up
that latter doctrine for the acceptance of the rational man—precisely
because it and its non-Realist alternatives constitute essentially entire
world views I can see no way to further argue the issues. To those who
value argued resolution above all else there remains the challenge:
find a neutral meta-language in which the issues between the alternatives don't reduce to value judgments among components of world
views (e.g., preferred epistemologies) that cannot be further argued
for (assuming each set of value judgments self-consistent). Incidentally, if I am right about this then it constitutes a strong argument for
what Feyerabend said long ago and everyone ignored (or failed to
grasp): the choice of an epistemology (enlarge this to world view) is in
some sense an ethical choice, (Hooker 1972).[2]

A second, larger revolution in philosophy of science is that now
being brought about by Feyerabend (1961, 1965a,b,c, 1969, 1970a),
Hanson (1963, 1965), Kuhn (1966), Lakatos (1970b), Toulmin (1963,
1965), and their ilk and by many other factors, cf. my comments on the
third revolution below. Traditional philosophy of science regards science as an abstract structure, specified in abstract linguistic terms. As
such it is entirely separated from any activity of the scientist *qua*
human being; one does not consider the psychology of discovery
relevant, only the 'problem of induction', one does not consider the
decision process for testing theories and choosing among them
(which involves all kinds of value judgments, as well as judgments of
other kinds), one considers only objective criteria of acceptance and
rejection. The consequence has been rational reconstructions of the
history of science which entirely ignore large segments of it (discovery

is irrational) and in which scientists habitually contradict the alleged canons of *Science* (e.g., by retaining a refuted theory). *Science* is not a human discipline, except accidentally. When we press this view on the issue of fostering insight into the course of science on this planet we discover a tacit ideology lying beneath it: the science of science should also be *Science*. But this leads to the exclusion of all that is importantly human from the account, since most of the human activity cannot be captured in the combination of basic descriptive statement plus logical machinery. Indeed, the approach fails on its own terms since, even behavioristically construed, specific scientific theories (e.g., of psychology) are needed to give an account of how science is possible for human beings, thus completing an epistemological circle in what was designed to be a rigorously logically (hence epistemologically) linear space, the space of scientific ascent to knowledge.

As against this abstractive approach the new revolution proposes placing (or re-placing) the scientist at the centre of the social-intellectual-ethical complex known as science. It proposes first studying the scientist, his knowledge and values, principles of rational action, ideological and social position, metaphysical beliefs etc. in order to understand *him* (or her!), then once a rational account of the lives of scientists has been offered we can turn to the task of asking in what measure an abstract notion of *Science* can be rescued from the collective participations of *scientists*. The detailed, systematic development of this approach lies in the future; what Feyerabend and Kuhn have done has been to offer us glimpses of the great power of this reorientation where e.g., what was irrational *vis-à-vis Science* (even though it affected its course profoundly) can now be seen to be rational *vis-à-vis* the *scientist*, where the profound links between the psychology of perception and linguistic usage in reporting can now be properly integrated with the logic of theory support and where the intimate interaction between scientific decisions, scientist's values and social and cultural conditions now receives a natural place with the proper importance.[3]

This essay is written with this new approach explicitly in mind. This is not to say that I explicitly reconstruct a *Science* from an account of scientists, for this concerns mainly methodology and the application of epistemology to the logic of acceptance. But I do attempt to construct a Realism which is ready to be grafted on to this account of science. In particular, the intimate role which the scientific account of perception plays in the establishment of an epistemology and semantics, indeed the way in which the theory of rationality and epistemology are made to learn from psychology, are designed to make way for a 'humans at the center' approach. Elsewhere I have been concerned with the application of this view to the future of scientists (see Hooker 1975b).

It is precisely the shift to a naturalistic epistemology and theory of rationality that constitutes the third revolution. To repeat: it is an indisputable fact that over the course of the development of science our philosophical theories have also been changing in response to scientific discovery. One only has to look at the philosophy of Bacon, Descartes and Locke, for example, to realize that what was at stake there was nothing less than the intellectual rationalization of the triumph of reason in science over faith. The foundations for the future course of Empiricism, and later of Conventionalism, were laid here as part of the programatic attempt to comprehend and integrate the 'new' way to knowledge and the picture of man that was emerging from it, just as Instrumentalism had earlier emerged from the debate in astronomy. And so it has been ever since. Recent research in perception has taught us much concerning the extent of the 'interpretation' the mind introduces, it has rendered ludicrous the notion of pre-occurring conceptualized data; recent advances in physics have destroyed the synthetic *a priori* of Kantian space (cf. Hooker 1970a, Reichenbach 1965). The advent of quantum theory has cast doubt on the nature and applicability of classical logic (cf. the status of geometry *vis-á-vis* relativity theory). Advances in neurophysiology and psychiatry, and even purely formal advances (e.g., in decision theory) have modified our concept of rational behaviour. And so one could continue.

And yet ironically Empiricism and Conventionalism themselves are not able to cope with this feedback from science to philosophy. For they assume a rigid intellectual hierarchy in which philosophical doctrine stands above and before empirical discovery and cannot be touched by it; rather, it is the *a priori* touchstone for understanding and evaluating empirical discovery. Thus logic, induction (read confirmation theory), semantics, etc., were all assumed given *a priori* in philosophy. *A fortiori* epistemology and theory of language and rationality were assumed provided *a priori* in philosophy. It is not therefore possible for philosophy to learn from science. This rigid hierarchy had one great advantage, no question of epistemological circularity arose. It has two disadvantages, it did not match experience and it gave no plausible answer to the question of the origin of *a priori* knowledge.

But there is abroad now another, contrasting conception of the situation which takes seriously the contributions of those sciences which apply to human beings. We might call this the 'new epistemology' and 'new rationality'.[4] The central contention of both doctrines is that the philosophical theories involved here are in no better position than our best scientific theories of the relevant human capacities. Rational minds are well-functioning minds where the latter term belongs to the (ultimately) unified science of neuro-psycho-physiology. Similarly what human beings can know and how they come to know it are questions belonging to the same theory.

According to philosophical tradition after Descartes, i.e., when the 'epistemological turn' began, epistemology was prior to science. Unhappily, the progress of science revealed that such epistemologies were almost invariably based on poor armchair psychology—and no wonder, given our self-ignorance during most of the period. In similar fashion, philosophy made the attempt to dictate what is rational in advance of understanding how the mind works.

It will be well to also bear in mind the changes which this shift brings with it. First of all, there arises the necessity for a clear account of the dynamic interaction between normative and descriptive systems. Where epistemology and rationality belonged to first philosophy this was unnecessary since the relationship was strictly asymmetrical—First Philosophy was a critic of science; but now that the two interact we must inquire how it is that human beings may alter their principles of action rationally, even their criteria for rational action, in the light of experience. This great task lies outside the scope of this paper, but I want to point out that this forms a second bridge between epistemology (and rationality) and ethics, for in each case we have normative systems in dynamic interaction with experience. Likewise in the spirit of unity, epistemology and the theory of rationality come much closer together. In the traditional philosophy it was supposed to be rational to reason in the fashion epistemology dictated, to be sure, but the effective integration of the two notions was small indeed. Now we have an entirely new setting for these issues: a man will have a variety of goals and various utilities attached to them and to the consequences of the various means to achieve them, and these will include epistemic goals; what it is rational for him to do will be determined on the one side by the general nature of human beings, their capacities, etc., and the circumstances in which he finds himself and on the other by some decision principles, such as the maximization of utilities. This model will hold for actions to realize epistemic goals (e.g., creation of a scientific theory) as for others. Which epistemic goals it is rational to choose will of course in its turn be a function of our nature and circumstances on the one side and critical reflection

on the process of acquiring knowledge (in the light of historical experience and theory) on the other. In this context many of the traditional concerns of philosophy are radically recast. Perhaps the most
important change is that in our approach to observation. Whereas
traditional philosophy placed great emphasis on the *a priori* analysis
of sensation because of its epistemological role, this pressure is entirely absent here and with it goes any special concern over sensory
atomism versus gestalt wholeness, or pure sensation versus interpretation by the mind—rather we are free to accept the findings of psychology as to what to count in any circumstances as observable. Correlatively, the notion of an observation sentence and its relation to
theory is freed, to await informing by psychology and history; in
principle all positions from a factual empiricist-style permanence to
Feyerabendian pragmatic adjustment are open (cf. below). This in
turn opens up a range of possible semantical positions concerning
theory, depending upon the deliverances of psychology concerning
human thought processes and the nature (if any) of meaning.[5]

In future, any interesting epistemology and theory of rationality for
science will have to take the feedback from science into account. What
we have is the logical form of a circle from an empiricist point of view;
actually, it is a spiral extending along the historical time axis: epistemological theory evaluates scientific method, scientific discovery informs epistemological theory. A similar spiral operates for our conception of rationality. As I pointed out earlier, one of the consequences of
adopting this line is the rejection of the old empiricist dualism between abstract philosophic criteria of justification for scientific theories and psychological accounts of individual scientists devising and
defending those theories. The present view dovetails with the development of a naturalistic epistemology and theory of rationality that
would unify the account of science.[6] Another consequence is that the
unit of empirical significance must now be considered as not just the
whole of science and metaphysics, but the whole of philosophy and
science. Given that our world view is at all coherent, and apriorism
rejected, we might have expected these consequences.

The tools for forging the new theory of the scientific enterprise are,
however, already being formed; we are developing decision theory,
general systems analysis, policy science and related areas, and the
psychology of perception and correlative theories of linguistic usage
are now increasingly well understood—for more comment and reference material see Hooker 1975b, cf. Ziman 1968. I digress here long
enough to remark on the particular application of this new orientation
to another old problem in the formal philosophy of science, the prob-

lem of induction. The inductive enterprise seems to have evolved through three stages. In the first stage a quasi-logical machinery was sought such that, upon being fed 'the facts' at one end, it would generate the true theory of them at the other (or, in a later modification, the truest theory of them). In the second stage this goal was given up as impossible and what was substituted was the goal of specifying a calculus of confirmation of some sort that would attach a degree of support or confirmation of some sort to theories. In some versions (e.g., Carnap's) acceptability meant probability of truth, in others (e.g., Popper's) not; in all quantitative versions I happen to have looked at, the inductive calculus was essentially a set of probabilistic inference rules of some kind. The more sceptical inductivists of this stage two mold decided that the most that could be achieved by this means was a comparative assessment of relative acceptability between theories rather than an absolute acceptability. Stage three appears when this approach is set aside as too specialized and the problem reformulated as a decision problem for *scientists* rather than a formal problem for *Science*. This issue now becomes "Given my pres ent circumstances and utilities, which theories should I accept (1) for belief and practical reliance, (2) for testing next?" Here one assumes that epistemic circumstances and utilities will play a key role. (Notice that the two decisions called for may concern very different theories—a point often overlooked in the presentation of methodologies!) In this new context formal methods of assessment constructed for the earlier problem may again play specialized roles as the occasion demands. Here too, one can obtain a more unified approach to the various so-called paradoxes of support (paradoxes of confirmation, inductive inconsistencies, lottery paradox, Goodman's new riddle of induction) by seeing them as all placing constraints upon the consistent formulation of a theory of rational action, especially the subtheory of rational acceptance. In what follows I shall say no more about the problem of induction, the reader will understand that, whatever the final form of a theory of rational decisionmaking we are able to formulate, my Realism assumes a stage three formulation of the issue.[7]

This essay is written then against the backdrop of these three recent revolutions in philosophy of science. In a sense, the most important part of the essay has been written, the rest being detail. The reader is forewarned that this larger context at times affects the canons of acceptable attack and defense considerably. (E.g., it is too easy, on occasion, to mistake a legitimate rebuttal of framework for an attack *ad hominem*.) It is my hope, though it is perhaps unlikely, that the specific Realist doctrine to follow will do justice to the breadth and unity of these three large-scale changes, which promise so much.

2.2 THE EMPIRICIST ALTERNATIVE

Since historically Realists have been put on the defensive by the domination of the empiricist tradition, it is appropriate to digress at the outset to characterize briefly the empiricist approach, the better to appreciate the origins of the chief objections to Realism.

Historically, the central dogma of Positivist-Empiricism (*P*-Empiricism) was the Lockean doctrine of ideas, and specifically that all ideas originated in either sensation or reflection. Let us call this the first dogma. This doctrine gave rise to the second dogma, that all claims can be exclusively and exhaustively divided into empirical and analytic claims (their origins, but more importantly, their justification, being grounded respectively in sensation and reflection) and to the third dogma that all empirical concepts (i.e., concepts putatively descriptive of the world) be analyzable without remainder in terms of the class of simple, ostensively defined concepts given directly in observation. These latter two doctrines, which state the semantical core of *P*-Empiricism, then serve as the foundation of the epistemological core of *P*-Empiricism, namely (fourth doctrine) that all empirical knowledge is grounded in indubitable, simple observational claims and all analytic knowledge *a priori*. It is an immediate consequence of these doctrines, especially of dogma 2, that inductive support is a purely logical relation holding between evidence and hypothesis.[8] This foundational epistemology is a (is the) most important instance of the 'Doctrine of the Given' and *P*-Empiricism is completed if we add the fifth dogma of Phenomenalism: the referent of the simplest observational descriptions are the simple sensory ideas in the mind (or sensations, or more recently, sense data).

Behind the dogmas lies a tacit psychology, the 'arena for sensations plus logical machine only' view of mind and the correlative 'up from tabula rasa via sensory imprinting and logical manipulation' theory of concept and belief acquisition. Hume brought the view to its logical completion with his noncognitivist theory of ethics and aesthetics, agnostic theory of religion, dissolution of the person and inductive scepticism.

The power of this position lies in its presentation of a clear-cut semantics and epistemology of science, but supremely in its avoidance of epistemological risk—for from the above doctrines it follows that, for every empirical claim, the truth conditions for the claim coincide with the epistemic conditions of acceptance for that claim, and both lie in the realm of simple observation. Let us call this latter, powerful result the Coincidence Theorem of P-Empiricism.

The dogmas of P-Empiricism are not mutually entailing, so it is open to a person to adopt fewer than all; as a matter of fact there has been an historical tendency to divide between dogmas 1, 3, 5 and dogmas 2, 4.[9] More recent Empiricism has dropped all but dogmas 2 and 3 and a weaker version of 4 that follows if the analytic-synthetic distinction is retained but either of the indubitability and/or aprioriness claims dropped (although the latter is more likely to be defended than the former.) A weaker version still (W-Empiricism) replaces the 'be analyzable without remainder in terms of' in dogma 3 by 'attain whatever semantic content they possess through their logical relations to the members of'. (There is a further weakening of dogma 3 that would add to this last clause 'and/or through implicit definition by the theoretical postulates', but to the extent that this notion is clear at all it endangers the empiricism of Empiricism.) The beauty of the full-blown doctrine is its comprehensiveness and unity, the more one weakens the position the less philosophically interesting it becomes, it becomes in fact a fragment in search of a 'worldview'.

Any of these versions of Empiricism provide sufficient grounds for introducing the observational theoretical distinction as fundamental to the analysis of science. They differ only in the conservatism with which they treat the specifically theoretical part of theories: P-Empiricism and Empiricism reduce this part entirely to the observational part, they support in this context the 'Verifiability Criterion of Meaning' (dogma 3 restated); W-Empiricism does not reduce away the theoretical part but leaves it as an in-principle second-class superstructure parasitic on the observational part for sense and function—an inviting target for would-be Instrumentalists. (P-Empiricism and Empiricism essentially admit only one inductive argument, that of generalization from instances, W-Empiricism has a much richer, if more problematic, inductive structure.)[10]

All variants of Empiricism support the accretion model of the history of science, for the continued existence of educated humanity means the continued accumulation of sensory experience and Empiricism holds the assertions describing these to be established beyond theoretical criticism (they are used to criticize theories, not vice versa). Theories amount simply to increasingly effective organizations of this accumulating data and to prediction machines for data to come.

The foregoing remarks suggest (but do no more than this) the way in which the Empiricisms also find their place in a coherent world view, (one has a semantics and epistemology, but also a psychology, which determine the basic outline, if not the detail, of a detailed model of man's evolution and functioning), one opposed in very important respects to that of Scientific Realism as I shall expound it. It is in this opposition that the real bite of the dispute begins to be felt.

2.3 The conventionalist alternative

Conventionalism is the view that the theories of science are systems of conventions, without literal significance, whose use is justified by the way in which they organize the data of science. Since it constitutes the other major opposition to Realism I shall briefly outline the position.

Conventionalism then also introduces a fundamental theoretical/observational dichotomy; for this reason it has often drawn succor and support from much the same doctrines as back *P*-Empiricism. But the special impetus for the doctrine lies elsewhere for, unlike the Empiricisms, Conventionalism does not attempt to reduce away part or all of the theoretical hierarchy in terms of the observational level, it simply shifts the status of the entire hierarchy without being especially interested in altering its detail.

The root source of the conventionalist urge, like that of the Empiricisms, is the epistemological agnosticism to which Scientific Realism is heir (see Section 2.4). If theories can neither be verified nor conclusively refuted then are we not justified in regarding them only as convenient fictions, elaborate *facons de parler* to organize data? And is not this the only justified view? Moreover this point of view apparently obtains some backing from experience in mathematics where one has mathematically consistent systems each claiming to satisfactorily realize subject matter (e.g., geometry) and which primarily differ only in some of the root definitions (e.g., that of straight line). This was, e.g., the route that led Poincaré to the position (see Wisdom 1971).

Recently pro-Conventionalist thought has been given some impetus by two consequences of a contemporarily fashionable Realism, that expounded by Feyerabend and others (e.g., Kuhn, Lakatos in many respects). For this view claims that the semantic content of the observation language stems from that of the theoretical language and not vice versa and that theory determines semantic content in such a way that conflicting theories are semantically 'incommensurable'. But this suggests that there is no area of science where a simple matching of human thought and nature is possible and that disputes between theories are not factual in the 'hard', straightforward way Realism seems to require. Theories then seem more like initially arbitrary creations of the human mind which float free of the world except insofar as we use them as conveniences to organize our lives. Whatever this support amounts to it is not compelling (otherwise we would have a *reductio* on this form of Realism), rather must it be combined with certain philosophical principles stating a preferred world view (in particular, a preferred epistemology) before it supports a shift away from Realism—but for those who hold such preferences the belief that this was the only acceptable form of Realism (a view I shall counter below), like the perception of the epistemic agnosticism of Realism, would constitute a strong motive to look for an alternative world view. (It hardly follows that it *must* be the Conventionalist view.)

It is clear enough that Conventionalism fits yet another world view, one which would share some basic features with empiricist world views but in which there would be a rather different account of the significance of the evolution of the neurophysiological equipment of the human being, the significance of language use and thought as well as in epistemology and semantics. (E.g., presumably conventionalists would want to give an evolutionary account of speculative thought which makes it clear why the operative mechanisms made plausible the conventional status of theoretical talk; just as Empiricism, when it is not Idealist, must offer an account of the neurophysiological mechanisms backing the reduction of every concept to certain simple, impressed concepts.) It is, however, neither my responsibility nor my interest to elaborate that view here (and one does not readily find it done by conventionalists themselves).

Instrumentalism, the view that theories have no truth value status at all but are merely convenient calculational recipes, I regard as a 'last ditch' version of Conventionalism (cf. Section 2.4.4.)[11]

These are the doctrines which form the systematic background for attacks on Realism.

2.4 Epistemology (I): general considerations

2.4.1 The Central Argument

The attack on the Realist comes in many forms but the underlying, basic theme is always epistemological, the basic attack is always the same: "But you cannot *know*—*cannot* know—which of your theories is true, or even which is near the truth, so what sense is there in saying that they are to be taken literally?"

I unreservedly concede the premise of this argument, that epistemological concession follows from even a superficial characterization of the logical structure of science.[12]

The general sense of this objection is that it is *not reasonable* to adopt Realism in the face of this epistemological fact. The retort to be answered is "Why not? What is the *argument* that leads from epistemological uncertainty to rejection of semantical theory?".

2.4.2 A Strong Form of the Argument

The strongest case that could be made would be one that terminated the argument with the conclusion that Realism was semantically void or incoherent, i.e., literally made no sense. To achieve a valid argument we clearly require a premise that passes from epistemological status to semantical status. The weakest appropriate premise would be one of the general sort: those proposistions whose truth values one can be confident of not knowing for certain can also make no sense. I shall call this assumption the Epistemological Dogma. Of course stronger assumptions will also suffice. One of the strongest is: those putative propositions whose truth conditions we cannot be certain of knowing (verifying) also make no sense. This I shall call the Security Dogma. Other positions fall between these extremes, the most common probably being: those putative propositions instances of whose truth conditions . . . etc., as for the Security Dogma—this I shall call the Verifiability Dogma.

There is only one kind of general doctrine I know of that is capable even in principle of supporting any of these claims and that is Empiricism in some form. Empiricism then is a general presupposition of the plausibility of this general kind of attack on the Realist. Empiricism has, of course, been under increasingly severe attack for several decades. What emerges from a careful consideration of that criticism, however, is that empiricism, despite the heavy criticism (justified in my view), is at its best a comprehensive philosophical doctrine which can only be adequately answered by another equally systematic (comprehensive) doctrine (otherwise the arguments against Empiricism largely become question begging). Such must Realism be—for it is sure that Realists must reject the dogmas of Empiricism (except perhaps a weakened dogma 3) since they leave no possibility in the account of the world for a serious role for the specifically theoretical in its own right.[13]

Whereas Realism and Empiricism seem at least to be able to come to

grips over specific arguments, Conventionalism seems best represented as simply offering an alternative view of the world which one
does not argue to from Realistic epistemology but which one might
find attractive if one did not relish some features of Realist epistemology. (Actually, Empiricism could also be presented in this way.) What
are we to say of it?

The first thing to be said is that Conventionalism shares many
features with Empiricism and to that extent is open to the same kinds
of criticism. Thus the conventionalist is committed to some form of
the observational-theoretical dichotomy (since primary empirical content is confined to a class of privileged, observational terms—though
there is perhaps a secondary empirical content expressed in the form
"It is a fact that the conventions C allow an adequate construction of
empirical knowledge") and to a corresponding psychology of perception and reflection (the latter with a conventionalist twist) to back the
view. But this dichotomous approach has been severely criticized in
its empiricist guise and the Realist will judge the criticism no less
relevant here.

Moreover, Conventionalism unsupported is, as Wisdom remarks,
on somewhat shaky ground for the following reason: it is not at all
obvious that a suitable set of conventions will be forthcoming that will
secure just those sentences a given theory requires. E.g., that the
empirical differences between Newtonian and relativistic physics
might be recaptured by suitable changes in geometric conventions
concerning the notions of time, straight line, etc., is, if it succeeds at
all, a brilliant piece of theoretical insight and not at all a superficial
linguistic manoeuvre. To render every scientific change as a change in
conventions will undoubtedly require considerable stretching of the
notion of a convention. In the long run the position must be forced to
no more than this: to change conventions is just to change the meanings of terms. This position is distinguishable from Realism only if the
meanings of terms are so chosen that the theoretical claims come out
analytically true under the semantical conventions (they become true
'by convention').The conventionalist is then faced with three problems: (1) how to make it plausible that fundamental assertions of
actual theories are indeed analytically or conventionally true; (2) how
to give a plausible account of the derivation of empirical generalizations (at least of those which differ from theory to theory, i.e., the
nontrivial derivations) from such theories; (3) how to give a plausible
account of theory change.

The instrumentalist, as I view him, steps into this situation and
offers to relieve the conventionalist of this burden by construing the-

ories so as to be devoid of semantical content. (There is a metatheoretical language of inferences that has semantical content, but this is an entirely different issue.)[14] The instrumentalist then is the least committal of all—he also takes the intellectual life less seriously, even the triumphs of applied non-Euclidean geometry are written off as nought but a successful pragmatic switch in calculation technique.

Even so, this extreme move can certainly be made in order to protect the position. For that matter I have no doubt that a consistent conventionalist treatment of science could be offered, sufficiently hard-nosed to mold science to suit it rather than vice versa. Conventionalism, like Empiricism, can be turned into a sufficiently elaborate worldview and has enough initially plausible contact with the world to be defensible by sufficiently hard-nosed techniques. The Realist then can only pit against this his own systematic position. It behooves me therefore to present a Realistic epistemology to replace that of Empiricism.

2.4.3 A Realist Epistemology

Now, and I cannot stress this too heavily, *whether or not a Realist gets into difficulty here depends largely upon the epistemology he chooses.* If, e.g., he chooses to adopt the Doctrine of the Given (dogma 4), i.e., a foundational epistemology, then he will be hard put to it not to plausibly choose the given from the domain of the sensorially experienced; if we now add (1) that theoretical concepts are not instantiated as such in this domain and (2) that the theoretical description and the initial observational description (the 'scientific image' and the 'manifest image') of the sensorially accessible situations are in general in conflict (both plausible claims) then we must conclude (twice over) that theories are relegated to a status where they can never function as literal descriptions. Dogma 4, therefore, had better not serve as part of any Realist epistemology.

Before we go any further it will be well to state more exactly the consequences of rejecting a foundational epistemology, for such a rejection may be, and usually is, associated with a more general philosophical position of a sort considerably more 'radical' than the rejection actually requires. Precisely, I want to point out that the rejection of a foundational epistemology does *not* entail (1) that one cannot draw a legitimate observational-theoretical dichotomy, and does *not* entail (2) that there are no epistemological asymmetries among the claims of science, so that these claims can be ordered in respect of epistemological primacy or acceptability (in particular along some axis which might correspond to an observational-theoretical hierarchy), and does *not* entail (3) that semantic content is purely nonostensive and that the notion of ostensive definition must be given up. (The leeway opened up here is important for a discussion of Realist alternatives.) Now we are ready to proceed.

There seems to be just one epistemology for the Realist and that doctrine is dictated by experience, namely a naturalistic, foundationless epistemology of ignorance. By this latter I mean (1) that epistemological theory is strongly determined by our scientific view of the world and our place in it,[15] (2) that with respect to justified belief man commences from total ignorance and approaches the truth only through imaginative guesswork and trial and error, and (3) there is no class of beliefs having the privileged status of unrevisable truths (in the historical process of critical inquiry all beliefs may be subject to revision, however 'fundamental'), there is therefore no class of accepted truths that could serve as the foundation of empirical knowledge.

The Realist is pledged to take his science seriously, in particular, therefore, the sciences of Biology, Anthropology, Psychology and the History of Science itself. The former two sciences inform us of the evolution of man from more restricted origins, the initial ignorance is well attested—even information built into neurological structure through evolution in the form of dispositions, etc., can be called in question when it appears at the conceptual level and anyway could not merit a role as foundation for knowledge on those grounds. (Though there is an important role for such pre-experiencial structuring—cf. Hooker 1973d.) Psychological research increasingly undermines the relevance, hence plausibility, of the phenomenalistic approach to perception. In its place I insert my own Realist view of perception, designed to harmonize with the scientific findings; for clearly if the phenomenalist analysis of knowledge is accurate there is no place for Scientific Realism—Realism in science includes psychology, hence the theory of perception, and so requires a Realist philosophical doctrine of perception also.[16] My Realist doctrine is unsympathetic to any Doctrine of the Given, i.e., to a traditional foundational epistemology. (For the detailed argument see Hooker 1970a.) The history of science supports the view that even the most fundamental assumptions (even the laws of logic, let alone the fundamental ontology types, the nature of space and time etc.) may be opened to challenging revisions.[17] Hence the doctrine.

So, man is born in ignorance and has only his pitiful senses and his imagination as aids to truth. No theory can be known or be guaranteed to be true—neither by observation nor by other means; the history of science teaches us the overwhelming likelihood that today's theory will not be tomorrow's. Theories are only *intended* true descriptions. Moreover they are intended truths for which we must admit that there are infinitely many incompatible alternatives, we must even admit that there are infinitely many experimentally indistinguishable incompatible alternatives. And the Scientific Realist must admit that the reality which he claims science intends to accurately describe is known only through these attempts at theoretical description; there is no independent access. Thus one must face each theory with a degree of critical or sceptical distrust—a generalized agnosticism is the order of the day.

Let us face his bogey right here. According to the Realist, every time one does serious science one sticks one's philosophical and scientific neck out, one runs the risk of being wrong (without, I think, knowing what the odds of error are). It is no use pointing to that conclusion expecting the Realist to capitulate in horror and stomach ulcers once it is clear how wide the scope of his agnosticism must be. (Without reasonable doubt, every decent extant scientific theory is false and pretty obviously so.) For the Realist revels in this situation! Remember Popper's dictum: the more risks you run, the more interesting and imaginative your theory is, the more you stand to learn through its failure.

On the other hand, in the face of these uncertainties many philosophers turned away to look for more comfortable truths. Various shades of Empiricism, of Instrumentalism, of Phenomenalism offer to take the uncertainty out of epistemic life by reducing theories to harmless parasitic nonentities of convenience, or by reducing them away altogether. (However clad in impressive theories of concept formation, etc., this is the truest function of the foregoing positions.) Scientific Realists, however, gladly accept these uncertainties and their consequences—for they have a *realistic* picture of man, they know the poverty of his ignorance, the slight riches of imagination and the limited reach of science. By comparison, the alternatives succeed, ironically, only in stripping man down to a meagre stature— too meagre even to provide a plausible account of his activities. This much we have already seen in the brief comparison of empiricist dogmas with the scientific view of man. And we shall see it reinforced when we compare the empiricist structure of science itself with a more realist version.

According to this Realist analysis the epistemological dogma is too restrictive twice over. In the first place there is the assumption that it is of the essence of informative, communicable content that it be possible to be certain of knowing it; this the Realist denies citing as the outstanding counterexample precisely the contents of scientific theories.[18] In addition, there is a tacit assumption that knowledge essentially demands certainty and this the Realist also denies, for it represents an impossibly high goal. (On this criterion, even the logical form of the world would be excluded from knowledge.) We may insist on this criterion of knowledge if we wish, but we shall then simply call forth a new word to refer to all those things of importance to us which are not 'known'. What the Realist may assent to (this Realist would anyway) is that knowledge does demand simple truth, and then claims to knowledge can still only be tentatively accepted. For Realism, knowledge does not turn out to be a very important category— and sure to certain knowledge a completely insignificant category— the interesting category is tentative knowledge and conjecture. This result may seem ironic, even paradoxical, to many philosophers who would regard Realists as overbold about their claims for man's abilities (e.g., the ability to transcend sensory experience), but actually it expresses a natural agnostic modesty which flows precisely from taking man's ability to theorize seriously.

A littler earlier I pointed out that the real power of *P*-Empiricism stems from the fact that its reductionist principles collapse truth conditions into knowledge conditions, so that no epistemological agnosticism was necessary. The Realist rejects such semantics. Here we set down the first two semantical distinctions of Realism:

(D$_1$) The truth conditions of a proposition are distinct from the conditions for its having a coherent semantic content (i.e., for its meaningfulness).

(D$_2$) The conditions under which a proposition is true (respectively, false) are distinct from the conditions under which it is known to be true (respectively, false).

These distinctions are *theoretical* distinctions; of course a single set of circumstances may *in fact* yield even all three sets of conditions (e.g., the circumstances of our world) but even here it is a rare thing for the *minimal* sufficient conditions of each sort to have any significant overlap, let alone coincide.[19] Now the Realist is faced with a task: specify the semantics of scientific theories. I shall return to this task later in the chapter.

2.4.4 A Weaker Form of the Argument

It is time now to return to the original argument and, having rejected the stronger versions of it (where the valid conclusion was literal senselessness of Realism), consider a weaker, but more plausible version. Now the argument runs: since no theory can admittedly be known to be true, since in fact all those that we have are almost certainly false, and since we change theories continually, is it not prudent . . . wise . . . reasonable! that we take a more conservative line than Realism over their significance? (And this is just what Conventionalism-Instrumentalism does—it identifies the semantical nature of theories with one of their useful nonepistemic functions, as convenient calculation devices.)

The Realist ought to be quite candid about this point: there is nothing in the realm of the 'hard data' of individual theories that could possibly distinguish his position from the Instrumentalist alternative with respect to those theories. From this *highly restricted* point of view the most that can be done is to point to the central role which theoretical structure plays in guiding research, modifying and changing scientific beliefs, *forming hard data from phenomenal data,* etc. The hard-nosed opponent, however, can simply treat this as heuristics.

But we can enlarge the battlefield. The point of Realism is to support a naturalistic world view. In this world view objects, geometry, man, the universe at large, are taken seriously as science knows them—and science knows them basically in terms of its theories. The instrumentalist, on the other hand, must restrict himself to organizing observable data, he can't take this view of the world seriously, the only things he can take seriously are the little partial glimpses of it that come to man through his senses. The final protest that the Realist makes then is to point out the implausibility of the resulting anthropomorphism that takes only things at a man-sized level seriously, the likely unhealthiness behind the insistence on epistemological security, the in-built tendency towards solipsist phenomenalism and so on. But exactly the point of being hard-nosed is the willingness (I am tempted to say, the *ability*) to ignore these charges. And so at last we run up against differences of philosophical temperament. The conservative, the Instrumentalist, is willing to write off these reasons for taking theories seriously as literal descriptions as mere *appearance* against the gain (for him) of taking no epistemological risks with theories—which are so manifestly risky—while still giving their skeletons something to do in science. The Realist on the other hand finds that the risks only add interest to a view already satisfying because of the way it comes fairly to grips with the unfolding intellectual drama of the human race. He would like an *argument,* some specific feature of science that could be adduced as a reason for not taking a straightforward view.

There are only two additional arguments I can think of. The first runs as follows. The simple schematic Empiricist model of science

(Note 12) places no restrictions on what can go into the topmost layers, but without restriction it would be possible to trivially explain anything. In fact science employs a host of selection principles which operate at this level to severely restrict the kind of theory admissible— the most important of these are simplicity in all its forms (often incompatible forms[20]), retention (in a generalized way—e.g., as a limiting approximation) of as much of the preceding theories in a field as is possible, preferred kinds of development to suit preferred onto- logies (e.g., to suit atoms + void, or field, ontologies). But these principles clearly have no independent justification in nature, they are empirically arbitrary (though they are not pragmatically arbitrary) restrictions brought down to make the job of theory construction manageable. But if theories in science are to be governed by such obviously anthropomorphic rules how can they, should they, be taken seriously as literal descriptions?

To this there is no reply but "Why should they not be?" It is true that restricting our theory construction in these ways is reason for greater scepticism about our theories, but why should it be anything more? Moreover, we still stand a chance of discovering whatever there is to discover in the world at the level of the simple mathematical forms with which we operate. One might as well argue: The only empirical information available to us comes via our pitifully limited senses and the instruments we can construct which are restricted by our pitifully limited resources and information; hence it is useless to take such anthropomorphically grounded theories seriously. Our information is indeed severely limited but if anything is necessary in a guide to the truth, our sensory and instrumental experience is.

Thus this well-known move against Realism also fails. We have instead another Realist distinction:

(D3) What is useful in a particular respect in science is distinct from what is meaningful in science.

Moreover, the premise of the preceding argument is not obviously true. I am of the firm opinion that it *is* possible to be critical of one's preferred metaphysics in science, as critical of it as we can be of anything in science.[21] Though the story is complex, the elements will be sketched a little later.[22] Of course this means that, consistently with the Realist epistemology enunciated, there is ultimately no preferred metaphysics (just as, in this sense, there is ultimately no preferred logic, or preferred anything else of *this* sort). Moreover since I hold the mathematical structures of science to embody a metaphysics, the con- tinual preservation and development of a mathematical formalism is as critically justified as is the exploration of the potentialities of a metaphysics. Finally, there are considerations of the sort Popper offers[23] to believe that there is some justification for choosing to explore the simplest theories first (though this defence is easily in the worst shape of all).[24]

There is of course another, well-known argument for not taking the straightforward view. It is based on the ability to deal exclusively with the purely observational part of a theory (with levels 3 and 4 only). The method of capturing just the observational part of a theory is due to Craig. The argument then runs: either the theoretical terms of a theory serve their purpose in leading to the establishment of a network of connections among observable terms and then they are unnecessary for the empirical purposes of science, or they fail to serve this purpose in which case they are to be rejected as useless; in either case theoretical terms serve no useful purpose in science (Hempel 1965). But this possibility poses no threat to the Realist, from the fact that such a separation of theory and observation is possible *nothing* follows about the semantical status of the terms of the separated components (whether theoretical or observable)—one could obtain a conclusion of the sort opponents of Realism wish *only if* an additional premise was added to the effect that what is not necessary to the sense-confirmable portion of science has no semantic content, but this premise simply recapitulates the empiricist-positivist dogmas and will be rejected by the Realist, precisely because of the anthropomorphic, implausible world view to which they lead. It is important to understand this point: this attempt is not rejected because it has a defect (that would constitute additional reason) but because of the general world view necessary to give it force.[25]

These arguments both fail and they are the only arguments I know of. I conclude that there is nothing but philosophical temperament left with which to decide the issue—except a reasonable assessment of the pluses and minuses of each side, and for a *realistic* view of the world I'll back Realism. (The aim—the *fundamental* aim—of science is discovery and understanding, I think, not pragmatic convenience of control, nor power, nor security.)

2.4.5 A Second Objection

The next objection hinges precisely on the tendency for theories to change radically. If they do so then the presumed fundamental ontology of the world may change, not just particular putative entities may now be denied existence, but entire putative categories of entities, indeed all putative categories of things, may now be denied existence. (This latter would happen if, e.g., physics in general switched between a field-plenum and particle fundamental ontology.) Moreover, so the objection goes, the semantical contents of such disparate theories will also be radically different—even where many of the same phoneme groups are employed. Moreover, it may well be the case that theories of these disparate types are experimentally indistinguishable from one another. But if this is the case how can any theories be taken as literal descriptions when the kinds of world the various possible theories describe differ so radically from one another? Or again, don't the radical semantical shifts that can occur show that theories are only implausibly viewed as intended descriptions of a single real world and more plausibly regarded as heuristic linguistic devices?

The short reply to both questions is: Why? Where is the valid argument that leads from the premises to the conclusion(s)? There is nothing very strange, given our Realist epistemology, with changing our minds radically about the nature of the world; and what semantical shifts there are follow on from that change of mind, as we attempt to express it. To make the reply more sweetly reasonable, and a little longer, the Realist can point out that one can have many kinds of mutually radically disparate maps of the one stretch of land—and language is like a complex map. (It is the mapping view of descriptive language which explains why even at our simplistic level of concept formation and mathematical skill we might still expect to discover some truths concerning the world.)

2.5 EPISTEMOLOGY (II): THE STRUCTURE OF SCIENCE

Our considerations concerning the structure of science begin with yet another objection. The first premise of the objection is that many, indeed all, of the mathematically sophisticated mathematical theories of science deal only in mathematical idealization (point masses, instantaneous rates of change, etc.). The second premise is that no such idealization is ever realized in nature and the conclusion is that no Realist interpretation of these theories succeeds. A weaker, but still sufficient claim would be that not all such idealizations to which the theory was prima facie committed can be realized in nature, and the conclusion retained in its present form.[26]

Certainly the Realist concedes at least the weaker second premise and corresponding conclusion—with the important proviso that the word 'naive' qualify 'Realist' in the conclusion. But this is an objection of the sort the Realist cherishes for it permits a complete turning of the tables on the objector.

Let us begin by noticing that the empiricist is equally at a loss to cope with this feature of science. Since we never observe such idealizations in nature they must be theoretical entities, but then the theories in question are patently 'about' such entities, rather than about the observable world, which is their only legitimate subject matter according to Empiricism. The simple empiricist structure outlined in Note 12 simply cannot accommodate such entities, they remain anomalous.[27] (On this score, only the conventionalist has a superficially plausible account.) But it is when we begin searching for a Realist reply to this objection, which takes the form of a more adequate Realist reconstruction of the structure of science, that we see both Empiricism and Conventionalism are bound to offer an inadequate view of science and to ignore the profound complexities revealed therein.

Chapter 4 offers a preliminary investigation of what I termed the 'global theories' of science, and argues that most of the theories of quantitative science were global theories in both these senses.[28] Empiricism, precisely because it treats theories in isolation from one another, and because of its necessarily simplistic epistemology for science, cannot accommodate these basic characteristics of scientific theories. (A striking example of this is found in the fact that P-Empiricism and Empiricism, precisely because they reduce all theoretical assertions to logical combinations of indubitable sensory reports, cannot erect a truly critical theory of perception and hence cannot give a realistic account of psychology, for it is the business of a global psychological theory both to explain how man behaves *and* how he comes to know what he does about what he does.) For the structural schema for science which I suggested as a replacement for the empiricist scheme see Figure 4.2, p. 119. This schema has at least seven respects in which it differs from, and improves upon, the empiricist schema.[29]

(1) The external global characteristics are explicitly recognized in the structure. The schema recognizes explicitly that two sets of additional theories are in general an essential part of any scientific situation: (a) theories needed in order to apply a given theory to a certain *kind* of situation, (b) theories needed to work out a theory of the specific *kind* of experimental situation envisaged. Finally, in order to know how to process instrumental outputs the theories of these instruments must be set down and related to the various features of the theoretical situations which may arise. These theories therefore have direct inputs into which instruments are chosen (sometimes indeed even an influence on which system [type] is chosen for investigation) and how the data is prepared and processed (including, in particular,

the estimates of its reliability). In addition, the structure includes the general 'background' theories—the various theories of mathematics and psychology, and whatever else may need to be assumed to obtain the *ceteris paribus* clause always invoked.[30]

(2) The internal global characteristics are explicitly recognized in the influence that the theory nominally under test (T_0) has on these same features of the situation, the selection of system and instruments, the preparation and processing of data. (I say 'nominally' under test because there is no severe asymmetry of roles between T_0 and the other theories in these respects.)

(3) The structure explicitly recognizes the important role of mathematical models in global theories. The mathematical theories of science that I have been discussing all model the real world using various mathematical models (e.g., differential geometry, point masses, instantaneous velocities, etc.) and often these are known to be idealizations (e.g., point masses). In most cases the transformation from the actual crudely observable properties of actual systems to the corresponding properties of the model is a very complex one, requiring various 'corrections' and 'adjustments' to the crudely described system until the model system properties are approached.[31] And the further transformation from the real system behaviour now described in the technical terms of the model to that of the model behaviour may be just as complex, since real systems, however described, do not behave exactly as idealized models.[32] The distinction between these two kinds of transition is important in establishing the character of two distinct kinds of correspondence rules—cf. (5) below.

I emphasize that it is not description in common sense terms alone that requires the complex transition to theory discussed above. Even descriptions couched in such technical terms as 'Wilson cloud chamber', 'ionizing particle trajectory', 'flip-flop pulse out-put' and so on still require the same kinds of transformations before the relevant theory of these systems can be brought to bear.

It is only when data are presented at the level of, and in the form of, the theoretical model that we can obtain an experimental verdict on the theory (or, if you prefer, it is only when the theoretical model can be linked to the simplest level of observational description via the theory of the experimental situation, that the theory can be confronted by experiment).

Thus the appearance of the 'model-system filter-transformer' in the schematic diagram. All connections between theory and experiment pass through this filter-transformer which has the task of commencing with an identification of the objects in the experimental situation (system under test plus instruments)—whether in common sense or technical terms makes no essential difference when the goal is hard data (it only adds or subtracts a step or two)—and tailoring their behaviour to fit the best theoretical models of them. Clearly it is this complex procedure which determines just how we prepare and process the data (as well as having the prior function of influencing the choice of system and instruments). As Sellars remarks, the empiricist reconstruction of science, however, sees no *essential* function for models at all (see 1965a, p. 178).[33]

(4) There is a little-observed feature of the scientific reasoning process, namely that *often not even the derivation of observable results is deductively valid*. Traditional Empiricism assumes a fully deductive structure. The situation as envisaged here, however, is to explicitly allow the theory/data transitions appearing therein to include nondeductively valid arguments as well as deductive arguments.[34]

(5) The nature and role of the so-called correspondence rules is radically different and much more complex than that envisaged in the empiricist model. Here there are two distinctively different kinds of linkages between theory and the world.

The first of these are linkages between theory and hard data. These are the connections usually considered by working scientists. But there is also a second kind of linkage included, that between model and the phenomenal data and identification level. These are the linkages that connect model theoretic assertions to commonsense descriptions.[35]

Note that both types of linkage may contain inductive as well as deductive components, again a departure from the traditional model.

(6) The present schema explicitly recognizes the presence and importance of a 'supra-theoretic' level of proto-theories and beyond those again a further level of metaphysics. It is hard to over-emphasize the importance of this level. Suffice it to say that I believe that the entire history of physics can, in effect, be seen as the competition of two incompatible metahysical schemes—the atoms + void and the plena + no void schemes.[36] Also of considerable importance are the 'proto' theories (see Bunge 1967b.) These are the theories that express the assumed general structures of some of the quantities entering the formulation of scientific theories, and of some of the methods employed in their application.

(7) Finally I draw attention again to the role accorded a 'phenomenal' or common sense level in the structure of science. We have already seen how the role might be criticized, indeed how in principle it might be eliminated, and how it is in any case not the chief linkage which appears in scientific accounts. In both of these ways it differs

radically from the Empiricist analysis. A little later on I shall briefly describe my own current views on its ultimate fate.[37]

Returning now to the objection with which this section began, namely why it is that the idealizations occurring in a theory do not render Realism untenable, we see now how a realistic analysis of science copes with the problem. Those espousing this argument emphasize that a theory's sentences do not in general accurately match the phenomenal system behaviour (a few low-level generalizations aside) and of course this is sometimes accurate. But to conclude from thence (as e.g., Suppe 1972a does) that the theory is false of the world is to move too fast. First we need to separate out those cases of conflict between theoretical and phenomenal level, if any, which are to be resolved on the side of theory. Such conflicts can arise in situations where there is a fundamental conflict between the conceptual structure of the theory and that of the phenomenal level (analogy: statistical mechanics vs. 'phenomenological' thermodynamics). In these cases it is probably the phenomenal concepts which must be given up as conceptualizing mere appearance (unless the theory has nothing else going for it), to do otherwise would be to offer too much respect to concepts at the phenomenal level. In most cases of straightforward conflict, I venture to suggest, there is no direct conflict between phenomenal and theoretical concepts (c.f. below), it is just that some beliefs formulated at the phenomenal level must be rejected.[38] In all these cases the Realist position is unscathed, the theoretical terms offer the fundamental description of the world and it is the phenomenal level which must be corrected to meet it.

That leaves us with only those cases in which there are theoretical reasons for believing that the theoretical idealizations cannot be realized at *any* level. In this last case there are again two subcases—that where there are grounds for believing that a particular idealization logically could not apply at any level and the remainder where we have grounds for believing that as a matter of fact it does not apply to our world (e.g., respectively lines of force, frictionless surfaces). In the latter case we can say that a theoretical claim is counterfactually true of the world, i.e., it says how the world would really behave if the appropriate conditions were realized. Contrary to those espousing the anti-Realist argument (e.g., Suppe 1972a) this circumstance is precisely compatible with Realism, it is in fact to say how the world really is in certain essential respects (and that these respects are merely complicated by additional conditions). If we wish to show this explicitly we may reformulate all relevant sentences of the theory so that they take the general form, 'As the circumstances C approach C_1

(the ideal circumstances) the behaviour of the system approaches B_1 (the theoretically specified behaviour)' where we assume the limiting process to be quantitatively specified. This leaves us with only the logically inapplicable idealizations. These are fewer in number than people suppose.[39] A Realist must insist on rigorously eliminating them from theory. I know of no case where this cannot be relatively simply done. And there are the strongest logical reasons for doing so (namely, there are logical grounds for asserting their ontic inapplicability). In short they can be seen to be patently devices of heuristic or convenience that can be done without. Thus, with one or two insubstantial modifications (clarifications) of theory, Realism emerges from the argument not only unscathed but strengthened.[40]

2.6 SEMANTICAL CONSIDERATIONS

2.6.1 The Theory of Truth

The Realist is clearly committed to a Correspondence Theory of truth. Whether this in itself brings with it any special semantics is not easy to say. Certainly Tarski's semantic theory of truth will be adopted; but, contrary to Tarski's own view, I do not believe that this is an explication of a peculiarly correspondence theory of truth, the coherence theorist might—and I believe *ought*—equally well take it over, for it forms a general account of part of the semantical structure of *any* language rather than an account of a specific theory of truth. While the correspondence theory is clearly connected with Realism, the coherence theory is connected with Conventionalism and Instrumentalism where the ordering of data is emphasized.

2.6.2 An Objection to the Theory of Truth

These remarks carry me to a correlative objective. Look about you, this objection runs, when does the scientific community count an assertion as true? Just when it coheres with all of the data available and with the best theory available. And what is the strongest operative criterion in the preferring of one theoretical description to another? Why, aside from compatibility with the data, the inner coherence and comprehensiveness of the theory. Surely then if any criterion of truth is relevant to science it is the coherence criterion, so that one ought to adopt this view of truth rather than the correspondence view. In any case the foregoing epistemological considerations have shown that for a Realist the correspondence theory would be effectively inoperative—it has already been conceded that we cannot choose our theories on the basis of their correspondence with the world, but precisely on the coherence criteria outlined above. Once you leave *all* claims open to revision the only criteria remaining are coherence criteria.

Once again the Realist must candidly admit that such coherence criteria dominate in science, and for just the reasons given in the objection. But these criteria are criteria of *acceptance*, not of truth. The foregoing objection simply confuses acceptance and truth and in so doing collapses. For the Realist to accept a claim or theory is a *pragmatic* decision to act, for the time being, as if the claim or theory were true; for the claim or theory to *be* true is a nonpragmatic semantical state of affairs in which the theory in some sense accurately mirrors the world. Thus we have the fourth distinction important to Realism:

   (D4) The conditions for accepting a scientific claim or theory are distinct from the conditions for the truth of that claim or theory.

Again (D4) states a conceptual distinction; most of the time the two sets of conditions will in fact also be distinct but various degrees of overlap may occur.

2.6.3 Realist Semantics (I): The Issues

But now the central semantical challenges to the Realist are unavoidable: (1) Say in what the meanings of theoretical terms consist, i.e., explain the basis of the semantical contents of theories; (2) Show how it is possible for theories to mirror the world, i.e., show how this semantical role for theories is possible.

2.6.4 Realist Semantics (II): From Whence Meanings?

With respect to the first challenge I must admit that I have no satisfying theory to offer. Indeed, this seems to me to be one of the outstanding trouble-spots for Realism. But since, as it also seems to me, no one else has anything more satisfying to say than what I shall say here, this *is* an outstanding problem for the Realist, but *not* a peculiar embarrassment for him.

As a Realist it seems to me at this point in time that I have available a spectrum of choices for a doctrine of semantical content, from a radical position, say Feyerabend's or Quine's, through more conservative doctrines (e.g., Sellars) to a conservative doctrine quite close to the empiricist tradition (Maxwell). I shall briefly elaborate these doctrines and then state my own view of the most plausible position in the spectrum.

2.6.4.1 Quasi-Empiricist Realism. I shall begin at the conservative end, for that seems to be the least likely defensible Realist position. Essentially, Maxwell takes a Ramsey treatment of theoretical terms[41] seriously. Roughly speaking, theoretical terms are treated as if they were bound variables, thus a sentence of the (simplest) form

$$(x)\ Tx,$$

is 'transcribed' to

$$(\exists t)\ (x)\ tx,$$

and so on for more complex sentences. As a matter of fact, though not of necessity, this treatment is not extended to the observable terms of a theory and so this approach presupposes, and enhances, an observational/theoretical dichotomy.

It is clear that this approach has the intention of treating the observational and theoretical levels quite differently; roughly the intention is to grant observational terms a 'full status', they are to have *connotations* (a sense, intentional content or what-have-you) as well as denotations (extensions), whereas theoretical terms are merely predicates, we know-not-of-what-content, which stand in certain extensional relations to each other and to the observational terms.[42] Maxwell regards the observational terms as essentially achieving their connotations through ostensive definition (he speaks in terms of Russell's knowledge by acquaintance and knowledge by description). Moreover, in this exposition of a theory, the observational level has epistemological priority for purposes of acceptance or rejection of the theory. Thus this view builds in much of the character of the empiricist view of theories—the issue is whether it builds in too much to be acceptable to the Realist.

First let us be clear that a number of immediate criticisms of this approach do *not* succeed: (i) deductive systematization is preserved and (ii) it can even be plausibly maintained that inductive systematization can be preserved[43] (in any case this latter objection is not decisive against someone who abandoned induction altogether in favour of the hypothetico-deductive approach—again the Realist, *qua* Realist, may be non-committal on this latter choice); (iii) that alternative models satisfy the Ramsey formalism is irrelevant; (iv) a Maxwell Ramseyan is *not* committed to the doctrine of the given (to dogma 4 of Empiricism), for nowhere is it asserted that the observational level claims are not open to revision and nothing has been said about concept-percept formation; (v) finally note that this position is not committed to the analytic-synthetic dogma, for a sharp observational/theoretical dichotomy is neither a necessary, nor sufficient, condition for this dogma (the one is semantical, the other epistemological), so that the way is still open here to regard logic as empirical if one desires (and this Realist desires to).

In fact, Maxwell claims that the Ramsey approach does *not* eliminate theoretical *roles*, for they have extensional roles not reproducible from the resources of the observational level. If ontology then is, roughly, what we must quantify over to have our assertions come out true, then the *intended* ontology of theories includes theoretical entities. Actually, I believe he is strictly able to assert only that *very probably* the Ramsey approach does not eliminate theoretical *entities*, for it is just possible that the objects satisfying the existential claims are non-theoretical objects, though this is so unlikely to be true that Maxwell's position is worth pursuing.[44] Moreover, this approach can consistently be conjoined with a Realist doctrine of perception and with the denial of the given to recapture the essence of the Realist epistemology adumbrated earlier. That observational terms are, *de facto*, semantically and epistemologically privileged counts nothing against Realism so long as observational claims are equally open to criticism in the light of experience and theoretical advance. (That the 'nothing' here is strictly warranted is controversial, cf. my treatment of Sellars' argument below.)

Indeed, Maxwell has a persuasive argument for his position. The argument runs as follows: (i) Beyond some level of some reasonably direct observational acquaintance we could really only know about the nature of the physical world through its causal consequences for those features of the world which are included in the directly observable level, and (ii) that the only such deeper-lying features which appear on this 'observable surface' are the structural relations and causal relations among the unobservable entities (simply because such structural and causal relations can be mediated through causal or nomic connections whereas the intrinsic properties themselves cannot be mediated in this fashion); it follows, therefore, that theoretical terms can significantly only stand for such relations and hence that they will be essentially structural in form and without qualitative content semantically.[45]

And there is a correlative argument for the observational/theoretical dichotomy which runs: Scientific theories are developed to explain and predict events in our observable world; however, because of the poverty of our senses such theories typically must employ unobservable entities, i.e., theoretical entities, in providing powerful explanatory and predictive systems; accordingly, the observational/theoretical dichotomy is an integral part of the scientific endeavour and arises quite naturally out of our sensory limitations.

The premises of these arguments seems to me to be entirely plausible and the arguments are surely valid. Together they constitute a powerful prima facie case for this quasi-empiricist position (indeed, for the empiricist position itself).

I turn now to an important argument of Sellars (see especially 1963 and 1965a). Sellars argues that terms have 'first class semantical status' only when they belong, or could belong, to the picturing language, i.e., only when, in some sense, they literally mirror or picture the world; but they can only have this semantical role if they occur, or could occur, in the observational vocabulary. Therefore, any analysis of science, e.g., Empiricism, which relegates theoretical terms to an *in principle* non-observational role necessarily prevents them from being taken Realistically. It looks as if this argument will apply equally against Maxwell's position.

Leaving aside the first premise, which is not strictly necessary (though I am inclined to accept Sellars' semantical account of what is peculiar to the correspondence doctrine of truth anyway), the Realist ought to grant the other premise, and the validity, of the argument. Indeed the recognition that, to be taken seriously (Realistically), the theoretical terms must, *in principle*, be capable of playing an observational role is one of the greatest of the post-Positivist lessons learned, primarily through the efforts of a mild epistemological conservative (Sellars) and an epistemological radical (Feyerabend). Roughly the idea is that, from a God's Eye perspective, the world must be exactly as (true) fundamental theory says it is and so one can in principle conceive of a sentient with sufficiently rich sensory equipment to observe all of these characteristics. (Notice though that this doctrine *does not* require commitment to any empiricist belief that observational terms have a special semantical content, it is entirely independent of that doctrine.)

But the further conclusion that the argument applies equally against Maxwell's position as against Empiricism is too hasty, on two grounds. (1) The argument is valid if, but only if, the 'in principle' is construed as 'logically possible'. In particular, the argument does not support the conclusion that it must be *physically* possible for theoretical terms to play an observational role, let alone that this role be actually realized. After all, whether or not this latter occurs depends, at least in important part, on the actual physical structure of our sensory relations with the world and on the structure of our central nervous systems (the former governing which information is accessible to us and the latter the possible developments of our conceptual-perceptual response apparatus). It is consistent with Realism, therefore, that the *de facto* epistemological privileges which some terms enjoy should, as a matter of fact, be unalterable, as long as they are *in principle* replaceable by theoretical terms (and the corresponding claims open to criticism, etc.). And something of just this sort seems to be Maxwell's position.[46] (2) The position as Maxwell states it, though already an elaboration of Ramsey's approach, can be elaborated still further. E.g., it is open to the Realist to claim that at some point some of the theoretical terms either (i) actually, or (ii) may in physical principle, or (iii) logically might enter the observational vocabulary, just as Sellars claims they must.[47] I shall label these positions, respectively, radical, mild radical and conservative quasi-Empiricism.

To see how even the mild-radical and conservative quasi-empiricist Realists can reply to this objection, note that they too are committed to the view that it is the satisfying substituents of the bound variables that are the theoretical entities, hence they will claim that there are genuine theoretical terms, namely chosen constants which designate these substituents, it is just that these constants have only denotations and no connotations. Of course scientists speak and feel as if their theoretical terms have connotations, but the quasi-empiricist has several moves he can make here; whether these suffice to construct a genuine connotation (at least one of these certainly improves the Ramsey approach) or explain the situation away as 'merely psychological' is of lesser interest.[48]

A presupposition heretofore has been that terms receive a connotation of the sort that counts only if instances of them are observable. The former of the foregoing alternatives would break with this assumption (and rightly so it seems to me, I can see nothing but old empiricist prejudices to recommend it). It has to be admitted, however, that if this assumption is allowed to stand then full-blown theoretical terms fade beyond our actual reach to the realm of mere (logical or physical) possibility. In this case the empiricist bite of these positions would make itself felt. The hard-nosed Realist can, however, either choose to grasp this thorn (it is not quite a nettle) and continue with his exposition of theoretical advance and change eschewing all use of full-blown theoretical terms, or, as I said, simply deny the supposition and choose the modified Ramsey approach.[49]

If, on the other hand, a more radical line is chosen and it is conceded that theoretical terms may be created and can actually usurp the role of the observable terms, then the last of this collection of problems disappears. Here once again observation as the source of connotation may be safely maintained. There remains, however, to give an account of exactly what is involved—conceptually and psychologically—when the transition happens.

The entire range of positions, however, must also face the following

problem: What is the relation between the existing observational concepts and claims made in terms of them and the possible or actual
replacing theoretical concepts and corresponding claims? Many people have argued, and there seems strong grounds for believing it, that
the world of simple observation and the theoretically described world
are incompatible, that the conjunction of all the ordinary descriptions
acceded to by common sense and all the theoretically adequate descriptions cannot be simultaneously true (e.g., Sellars—the 'manifest'
and 'scientific' images clash; Feyerabend—common language embodies a false theory). This conclusion would leave the conservative
and mild-radical stuck with an observation language for science
which is admittedly conceptually inadequate but which they cannot
get rid of. However, if it became absolutely necessary, this thorn too
could be grasped. On the other hand a distinction might be made
between the adequacy of the concepts of the common sense conceptual framework themselves and the truth-or-falsity of the beliefs formulated in terms of those concepts—especially if one continued to accept
the analytic/synthetic distinction. Now it is not *obvious* that in some
deeper sense the concepts of the common sense conceptual framework are inadequate, i.e., quite incapable of being used to formulate
true—or at any rate experience-supported assertions, as opposed to
many deeply embedded common sense beliefs being in fact false. (Of
course the common sense conceptual framework *is* inadequate to formulate the deeper intended truths of science, but this is compatible
with its possession of adequate concepts for the formulation of shallower truths.) Moreover the sense of 'replacement' of common sense
by theoretical concepts would now be a rather benign one, indeed
'addition' might often be the more appropriate description. But if this
latter alternative holds then the conflict (though not the difference)
between the two conceptual frameworks is removed (though also not
the difference in beliefs) and the painfulness of the clash evaporated.
In any event this is a line of response at least initially open to the
quasi-empiricist, for it does satisfy Sellars' demand that theoretical
terms should in principle take on an observational role (one which I
shall explore further below). What all positions are forced to admit is
that, whether in practice or only in principle, the observational language is to become dominated by theoretical predicates when it
comes to an objective description of the world.

At this point the further radical alternative of denying the observational language any special semantical privileges (by denying the
existence of observationally conferred connotations) seems increasingly attractive, since by removing any distinction in status between

the two sets of terms, except for the pragmatic one of being the terms in which we habitually couch observational reports, we (1) remove the sense of any special breakthrough occurring when theoretical terms enter the observational level (a man is simply re-educated and his choice of observational terms change) and (2) open the way to saying that the clash, if conceded, between the two sets of terms is essentially just a clash between two trial-and-error attempts to describe the world, i.e., only a generalized version of a clash between two theories. In the further account now required of the origins of observational and theoretical concepts the variant claims would run roughly as follows: the conservative and mild-radical variants would claim that of physical necessity, or in fact, the world conditioned in us responses requiring just (terms for) the privileged extensions, while the more radical variant would claim that our conditioned responses are actually, and not just in principle, open to conceptual alteration.

It should be appreciated that denying any special semantical status to observational terms (1) does *not* entail a denial of the analytic/ synthetic distinction (cf. Note 28) and (2) does not entail rejection of the notion of ostensive definition. Once again this is worth emphasizing because these rejections, although congenial to a radical semantical position and often found together (e.g., in Quine) do not *inevitably* go together.[50]

There is here then a rich variety of quasi-empiricist doctrines compatible with Realism. I have elaborated them at some length because their compatibility with Realism, and their richness, seems to be insufficiently appreciated.

2.6.4.2 Anti-Empiricist Realism. Paul Feyerabend stands empiricism on its head.[51] In the first place, as I have noted, he regards observational terms as simply pragmatically determined by various conditioning processes (cf. 1958). But then one can ask "From whence are these terms drawn?" Feyerabend's answer is: From theories—a (sufficiently general) theory determines its own observational language. Correlatively, every observation language becomes 'theory laden'—even so-called natural languages are regarded as embodying primitive theories. Not only is the doctrine of the given denied, any 'natural' observational level is also denied. The observational/theoretical dichotomy disappears from semantics, and nearly from epistemology, into pragmatics, where it is of relatively little importance.

It follows that for Feyerabend theories must determine their own semantic content, hence also that of their observational sublanguages.[52] This suggests the notion of *implicit definition*—an obscure and difficult concept, though some sense can certainly be made of the idea that the syntactical structure of theoretical postulates restricts the range of possible physical models for the theory and in this sense contributes to the relations among the terms. Feyerabend himself has proposed a syntactical ('structural') approach to internally determined semantical content (cf. 1965) though not, I think, very successfully (cf. Achinstein 1964).

Attempts to state clearly a plausible and viable notion of implicit definition are fraught with difficulty. One of these is the danger of collapsing the notion into that of explicit definition. In the present context this would amount to reducing implicitly defined terms to observation terms *à la* Empiricism. For Beth has proven an interesting theorem to the following effect: under certain general assumptions a predicate is implicitly definable if and only if it is explicitly definable.[53] It seems to me that Beth's theorem deals a serious blow to any plausible notion of full-blown implicit definition. Serious, but not in itself deadly. There are essentially two ways around the theorem: reject the criterion of explicit definability as too weak, or that of implicit definability as too strong. *A propos* of the latter, one could go on to talk of *partially* implicitly defined predicates which were not required to satisfy so strong a condition as Beth's and so avoid his theorem but, so far as I can see, this is then to say no more than the range of models is partially restricted by the axioms. Conversely, one might insist that explicitly defined terms be expressed by something stronger than an entailed material equivalence, but the possibility of this of course depends upon the resources of the language, in most cases nothing stronger will be available. This suggests that we need the resources of a meta-language, and indeed there is a strong tradition concerning the nature of implicit definition that formulates its approach meta-linguistically; ironically, it leads to equally great difficulty of an opposite sort.

For in the commonest tradition the notion of internally determined semantic content is in constant danger of reducing to zero the empirical content of a theory by rendering each of its fundamental postulates as an (implicit) tautology. It suggests that a theoretical concept is, in outline, the concept of a set of entities standing in certain relations (specified by the theory) to certain other sets; but if this is the analysis of every term in an assertion (or even of only an appropriate subset of the terms) the assertion must become effectively tautologically true.[54] Ironically, this analysis offers a restricted semantical content to theoretical terms which is virtually indistinguishable from that offered by the Ramseyan analysis in the quasi-empiricist approach.

It begins to appear that an account of wherein 'implicit definition' consists can only itself be explicitly given on pain of either reducing theories to tautologies or of reducing all implicit definitions to explicit definitions.[55]

2.6.4.3 A Middle Way. Feyerabend and Sellars agree that ultimately theory must be able to determine the observational level, they agree that the conceptual framework of common sense and theory clash, and they agree that in some cases the displacement of common sense observational terms by theoretical terms is actually happening (cf. Sellars 1965a, b). They disagree only about the actual nature and role of natural language in science up to, and including, the present. For Sellars the conceptual structure of natural language is, roughly, constitutive of the objects of common sense, as well as providing the resources for formulating additional theories concerning them—in the sense in which a theory, in the usual sense of the term, has an observable domain, described independently of it (namely, in the natural language) and which it is about, natural language is not a theory.[56]

Correlatively Sellars disagrees with Feyerabend's claim that natural language, more precisely the level of common sense observation terms, can already be dispensed with, for Sellars argues that science has not yet provided a sufficiently complete conceptual schema with which to replace it. In the meantime the natural observation language acts in a de facto epistemologically privileged role as the basis for theoretical acceptance and rejection (1965a, p. 186f.).

The disagreements here are not just quibbles on Sellars' part, a mere matter of fine judgment of historical timing, for Sellars has a different answer from Feyerabend to our semantical question "Whence comes the semantic content of theories?" According to Sellars, theoretical terms—and here, as with Feyerabend, they are full-blown terms, i.e., predicate constants with connotation and denotation, or at any rate will eventually be so (cf. below)—have two sources of semantical content. (1) There is implicit definition construed as contributing only via the reduction in the range of possible physical models and (2) there is *analogical* transference of meaning from common sense concepts to theoretical concepts, this transference being mediated by the specific model or models of the theory (roughly, the theoretical concepts and the common sense concepts, though distinct, are said to share a range of higher order attributes in common).[57] It is this latter component which is all-important, for implicit definition alone is not sufficient to grant a full measure of meaningfulness to predicate constants, instead, qua implicitly defined, they are only would-be constants (1965a, p. 176), whereas "the distinctive feature of the use of models and analogies in theory construction is that the conceptual framework of the theory is *generated* by specifying the analogies which are to obtain" (1965a, p. 181). Component 2 grants fullness of meaning to the would-be theoretical predicate constants.

It is the eventually-to-be-abandoned observational language of common sense that is itself the external source for the generation of semantic content to the successor scientific world view. And "Only if we recognize that the anology. . . of the model is not to be construed in terms of the identity or difference of first order attributes, can we appreciate how the use of models in theoretical explanation can generate *genuinely new* conceptual frameworks and justify the claim to have escaped from the myth of the given" (1965a, pp. 183–4).

Notice that, apart from a more complex account of the relations between common sense observation and theory, Sellars' position is very close to that of the mild-radical quasi-empiricist.

What Sellars first owes us is an account of analogical transference of semantic content. This is nowhere spelled out in the detail required to cope with an actual theory of science, though it is clear from Sellars' writings that some form of modeling is central to the process and internal logical relations also play an important role.

What Sellars *now* owes us of course is an account of how the common sense conceptual framework acquired its semantic content. Any attempt to introduce a succession of frameworks related to one another as theory is to common sense not only does not answer the question, but merely postpones it, while at the same time forcing us back on Neanderthal concepts (if any) as the basis of contemporary semantics. Any attempt to stop the regress at some language by insisting that meanings in it were directly conferred in observational experience is in danger of returning us to the worst of the empiricist dogmas. Sellars is aware of this and attempts to provide a somewhat different account of the emergence of the common sense conceptual scheme. This account is the famous story of our Rylean ancestors who possessed only crude behavioural concepts at first without any explicit concepts of semantic rules but who gradually enriched their language to achieve the full-blown conceptual scheme we have today (see 1963, Ch. 5). Though the general idea of an evolving conceptual scheme is surely correct, Sellars' account is still clouded by the empiricist's insistence that observation brings something special to concepts, the mechanisms of the semantic 'bootstrap' by which evolution occurred are vague and do not seem to avoid the pressure toward a regressive language as seeking a pure behavioural reductive base.[58] Perhaps if Sellars had given us an account of the origins of the meanings of especially the general concepts of the common sense framework we should have a clearer understanding of the matter.

2.6.4.4. The Problem of Semantical Determination. The advantage of quasi-Empiricism is its obvious bowing in the direction of the observation framework of common sense that we all in fact use and its consistency with our intuition that unobservables can only deal in causally mediated structural features of the world whereas perceptibility confers an additional qualitative content to concepts. Even Sellars accepts these features. Its disadvantage is that it seems to restrict theories to a much more poverty-stricken role than we are inclined to give them, for whatever our doubts about them, historical experience tells us that theoretical ideas have dominated the course of scientific knowledge almost everywhere and that, whatever their semantic defects, theories do seem to provide a 'picture' of the true nature of the world. Sellars accepts these features too. The Feyerabendian position at the opposite extreme to quasi-Empiricism has the advantage of taking theories seriously enough; if anything it has the disadvantage of taking them so seriously that they cannot fulfill the role then demanded of them (and the role of an observational language is perhaps taken in too cavalier a fashion). The mid-way position occupied by Sellars seems to retain the attractions of the extremes but actually it also seems to possess transpositions of their respective weaknesses. Theories are restricted, ultimately, to logical combinations of would-be predicates (the replacement of the common sense world has yet to occur) depending for their content on analogical transpositions of what are ultimately crudely observational concepts. (Yet if theories are to be truly semantically transcendent the origin of the additional semantic richness escapes us after all, or is itself reduced to observation.)

We seem left then hanging somewhere between empiricist observationally conferred content and pure implicit definition, with perhaps a third kind of source, as yet unspecified, thrown in (pure imagination perhaps?), to account for the semantic content of theories. And this is, essentially, where I shall be forced to leave the issue. To become any further engrossed in the detail of contemporary proposals for the analysis of semantical content would take us altogether too far afield. The point I wish to stress again is the rich range of these positions which are compatible with Realism.

2.6.5 Realist Semantics (III): The Criteria of Realism

Our second challenge, it will be recalled, was to show how Realism was possible, i.e., to show how that semantical role for theories was possible. This challenge turns out to have no better answer than we can provide to the first. For it is perfectly clear now what must be shown, namely just how theories can come to dominate the observational level—at least in principle. But the mechanism offered for this process will clearly depend in a general way upon the accounts offered of the origins of semantic content for theories canvassed in the preceding. For Feyerabend observational languages are simply replaced *tout court* when theories replace one another—the satisfaction of this criterion offers no special problem, it is assumed satisfied from the beginning. Sellars offers us his complex mechanism of analogical transference from the common sense framework, but does not actually say just how theoretical terms acquire a 'reporting role' from there, perhaps the training mechanism is not unlike Feyerabend's (see Feyerabend 1965a and Carnap 1956a, pp. 211-218; cf. Hooker 1972). The quasi-Empiricist account as I have developed it has nothing to say on the matter, not surprisingly since for all but its radical extreme it is not a matter of actual occurrence; still it owes us an account of how the transition might go *in principle*, this will however be of a somewhat different sort from the earlier possibilities canvassed here since we would presumably be discussing a counterfactual situation in which the constitution of *homo sapiens* and/or that of fundamental physics itself is significantly different from what it actually is.

What emerges then is an unanimous silence on the details of the actual mechanism of replacement. In part this silence is surely warranted since it must be a matter of psychological investigation how observation terms actually get replaced or enriched, and whether piecemeal or by entire conceptual schemes. On the other hand there is a corresponding semantical dimension and we seem not to have any but crude accounts of this—we can choose between replacements *tout court* (and never mind about the relations between successor languages) and some transitional semantic process (e.g., Sellars' analogical transference), possibly together with the theory of observation terms as pragmatically conditioned responses to sensory nerve bombardment. Despite this unsatisfactory state of affairs, the important positive definite thing I wish to emphasize is the Realist criterion of success, namely ultimate theoretical domination of the observation language, in principle.

2.6.6 Realist Semantics (IV): A Second Middle Way

2.6.6.1 *Statement.* In this section I am going to briefly set down my own tentative selection of doctrines from among those presented in the foregoing. It seems worthwhile to do only because that selection differs a little from those I canvassed there and because it is intended to represent a comfortably sane position (to be contrasted with the heroism of the extremes). I have labelled it a second middle way.[59] I would not be overly disturbed to be persuaded that, really, it was essentially a version of radical anti-Empiricism with a mildly modified 'network model' of theories.

It should by now be clear that I agree with Sellars that, at least in principle, theoretical terms can acquire an *observational* role and that theories, ultimately, provide us with our truest characterization of the world. I even agree with Feyerabend (and to the extent to which Sellars accepts Feyerabend's cases, with Sellars) that many theoretical terms have already acquired a *reporting* role in observation. I agree with Sellars that the terms of the common sense framework are in an epistemologically favoured position and I even agree that there is something semantically distinctive about such observational terms. But here agreement stops.

2.6.6.2 *A Distinction.* First let me draw a distinction between a term's acquiring an *observational role* and its acquiring a *reporting role in observation*. The first of these achievements I construe as follows: A particular concept achieves a status such that the neurological processing structures that are the (correlates of the) possession of that concept are habitually active in the perceptual process, i.e., we normally process the incoming sensory information using those structures, i.e., using that concept (among others). I have spelled out this view of perception in detail elsewhere (Hooker 1970a) but what this amounts to is that we habitually (i.e., normally) conceptualize our perceptions using this concept. The concepts of the commonsense framework typically have this status.[60] By 'acquiring a reporting role in observation' however I understand only that we respond to perceptual stimulation, in an appropriate set of circumstances, with reports (= descriptions, claims, identifications, etc.) that contain the concept in question.

These two statuses are quite distinct, for on the one side there may be ranges of circumstances where we habitually do not employ our perceptually active concepts but only those that have acquired a reporting role and on the other side concepts may acquire a reporting role in observation and yet play no natural part in perceptual processing. The latter alternative comes about through training and education. The most striking examples are probably provided by working scientists. These people are educated to respond directly to laboratory situations with reports couched in the technical language of theories. In fact this is exactly how the 'hard' data, or at any rate, the prepared data, are reported, they are 'read' straight off the instruments and this behavioural fact is what gives the overwhelming impression that this is the only significant observational level in science. There is no doubt that psychologically scientists do respond *directly* in normal circumstances, i.e., there is no hidden psychological inference process involved which moves from the 'real' observation reports, couched presumably in the 'real' observational terms, to reports couched in theoretical terms. Nonetheless there is an important sense in which even these people continue to perceive fundamentally in common sense terms *even in those situations where they are not reporting in those terms*.[61] What has happened is that through training and education these people are conditioned to respond directly to stimuli with *reports* couched in terms other than those in which they fundamentally *conceptualize* those stimuli in perception. The situation is rather like (though to be distinguished from) perceiving situations *as* theoretical states of affairs.

This distinction is largely unappreciated in the philosophy of science.[62] Once it is made we can see the elements of truth (but also that of error) in both the empiricist and radical anti-empiricist extremes. Feyerabend is right to think that scientists are not limited to common sense vocabulary for their observation *reports* but react directly to perceived situations using the terms of theory because of a pragmatic conditioning process. He is wrong to believe that they leave the common sense terms behind, or that the observation experience changes conceptually, and for that reason he is wrong to say that the observation language has changed *tout court*, rather has it been enriched (and perhaps also been modified a little, cf. below).[63] Moreover the grain of truth in the empiricist position is, roughly, that we are stuck with the perceptually active concepts we have because these arise from the deeper structure of the world at large and our particular human neurophysiology—and we retreat to this level whenever we wish to make epistemologically less daring claims. But note that epistemological caution does *not* equal indubitability, nor does it even mean exclusiveness of observational role, much less exclusiveness of semantical role, nor does it demand to operate at a phenomenalistic sense data level—these are empiricist errors.[64]

2.6.6.3 The Nature and Role of Common Language.

An untheoretical language. The distinction just discussed opens the way to admit to science an observational vocabulary that is theory-independent. Consider the perceptually active concepts; there is good neurophysiological and historical-anthropological reason to suppose that these have not changed significantly for millenia. (Aristotle was just as capable of perceiving a shining orb in the blue sky as was Einstein, and they would have agreed on that much despite their distinct theoretical descriptions of the situation.) Moreover, a single scientist may switch belief between totally disparate conceptual-onto-logical schemes, e.g., between field and particle theories, without any shift in his perceptions and commonsense conceptual schema. These claims constitute strong grounds for introducing such a level. Thus these concepts, and the simple general truths that may be stated with them, are common between all the theories of western science, they thus count as theory-neutral or independent in this specific sense.[65] The terms of this language represent the perceptually active concepts, they belong to the natural language (the common sense level) and they have been with mankind for millenia, they remain as theories come and go.

It is also true that this sub-language has become increasingly irrelevant to science, because the concepts of scientific theories are increasingly removed from the common sense level. (Remember that only hard data descriptions confront theory.)

Semantic ambiguity. Understanding the situation here is complicated by the fact that often the same sign has two (or more) distinct uses, one (or more) at the theoretical level and one at the untheoretical level (e.g., particle, space, exchange). Thus one particular token of the sign-type may be heavily theory-laden, another untheoretical.

Theories and commonsense language. Quite aside from the theories that can be specifically formulated using common sense concepts, these concepts often have an additional theoretical load built into their semantic content.[66] This is what partially justifies Feyerabend in referring to common sense language as embodying false theories (*in even his opponent's sense of theory*).

Common sense language: is it conceptually inadequate? You will recall that the claim was that the common sense conceptual framework clashed irrevocably with that of science. The implication was that it would have to be abandoned. I proposed denying this latter conclusion. Let us consider the case of a table, described as a solid wooden brown object and perceived in corresponding terms. According to the usual account, the commonsense conceptual framework commits one to the existence of a continuous, coloured, impenetrable object with sharp boundaries, but in fact none of these attributes is strictly true of the object before one according to fundamental theory, hence that object must be discarded *in toto* as mere appearance. In fact, though, fundamental theory and common sense agree that there is an object present at very accurately the perceived location of the table, with boundaries that are very nearly sharp, which does in fact resist penetration from other macro objects to a very high degree and whose interstices are each very small compared with macro magnitudes. If this were not the case it would be a very remarkable world indeed in which theory could explain macro appearance and behaviour. Suppose then that we construe the common sense observation report along these lines "There is a table present which has no visible interstices or breaks at its edges and which permits no perceivable penetration by other macro objects . . . " and construe the further claim, whenever it is present in the speaker's meaning, that the table literally is interstice-free, with sharp boundaries and totally penetration-resistant as a further (unwarranted) primitive explanatory attempt to be exorcized from the commonsense scheme—then we obtain a commonsense claim that even fundamental theory agrees is true. It is clear that the common sense scheme is capable of drawing this distinction internally to itself. I do not claim that the 'purified' common sense scheme thus obtained must of necessity be compatible with fundamental theory in this fashion,[67] what I do claim is that in our world we do have this compatibility.[68] But this does not extend in quite the same fashion to the secondary qualities, for I believe, contra Sellars, that objects are not e.g., literally coloured at all, though they appear to be. Judgments of this kind must be exorcised from the corpus; what need not be removed are the various true claims that are instances of the general claim that objects possess properties in virtue of which we sense objects in the qualitative fashion we do.[69] A very great deal of the common sense scheme remains after these modifications, especially outside of the secondary qualities. (I have not discussed numerical concepts, relational concepts, identity concepts and a host of other dimensions to the commonsense scheme; in general all of these aspects will be less in need of modification than those I have discussed.) All that has been done is to render that scheme epistemologically more cautious. It is true that this has destroyed the rich theoretical and quasi-theoretical conception of common sense objects tacit in the scheme, but it has left a large portion of what we wish to say of them intact.

In sum, I claim that if we rid commonsense language of its explicit theories and the implicit theorizing built into semantic content we are left with a theory-neutral scheme whose observational concepts are exactly the untheoretical concepts of the beginning of Section 2.6.6; but these concepts do not clash with theory, they are simply not very relevant as they stand to specific theories from the point of view of testing them. Nonetheless they are *a* fundamental part of observation and science. This neutral scheme acts as a framework within which all members of a community may orient themselves to one another, irrespective of their theoretical beliefs. Within this common macro world the most important role for science which these untheoretical concepts play is in the keying in of students of a theory to the situations in which they are to apply the theoretically-loaded observation terms, i.e., in the process of acquisition of vocabulary with a reporting role. Finally, the scheme has an historical importance as being that out of which science grew (though its semantic role in that process is obscure). Theory *enriches* this neutral observational vocabulary with its reporting roles, it does not replace it, *though in principle it could do so* (i.e., the appropriate changes in neuro-physiological perceptual processing will be possible, in principle, if the theory is true—though the transition is very probably not possible under normal human conditions). Theory does, however, criticize and reject old common sense theories and beliefs (where they are false) and likewise for common sense concepts having false theoretical assumptions built into their semantics—here the clash indeed occurs. Since these latter conditions are reasonably widespread in common sense language there is a measure of truth in the usual view, though the error made by attending to it alone dwarfs this truth in importance.

The continuum of theory-ladenness. We find, then, as I earlier suggested, a roughly continuous progression from observational reports couched in untheoretical terms through the wide variety of 'halfway house' terms that abound in common language to reports couched in the technical terms of some specific theory. (Common language is full of terms, or particular word uses for a given sign, that are semi-theoretical, largely through a slow osmotic transfer process from earlier theories. E.g., metal, acid, vacuum, level. These terms come to be integrated into the commonsense conceptual structure.)

Why untheoretical? There are two senses in which even our common sense perceptually active concepts involve a *theory-like* commitment.

To see what the first sense is, we begin again with the doctrine of perception. That doctrine informs us that a logical prerequisite of perceptual experience is the possession of a perceptually active conceptual scheme, i.e., the possession of the appropriate cortical processing structures. (Physically, the possession of these structures is a corequisite of perception.) But in a very general way the conceptual scheme which is perceptually active embodies a metaphysics (it may in fact be capable of embodying several distinct metaphysical schemes). Thus the categories of perception themselves will reflect a very general commitment to a metaphysics for the world. In our own case, for example, we habitually perceive the world in terms of individuals located in a three-dimensional space and changing in time, though the four-dimensional space-time world of relativity theory and the continuous plenum world of field theory represent two logically possible alternative metaphysical schemes which might have been our perceptually active scheme. In this sense then our habitual categorizing in perception involves a very general commitment to a view of the world as made up in a certain way. Since I hold that even general metaphysics is ultimately open to criticism in an exactly similar fashion to which theories are criticizable (except for the time scale of criticism), this commitment can properly be said to be a theory-like commitment.

There is a second, much more direct, sense in which the concepts of the common sense scheme, *a fortiori* those of the untheoretical scheme, contain a theoretical component, namely, it is simply not possible to teach those concepts or guarantee the publicness (intersubjectivity) their social use demands unless they are understood (whether tacitly or explicitly) to function in some laws (cf. e.g., Hesse 1970, pp. 44f).E.g., one only has to think of the network of geometrical laws in which shape and size predicates are imbedded. The realization of this is anyway immediate once one reflects upon the complex array of laws that must be tacitly understood before even ostensive definition can be made to work. (Pointing as a human act must be understood, the behaviour of sight in relation to the body, the kind of thing being pointed out etc., etc.)[70] Most of the laws involved are tacitly understood and seem only partially reflected in the semantics of the scheme (how deeply imbedded is the law that a spherical body will roll on a flat surface? roll forever?—cf. locally Euclidean but globally non-Euclidean geometry), though the laws could be stated within the common sense frame if necessary.[71]

It would appear that one cannot easily make a sharp distinction here between tacitly held and semantically integral laws, nor easily between theoretical extrapolation and untheoretical perception. To claim, e.g., that a spherical object will roll forever on a flat surface seems clearly a theoretical extrapolation from common sense experience; to claim only that an object rolls smoothly on the perceivable parts of a perceptually flat surface to the degree it is perceptually spherical, so long as one is not under illusion, is plausibly untheoretical. What this suggests is that stripping away the theoretical extrapolation from the common sense scheme may not lead to an obvious sharp demarcation of the untheoretical.

This is not a disaster because ultimately it will be recalled, the criterion of the observationally untheoretical is that of active role in perceptual processing. This latter can be determined, in principle, experimentally (irrespective of the outcome on the theory-commitment issue). There never was anything to *guarantee* that the stripping process for the common sense scheme outlined above would yield exactly the observable untheoretical concepts so defined or that these latter would forever remain theory-neutral.[72]

This discussion makes it clear that neither sense of theory-like commitment is logically different from straightforward theoretical commitment, the difference comes in the different processes by which the commitments came to be made (the one by a conscious, verbal process of theoretical postulation, the other through unconscious neurophysiological adjustment), and the different epistemological roles they play in the philosophy of science (the untheoretical plays an ultimately dependent, but critical, role in the inter-theoretic orientation of the human community).[73] Certainly the untheoretical scheme, like the theoretical scheme, has been (and probably still is being) elaborated over time in the light of experience, though again by different processes. Like our theories, this elaboration might go wrong (though it would have to do so in systematic ways to allow survival). As I have said, one could imagine circumstances under which fundamental theory informed us that many or all of our perceptually active concepts did not apply—we were under systematic illusion. Nonetheless we have excellent reason to believe that nothing has gone wrong in the process grounded on (i) general considerations concerning what is known of the mechanisms of neurophysiological processing adjustment, (ii) historical evidence, (iii) the agreement of fundamental theory with untheoretical common sense.[74] I regard it therefore as a reasonable thesis that throughout the history of Western science there has existed an untheoretical conceptual scheme, that its observational component is made up of exactly those concepts active in perceptual processing and that it can be arrived at very closely by stripping commonsense concepts of their overt and tacit theoretical commitments.[75]

2.6.6.4 The Semantical Content of Theories. I have no more informative account to offer of the sources of semantic content for theoretical terms than that with which I concluded the previous Section.

It does seem to me however that, bearing in mind the information-processing model of conceptual activity, the imaginative roles of what we call association of ideas, analogy, and very probably many transitions for which we presently have no useful name, should not be underestimated in their contribution to a conceptual and, derivatively, a linguistic, framework because of a precommitment to some 'origins' doctrines of meaning where every concept has to be built up logically from some privileged class of initial concepts.[76]

2.6.6.5 Why Realist? Recapitulation. The reader will recognize the foregoing account as a form of mild-radical quasi-empiricist account of the observation language, with perhaps a more liberal view of the possible sources of semantic content for theoretical terms.[77] The compatibility of this view with Realism I have already argued. I simply remind the reader that to this position must be added the epistemology and structural view of science of earlier sections.

2.7 A REALIST ALTERNATIVE REJECTED: THE LEVELS HYPOTHESIS

In a recent, important book J. C. Graves (1971) has defended a form of Scientific Realism which I shall call the levels hypothesis. I shall endeavour to explain the view and then give my reasons for rejecting it as a serious alternative open to the Realist.[78]

Despite Graves' rejection of Empiricism, and that of the epistemological tradition in which it stands, the notion of a *level* for Graves is first an epistemic one: Graves introduces cognitive levels (p. 17), only later do we slip into ontological levels. The reason for this priority seems to be that Graves thinks of levels as tied to theories and theories, Graves reminds us, are obviously epistemic affairs (p. 19). Actually, the closest we come to a definition is this: A level is the range of validity of a theory (p. 19). This definition no doubt accounts for Graves' willingness to countenance many different types of levels, e.g., that specified in the size hierarchy of physics, the order of evolution of complexity (whether chemo-biological or social) and so on (pp. 18–19). Intuitively, Graves seems to have in mind that a theory (or at any rate a sufficiently general one—whatever that may come to) typically either concerns a class of phenomena described in terms more or less unique to itself (cf. molecular chemistry versus cybernetics) or pretty clearly is concerned with the world only within some delimited domain (cf. quantum molecular theory vs. general relativity). Obviously there is some truth to this claim.

Before pressing on from epistemology to ontology, let us pause to consider the notion of a cognitive level. Even definitions using epistemic components may not define epistemic entities. Such is the case with Graves' definition of a level. For a Realist, the range of validity of a theory selects an objective subdivision of the world; though a theory may be epistemic *qua* constructed by man seeking knowledge, its truth conditions are non-epistemic states of affairs (though of course any description we give of them will be in the terms of some theory). Moreover, the definition is not easily understood clearly, because no theory defines its own range of validity. This is always a question of combining experience with mathematical meta-theorems (i.e., meta to the theory). But how experiments are interpreted and combined with such mathematics is itself a matter for theory, and not usually just the theory in question but others also, and even an entire world view as well.

Nonetheless, there is a certain plausibility about the notion of cognitive levels; we do seem e.g., to know about tables and their putative atomic constituents in fairly different ways, or anyway different contexts—certainly the descriptive languages are different. But taken only thus far the idea is of minimal philosophical interest, it expresses no more than a rather obvious reference point for all philosophy of science. Notoriously, nothing follows for ontology from such epistemological remarks, for a Realist. How then does Graves arrive at ontological levels?

By following the empiricist order of proceeding again: from epistemology to semantics. The different cognitive levels will in general have, as I just said, somewhat different concepts associated with them. Graves takes this to yield prima facie distinct ontologies for the various levels. Graves concedes the possibility of reduction of one ontic level to another but offers a number of arguments for believing that many levels are and must remain, ontologically distinct. So then, the levels hypothesis turns out not to be merely an innocuous superficial description of science but a serious claim concerning the structure of reality. Now we can reverse the procedure and claim the ontological levels structure as grounding the various epistemic-descriptive levels. I shall not recount here all of the advantages Graves lists for this approach, none of them are guaranteed unique to the levels view, though certainly Graves is saved a lot of work on the relations among theories that someone who believes in only one level is in for.

The alternatives which this hypothesis foists on one I find totally unacceptable in the light of experience to date. Let us assume first P: No two material objects can be in the same place at the same time, and second Q: The spatio-temporal world structure consists of a single four-dimensional spatio-temporal manifold. Now consider any two ontic levels which Graves believes distinct, e.g., the common sense level and the atomic level. Suppose we consider a table T and the corresponding collection of atoms t_i ($i = 1,..., \sim 10^{24}$). Let the table occupy the volume V at time t and the atoms respectively the volumes V_i at time t. Now if the table T is ontologically distinct from the *structured* collection of atoms T', then either P is false, or Q is false or R is false, where R is: Position measurements indicated that $V_i \subset V$, most i. On the assumption that R is an experimental truth—no one to my knowledge doubts that the structured collection of atoms is located where the table is located (actually, all I need is the weaker $\exists\, V_i : V_i \subset V$, which takes care of 'fuzzy edge' arguments)—P or Q must be false. But I can see no reason to believe either that we live in a world with multiple spaces of which we are all somehow simultaneously conscious, or that two distinct objects can occupy the same place-time.[79]

Graves in fact offers three arguments for the claim that, irrespective of the consequences, levels must be considered ontologically distinct.[80] None of these arguments withstands examination.[81]

I can therefore see nothing to recommend Graves' position. It would appear that he is a victim of precisely that order of priorities adopted by Empiricism, which he criticized so sharply. (How few confessed anti-empiricists truly escape empiricist assumptions!—A caution to the reader of this chapter.) The goal of Realism is nothing less than the construction of the true model of reality, a unified account of the world, including its reasoning inhabitants. Graves' pluralism of levels—cognitive, linguistic and ontological—destroys that unity and the motive to seek it.

2.8 Methodology

The three revolutions (Section 2.1) are reflected also in methodology. Methodology I take to be a branch of pragmatics, roughly it asks and answers the question "Given the existing circumstances, which strategy best furthers the development of knowledge?"

Empiricism construed 'the existing circumstances' narrowly to include just the known facts and theories preceding the time in question (and it construed 'knowledge' equally narrowly to mean a collection of propositions formulated in the favorite formal manner).[82] Feyerabend and Hanson especially have attacked this methodology vigorously.[83] Though neither of these writers seems to have explicitly formulated the full-blown alternative to the empiricist program adumbrated above both instinctively attacked the empiricist's *science* and attempted to replace it with a rational account oriented towards *scientists*. In this context the full force of methodology as providing a *strategy* for increasing knowledge is evident—each scientist faces the full culture of his time and must act in the light of all the likely repercussions of any given action. Feyerabend has illustrated this point brilliantly in his study of Galileo (and he was making points primarily about *epistemic* strategy, not simply about Galileo's personality, though we must begin back there for a full-blown explanation of the actual course of science).

The methodological conclusion to be drawn from an epistemology of ignorance, in the light of the revolutions in philosophy of science, is that a vigorous pluralism is called for. When it comes to theoretical ideas 'let the hundred flowers bloom'. The reasoning is simple enough. Since we begin in ignorance and with very limited sensory equipment, we have only our native wit to help us to an imaginative conceptual grasp of the world; experience shows that the most effective way to develop such insights is in the constant critical play of ideas against one another. Within the empiricist tradition one had such reverence for the domain of 'facts' that they were endowed with large powers, e.g., the power to point out the path of theoretical progress (if one countenanced such at all seriously), but once that myth is abandoned in recognition of the pitiful limitedness of our senses the way is open to concentrate on a use where experience can be of moderately powerful service, as a judge at the sensitive empirical meeting points of incompatible theories.

How vigorous the pluralism is depends upon other factors in one's philosophy.[84] In my own case I am at liberty to exploit the approximate sameness of the phenomenal level for all scientists, despite the possible incommensurability of the hard data claims. But in addition I believe that Feyerabend has seriously overemphasized and oversimplified the semantic disparities between general theories because of his neglect of the complex roles of models and so-called auxiliary theories. Even for our most general theories, submodels of theoretical models may coincide. More importantly, a powerful theory can model in its modelling resources the models of another theory (thereby explaining why they broke down and the degree of the failure). It will also generally be necessary that incompatible theories share a range of auxiliary theories in common.

Methodology is a branch of pragmatics for the Realist, its methods dictated (in part) by semantics and epistemology; it is not necessary here that I go into great detail. My own view is that every case of the clash of theories needs detailed analysis as to the semantics of the two theories, the range of models constructible and the relations between hard data reports and phenomenal experience before any verdict can be given as to the precise locus of the clash—so far as I can see, every (important) case differs in philosophically important respects.

2.9 EPISTEMOLOGY (III): THE HISTORY OF SCIENCE

With respect to the history of science we are faced with two extremes. On the one side is the empiricist's account where we have an ever-accumulating pile of facts with theories representing increasingly good organizations of them. Theories then supercede one another according to the objective criterion of adequacy to organize the data, they are mutually compatible where they overlap, indeed earlier theories are just for this reason reducible to special cases of their successors. The history of science presents a superbly rational front. At the other extreme alternative theories determine their own semantic content and that of the observation language and the domain of theory-neutral facts is entirely destroyed. In this case we cut ourselves off from any rational account of the history of science as a continuous process. For then a change of scientific theory becomes a fundamental semantical shift of the entire vocabulary, it is therefore impossible to meaningfully compare theories, and therefore impossible to give any rational account of progress from one theory to another. Both extremes are unacceptable.[85]

Ultimately, what account we offer of the history of science must depend upon the account we offer of human beings. Both extreme views, in their several ways, simply bring their *a priori* assumptions concerning rationality and epistemology (especially observation) to bear upon history forcing it into the necessary mold.[86] Let me now elaborate briefly the sources of continuity in the history of science which I have still allowed myself, though we can expect the account to be elaborated and probably modified as more information becomes available.

First of all there is the existence of an essentially untheoretical observational level which provides for a source of common experience to the scientists of an entire culture and therefore for the scientific tradition throughout an entire culture (e.g., that of Western man during the last 2500 years). Since each theory must confront such elementary observational experience, however tenuous this connection be, each theory can be compared in point of its success in this regard. As we have seen, however, such comparisons will not bear great weight in the decision among theories because of the necessity of the transposition of such experience into a form suitable for direct confrontation with the theory in question.[87]

Second, and at the opposite end of the scale, as it were, I have suggested that there are broad metaphysical conceptions of the world, and correlative to them broad conceptual descriptive schemes for the world, which have been carried essentially unchanged through the entire history of science. These very general conceptions of the world therefore also represent an element of continuity in the scientific process.[88] Intimately connected with such broad descriptive schemes lie certain broad mathematical structures which also run continuously through the history of science.[89]

Within this limited continuity provided at the extreme ends of the scientific structure, however, I believe we must admit that wholistic changes in scientific theories have occurred through imaginative 'leaps' on the part of individual scientists which can be followed only at the individual level and probably cannot be given a rational reconstruction within *Science*. My general conclusion is that the history of science is one of continuous creation under the careful constraints of a rationally reconstructable continuity.

Finally I raise the question of whether these culture-wide aspects of science cannot themselves in some way be opened to critical examination. I suggest the view that ultimately both of these aspects are open to the same kind of critical reappraisal as are any other elements in the structure of science—it is just that the reappraisal time is so much longer than for other elements and the reappraisal process so much more complex and difficult to realize.

In respect of the perceptual level it is difficult to imagine that our perceptual organization would have even this much flexibility, precisely because it is so clearly determined in large measure by our neurological make-up, and we have reason to believe that this was acquired only after millennia of evolutionary experience. Nevertheless, there is reason to believe that this neurological make-up has some degree of flexibility built into it (cf. Hooker 1973a) and one cannot help but at least consider it possible that over the course of a much longer period of time (perhaps millennia) the conditions under which man operated, cultural and perhaps also neurological, could so change as to alter his fundamental perceptual organization, i.e., to alter the concepts active in perception and/or the manner in which they function together. Indeed there is talk of an 'evolutionary epistemology' (Campbell 1959, 1973), if so it will be a naturalistic epistemology, one whose course is critically understood within science.

POSTSCRIPT

The reader will recognize that it is not possible to do more here than provide a sketch of many of the aspects of a systematic Realist position—in particular, this is true of an account of scientific discovery and scientific change, reduction and the unity of the sciences, the nature of values and their roles in the sciences and the relations between the pursuit of science and cultural activities generally. For the same reason the notes often contain more substantive material than their conventional role would justify. Even so, the space this essay occupies is substantial and I wish to express my gratitude for the generosity of Prof. Jaakko Hintikka and *Synthese*.

CHAPTER 3

Philosophy and Meta-Philosophy of Science: Empiricism, Popperianism and Realism

INTRODUCTION

In Chapter 2, I introduced and argued for the view that philosophies of science going by the usual labels (eg., empiricism, conventionalism, realism) had in fact to be construed as offering complete, systematic world views if the arguments between them were to be perceptively understood and intelligently evaluated. (For example, I remarked that the realist position in philosophy of science might centrally be construed as a semantical thesis concerning the semantical status of theoretical terms and yet the arguments against the position found in the literature and stemming largely from the empiricist and conventionalist positions are almost all of them based on epistemological and/or psychological assumptions; the relevance of the latter two to the former cannot be understood except by placing the arguments in the larger context of a systematic world view.)

In this chapter I want to sharpen the statement of that thesis a little by explicitly introducing meta-philosophy and by offering schematized characterizations of both the philosophy and meta-philosophy of the major empiricist positions and of my own realist doctrine. (The major empiricist positions I take to be early positivism, mainstream (Carnapian) empiricism and Popperianism.)

The meta-philosophy of a philosophy of science is the place where the peculiar character of the world view associated with that philosophy of science becomes most clearly evident. Hence if we are to gain any perceptive insight into the real sources of divergence between the major philosophies of science, and also if we are to be able to assess the degree of similarity among what I have described as the major variants of empiricism, we must be able to obtain some grasp of the accompanying meta-philosophies.

Correspondingly, if we are properly to understand and evaluate the arguments launched by the one position against the other we shall have to have a grasp of the corresponding meta-philosophies for, it turns out, most of the important arguments (e.g., all of those which I consider in Chapter 2) hinge crucially on features of the meta-philosophy of the position from which they stem whereas adequate responses to them hinge crucially on the corresponding meta-philosophy of the opposing position.

(I might add that, in the light of these claims, supposing the subsequent text to bear them out, I am increasingly surprised that there is not considerably more explicit discussion of meta-philosophy in the literature. In my reading of the standard literature I have yet to come across a single article which states the relevant meta-philosophy explicitly, though in every article it is there lurking behind every paragraph; one is left, however, to dig it out by hint, innuendo and tacit implication.)

The reader is warned in advance that what follows are only brief, *schematic* presentations of the philosophies in question. The historical truth is that there has been a bewildering variety of individually idiosyncratic variations even among those who would generally be held to fall centrally under the labels empiricism and realism. Nonetheless, for the purposes of my argumentation, if I can succeed in abstracting a roughly common core to these positions then I shall have a sufficient basis for accomplishing my programmatic objectives. Thereafter, particular positions of particular philosophers would have to be fleshed out on this schematic skeleton.

3.1 VARIANTS OF EMPIRICISM SCHEMATICALLY PRESENTED

3.1.1 Philosophy of Positivism (Logical Empiricism)

Positivism is understood as a severe or austere empiricism with which we associate rejection of all cognitive claims except those empirically based in the positivist-empiricist sense. It would be natural to present this doctrine beginning with its epistemology since this latter is pretty clearly the motivating core for the choice of other doctrines; however, I shall present its philosophy in a somewhat different order in order to briefly develop the relations among the component doctrines.

First I shall be concerned with positivist *philosophy* of science, then I shall turn to positivist *meta-philosophy* of science.

3.1.1.1 Theory of Rationality. This may be summarized in two doctrines. (D_1) The epistemic goal of a rational man is the acquisition of knowledge which latter is to be understood as certain truth. (D_2) Rationally acceptable argument is restricted to the domain of deductive logic. (Note: since it will turn out that there is no cognitively significant positivist ethics, aesthetics, religion, etc. there is in fact no need to cover myself by claiming that I here offer only a fragment of the theory of rationality, the fragment restricted to that pertaining to science.)

3.1.1.2 Philosophy of Language (I): Semantics. Positivist doctrines of semantics may be presented thus: (D_3) Every cognitively meaningful sentence is a finite truth function (plus predication) of cognitively meaningful descriptive terms. (D_4) Every cognitively meaningful descriptive term may be logically analyzed as (is logically equivalent to) a finite truth function of immediately given (ostensively defined) descriptive terms, where an immediately given descriptive term is one whose meaning and reference are acquired directly in sensory experience. (D_5) The cognitively meaningful empirical language comprises the class of cognitively meaningful sentences together with logical theory (restricted to the theory of truth functions).

Notice that this characterization of the positivist language already is capable of yielding the characteristic sharp distinction between analytic and synthetic sentences, the analytic sentences being those which are capable of being transformed, upon allowable substitutions, into the forms of truth functional tautologies. Notice that it also follows that every cognitively meaningful sentence of the empiricist language can be ultimately transformed, via allowable substitutions, into a finite truth function of sentences each of which contains only a finite number of immediately given (ostensively defined) terms.

3.1.1.3 Epistemology. (D_6) All analytical knowledge is *a priori* and not empirically significant. (D_7) All cognitively meaningful knowledge is empirical knowledge and ultimately founded upon direct knowledge grounded in sensory experience. (D_8) Direct knowledge grounded in sensory experience comprises the class of logically simple sentences issued as immediate serious reports of sensory experience; each such sentence is indubitably (or certainly) true.

The way in which the doctrines of rationality and semantics prepare the ground for the support of the central doctrines of epistemology should now be clear. The semantics provide first of all the necessary analytic/synthetic distinction which is at the basis of the doctrine D_6.

Secondly, the possibility of 'founding' all of empirical knowledge on sensory experience is provided for through the analysis of terms (and so sentences) into finite truth functions of the simple sensory experience terms. In fact, if we now combine doctrine D_3 with doctrines D_7 and D_8 we obtain the conclusion that the scope of empirical knowledge is the class of all finite truth functions of reports of immediate sensory experience. It follows immediately that, for every empirical claim, the truth conditions for the claim coincide with the epistemic conditions of acceptance for that claim, and both lie in the realm of simple observation. From which it follows immediately that the truth value of every empirically meaningful sentence is knowable in a finite number of steps. Finally, it is now clear (i) why we are able to restrict ourselves to deductively valid arguments, for from Pa, Qb (assuming them for the moment to be sensory experience reports) the truth functions $Pa{\cdot}Qb$, $Pa{\vee}Qb$ follow validly and hence we can obtain all the remaining interesting truth functions also, and (ii) how it is that this whole schema is aimed at the acquisition of certain truth.

The epistemological doctrines have been somewhat awkwardly worded, using the epistemologically and psychologically vague phrase 'report of sensory experience'. I have done this deliberately because of the dispute which has raged among proponents of these foundational epistemologies as to whether the ultimate referents of such reports are mentalistic items (eg., phenomenalistic sense data) or are special logically simple components of a neutral monist ontology or even simple features of an external macroscopic world. From the point of view of my argument in this chapter it is not crucially important which of these alternatives is chosen, though it should become clear in the sequel that I do not believe that the third position can be made consistent in any deep sense with the positivist doctrines (and possibly not the second position either). In any event in what follows I propose to use the vague term 'observation report' (or 'observation sentence') to characterize the class of sentences and to leave the question of their ultimate referents open. Nonetheless, a completed account of positivism would include a doctrine settling this issue.

Equally, positivism denied that simple sensory experience disclosed any aspects of the world beyond those dealt with in the physical sciences. (In the pragmatist tradition Dewey was prepared to include moral and other aspects in the directly experienced in such a way as to be in the scope of the cognitively meaningful, and before him Reid vis-à-vis Hume.) This doctrine too needs to be added to complete the positivist account.

Thus we add, for the 'severest' form of the doctrine:

(D_9) The ultimate referents of sensory experience reports are mentalistic contents of the experiencing mind.

(D_{10}) Simple sensory experience discloses no features of the world than those that fall in principle under a unified physical science.

3.1.1.4 Theory of Science. Aim: The aim of science is the maximization of the class of certain empirical truths (empirical knowledge). *Demarcation:* The sentences of empirical science are all and only those of the language characterized in D_3 above. *Scientific Language:* The language of D_3 above. Call this language L. *Scientific Theory:* A deductively axiomatized class of sentences in L. *Scientific Data:* The class of logically simple sensory experience reports in L. *Criteria of Scientific Acceptability:* Truth of theory; a theory is true if and only if the scientific data entail the theory. *Methodology:* Maximize scientific data, accept all true theories that result. *History of Science:* Continuous expansion of scientific data, acceptance of progressively more general and successively inclusive theories.

The emphasis on deductive logic as the principle constructional tool (see also the meta-philosophy below) certainly makes the alternative lable *Logical Empiricism* apt, but I have chosen to use *Positivism* in order to distinguish the use of logic clearly from that arising in *Empiricism* (see below).

The foregoing is a very brief sketch of the positivist reconstruction of science. One or two further points are worth noting. The characterization of methodology is determined on the one side by the theory of rationality and on the other side by the theory of science (itself determined by the semantics and epistemology): methodology is simply the maximally efficient pursuit of the aims of science within whatever other constraints are imposed. (This characterization will hold good of all philosophies of science.) It turns out that for positivism what I have elsewhere, Hooker 1972b, called retrospective methodology (that is the criteria of justifying a scientific theory in the light of the evidence) coincides with prospective methodology (i.e., the criterion of which theory is to be introduced and pursued next). Notice that on this account of science there is, in effect, no interesting structure to science, for whilst a scientific theory is a deductively axiomatizable set of sentences in L we learn from D_6 and D_7 that every such sentence in L can be replaced by a finite truth function of simple observation sentences and so every theory is reducible without remainder to what would ordinarily be called the level of simple observation. This leads immediately to a Humean account of laws in its severest form: there are no law statements admissable in the scientific language L, only collections of simple observational sentences; that they form regular sequences is statable only in a meta-language (cf. Section 3 below). Correspondingly, there are no inductive inferences of any sort (cf. D_2) and the theory of explanation is trivialized to subsumption under Humean regularity.

It is clear, though most positivists do not discuss it explicitly, that motivating these positivist doctrines and, correspondingly, supporting them, is a positivist model of man. The origins of positivist psychology can be traced back fairly explicitly at least to John Locke and his doctrine that all ideas (conceptions) originated in either sensation or reflection. Thus we shall add:

3.1.1.5 Psychological theory of man. (D_{11}) Man is a sensory experience reception chamber plus deductive logic machine. The function of the sensory experience reception chamber is to receive the empirical world one logically simple unit at a time and to transcribe the conceptual content of that unit into the memory. The function of the logic machine is to create all possible truth functions from such unit memories, to define new terms in terms of truth functions of the old and so build up theories etc. We now endow this unit collection and truth-function-forming machine with the goal of maximizing knowledge (certain truths) and set it running, the result is science.

The result is also language, and it is at this point that we could go on to elaborate the remainder of a positivist theory of language. In the following, I shall attempt only a fragment of this task.

3.1.1.6 Theory of Language (II): Origin, Scope and Significance. (D_{12}) Every empirically significant concept is derived directly from specific sensory experiences. (D_{13}) The remainder of language comprises two disjoint components, the logical and the social-emotive; the logical framework for a language is a conventional construct of the human mind, devoid of empirical content—it may be chosen arbitrarily but in general questions of convenience of expression will decide the choice; the social-emotive component of language consists of pseudo terms and pseudo sentences (i.e., recognisable linguistic units which behave as if they had the syntactical, perhaps even semantical, properties of terms and sentences) which serve to arouse emotion, threaten, cajole, etc., but which are also devoid of empirical content. It follows from all of this that human beings acquire the empirically significant component of language through increasing sensory experience and the operation of the logic-machine mind upon the resulting imprinted concepts and acquire the socio-emotive component through the non-rational (Skinnerian?) process of socialization in the human community. It further follows that positivists offer no cognitive content to ethics, aesthetics, religion, metaphysics, or indeed to philosophy itself (ultimately, philosophy becomes linguistic therapy).

The literature on positivism is immense and the reader must be left to consult it for himself in order to decide whether I have painted an even roughly accurate picture I include in the bibliography a sample selection of useful works (Achinstein/Barker 1969; Aune 1970; Ayer 1940, 1946, 1959; Bergmann 1954; Bridgeman 1927, 1936; Carnap 1928, 1932; de Santillana/Zilsel 1941; Feigl 1943; Goodman 1951; Hempel 1950, 1952; Joergenson 1951; Mach 1959, 1960; Morick 1972; Neurath 1932, 1952; Neurath et al. 1970; Pap 1963; Popper 1934; Quine 1951b; Reichenbach 1938, 1951; Russell 1924a; Schlick 1938, 1949; Von Mises 1951; Weinberg 1936; Wittgenstein 1951) with which the interested reader may begin. These range all the way from the very early Wittgenstein and Carnap, which share the reductive analysis of language (Carnap also displaying the turn toward phenomenolism) to a much later essay by Carnap which still reiterates the notion of the logical framework of language as being conventional—in between there are the historically intermediate works and an increasingly rich range of commentary. (Again, I repeat my relative surprise that this burgeoning literature does not seem to contain an explicit analysis of the philosophy and meta-philosophy in the kind of schematic form in which one can obtain a clear overall picture of the position.) In perusing this literature it will become clear to the reader that no one historical figure, let alone any collection of historical figures (e.g., those original members of the Vienna Circle) instantiates exactly the foregoing doctrines. For example, neither Neurath nor Popper could accept the notion of indubitably given empirical knowledge and experience though they shared much else in common with positivism (on Popper see below), and Carnap and his followers did not long stay with the strictly positivist analysis of language, especially of theoretical terms (cf. Empiricism below), nor did even the early Reichenbach treat the problem of induction as vacuous (though at the time Schlick and others were treating laws as empirically vacuous heuristic guides), and so one could go on and on; nonetheless, as I said before (defensively), it is worthwhile to single out an artificially sharpened position in order that one can more clearly understand its variants and its major opponents. I shall now turn forthwith to meta-philosophy.

3.1.2 Meta-Philosophy of Positivism (Logical Empiricism)

I can only offer a tentative statement of meta-philosophy for positivism. Since positivists, in common with the remainder of philosophers, don't explicitly state their meta-philosophy one can only ask 'what meta-philosophical principles must they defend in order to defend effectively their philosophical doctrines?'. The six doctrines now to be presented constitute my tentative answer to this question.

(M_1) There exists a First Philosophy which includes theories of epistemology, rationality and language. A First Philosophy is logically and epistemologically prior to, and hence normative for, all other statements in the admissible structure of human knowledge and (in some appropriate sense) constitutes a necessary framework for the expression of the content of human knowledge.

(M_2) All acceptable sentences, whether philosophical or empirical, are expressible in a language $\bar{L}$, where $\bar{L}$ is a logically and semantically clear and precise language. Theories of epistemology, rationality, semantics and of science itself are to be characterized in terms of logical structures in $\bar{L}$.

(M_3) The theory of epistemology is the analysis of the foundations of human knowledge; an epistemological foundation is adequate if and only if it provides grounds for epistemic certainty. In the construction of epistemology it may be assumed that the mind is epistemically transparent to introspection.

(M_4) The scope of the theory of rationality is confined within the domain of the empirically meaningful; that part of the theory of rationality pertaining to the pursuit of truth is logically independent of any other component of the theory (if any).

(M_5) The doctrines of philosophy and meta-philosophy must be logically consistent; hence it follows in particular that both sets of doctrines are conventions, devoid of empirical content, which in some sense constitute successive logical frameworks for the construction of empirical knowledge.

It follows that

(M_6) First Philosophy (and of course meta-philosophy) is logically and epistemologically prior to, independent of, and normative for theory of science.

The philosophy and meta-philosophy together form an intricately interlocking unity. For example, if one adopts the positivist conception of man (D_{11}) there is no choice but to construe philosophical theory as purely logical construction (M_2), thence consigning logic to the conventionally chosen (D_{13}) consigns philosophy to the empirical-ly vacuous (M_5) and vice versa in each case. One could go on pointing out interrelationships of this sort for a long time—it is what gives confidence in the statement of the meta-philosophy. More precisely:

I would defend the choice of these meta-philosophical doctrines by arguing that (a) they offer a view of the nature of philosophizing which indeed leads to positivist philosophical doctrines, (b) they offer a view of the nature of philosophizing which is itself a natural exten-sion of the positivist world view (as presented in the philosophy), (c) for these reasons they seem the natural (and essentially only) doc-trines that positivists would fall back upon when required to defend their philosophical doctrines.

The reader can best judge this latter for himself by considering typical attacks on positivist doctrines and the ways in which positiv-ists might most consistently and powerfully respond to them. (E.g. [1] Suppose it is argued that positivist theory of science offers a hopeless-ly inaccurate reconstruction of the actual beliefs and activities of scien-tists, what is the positivist to say? One strategy, of course, is to argue that the appearance of inadequacy is only appearance and that there is a plausible re-presentation of scientist's beliefs and activities which shows them to be positivists—this strikes me as the heroic, not to mention downright foolish, course. The more appropriate course is simply to reject the implicit *meta-philosophical* judgement that philo-sophical doctrines which do not use adequate reconstruction of the actual behaviour and beliefs of people, scientists included, are on that ground to be rejected—to reject this latter doctrine and simply to argue that First Philosophy is prior to and normative for theory of science and that the facts presented simply serve to show that scien-tists have a misconception of the nature of their own discipline. E.g. [2] What is the positivist to make of the argument that we surely do not have any access at any time to indubitably certain knowledge based on experience, that human experience is really much more complex, both biologically and epistemologically, than the positivist doctrine acknowledges? Again, there is the heroic course of attempt-ing to show that contemporary biological and psychological doctrines can be reconciled with a positivist epistemology and theory of man. But the more consistent positivist position, and the more powerful one, seems to me to be this: to argue that having a view on these matters at all necessarily presupposes having a clear conception of the nature of human language and knowledge within which to state these views and that the only such clear conception is the positivist one;

moreover, that the unconditionally given aim of epistemology is the analysis of the foundations of human knowledge and that anyone who attempts to introduce biological and psychological consider-ations at this point is simply confused about the priority relations between theory of epistemology and the theory of biology and psy-chology, for the latter are ultimately to be constructed through the theory of science which itself emerges from philosophical doctrines of epistemology, language and man. The strategy of this second exam-ple, like the first, requires a number of meta-philosophical doctrines to justify it and indeed these two examples provide what seem to me to be the general kind of strategy which a positivist will always em-ploy under attack, namely to appeal ultimately to his meta-philo-sophical principles for the construction of an adequate philosophy in order to justify the adoption of his philosophy and the adoption of it prior to the construction of the theory of science and, hence, prior to offering an account [a reconstruction] of actual human beliefs, experi-ence and behaviour. *In this way, meta-philosophy enters essentially into the structure of every adequate defense of a philosophical position.*)

3.1.3 Philosophy of Empiricism

The development of core, twentieth-century empiricism out of posi-tivism can be conveniently followed in Carnap's historical develop-ment from his early shift from a phenomenalistic to a physicalistic language (1928, 1934), the successive weakening of the strict positivist criterion of verifiability (1936-7, 1962) and the increasing liberalism of the criteria for the admission of empirically meaningful terms, culmi-nating in his 1956a. Carnap was not alone of course, ever since the early thirties the field of scholars has been expanding and the relevant literature expanding nearly exponentially (the bibliography contains a smattering of key items, e.g., Achinstein/Barker 1969; Aune 1967, 1970; Ayer 1940; Bunge 1964; Campbell 1957; Capek 1961; de Santilla/ Zilsel 1941; Feigl/Brodbeck 1953; Frank 1957; Hempel 1952, 1965; Hooker 1972a; Joergenson 1951; Margenau 1950; Maxwell 1962, 1970; Morick 1972; Nagel 1961; Neurath et al. 1970; Pap 1963; Popper 1934; Quine 1953; Radnitsky 1970; Reichenbach 1938, 1951; Russell 1927; Schilpp 1963, 1973; Schlick 1949; Sellars 1963; Suppe 1974a) until to-day the variations on this general theme overlap with realism to the extent that it is very difficult to untangle systematic positions. (In-deed, one suspects that most writers on philosophy of science do not have such a position and write from the tacit presupposition of a miscellaneous collection of fragments from various positions.) I describe the position as *core* empiricism because it revolves around essentially the same epistemological doctrine, *but more especially because it retains essentially the same meta-philosophy.* The statement of its philosophy will appear then as a modified positivism.

3.1.3.1 Theory of Rationality. This may be summarized in two doctrines (D'_1) The goal of a rational man is the acquisition of knowledge, which latter is to be understood as (something like) justified true belief. (D'_2) Rationally acceptable argument is restricted to the domain of generalized logic.

(By *generalized* logic I mean to refer to the intuitively recognizable class of formal systems of reasoning which are like formal deductive logic in that the class of acceptable argument forms can be stated precisely, the relations between the argument forms and truth, probability, etc. can also be stated precisely and so on. While historically and *vis-à-vis* positivism the primary additions to the theory of truth functions is the introduction of the first order predicate calculus and systems of what are called inductive logic, these days we consider also N-order predicate calculi, various forms of modal logics, many-valued logics and there is, so far as I am aware, none but an intuitive way to describe the class of all such potentially admissible systems. I propose to include all such purely logical extensions of the scope of admissible reasoning under the heading of empiricism.)

It will turn out that so long as a doctrine of the sort D_{10} for positivism is also retained here there will be no other component to the theory of rationality than that stated above.

3.1.3.2 Philosophy of Language (I): Semantics. (D'_3) Every cognitively meaningful sentence is a generalized logical function of the class of observationally basic sentences. (D'_4) Every observationally basic sentence is a sentence of the positivist language L, as described in doctrines D_3 and D_4. (D'_5) The cognitively meaningful empirical language comprises the class of cognitively meaningful sentences together with generalized logical theory. (By a generalized logical function I obviously mean an admissible function in generalized logical theory, in just the way that a truth function is an admissible function in the propositional calculus.)

Equivalently, we may construe these doctrines in the following form: (D''_3) Every cognitively meaningful sentence is a well-formed formula in some generalized logical calculus such that each nonlogical term is empirically admissible; (D''_4) A non-logical term is empirically admissible if and only if it can be reduced to some generalized logical function of positivistically admissible terms—where a term is positivistically admissible if and only if it occurs in the positivist language *L*.)

Notice that in these generalized formal languages we may hope to retain the analytic synthetic distinction but the positivist goal of restricting cognitively meaningful sentences to finite truth functions of sentences containing only finite numbers of immediately given terms has been abandoned. The question is: what exactly are the consequences of this logical liberalization?

3.1.3.3 Epistemology. (*D'₆*) All analytical knowledge is *a priori* and not empirically significant. (*D'₇*) All cognitively significant knowledge is empirical knowledge and ultimately founded upon direct knowledge grounded in sensory experience. (*D'₈*) Direct knowledge grounded in sensory experience comprises the class of logically simple sentences issued as immediate serious reports of sensory experience; each such sentence is indubitably (most certainly) true.

As for positivism, the doctrines of rationality and semantics prepare the ground for the support of the central doctrines of epistemology. Here, however, the notion of the 'founding' of empirical knowledge on sensory experience is to be analyzed not in terms of reduction to finite truth functions but in terms of reduction to a preferred class of generalized logical functions (whatever they are chosen to be). But now the coincidence between truth conditions, epistemic conditions of acceptance and observationally accessible conditions, which held for positivism, must be given up. The 'problem of induction' is the problem of specifying the class of preferred functions.

As for positivism, there is the possibility of choosing to replace the vague phrase 'report of sensory experience' with something more precise ranging from a thoroughly phenomenolistic doctrine to one referring to a simple macroscopic physical world. Whereas the positivist had almost no logical machinery available to ascend from his solipsistic trap to the intersubjective world the empiricist has (in principle) all the possible kinds of logical machinery available to do this and so can make his attempt correspondingly more plausible, see e.g., Goodman 1951 for some beginnings. (In this context Sellars' objection against phenomenalism that it cannot reconstruct an intelligent notion of physical possibility and of natural law would surely fail as would many similar objections really based on the simple inaccessibility of a sufficiently rich logical machinery. For all that, I do not think that this liberal form of empiricism is ultimately convincing *in its own terms,* let alone in terms of its overall world view.)

On the other hand, empiricists certainly still seem committed to the view that simple sensory experience discloses only physical features of the world.

Hence, for comparison with austere positivism, we add the following two doctrines:

(D'_9) The ultimate reference of sensory experience reports are mentalistic contents of the experiencing mind.

(D'_{10}) Simple sensory experience discloses no features of the world than those that fall in principle under a unified physical science.

3.1.3.4 Theory of Science. Aim: The aim of science is the maximization of empirical knowledge, i.e., of maximally justified true belief. *Demarcation:* The sentences of empirical science are all and only those of the language characterized in (D'_3) above. *Scientific language:* The language of (D'_3) above. Call this language L'. *Scientific Theory:* A deductively axiomatized class of sentences in L'. *Scientific Data:* The class of basic sentences in L'. *Criteria of Scientific Acceptability:* Adequate evidential support (as specified in the generalized logical theory). *Methodology:* Maximize scientific data, accept all theories that are adequately evidentially supported by the data. *History of Science:* Continuous expansion of scientific data, acceptance of progressively more general and successively inclusive theories.

By comparison with positivism one of the gains for empiricism is a much more interesting account of the structure of science. For the richer logical machinery will permit us to introduce empirically meaningful terms and empirically meaningful sentences which are not respectively reducible to or replaceable by, *salva veritate*, any truth functions respectively of the immediately given terms or of the basic sentences. Moreover, the resulting structure of science which is offered has the characteristic dichotomy between observational terms and theoretical terms which has been one of the dominating features of empiricism. And it is well known that in terms of this traditional empiricist structure for science (see e.g., N. Campbell 1957; Carnap 1956a; Hempel 1965, 1966; Nagel 1961; Pap 1963) interesting theories of laws, explanation and induction can be offered. This gain in structural richness for the account of science is the chief motivation for liberalizing the positivist restrictions on logical machinery. On the other hand, prospective and retrospective methodology once again coincide. In fact, it should have become generally apparent that the doctrines of empiricism as I have presented them are essentially identical with those of positivism except for the matter of a liberalized logical machinery.

It will follow therefore that the empiricist is motivated by an essentially similar conception of man as is the positivist. Hence we add:

3.1.3.5 Psychological Theory of Man.

(D'11) Man is a sensory experience reception chamber together with a generalized logic machine. The description of man's functioning is essentially the same as it is for positivism.

The result of turning the sensory receiver/logic machine loose is also a development of language and so we have, in parallel with positivism:

3.1.3.6 Theory of Language (II): Origin, Scope and Significance.

(D'12) Every empirically significant concept is derived directly from specific sensory experiences. (D'13) The remainder of language comprises two disjoint components, the logical and the social-emotive; the logical framework for a language is a conventional construct of the human mind, devoid of empirical content—it may be chosen arbitrarily but in general questions of convenience of expression will decide the choice; the social-emotive component of language consists of quasi-terms and quasi-sentences which serve to arouse emotion, threaten, cajole, etc., but which are also devoid of empirical content.

It follows from all of this that human beings acquire the empirically significant component of language through increased sensory experience and the operation of the generalized logic machine upon the resulting imprinted concepts and acquire the socio-emotive component through the non-rational process of socialization in the human community. It further follows then that empiricists, like positivists, offer no cognitive content to ethics, aesthetics, religion, metaphysics, or indeed to philosophy itself (and once again philosophy ultimately becomes linguistic therapy—people must simply be brought to see how to think in a clear and coherent fashion).

The literature on empiricism is even more immense than that on its more austere subcategory (positivism) and once again the reader must be left to consult it for himself in order to decide whether I have painted an even roughly accurate picture (see citations above). Once again I remind the reader that specific historical figures may only be concerned with one or two doctrines of empiricism, may hold some of its doctrines in combination with fragments of substantially different systematic philosophies and in general may not be concerned about systematic philosophy at all. I leave the reader to construct his own variants of empiricism.

3.1.4 Meta-Philosophy of Empiricism

As for positivism, I can only offer a tentative statement of meta-philosophy for empiricism since by and large the doctrines are not explicitly discussed as such. But it will be already clear to the reader that since I have presented empiricism as essentially a version of positivism with a liberalized conception of logical apparatus, the meta-philosophy will remain substantially unaltered. (For example, it is clear that empiricists also work thoroughly within the tradition representing philosophical doctrines in clarified form through the medium of logical structures just as positivists do.) Thus I propose the following doctrines:

(M'_1) There exists a First Philosophy which includes theories of epistemology, rationality and language. A First Philosophy is logically and epistemologically prior to, and hence normative for, all other statements in the admissible structure of human knowledge and (in some appropriate sense) constitutes a necessary framework for the expression of the content of human knowledge.

(M'_2) All acceptable sentences, whether philosophical or empirical, are expressible in a language $\bar{L}'$, where $\bar{L}'$ is a logically and semantically clear and precise language. Theories of epistemology, rationality, semantics and of science itself are to be characterized in terms of logical structures in $\bar{L}'$.

(M'_3) The theory of epistemology is the analysis of the foundations of human knowledge; an epistemological foundation is adequate if and only if it provides grounds for epistemic certainty. In the construction of epistemology it may be assumed that the mind is epistemically transparent to introspection.

(M'_4) The scope of the theory of rationality is confined within the domain of the empirically meaningful; that part of the theory of rationality pertaining to the pursuit of truth is logically independent of any other component of the theory (if any).

It follows that

(M'_6) First Philosophy (and of course meta-philosophy) is logically and epistemologically prior to, independent of, and normative for theory of science.

I would defend the choice of these meta-philosophical doctrines by arguing that (a) they offer a view of the nature of philosophizing which indeed leads to empiricist philosophical doctrines, (b) they offer a view of the nature of philosophizing which is itself a natural extension of the empiricist world view (as presented in the philosophy), (c) for these reasons they seem the natural (and essentially only) doctrines that empiricists would fall back upon when required to defend their philosophical doctrines. Indeed, I would argue that the strategy of empiricist defense against criticism (and the same kinds of criticisms as are levelled against positivism at that) will be exactly the same as it is for the positivist.

It will not have escaped the reader's attention that a doctrine corresponding to the positivist meta-philosophical doctrine M_5 is missing in the above. In my view, the strictly consistent corresponding doctrine is that of M_5 once again, hence I shall here add:

(M'_5) The doctrines of philosophy and meta-philosophy must be logically consistent; hence it follows in particular that both sets of doctrines are conventions devoid of empirical content, they in some sense constitute successive logical frameworks for the construction of empirical knowledge.

An alternative doctrine might be substituted, one Kantian in flavour and currently 'in the air', which might be formulated roughly as follows:

(M'_5*) The doctrines of philosophy and meta-philosophy are necessarily universally descriptive of intellectual structure.

The idea behind (M'_5*) is that one may certainly build up one's conceptual structure in the empiricist fashion indicated but that, upon reflection, we come to see that for creatures of our construction there is necessarily no alternative but to think according to the foregoing principles if we are to think clearly at all. It is Carnap with his conventionalist views of the choice of language frame which inspired (M'_5) while it is Kant (and Kohlberg 1971, 1973a) and others that suggest (M'_5*). I leave a discussion of (M'_5*) until a little later in the paper.

3.1.5 The Philosophy of Popperianism

Popper's early views are certainly closely tied to the roots of 20th-century empiricism, even if his views were formed as much in reaction against the more austere positivism of the Vienna Circle as they were in relation to those doctrines. Indeed, for many it may come as something of a shock to see Popper's views classed as a variant of empiricism, for he certainly held some views which were radically at variance with traditional empiricism (as presented above) and which he made very explicit were at radical variance with traditional empiricism. Nonetheless, I hope to be able to show that Popper must hold almost the entire meta-philosophy in common with empiricism and much of the philosophy besides. (One of the advantages of this kind of systematic, schematic, analysis is that one is able to achieve some perspective on the actual degree of difference among seemingly substantially different view points—e.g., it has already turned out that empiricism and positivism are not substantially different in either their philosophy or their meta-philosophy.)

It is also the case, so it seems to me, that Popper has significantly shifted his ground in the years following the publication of *Logik der Forschung*, this shift is particularly noticeable in his most recent book *Objective Knowledge*. I shall make one or two comments about the evolution of Popper's doctrines, as I see it, in what follows below but for the moment let me suggest that the reader accept the philosophy now to be offered as essentially that of the *Logik der Forschung*.

3.1.5.1 Theory of Rationality. (D''_1) The epistemic goal of a rational man is the maximatization of the depth and scope of understanding. (D''_2) Rationally acceptable argument is restricted to the domain of deductive logic.

The formulation of the objective of science as understanding in depth comes naturally to the reader of *Logic der Forschung* (*L.d.F.*) but looks increasingly to be a case of mistaking means for ends as one passes progressively through *Conjectures and Refutations* (*CR*) to *Objective Knowledge* (*OK*). In the latter work Popper explicitly commits himself, or so it seems, to the view that the primary goal of science is the pursuit of truth. Now since Popper certainly hasn't changed his mind about the methodological principles he enunciated in *L.d.F.* we are able to conclude that whatever 'pursuit of truth' might mean Popper certainly does not mean that we can ever actually attain the truth (except accidentally perhaps and then not know it if we did), nor does it entail that one should aim at the theories most likely to be true nor even that one should aim at theories which have the greatest amount of positively relevant evidence in their favour. To the contrary, Popper's methodology requires us to aim at theories which are least likely to be true and this precisely because they have the greatest content and hence lead to greatest depth in understanding. One cannot therefore say that the rational succession of theories in the Popperian view of science corresponds to a sequence of theories which are closer and closer approximations of the truth in any of these senses. At any event these theories are increasingly unlikely to be true (because they have increasing content) and although Popper did try to capture a sense of closeness to the truth with his conception of 'verisimilitude' this conception has recently been subject to a devastating attack by Miller (1974, 1975). In the light of all this I propose to retain (D'_1) as is and leave later students of Popperianism to clarify the sense, if any, in which the metaphysical idea of truth is related to the pursuit of Popperian understanding (but cf. also Section 10 below).

3.1.5.2 Philosophy of Language (1): Semantics. Like the positivist and the empiricist Popper still wishes to retain a doctrine of empirical content which is formulated in terms of a distinguished class of sentences, the basic sentences. (D''_3) Every empirically meaningful sentence has in its consequence class the negation of at least one basic statement; where a basic statement is a singly quantified existential assertion. (D''_4) The cognitively meaningful empirical language comprises the class of empirically meaningful sentences together with logical theory (restricted to deductive logic).

Popper offers no explicit doctrine of the meaning of descriptive terms. He does say two things explicitly which rule out any empiricist account of the meanings of descriptive terms. He says that all descriptive terms within the sciences have a complex semantical content, they are all 'theoretically laden'; put another way, he says that the consequence class of any sentence of empirical science, including the basic sentences, is essentially infinite. And he also says that the non-logical terms of other subject matters, such as ethics, aesthetics and religion, but also philosophy itself, are perfectly meaningful though they are not empirically meaningful in the sense which he wishes to delineate. This latter doctrine makes it implausible for him to adopt any simple empiricist account of the construction of concepts out of experience and the former doctrine backs this up by explicitly under-cutting any notion of a linear semantical hierarchy of descriptions within the sciences beginning at the simple observational level (which would presumably have been the level of basic sentences) and ascending to increasingly theoretical realms. There is therefore no semantical doctrine corresponding to (D_4) for positivism, though the Popperian philosophy of language will ultimately need one for its completeness. (This is a problem Popper shares in common with all those who reject an empiricist account of the construction of language and its solution will not be easy—cf. my discussion in 1972a and in Chapter 2 above.)

Epistemology. (D''_5) There is no given foundation for human knowledge. (D''_6) The criterion of epistemic acceptance is not inductive proximity to the truth but logical content (*qua* measure of contribution to depth and scope of understanding) modulo severity of tests applied and passed. (D''_7) The scope of empirical knowledge is confined to the sentences of the meaningful empirical language (see D''_4).

There are essentially three components to the foundationalist epistemological doctrine advocated by positivism and empiricism: (f_1) There exists an epistemologically distinguished class of sentences which form the given foundation for empirical knowledge (these are the reports of sensory experience), (f_2) every epistemologically acceptable sentence is some inductive logical function of members of the epistemically distinguished class, (f_3) membership in the epistemically distinguished class is completely and exhaustively determined by sensory experience. A thoroughgoing foundationless epistemology would deny all three doctrines and this I believe Popper does. But whereas Popper's denial of the doctrines f_1, f_2 is vehement, Popper (*L.d.F.*) would I think be inclined to accept a milder version of f_3 in which experience was the only relevant source for the selection of basic sentences though it might not determine their selection unambiguously or irrevocably.

3.1.5.3 *Theory of Science.*

Aim: The aim of science is the maximization of the scope and depth of human understanding. Demarcation: The sentences of science are all and only the falsifiable sentences as described in the semantics above. Call this language *L"*. *Scientific Language: L"*. *Scientific Theory:* A deductively axiomatized class of sentences in *L"*. *Scientific Data:* A class of basic sentences in *L"*. *Criteria of Scientific Acceptability:* Degree of logical content (qua measure of degree of falsifiability, i.e., qua measure of degree of contribution to understanding) modulo severity of tests actually applied and passed. *Methodology:* Maximize creation of theories with highest logical contents (as above), maximize severity of tests applied to these, provisionally accept those not eliminated. *History of Science:* History of the rational evolution of scientific problems qua relevant to the development of the scope and depth of scientific understanding.

Popper's philosophy of science avowedly eliminates inductive inference and hence offers no account of that procedure nor of the corresponding notions of evidential support and closeness to the truth. On the other hand Popper's semantics certainly permits him a rich reconstruction of the logical structure of scientific theories, for though it is logically more austere than that accessible to empiricism (because of its rejection of inductive logic and its restriction to strictly deductive logic) it is also not constrained by a strict observational/ theoretical distinction among scientific terms with the latter in some sense constructed out of the former and the former theoretically 'simple'. In fact Popper is able to have a two-way intercourse between the level of theory and the level of basic sentences—each level can criticise the other and eliminate member sentences from the other. (The intercourse is truly one-way in the case of positivism and empiricism.) Moreover, since all three doctrines agree on presenting science as a deductively organized hierarchy of sentences (though there is no natural 'bottom' to the Popper hierarchy and the interconnections make it look more like Quine's network model than the pyramids of positivism and empiricism) Popper clearly has open to him all of the usual kinds of accounts of laws, explanation and the like. (And in fact he has offered a rather rich theory of the nature of laws—see Popper 1934, appendix *x.)

On the other hand Popper explicitly rejects any 'psychological' elements in his philosophy as a confusion between normative and descriptive. In particular, Popper explicitly denies that there is any rational philosophical account of theory construction—so that Popper offers no prospective methodology of acceptance. Despite this point of view, I do believe that there must be a conception of man, of his nature and abilities, operating behind Popper's doctrines and I believe that it is rather like the positivist conception of man.

3.1.5.4 Psychological Theory of Man. (D''_8) Man is a sensory information reception chamber together with a deductive logic machine and a non-logical concept generator. (The concept generator is a necessary addition to the positivist conception since for Popper the empirical language is not constructed by logical manipulation on imprinted concepts—cf. the semantics—and indeed the construction of new concepts cannot be any logical process since if this were the case we assuredly should be able to work out a rational theory of theory invention, which Popper expressly denies.)

For the same reason we cannot simply say, as we could for positivism and empiricism, that language is the result of turning on the sensory receiver/logic machine. We can of course say that language is the result of turning on the sensory receiver/logic machine/concept generator but until a great deal more is said about the nature of the latter component (the concept generator) no clear theory of the origin, scope and significance of language can emerge. On the other hand, the Popper of *L.d.F.* is certainly in strong sympathy with the empiricist view that philosophy, and I think at least also ethics, has essentially the nature of a series of conventions, devoid of empirical content, in some sense useful for the guidance of the intellectual and practical life but not on an epistemic par with science. Thus while there is no doctrine corresponding to D_{12}, we may add:

3.1.5.5 Theory of Language (II): Scope, Origin, Significance. (D''_9) The remainder of meaningful language over and above L'' comprises a collection of conventions, devoid of empirical content and empirical significance, but whose adoption is presupposed by the achievement of an intellectually clear and coherent life.

Popperianism as I have presented it shows two substantial deviations from empiricism and positivism, these are set in a context which is otherwise very close to the empiricist-positivist position. The first deviation is the replacement, essentially, of verificationism with falsificationism. Viewed systematically, this difference occurs essentially in the semantics, it reappears in the epistemology in doctrine D''_7 and so finds its way into the methodology of science. (Historically, it may well be that Popper worked backward along this chain.) The second major deviation is the rejection of a foundational epistemology (doctrine D''_5). It also reappears in the methodology of science.

So far as I can see, these two modifications of empiricism are essentially independent of each other. It seems perfectly possible to adopt a falsificationist semantics whilst adopting a thoroughly foundationalist epistemology. Correspondingly, it seems perfectly logically coherent to deny a foundationalist epistemology whilst retaining a thoroughly inductivist semantics and methodology of science. I shall not trouble to sketch out the hybrid philosophical positions here but rather leave them for the reader—I do not see any objection in the road to carrying them out consistently.

These two Popperian modifications become inextricably intertwined both in the expression of the theory of rationality (to pursue understanding) and in the methodology of science—this probably explains why it is very hard to get clear about the relation between them from reading the literature and why it may come as something of a surprise to realize that they are actually logically independent of one another. (Of course I should add that Popper came to epistemology with different problems, namely a concern with questions about how scientific knowledge grows rather than with the question of how exactly reliable it is at any one time—cf. Skolimowski (1973) on Popper—and Popper identifies epistemology with the theory of scientific method (Popper 1934, p. 49). All of these things are natural things to say in the light of the doctrines sketched above, but I believe that the structure of that sketch is more conducive to insight into the Popperian position than the usual phrasiology.)

The Meta-Philosophy of Popperianism

When we stop to ask ourselves what meta-philosophical doctrines control the development of the Popperian philosophy of science I believe we reach a striking conclusion: the objective of epistemology aside, Popperian meta-philosophy is essentially identical with the meta-philosophy of empiricism-positivism.

It is certainly the case that Popper is committed to defending the view that philosophers propose normative accounts of the nature of science and of epistemology and rationality itself. Moreover in *L.d.F.* the dominant conception of the theories thus proposed is that they have a status which is logically prior to science, i.e., Popper seems also to subscribe to the view that if a theory is normative then it is thereby separate and 'higher' in status than the subject matter for which it is normative. Moreover, in *L.d.F.* Popper seems clearly to accept that philosophical theories cannot be affected by science, in the sense that what is normatively justified is so independently of any appeal to the particular content of science. Of course this is compatible with the view that problems in normative theory are *suggested* by science, i.e., with the view that the history of science informs us as to which problems have to be solved, for the point is rather than their solution does not involve any appeal to the detail of scientific theory (hence this view is compatible with essays of the former theme in *CR*). Thus far, then, Popper seems committed to a metaphysical doctrine of the form M_1, and so also to one of the form of M_6.

Moreover Popper seems clearly to aim at the presentation of his major philosophical doctrines in terms of logical structure. (Consider eg. his account of the content of theories, the nature of laws and explanation, the structure of scientific method and so on.) Thus it seems that Popper is also committed to a doctrine of the form M_2. And while it is less obvious I think it no less clear that Popper too wishes to confine the scope of the theory of rationality to within the domain of empirically decidable sentences (at least in so far as rational procedure in science is concerned), thus a doctrine of the form M_4. Thus I propose the following meta-philosophical doctrines for Popperianism:

(M''_1) There exists a First Philosophy which includes theories of epistemology, rationality and language. A First Philosophy is logically and epistemologically prior to all other statements in the admissible structure of human knowledge and (in some appropriate sense) constitutes a necessary framework for the expression of the content of human knowledge.

(M''_2) All acceptable sentences, whether philosophical or empirical, are expressible in a language $\bar{L}''$, where $\bar{L}''$ is a logically and semantically clear and precise language. Theories of epistemology, rationality, semantics and of science itself are to be characterized in terms of logical structures in $\bar{L}''$.

(M''_3) The aim of epistemology is to explain how science is possible; in particular to explain how an evolving, improving science is possible.

(M''_4) The scope of the theory of rationality is confined within the domain of the empirically meaningful; that part of the theory of rationality pertaining to the pursuit of truth is logically independent of any other component of the theory (if any).

It follows that (M''_6) First Philosophy (and of course meta-philosophy) is logically and epistemologically prior to, independent of, and normative for theory of science.

Once again I would defend the choice of these meta-philosophical doctrines by arguing that (a) they offer a view of the nature of philosophizing which indeed leads to Popperian philosophical doctrines, (b) they offer a view of the nature of philosophizing which is itself a natural extension of the Popperian world view (as presented in the philosophy), (c) for these reasons they seem the natural (and essentially only) doctrines that Popperians would fall back upon when required to defend their philosophical doctrines. Indeed, I would argue that the strategy of Popperian defense against criticism (and the same kinds of criticisms as are levelled against empiricism at that) will be exactly the same as it is for the positivist and empiricist.

But there was always an evolutionary strain in Popper's thought, even in *L.d.F.*, though this was not really emphasized until *OK*. The evolutionary approach is hard to reconcile with the doctrines M''_1 and M''_6; for surely philosophy too should evolve with our evolving understanding and then it becomes implausible to talk about normative doctrines which stand aloof from the evolutionary historical process of the accumulation of knowledge concerning the world. In *L.d.F.* the evolutionary remarks were sparse and applied only to science and not to philosophy itself, which latter was taken to be a merely conventional framework, evidently in something like the empiricist sense, and even in *CR* the theme is not elaborated for all of human knowledge. But in *OK* it is and this marks the second significant change of Popperian doctrine from *L.d.F.* (the first being the development of the theory of the Third World). In such a setting the title of a paper such as 'The Nature of Philosophical Problems and Their Roots in Science' would have to be taken far more seriously than would be indicated by a doctrine of the mere suggestion from the history of science of problems for normative theory. But I see no sign in Popper anywhere of abandoning M''_1, and M''_6, to the contrary the doctrine of the 'third world' as elaborated in *OK* reinforces these meta-philosophical positions. (Later I shall elaborate a truly evolutionary doctrine which does abandon M''_1 and M''_6.)

It will not have escaped the reader's attention that a doctrine corresponding to the empiricist meta-philosophical doctrine M_5 is missing once again, hence I shall here add:

(M''_5) The doctrines of philosophy and meta-philosophy must be logically consistent; hence it follows in particular that both sets of doctrines are conventions, devoid of empirical content, which in some sense constitute successive logical frameworks for the construction of empirical knowledge.

An alternative doctrine might be substituted, one Kantian in flavour and currently 'in the air' which might be formulated roughly as follows:

(M''_5*) The doctrines of philosophy and meta-philosophy are necessarily descriptive of intellectual structure.

If (M''_5) represents the doctrine of *L.d.F.*, the Popperian position at the time when Popper was still very close to empiricism, (M''_5*) represents, I believe, the motivating doctrine behind the later Popperian doctrine of the Third World found especially in *O.K.* Since both doctrines fit well with the other meta-philosophical doctrines, though they give somewhat different slants to the overall meta-philosophical position, and since (as we shall see) the replacement of the earlier by the later doctrine will offer both the Popperian (and the empiricist) a more plausible response to certain meta-philosophical questions, it is not hard to see why Popper should have made the transition between the two and now seems to be defending a rather more platonic-looking rationalist position. Moreover, the doctrine of the Third World is able to accommodate Popper's evolutionary remarks without abandoning the meta-philosophical doctrines (M''_1) and (M''_6), indeed while reinforcing them—the evolution occurs in the Third World and Popper thus seems free to subsume philosophy also under the evolutionary process whilst maintaining its quasi-platonic distinctiveness and independence as characteristic of its normative role. Apart, then, from the changes in the meta-philosophical account of epistemology, which represents a thoroughgoing and radical overhaul of the empiricist-positivist approach to epistemology, Popperianism emerges as remarkably similar to empiricism-positivism at the meta-philosophical level and there are still important similarities at the level of philosophy. This is essentially why I have cast it as a variant of empiricism.

3.2 Meta-philosophical questions

3.2.1 Remarks on the Adequacy of the Variants of Empiricism

There is no doubt that each of the three variants of empiricism which I have presented above is internally consistent and highly coherent (integrated) and no doubt that each offers a more or less complete account of the nature of (the relevant aspects of) philosophy and the theory of science. In these respects I find nothing to choose between the three variants. Nonetheless, these are not all the questions which a systematic philosophy might be asked to settle. Prima facie at least, we might press on with the following two meta-philosophical questions:

> Why is the epistemology chosen in the philosophy the most appropriate one?
> Why are we rationally justified in choosing this epistemology?

In order to make the point we could ask ourselves, for example, whether the epistemology is an appropriate one for God, or for a class of possible creatures whose minds are in direct communion with God and whose knowledge comes directly therefrom. We could ask whether it is an appropriate epistemology for a class of possible creatures who have no sensory organs as such but upon whom the patterns of the universe impress themselves directly upon their intelligent functions (e.g., by direct, global physical interaction with their thinking processes or by some more mysterious means which we might label 'telepathy'). What is being urged here is that one might plausibly expect the details of a defensible epistemology to be related in some fashion to the actual facts pertaining to the species to whom the epistemology applies. And what the nature of the philosophy suggests, and the meta-philosophy makes explicit, for each of these variants of empiricism is that they hold to the (common) notion that a philosophical answer to a philosophical question, once given, is of such a nature that accepting it one accepts also that there is no coherently conceivable alternative—if philosophy applies to us at all then it necessarily applies to all rational creatures irrespective of their circumstances.

This latter characteristic has traditionally been taken to be the central usable characteristic of normative theories. The three philosophies of science which I have sketched all agree in this matter—it is the nature of philosophy in general to be normative precisely in providing doctrines which apply, if at all, necessarily to all rational creatures. About the nature and sources of normativeness, however, there may be substantial disagreement. For positivist philosophical doctrines are normative only in the sense that they constitute the only appropriate framework from within which clear thinking can be conducted; since these doctrines do not possess a cognitively significant content there is no further problem concerning the sources and nature of their normativeness. The empiricist too may accept this account but he may equally accept the alternative quasi-Kantian account to the affect that their normativeness resides in the recognition of their being necessarily universally true descriptions of the intellectual structure of rational minds. There are of course other accounts of the nature of normativeness, for example that it consists in the property of being commanded by God, or that it is a transcendental truth (or an ordinary truth from a transcendental world) revealed to man through a special intuition or rational faculty, and there is the doctrine (to be elaborated below) that the normativeness of a doctrine consists in its belonging to the best available theory of the time, and no doubt there are still yet others. It suffices here to remark that all three of the doctrines which I have sketched agree on adopting one or other of the first two accounts of the nature of normativeness, in particular that both the empiricist and Popper seem to be either too positivist or too rationalist to adopt the last mentioned naturalist account.

All but the first account of normativeness which I mentioned have their distinctive sources which account for the acquisition, by *Homo sapiens*, of knowledge of the normative doctrines. Thus if being normative amounts to being commanded by God then it is God's special revelation which makes possible our knowledge of the normative doctrines; if the normativeness of a doctrine consists in its transcendental truth then it is by a special faculty of the mind that we have epistemic access to the normative, while for the quasi-Kantian account and for the naturalist accounts it is by whatever procedures that we come to hold, respectively, necessarily universal descriptions of intellectual structure or a currently most satisfying theory that we have access to the normative. (The accounts of this process will be somewhat different as between the empiricist who must use an empiricist account of the evolution of language and knowledge, and the Popperians and naturalistic realists who are not thus restricted.) So that for all of these positions there is another naturally posed meta-philosophical question:

> How is it that the philosophy and meta-philosophy is known as the normatively correct one?

to which each of these doctrines provides its own distinctive answer.

And not even the positivist (and those empiricists which share the positivist position in this respect) can avoid facing a version of the same problem. For the fact is that they too claim that their account is applicable to all rational creatures and they succeed in avoiding the rationalist spirit of this claim only by also claiming that philosophical doctrines are devoid of cognitively significant content and in some sense constitute only a conventional framework for clear thinking. Nonetheless, this only diverts our attention from the fact that the mind must evidently at least have the power to think clearly and to clarify itself when it is thinking unclearly and this in turn rather strongly suggests that the mind must have yet a third capacity, one which positivism cannot strictly allow it, namely to know exactly when it is operating in a clarified fashion and to know what the possible range of appropriate conventional representations of that clarified mode of operations actually is. An account of the nature of the human mind which did justice to these issues would surely amount to an answer to the foregoing meta-philosophical question.

In point of fact it is clear on reflection that the alternative, quasi-Kantian position is also in difficulty over much the same issue when stated within the empiricist framework, for not only must the mind be able to construct language and theories in the empiricist fashion but it must be able to recognize the necessarily universal when it is constructed and of this mental capacity the doctrines of empiricism can have nothing to say.

In point of fact neither the positivist nor the empiricist account of man is adequate to explain the possibility of the remainder of its philosophical doctrines. (The positivist, and the empiricist who also accepts a version of the doctrine M_5, might attempt to escape this indictment, with what degree of plausibility I will not argue, by asserting that within their framework none of these putative questions can be meaningfully formulated and hence none requires an answer.) From within the empiricist framework the point of shifting from the positivist doctrine M_5 to the quasi-Kantian doctrine M'_5 was precisely that this move allowed some attempt at an answer to the first two metaphilosophical questions. Unfortunately, I have argued that it runs directly into difficulty over providing an answer to the third meta-philosophical question.

It is clear that Popperianism under the version in which it adopts the doctrine M''_5 is subject to the same criticisms as was positivism and the M'_5 versions of empiricism. On the other hand, it is not so clear that Popperianism in the version which it takes the doctrine $M''_5{}^*$ is subject to the same criticism as was empiricism under this quasi-Kantian alternative, because it is not clear what precise limitations there are to the account of the mental capacities of *Homo sapiens* within the philosophical world view of Popperianism. The potential ability of Popperianism to provide reasonable answers to all three meta-philosophical questions when it takes the doctrine $M''_5{}^*$ is an obvious, and I think the major, reason for adopting that doctrine (cf. Popper's philosophical development, eg. as discussed in Feyerabend 1974, Jeffery 1975, Schilpp 1973, Skolimowsky/Freeman 1973).

There are of course many other ways to answer these meta-philosophical questions through the construction of systematic philosophical and meta-philosophical doctrines. It is not the purpose of this paper to discuss them all. Rather, it is my purpose to present my own version of what I call *Naturalistic Realism,* using the foregoing doctrines as contrasts against which to state my own position.

3.3 A RADICALLY NON-EMPIRICIST POSITION OUTLINED

3.3.1 Meta-Philosophy of Naturalistic Realism

Contrary to the mode of presentation in the foregoing, I shall first discuss meta-philosophy and then discuss philosophy.

(*MNR₁*) There is no First Philosophy (in the traditional sense).

Commentary. According to naturalistic realism (hereafter NR) there are no philosophical doctrines which are either epistemologically prior to, or independent of, all other statements in the admissable structure of human knowledge. Moreover, there is no transcendent source of normative force. Although there may be logical priority among sets of doctrines in the sense in which philosophical doctrines are in some sense both more general assertions than those of science, include the doctrines of science among their subject matter and even in some sense constitute a framework for the expression of scientific knowledge, they are in no sense immune from criticism emanating from the development of the science. Indeed, philosophical doctrines are held explicitly to evolve in dynamic interplay with the evolving scientific world view itself. From all of which it follows that a quite different account of the normativeness of philosophical doctrines must be offered.

(*MNR₂*) The normativeness of philosophical doctrines consists in this: they stand in the same relation to the theories of science as theories of science do to their own data fields.

Commentary. It is now theories, at all levels of generality and abstraction, which are the essential carriers of normative force. According to this account a theory is normative for its domain precisely and only because it can be used as a framework for the criticism of the elements of the domain. Thus it is that scientific theories can be used as a framework for the criticism of putative scientific data—on many occasions we both criticize data presented on theoretical grounds and even go about forming of data according to the dictates of theory, the very same theory in both cases as is meant to be confronted by the data (see Chapter 4). The scientific theory is normative for the acceptance of scientific fact in the domain or field of the theory. Similarly, philosophic theories are to be accounted as normative for their domains or fields precisely because they constitute a framework from within which their subject matters, e.g., scientific theories, scientific procedures, may be criticized, evaluated and possibly even rejected.

On the other hand, scientific theories are confronted by the data in their field and it is on the basis of this confrontation that we continue to accept, or reject, the theory in question. Similarly, this account holds that philosophic theories are to be confronted by their own field of application and that it is ultimately in terms of the adequacy of philosophical theories to give a coherent and penetrating account of the structure of their field that we shall accept or reject these theories. (Cf. *MNR₁*).

Thus it is that the evolution of science is a very delicate and extremely intricate interaction between the theoretical critique of experimental procedure and presentation of data on the one side and the data-based critique of theory on the other. And so it is similarly that the evolution of philosophy of science is a delicate and extremely intricate interaction between the criticism of the development of scientific knowledge on the one side and the criticism of philosophic theories on the basis of the historical evolution of scientific knowledge on the other.

There is an important contrast between this doctrine concerning the nature of normativeness and the other doctrines discussed above. Alternative doctrines place an unbridgeable gulf between normative and descriptive, a gulf usually made clear by the choice of source for the normativeness. This is inevitable on the view that normative doctrines necessarily apply to all rational agents, since no merely empirical source for normative theories and no merely theoretical status for them could sustain this role. On this view no rational account can be offered of the influence, across this gulf, of the descriptive on the normative (though it might influence the might-be-normative of the quasi-Kantian alternative). The present naturalistic doctrine also specifies a 'source' for normative theories—experience and imagination—but gives up the claim that theories now accepted as normative are necessarily so for all rational creatures, or for all time. In this way it is able to claim that it is precisely a theory's *descriptive* (explanatory) success that justifies its use as *normative* thus providing for a dynamic normative/descriptive interaction and so closing the gap, as far as it properly should be.

Since normative doctrines are theories about rational action, rational belief, the form of morality, etc. (this naturalistic account applies to all normative domains), we can argue that such theories develop in the same way that descriptive theories do, a generalized evolutionary process of selection among alternatives. And this is necessary on any seriously evolutionary account of *Homo sapiens,* we cannot specify our values in advance; as for the facts, we are born in ignorance of them. (Incidentally, it is not too difficult to see why empiricism and Popperianism shyed away from this account of normativeness, for it leads inevitably to some such doctrine as MNR_1 and hence would entail the rejection of practically all of the meta-philosophy and philosophy of those two doctrines. In *OK* Popper tried to bridge the normative/descriptive gulf with which his account leaves him—the gulf between world 3 rational dynamics and world 2 psychological dynamics—by introducing ad hoc a 'principle of transference' which says that what is valid in the normative realm is psychologically valid also, but the basis for this assertion must forever remain a mystery in Popper's system.)

(MNR_3) The aim of epistemology is to offer a general theory which will explain how science is possible (in particular, explain how an evolving, improving science is possible), what the scope of scientific knowledge is, how that knowledge is acquired and what the relative epistemic status of various components of that knowledge is.

Commentary. First-Philosophy style epistemology is characterized by an allegedly a prioristic analysis of knowledge claims—syntactic-semantic issues are held to dominate (actually a great deal of armchair psychology is involved); only after the analysis of 'X knows that P' is complete are scientists able to go on with the task of investigating how X actually comes by P at all. What the scope of such P's is and what the relation is between the coming-by relation and the epistemic status of P are left, as left they must be, uncommented on and obscure.

When an evolutionary view of *Homo sapiens* is taken seriously these latter questions move into the forefront. We do not know in advance what is the potential scope of human knowledge, any more than we *know* anything else in advance, this is something we learn as we study ourselves and form theories concerning the possibilities for life in this universe. We do not know in advance how we know anything, how accurate or inaccurate our senses are and in what respects, how intuition works and whether it is reliable, whether mental telepathy is a real occurrence and so on. We may well discover (= come to accept a new theory about) the systematic biasedness of our senses (already actualized e.g., in the theory of illusion), the systematic degeneracy of our logical inferences (already suggested strongly by studies of 'quantum logical' theories), the existence of a new sense based on a new form of energy, the reality of pre-science. And the theory of our brains too is relevant; suppose e.g., that we discovered that in certain conditions the sentences formulated only bear a statistical truth relation to the actual information representations in the cortex, though the condition was sufficiently rare and/or complicated for it to be hard to notice intuitively. And these realistic possibilities only scratch the surface of what we can imagine (theorise) concerning the powers and properties of other life in the universe.

In sum: The justification of a certain epistemic status to a certain class of propositions is to be given by the scientific account of the circumstances under which such sentences come to be formed and seriously affirmed. In this account the epistemic evolution of the individual plays a key role (cf. Piaget's genetic epistemology 1970, 1971a). The same general theories of our constitution then also provide an account of the scope and limitations of human knowledge.

Conversely, epistemology is the best theory we can raise, taken in the light of the scientific findings concerning the scope of human knowledge and, within its scope, what it is rational to accept and for what purposes and why, in particular what it is rational to believe and to what degree and why; how one changes acceptance rationally in the light of changing evidence (largely theoretical), and so on.

A central part of epistemology is thus a critical theory of scientific knowledge, in particular what measures and methodology lead to its growth and what are the limitations and defects (if any) of these methods. Such a theory fully takes into account the actual constitution, both psychic and physical, of *Homo sapiens*. In particular it must deal, not only with their intrinsic individual makeup, but with the question whether science is necessarily a collective enterprise, as opposed to possibly an individual enterprise and, if so, in which respects and why (cf. 'demarcation' below). The history of science, modulo our theories of possible (and not merely actual) human behaviour, is central to the evidence for this theory. (The account of normativeness offered above resolves at a general level the question of the relation of the factual history of science to the normative methodology of science.) The historical evolution of science will be intimately related to the evolution of the individual, both together forming two coherent central planks in a systematic scientific account of *Homo sapiens*.

Equally important to the assessment of epistemology is the theory of language. What account is offered of the nature and significance of language will intimately affect what is said of the epistemic status of certain classes of assertions. Traditional 'First Philosophy' apparently treats language as given, logically and epistemologically clear (or at any rate clarifiable) to be used unproblematically in the statement of philosophical doctrine. *NR* must believe otherwise.

(*MNR₄*) The theory of language is founded on the scientific account of *Homo sapiens*; the use of symbolic forms, in particular formal or natural languages or fragments of them, for certain purposes is to be justified on the basis of this latter account. In particular, there is no pre-determined preference for formal languages, nor any initial assumption concerning either their greater adequacy in all or any particular respects, or their universal applicability—their specific use is to be justified as above—and conversely for natural languages also.

Commentary. This meta-doctrine is thrust upon one once the evolutionary view is taken seriously, for language cannot be expected to be given in advance, rather it will be a social creation for certain purposes, thus sharing in a myriad defects and biases ideosyncratic of human's kind general constitution and specific social functions. (Witness the varieties of human language and the wider varieties of other signalling systems, e.g. by dolphins, and the even wider variety of theories concerning possible kinds of language systems. Incidentally, the question of expression of such theory within our language need not be a problem if (a) notice is taken of the view of language I later propose and (b) it is remembered that for sufficiently rich languages, each of two such languages may be able to represent the other even though they have radically different structures.)

If it later turns out, as it will, that linguistic meaning is irrevocably vague, that language 'points' to what is richer, and partially apprehendedly richer, than its expressive power can capture (cf. Campbell 1973, p. 433 and Section 5 on the evolution of language, my 1975d and Section 3.3.2.2 below), then in a certain (Buddhist-like) sense all assertions are to be understood as distortions of reality and qualified epistemically as such.

(*MNR₅*) The concern of a theory of rationality is the construction of the most adequate theory of the well-functioning mind, where 'well functioning' is a term whose content is to be informed by scientific theory.

Commentary. There have always been two apparently utterly distinct kinds of criteria for rationality; the one descriptive: survival, evolutionary success; the other normative, e.g., logically consistent, truth-preserving, critical (Popper-style). Traditional philosophy could never bring the two kinds together, because of the normative/descriptive gulf, yet there always seemed as if there should be a connection. What *would* one say of an alleged universe in which evolutionary creatures had to be systematically irrational to survive? That it was mis-described? (Notice the difference between a universe of rational creatures confronted by a cartesian demon who made rational science practically impossible and the universe allegedly being contemplated here.) What *other* evidence can we ultimately have for what rational behavior (including epistemic acceptance) consists in except the accumulated historical experience of the species (especially its history of critical enquiry)? The *NR* conception of a normative theory, by contrast, permits the two kinds of criteria to be brought together. Our normative account of rationality is a theory about how sane human beings function, a theory that utilizes a variety of theoretical criteria (at any particular time), but the theory itself is to be justified by its explanatory adequacy in *accounting* for the actual development and specific behaviours of *Homo sapiens* and, for that matter, of other intelligent species we may run across.

The last clause above raises an interesting question, one already of great interest for *Homo sapiens:* What is the best way to describe a well-functioning, i.e., rational, mind? Traditional philosophy, true to its a priorist armchair spirit, has assumed that rationality is bound up with linguistic rules. But modern science teaches us that language is only the surface reflection of much more complex information processings in the cortex, an abstracted portion of these activities fed to the tongue and the hand for social purposes (cf. *MNR₄* commentary). We can hardly expect, then, that either in ourselves or in any other intelligent species will a linguistic form provide the most significant characterization of rational processes. The *NR* meta-philosophy expressly opens the way for alternate characterizations in the terms disclosed by existing scientific theory as most suitable (see e.g. my 1975d and below).

(*MNR₆*) The content of a philosophy of science comprises a theory. This theory is of the same kind as those of science in every philosophically relevant respect except logical role, insofar as the subject matter of the philosophy is science itself.

It goes without (further) saying that we do not now have all of the theoretical framework necessary to carry out the detailed justifications alluded to in the foregoing. We do not, e.g. now have a sufficiently strong theory of linguistic development in the context of general cortical information processing functioning to be able to make very many penetrating observations on the legitimate roles of abstract logical formalisms. We do have some limited 'internal' criteria that are relevant (e.g. truth preservation under inference) and some comparative experience with the expressive resources and quirks of various systems, but this hardly amounts to an interesting case for either their free use or their abandonment. Let us by all means use such calculi according to our present lights, but let us call our claim to clarity and certainty concerning their superiority, exhibited in the erecting of their alleged superiority into a meta-philosophical commitment, let us call this for what it is: whistling in the wind. The same applies to all of our other pieces of fundamental guesswork.

Incidentally, it should be clear why for NR it is preferable to state the meta-philosophy before the philosophy. MNR_1 e.g. informs us that philosophical doctrine is not to be constructed *a priori*, with some intuitively fixed goals (fixed e.g. in terms of their 'neatness', completeness, security-making etc.) which are set in advance, but rather it is to aim at capturing our current understanding of ourselves and our world as contained in common experience and refined in science. This orientation may make the statement of those doctrines less precise, more programmatic, certainly less final, than is customary in philosophy, and of a distinctive content. Unless we are told this in advance and told how the various constructions hang together, it will be difficult to fully appreciate the philosophy.

The reader will observe that the meta-philosophy of NR is maximally opposed to that of positivism-empiricism, indeed every meta-philosophical doctrine of those positions finds its *negation* among the meta-philosophical doctrines of NR. The same is true of Popperianism *vis-à-vis NR*, except for the approach to epistemology. The Popperian epistemological inspiration is acknowledged. (This is because it is, as Campbell notes, an evolutionary epistemology. Moreover in NR Popper's doctrines are set in the wider naturalistic evolutionary context which he shunned.) Recalling my argument to the effect that every attack on, or defense of, a philosophical doctrine requires recourse to at least one meta-philosophical doctrine, it will not be hard now to understand why the traditional philosophic attacks on realism are not telling against a systematically formulated position—they inevitably require the realist to accept a criterion inimical to his own approach to philosophy (to his meta-philosophy). Much of my earlier 'Systematic Realism' was devoted to this point (see Chapter 2).

3.3.2 Philosophy of Naturalistic Realism

As I earlier remarked, what follows under this heading can only be the merest sketch since a full account would necessarily involve, among other things, the setting out and defence of a complete version of the current scientific world view. Rather I shall try only to inject comments on each topic selected for their relevance and 'flavor'.

3.3.2.1 Theory of Rationality. A rational person so acts as to maximize human potential (his/her own primarily, but also that of the species in the longer run) and the relevant potential is defined, to a degree specified by science, as perceived or accepted potential; moreover he/she so reasons as to be a maximally efficient information processor.

Commentary. To develop and defend this view at length would take me too far afield. The notion of human potential is clear enough by example, if unspecifiable in advance (cf. Popper's argument for the unpredictability of the growth of knowledge). A human being e.g., has the potential for language, mathematics, culture, though he/she may never exercise it, or never fully exercise it, if not reared in the appropriate environment. Collectively, we have the potential for developing science and technology, cultural achievements of great refinement, perhaps even control of our own evolutionary destiny (etc.), though to what extent we shall realize any of this potential is an uncertain function of our existing cultures. Certainly the extent of this potential is presently unknown, and equally certainly our present cultures suppress too large deviations from 'normalcy'. That healthy persons seek to maximally realize their potential, within the confines of their culture, is a truth increasingly attested to by modern psychology and indeed in danger of becoming a tautology. Of course realizing 'higher level' potentials is dependent upon having basic needs satisfied, so that this point of view is compatible with a 'hierarchy of needs' conception of the well functioning human (e.g., Maslow's), and equally compatible with the view that some unfortunate persons so find themselves in alien circumstances that to protect their own personalities they become what we are pleased to label as 'psychotics'.

Of course such a characterization suggests that there is some rational ordering of values (read 'utilities' for the game-theoretic version), some ordering of utilities that can be rationally defended. I have much sympathy for this view (though I must believe that such orderings are only conjectured, theorized to be rationally preferable—increasing experience can be expected to constantly modify our rankings of ends); but the paucity of literature, convincing argument, and even of current research, forces replacement of argument with a promissory note to defend the view (on naturalistic contingent-scientific, fallibilist grounds).

Whatever else may be said, this much is sure: it is the *collective, historical* human experience which counts. This is so on two counts: (a) The development of theory in these respects centrally involves the development of suitable cultures that foster the development of human beings, individually and collectively. One very important (if thoroughly partial) aspect of this is the notion of a critical culture (cf. chiefly Popper's exposition), and critical not just with respect to factual belief, but with respect to values (ends), means, conceptual schemes—everything. The theory of human ends is at least a theory of human cultures. But cultures are collective creations. (b) Moreover, the adequate testing of cultural theories may require millennia rather than years. (Are we really historically in a position to decide between a Zen Buddhist or Tibetan culture and our own?—even with respect to exploration of the real nature of the universe?) Certainly it will typically require temporal spans much longer than an individual lifetime. The more so, since there is scarcely an extant (or past) culture that has tolerated critical enquiry to any significant degree yet (one of the reasons why we have never attempted a 'meta-cultural' rapport with Zen Buddhist or Tibetan culture in the spirit of critical, comparative exploration.) We are only just beginning, as a species, on the exploration of cultural, and hence value, theory—and beginning blindly at that.

As to means, the position is simpler to state (vaguely): we theorize that the rational mind so processes information that the resulting sequence of states represents a dynamically optimal path from initial (epistemic) condition to choice of action. (A 'dynamically optimal path' is intended to capture the notion of a most efficient sequence of information processing states, where efficiency itself has to be evaluated against the ultimate values of the organism.) In appropriate circumstances an abstracted gloss on this process may be adequately representable as a deductively valid argument, or perhaps an inductive one, in some formalized language. E.g., recent work in rational belief change postulates a 'minimal change principle' for changing beliefs, and degrees of credibility attached to beliefs, in the light of new evidence—such minimal actions will be clearly related to dynamically optimal paths for information processing. Moreover, the formulation is designed to incorporate the decision-theoretic model of strategy choice as choice of utility-maximal, or perhaps satisficing, path. In most cases there is reason to believe that not even the simplest such reasoning process is really one of these incredibly simple, abstracted linguistic transitions. (Here is the place where 'intuition', 'analogy','association of ideas', even feelings, can be rehabilitated as part of rational function.)

The same must be true of the rational evaluation and choice of ends. Indeed, reflection suggests that rational models of belief change and value change should be intimately related—and especially so on the present view since both factual beliefs and chosen values have essentially the same epistemic status (conjectural theories), the same evolutionary history and the same normative/descriptive roles. Again I refrain from offering further development.

Finally, as the decision theoretic version suggests, choice of action will be choice of a compromise among various ends, between long and short range ends, even on occasion between information processing efficiency and development of potential, such that the net resulting benefit (however complexly defined) is maximal or anyway satisfactory.

What these comments make clear is the internal complexity of a complete theory of rationality. Such a theory must not only deal with rational acceptance of ends, beliefs and means in science and living generally, but also with the rational critique and change of those ends, beliefs and means, with the rationality of those critical procedures themselves and with the rationality of accepting the philosophy on which those critiques are based, with the rational critique of those meta-philosophical considerations, and so on up, perhaps indefinitely. Within the traditional framework, where the intellectual transparency of the world of philosophy was somehow assumed, this inner complexity was obscured, theory of rationality was focussed on the first task alone (and then usually restricted to problems of belief alone). But within *NR* its full scope is unavoidable because of the naturalistic, fallibilist setting and the rejection of the primacy and transparency of language. Nor is the added complication trivial, for it is essential to a clear discussion of the distinction between accepting an entire schema (e.g., a conceptual scheme or culture) and accepting more particular ends or beliefs within such a schema. (Cf. Carnap's trivializing this distinction by making the former a non-cognitive, non-rational 'conventional' affair—a doctrine required by empiricist metaphilosophy, but certainly not the only meta-philosophy, or even the only notion of 'convention'.)

3.3.2.2 Theory of Language . . . (Given by an account of neurophysio-logical-cum-mental information processes.)

Commentary. Neither the understanding of our neurophysiology, nor of generalized symbolic systems, nor of the evolution of communication is yet sophisticated enough to offer a detailed account—and what is known would take far too long to set down here. (Cf. e.g. Arbib 1954, 1972, Sebeok 1972, on the brain; Piaget 1954, 1970, 1971a, on the ontogenesis of the conceptualizing, communicating individual; and my 1975d on the impact of this point of view on philosophy generally.) But the following points might briefly be made.

Language will surely be seen as a surface abstraction of much richer, more generalized information processes in the cortex, a convenient condensation fed to the tongue and hand for social purposes. The cortical processes themselves, it seems, will be much richer in content than natural language captures. Yet even these constitute transformations, and inevitably simplifications, of total stimuli.

It follows that the primary function of language is to indicate or point to a world (including the cortex itself) much richer and only partially captured in symbolic code. We should expect, then, that meanings will be systematically illusive and will in any case be functions of the total history of the person concerned and of the culture in which he/she lives. Semantics as the study of meanings (as if they were definite objects of some sort) will hold out little promise. (Formal semantics clarifies logical structure and as such remains a valuable tool.) What can be done is to continually widen the network of elucidation, in order to improve 'pointing'. (Note: pointing is not like naming—unless it be a causal-history account of naming—not when pointing is shorthand for a complex of relationships between a word, phrase, sentence or whole paragraph and an historical sequence of experienced situations in which similar words, phrases, etc., were employed for orienting the organism to the situations in distinctive ways.)

There are roughly three ways in which the word 'realism' is used in the literature: (1) to name a thesis concerning the nature and foundations of mathematics; (2) to name the thesis that there are real properties, real kinds in the world; (3) to name a thesis concerning the ultimate (intended) referential status of theoretical terms. *NR* is committed to realism in senses (2) and (3); sense (1) realism seems to be a logically independent issue about which I say nothing here (though I incline to some form of logicism, with logic empirical). The remarks on meaning complicate the specification of the commitment to (2);

roughly, it is theory that will tell us how knowledge is possible on the basis of natural kinds, which kinds (we conjecture) there are, and how interaction with them is related to our concept formation.

Finally, as these remarks make clear, the account of language should be powerful enough to explain how it is possible, and why it is legitimate, nonetheless to erect a theory of language, in language, that tells us all of this (rather than take the positivist's 'therapy' way out).

3.3.2.3 Epistemology. Man is an epistemic engine. The system of information held by this engine at any one time and classified as knowledge is foundationless and irrevocably theoretically conjectural (whether linguistically formulated or not). Knowledge schemes evolve from ignorance through conjectural creations of conceptual schemas and theories within these—rational evolution is evolution under criticism in the light of chosen human ends (utilities). The scope of knowledge is undecided in advance, at any one time it is at least equal to that of science + philosophy + meta-philosophy.

Commentary. An epistemic engine is a device whose current states are at least partial functions both of its past states and of its current environment. In this respect *Homo sapiens* is different in degree but not in kind from almost any other physical system. A beach is an epistemic engine of very low degree. (Cf. Churchland 1979, from whom I borrowed the term.) How such engines work, including the human engine, what is the variety of their possible realizations and which ones are most effective for which purposes, is an open question for theoretical science.

We may speak then of an evolutionary epistemology, an epistemology which provides a theory of method by which creatures in evolutionary ignorance may progress epistemically, if epistemic progress is possible for them. (There will be no guarantee that it is.) Moreover, the best theory of such methods yet proposed, a modified version of Popper's theory (see below), itself turns out to specify an evolutionary process with deep similarities to the process of biological evolution—a resemblance recently made much of by Popper in *OK*. This is as it should be, for there is something deeply uneasy for a unified conception of evolving man in suggesting one process of evolution for his body and another for his mind, considering the deep integration of communication with other biological processes and its evolutionary emergence (cf. e.g. Lenneberg 1967, Masters 1970, Mischel 1971, Pattee 1973, Sebeok 1972, Smith/Miller 1966, Wimsatt 1974). Note however, that this unification has its foundation in a unified naturalistic ontology, one which is therefore diametrically opposed to Popper's ontological pluralism. (For a critique of Popper along naturalistic lines, see Feyerabend 1974.) Thus we will have processes of elaboration and selection going on at a variety of levels: biological, scientific, philosophical, meta-philosophical. But it looks likely that this unified evolutionary perspective can be deepened still further (see paragraph 4 below).

The evolutionary, naturalistic perspective forces the conclusion that in the beginning was an epistemic vacuum, neither specific knowledge, nor language, nor even conceptual schemes. We evolved from total ignorance on the conceptual level, inventing as we went. Hence the pervasiveness of conjecture (admirably confirmed by developmental psychology) and the absence of any guaranteed foundation for knowledge. It follows that the only rational epistemology to choose is one whose *methods* are suited to this evolutionary situation—it is no accident that it will be heavily Popperian in form (cf. Campbell 1973, Toulmin 1962, 1972).

From an evolutionary perspective, there are two central problems for human method in science: (i) What to do when a data/theory clash occurs? (ii) How to allocate human resources, individual and collective, between the pursuit of individual epistemic ends and the pursuit of collective epistemic ends? Empiricism trivialises the first problem by treating data as absolute, or, with Popperianism, leaves the answer a mystery *vis-à-vis* rational procedure. Both empiricism and Popperianism tacitly assume that science is an individual enterprise and so preclude themselves from having anything interesting to say on the second question. Instead, both focus on degenerate forms of the first question (what to do in the absence of data, or in the absence of theory?) and make dogmatic pronouncements on a third important question: (iii) How should human ends, in particular epistemic ends, be ordered?

So that while epistemology is concerned with critical method *à la* Popper, and Popper himself has broadened this conception from *L.d.F.* to *OK*, I do not want to confine epistemology to Popper's dicta for, to repeat, since nothing is given in advance I find it unacceptable to divide off the realm of science from the rest of human history in the way that Popper continues to do. Rather, I want to place epistemology in the wider, more historically adequate context of the evolution of entire cultures. I shall say then, following the decision-theoretic framework suggested under the theory of rationality, that acceptable epistemic method is a function of a relevant utility ranking and that from a collective, historico-cultural point of view it is optimal for the development of human potential to have a range of utilities operative within the culture.

To illustrate: (a) Suppose that human understanding in roughly the Popperian sense is the dominant utility, then epistemic acceptance is acceptance for testing. In this case criteria such as content, falsifiability, etc. dominate. There are even collective phenomena for, Feyerabend has convincingly argued, a rational person also promotes radical theoretical pluralism under these conditions (cf. Hooker 1972b, 1973d; Lakatos/Musgrave 1970; N. Maxwell 1974; Suppe 1974). (b) Suppose instead that technological reliability is the dominant utility. Then epistemic acceptance is governed by something like degree of inductive support (of the kind attesting to reliability). One might e.g., use methods of statistical inference. And there are other human utilities for doing science: technological power, intellectual coherence and unity of understanding, future fecundity, etc. Even truth—though it is clear that in any extant culture we habitually trade off this latter goal against others.

The decision-theoretic construal of method might seem to take us further away from a unified evolutionary view, but I do not believe that it is so. Using critical method we elaborate and select among theories, historical experience with such methods leads to elaboration and selection among critical methods. Such selection involves choices among differing orderings of the utilities in question and (see below) different cultures in which the institution of science is embedded. At this level evolutionary selection operating on philosophies merges into evolutionary selection operating on entire cultures. That is the first unity achieved (see further below). But further than this, recent work strongly suggests the fruitfulness of the reconstrual of the biological evolutionary process itself in decision-theoretic terms (see Lewontin 1961; Marchi/Hansell 1973; Templeton/Rothman 1974), so that a direct union of theoretical description may become possible. (As long as we rid ourselves of the notion that rational method ought to guarantee success, or ought to prescribe for more than the incremental short term, and correlatively rid ourselves of the image of Darwinian evolution as a kind of crude, narrowly construed functionalist trial-and-error process, then the way is open for this unified viewpoint.) At the very least a single theory of evolution ought to encompass all these levels as integrated special cases. This is the second unity to be achieved. Beyond this, there is the possibility (admittedly speculative) of understanding all of these processes in thermodynamic terms—biological evolution (Morowitz 1968), economic dynamics (Georgescu-Roegen 1971) and through these two, via the preceding literature, all evolutionary processes describable in de-cision-theoretic terms. This would provide the third and strongest naturalist evolutionary unity.

Let me return now from these speculations on evolutionary unity to the question of embedding epistemology in a wider cultural setting, and to the spread of competing utilities for science in particular. The spread and conflict of utilities is particularly clear in the social sci-ences whose object of enquiry is not an (ostensibly) fixed, value-neutral physico-biological order, but society itself. Here there is an intimate interaction between theory and reality since the social world is itself a human artifact created, within constraints, according to our (theoretical) images of ourselves. The creation of social theory be-comes a reflection of values and conceptualizations chosen and, vice versa, the cultural evolution of a society becomes a (partial) function of theory developed. Here we need a sharply different model of meth-od from that customarily proposed for the natural sciences (though I have argued that that too is too simple-minded and narrow), one of the sort proposed where a multiplicity of utilities is operative and the collective, historically long term choice of optimal balance among them is a distinctively different issue from any attempt, at the indi-vidual level, of a once-for-all justification of a single ordering (which is how the customary accounts present the situation).

In point of fact this is as true for the societal interaction of the natural sciences, since they have a profound impact on the develop-ment of culture and social structure and vice versa.

I emphasize this setting for epistemology not only because of its manifest appropriateness but in order to secure a particular objective which I consider of great importance: To show that, and how, the roots (normative and descriptive) of societal science policy and of scientific method are *the same* and hence to unify decision making *for* science and *within* science in a single model that will more accurately reflect the intimate interactions between the two.

The last step in securing the possibility of this goal is to theorize that what demarcates science from non-science is the critical cultural-insti-tutional framework in which enquiry is conducted. What makes a line of enquiry distinctively scientific is the criticalness with which it is pursued—so much Popper taught us. Moreover, we must enlarge the schema of criticism to include (a) criticism of particular fact, techno-logical procedure; (b) criticism of specific theory, (c) criticism of kind of theory (eg., of atomic ontologies); (d) criticism of deeper, more general levels of conceptual framework; (e) criticism of allocation of societal resources among these areas of criticism and to pursuit of creative conjecture at all these levels (i.e., criticism of utility ranking), (f) criticism of the currently institutionalized structure of research and criticism. The time intervals for significant exploration and testing increase through these levels of criticisms until at the last what is at stake is nothing less than the appropriateness of an entire cultural and scientific tradition, extending perhaps over millennia (cf. concluding remarks in Hooker 1973d).

Moreover, there is a profound interconnection between cultural-institutional setting, individual personality and scientific practice. Critical practice requires absence of distorting ego involvement, a self-conception not defined in terms of the details of the external status quo, etc.; such personalities can only develop in a critical culture. Conversely only a critical culture can develop the institutional structure necessary to practice science. And it is the practice of critical enquiry, among other practices, which leads persons to thus understand and accept themselves and to improve that understanding and acceptance.

Nothing less than a cultural and institutional setting which realizes critical evaluation at all of these levels can count as a culture which practices science; the naturalistic realist must admit the possibility of error at each of the levels indicated above (the higher the level the more subtle the error), any level of criticism missing constitutes an unacknowledged and baseless dogmatism. But it is equally clear that the network of criticism extends unbroken from the individual scientist to the societal governor. A theory of science must centrally include a theory of a critical culture, the milieu of framework within which the specific acts of science take place.

All of this can be restated in an abstract decision-theoretic and institutional framework roughly as follows. Institutions have systematic design (characterized in part by their information and decision flow structures). These latter designs profoundly influence the *kinds* of problems that can be formulated and the *kinds* of policies that can be developed in response to these problems. A theory of institutional design would relate problem/policy formation kinds to systems designs. An appropriate institutional model might represent institutions as nets of matrices over which information and decision flows are defined. (The matrices are decision matrices, transforming incoming information and decisions into outgoing information and decisions. The theory of matrix structure is determined by decision theory, and psychology.) In this sense an institution can be represented as an ecology—this yields intra-institutional ecology. The collection of institutions also interact among themselves in ways analogous to the species of an ecology—they exhibit competition, parasitism, symbiosis, etc. and they, like real ecologies, together form a single, multiply connected net—this yields inter-institutional ecology. Decision making takes place throughout the total net. In various institutional locales it is called by different names—methodology, policy formation, business management. And the structure of the matrices change across the net (different sub-nets have different credibilities attached to beliefs and differing utility orderings). But in every locale the decision making framework is the same, the field of utilities is the same, the network of potential interactions to be taken into account is the same. The unit of real significance is the evolution of the total net, for it is this net that contains accrued wisdom and it is its 'shape' which either constrains or develops the full panoply of future possibilities. Adequate human policy must be fundamentally whole-network policy, constructed in delicate interaction with the rational demands of sub-nets.

Now let me briefly state the *NR* account of science.

3.3.2.4 Theory of Science. Aim: Maximization of human epistemic potential. *Demarcation:* Method of enquiry characteristic of a critical culture and institutional structure. *Scientific Language:* No preconceptions, whatever choice is best supported by experience and theory of language—cf. Hooker 1975d. *Scientific Theory.* An account of a model for the world, or some aspect or fragment of it,—cf. Chapters 2 and 4. *Data.* Theory-processed behaviour of instruments (human, non-human, natural or artifactual)—cf. Ch. 4. *Criteria of Scientific Acceptability:* Utility—maximal or satisficing choice (see above). *Method:* Class of utility-maximal or satisficing strategies—see above, cf. Chapter 2. *History of Science:* Evolution of theoretical conjecture within evolution of human cultures—cf. above and Chapter 2, Section 2.1, Hooker 1973d.

Popper (1934) made much in *L.d.F.* of Fries' trilemma (see §§26-29). Fries argued that if our accepted statements must be justified we are faced with a trilemma, for we must choose to accept either dogmatism (refusal to admit the need for justification), psychologism (the doctrine that some statements are fully justified by experience) or an infinite regress of justifications. Fries chose psychologism, in company with most late nineteenth philosophers of science and the twentieth century positivist-empiricist epistemological tradition. It is clear that *NR*, which espouses an evolutionary, totally fallibilist epistemology, is committed to rejecting both the dogmatist and psychologist alternatives and that, with Popper, it must grasp a version of the infinite regress alternative. Popper says that criticism is extended as far as is practicable, the *NR* formulation is that criticism is extended as far as the operative utilities dictate (thus allowing for a more detailed scrutiny of theories of testing in a decision theoretic framework and for variation in method from situation to situation).

But it is also the case that sensory experience can be given a respectable role within this fallibilist framework by distinguishing between the acceptance of a theoretical framework and acceptance of statements within it. (Contrast Popper who rejects experience as essentially irrelevant.) Once a psychological theory of experience (perception, cognition and communication) is sufficiently advanced we will have *theoretical* criteria for conditions under which experiences of certain types are indeed sufficient conditions for the truth of certain statements, and when these experiences are accurately reported. (None of this is a simple matter, consider the roles of conceptual filtering, illusion, bias, etc.) In this case the reports of the experiences will be taken as sufficient conditions for the truth of those statements. But at any time the psychological theory is open to criticism and with it all of these statements accepted on the basis of experiences, these acceptances are relative to accepting the theoretical framework.

These same considerations are relevant to another criticism of *NR*. This criticism is to the effect that once the evolution of science is tied into the evolution of culture the history of science becomes systematically epistemologically ambiguous. To wit there is no guarantee for any culture that it will not suffer from the following twin defects: (i) a systematically wrongheaded scientific tradition, (ii) a cultural environment which precludes either thought or recognition of this fact. Therefore no one is justified in reposing any positive degree of rational belief in any scientific tradition, no matter how long and glorious. I concede that under the *NR* account of science, the history of science is indeed systematically epistemologically ambiguous in just this way. This seems to me to be an accurate reflection of the human condition—development of our cultures, just as much as of our sciences, are risks which we take in the hope that they will lead toward increasing understanding, freedom, etc. (i.e., that they will fulfill humankind's potential) and risks taken in the knowledge that we are in uncharted seas and could be led subtly but disastrously astray at any time.

But it seems to me that *NR* is committed to at least this systematic fallibilism for science, irrespective of its cultural foundations, as soon as it is conceded that the world is not experienced as already understood in a fixed mode once-for-all, but rather that we grasp our experience, and through it the world, via the imaginative development of conceptual schemes and theoretical systems. For the world could be 'plastic' in this sense: What it is, is a function of how we conceive it and what we believe of it. This is not meant as an elliptical rephrasing of the general truth that every truth is expressed in created concepts, but a stronger statement that in a 'super-theory' constructed by God, what is actually true of the universe is a function of the epistemic states of *Homo sapiens*. There can be degrees of plasticity and I see nothing incoherent or impossible about any of them. (Incidentally, positivism and empiricism only avoid their impact by having semantics which prevent the stating of any of the possibilities.) The cultural foundations for science only adds a further dimension to the possible causes of epistemic ambiguity.

But with all of this admitted the sceptical conclusion, i.e., that it is unreasonable to repose any positive degree of rational belief in any scientific statements, by no means follows. For we may distinguish between acceptance of frameworks and acceptance of sentences relative to acceptance of frameworks. The structure to the theory of rational acceptance which *NR* proposes is this: at the *meta-meta-philosophical* level a healthy agnosticism concerning all scientific traditions, no matter how glorious (indeed, concerning all traditions); the choice of the pursuit of critical science, and so of *both* an *NR* philosophy *and* meta-philosophy of science as the most satisfying form of life and most explanatorily adequate position; within the scientific tradition the (conditional) acceptance of what method dictates and even the acceptance of a class of claims to the effect that certain well-supported claims of science (or commonsense) will never in fact have to be rejected—but acceptance of all of these latter modulo the degree of criticalness of our scientific tradition. Thus we have agnosticism on one level, but compatibly with positive acceptance at the level of practical action. (This structure is a rephrasing of Campbell's levels of variation and selection, this is the appropriate structure of belief because we acquire beliefs in a nested hierarchy of evolutionary selection processes—see Campbell 1973, pp. 421–2.)

Nor is it the case that pursuit of truth, though almost certainly unattainable, except possibly in a partial fragmentary way (because of ideosyncratic concept formation and range of experience in *Homo sapiens*), and certainly not demonstrable as such if attained, is irrelevant to the philosophy of science. For just as action everywhere is guided by ideals (maximally valued, though unrealized, situations) so the search for truth can function as a guiding ideal for science. (And do so without defining it, in the pragmatist fashion, in terms of the ultimate end-products of scientific method.)

Finally, need I remark further on the degree to which *NR* is so formulated as to yield explicit, specific answers to the meta-philosophical questions? The commentaries on the *NR* doctrines and these latter remarks on science were offered with these questions specifically in mind.

CONCLUDING REMARKS

I have tried to set out clearly something like a complete framework for a naturalistic realism as a philosophy of science (or anyway a more complete framework than is typical of extant literature). I have tried to show the distinctiveness, strengths and weaknesses of the position by contrasting it with frameworks for variants of empiricism.

I believe that this framework offers the only real possibility for reconstructing an adequate and serious sociology of knowledge (of scientific knowledge in particular). I believe it to be the proper context from which to view the pronouncements of Feyerabend, Kuhn and the like, the proper framework to reconstruct what seems insanely radical so that it makes perfectly sound sense, the proper framework from within which to dis-ambiguate the ambiguity and clarify obscurity in their writings. But these are tasks for other occasions.

Tasks equally for other occasions are the presentation and defense of detailed theories of explanation, rational acceptance, method, etc. Here, as I said, there is space only for a general outline of the overall conception. (For some of the detail see Chapters 2 and 4, this work; Hooker 1973d.)

It has also been suggested to me that (i) my remarks on demarcation, method and critical culture constitute an English-language version of a framework for the contemporary continental research on research (see e.g. Althusser 1965; Ficant/Pecheux 1969; Habermas 1968; Radnitzky 1970, 1971; Stachel 1973, Tornebohm 1969, 1970), (ii) the account of *NR* is in many (not all) respects pragmatism recapitulated (though, charitably, perhaps in more explicit, more systematic form!). I find both of these suggestions congenial and plausible, but arguing them, too, comprises tasks for other occasions.

CHAPTER 4

On Global Theories

4.1 INTRODUCTION

The basic conception of a scientific theory put forward in the standard literature on the subject is a relatively simple and straightforward one. Individual theories are treated in isolation from the rest of science. Each theory is conceived of as a collection of sentences which are descriptive of the world and which are usually assumed to be ordered in a deductive hierarchy. At the bottom of the deductive pyramid lie the so-called observation sentences—those sentences whose truth can be checked experimentally—whilst at the apex of the pyramid lie the most general theoretical principles of the scheme.[1] Just exactly where and how the twin elements of theory and observation permeate this structure is a matter of contemporary controversy but is not of immediate concern to us in this chapter.[2]

This structure had its origins in the Empiricist-Positivist analysis of science and it reflects the dogmas of that approach. What I wish to stress is that *in that conception of a scientific theory the primary business of theory is to make assertions at the observational level.* The specifically theoretical part of theories is either eliminated (Positivism) or reduced to a merely heuristic role (Instrumentalism) or at the least left hanging for its semantic life by the threads connecting it to the base of the pyramid (later Empiricism). All other elements which are necessary to provide a complete account of the scientific process are assumed to exist independently of the theory in question. Thus the use of experimental laboratory equipment, the analysis of data, the rules for establishing the degree to which given data supports the theory, the description of the initial data and so on are assumed to be matters which are settled externally to the theory itself—indeed, to be settled externally to the entire class of scientific theories. *That,* it is covertly considered to be the business of philosophers of science to settle. The attractiveness of this kind of model of the scientific enterprise is at least two-fold: (a) the various components of the scientific process can be isolated and studied separately in their own right, thus simplifying problems considerably; (b) any appearance of circularity in the justification of scientific theories is thereby avoided.

In what follows I want to argue that this traditional conception of a scientific theory and this traditional division of labor in the scientific process does not in fact capture theories as they actually occur in science, that its inadequacies lead to a crucial blindness as to the nature of the scientific enterprise and that an attempt to do even philosophical justice to science as it actually occurs requires a quite radical revision of many of our conceptions of the component areas mentioned above.

4.2 THE REAL SITUATION (I): INTERNAL GLOBAL CHARACTERISTICS

To see what scientific theories are actually like, let us begin by examining a particular case—quantum theory. Central to quantum theory is a theoretical description of how, *fundamentally,* the world is. (That we are having enormous difficulty figuring out how exactly this is, is beside the point here; cf. Hooker 1972b, 1974c.) In addition there is, of course, a large range of experimental data which is directly connected to the degree of assuredness with which scientists accept the theory. Are these then the only aspects of significance in quantum theory? The answer is clearly "no."

Quantum theory, being a *general* theory of the physical world, must also provide a theory of our measuring instruments, of our general experimental laboratory equipment. That is, quantum theory must— and indeed does—tell us which instruments will measure which quantities and under which conditions. For example, we need quantum theory to inform us that we may analyze the intrinsic spin of atomic or subatomic particles using a Stern-Gerlach apparatus.

In addition, quantum theory not only tells us when our measurements are appropriate but it also describes the conditions in which we may expect errors, and the degree of reliability of the information which we do gain. Thus, we may analyze the spin of a stream of hot silver ions in, say, the z direction using an appropriate Stern-Gerlach apparatus, but if we then attempt to add to that apparatus an additional stage which is intended to analyze the spin in the x direction of the *original* stream of silver particles then quantum theory informs us that we shall gain no significant information from the further outcome. Again, there are some measuring processes for which quantum theory informs us that there is a certain probability that the result of the measurement will be unreliable, as an indication of the property in question—and this even in circumstances where the method of measurement is the most appropriate one to the occasion.[3]

Moreover, quantum theory influences our evaluation of experimental data in the following fundamental sense: it specifies which kinds of processes are expected to be causally connected, which are expected to be statistically, though directly, connected and which are expected to be merely accidentally connected. Thus it informs us that the correlations exhibited by a set of counters counting the products of two independent radioactive sources will be merely accidental, that the correlations observed among the photons of two interfering laser beams will be statistical, though connected, and that there will be a causal relationship between the decay of a neutron and the subsequent appearance of a photon and an electron. Because of these different statuses to the various connections, experimental evidence in respect of them will be assigned different weights when we are assessing the degree to which they support corresponding generalizations concerning these processes.

But quantum theory also plays other important roles. It not only concerns itself with the means and the reliability of our observations, it also specifies what can be observed (and, of course, under what conditions). Thus we know from quantum theory that electrons and other fundamental particles cannot be observed in the sense in which macroscopic objects may be observed and we know that we can only observe certain features of a crystal-ionic lattice (e.g., the spatial distribution of the ions but not the detailed trajectories of the electrons in the crystal gas) and then only under certain specified conditions (e.g., not with using photons of wavelength significantly larger than the ion separation distance, nor with wavelength so small that they significantly perturb the ions).[4]

Furthermore, quantum theory prescribes in a general fashion the kinds of descriptions that will count as data in the domain of quantum physics. Thus we are allowed to describe our results in terms of particle localizations, energy exchanges and interactions, state transitions and so on but we are not allowed to describe our data in terms of continuous fluid flow, continuous energy absorption, etc.[5]

The general picture I am trying to build up, then, is this: quantum theory not only provides us with a theoretical description of the world, it also (a) prescribes the general terms in which we are relevantly to describe our observations, (b) specifies what is and what is not observable, (c) specifies the conditions under which what is observable, is observable, (d) specifies the instrumental means by which what is measurable is measured, (e) specifies what is causally, statistically and merely accidentally connected, and (f) specifies the degree of reliability of those measures (building upon (d)). My conclusion is that a general theory of a given domain worth its salt is a much more general, encompassing affair than the traditional simple model would have us believe—it has *global* properties, it covers every aspect of the domain.

The global character of fundamental physical theories that I have picked out here is an actual feature of science. It is illustrated in various degrees in Newtonian mechanics, Psychological Behaviorism, the Phlogiston theory of chemical elements and compounds and the Darwinian theory of evolution. I briefly outline another illustration—general biochemical theory of organisms—in **Appendix 1.** Being part of practice, it is not easy to define in the theoretical terms currently available to philosophers of science and I have no neat definition to offer here. The components of internal globalness which I have singled out range all of the way from a redescription of the experimental situation (instruments, laboratory, etc.) in terms of the theory to methodology and the assessment of weight of evidence, and further still to prescriptions for factual description. The proximate end of this chain stands near enough to theory in the restricted sense of the standard version but the other components stretch increasingly further away. The fact is, I believe, that the fundamental intellectual entity in science is the *theoretical-world-view* (more realistically, the partial world view—cf. below); this is something like a tightly interconnected ("coherent") set of conceptual categories for grasping the world, finding expression at the most general level as a systematic metaphysics (systematic ontology) then a more particular application as a fundamental theory (standard sense), next as forging links to other important theoretical areas as necessary (e.g., to the psychology of perception, theory of methodology, justified acceptance and so on) and finally all of this as applied to specific experimental situations (instrument analyses, factual description). The reader may gain a better idea of the levels of function and their interconnections if he glances at the structure of Figure 4.2 (p. 119). Though it is nonstandard terminology, I am using the term *theory* to stand for *theoretical-world-view* and to distinguish this usage I shall italicize it hereafter.

It is not easy to say what the criteria are for theoretical-world-views (*theories*, partial or complete) and I will not attempt to offer any here. I note, however, that they correspond in a natural way to *tightly, conceptually integrated* varieties of Shapere's *scientific domains* (with perhaps more emphasis on description and less on problem than with Shapere 1964, 1974); have close similarities at the higher reaches to Wisdom's embedded ontology and *Weltanschauungen* (see Wisdom 1971, 1972), and begin to capture what Feyerabend evidently must mean by a "sufficiently general theory," (cf. my comments at the end of Hooker 1972b). It is probably closely related to a descriptively oriented component of Kuhn's *paradigm*. However these relations run in detail, the central unifying structure to my conception of a theoretical-world-view (*theory*) is its conceptual (categorial) structure operating at many structural levels in the analysis of science and I believe that the best analysis of science in the future will have precise, detailed versions of these intellectual units at its heart.

Realistically, it is better to speak of *partial* theoretical-world-views (*theories*) since in actual practice we fragment our basic conceptual structures in various ways (corresponding, roughly, to subsets of the now traditional disciplines).

Theoretical-world-views can be regarded as partial in another sense also. I tend to view the fundamental theory (standard sense) as the most easily recognizable core element of a *theory* and I individuate *theories* by reference to them. But many (most, all?) *theories* are not completely internally global, they do not specify everything. If we said that a *theory* was complete$_2$, or was a complete$_2$ partial$_1$ *theory* of its domain (or that a theory generated a complete$_2$ partial$_1$ *theory*) only when it covered everything in its domain, then most *theories* are only partial$_1$, partial$_2$, *theories* of their domains. See Appendix 1 for discussion of the examples I use here. I do not think that anything very exciting hinges on precisely how one develops the theory of theories, *theories*, and domains, though there is doubtless a great deal of aesthetic pleasure to be gained from ploughing straight furrows through virgin territory. In particular, the philosophical problems raised by the internal global characteristics of *theories*—hitherto virtually ignored by the standard philosophy—are not in anyway mitigated by this extended notion of *theory* (cf. Sections 4.5 and 4.6 below).

4.3 The real situation (II): external global characteristics

Let us consider quantum theory again, this time paying more careful attention to its experimental application *vis-à-vis* other theories. Suppose, for example, we are studying high energy nuclear collisions by looking at the distribution of "fundamental" particles in the showers of these in the lower atmosphere caused by a high energy collision high in the atmosphere. How do we go about designing the experiment?

(a) First there is the consideration of what aspects of the quantum theory of high energy collisions are really worth investigating: collision cross-sections as a function of energy, perhaps, between protons and other heavy particles (not between electrons) and so on. All of the relevant theoretical considerations here are determined by the quantum theory and even the actual judgment of relative interest made by the experimenter, though based on his intentions and not codifiable at present, are heavily influenced in some complex way by the structure of the theory under test (i.e., quantum theory again).

(b) Second, there is the question of what investigable features of air showers are related to the interesting aspects of high energy collisions and in what ways. This is a job for quantum theory, together with the kinetic theory of gas dynamics (a branch of statistical mechanics). Random motions of air molecules, systematic wind-streaming and the exponentially increasing air density are all taken into account using parts of the latter theory with quantum theory being used to analyze the outcomes of the various particle/air molecule collisions that actually occur.

(c) Then some way must be devised to determine satisfactorily these features of the air showers. For example, if it is the spatial distributions and relative number densities of the "light" particles (electrons and pi mesons) that are of interest, then some kind of particle counting devices, such as geiger counters or scintillation tubes, will do the trick. If the energies of "heavy" particles (e.g., protons) in the core is of interest, some energy measuring device, such as a photographic emulsion block, is used. Why these instruments? Because the theory of the instruments tells us that these are the appropriate devices. Thus quantum theory itself tells us that length and ionization rate of track in an emulsion is a measure of energy and chemistry relates that ionization to the transformations that will occur on development. In the case of counters, quantum theory and electrical theory explain just how counters work (not simple!).

(d) Then the data furnished by these instruments must be collected and put through a preliminary processing. This processing means, in the case of the counters, converting the outputs of the counting devices into usable electrical signals whose characteristics are related to the interesting features of the air showers—this is done with the help of electrical circuit theory. In the case of the film emulsion it means developing the film to reach the same stage. This requires a knowledge of the chemistry of emulsions, not only to know *how* to develop it, but to know that *what* appears is related in a particular manner to the proton track.

(e) A second preliminary analysis of the now processed information is then undertaken—this time a mathematical analysis designed to compute from the processed information the quantities of interest. This is especially important in the case of those instruments where what you receive from the instrument is only statistically related to the features which the instrument is measuring. (Both particle counters and emulsions are in this class.) The kind of analysis undertaken is determined jointly by a variety of mathematical theories (e.g., theories of statistics) and by the theories of the instruments. This level normally involves computers and other processing devices and so also involves an indirect appeal to the theory of these instruments (electronics, mechanics, etc.).

(f) Finally, the now fully processed information—we might say "the data"!—is confronted with the theory.

This, in barest outline, is the six-stage design structure of the air shower experiment. It is typical of experiments employing rich scientific theories, theories that have internal global features. And what I want to draw attention to here is the involvement of *other theories* in the design structure. In the present case we uncovered reliance on statistical mechanics (and/or macro-gas theory), electrical circuit theory, chemistry and classical mechanics—as well as a wide range of mathematical theories.

In fact, there are two further important ways in which a typical scientific experiment relies on other theories which haven't yet been mentioned. First, there is always the tacit *ceteris paribus* assumption concerning the experimental situation: there are no other physically significant external disturbances. That is, the results (suitably processed) which the instruments give truly reflect the actual situation in the ways we have supposed in our theories of them. Why do scientists accept such sweeping clauses? Because their *theories* tell them it is all right to do so. These theories are themselves backed by experience, of course, and the assumption can always be tested in *some* respects in any given situation but (i) it cannot in any situation be tested in *all* respects, (ii) which aspects of it a scientist actually tests is determined in practice by his time and money and by whether the *other* theories he believes tell him there are likely to be any suspicious circumstances around. In general, no test is made of the clause until something *theoretically* (!) unexpected happens. Second, we should, to be complete, recognize the tacit reliance upon a variety of psychological theories concerning the performance reliability of rational human minds, the prevalence of rationality among scientists, the conditions of reliability of normal perceptual experience and so on. Crude and unformulated as these theories may be (outside—and, perhaps, inside—of psychology departments) and as obvious as we may feel the failures of normality to be, reliance on them is heavy and crucial to science.[6]

An important characteristic, then, of rich theories is that their application to experiment relies upon a wide range of theories external to them. Let us consider briefly another example: suppose that we wanted to test pair-production theory (i.e., the theory of the transition $\gamma \rightarrow$ $e^+ + e^-$) or similar particle reactions using a Wilson cloud chamber. Then we must know how the chamber operates—i.e., we must know that a mechanical valve can be triggered at a known time so as to reduce rapidly the gas pressure in the chamber and produce a supersaturated gas, that supersaturated gas will form condensation droplets preferentially around such "impurities" as ionized gas atoms and dust particles and that, the rate of formation being what it is, if a short-exposure photograph be taken of the chamber very near (but shortly after) the valve activation, a relatively spatially well defined set of droplets will be distinguishable in the photograph. To know all of this requires classical rigid body mechanics, gas theory, thermodynamics, fluid mechanics, optics and chemistry. The chamber is normally activated by an entering charged particle which triggers a particle counter which in turn electrically activates valve and camera. We must also know the kind and rate of ionization in the chamber that the particles we are interested in are likely to produce. Finally, in order to determine energy and momentum of the particles a magnetic field is usually introduced and the curvature of a particle's track, which is related to its momentum, is measured off the photographs. Thus we require electronics, quantum theory of collisions and electromagnetic theory to be added to the above catalogue of theories relied upon in designing the experiment. Then we must add whatever is necessary to ensure our satisfaction with the *ceteris paribus* clause and theories of human psychology and perception. We wind up relying upon a goodly part of the entire remainder of science in testing this one aspect of particle theory![7] For the benefit of the reader, the situation here is outlined schematically in **Appendix 2.**

My aim has been to show the intricate mutual interdependencies of the sciences not at the level of pure theory, where it is customary to search for relationships, but at the level of testing and experiment. My aim has been to show, indeed, the fundamentally misleading nature of a model of scientific theories that treats each theory in isolation from all others. For such a model tends quite naturally to ignore the complexities of actual applications of theories, especially those involved in experimental design. In so doing not only does it miss the important inter-theoretical relationships illustrated above, but it arrives, in consequence, at an inaccurate formal model for the deductive sciences and hence at inadequate evaluations of scientific methodologies.

Internal globalness and external globalness are incompatible features of a *theory*. Just to the extent that it is internally global to that extent it escapes external dependence. The final, true science—for those who believe in such a thing—is presumably a fully internally global *theory*, the ultimate in unity. What we often have in practice is a partially internally global theory that has something to say on every component and structural level of its domain but covers few or no aspects completely, hence is also thoroughly externally global also.

4.4 THE STRUCTURE OF GLOBAL SCIENCE

Although its details vary, depending on who is elaborating it, the basic structure of a scientific theory according to the traditional view is the four level affair indicated diagrammatically in Figure 4.1

Level	Type
1.	(x) (. . . . T . . . .)
2.	(x) (. . . . T, 0 . . . .)
3.	(x) (. . . . 0 . . . .)
4.	. . . . 0, a . . . .

Figure 4.1

As indicated in Figure 4.1, Level 1 is the purely theoretical level at which unobservable theoretical terms are linked to one another; level 2 contains links among theoretical and observational terms—this is *the* so-called level of correspondence rules; level 3 consists of all those generalizations, containing observational terms only, deductively derivable from levels 1 and 2 combined; level 4 contains singular statements involving only observational terms and names of individuals (objects, events, locations, etc.). Some of these latter, when conjoined with the generalizations of level 3, deductively imply some others of level 4, these being the events to be predicted (or, if the deduction occurs *ex post facto*, to be explained). However the Empiricist system is elaborated, it is always an elaboration within this basic schematic structure.[8]

It should now be clear that this model is a quite unrealistic treatment of the structure of science. It fails to do justice to the global features of scientific theories and to the complexities of experimental design as adumbrated in the foregoing.

A schematic structure for science that is much closer to real science is that offered in Figure 4.2. There are at least seven significant ways in which this structure differs from, and improves upon, the simple Empiricist model.

(1) The external global characteristics are explicitly recognized in the structure. The schema recognizes explicitly that two sets of additional theories are in general an essential part of any scientific situation. Such theories appear at two levels: (*ia*) there may be additional theories needed in order to apply a given theory to a certain *kind* of situation (e.g., classical and quantum mechanics of individual interactions must be supplemented by classical and quantum statistical theory respectively before they are adequate to handle practical applications to gases, liquids, and solids); (*ib*) having obtained the right *general* kind of theory, additional theories still will often be needed in order to work out a theory of the *specific* kind of experimental situation envisaged (e.g., to the quantum theory of pair formation must be added the quantum theory of gaseous ionization and electromagnetic theory in order to get a theory of the behavior of such fundamental particle pairs in a general experimental environment of a gas immersed in an electromagnetic field); (ii) finally, in order to know how to process instrumental outputs, the theories of these instruments must be set down and related to the various features of the theoretical situations which may arise. These theories therefore have direct inputs into which instruments are chosen (sometimes, indeed, even an influence on which system (type) is chosen for investigation) and how the data is prepared and processed (including, in particular, the estimates of its reliability). In addition, the structure includes the general "background" theories—the various theories of mathematics and psychology, and whatever else may need to be tacitly assumed to obtain the *ceteris paribus* clause always invoked.

(2) The internal global characteristics are explicitly recognized in the influence that the theory nominally under test (T_0) has on these same features of the situation, the selection of system and instruments, the preparation and processing of data. (I say "nominally" under test because there is no severe asymmetry of roles between T_0 and the other theories in these respects.)

(3) The structure explicitly recognizes the important role of mathematical models in global theories. The mathematical theories of science that I have been discussing all model the real world using var-

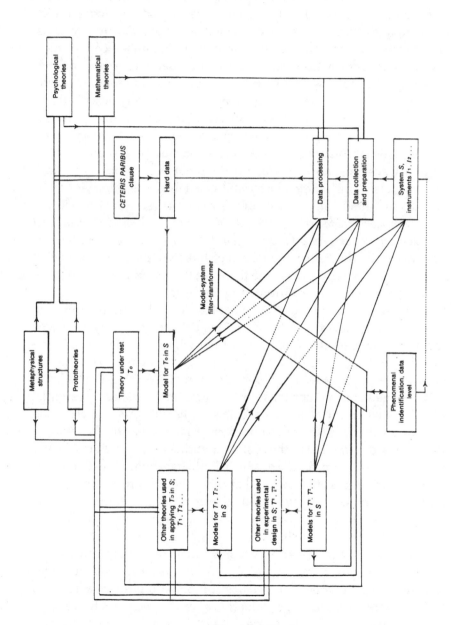

Figure 4.2

ious mathematical models (point masses, instantaneous velocities, etc.) and often these are known to be idealizations (e.g., point masses). From a formal point of view the theory is directly about the behavior of these model systems, not the real world systems. Indirectly, though, these models are seen as models of the real world systems, adequate in the relevant respects in certain circumstances. In most cases the transformation from the actual crudely observable properties of systems to those of the model is a very complex one, requiring various "corrections" and "adjustments" to the crudely described system until the model system is approached. Indeed, even the transformation from the real system behavior described in the technical terms of the model to that of the model behavior may be just as complex, since real systems, however described, do not behave exactly as idealized models. (This point is important in establishing the character of two distinct kinds of correspondence rules—cf. section 4.5 below.)

It is only when data are presented at the level of the theoretical model that we can obtain an experimental verdict on the theory (or, if you prefer, it is only when the theoretical model can be linked to the simplest level of observational description via the theory of the experimental situation, that the theory can be confronted by experiment).

Thus the appearance of the "model-system filter-transformer" in the schematic diagram. All connections between theory and experiment pass through this filter-transformer which has the task of commencing with an identification of the objects in the experimental situation (system under test plus instruments). Whether this identification is made in commonsense or technical terms makes no essential difference when the goal is hard data (it only adds or subtracts a step or two). In any case, the filter-transformer must tailor the behavior of the objects identified to fit the best theoretical models of them. Clearly it is this complex procedure which both determines just how we prepare and process the data and also has the prior function of influencing the choice of system and instruments. By contrast, Sellars remarks, the Empiricist reconstruction of science sees no *essential* functions for models at all.[9]

(4) The example in **Appendix 2** instances a little-noted feature of the scientific reasoning process, namely that *often not even the derivation of observable results is deductively valid.* Traditional Empiricism assumes a fully deductive structure. The situation as envisaged here, however, is explicitly to allow the theory/data transitions appearing therein to include nondeductive arguments as well as deductive arguments. Sometimes, for example, scientists argue after a form "If T and E then with probability p (near 1) S, so assume S; now if S . . . ." and some-

times they argue "if *S* then *T*, assuming *T* we shall also assume *S*; now if *S* . . . ." when predicting how things will go, as well as when assessing the degree of support a theory possesses. Of course many far more complex argument forms than this appear as well in actual practice. In many, many applications of a scientific theory one cannot say for certain, given the theory under examination, precisely what the experimental conditions are, though one can usually know very probably what they are. Unlike the Empiricist structure, therefore, which segregates deductive and inductive arguments, the present model permits both types of argument to occur in all theory/data transitions.

(5) The nature and role of the so-called correspondence rules is radically different and much more complex than that evisaged in the Empiricist model. Here there are two distinctively different kinds of linkages between theory and the world.

The first of these are linkages between theory and hard data. These are the connections usually considered by working scientists. In this case the linkages are extremely complex, since they must properly be traced down through the filter-transformer and back up through the data processing and preparation chains. Notice, though, that the end result of this chain can be expressed as a direct theory-hard data linkage. (E.g., for quantum theory we might have (very roughly): "An electron-ionized track intersecting a positron-ionized track in a Wilson cloud chamber gives off a particle producing no ionization until . . . etc.") The temptation to resort to this expression *alone* is fatal, however, because it suppresses all of the complex and novel features of these linkages. (*i*) It tends to suppress the distinction between hard data and phenomenal data (cf. below). (*ii*) It suppresses the *role of models* in developing the correspondences. (*iii*) Even more importantly it suppresses their character as *multiply theory dependent*. (I daresay there is not a single correspondence rule connecting any real life global theory to hard data which is not thus dependent upon other theories as well.)

But there is also a second kind of linkage included, that between model and the phenomenal data and identification level. These are the linkages that connect assertions couched in the descriptive terms of the model to commonsense descriptions. (Thus: "A Wilson cloud chamber (technical model theoretic name) is a vacuum sealed box capable of providing supersaturated vapor by . . . ," and even further than this quasi-technical description: "A Wilson cloud chamber (same use) is a black metal box with a little plunger that . . . ," and perhaps we are still not sufficiently "far down" into commonsense terminology.) At all events we are dealing with a continuum of cases here whose bottom is "pure ordinary English," whatever that is—cf. below. The scientist habitually makes use of such connections to tell his technicians, or the storeman, what to do, but they never enter his account of science. They are, on the other hand, what the epistemologically self-conscious philosopher typically has in mind, though they are often confused with the former rules.[10]

Finally, note that both types of linkage may contain inductive as well as deductive components, again a departure from the traditional model.

(6) The present schema explicitly recognizes the presence and importance of a "supra-theoretic" level of proto-theories and beyond those again a further level of metaphysics. These elements, which are almost without exception only tacit in the exposition of theories, are also almost universally ignored by philosophers. Positivist-Empiricists were an exception; they actually dismissed the crucially important metaphysical level! It is hard to overemphasize the importance of this level. Suffice it to say that I believe that the entire history of physics can, in effect, be seen as the competition of two incompatible metaphysical schemes—the atoms + void and the plena + no-void schemes. This remark is elaborated briefly in **Appendix 3.** In view of this history one need hardly emphasize the thoroughgoing way in which our descriptive conceptual schemes contain and reflect these fundamental structures. Indeed, I have recently argued in some detail the thesis that the deep mathematical structures employed by theories of mathematical physics are chosen so as to reflect the preferred metaphysics that the theory is expressing (and further that this approach offers the only hope of unravelling the mysteries of quantum theory).[11] The metaphysical schemes lay down the most fundamental general principles governing the conceptual structure of a coherent description of the *kind* of world—it is no wonder therefore that they have a fully pervasive influence on the form and content of the theories that express them. It has been a great loss to philosophy of science to ignore their presence and importance for so long.

Also of considerable importance are the "proto" theories (Bunge's term; he first drew my attention to them; see 1967a, b). These are the theories that express the assumed general structures of some of the quantities entering the formulation of scientific theories, and of some of the methods employed in their application. Thus we include here a theory of the structure of the time continuum (a set, ordered by an antisymmetrical, transitive, irreflexive relation, etc.), space, abstract measurement theory, etc. (The reader should consult Bunge for details—but beware of reading too much into these proto-theories, cf. Hooker 1971b.) Such theories could be assumed absorbed into the expression of each specific theory (as I suppose we ought charitably to assume the Empiricists to do), but it certainly is not so in *typical* expressions of a theory and their special role has been largely overlooked. Of course they serve as an initial filling out of a metaphysics, hence their position in the schema.

(7) Finally, I draw attention again to the role accorded a "phenomenal" or commonsense level in the structure of science. We have already seen how that role might be criticized (indeed, how in principle it might be eliminated) and how it is, in any case, not the chief linkage which appears in scientific accounts. In both of these ways it differs radically from the Empiricist analysis. In section 4.6 below, I shall briefly describe my own current views on its ultimate fate.

These then are the seven ways in which this schema for science differs from, and improves upon, the traditional Empiricist model that has been so influential. Now it is time to look at some of the other general issues raised by the recognition of the existence of global theories.

4.5 PROSPECT FOR CONFIRMATION THEORY

I believe we can say this: if anything like full justice is to be done to the actual structure of scientific reasoning then the older, simple picture of the place of confirmation theory in the scientific process must be abandoned, at least initially. In this older conception the theory of confirmation was seen to be independent of, and supervenient upon, the core structure of science. Operating, as it were, solely at a metascientific level, the theory of confirmation applied equally to all scientific theories and was thus independent of any one of them. We have seen in the above, however, *that actual judgments of relevance and confirmation in science are not independent of, indeed are heavily conditioned by, the very theories with respect to which the judgments of relevance and confirmation are made, and possibly to many other theories besides.* (Thus quantum *theory* affects the theorist's judgments of the relevance and support of observational data to statements *of that very same theory.*) How are we to cope with this situation?

Initially, we may propose relativizing statements of confirmation to a *theoretical* context. Thus, instead of trying to erect a theory of confirmation under which, for example, the degree of support afforded a *theoretical* sentence by a set of observational sentences depends only upon the predicates and syntactical structures occurring in both types of sentence, we may attempt instead to construct confirmational relations in which the degree of support is a function not only of the supporting sentences and the supported sentence but also the *theoretical* context pertinent to both. We must then face the fact that judgments of support between *T* and *E* (*theory* and observational claim) will themselves be functions of *T* (as well as of other *theories*). What such a confirmation theory will be like exactly I cannot say but, as we shall see in the discussion of epistemology below, there need be nothing vicious in the feedback occurring here.

Moreover, the complexity of judgments of support is indicated by the complexity of the transformational chains that get us from *theoretic* models "down" through the filter-transformer and "up" through the data preparation and processing to the hard data. The "distance" between experimental event and *theory* confrontation is considerable and every step in covering it compounds the complexity.

But there is, of course, a distinction between what science in fact is, or has been, and the theoretical ideals towards which philosophers should work in their analysis of science. In the spirit of this distinction we may still work toward obtaining a logic of confirmation which is less dependent on the details of particular scientific *theories* than is the tentative suggestion immediately above. We may begin to see our way clear in this area by asking "Why is it that scientists make the particular judgments of confirmation which they do in the light of the *theories* which they have?" Answers to this question will be of the sort "Because, according to the *theory T*, the connection between the *theoretical* statement *S* (belonging to *T*) and the outcome of experiment *E* is e.g., causal (or statistical, or merely accidental), so the degree of support which a positive outcome for *E* provides for *S* is high (or moderate, or nil)." We would then be in a position to extract from the answers to such questions *theory*-neutral statements of confirmation of the form: If the relationship between observational statements *E* and the *theoretical* statement *S* is thus and so, then the degree of support which positive instances of *E* provide for *S* is thus and so. Such statements of confirmation would then be independent of any particular *theory* and could be applied to a *theory* "from without" so to speak, rather than each separate *theory* having its own set of confirmation rules operating "from within." Such statements, together with the statements of the *theory* concerning the relationships which in fact obtain, would yield derivative confirmational statements concerning the actual relationships between a given *theoretical* sentence and given observational data.

We should notice, however, that this task still awaits completion, for such judgments of confirmation are in general richer than those now considered in formal theories of confirmation. We need a theory of confirmation which is capable of taking into account the detailed and complex relationships which can exist between the *theoretical* sentences and observational sentences according to contemporary theories.

I do not believe, for example, that there are any actual scientific situations which are as simple as the relationship between a number of observed white swans and the generalization that all swans are white. Indeed, in this particular case we have in actual science the more complex judgment that swans observed, even in number, in any one particular location on the earth will in general (depending upon the climate) be an unreliable indication of the color of swans in general, *given our general biological knowledge of the internal constitution of birds*. The actual judgment of confirmation, therefore, concerns not merely the number of positive instances of the generalization, it is a much more complex judgment concerning the degree of support which certain classes of positive instances are capable of providing for the generalization in the light of our general biological knowledge of birds.[12]

Indeed we can now see a second reason why the above program in confirmation theory has not been carried out; not only are the confirmational judgments not yet sufficiently rich and detailed to be able to take account of the examples which actually occur in science, but the analysis of any particular scientific *theory* in order to isolate how, precisely, it determines judgments of confirmation has never in fact been carried out. The prospect of analyzing our general biological theories of the constitution of living organisms in order to isolate precisely the role which the statement of the possible variability of color with climate would play in that theoretical complex should already indicate to the reader the enormity of the task that would be involved in completely analyzing the judgments of confirmation of any actual scientific theory.

Moreover, we should not lose sight of the fact that there is an inherent danger built into this aim for confirmation theory. For the confirmation claims envisaged here are conditional in form and *the antecedent of the conditional makes an empirical claim*, hence we are not in a position to apply this theory *a priori*, as we are with traditional confirmation theory, but must use *theory* to sanction these claims. The temptation to forget this and so to obscure the new epistemology of confirmation is as good a reason as any not to pursue this ideal but to display openly the new epistemological structure of the situation by making our confirmational claims explicitly *theory* dependent. This view is reinforced when we observe that the *general form* of such judgments will also be metaphysically dependent as well (according to my structural schema for science).

4.6 EPISTEMOLOGY

Here I concentrate only upon those epistemological issues directly raised by the occurrence of global theories. Already some of the general epistemological issues have been raised in Section 4.4 on the general structure of science and a specific issue in confirmation theory was raised in the immediately preceding section.

The prospect of having global theories at once raises the specter of having theories which are not open to independent criticism—i.e., to criticism independent of the *theory* in question. And if this is so then we face the prospect of having *theories* which are essentially unfalsifiable, for they may so regulate the criticism which they allow that it, essentially, does not place them in jeopardy. One can see from the above account several points at which such a possibility seems to open up. (a) Thus if a *theory* could, indeed, totally prescribe the kinds of descriptions of relevant observational data which were permissible, or if it could insinuate its way into the meanings of the terms in the observational vocabulary in a sufficiently thorough manner, then we should fear that it might prescribe their occurrence or their meaning in such a way that no observational reports could be produced which would be incompatible with the principles of the *theory*. (b) Again, if it is the *theory* itself which is used to provide the analysis of the experimental instruments which are used to provide experimental tests for the *theory* then we may fear that the prescriptions for experiments which it offers us are so designed that those experimental outcomes could never embarrass the *theory* itself. (c) And, finally, we may suspect that if judgments of confirmation, concerning the degree of support which experimental evidence provides for a *theory*, are themselves mediated by the *theory* then the *theory* itself might so determine the rules of confirmation that no observational evidence could undermine the *theory*.

To what degree are our scientific *theories* involved in this kind of epistemological circularity and what have been philosophers' reactions to it?

(a) With respect to theoretical influence on the observation language, philosophical reaction has ranged from the empiricist extreme—under which the observational language shows no theoretical influence whatever and remains independent of, and common to, all acceptable theories—to the opposite extreme (under philosophers such as P.K. Feyerabend) according to which the observational language is totally dominated by *theory* and changes when the *theory* changes—as do also our perceptual experiences.

This is a complex matter but, following an analysis of it I have given in Chapter 2 (see also 1973d), I shall take the following position: In the sense of *theory*-influence normally intended there is a level of observational vocabulary which is *not* appreciably *theory*-influenced or *theory*-dependent. This is a *subset* of the phenomenal data level. There is, however, a level of observational vocabulary, *often employing the same signs as the former level*, which *is* dominated by *theoretical* conceptions and which is the normal vocabulary of the scientific laboratory. This vocabulary operates at the level of preparation and processing of data. Roughly speaking, then, I believe that there is a continuum of *theory*-domination visible in actual language and that there is a "bottom" to this continuum that is essentially *theory* free. I incline, therefore, to that peculiar combination of strands of Realist thought which holds, on the one hand, the conservative view that there is a subset of our commonsense concepts which will survive *theory* change (within the Western scientific tradition hitherto—cf. below) and on the other hand, holds the radical view that many of our commonsense concepts are *theory*-laden and should be rejected and that much of the *theory*-laden observational vocabulary is *actually*, and not just potentially, being replaced with vocabulary dominated by the newer *theories*. (I hold in addition the Realist rejection of any "givens," i.e., of any level of indubitability.)

In addition, there is another sense, distinguishable from the foregoing sense, in which even the first mentioned level of observational vocabulary is infected by *theory*—though this infection becomes visible only when one considers entire cultures. It is *theory*-dominated in this sense: its fundamental conceptual structure is dominated by the metaphysical structures it expresses, and I regard all metaphysical structures as ultimately open to criticism just as is *theory*, hence as theory-like (though the historical scale of the criticism may be measured in centuries and cultures).[13] In this latter, but *not* in any former, sense the most general *theoretical* component does effect our perceptual experience. *Within* our Western culture, therefore, the scientific enterprise is not, I believe, seriously endangered by the prospect of epistemological circularity in virtue of its domination of the observational vocabulary in the sense understood by current philosophy. At the wider level of an entire culture, or perhaps even of the entire species, we may have cause for concern that the scientific enterprise operates within some broad confines imposed by the fundamental (neurological?) constitution of its human protagonists.

There is, in addition, a second way in which a degree of epistemological circularity may enter in respect to the observational level which needs to be considered. I pointed out in the first section of the paper that a scientific *theory* does prescribe the kinds of terms in which the observational data may be described when it is being transformed into hard data for that *theory*. (I gave the example of how quantum theory teaches us to talk in terms of energy transitions and interactions, particle localizations and so forth, rather than in other terms which we might have chosen for the expression of our processed experimental data.[14]) Both of these sorts of effects operate, however, at the second, and *theoretically* laden, of the two levels of observational vocabulary distinguished above. The point of the restrictiveness comes, therefore, in the specification of the rules by which the *untheoretical* observational descriptions are translated into the *theoretically loaded* observational descriptions in preparation for their confronting the *theory*. There seems to be no doubt that these rules are indeed heavily determined by the *theory* in question and that in some respects they do indeed constitute a *prima facie* selection in favor of the kinds of descriptions favored by the *theory* itself. The degree to which this selectivity operates can only be judged by detailed analysis of actual examples from the history of science (e.g., the quantum interpretation controversy *vis-à-vis* the phraseology mentioned in Note 14).

(b) In respect of the role which *theories* play in analysis of the experimental situations which are set up to test *themselves* there seems less immediate danger of circularity. For, in the first place, so long as *theories* have something definite to say about the functioning of experimental instruments such statements can be conjoined with other statements of the *theory* to yield definite predictions for the outcomes of such experiments and the *theory* is therefore open to criticism. Furthermore, and equally importantly, *theory* cannot, in any simple way, adjust its statements concerning the functioning of experimental instruments in the light of experimental results which conflict with its predictions so as to remove the conflict. For, since the *theoretical* account of the functioning of such instruments concerns the general dynamical characteristics of the fundamental *theoretical* quantities involved in the entire domain over which the *theory* ranges, any alteration in that account for the benefit of any given particular experimental arrangement cannot help but have systematic repercussions throughout the entire domain and will therefore itself be open to experimental criticism. (At least, this analysis shows that it is desirable to place a methodological premium on construction of *theories* which have this degree of "coherence" or generality.) It seems highly improbable that an entire domain of science should have the requisite symmetries required for preserving a *theory* from experimental criticism by the *ad hoc*, but systematic, alteration of its account of the fundamental functioning of such instruments. Nonetheless, the history of science shows that there are many cases where what are perceived at the time to be relatively isolated negative results are indeed set aside, often on the grounds that we do not yet have an adequate *theoretical* understanding of the situation in which they were obtained, only later to be resurrected and made the foundation of an alternative account of the entire domain (diffraction phenomena in the seventeenth century, perihelion of Mercury, etc.). We cannot therefore entirely set aside this aspect of *theories* from consideration concerning how theories are, and may be, criticized.

(c) Because the field of confirmation theory as discussed above is yet so indefinite I am not able to form an opinion as to the possibilities of juggling judgments of confirmation so as to keep a *theory* immune from effective criticism. There is no doubt, of course, that so long as there were *no* limitations placed upon the way in which such judgments could be altered these alterations would indeed suffice for that purpose. But judgments of confirmation must after all be reasonable and so they cannot be altered without limits. Indeed, one can only hope that the systematic analysis of confirmation as envisaged above will lead to a sufficiently precise theory of confirmation to support our intuition that we can eliminate this possibility as a source of epistemological bias.

Despite our careful restriction of the global properties of *theories* as indicated in the above paragraphs there is no doubt that such properties of *theories* raise a severe problem for any rational account of the progress of science. One of the great advantages of the empiricist view of science is that it not only provided a firm, theory-neutral foundation for scientific knowledge but also attempted to provide a systematic procedure by which new theories could be erected in the place of older theories which proved incompatible with observation, theories which would be more adequate—these methods were the so-called methods of induction. On the other hand once we recognize the global character of scientific *theories* we realize the impossibility of determining any such theory on an inductive basis. It is difficult to see how inductive arguments—even if accepted—could lead us to the establishment of rules of confirmation for the theory in question.

Moreover, it is nearly impossible to see how such arguments could lead us to a theory adequate to analyzing the very experimental techniques by which the data which formed the basis of such arguments was obtained (experimental data is already a highly selected aspect of the investigable world and it is selected on the dictates of *theory*). Not only is all of this the case, but it is in principle impossible to see how such arguments can lead to the establishment of a unique set of rules for translating phenomenal observational data into a form that is relevant for its confrontation with *theory*, or could lead to a unique specification of *theoretical* terms, forms of description and laws which are required. It follows then that global *theories* give to scientific theories a certain "holistic" character; one seems forced to say that one either lays down the *entire theory* at a single blow (i.e., *theory* proper, supporting *theories*, forms of description and rules for analyzing data, analysis of experimental situations and confirmation rules all included) or one has not laid down a unit which can operate effectively in science at all. It gives support to the Quinean contention that "the unit of empirical significance is the whole of science." Nonetheless, the two great background metaphysical-conceptual schemes and their corresponding ontologies, discussed earlier, together with the elementary observational level, form two elements of continuity in the history of science.

Within this limited continuity provided at the extreme ends of the scientific structure, however, I believe we must admit that holistic changes in scientific theories have occurred through imaginative "leaps" on the part of individual scientists which can be followed only at the level of psychological analysis and probably cannot be given a rational reconstruction solely in objective, Popperian, Third World terms (cf. Popper 1973) though the actions of individual scientists might well be given a rational decision-theoretic analysis where the full range of human utilities is involved (cf. Chapter 5, this work). Nevertheless, we should not underestimate the force of the above two sources of continuity for I believe that such imaginative leaps as there are have always arisen out of a detailed controversy concerning certain specific characteristics or defects of an existing *theory* (the controversy usually linked to the metaphysical-mathematical continuity level—e.g., Einstein's remarks on the equivalence of inertia and gravitational mass) and the particular solutions which have been adopted have always been adopted with an eye to conforming to the fundamental metaphysical-conceptual schemes of the culture and (as far as possible) to the fundamental mathematical structures of the preceding *theory*. To what extent the theories may be compared in detail on this view in the history of science, i.e., to what extent the meanings of theoretical terms are theoretically determined, and to what extent there is any common sharing of ontologies between competing theories, I shall leave as open questions.

What I want to draw attention to here, however, is the fact that this constancy need hold only within the confines of a general culture. One can perfectly well imagine that other cultures may have adopted a different fundamental ontology, for example, a process ontology, and with it different fundamental conceptual descriptive schemes. One can even imagine—though it is less likely—that a different culture established conditions where the perceptual learning of children was such that the world was perceived in different terms from those that are active in our own perceptual processing (one can't help but feel that there must be some differences even in a culture which adopted a fundamentally different metaphysics from ours but one can also imagine more radical differences such as, for example, the adoption of a four-dimensional space-time perceptual organization—cf. my discussion in 1970a, and Bohm 1965, appendix).

We must now raise the question whether these culture-wide aspects of science cannot themselves in some way be opened to critical examination. I suggest the view that ultimately both of these aspects are open to the same kind of critical reappraisal as are any other elements in the structure of science—it is just that the reappraisal time is so much longer than for other elements and the reappraisal process so much more complex and difficult to realize. If a culture presses a particular descriptive scheme and its correlative ontology over a long period of time (e.g., many centuries), constructing within its confines many different successive theories, each one designed to cope more adequately with those areas of experimental experience where the former theories ran into difficulty, and if at the end of such a long process these difficulties were not clarified but seemed only to deepen in their embeddedness in the fundamental theoretical structure, then it may force that culture to a re-evaluation of its fundamental descriptive scheme and ontology and to seek to create alternatives to it. This thesis really applies Lakatos' notion of a "research programme" to the level to which it is most suited, the level of general metaphysics, the top level of *theory* (see Lakatos 1968b).

As a matter of fact, I believe that we in western society are precisely in this position in the twentieth century where the two great conceptual schemes mentioned above have twice met—leading to the creation of relativity theory and quantum theory respectively. That we are now discovering that difficulties involved in the use of those two schemes, and especially in the attempt to combine them, suggests that very fundamental revisions in the basic structure of our description of the world are required. Under these circumstances we may well be forced and encouraged to look around for alternatives to these two schemes.[15]

APPENDIX 1

Partially Internally Global Theories, An Example:
General Biochemical Theory of Living Organisms

We now have a *general* (though not always detailed) biochemical theoretical description of the constitution of living organisms and this description is certainly related to, and supported by, a vast network of experimental data. Now let us run briefly back through the six aspects of quantum theory mentioned above—in addition to the theoretical-observational core—which gave it its global character and see to what extent they are reflected in this situation.

(i) As to the mode of description of data, we are to describe the functionings of an organism in terms of chemical rates of exchange, permeability of membranes, blood pressure and so on but not in terms of vital spirits, life forces or sympathies. One of the key kinds of descriptions of organisms is in functional terms, but what is to count as a function in biology is itself prescribed by biological theory. Thus the heart's pumping blood to the brain will be a biological function, though a man's living in order to listen to Beethoven's music will not in general be counted as a biological function (not *yet* at any rate, for the future nature of psychology is still a matter of dispute—and even then, not ever under *that* description).

(ii) The biochemical theory certainly specifies the general category of things which will be observable. Thus it informs us that biologically key microorganisms such as viruses will not in general be observable, neither in superficial observations of a larger living organism, nor in unaided observation of its innards, no matter how attentive; but that they will be observable under a sufficiently powerful microscope in certain circumstances. We are informed that genes may not even be observable under these circumstances, though their effects, e.g., red hair, certainly are open to even superficial observation in many cases.

(iii) Our biological theory tells us, for example, the conditions under which the key hereditary structures of an organism are observable (in some cases under an electron microscope, etc.—see also (ii) above) as well as those under which cell reproduction is observable.

(iv) Insofar as biological instrumentation is used for observation—e.g., cell staining techniques—and insofar as the interactions of biological and physical instrumentation must be analyzed before experimental results can be evaluated, the biological theory is clearly involved in the specification of what instrumentation is appropriate for the making of observations and the conditions under which the observations may be made. Thus you can stain cells if you wish to examine the length of sperm tails but not if you wish to examine the flow of material through the semipermeable membrane of the cell wall.

(v) According to our biochemical point of view the appearance of excess fat tissue in an organism would be causally related to the malfunctioning of the glandular system, the appearance of blue eyes in an offspring will be only statistically related to the eye colors of the parents, whilst the correlation in color between polar bears and albino budgerigars is accidental.

(vi) And finally it is clear that it is the biological theory which must help us to assess the reliability of observations which are carried out for the purpose of supporting theoretical biological generalizations. Thus, for example, biological study of the composition of blood plasma in a leukemiac will not provide reliable information on the dynamics of the disease if the patient is also diabetic or is suffering from a significant iron deficiency. And clearly the evidential supports of appearance of excess fat tissue for glandular malfunctioning, of blue eyes in an offspring for parental eye color and of polar bears for the existence of albino budgerigars will be very different from one another and conditioned by the information contained in (v) immediately above.

In the case of at least this example the global characteristics of the theory are not complete—the theory does not dictate *every* aspect of its domain. (i) Thus, for example, biochemical theory does not dictate completely the vocabulary of observation for the domain in question. (Whether, as an extension of the technical issue of Note 5, there is a primitive observational vocabulary belonging to "natural language" which quantum theory may absorb but does not dictate is a difficult question which I do not attempt to answer in detail here. It is part of the general issue of the impact of the theory itself on the meanings of the terms in the observational vocabulary; see Chapter 2.) But the drive of the above comments was not the so-called "theoretical loadedness" of the observational vocabulary; rather, that the theory restricted the observational vocabulary to sets of appropriate observational terms (thus description in terms of discontinuous processes rather than continuous processes). (ii), (iii) Neither biochemical theory, nor quantum theory for that matter, specifies purely internally to itself what is and is not observable; for observing X, as opposed to X's merely being of macroscopic size, is a matter for the psychology, as well as the physics, of perception. What each theory does is to tell us how big or small its entities are and what relations they may stand in to such things as light waves, geiger counters, electron beams or whatever. This information, allied to a theory of perception (implicitly assumed), then specifies what is observable. Both of these theories are fairly exhaustive in their specifications of sizes, but biology needs supplementation by quantum theory to specify the relations its entities can have to various probing media (light, etc.). For quantum theory is, at least in principle, a theory of the constitution of *all* physical systems, whereas biological theories make no such claim and hence must borrow from other physical theories in appropriate domains (e.g. for the treatment of the mechanical aspects of organic functions and for the analysis of the workings of much of the laboratory equipment).

These intimate involvements of a theory with other theories already takes us into the second dimension of global characteristics. (iv) Both theories are again more or less exhaustive. With biological theory, however, there is always only the specification of the biological function which an appropriate measuring instrument must be able to play, the physical details being left to other theories. (v) Both theories are also exhaustive in their specifications of the kinds of relations holding among kinds of events (causal, statistical, etc.— though I remain more certain of this in the case of quantum theory for obvious reasons, but one would expect this exhaustiveness of a completed biochemical theory at any rate). (vi) Again, neither theory provides all of the rules for evaluating the weight of evidence for or against a given statement, but both theories provide significant statements concerning the values of the relevant observational data. But over and above all of this, not every theory—indeed not any theory so far—makes fully explicit all of the assumptions concerning the general character of the physical world under which it operates and which guide the construction of the theory: assumptions concerning the nature of individuals, of space and time, of causality, of continuity and discreteness, and so on. But nonetheless such assumptions are operative, I believe, in a scientific process and we must make them explicit if we are to come to a richer understanding of the nature of scientific theories. (For an examination of classical and quantum mechanics see Hooker 1973c.)

APPENDIX 2

The Structure of Science, An Example: Electron Paths in Cloud Chambers

What follows will be a *fairly rough*, but indicative, analysis of a typical experimental situation. In particular, the data preparation-processing structure is not made explicit, the model concentrates only on the structural role of other theories in the experimental design.

A cloud chamber is, essentially, a box within which air can be supersaturated with water vapor. Under this condition, any disturbance of the air will cause water vapor to condense out and form water droplets.

An electron is a small charged particle, and charged particles, if they are travelling fast enough, can knock other electrons off gas atoms (ionize them). Thus an electron moving in a cloud chamber leaves a trail of ionized gas atoms (ions). These ions act as disturbances around which water droplets form. Consequently, an observer sees a cloudy trail in the chamber where the electron has been.

Electrons, because they are electrically charged, experience forces in the presence of electric fields. So you can tell whether the particle in the chamber is an electron by how it moves, that is, by how its track looks, when an electric field is applied. For example, looking at the chamber side on:

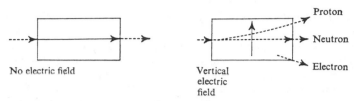

How do we know all of this? Because of the fundamental theories which we have.

1. The *Atomic Theory* tells us that everything is made of atoms and that atoms have a central nucleus surrounded by electrons.
2. The *Electromagnetic Theory* tells us under what conditions electrons can be stripped off atoms.
3. The *Heat Theory* tells us how we may satisfy these latter conditions and obtain a supply of electrons from a hot filament.
4. The *Electromagnetic Theory* then tells us how to use electric and magnetic fields to force electrons to enter the cloud chamber.
5. The *Theory of Gases* (a branch of *Atomic Theory* these days) together with *Heat Theory* tells us how supersaturated gases are produced and how they behave.
6. The *Theory of Mechanics* tells us about an electron's collision with gas atoms, and
7. The *Electromagnetic Theory* then tells us whether the electron will ionize (knock an electron off) the gas atom.
8. *Atomic Theory* and *Heat Theory* (see 5) then tell us about the formation of the water droplet trail.
9. *Electromagnetic Theory* tells us how to produce an electric field in the chamber and
10. *Electromagnetic Theory* and the *Theory of Mechanics* tells us what shape the electron's path, and hence the cloud trail, will be.

(Note that some of these theories will have to take their quantized forms.)
Let us see how the example might be *very roughly* formally constructed. Let:

T_1 stand for Atomic Theory
T_2 stand for Heat Theory
T_3 stand for Electromagnetic Theory
T_4 stand for Theory of Mechanics

(i) $(T_3 \cdot T_4) \supset (x)$ ((Particle $x \cdot x$ is negatively charged $\cdot x$ is in a vertical electric field $\cdot x$ has a nonzero horizontal velocity initially) $\supset x$'s path is a downward curve with geometrical characteristics $C_1 \ldots C_n$).
("T_3 and T_4 together imply that all negatively charged particles in a vertical electric field which have an initial nonzero horizontal velocity travel along paths which are downward curves having characteristics $C_1 \ldots C_n$.")
Call the *consequent* of this remark H_0.

(ii) $T_1 \supset (x)$ (Electron $x \supset$ (Particle $x \cdot x$ is negatively charged)).
("T_1 implies that all electrons are negatively charged particles.")
Call the *consequent* of this remark H_1.

(iii) $(H_0 \cdot H_1) \supset (x)$ ((Electron $x \cdot x$ is in a vertical electric field $\cdot x$ has a nonzero horizontal velocity initially) $\supset$ x's path is a downward curve with geometrical characteristics $C_1 \ldots C_n$.)

("H_0 and H_1 together imply that all electrons travelling with an initial nonzero horizontal velocity in a vertical electric field travel along paths which are downward curves having characteristics $C_1 \ldots C_n$.")

Call the *consequent* of this remark H_2.

(iv) $(T_1 \cdot T_2 \cdot T_3 \cdot T_4) \supset (x)$ ((Particle $x \cdot$ charged $x \cdot x$ has a velocity larger than V $\cdot x$ is in a supersaturated gas) $\supset$ water droplets form at each point of x's path).

("T_1 and T_2 and T_3 and T_4 together imply that all charged particles having velocities larger than V and moving in a supersaturated gas leave water droplets at each point of their paths.")

Call the *consequent* of this remark S_1.

(v) $(T_3 \cdot T_4) \supset (x)(y)$ ((x is a vertical electric field $\cdot$ y is a voltmeter in good condition $\cdot$ y is at the same location as x) $\supset$ y shows a positive reading).

("T_3 and T_4 together imply that all voltmeters in good condition and in the presence of an electric field show positive readings.")

Call the *consequent* of this remark S_2.

(vi) $(T_1 \cdot T_2 \cdot T_3 \cdot T_4) \supset (x)$ ((x is a hot filament $\cdot$ x is in the presence of electric and magnetic fields E and B) $\supset$ x emits electrons with an initial horizontal velocity larger than V).

("T_1 and T_2 and T_3 and T_4 together imply that all hot filaments in the presence of electric and magnetic fields E and B emit electrons with an initial horizontal velocity larger than V.")

Call the *consequent* of this remark S_3.

(viii) $T_3 \supset (x)$ (x is a collection of batteries and circuits of type $M \supset (\exists y)(\exists z)$ (y is an electric field $E \cdot z$ is a magnetic field $B \cdot y$ is located at $x \cdot z$ is located at x)).

("T_3 implies that collections of batteries and circuits of Type M always produce electric and magnetic fields E, B respectively.")

Call the *consequent* of this remark S_4.

Notes: H_0, H_1, and H_2 are the particular *theoretical* generalizations which we wish to cull out of the four theories as being of particular *relevance* to this problem.

S_1 through S_4 are the statements which we need in order to *connect* the *theoretical terms* appearing in H_0, H_1, and H_2 to what is *observable*.

S_1 and S_2 state *observationally necessary conditions* for theoretical terms to hold. S_3 and S_4 state *observationally sufficient conditions* for theoretical terms to hold. They are all themselves conditional in form. What is the relevant observational evidence?

> E_1: That a certain cloud chamber A with supersaturated gas in it is present, and
>
> E_2: That A has attached to it a collection of batteries and circuits of type M on one side of A and facing into A, and
>
> E_3: A has a hot filament attached where the batteries and circuits are.
>
> E_4: A voltmeter V in A shows a positive reading when connected vertically, and
>
> E_5: So far as examination can tell V is in good condition, and
>
> E_6: There is a curve of water droplets in A, and
>
> E_7: The curve of water droplets has characteristics $C_1 \ldots C_n$.

How might we bring the evidence to bear on the problem?
First, we begin with S_3 and S_4.

> From S_4 and E_2 we *deduce:* C_1: There is an electric field E and a magnetic field B at one side of A, where the batteries and circuits are.
> From S_3 and $E_3 \cdot C_1$ we *deduce:* C_2: The hot filament emits electrons into A with an initial horizontal velocity greater than V.

Second, we apply S_2.

> From S_2 and $E_4 \cdot E_5$ we *induce:* (Very probably) C_3: A has a vertical electric field in it.

Now we have established what we need to apply H_2.

> From C_1 and C_2 and C_3 and H_2 we *deduce:* C_4: Electrons travelling in A follow downward curves with characteristics $C_1 \ldots C_n$.
> From E_1 and S_1 and H_1 we *deduce:* C_5: Electrons create curves of water droplets in A over their paths.

Finally from C_4 and C_5 we obtain

C_6: There is a curve of water droplets in A having characteristics $C_1 \ldots C_n$. C_6, the prediction, is tested by observation; and according to E_5 and E_6 the prediction is confirmed. The structure of the example looks like the figure below.

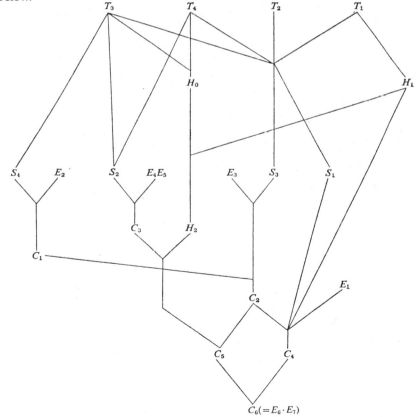

Appendix 3

Metaphysics and The History of Science

Western metaphysics is dominated by the conception of the world in terms of substance in space and time. (I also include logical structure, as well as the laws of identity, the causality/harmony conceptions and the categorial structure of attributes within metaphysics.) There have been two specific realizations of this general conception that have, as I say, dominated the history of science: (i) atoms and the void, (ii) plena and no void. The Greek philosophers debated the merits of these two models and they have been with us ever since. The atomic hypothesis reappeared in the sixteenth century after a virtual absence of 1800 years (as a corpuscular scheme), only to be met by the Cartesian plenum, a descendent of the Platonic and Aristotelian plena that had dominated scientific thought since its inception. When the atomic hypothesis became a serious empirical contender at the time of Dalton it developed alongside of, first, ether theories and then field theories. In the twentieth century these two great metaphysical schemes and their correlative conceptual and logico-mathematical structures met twice, in optics and in atomic theory.

The *first* interaction occurred when light was found not to behave as a wave should (unique velocity relative to its *plenum of propagation*—the ether) nor yet to behave as a particle (the ballistic hypothesis was refuted). Out of this situation relativity was born (though I intend no suggestion here that Einstein first studied the experimental results and then produced his theory). And we discover that the change from the Galileo space-time group to the Lorentz space-time group necessitates a change to a local theory where all mechanical action is continuous and the field is the natural ontology. Indeed, the incorporation of the particulate or atomistic aspect of matter is still a chief stumbling block to Einstein's unified field program.

The *second* interaction occurred in the atomic domain and centers around the "duality" of matter and light, i.e., around the fact that matter and light behave in ways which can be partially, but only partially, incorporated into the atomistic framework and partially, but only partially, incorporated into the plenum framework. Out of this circumstance quantum mechanics was born. In the quantum theory, what with its wave (plenum) equation and statistical (atomistic) interpretation, we find the latest (and the ultimate?) confrontation (or union?) of atomistic and plenum (wave, field) concepts of global theories.

CHAPTER 5

Methodology and Systematic Philosophy

5.1 INTRODUCTION

Method describes a sequence of actions which constitute the most efficient strategy to achieve a given goal; *Methodology* describes the theory of such sequences.

This statement above is neither a usual formulation, nor agreed to, in the extant literature, but I am going to argue both that it is nonetheless an accurate description of otherwise conflicting approaches to methodology and that it opens the way for a new and much more powerful approach to methodology.

According to the dominant English-speaking philosophic and scientific tradition, method is determined by theory of science and more particularly by epistemology. According to another tradition, method defines the scope of epistemology and determines the form of the theory of science. With the former view we associate the empiricist mainstream of this century, with the latter the pragmatists (e.g., Dewey) and Popper. Both approaches can accept the dictum that it is method which distinguishes the practice of science from, say, myth.

I shall later defend a modified version of the science-as-method view by arguing that this is the only acceptable approach for a coherent, systematic realism. But my account of realism will also make it clear how far the conception of systematic methodology required by an adequate realism must transcend the extant conceptions of method and what a more adequate, if more complex, relation to epistemology would consist in.

5.2 RECAPITULATION: METHOD IN AN EMPIRICIST FRAMEWORK

In Chapter 3 I have presented a more detailed construction of the philosophy and meta-philosophy of empiricism (and of positivism as a more restricted variant—namely, with logic restricted to finite truth functions only). Rather than re-present the abstracted, axiomatized system, I shall summarize the pertinent features as follows: Empiricists aim at the maximal accumulation of maximally justified true beliefs; these latter are to be expressed in a logically clarified language comprising logical terms and whose only meaningful descriptive terms are those which are analyzable into immediately experienceable terms and logical terms. The logical machinery here is not restricted in complexity, though historically the first order predicate calculus has been the dominant system. Call this language L. This language grounds the well-known empiricist epistemology. There is a supporting meta-philosophy which requires a foundationalist epistemology and the statement of philosophical doctrine in terms of the logical structure of a logically clarified language together with the claim that epistemology, theory of language and rationality are independent of, prior to and normative for the remaining structure of human knowledge. Taken together with other elements of a complete doctrine it leads to the following theory of science. *Aim*: The aim of science is the maximization of empirical knowledge, i.e., of maximally evidentially supported true belief. *Demarcation*: The sentences of empirical science are all and only those of the language L. *Scientific language*: L. *Scientific theory*: A deductively axiomatized class of sentences in L. *Scientific Data*: The class of basic sentences in L. *Criteria of Scientific Acceptability*: Minimally adequate evidential support (as specified in the generalized logical theory of inference). *Methodology*: Maximize scientific data, accept all theories that are at least minimally adequately evidentially supported by the data. *History of Science*: Continuous expansion of scientific data, acceptance of progressively more general and successively inclusive theories.

The meta-philosophy and philosophy of empiricism commits it to its conception of methodology, as sketched in the theory of science. Empiricist epistemology presents an absolute foundation for knowledge and the meta-philosophy demands the construction (and reconstruction) of science on its terms; precisely how this reconstruction is to proceed is given on the one hand by the aim of science, itself fixed by the theory of rationality, its nature in turn constrained by the meta-philosophy, and on the other hand by the theory of language which specifies the class of admissible constructions. The details are less important than the overall form, every empiricist position asserting a foundational epistemology with a supporting semantics and meta-philosophy is committed to reconstructing methodology in this form.

5.3 THE ROLE OF METHOD IN AN EVOLUTIONARY APPROACH: NATURALISTIC REALISM

Once we 'saw' dimly through the 'eyes' of a protozoan, as Campbell (1973) says, and no revelation has been granted us since. Evolution since that time has been total, an evolution of capacity to see, of the capacity for symbolic processes, thought, language. However we came by our philosophy, our science, our culture, we came by it all in the same manner. Humankind emerged from the evolutionary background and was capable, eventually, of all of these things; there has been no revelations, inner or outer. The brain of *Homo sapiens* may have been designed through natural selection to fit with the world in some ways, more or less imperfectly, but no one told us that authoritatively, neither an external deity nor an inner voice of reason. Language emerged only gradually, a bewilderingly complex abstraction from the processes in the nervous system, which produces a usefully simple result for social action in the commonsense world, we understand its nature and status even now only very imperfectly; there are no givens here, no revelation. We came by everything then in the same manner; which manner? By trial-and-error guesswork, by throwing out a framework to grasp the world and modifying it as we went along, by blindly experimenting with the creation of societies, language, cultures, driven by ecological pressures and inner needs, learning only painfully slowly what 'works'. And this too is how we came by philosophy—by epistemology, ethics, metaphysics and the rest—through blind guesswork and selective elimination, by something like the same process of natural selection which forms the basis of biological evolution itself.

In such circumstances method becomes central to defining epistemology, for method is all that we have. If one knows in advance the nature of true knowledge (e.g., that it is grounded in sensory givens, or in mystical access to Platonic heavens) then an epistemology may be erected in these terms (using this knowledge!) and method deduced as the most efficient means to maximise knowledge thus understood. But if one knows nothing in advance, not even what it is to know, then the only thing that can matter is a study of the methods of relieving ignorance. Of these latter there is only one in a universe which is not given to its organisms once-for-all, the method of conjecture and refutation.

And this method is 'natural' to our universe, for we have increasing reason to believe that it is but a representation, at the abstract symbol-using level, of a basic biological development process that extends throughout the spectrum of living organisms, from the amoeba to humankind; that it is the fundamental problem-solving mode of evolving life. Campbell (1973) has argued this, following Popper (1973) and a host of others (recently see e.g., Lorentz, 1976; Geist, 1976; Wilson, 1975).

Now epistemology becomes defined in terms of this method. How is it possible to know? Answer this: How is it possible to pursue such a method? What is the scope of knowledge? That depends on the potential scope of the method. When do we know? What does the method tell us about the conditions under which it works? What do we know best? What does the method say about unrevisable results, the relative status of theory and observation, etc.?

Epistemology is defined in terms of the method, but not reduced to it. There is a great deal else that one must know before answers to these questions can be given. What sort of creatures are we? What capabilities have we? What is the nature of societies and cultures? What role do they play in the development of science? Until we know a great deal about our perceptual systems, brain functioning, languages, social interactions and so on we cannot say much about the nature, scope and conditions of human knowing. All of these things lie outside of method, they belong first to science proper and then to a fully developed epistemology as a theory of knowing for creatures such as we are.

There is much science that must be known before epistemology can be adequately developed, many results of method must be in hand before the nature of the method itself is understood. Is the form of a circle apparently detectable here objectionable? Not at all. Historically we are faced with the simultaneous emergence of both science and epistemology, conjectural theses in dynamic interaction with each other, more a pair of interlocked spirals than a circle. That is how it is for those who evolve from ignorance.

But many more questions ought to be asked concerning such a conception of the role of method. An adequate preparation properly requires an explicit statement of philosophy and metaphilosophy of an Evolutionary Naturalistic Realism (ENR). This has been done in Chapter 3 of this work. Briefly, ENR denies the existence of any 'First Philosophy' and claims that the purpose of philosophy of science is to provide a critical theory of theorising with the same epistemic status as any scientific theory. It is in its critical role that its normative status lies. The rational person so acts as to maximise her potentials and the rational society acts so as to maximise its collective potentials. Science is a principle means for the achievement of both types of ends. Science is thus to be viewed as a socially realised (institutionalized) collective method for the enhancement of the potentials of the species. It is one of our survival strategies, to be integrated with both ethology/evolutionary biology and brain function.

From the species standpoint, it is the *collective, historical* human experience which counts. This is so on two counts: (1) The development of theory in these respects centrally involves the development of suitable cultures that foster the development of human beings, individually and collectively. One very important (if thoroughly partial) aspect of this is the notion of a critical culture (cf. chiefly Popper's exposition), and critical not just with respect to factual belief, but with respect to values (ends), means, conceptual schemes—everything. The theory of human ends is at least a theory of human cultures. But cultures are collective creations. (2) Moreover, the adequate testing of cultural theories may require millenia rather than years. (Are we really historically in a position to decide between a Zen Buddhist or Tibetan culture and our own?—even with respect to exploration of the real nature of the universe?) Certainly it will typically require temporal spans much longer than an individual lifetime. The more so, since there is scarcely an extant (or past) culture that has tolerated critical enquiry to any significant degree yet (one of the reasons why we have never attempted a 'meta-cultural' rapport with Zen Buddhist or Tibetan culture in the spirit of critical, comparative exploration). We are only just beginning, as a species, on the exploration of culture, and hence value theory—and beginning blindly at that. How this view integrates with the general theory of method will shortly become even more obvious.

5.4 METHOD AND JUSTIFICATION:
THE DIVERSITY OF SCIENTIFIC AIMS

There is an intimate connection between the theories of methodology and justification in science, whatever the view of science. The general strategy of the connection is this: if method is the most efficient route to the goal of science and a scientific theory is justified or not on the basis of its achieving that goal, then the core of any justification will be its appeal to method correctly carried out (with the theory in question as result). However, the particular connections established in the cases of empiricism and ENR are radically different in nature.

Within an empiricist framework, there is apparently only one goal of science, empirical truth. When this is cashed out in detail, it comes to acquisition of evidentially supported empirical theories. Methodology is a theory about the obtaining of maximally informative and unbiased empiricist data from various situations, together with the appropriate inductive theory. A theory is justified if the relevant data have been acquired in accord with the method and it turns out after proper application of the inductive logic that the theory is sufficiently evidentially supported (whatever this amounts to). In the case of positivism the appeal to method is at once very clear—it concerns only the acquisition of basic data (nothing is left above this but the formation of truth functions)—and very obscure because it requires the introduction of some theory of the process of acquisition of basic statements, about which positivists have had little or nothing to say. (It requires introducing either a psychology of observation, which is anathema to their meta-philosophy, or a theory of conventional choice, which must remain a mystery on their meta-philosophy.) Empiricist methodology is faced with the same problem, to give an account of the foundations of their methodology which is itself rationally justified and consistent with their meta-philosophy (cf. Hooker, 1981b and Chapter 3, Section 5). In addition, empiricist methodology must include a theory of inductive support and criteria of sufficient inductive support to warrant rational acceptance as knowledge—these too are controversial and hitherto uncompleted tasks.

For ENR methodology is not dictated by an already fixed epistemological goal, rather method follows from a specification of the life-goals we have for science: individual, national and for the race; it serves as part of a theory of epistemology. By contrast with empiricism (and most other philosophies of science, e.g., Popper's), ENR (1) counts the goals for science as strictly on a par with all other life-goals, indeed as inextricably bound up with them and therefore (2) explicitly recognizes a multiplicity of genuine goals for the scientific activity. Both differences are worth elaborating upon.

On (1). Rational individuals and communities, and the race as a whole, can be regarded as possessing systems of goals which entail 'life strategies'. (Or at least they behave in such a manner as is economically explainable in this fashion; clearly the notion of rational choice which is at the back of these conceptions becomes increasingly subtle and indirect as one proceeds to numerically larger communities and longer time spans and its connections with biological evolution become increasingly important—cf. Section 5.3 above.) Amongst such goals will certainly be relief from ignorance as an epistemic goal unto itself, but we will also find such goals as survival (security)—

short and long term—technological mastery, self-expression, theoretical fecundity, excitement, sensual satisfaction, linguistic economy, control (power), etc. We can introduce some order into this bewilderingly complex array of goals by pointing out that some of them are derivative upon others (e.g., the desire for technological mastery as means to achieve control and control as a means to achieve security) and hope to arrive in the end at some hierarchical ordering of goals (as e.g., Fried, 1970).

But this ordering will not be simple, because many of the goals will conflict with each other in a variety of ways; e.g., I might seek technological mastery in order to enlarge the means of my self-expression, so long as the latter doesn't conflict with the achievement of a certain level of excitement and the avoidance of unchallenging labour; for the latter I aim at highly economical theories, so long as they are aesthetically pleasing as a means of self-expression and theoretically fecund and so exciting, though these theories must also lead to technological mastery, etc. (Just how complex these orderings may be can be ascertained from recent discussion, e.g., Hooker *et al.* 1977c.)

The interrelations among these goals are such, it seems to me, as to preclude separating them out in any nonarbitrary fashion as goals specifically pertaining to the pursuit of science and other goals. Science may be pursued with almost any goal ultimately in mind, from the contemplation of the creator to the lust for criminal wealth; conversely, every epistemic goal inevitably leads to the pursuit also of some nonscientific activities (e.g., the cultivation of certain social forms as conducive to the activity of critical enquiry). Moreover, within the system of goals it always turns out that there are trade-offs to be made both among epistemic goals and between these and other goals. To attempt nonetheless to separate off a goal or goals for science is surely just to ignore science as a human social endeavour.

The dominant philosophical tradition, however, still regards science as a separate unique endeavour and one, moreover, to be defined quite abstractly. (Positivists, empiricists and Popperians all agree on this.) Science becomes a practical social activity only in an attenuated theoretical sense and a distinctively human activity in no sense at all. (*Would* all possible intelligent creatures in the universe practice science as we do?) The inevitable result is the attempt to segregate the goals of science so as to achieve a characterization of scientific method independent of all other considerations.[1]

The conventional isolationist view of science leads to the formalist approach to the problem of induction (e.g., Lakatos, 1968b). I advocate a formulation of the problem in which the system of life-goals and a given data base (together with its scientific history) are fed as input to decision theory and a strategy of acceptance generated as output. The strategy may include more than one theory, include the criticism of the initial data base and concern a group of persons rather than an individual (cf. the discussion in Section 5.5). The possibility of criticism of the data base shows the need for a feedback loop from output to input, via a detailed theory of science so that output can modify input. The loop is activated until a steady state is reached and reactivated each time the data base is changed—cf. Harper (1977). In this fashion the multiplicity of the goals of science leads to a corresponding complexity to the structure of acceptance, for acceptance is always acceptance for certain purposes, relief of ignorance is always relief in certain respects.

If we construe both orthodox empiricist inductive theory and Popperian methodology as offering decision-theoretic accounts of rational choice in science then we can begin to see how to reconcile, or at any rate relate, the two. Both approaches offer goals for science, but these goals turn out to be distinct. Empiricism offers cautious generalization on the evidence, consistency, completeness and the like as criteria, criteria aimed at predictive reliability, technological security and control as goals; Popperianism offers degree of content, falsifiability and the like as criteria aimed at theoretical depth, fecundity and explanatory power as goals. These goals may be incompatible in the sense that in general a given decision could not be optimal for both kinds of goals simultaneously, but there is also nothing to stop a species pursuing them both through different members or the same person pursuing different goals at different times—cf. below. Of course both orthodox empiricism and Popperianism agree on *truth* as the ultimate goal, in some sense, but this turns out to be innocuous; it is not the infinitely long-term goal that counts but the more immediate goals to be pursued in the hope of truth that characterizes the differences between the two. If there is direct conflict anywhere, it lies in conflicting claims as to the most efficient strategy to achieve truth (or anyway approximate truth, an important improvement of the Popperian tradition over orthodox empiricism, if the notion is workable, cf. Miller, 1974, 1975); though I should prefer to reconstrue the conflict as one over what should be the dominant utilities of science, for within the domain of *truth* there is surely superficial or 'low level' and deep truth, a species could aim at both. Nor, of course, need there be any other conflict than this over how to account for historical decisions; if now one now the other approach seems to do more justice to a particular historical situation it will be because the scientists involved had different utility orderings for science and not because they were irrational.

Throughout the foregoing I have used justification in the traditional sense. It is time now to speak of its dual: discovery. The connection between method and justification which the decision-theoretic account builds can be put this way: the theory of justification is just the retrospective methodological theory of acceptance. But the decision-theoretic account also forges an inevitable connection between retrospective methodology and prospective methodology. Consider this claim: For any scientist S and any utility ranking R which S has, if S accepts theories of kind (character, type) T from among extant theories because doing so is utility-maximal for S in the circumstances, then whatever resources S devotes to theory testing should be devoted to T-kind theories and whatever resources S devotes to the invention of theory should be devoted to the invention of T-kind theories. For surely it would be irrational of S to devote resources to the testing or invention of theories which do not maximally advance the goals for science which S holds. Thus we have for ENR, as for empiricism, that retrospective and prospective methodology coincide. (All of this relativized to a particular time, because goals for science may evolve internally to science and they may be rearranged as circumstances alter, i.e., as a function of the larger cultural setting.)[2] Once again the diversity of utilities leads to a diversity of resource investment in research programs.

Perhaps the central problem of classical economic theory is that of the allocation of scarce resources among competing claimants. Once the diversity of goals for science and the coincidence of retrospective and prospective methodology are realized, a similar problem arises in the allocation of scientific research resources. An individual, society, species must adopt by some means some allocation of resources among the various possible, generally competing, research strategies. Just as in economic theory the optimal solution is in general not the allocation of all of a scarce resource to one individual, so in scientific research we cannot expect the optimal strategy will be to do only one thing. Thus we can expect that the normal, rational situation in scientific research to be one in which a diversity of scientific researches are being actively pursued simultaneously. This conclusion holds surely even if the range of admissible goals for science is imagined restricted to something approximating the purely epistemic, for an optimal allocation of resources would still require e.g., that at one end of the methodological spectrum some scientists work on the incremental elaboration of the most acceptable theory of the day while at the other end others work on radical alternatives to it. Feyerabend (and others) have provided special reasons why this methodological pluralism is reasonable (translation: is necessary for an optimal strategy), these have to do with the explanatory flexibility of explanatorily powerful and general theories (see e.g., Hooker, 1972b).[3]

The conception of method considered here for ENR is just that needed to display the internal complexity and subtlety of scientific choice. Consider the operative levels of scientific practice (cf. Chapter 4): there is the level of applied theory, including theory of instrumentation, where detailed models are constructed for specific situations; next the level of general theory, wherein the general principles of a theory, not situation-specific, are systematized and developed; next the level of proto-theory at which those background theories too fundamental to normally be questioned are explicitly developed (e.g., the linear theory of time, theory of continuous space); next the level of abstract theoretical framework at which abstract mathematical or logical structures are delineated (e.g., Hilbert space theory, theory of relations); finally the level of systematic ontology, wherein the fundamental forms assumed for the world are made explicit (e.g., atomic, plenum or process systematic ontologies). Although one asks the same kind of question at each level, "In the light of all of the available information, do I accept or reject this theory?", each of these levels involves somewhere different decision-making problems.

At the first level of detailed applied theory where everything in a model situation is specified, the major question is: "What is the relation between the data as constructed and the predictions of the theory?" Other considerations have to do with the possibility of arriving at the correct predictions for the wrong reasons (e.g., construction of data using a faulty theory, gratuitously cancelling effects) and the availability of alternative, equally empirically adequate, applied theory. As soon as one passes to the more general level of pure theory a host of additional problems present themselves, especially when the results are negative for the specific applied theory: Could we alter the theory of the instruments?, or of the data construction?, or deny the ceteris paribus clause?, or reject one of the auxiliary theories?, etc. And if the results are positive, there are still the same kinds of additional questions as appeared at the applied level, together with the question of how the support is to be distributed among the various components of the applied model which incorporated the general theory. This latter question reappears even more urgently when a class of situations have been tested in each of which the general theory is embedded in an applied theory. At the next higher level one is required to test a variety of general theories in which various proto-theories are embedded before any reasonable decisions can be made, each general theory in turn requiring the testing of a sequence of applied theories. And so on up. Thus, as one ascends still higher toward the increasingly abstract and general, these considerations multiply and the number of research avenues which must be explored, each requiring the conducting of long sequences of tests before any kind of reasonable decision can be made, increases sharply.

Thus on this view each of these levels of science is open to testing and rational decision making; the obliqueness of the relationship between data and theoretical level, however, increases sharply as one moves through this list of levels with the consequence that the time period required for the elaboration and testing of a theory at each level also increases sharply. The time frame for coming to an adequately supportable decision on some highly detailed applied theory might be five minutes, and typically of the order of a year or less, the time frame for adequately exploring the appropriateness of, say, the atomic ontology as the fundamental form for physical theory is certainly longer than two thousand years in our particular case (though none of our cultures have been critical) and could be expected to be of this order of magnitude, even in a critical society. (On the latter notion cf. Section 5.3 above and further below.)

This internal complexity in the structure of time frames for testing various levels of scientific theorising leads to a corresponding complexity in the structure of rational research resource allocation problems and a sharper statement of the conflict between various goals for science. For a society (e.g., a nation or group of nations) there is the problem of how to allocate resources over time, perhaps over generations, to the various levels of research programs that it considers worthwhile pursuing. And for the species there is the issue of how to allocate resources over time, say millenia, to the exploration of alternative cultures embodying perhaps alternative conceptions of reality, alternative institutionalizations·of the activities of science and (therefore) alternative research programs at all levels. It seems safe to say that *Homo sapiens* has hitherto never approached the latter question and never at all seriously approached the former question, except perhaps for the last two decades and then only in embryonic form. We humans have never experienced a truly critical culture (cf. below Section 5.5). Such long-term goals clearly often conflict with the short-term goals of technological security and progress, explanatory enlargement and unification of science within existing theoretical perspective. They conflict also with the middle-term goals of elaborating theories of particular abstract types (e.g., phase space theories), which embody particular systematic ontologies (e.g., the atomic ontology).

It is certainly the case that hitherto the allocation of research resources has not taken future generations into account, nor yet alternative cultures, nor even alternative societies or institutions within a generation (as far as can be avoided), but rather has proceeded by dint of the strictly locally powerful both in time and social space. But this generates a generalized form of a 'Prisoner's Dilemma' game from the point of view of the species, for each institutional subculture pursuing its own goals will inevitably prove to be a less efficient basis for the allocation of research resources than the 'long-term cooperative solution' in which we all contribute optimally to a species strategy. A critical culture would be one which possessed a public rationale and corresponding institutional structure for solving this problem in a rationally justifiable way. (There may be many such ways corresponding to many cultures and many conceptions of the world and of the rational human.)[4]

5.5 Science methodology and science policy: evolution of the species

One of the important motivations of the decision-theoretic construal of scientific methodology is its permitting the unification of the normative foundations for scientific methodology and science policy. Of course I did not intend it to follow from this statement that there was never any distinction to be made between science and anything else, e.g., politics, or that political decisions should always be those that dominate in the pursuit of science, or that there never would be any rational conflict between the objectives of scientists and those of other segments of society. Just as the methodological policy of "anything goes" does not hold within scientific methodology it does not hold either for the interaction of a scientific institution with the remainder of the social structure.

Indeed, my intention in seeking this common foundation between methodology and policy is deeper-lying than an immediate concern for politics and the like.

A realist, I have argued, is required to give a complete naturalistic account of the species *Homo sapiens* in its full evolutionary setting. It is my increasing intuitive conviction that an adequate biological understanding of our species suggests that many of our crucial capacities are really collective or communal species capacities rather than intrinsically individual capacities. At the present time the question of group or communal selection processes within evolutionary dynamics is thoroughly controversial and at the forefront of research; nonetheless, we have very strong evidence for my point of view in the case of the structural features of the gene pool for *Homo sapiens*, since this pool is a species possession rather than an individual possession, for the ability to actually use language and for any number of other abilities which are clearly social in nature (e.g., the ability actually to solve differential equations). But I suppose that our possession of a concept of self and a correlative notion of reality, our conceptions of rationality, epistemology and the like are all equally strongly tied to being features of the socializing species rather than simply independent intrinsic properties of individual human beings. And in particular I should want to argue for the view (though not here) that the epistemic capacities of *Homo sapiens* are functions of the biological capacities of the species *Homo sapiens* for specific forms of social interaction. That we are capable of only certain forms of communication (e.g., speech and not telepathy) and that our evolutionary heritage strongly inclines us toward certain (rather primitive) forms of social organization (cities, voting schemes) has a profound influence upon the epistemological enterprises which *Homo sapiens* is capable of pursuing. (And, of course, to borrow Kant's point, a profound correlative influence upon the kinds of epistemic enterprise which *Homo sapiens* is capable even of conceiving of pursuing.) The same considerations apply to all of the other characteristics of *Homo sapiens* which I mentioned earlier.

Moreover, our learning about our capacities in this fashion is itself part of the growth of science. In the simultaneous evolution of scientific theory and theory of science (and theory of society) this is one of the strongest feedback links from scientific theory to theory of science (and society). It is one of those links which I wish, as a realist, to take very seriously. But if one does so one has to admit that a deep account of the nature and evolution of the scientific enterprise must make reference to the social structure of the organisms pursuing that enterprise. A penetrating account of the nature and history of the scientific enterprise on this planet must take into account not only the evolution of scientific theorizing but the evolution of the biological, institutional and cultural context generally within which the scientific enterprise has been conceived and operationalized. Moreover, from now on it will become increasingly important also to take into account the development of selfconscious theory of the design of institutional forms and cultural systems for the future evolution of the scientific enterprise.[5] For it is the distinctive feature of the twentieth century that we have become aware selfconsciously for the first time in the planet's history of the designs or structures or systems, biological and sociological, operative in our circumstances and we are for the first time in a position to debate the choice of our own future designs.

One consequence of this point of view is that there is not, and cannot be, what might be called a purely intrinsic characterization of, or demarcation of, the nature of science. What makes an enterprise a scientific enterprise has to do with the structure of the institution which realizes that enterprise and the structure of the culture generally (value systems, modes of communications, etc.) within which that institution is imbedded. There are more or less thoroughly critical, or scientific cultures and these have the capacity to pursue scientific enterprise to a greater or lesser extent, but it follows from the above that there will not be, cannot be, a characterization of that enterprise which makes no reference to the policies, procedures, communicational forms and so on which the institutions in question embody. In terms of purely internal characterization, e.g., I can see no way plausibly to make a distinction between the pursuit of science in western culture and the pursuit of a mythological-magical understanding of the world in some other culture; what seems to me to make the crucial difference is the nature of the social processes set in train by each culture for the pursuit of their point of view.[6]

The integrated approach to rational action described here opens the way for a reformulation of the problem of the social responsibilities of scientists. This problem cannot be adequately stated whilst ever an unbridgeable gulf separates methodology and policy. The scientist's rational behaviour qua scientist is separated and unrelated to his rational activity qua citizen. Under this scheme he is forced to choose between society and science and the choice will inevitably be judged irrational by the other party. In general then no rational reconciliation is deemed possible or, if it has somehow to be asserted, it is assumed achieved mysteriously in the depths of the scientist's spirit. The present framework suggests the following reformulation: In the light of the present total situation of the species (socio-cultural, technological, epistemological, etc.), is pursuing research strategy R likely to promote or confine the future developmental capacities of the species? The answer depends, obviously, on the evaluation of the full range of human developmental capacities. It is confined too by our ignorance of them. One part of the answer certainly has to do with the direct impact of pursuing R on the growth of knowledge. But another part has to do with the chain of consequences passing through the resulting socio-cultural, especially institutional, structure and technological/technique structures and reflecting on our future capacities to pursue understanding, mastery and all of our other goals. There is the most intricate interaction between these parts, in fact they cannot be separated off from one another at all. Whatever the imponderables involved, this is a much more adequate form in which to pose the problems than the usual schizophrenic conception of the issue.[7]

That these processes of decision embrace an entire culture is demonstrated by the very different approaches to the world taken by other cultures (e.g., Tibetan). Nor need alternative approaches be less critical, I think. Nor need it be obvious that western science is the only effective approach to reality, or the most fruitful in the long run. Indeed, in evolutionary perspective *Homo sapiens* has evidently just entered upon an experimental exploration of the resources and potential of differing cultures. This is as yet 'blind' exploration by uncommunicating individuals (i.e., individual cultures). The species has yet to face the challenge of entering the period of the critical exploration of fundamentally different conceptions of reality. Not only the result of such an experiment would be in doubt (for the tens of millenia it would take to accumulate relevant experience—these would be the longest time-frame experiments of all) but it is doubtful whether our species possesses the social and intellectual capacities to even attempt it. *A fortiori* the evolutionary result of our present experiment with western science is in doubt (cf. Chapter 4). At no other time in the development of the species has there been a more urgent requirement to understand the complex relations between methodology and policy and culture and to work towards a viable and humane culture.

CHAPTER 6

Surface Dazzle, Ghostly Depths: An Exposition and Critical Evaluation of Van Fraassen's Vindication of Empiricism Against Realism

To be an empiricist is to withhold belief in anything that goes beyond the actual, observable phenomena, and to recognize no objective modality in nature. To develop an empiricist account of science is to depict it as involving a search for truth only about the empirical world, about what is actual and observable. Since scientific activity is an enormously rich and complex cultural phenomenon, this account of science must be accompanied by auxiliary theories about scientific explanation, conceptual commitment, modal language, and much else. But it must involve throughout a resolute rejection of the demand for an explanation of the regularities in the observable course of nature, by means of truths concerning a reality beyond what is actual and observable, as a demand which plays no role in the scientific enterprise.[1]

6.1

The surface of the title is of course the empirical, phenomenal world, the alleged 'surface appearance' of things. The depths refer to the real entities and mechanisms 'behind' the appearances, causally giving rise to appearances and explaining them. Realists hold that the surface merely dazzles and should not beguile anyone into mistaking it for reality. Empiricists, contrariwise, hold that the depths are ghostly, having no independent rationale for their veneration beyond the surface through which they indirectly appear.

I am a persuaded realist. In this essay I shall critically examine a recent line of argument for Empiricism, with a view to defending realism. The argument line is presented in a recent book quoted above; I believe it to be the most important defense of empiricism for more than a decade. Van Fraassen calls his version of empiricism, *Constructive Empiricism*, hereafter referred to as CE. The essence of van Fraassen's challenge lies in this: whereas empiricists have traditionally argued for the non-existence of the depths, van Fraassen argues only non-committalness. (He plays the agnostic to the empiricist atheist.) This allows him much more scope to borrow realist insight while refraining from realist belief.

<h2 style="text-align:center">6.2</h2>

The general empiricist position is presented in Chapter 3. The formal language is the backbone of empiricism, everything else is structured by its expressive resources. Historically, the contemporary empiricist movement first clearly emerged as positivism, which espoused a very austere language, the simple logic of finite truth functions wedded to predication, names and a class of immediately observationally verifiable descriptive terms. In these terms, very little could be (cognitively) meaningfully said. Later empiricisms successively enlarged the logic but otherwise tried to leave the positivist framework untouched (although some alterations were inevitable). They hoped that richer logical structures would offer richer, hopefully more realistic, descriptions of science while leaving intact the essential positivist philosophical program for interpreting science.

The chief conventional objections to the positivist theory of science are (1) theories are not definitionally reducible to finitely, observationally verifiable assertions; (2) scientific method is not rationally confinable to entailment from the facts; (3) observation is not a fundamental, transparent category but a complex, anthropomorphic process, itself investigated by science; (4) historical intertheory relations do not fit the accumulative model; (5) accepted observationally-based facts do not belong to an eternal, theory-free category but are theory-laden and subject to theoretical criticism. To these I would especially add the criticisms that (6, 7) science is not isolated from the human individual and from society in the manner presupposed by positivism; (8) that method is not rationally universal either across scientists at a time or across history; (9) that logic does not have the privileged status given it by positivism but is itself open to broadly empirical investigation and (10) that there is not the gulf between the normative and the descriptive presupposed by positivism. (Besides Ch. 3, Bjerring/ Hooker 1979, 1980, 1981 and Suppe 1974a, see Achinstein/Barker 1969, Easlea 1973, Feyerabend 1965a, b, 1969 for these criticisms.)

The first five of these criticisms have overwhelming support and are now broadly agreed to by all sides. They forced an initial retreat to a richer logic, simple quantificational logic, which allowed richer, less direct and partial definitions of theoretical terms, of the theoretical ontology (hence of the observationally fixed, yet unobservable), and of intertheory relations. Ingenious logical constructions, such as Carnap's reduction sentences, were much manipulated. This did something to ease objections 1, 4 and 5, though it never really blunted them; removed objection 2, replacing it with a confirmationist program; but left objection 3 untouched. The confirmationist program soon gave way to an inductivist program proper, requiring a further enrichment of the logical framework, which has provided a rich methodological program. It also added two more traditional objections to replace 2: (2′) inductive logic is impossible (inadequate, incomplete) and (2″) it is impossible to distinguish true laws of nature from accidentally true generalizations.

These objections essentially received two kinds of response from those calling themselves empiricists (= positivists using quantificational logic): *first*, introduce pragmatic considerations, as empirically noncognitive, to settle questions left unsettled by the resources of quantificational logic and *second*, introduce still richer logical structures, such as Carnap's inductive calculi, modalities, probabilities. The virtue of this twin response was this: as long as the only accretions made could be argued to be either empirically non-cognitive or purely logical, empiricists could claim to hang onto the basic positivist philosophical and meta-philosophical position. Van Fraassen, as we shall see, falls squarely in this tradition.

For three decades (1930s through 1960s) most philosophers of science focused on the questions made salient by these strategies: What can pragmatics and richer logics do to ease the objections to empiricism? Is pragmatics really non-cognitive (empirically anyway) and can empiricists really accept the richer logics? Van Fraassen essays positive answers to his versions of both questions.

This rather stark strategic history of empiricist philosophy of science in this century is only slightly complicated by strands of conventionalism and operationalism running through it.[2] For internal reasons it was only slightly modified by Popper's early attacks (see Ch. 3 and Hooker 1981b for my claim here). For external reasons it was virtually unaffected by other, largely continental traditions (e.g., Phenomenology, Marxism, Hermaneuticism), yet it is these that ultimately kept alive the crucially important objections 6 through 10 above. These latter objections now rival the traditional ones (1 through 5, 2', 2''''') for philosophical attention. We must see what van Fraassen does with them.

<h2 style="text-align:center">6.3</h2>

> Recall the main difference between the realist and anti-realist pictures of scientific activity. When a scientist advances a new theory, the realist sees him as asserting the (truth of the) postulates. But the anti-realist sees him as displaying this theory, holding it up to view, as it were, and claiming certain virtues for it.
>   This theory draws a picture of the world. But science itself designates certain areas in this picture as observable. The scientist, in accepting the theory, is asserting the picture to be accurate in those areas. This is, according to the anti-realist, the only virtue claimed which concerns the relation of theory to world alone. Any other virtues to be claimed will concern either the internal structure of the theory (such as logical consistency) or be pragmatic, that is, relate specifically to human concerns. (p.57)

This quote and that with which this essay opens define the essence of van Fraassen's position. It is focused on the 'manifest image' alone, taking that image as a depthless surface without any but observable structure; all else in science is either explained as purely pragmatic, or explained away.

But note how much of what had hitherto been considered distinctively realist, or in any case beyond the reach of empiricism, van Fraassen claims to capture for CE:

(1) *On observation and theory* he says:

> If there are limits to observation, these are a subject for empirical science, and not for philosophical analysis. (p.57)
>   . . . observation has nothing to do with existence (is, indeed, too anthropomorphic for that). . . (p.19)

See also pp. 59–64 for detailed examples and discussion.

Traditionally, as van Fraassen himself acknowledges, the observation/theory distinction had been crucial to empiricism; the distinction had been drawn philosophically, as part of a conceptual analysis of the foundation of empirical knowledge. Realists, in contrast, have argued for the imperfectness, limitedness and radical idiosyncrasy of human observation, on general scientific grounds, and from thence to the conclusion that observability should be no criterion of existence, not even a factual one, let alone a semantical one. But all of this critique van Fraassen is able to grant, and still go on to affirm his version of empiricism (see quote opening Section 6.3).

(2) *On language and theory* van Fraassen agrees that:

> All our language is thoroughly theory-infected. . . The way we talk, and scientists talk, is guided by the pictures provided by previously accepted theories. This is true also, as Duhem already emphasised, of experimental reports. Hygienic reconstructions of language such as the positivists envisaged are simply not on. (p.14)

These remarks clearly signal an abandonment, not only of positivism, but of the entire twentieth century empiricist tradition up to and including later Carnap and fellow-travellers, for this entire tradition rested on a reconstruction of theoretical language in terms of logical constructions out of observation terms. This rejection of a schizophrenic attitude to the language of science is one of the planks in the realist platform and the semantic counterpart to rejecting a formal observation/theoretical dichotomy.

(3) *On truth and theory* he says:

> I would still identify truth of a theory with the condition that there is an exact correspondence between reality and one of its models. . . . And logical relations among theories and propositions continue of course to be defined in terms of truth. . . .(pp.197-8)

Traditionally, empiricists have wanted to deny meaningfulness to any parts of theory that would create ontic commitments to unobservables, or to reduce those unacceptable parts to the acceptable, observable core. The most liberal empiricists allowed only commitments to unobservable entities identifiable by definite descriptions using solely observable predicates (e.g., behavioural psychology's intervening variables). Although liberal enough to cause epistemological difficulty for empiricist principles, this latter criterion is still much narrower than van Fraassen's position. For as far as meaning, reference and truth are concerned, van Fraassen professes to treat theories literally, just as realists insist they should be. Once again the Realist critique is deflected as apparently indecisive.

(4) *On experiment and theory* he writes:

> For theory construction, experimentation has a twofold significance: testing for empirical adequacy of the theory as developed so far, and . . . guiding the continuation of the construction, or the completion, of the theory. Likewise, theory has a twofold

role in experimentation: formulation of the questions to be answered in a systematic and compendious fashion, and as a guiding factor in the design of the experiments to answer those questions.(p.74)

Again, the empiricist tradition has been a 'bottom up' account in which experimental results were the most important category and inductively determined everything 'above' them. (For the positivist it was even deductive determination of theory by experiment.) Van Fraassen notes approvingly Sellars' demolition of this naive picture (p.32). By contrast, traditional realism has tended to the opposite extreme, giving all the weight to theory, relegating experiment to theory testing. Only determined realists, trying to take humankind's evolutionary epistemic status seriously, have seriously started to explore the proposition that there are extremely complex two-way interactions and trade-offs between theory and experiment in the risky business of pushing science along. But van Fraassen calmly accepts the insights as his.

Of less theoretical importance, but still of interest, he says of the *rational scientific psychology*:

> . . . acceptance has a pragmatic dimension: it involves a commitment to confront any phenomena within the conceptual framework of the theory. . . That is why, to some extent, adherents of a theory must talk just as if they believed it to be true. It is also why breakdown of a long-entrenched, accepted theory is said to precipitate a conceptual breakdown. . .
> . . . commitment to a theory involves high stakes. The theories we develop are never complete, so that even if two of them are empirically equivalent, they will be accompanied by research programmes which are generally very different. Vindication of a research programme within the relatively short run may depend more on the theory's conceptual resources and facts about our present circumstances than on the theory's empirical adequacy or even truth. (p.202)

The overall picture van Fraassen provides of science then, has remarkable similarities to that promulgated as crucial by the strongest realists, myself included. But we know from the first two quotes in this section that there are deep differences and it is time to expose these.

First, it is clear that, despite the range of agreement, *there is a deep difference in the theory of rational commitment* espoused by the two theories. Van Fraassen gives as the defining conditions for realism and CE:

[Realism] Science aims to give us, in its theories, a literally true story of what the world is like; and acceptance of a scientific theory involves the belief that it is true. (p.8)

[CE] Science aims to give us theories which are empirically adequate; and acceptance of a theory involves as belief only that it is
empirically adequate. (p.112)

And later he elaborates as follows:

> . . . we can distinguish between two epistemic attitudes we can
> take up toward a theory. We can assert it to be true (i.e., to
> have a model which is a faithful replica, in all detail, of our
> world), and call for belief; or we can simply assert its empirical
> adequacy, calling for acceptance as such. In either case we stick
> our necks out: empirical adequacy goes far beyond what we can
> know at any given time. (All the results of measurement are
> not in; they will never all be in; and in any case, we won't mea-
> sure everything that can be measured.) Nevertheless there is a
> difference: the assertion of empirical adequacy is a great deal
> weaker that the assertion of truth, and the restraint to accep-
> tance delivers us from metaphysics. (pp.68-9)

But this cannot be all there is to acceptance for CE since it would not
motivate the CE scientist to take the non-empirical part of theories as
seriously as van Fraassen agrees they do. And it isn't, there is a
pragmatic dimension as well.

> *Theory acceptance has a pragmatic dimension.* While the only belief
> involved in acceptance, as I see it, is the belief that the theory is
> empirically adequate, *more than belief is involved.* To accept a the-
> ory is to make a commitment, a commitment to the further con-
> frontation of new phenomena within the framework of that the-
> ory, a commitment to a research programme, and a wager that
> all relevant phenomena can be accounted for without giving up
> that theory . . . Commitments are not true or false; they are vin-
> dicated or not vindicated in the course of human history. (p.88,
> v.F.'s italics)

See also the quote from p. 202 two paragraphs above; that quote
continues:

> The depth of commitment is reflected, just as in the case of
> ideological commitment, in how the person is ready to answer
> questions *ex cathedra*, using counterfactual conditionals and other
> modal locutions, and to assume the office of explainer. (p.202)

But of course modal locutions (possibilities, probabilities, counter-
factual conditionals, nomic necessities) and explanation are held by
CE not to add to the empirical content of theory—the quote concludes
with the paragraph quoted at the outset of this paper.

This brings us directly to the *second* and *third* major differences
between CE and realism, over the *theories of modalities and explanation,*
CE relegating them to merely pragmatic status and realism typically
taking them to be crucial substantive features of theories.

With respect to explanation, van Fraassen summarises the realist as involving these claims:

> [E]xplanatory power is something quite irreducible, a special feature different in kind from empirical adequacy and strength . . . what science is really after is understanding, that this consists in being in a position to explain, hence what science is really after goes well beyond empirical adequacy and strength. Finally, since the theory's ability to explain provides a clear reason for accepting it, it was argued that explanatory power is evidence for the *truth* of the theory, special evidence that goes beyond any evidence we may have for the theory's empirical adequacy. (pp. 153–4,v.F.'s italics)

Van Fraassen sums up his own pragmatic theory of explanation as follows:

> To call an explanation scientific, is to say nothing about its form or the sort of information adduced, but only that the explanation draws on science to get this information (at least to some extent) and, more importantly, that the criteria of evaluation of how good an explanation it is, are being applied using a scientific theory. . .
> . . . Being an explanation is essentially relative, for an explanation is an *answer*. . . Since an explanation is an answer, it is evaluated *vis-a-vis* a question, which is a request for information. . .
> Hence there can be no question at all of explanatory power as such (just as it would be silly to speak of the 'control power' of a theory, although of course we rely on theories to gain control over nature and circumstances). Nor can there be any question of explanatory success as providing evidence for the truth of a theory that goes beyond any evidence we have for its providing an adequate description of the phenomena. For in each case, a success of explanation is a success of adequate and informative description. And while it is true that we seek for explanation, the value of this search for science is that the search for explanation is *ipso facto* a search for empirically adequate, empirically strong theories." (pp. 155–7; v.F.'s italics)

Here the sense becomes clear in which a pragmatic feature of science adds nothing to the substantive content of science, nothing to the intrinsic cognitive content and status of science. The same treatment is accorded all modalities.[3]

These then are the main differences between van Fraassen's CE and realism. The last question to be asked is how he manages to take over so much of what has hitherto been held distinctive of realism and yet maintain these sharp differences. Specifically, treating, as he does, all terms as theoretically laden, theories as providing a nomic structure, observation as internally specified and truth conditions as specified by theoretical models, how can he still construct the empirical observable core of a theory, isolated from unobservables and modalities?

The secret lies in van Fraassen's abandonment of syntactical logical constructions and his adoption of model-theoretic semantical constructions.[4] Whereas traditional logic has historically been the recognised vehicle for the study of the syntactic features of formal and natural languages, including theories, the appropriate vehicle for semantics is formal model theory. Then 'Theory T is true' can be re-expressed as 'Reality exactly matches one model of T' (cf. the quote from pp. 197–8 above). Many other formal semantical features of languages or theories can be defined in model theoretical terms, e.g. consistency ($=$ has at least one model). The important point is that passage to model-theoretic semantics represents a further strengthening of the logical tools available to the empiricist. Everything that can be syntactically expressed can be expressed model-theoretically but there are semantical constructions that are inaccessible to the syntactical approach, for example relative semantical embeddability ('every model of T_1 can be mapped homomorphically into a model of T_2'):

> This sort of relationship [relative embeddability] which is peculiarly semantic, is clearly very important for the comparison and evaluation of theories, and is not accessible to the syntactic approach.
> The syntactic picture of a theory identifies it with a body of theorems, stated in one particular language chosen for the expression of that theory. This should be contrasted with the alternative of presenting a theory in the first instance by identifying a class of structures as its models. In this second, semantic, approach the language used to express the theory is neither basic nor unique; the same class of structures could well be described in radically different ways, each with its own limitations. The models occupy centre stage. (p. 44)

Van Fraassen goes on to give a devastating critique of the old empiricist approach which relied solely on syntactic methods to define its key structures (e.g., definitions of empirically observable and theoretical portions of theories, see pp. 53–6). As van Fraassen observes, it is possible to define and identify all manner of unobservable, theoretical entities using only observable empirical predicates and logical devices, so attempting to extract that portion of a theory (defined syntactically via theoremhood) stated in some observational sublanguage will never isolate the empirical observable content of the theory, rather it is merely "in a hobbled and hamstrung fashion, the description by T of everything." (p.55)

Well then, how does the semantical deployment of model theory work the trick of isolating an empirical core? Like this: the model 'models' everything in the theory; it models, therefore, the full theoretical ontology and its complete set of nomicly permissible processes. But it also thereby models that subset of processes within the theory which represents measurements or observations and the features of the theoretically specified model which are thereby measured or observed. In so doing a model has modeled the observable/unobservable distinction, as specified by the theory. The class of all thus modeled observable features forms the empirical core of the theory.

> To present a theory is to specify a family of structures, its *models*; and secondly, to specify certain parts of those models (the *empirical substructures*) as candidates for the direct representation of observable phenomena. The structures which can be described in experimental and measurement reports we can call *appearances*: the theory is empirically adequate if it has some model such that all appearances are isomorphic to empirical substructures of that model. (p.64, v.F.'s italics)

Why are these empirical substructures modality-free? Because if the theory picks out only what is observable in each circumstance then a catalogue of those features will be thoroughly 'Humean', modalities won't come out as observable in any one situation and across situations only correlated bundles of observable features will be listed. Even the modality-inclined realist must admit, if she is realistic, that modalities belong to theory and aren't among the observable features of the world, so no theoretical models of observability will assign them to their observable sub-models. Technically the matter is settled by building in these results to the models from the very beginning. Van Fraassen's theory of probability is a good example. Theories with irreducible probabilistic features are modeled by families of possible experiments, the relative frequencies of whose outcomes model the probabilities involved; of course only individual such experiments can be actual and only their identifying conditions (apparatus-type, etc.) and outcomes will be identified as observable by the theory; thus the empirical substructure of the theory is some actual finite collection of these identifying conditions and outcomes, no probabilities or possibilities occur therein.

It is time to take stock of the new situation in the realism/empiricism debate. Van Fraassen has managed to deflect many of the sharpest criticisms from realists by simply incorporating them into his own position. In doing so, he has had to forego many of the treasured dogmas of his empiricist predecessors, e.g., that there is any episte- mologically prior distinction between theory and observation, that theory is a 'dependent variable' only, either deductively or inductively determined by experiment, and that there is no semantical priority for observational terms. Nonetheless, van Fraassen claims through all of this to hold on to the essential core of empiricist doctrine and thereby to retain the essential disagreements with realism, to wit: commit- ment only to empirical adequacy, not truth; no modalities within the commitment; explanation is not an objective virtue. How is this liber- alized balancing act between concession and defence achieved?

First, by moving away from the twentieth century empiricist em- phasis on reducing the cognitively meaningful to the observable and convicting all else of meaninglessness, as a way of ensuring epistemic accessibility and security. Instead, van Fraassen takes an agnostic stance far more seriously in the limiting of epistemic commitment (cf. his explicitly religious analogy between Gods and theoretical entities) and in this sense places himself more clearly in the conventionalist- instrumentalist tradition (cf. Chapter 2). Second, through the wield- ing of powerful new logical tools van Fraassen is able to cut the boundary of empiricist doctrine more finely, closer to the core yet consistently defensible while consigning all of the new leftovers to non-cognitive pragmatics. Thus a recognizable historical pattern is repeated, van Fraassen is following exactly the strategy of his empiri- cist forebears (recall the discussion in Section 6.2 above).

Have we now, perhaps, reached the ultimate end of this process? Now, after the passage from finite truth functions to quantification, to quantification with definite descriptions, identity and various abstrac- tion operations, to various inductive calculi; now, as van Fraassen says, after each of these transitions has distracted a generation of scholars; now with the passage to model theory perhaps we may suppose there is at last a solid defensible core to empiricism and the issue with realism can be finally joined in less superficial terms than criticisms of logical inadequacy? I frankly suspect not, since I don't think that what divides realists and empiricists ultimately revolves around the empirical adequacy of either of the two philosophies of science.[5] But being the most recent in a long line of such manoeuvres, van Fraassen's empiricist position is certainly the most plausible and powerful version of the doctrine yet and the logic to which he has access makes it uniquely more powerful than its predecessors; his position deserves to be treated as such.

6.4

6.4.1 Central Argument.

The core of the difference between van Fraassen's CE and realists concerns what kind of epistemic attitude is rational where scientific theories are concerned. According to van Fraassen, CE says "Only accept theories as empirically adequate, no more", realism says "Believe theories as true, on the grounds of their empirical adequacy and explanatory power (and perhaps other virtues)."[6] Consider first the rationality of CE's epistemic attitude.

Van Fraassen says:

> On the view I shall develop, the belief involved in accepting a scientific theory is only that it 'saves the phenomena', that is, correctly describes what is observable. But acceptance is not merely belief. We never have the option of accepting an all-encompassing theory, complete in every detail. So to accept one theory rather than another one involves also a commitment to a research programme, to continuing the dialogue with nature in the framework of one conceptual scheme rather than another. Even if two theories are empirically equivalent, and acceptance of a theory involves as belief only that it is empirically adequate, it may still make a great difference which one is accepted. The difference is pragmatic, and I shall argue that pragmatic virtues do not give us any reason over and above the evidence of the empirical data, for thinking that a theory is true. (p.4)

I shall reserve for later discussion the question of whether the decision to "continue the dialogue with nature in one conceptual scheme" is pragmatic and, if pragmatic, also non-epistemic. The other question remains, why is it rational to epistemically accept a theory only as empirically adequate? I suppose for this ironical reason: it minimizes risk in the face of the very fact realists have often emphasised, namely that every actual theory is likely only to be an approximation to the truth, hence strictly speaking false. Faced with this 'realistic' assessment of the human epistemic situation, one withdraws to a less risky affirmation; for even if the theory is overthrown, surely its empirical adequacy *at the time* remains. Thus the tables are turned on a realist trying to be realistic.[7]

6.4.2 Reply.

This important argument invites two major responses: (i) the epistemic strategy recommended is a very poor one in itself, arguably less likely to advance knowledge than alternatives, and (ii) there is anyway no reason to suppose that van Fraassen's position *is* less risky than the realist's, hence risk-taking cannot be the decisive ground. I shall consider these two replies in order.

6.4.2.1 Reply (i) Epistemic Strategy. Why is it rational to limit epistemic commitment to observational adequacy out of caution? Popper taught us long ago that caution is a poor policy for creatures born in ignorance and trying to find the truth. Ultimate caution for an empiricist would require sticking just to the evidence as it comes in, risking no theoretical ideas about it at all, but in this case we would learn very little. In fact we would quickly become mired in dogma, for not only would few (if any) exciting new experiments be tried, but we would be incapable of criticising our existing experiments and data, our unnoticed biases and errors would quickly accumulate.[8]

Would one then always rationally wish to prefer the more empirically adequate scientific theory, i.e., the theory most closely in accord with the available data? I suggest not and for the reasons Popper has already pointed out: it may be explanatorily shallow or even self-confirming, descriptively idiosyncratic, internally fragmented, etc. Indeed, it is typical of scientists to prefer to explore what is judged to be the theoretically deeper theory, even if it has some empirical difficulties, over less theoretically insightful, if more empirically adequate, alternatives. Scientists aim at interesting or valuable truth, not simply truth.[9]

Although this disposes of the naive empiricist conservative, it doesn't dispose of van Fraassen, for he grants the necessity of bold theoretical conjecture and of theory-directed experimentation and evaluation, and he would be able to find a place for the other virtues of theory just considered—it is just that he insists that all of these factors and considerations are non-epistemic, they are merely pragmatic. They are to be understood in some way as merely satisfying our individual interests, or as mere heuristics in aid of scientific creativity and the like, thereby falling outside of empirical cognition proper.

Again I postpone consideration of the status of alleged pragmatic commitments, but wish to note in passing that no argument emerging here can actually force a realist to adopt the CE view. This is because, as is the case with Craig's theorem and the theoretician's dilemma (see Note 5) the assumed cognitive/non-cognitive division required for any such argument would be rejected by realists and so the argument would only succeed in begging the question. Van Fraassen himself concedes the same points in the Craig case (p.30, cf. an additional example at pp.21–2). But just so, too, with his own position here.

6.4.2.2 Reply (ii) Risk. Turning now to the second response to the argument for CE from risk reduction, I shall offer a three-stage argument that van Fraassen's position is no less risky than is that of realism. *First*, with respect to observation we have already noted van Fraassen remarking, "Even if observation has nothing to do with existence (is, indeed, too anthropomorphic for that), it may still have much to do with the proper epistemic attitude to science" (p.19). But if observation really *is* too anthropomorphic to be a safe guide to existence why is it rational to base one's epistemic attitude to science solely on it? Isn't this latter attitude therefore a very risky one, relying on a collection of senses known to be limited and idiosyncratic, and sometimes even suspected of deep error?

From an evolutionary point of view what is risky is cognition generally, whether concerned with observational or non-observational aspects. Our cognitive capacities include both abilities to perceive and abilities to theorize; both evolved in idiosyncratic ecological conditions from less complex life forms and both may be supposed to thereby inherit limitations and idiosyncrasies. Why reserve scepticism for just one? Indeed, from an evolutionary point of view theoretical thought has the impressive achievements of having grasped both mathematics (the simpler, linear part anyhow) and highly insightful formal theories for dynamics. By contrast, we have merely come to understand the quirks and limitations of human observation better over time without significantly enlarging its nature—why not then side with Plato and give theoretical cognition the primary trust? At the least, why not put the two risks on a par and proceed with a unified, realist account in which each risk is traded off against the other?

Second, there is a further risk with CE commitment, for empirical adequacy refers to a theory's fitting the observable phenomena *for all time*, and this can never be guaranteed by the evidence available now (see p.69, quoted above). Thus, if it is the mere underdetermination of a theory by its observational core that makes realism unacceptably risky, then CE ought also to be rejected since any empirical evidence available to us will in general radically underdetermine a theory's empirical adequacy. If it is the volatility of theoretical ideas and principles under criticism that favours CE, then observational terms and data have shown volatility as well (e.g., the starry dish above).

Third and finally, it is not as though accepting a theory à la CE is risk-free. There is the risk of committing oneself to confront nature in its terms and within its resources. Considering the very strong role which van Fraassen has theories play in the scientific process, these commitments are every bit as risky as are the corresponding realist commitments.

In sum, van Fraassen's CE risks are in fact exactly the same as are those of the realist. This seems to me to dispose of the argument for CE from risk. If there is to be an advantage for CE here, it must hinge on the pragmatic status CE accords most of these risks. So let us postpone this issue no longer but consider it directly.

6.4.3 Pragmatic-Cognitive.

Consider van Fraassen's account of the role of theory in experiment (see quote above). If theories are to structure the questions to be asked and to inform the experimental designs needed to pose them properly to nature, surely theories must be taken seriously epistemologically. How can scientists rely on them to this extent and remain committed only to their empirical adequacy?

Van Fraassen's answer is: by carefully distinguishing pragmatic use of the models of a full theory from the empirical core of that theory. Thus if in testing theory T_1 in some situation S, theory T_2 suggests a factor F in S which either T_1 might not account for, or which must be controlled for if a parameter crucial to T_1 is to be measured, then what is really happening is no more than this: the models of T_1 are extended in certain ways, viz. to include models of F drawn from models of T_2, and the empirical cores of the extended models are then compared with those of T_1 alone and with experimental outcomes (p.80)). Everything can be done with models and empirical cores, and the focus is on the adequacy of those cores, so a realist account is unnecessary. But, like the older use of Craig's theorem, this reply misses the point; why rely on these theoretical models so heavily if they have no cognitive significance? If it is unreasonable to believe that these models capture something of the structure of things beyond the observable, why the meticulous reliance on their detail?

Van Fraassen can consistently answer, as he does, that the only *cognitive* reason for reliance is empirical adequacy, that the remaining reliance is purely pragmatic and present only because we have no option but to take risks in the epistemic game. So let us revive again the two claims I suppressed at the outset of this discussion: Is the reliance on theory pragmatic and is the pragmatic non-cognitive? Van Fraassen adopts affirmitive answers to both questions, but what arguments does he offer for them?

So far as I can see, none at all, except for the following brief remark:

> . . . the requirement that our epistemic policies should give the same results independent of our beliefs about the range of evi-

dence accessible to us. That requirement seems to me in no way
rationally compelling; it could be honoured, I should think,
only through a thorough-going scepticism or through a commitment to wholesale leaps of faith. (pp.18–19)

Here van Fraassen is facing the objection that "observable" really
means "observable-to-us", but since other species may count our unobservables among their observables, observability is a poor criterion
of cognitive commitment. Van Fraassen doesn't deny the basis for the
objection, he simply argues that the alternative is worse: thoroughgoing scepticism or wholesale leaps of faith. If realist epistemology
could be spiked on the horns of that dilemma it would argue in favour
of van Fraassen's agnosticism. But it cannot, because we have just
seen that a good CE scientist will risk practical reliance on theory no
less than his realist counterpart. The risks are as great and, since a CE
scientist suspends belief in theory but is still forced to rely on it,
whatever the dangers involved, the degree of scepticism involved
must be at least as great. Beyond this I can find no argument in the
book.

And van Fraassen himself says that ultimately semantics, which
contains the notions of truth and empirical adequacy, is only an abstraction from pragmatics (p.89); in that case why claim that pragmatics is non-cognitive while semantics is cognitive? No direct answer is
given, but the answer van Fraassen's comments suggest is that pragmatics concerns relations of language or theories to users of the languages while semantic concerns relations of language or theories to
the world (p.89, cf. p.100). It is not clear what this distinction really
comes to, van Fraassen himself agrees that there is no neat way to
demarcate semantics within pragmatics (p.89).

In any case, why does this distinction render the pragmatic non-
cognitive? Even supposing explanation were a relation between a
theory and its human users, as van Fraassen claims, surely it is a
significant feature of a theory that humans can use it to explain and
predict. Indeed, whatever the limitations and idiosyncrasies of humans, it would be an objective feature of a theory that humans could
use it to map the world. Is this not a significant cognitive feature of the
world? More generally, it would be a significant cognitive feature of
any species, theory pair (S, T) that S's could explain and predict
successfully using T. Martian scientists might incorporate just such an
account of our activities in their science, and we of them. More relevantly, we are rapidly building a science of ourselves which is now
beginning to be able to reflect on our own species use of theories for
various purposes. Theoretical reflection on human perception, the

basis of empirical adequacy, and the subsequent theory-guided modification and extension of human perception, is an excellent case in point.[10]

A unified evolutionary account of intellectual development undermines any attempt to dismiss the relating of science to human purposes as merely pragmatic; at bottom all human purposes are understood to be at least partly cognitive (survival and life enhancement require information), and those connected with scientific activity (theory construction and testing, yes, but also technology development, development of epistemic institutions, meta-theories of explanations, methodology, etc.) deeply so.

I must conclude that van Fraassen's position is just that, a merely convenient position on the matter. This is reminiscent of an earlier empiricist, Carnap, who simply claimed that there were two kinds of questions, internal and external, and that the latter were pragmatic and so non-cognitive, also without giving any argument.[11]

6.4.4 Unmatched Advantages to Realism.

Are we then at a stand-off between CE and realism?, each with a consistent account of practice and no deciding arguments either way? I think not. To begin with, the realist is better able to explain why he didn't always choose to rely on the most empirically adequate theory. But there are other arguments to be marshalled.

From an evolutionary, naturalist point of view, there is a general argument from a unitary view of mind. As remarked, the human cognitive apparatus developed with both theoretical and practical abilities; without all of these abilities, and without their intimate interaction with each other, our cognitive capacity would be much less. What theoretical reason in cognition is there then to distinguish among these capacities, giving special status to some and not others? There is, e.g., a strong case for the role of theoretical capacities in perception itself.[12]

In the absence of counterargument the evidence favours treating all cognitive abilities on a par, within a single framework and, as suggested above, refusing to draw any basic cognitive/pragmatic distinction.

An important structural reflection in science of this deeply interacting cognitive unity is the now rapidly increasing interaction between scientific theory and normative meta-theory (see Chapter 7, Section 7.3). Indeed, such intense internal critical awareness and interaction is one of the hallmarks of the present stage of the development of science. Unhappily, empiricism really cannot make any sense of this crucial development.

And there is a further general argument for realism from the 'scientific image' itself. The fact is, science has confirmed the evolutionary, naturalist picture of humankind as mammals with complex nervous systems slowly building up their individual and collective cognitive representations of the world using all of the complex and idiosyncratic array of devices to hand: sensory perception, behaviour, language, technology, institutions, culture, etc. So realism in philosophy is confirmed by realism within science. For CE however, empiricism in philosophy is in tension with the picture of *Homo sapiens sapiens* presented in the content of science. The CE scientist is forced continually to play a schizoid game of pretend, to pretend that the theories in which he is immersed are informative and, because the information they convey contradicts his philosophical self-view, at the same time to be reminding himself to suspend belief, to treat science as, after all, only a game. It is possible to thus play games, our very theoretical or imaginative capacities make it so; fiction and drama would be impossible otherwise. The question is: is it *rational*? I suggest that it is not rational unless there are specific reasons for doing so (as there are in drama), but here we have none.

Finally, there are the continuity and conjunction arguments for realism, based on scientific methodology and the history of science. The continuity argument is this: Theoretical ideas and theoretical structures crop up in various contexts throughout the history of science, successively refined, modified or conditionalized in the light of further experience. If theories are merely empirically adequate there is no reason to expect this, unless it can be shown that such ideas are merely of pragmatic convenience. But it is not plausible to regard the correction of Newtonian physics in relativity theory of or Lavoisier's oxygen chemistry by electrochemical valence and that in turn by molecular quantum chemistry, etc. in this way. Hence the history of science demands that theoretical structures be treated seriously as grasping, albeit imperfectly, the unobserved structure of reality.

The conjunction argument is this: scientists regularly, and surely rationally, conjoin two theories to derive consequences unavailable in either; this practice is understandable if the theories are taken to be true, since if A is true and B is true, then (A & B) is true; but the conjunction of empirically adequate theories need not be empirically adequate, or even consistent; hence the justification of this practice as rational requires a realistic understanding of theories.

Van Fraassen is aware of the conjunction objection, devoting a special section to its discussion (pp. 83–7). His reply consists of three claims: (1) there are enough observable phenomena overlapping the domains of two or more theories to provide a sufficient empiricist case to explain the scientific desire to conjoin theories (pp.86–7), (2) much conjoining turns out to be correction of one or both theories and so falls outside the argument (p.83–4,87), (3) the real and anyway methodologically sufficient motive for conjunction is to test the empirical adequacy of the conjoined theories (p.85).

I believe van Fraassen wrong on all three counts. With respect to claim (1), it is granted that explanation of empirical phenomena often requires conjoining theories; indeed conjoining them far more powerfully than van Fraassen suggests, for laboratory phenomena typically require the conjunction of four or more theories to properly understand them, the passage from theory to observatism is typically *theoretically* complex (see Chapter 4). Even so, it seems clear that theory conjunctions have not always been motivated by appropriate observable phenomena, at least not in the direct sense van Fraassen has in mind. Relativistic quantum field theory of interior nuclear structure has no directly observable consequences in the way that van Fraassen's man on the moon requires conjoining terrestrial physiology theory and celestial gravitation theory. The relativistic theory was developed historically first and foremost to 'see how it goes', to gain *theoretical* insight; it would still be developed on this basis today. Such observational results as have emerged are quite indirect, requiring the mediation of several other theories to trace their causal claims 'up' to the observable surface. Much the same can be said for the development of the kinetic theory underpinnings and corrections to thermodynamics (it still cannot explain such obvious thermodynamic phenomena as phase transitions, but eventually doing so is expected to be a source of *theoretical* insight), of quantized general relativity theory and so on. Of course, van Fraassen has himself covered; he need only transform theoretical insight into structural knowledge of the models of joint theories and claim that enlarged empirical adequacy is the real long-run goal (cf. p.93) and he can claim to accommodate the attitude. What is at issue is not the logical consistency of the CE doctrine but its intellectual and empirical plausibility.

Second, and à propos claim (2), it is mistaken to appeal to theory correction at conjunction as rendering that conjunction irrelevant to the issue. The necessity for correction arises from another theorem concerning preservation of truth,

$$(A \rightarrow \sim B) \rightarrow \sim (A \ \& \ B),$$

if A and B are not consistent their conjunction cannot be true. So a main motive for correction must be truth. (We may follow scientific practice and set aside trivial entailments, e.g., through some notion of relevant entailment, hence holding that with respect to empirical adequacy the conjunction of two inconsistent theories might well be empirically adequate, for their nontrivial inconsistencies might be confined to their theoretical components).[13] In any case, the original form of the conjunction argument must apply to the corrected theories. Again, van Fraassen might consistently reply by appealing to enlarged empirical adequacy as the real long run goal and to consistent model structure as the intermediary. Thus whether conjunction involves correction or not makes no difference to the argument.

The third claim (3) begs the question. It is not denied that testing joint empirical adequacy is a primary motivation of conjunction. But enough has already been said in discussion of the first claim to indicate that basic theoretical understanding in the pursuit of truth can plausibly be looked upon as an independent (though interacting) factor, an equally important reason along with empirical adequacy for examining joint theories. Any attempt to rule out this latter motive would simply beg the question. Van Fraassen might agree, arguing instead that the theoretical motives were all pragmatic, hence not cognitively significant. This would only return us to an earlier argument, one where I believe the realist has a distinctive advantage.

There is no need to rehearse the continuity objection to CE further, it is clear that the argument would run a similar course to that of the conjunction argument.

In sum, neither objection is decisive, but both add additional weight to the argument that to support itself CE must advocate a strained and fragmented picture of science.

Recalling the dependence of observability and hence empirical adequacy on the epistemic community concerned, we may say that science itself theorizes its own epistemic community and on that basis modifies it.[14] In addition, humans meta-theorize (philosophize) science. This sort of complex internal and meta self-reflection can itself be understood from the point of view of an emerging scientific theory of humankind, the evolutionary theory of self-organizing cognitive systems.[15] The realist picture fits well together as a single, if complex, pattern. Again, it is possible to ignore this picture, gather up the apparatus of models, empirical cores and agnosticism and give an account in terms of joint models of theory and theorizer, and of meta-models of model making, etc. But unless there is a definite reason for it, why would it be reasonable to do so when the realist alternative gives a more unified, more deeply insightful theory of what is happening?

6.5

In all of this discussion the matter of meta-philosophical commitment has been set aside. The reader will recall my summary of empiricist meta-philosophical commitments in Chapter 3. It is now time to enquire of the corresponding commitments behind CE.

Van Fraassen never explicitly mentions meta-philosophy and, with his general aversion to speculation and commitment, might well eschew it altogether, perhaps along the conventionalist lines of M'5 for empiricism (see Chapter 3, Section 3.1.4)[16].

Certainly occasional comments reveal a lack of awareness of the often intimate relations between philosophical and meta-philosophical commitments. E.g., van Fraassen remarks that interpretation of science and methodology of science are two independent doctrines (p.93). But this is not even strictly true of empiricist meta-philosophy, for choice of empiricist methodology is heavily constrained by empiricist interpretation of science, cf. the bearing of M'2, M'3 on M'4, and it is strongly false of the realist meta-philosophy I shall shortly describe. (Nevertheless, the lack of interest in meta-philosophical matters and the assumption of interpretation/method independence are characteristic of empiricism.) However, and as with earlier empiricists, *we* can ask what system of meta-philosophical commitments makes most sense of CE, what would be needed to defend CE, whether or not these commitments occur explicitly in the text.

I think that two of the empiricist commitments very clearly stand behind CE as well, viz., M'2 and M'4. M'2 because van Fraassen's primary effort is devoted, as we have seen, to explicating key philosophical concepts and principles in terms of logical structure in a newly enriched formal language, that of model theoretic semantics. M'4 because the whole thrust of the distinction between cognitively directed action and pragmatic action is in line with demarcating the theory of the rational pursuit of cognitive ends from other components of rationality and within the former the sole focus of rational choice concerns the obtaining of empirical adequacy; other factors in theory choice are also pragmatic.

To my mind CE also embodies the spirit of M'3 and M'6. M'3 because the insistence on agnosticism about all beyond empirical adequacy suggests an attachment to perceptual experience as carrying an epistemological surety that the rest of science does not; correspondingly, empirical adequacy is appealed to as the ultimate ground of knowledge claims in science. However, the requirement of certainty must likely be relaxed; and there is no commitment to the last clause of M'$_3$ except insofar as the mind must serve as the intuitive source of doctrine satisfying M'$_6$ and M'$_1$. As for M'$_6$, van Fraassen's book is written on the tacit assumption that philosophers can provide a philosophy of science from within the resources of philosophy alone (which they can if M'$_2$ holds universally of philosophy) and that this doctrine should dictate the approach to science. This assumption only surfaces when it is contrasted with realism's strong denial of it (see below).

That leaves us with 'classical' empiricism's M'$_1$ and M'$_5$.[16] On both of these I remain agnostic as to CE's commitment. As remarked earlier, I tend to favour a form of M'$_5$ as most fitting CE and it is some version of M'$_1$ that sits best with the other doctrines, but there is too little evidence to argue the matter.

All told, CE shows the distinctive pattern of meta-philosophical commitments characteristic of empiricism. This is not surprising since van Fraassen sees himself as squarely in the empiricist tradition. What it does do, however, is open up a new front for the evaluation of CE; are its meta-philosophical commitments convincing? I hold that the realist view provides a much greater degree of coherence with the scientific image than does the meta-philosophy of CE, and that it thereby itself acquires a greater claim on our commitment. If we are, as science suggests, cognitively organised mammals, exploring the world from an original position of ignorance, why would one suppose that philosophic distinctions and capacities were as empiricist meta-philosophy suggests?

Consider the theory of intelligence, a subject which modern cognitive and computer studies have revolutionised in the past decade; can we confidently assert that epistemology has nothing to learn from it? The reverse is already the case, since cognitive science has been one of the important factors in the emergence of the class of "economic" models of knowledge in which knowledge claims are viewed as context-dependent, risky or uncertain commitments. This represents a profound break with traditional epistemology. Our cognitive resources are being invested increasingly in extrasomatic machines and institutions, all designed in line with our present theories but also thereby helping to transform those very theories. As this happens, who can confidently say what the future of cognition is?

Van Fraassen speaks easily of a "completed human biology" (p.17) but it is not clear that there ever will be such a thing. As science gives us greater scope to intervene in the genetic and physio-chemical functioning of our species, not to mention the intrusion of extrasomatic devices, the whole idea of a species biology becomes blurred and the future possibilities for *Homo sapiens* gape wide open—in vitro fertilisation (achieved), storage and genetic intervention (in process of achievement), and multi-cellular cloning (achieved) are but the beginning. Only the beguilement of the mind by the empiricist idea of a spectator model of science (in which we ideally simply record truth as it is presented to our senses) could lead to this ignoring of what is nowadays daily news. And if not a completable biology then not a completable perceptual structure and hence not a completable notion of observable or empirical—in everything, even van Fraassen's empiricist touchstone, we rely on spinning out a survivable order via our theorising. Nor will there likely be a completable theory of cognitive science, hence not a completable theory of rational cognitive strategy and thence not a completable philosophy of science. I cannot help but think that, measured against the real excitement and danger of the human adventure, empiricism has a meanness of vision, no matter how elegantly expressed; that it is rather like Blake's Newton gazing at the ground when overhead, unseen, the cosmos is ablaze with light.

But I recognize that this last sentiment is unfair, to van Fraassen anyway, for he aims to capture much of the rich complexity of science, and his anti-realism is promulgated in the interests of advocating the merits of caution and of protecting us from the excesses of speculation. This is, then, the time to say candidly that realism has had its excesses and has had to undergo modification to survive. The balance of the essay will be restored if these matters are frankly addressed, which I do in the next section.

6.6

Realism in science has no doubt often been fostered by a belief that in science we really do come to know the world once-for-all with a degree of surety that warrants the claim to knowledge. This naive realism has a sister theory of perception, naive direct realism, according to which we directly perceive the world exactly as it is. Both naive realisms have had to give way before our historical experience. We have today strong inductive grounds for believing that all of our extant theories of any given time will eventually be overthrown, possibly in favour of theories with substantially different structures which are more than mere refinements of them. And we have good scientific reason to believe that perception is interpretation-laden and replete with idiosyncratic features, all of which give rise to characteristic illusions and limitations. Thus naive realisms have to become critical or sophisticated if they are to remain plausible. All this was established a century or more ago.

Recently, U.S. discussions of realism have especially focused on the writings of Putnam, Boyd and others who have committed their version of realism to the following group of ideas and doctrines:

a. There is a general progression of science towards increasingly accurate and general theories; where theories have been successful in the past their successes have been, rightly, incorporated into succeeding theories, usually as limiting cases of the successor.

b. Successful theories are so because their theoretical terms really do succeed in referring to what there is and the theories assert true, or approximately true, relations among those entities.

c. b explains the historical achievement *a* asserts and also why the historical practice described in *a* is the right one and *b* offers the only plausible explanation of the success and history of science, which would otherwise be a mystery.

Unfortunately for this version of realism, many of these claims, or those that support them, are open to serious questions and van Fraassen and Laudan between them have levelled a very serious critique of them.[17]

In considering theories T_i from the history of science, Laudan e.g., makes the following points: (1) the mere fact that a $T_i's$ terms succeed in referring doesn't guarantee or explain its empirical success and vice versa, $T_i's$ empirical success doesn't guarantee or explain referential success for $T_i's$ terms, the history of science being replete with theories successful at a given time and now judged to be non-referring; (2) $T_i's$ being approximately true doesn't guarantee that $T_i's$ terms refer and vice versa; moreover, even were it given that no T_i whose terms failed to refer could be approximately true, approximate truth would not be guaranteed by empirical success; and finally no realist has furnished a workable definition of approximate truth; (3) historical intertheory relations in general do not exhibit the subsumption-as-limiting-case relation; further, that relation, even if it held, would guarantee neither reference for the subsumed $T_i's$ terms not even approximate truth for the subsumed theory, and no other plausible realist intertheory relation holds historically. Van Fraassen also levels some of these criticisms indirectly, adding directly that it is equally possible to explain the success of theories in quasi-Darwinian fashion as simply the elimination of empirically unsuccessful by empirically more successful theories, avoiding any reference to theoretical terms or more global approximate truth.[18]

Many of these points are quite valid, and by no means confined to critics of realism. I have myself, e.g., emphasized the complexity of historical inter-theory relations, that retention-as-a-limiting-case does *not* guarantee any substantive reduction relation, that empirical success does *not* either reference or many versions of approximate truth.[19] At the same time I have argued at length for realism.

But before turning to other doctrines of realism, let us briefly consider where these criticisms leave the Putnam et al. realism. *First*, though it leaves this version of realism in a greatly weakened position, it is not quite so weak a position as Laudan makes out. Partly by prejudicial formulation[20], partly by overstatement[21], Laudan makes a stronger seeming case than his argument sustains. *Second*, it must be admitted that these criticisms do undermine important parts of the doctrine, e.g., at least the second part of a, all of b as it stands and, on any acceptable version of b, c clauses two and three. However, *third*, there is a version of b which I think defensible: b^1. Successful theories T_i are so because their basic (presumably theoretical) terms either (i) really do refer or (ii) while not referring as intended, there is a true theory in which the T_i theoretical descriptions can be approximated (the T_i entities can be 'aped') and (iii) T_i asserts true or approximately true relations among them. Moreover in my view b^1 is connected to the structure of understanding in explanation and it is suited to the use of Sellars' version of intertheory relations, which Laudan has done nothing to refute.[22] And this complex of doctrines *does*, I still think, explain the success and history of science, though, as van Fraassen's alternative makes clear, not uniquely so.[23] Finally, *fourth*, this leaves the realist with a substantial framework within which to address the dynamics of science, but not the argument for realism which a through c was intended to provide. So be it.

If other realists run afoul of these criticisms, then it should be recognized that by no means all versions of realism are involved. The historical record which Laudan cites to such effect is damning of simple structural models of the dynamics of science, but I have long argued that this only represents one more naiveté to be surpassed in the passage to an adequate realism.

However, there are in addition specific features of contemporary science which seem, or have seemed, especially recalcitrant to realist analysis, but reflection suggests that the evidence is quite ambiguous. Earlier this century relativity theory was often hailed as a triumph for the empiricist operationalist method. Einstein himself occasionally dressed it up that way. Recent analyses have shown that, to the contrary, a realist analysis is both possible and plausible; indeed, the drift in the evolution of the theory is toward an objective absolutism (of a relativistic kind).[24] Of course van Fraassen can side-step all this as already indicated, but the move to remove the presence of a substantive space-time from the models of the theory has faltered and will likely fall.

Another case often cited in this same connection is modern quantum theory. The theory is strikingly empirically adequate, as well understood mathematically as any other theory (i.e., modestly so), but poorly understood conceptually and ontologically. If CE was the rational position to hold then quantum mechanics should be a paradigm of a successful, satisfying scientific theory. Some scientists do take the empirical success of the theory, combined with its interpretational obscurity, as proof that empiricism is the correct attitude, but this has not been widespread. In fact, no theory has drawn more interpretational discussion in the history of science, and not just (or even mainly) by philosophers but primarily by scientists themselves seeking theoretical understanding. There are also many scientists, it must be admitted, who point to the empirical adequacy and say "enough, get on with experiment", but these scientists have really dismissed the interpretational issue rather than decided it, and they are seen to have their pragmatic motivations. These scientists will be satisfied by crude empiricist renditions like that of the physicist Ballantine[25] and they ought to be satisfied by the elegantly worked out, but ontologically noncommittal models van Fraassen himself has provided.[26] The irony is that, for all its elegance, van Fraassen's interpretation is being, and is bound to be, largely ignored by scientists just because it doesn't treat the theoretical problems seriously in the sense required.[27] With few (any?) exceptions, all of the outstanding scientists of this century have worried the problem, seeking theoretical insight.

It must be admitted, however, that relativity and quantum theory still pose difficult unresolved problems for realism. Added to the retreat from naive forms of the doctrine documented above, it makes it pertinent to ask for the surviving distinguishing core of the position.

In Chapter 2 I cited as the distinctively realist claim the thesis that ". . . the intended and proper sense of the theories of science is as literal descriptions of the physical world . . ." This should be compared with van Fraassen's version, quoted above. It is now clear that the semantical thesis by itself may be necessary, but is not sufficient, for as already noticed, van Fraassen too adopts a position in which the full theoretical content determines truth conditions (see above). For van Fraassen the conflict with the realist comes over rational commitment, and, correlatively, over the (rational) aim of science.

I think it is correct to locate one locus of the dispute at this level and here the distinctive tenets of realism are surely these: (1) that there is a reality independent of our intelect and sentience with which we interact and represent to ourselves in theories, (2) that observable and unobservable features of a theory are on an equal footing ontologically and epistemologically, and hence that (3) it is the overall value of a theory, of which empirical adequacy is but one component, which should determine our commitment to it and that (4) our most valuable theories are our most acceptable guides to the nature of that reality.

These are propositions which are not relinquished in the retreat from naiveté and which CE must deny. (One might add: CE is committed to this denial however much of the resulting realist account of science CE claims to mirror within itself. Indeed, part of the burden of argument in Section 6.4 is that CE gives recognition to all too much of scientific practice to remain plausibly empiricist.)

In spelling out realism, however, it is also necessary not to be naive about realist rational commitment. As van Fraassen remarks of his own formulation "It does not imply that anyone is ever rationally warranted in forming such a belief." (p.9) Van Fraassen had in mind someone who only ever attached probabilities less than one to scientific theories, but in Chapter 5, Section 5.4 I suggested a context-dependent formulation which I still find more fitting to our actual circumstances: there is a complex of epistemic contexts, rational commitment is always commitment relative to one of these.

Relevant contexts are: a 'commonsense' (theory) specified practical setting (e.g., carpentry), a theory specified practical setting (e.g., laboratory experiment), a theory-field (or paradigm?) specified setting (e.g., 'normal science' in any discipline), an epistemic institution specified setting (e.g., arguing competing gravitational theories within the codes of argument currently specified as scientific), a cultural or perhaps transcultural setting (e.g., debate about the limitations of science as a way to knowledge, debate about the idiosyncrasies of human intelligence). For some purposes it may be useful to draw finer distinctions, and these are probably not the only sorts of context involved; but they suffice to indicate what is intended. Commitment to a proposition P is relative to acceptance of a context S.

It would be wrong to adopt a simple hierarchical structure to contexts to express the structure of context acceptance. Contexts exhibit complex cognitive interrelations for, as indicated in the realist metaphilosophy (Section 6.4), commitments in one context can influence commitments within, and acceptance of, other contexts. (E.g., commitment to a theory of human intelligence may well affect acceptance of science, in some theoretical characterisations, as the best route to knowledge.) The distinction among contexts is like Carnap's internal/external distinction pluralized, except that the realist holds all acceptance and commitment decisions to be cognitive and mutually influencing. Or, since Quine demolished the formal significance of Carnap's distinction, like epistemic propositional attitudes partitioned across Quine's web of belief.[28]

With respect to realist attitudes to commitment/acceptance then, the position I have been sketching earlier suggests the following structure: in all theory-specified contexts, the theory is accepted as literally true and the commitments, whether to belief or action, are as determined by the theory; (but) in all theory-field specified contexts the general theoretical propositions underpinning the research program are accepted as true and theory commitment is only to what follows from these, while the details of subprograms for particular problems may be practical commitments only (though context acceptance might dictate commitment as true); (but) in epistemic institution specified contexts the acceptance is of scientific procedure and commitments in this context are thus constrained, but are compatible with agnosticism or scepticism about the successfulness of any one theory or research program, . . . and so on. In sum, commitment at one level is compatible with scepticism at another, but not necessarily 'higher' level. (E.g., one may be committed to a particular theory of human intelligence and hence be relatively more sceptical of science as theorized in a certain way.) The whole interacting 'web' of acceptances, agnosticisms, scepticisms and commitments is then juggled in the light of the evolving totality of theoretical insight and practical experience. I have no good theory of precisely how this is ultimately done, and there may be none.[29]

As remarked, none of this is essentially new. But with respect to realism it allows two important points to be made: This debate on the structure of acceptance/commitment does not touch the core propositions of realism. Hence realists are not forced into the naive position of not being able to be critical of science, even radically critical, just because they are realists. To try to impose some sort of hierarchical subsumption structure on acceptances is just to ignore the introduction of risk and trade off to epistemology, to deny an 'economic' theory of knowledge and insist instead that logic suffices to structure epistemic attitudes.[30]

We have now touched on the final locus of realist/empiricist difference, the one not addressed by van Fraassen: the conflict over meta-philosophical commitment. It is clear that realism as conceived here differs fundamentally with empiricism over the aims of epistemology and rationality theory. The two also conflict over the significance and role of logic in philosophical theory and normally conflict over the status of philosophical theory (though in the case of van Fraassen's CE, it's hard to tell). But behind these differences lies a more general and more fundamental difference: realism insists on informing the basic content of philosophical theory with the scientific image, empiricism maintains the separation of philosophy and science. This is the basic difference because it leads to the general differences over the aims of philosophical theory just mentioned and, via them, to the other conflicts over theory of science already discussed.

These are, then, three loci of difference between empiricists and realists, (1) meta-philosophical commitments, (2) general philosophy of science, e.g., of rational commitments in science, the correlative aims of science, the metaphysics of truth, and (3) specific philosophic theories, e.g., of rational commitment. It is idle to hope that the differences will fade as empiricism enriches its logic and realism sheds its naiveté, although some differences in their specific descriptions of science may be removed in this manner. It is idle to hope that either position will be broken simply by poking holes in their respective theories of science, although doing this may force change upon them, and indirectly weaken their claims on our commitment. Because it fosters the foregoing two hopes, it is misleading to focus the issue solely at the level of their theories of science. Both have survived the criticism flung at them and evolved into more vigorous forms under its selective pressure; but the one with the greater claim on our commitment is, I still think, realism.

I shall now test this conclusion once more by expanding the context beyond the 'interior' of science to include the scientific process in its wider social setting.

6.7

The basic divergences between realism and CE have been delineated, but this does not exhaust the potential areas of mutual opposition. A last area of dispute remains, the relations between philosophy of science and the larger role of science in the human evolutionary process of the planet, i.e., disputes concerning the social, political and cultural place and significance of science. I have substantial enough commitments in these areas, as will shortly become clear, and regard the issues as very important. However, there is presently so much controversy about the intellectual significance of the connections I shall discuss that I have deliberately segregated the discussion so that criticisms of CE levelled here can clearly be distinguished from the assessment concluded with Section 6.6.

Science is concerned with creative cognitive construction in the face of evolutionary ignorance. The philosophy of science is itself an example of this process—hence the relevance of meta-philosophical considerations to the assessment of realism (Section 6.5). But science is also the leading edge of the intrusion of cognitive organization into every area of human life, and philosophy of science, broadly construed, has a central part to play in this process—hence the relevance of asking whether CE forms an adequate basis for understanding these social processes.

As to the process itself, I can summarize my own view (cf. Chapter 7) in this way: the human species has been undergoing a slow but fundamental reorganization around human cognitive organization, a process which has evidently accelerated this century. This process can be conveniently, if artificially, divided into two dimensions, science as remaking the world at large and science remaking itself. The net effect is that not only is more and more coming within the object of scientific enquiry but those objects are being increasingly transformed into human artifacts. Artifacts, however, are only partially natural objects, for they exhibit human designs which imbed human values, reflecting human choices from among what is possible. Correlatively, the focus of theory shifts from a description of what is to a theory of what is possible. I shall argue that these fundamental changes in the nature, scope and human significance of science do not sit well with CE, but that they do find a natural framework for their understanding within the kind of realism I have been defending.

The fact that science is remaking the world around it hardly needs emphasizing. From our impact on the global climate, forests, ocean ecologies, hydrology and so on to the explosion of urban megalopolises, man-made agricultural species and electronic communication networks, and in a hundred other like ways, science-based and organized technological development has been transforming the biophysical world in quite dramatic ways into a human artifact in new patterns. These patterns have not been universally approved, far from it, but they are human designs nevertheless. At the same time the social and personal conditions of human life are being similarly transformed. At the personal level we now have neurosurgical intervention, deep drug therapies and psychotherapies, behaviour modification and so on, all of which make the very boundaries of the self problematical, though in addition there is role model and social learning theories and the like which make the social conception of the individual problematical. And medical intervention now encompasses *in vitro* fertilization, genetic engineering and cloning, the ingredients of transforming any species into an artifact. At the social level, to take but one example, new developments in electronic communication and information processing are transforming public and private media, work role distributions, work/leisure relations and the basic concepts of money/wealth and of the political process. New planetary institutions have emerged on a scale undreamt of a century ago, made possible, and necessary, by modern science and technology, designed and managed, at least in part, through the use of scientific theories.

It is perhaps less obvious that science has been transforming *itself* in a fundamental way, but this is so. *First*, there is a growing internal scientific self-consciousness which is transforming the conduct of science. There are several aspects to this, of which philosophy of science is obviously one, for it raises the self-consciousness of scientific methodology, including theory construction and testing, intertheoretical relations and so on. Another important dimension has been the growing sensitivity to the history of science with its perspectives on long term developments in science, the history of scientific concepts, changing relations of science to mathematics and technology and so on. And finally there has been a growing mathematical sophistication concerned with the general foundations of scientific description which has for the first time led to the formulation of major alternatives to basic scientific assumptions.[31]

Second, there is a rapidly developing scientific interest in the institutional nature of science and in its social relations. Historical studies already called attention to the social context for science but there has been a recent explosion of work in the sociology of knowledge, economics of research and development, science and technology policy and related areas.[32] At the same time science itself, and of course technology development, has been institutionalized on a scale that would have been scarcely comprehensible a century ago. Research strategy has a global structure, journal articles number in the millions (even in a single discipline), specialization has reached the point where not even sub-sub-disciplines may be able to communicate. The cognitive characteristics of science are increasingly influenced by its institutional structure. Social studies of science and technology have become increasingly aware of this development. Finally, science itself has given birth to a collection of new theories, distinctive of the twentieth century and directed at the management of complex systems (including science itself and its immediate social and environmental relations): systems theory, decision theory, operations research, cybernetics, artificial intelligence, irreversible and network thermodynamics, control theory and so on. The net effect of these three synergistic processes is that science is increasingly redesigning itself in its own image, even while it is transforming the world around it.

Taking both the external and internal transformations of science together allows one to see the depth of the transformation that has occurred over the past three centuries in the role which science plays in human affairs. In the seventeenth century science might reasonably have been regarded as an intellectual tool, (1) of individuals, (2) for the objective (because non-interfering) description, (3) of the autonomous workings, (4) of a given natural object, the world. Beyond that, if science could be applied in humankind's service it could be understood as a tool like any other, subject to the prior interests of policy, economy, community and individuals. Today, the image of science as a simple tool, intellectual or utilitarian, must be replaced by the concept of a powerful self-organizing and environment-organizing system. The non-interfering description has been replaced by redesign on a massive scale, the individual by something rapidly approaching a species-wide organization, the autonomous object by a human artifact and the various prior interests are now increasingly moulded by the available images and designs. That this process of species 'encephalisation' enhances the scope for disaster and the delicacy of survival conditions argues not against either its existence or importance.

What then are we able to make of it from within CE? What approaches does CE offer for its understanding and assessment? I believe CE serves only to obscure both the process and what is at stake for humanity in it. CE retains the empiricist view that science is at bottom value-neutral and separate from social processes as such and it emphasizes fact and logic as the sole cognitive determinants (though not perhaps the sole determinants) of science. These characteristics introduce, in my terms, two profoundly distorting effects.

1. They deflect attention away from the object of science as increasingly an artifact, obscuring the understanding of the nature-to-artifact transformation. Artifacts are not value neutral. CE must relegate treatment of their evaluative components to some extrascientific realm, say politics. But is this the most helpful way to understand the process? Correlatively, CE encourages an image of pure science as separate from applied science or technology, insofar as the latter is

bound up with the pursuit of human interests not determined by fact and logic. (The pure/applied distinction is but an application of the fact/value distinction.) However, the pure/applied distinction cannot be sustained when the object of theorising is itself an artifact and when technology plays so fundamental a role in experimentation and even conceptual evolution (cf. Chapter 7, Note 2). The point here is not simply to repeat internal criticisms of CE but to draw attention to ways in which the inherent structure of CE represents a barrier to really coming to grips with the actual character of human cognitive processes.

In particular, CE discourages any value-based critique of 'pure' science, defending its neutrality with entrenched distinctions. In specific cases it may well be appropriate to defend science in this way, e.g., against wanton political intervention.[33] But in a world in which increasingly the objects of scientific study are themselves human artifacts, it is important to be able to subject the general directions of all science to evaluative scrutiny. For example it is at least conjecturable that humans might well be so structured as to make some scientific models of them self-fulfilling prophecies if universally applied. (One is tempted to think of sufficiently crude behavioural models or models of political governance here.) Such a circumstance would require a carefully integrated normative-factual evaluation. It is also important to be able to subject the details of science to the same scrutiny as one now more easily applies to technologies.[34]

The really critical questions for our century are (a) how to decide when science is to be defended and when it is to be criticised and (b) how to institutionalize these processes compatibly with proper cognitive and political freedoms. These are difficult and urgent questions in our cognitive and political circumstances. CE's absolute dichotomies reduce their allowable answers to disastrously simple-minded proportions.

2. Historically, empiricism has been associated with the relegation of extrascientific thought and behaviour to a cognitively inferior status. In its most extreme form only causality, not cognition, operated outside science, all extrascientific belief and behaviour was to be explained causally, e.g., via Skinnerian reinforcement schedules, but not to be expected to exhibit an intrinsic cognitive aim and rationale. Hobbes at the opening of the modern liberal-empiricist tradition, and the twentieth century positivists at its apogee, all held some version of this doctrine. But this view leaves no distinctively ethical-spiritual, social or rational structure to extrascientific life, after all the major substance of life. The only operative terms that can be rescued for

theory construction, besides cause, are power (wealth/force), persuasion, desire satisfaction and their cognates socio-politically, and efficiency and cognate terms economically. There is a correlative theory of rationality, holding that outside of logic there either is no rationality or rationality is purely economic, restricted to choosing efficient means to satisfy desires.

My view that this schizoid conception of cognition and of rationality is internally unsatisfactory has already been explained. But I also hold the view that widespread adoption of this position would be a historical socio-political mistake for humans and not simply an intellectual one. It would be a mistake because it would reinforce a self-interested and cynical conception of social and political life at a time when we desperately need a more humane vision of its possibilities and a more humane practice for our present tenuous civilizing institutions. It would help to demean human culture, giving an unwarranted legitimacy to fashion, sophistry and propaganda in the hands of the merely powerful. It would aggrandize narrowly economic assessments of courses of action, where efficiency is ultimately dominated by the wealthy and otherwise powerful, when humans badly need a more ecologically and socially sane process of social choice. The cultures of western nations already suffer enough from these distortions of an extreme liberalism reinforced by positivist social sciences, without masking them with a plausible-seeming theory.

Van Fraassen might well reply that these criticisms reflect a self-righteous, moralising approach to socio-political life and culture, an approach that exhibits an inevitable tendency to authoritarianism and ultimately to totalitarianism. However, he would certainly add, it fails to reflect our real and basic capacity to be sceptical, to enter lifestyles and discourses experimentally or even pragmatically, to change our commitments. And I would concede that authoritarianism is a danger of the position I have been outlining, though not an inevitable outcome of it. I would also agree that we do have the capacities just mentioned, at least within limits. And I would join van Fraassen in opposing authoritarianism and in insisting on recognition of basic human experimental and sceptical capacities. But though I have no utopian formula for the culture well balanced between individualist anti-authoritarianism and social value-commitment, I am equally sure that it lies to the commitment side of van Fraassen's position. And though I have no insightful formulae to capture the proper balance between scepticism and commitment I am sure that it lies well to the commitment side of always playing at accepting theories and practices. (There is a tendency in van Fraassen's approach to encourage a nihilist theory of lifestyle.)

Van Fraassen might well reply that these areas of dispute lie well beyond the philosophy of science and that it is unfair to assess his view in a perspective much vaster than the one to which he confined himself. He might go further and claim that it was a straight intellectual blunder to attempt this kind of assessment. I am sure that the latter claim would only be begging the question and fairly confidently conjecture that it is false. Hence I conclude that the first claim is unwarranted. But I have no neat account to offer of how we intelligently juggle narrowly epistemic and broadly evaluative commitments, I am only sure that we do and that it seems to be of the essence of our circumstances and natures that we do so. For myself, I am inclined to regard the evaluative dimensions as also cognitive, properly understood, and to attempt to see the process as some kind of unified cognitive exploration strategy (see Chapter 5). But we are now well into controversial and speculative waters, I rest content with the insistence that a more complex, more integrated theory than CE's dichotomies will permit is required if the character of evolutionary strategies are to be understood and the challenges of our present circumstances are to be met.

CHAPTER 7

Understanding and Control: An Essay on the Structural Dynamics of Human Cognition

7.1 STORIES TO DISTURB THE TRADITIONAL IMAGE OF SCIENCE

Let us imagine ourselves advanced far into the future, far enough to give the human species access to enormous energy resources, energy resources on a cosmic scale. This idea does not appear to be in itself theoretically problematic; it can be regarded as an extrapolation from past history. The history of mankind's evolution on this planet has had, centrally to it, a history of continually increased access to energy resources; at each stage of our development, access to new energy resources has been part of a thorough transformation of the structure of civilization. We imagine then a future time where our species controls the pattern of energy flows on a vast scale.

Let us further imagine that, in the currently fashionable cosmology, the universe commences from some 'big bang,' expands against gravitational attraction for a time and then falls back upon itself, only to re-create the next 'big bang.' Let us further agree that the nature of the expansion and contraction processes, which in turn dominate the formation of stars and planets, the conditions for the evolution of life and so on, is heavily influenced by the pattern of distribution of energy, in its various forms, throughout space-time.

Granted this scenario, it becomes thinkable that our species might someday intervene in the cosmic process on a cosmic scale. We might, for example, intervene to reverse a contraction in favor of an expansion, or to prevent a contraction from becoming a highly concentrated 'big bang,' perhaps in the interests of altering the subsequent evolution of the universe in favour of life forms of our type. Marvellous science fiction stories could be woven around the theme, but the point is not to develop these but to raise the following question: Could not the time come when the cosmos itself becomes, at least in principle, a humanly designed affair? Can we not consistently contemplate the idea that cosmological structure, and life forms on a cosmic scale, should become human artifacts? But cosmology is surely one of the great natural sciences; radio and optical astronomy, astrophysics and general relativity all have respectable positions within physics, the 'king' of the natural sciences. However, under the conditions we are imagining, would cosmology become more like engineering perhaps, or even political science, or even music?

The story may give us pause to reflect: may the dividing line between the natural and social sciences not have more to do with the quantities of energy and information to which we have access than it has to do with the intrinsic nature of the subjects? Could it be that because we have emerged from evolutionary ignorance with only a predator's access to ecological energy flows, the fundamental structure of our sciences are as they are? Let us press the question with another story.

In biology, Darwinism is transcendent. I mean the neo-Darwinian synthesis which combines Darwinian selection with genetic theory. The basic Darwinian scheme is elegantly simple: each organism, and each population of organisms, is represented by a genetic structure; from generation to generation these structures exhibit random variations (mutations); each such variation may be thought of as a trial, an experiment in survival in the environment; the environment, conceived as a system of external causes, determines the success or failure of these trials or experiments, exhibiting their outcome in the survival, or in the death, of the organisms and populations concerned (or, more sophisticatedly, in the proportions of progeny which survive each organism, or population-at-a-time); the overall evolution of life on the surface of the planet is understood as the dynamic development of this system. Darwinism has the attraction to science of providing a framework for a purely causal account of the development of living forms on the planet without any need to appeal to intelligence and teleology (purpose) as transcendent driving forces.

The account works very well indeed at the level of primitive organisms such as viruses and amoebae. Here the primary impact of the environment is through its chemical structure acting directly on that of the organisms themselves. But by the time we reach even so lowly an object as the white mouse it is clear that the initial picture I have painted is too simple in at least two significant ways. First, white mice are capable of modifying their environment, for example through burrowing, and they are thus able in some small degree to *preselect* the environment which is to select them. Second, white mice are also capable of learning, both individually and as a population. Environmental selection acts on the mature adult, the developed phenotype, and not directly on the genetic structure. Thus the genetic effects of the environment are mediated through phenotypic characteristics, including learned behavior. In this manner white mice are able to *preselect* the intermediary causal structures through which the environment acts selectively on their genetic structure. With these two modifications explicit, the locus of evolutionary action has now shifted significantly from a simple environment-genetic causal interaction, to an interaction mediated by the behavioral ability of the organisms in question. In white mice, one may be inclined to accept that most of the significant behavioral abilities are genetically inherited, though clearly at least some are learned. And of course as we move back 'down' the evolutionary scale toward ever simpler organisms, the importance of behavioral abilities generally, and of learned abilities in particular, steadily diminishes so that the simple causal account becomes increasingly adequate. However, as we move 'up' the evolutionary scale toward more recent species with their ever more complex nervous systems, the importance of behavioral abilities, especially learned behavioral abilities, increases sharply.

In the case of ourselves, *Homo sapiens sapiens*, we are able to modify the environment, to preselect it, on a vast scale, at least by comparison with any of our predecessors. Indeed, extrapolation of very recent developments suggests that we shall soon be able to deliberately plan major features of the global climate, other major geophysical features (such as fresh water systems), major features of the plant ecologies and fisheries on the planet and other major components of the environment on a planetary scale. These vastly augmented behavioral abilities of ours are no longer governed by instinct, by genetically inherited patterns, but are dominated by cognitive control. And it is clear that this same cognitive control is intimately involved in our vastly richer tapestry of learned behavioral abilities which express themselves in such genetically relevant structures as courtship and marriage cultural patterns, modern medicine, the road toll and nuclear weapons. Thus in the case of our own species we exhibit preselection both of the environment and of the phenotypic mediation of environmental selection on a hitherto unprecedented scale, all of it dominated by our cognitive control structures.

Furthermore, if we project ourselves but a little into the future and imagine a developed genetic engineering science then we can see ourselves as having the ability to preselect the very genetic structures themselves on which, according to Darwinism, environmental selection is to work. To some extent this is already the case with the now widespread development of genetically selected plant and animal species, though the methods used are most often still more indirect than we can expect them to be in the future. Certainly our recently developed capacities for *in vitro* fertilization of mammalian embryos, of elementary mammalian cell cloning and of the direct manipulation of genetic material, furnish grounds for the belief that we shall in the near future be developing hitherto undreamed of abilities to both intervene in the genetic structure and history of species and to mold entirely artifactual species. We may speculate further; perhaps armed with these more direct manipulative techniques, we shall acquire the ability to preselect the nervous system's ability for developing cognitive control structures, structures which are themselves to mediate the cognitive capacities through which environmental selection is to be felt. They would also mediate the capacities through which the ability to develop yet new structures in the future of the same sorts will be felt.

In this case, may we not reasonably claim that the locus of evolutionary development is now shifted decisively from a simple causal environmental-genetic interaction to a model in which human cognitive control capacity stands at the very center of the process and in which the human preselection of the future as a deliberate cognitive and normative act is of decisive importance for the structure of the process? Where then, we might ask, is the locus of evolutionary development? Is the process causal or cognitive, natural or normative? Is evolutionary biology, then, to become more like engineering, or perhaps political science, or perhaps music?

I have been pointing to some unique characteristics of the human process on this planet. The evolution of species has come to focus more and more intensely upon the cognitive control structures and resulting behavioral capacities involved. On the one side we humans have to come socially to grips with this historical transformation as a set of practical problems posed to us, from nuclear weapons and environmental disruption to jet travel and genetic intervention. On the other side we must equally come to terms with the transformation cognitively, as a profound challenge to the traditional conception of the nature of science and of its relation to human values and human identity.

7.2 THE QUIET REVOLUTION OF SCIENCE (I):
THE EXTERNAL ECOLOGICAL ROLE OF SCIENCE

The fact is, science and technology have transformed the shape of human life beyond all recognition by our forebears. Moreover, the very nature of science and technology itself is being transformed in the process. In consequence, the theoretical accounts of science and technology, and much other theory besides, that seemed comfortably appropriate as little as fifty years ago, have in fact proven irrelevant and even dangerous.

Many people distinguish sharply between science and technology. I do not. I do not believe that, at bottom, a principled distinction can be made. Technology is to science at the very least what crawling and hands are to the conceptual development of the young child.[1] There are important differences between science and technology but these concern differentiation within a complex institution; they are relatively insensitive to the larger issues of which I shall speak here.[2] So, for want of space for a finer treatment, I shall use the word science to cover both. If any reader feels this leads to blunders in what follows, he or she is welcome to keep the two explicitly in mind and reformulate what I say according to his or her account of their differences.

To obtain a focus on the problem I shall start with a simple abstraction of the main elements of the transformation of the conditions of human life—the 'external' problem—and then consider an equally simple model of the 'internal' problem, the self-transformation of science.

Consider, by way of example, energy use. The pattern of energy flow is a fundamental feature of human life. Living itself is basically extracting and using food energy. And each transformation of human life has been associated with the exploitation of new energy sources. Early hunters and gatherers had only what they could find. Settled agriculturalists systematically reduced plant and animal variety, channelling the energy in the surviving food chains directly to human use. As the energy flow increased, so did the opportunity for increases in population, urban life, and learning. From then until 1500 A.D. the first nonfood energy subsidy was developed, i.e., wind, water and wood energy. This additional subsidy provided the framework for the initial development of science and technology. Then came fossil fuels: coal, gas, oil. Coal, coupled with the steam engine, formed the backbone of the Industrial Revolution. Later came oil and natural gas as energy demand increased, fuelling the explosion of scientific development this century. A direct result of that development has been a beginning of the exploitation of the last energy subsidy: nuclear energy. Many see nuclear energy as a necessary base for the scientific revolutions of the twenty-first century. Others advocate a return to our older energy subsidies, solar heat, biomass fuels, wind generators, focusing on them our new scientific abilities.[3]

In sum, our increasing exploitation of energy has been associated with radical transformations in our way of life until, today, our entire social order is critically dependent on its pattern of energy flows. Such important social qualities as independence and privacy, freedom of association and communication and the amenities of city living are based on mobility, effective communication, specialized/mechanized production and the like. These in turn depend crucially on our energy flows and on the technologies which exploit these flows.

The increased energy flows have, however, been bought at a price. The most visible part of the price lies in the negative environmental and medical impacts of energy exploitation, and in energy-induced world inflation and conflict—coal mining accidents, invasion of waterways and farmlands by electricity systems, the crippling price of world oil to Third World nations, Middle East conflict and so on.

Yet there is another, less visible, dimension to the price; namely the transformation of the public policy-making problem for energy. The *spatial scale* of energy decisions has increased rapidly until now they span the globe. The *time scale* of energy decisions has increased from years to centuries. The *resource scale* of energy decisions is now critical; for the first time in human history resources on a planetary scale are being exploited in a single lifetime. The *social and intellectual intricacy* of the decisions is increasing rapidly. Whether certain energy policy options—e.g., fuel-cell, photo voltaic, fusion energies—will be available two decades hence will depend critically on the research effort funded now, the development of technological infrastructure in a decade, the evolution of appropriate legal frameworks, urban and support infrastructure at the time, etc.

These four features to energy policy are all essentially unique to the twentieth century and they give energy policy a special urgency and complexity. They are not, however, unique to energy policy. All public policy areas of any general structural importance—for example communications, transportation, education, health—display the same features. This is what lends a sense of urgency and importance to the development of a general approach to public policy making for the era in which we live.

Transforming the conditions of public policy making is my first dimension to the science-based transformation of the conditions of human life. As a result, quite extraordinary demands have been placed on political institutions, demands for which their history did not prepare them. And science itself has not yet provided itself with the institutional means to responsibly relate its development to society. Rather science developed opportunistically and competitively, often agreeing only on claims for support and autonomy. On the other hand, it must in justice be added that society equally failed to develop adequate institutions for relating to scientific advances, also preferring opportunistic seizure of profitable results and piecemeal after-the-fact response to difficulties. Now, under the lash of historical development, all advanced societies are scrambling, mostly in piecemeal fashion, to plug these gaps. But before further developing these ideas, let me briefly catalogue some other dimensions of the transformation.

Science is *transforming the ecological/environmental conditions* of human, and all, life on the planet. Before 10,000 B.C. the dominant time scales were those of nature, there being little, if any, human-induced change. Today, humans have the capacity to introduce major changes in a generation. The removal of the great original southern hemisphere forests, the decimation of the whale populations, the replacement of many natural grasses and grains by a few commercial species, the damming and redirecting of river systems, the ejection of fluorine into the protective ozone layer of the upper atmosphere—these are a few examples of the transformation of the Earth. This transformation is proceeding at a pace and on a scale which far outpaces the natural rhythm of change and introduces genuine future uncertainties, e.g., in global climate, ocean productivity, desert expansion and plant disease patterns, to name only some of the impacts. Who has knowledge of the design of the Earth? Who selects the future design? It is an act of arrogance, properly speaking, to attempt these changes with any confidence of the outcome, or without concern for the outcome. Science pushes us on to enlarge still further our transforming powers.

Science is rapidly *transforming the social conditions of human life* on the planet. Not long ago humanity was split into thousands of local cultures, each interacting with most others weakly or not at all. Each culture was, in effect, a separate experiment in survival and in what it was to be human. Now scarcely one local culture remains intact and most have been transformed out of all sight of their origins. In the past fifty years cultures have become extinct much faster than have species. Science has played a central role in the transformation; it has aided it even in the very attempt to study the ancient cultures and understand their transformation. (In Canada it is said that the typical

Eskimo family consists of grandmother, husband, wife, children, husky dogs and an anthropologist.)

Perhaps the creation of a global culture enhances our chances of long-term survival, e.g., by concentrating intelligence; perhaps it ensures our ultimate destruction, e.g., by reducing our cultural variety and creating unmanageable problems. Who has had time to reflect on the matter?

Science is also busy *transforming the self-hood conditions for human life.* Our forebears found it more unproblematic to say what a person was: overwhelmingly he was a normal member of his cultural group, hunting, farming and dancing with the rest. Now it is much more difficult to say what is normal. Is a person with a commisuterotomy—one whose right and left brain hemispheres have been severed at the cortical level—a person? Commisutored patients are certainly not normal; they often act as if they were two different people. How much of a person's neural equipment can be excised before he or she ceases to be a person? And if we intervene psychotherapeutically, or with behavior modification techniques, to 'de-construct' a troubled or troublesome personality and 're-construct' a less troubled or less troublesome one, what is normal for that person? What is a normal outcome? Would Blake have survived? Would Jesus?

B. F. Skinner, a great scientific psychologist, tells us that we humans, being what we are, can have freedom or dignity, but not both; and perhaps not either if we choose poorly politically. Is he correct? How shall we respond, politically as well as personally, to this radically different conception of the normal person from that of the Judeo-Christian tradition?

We are now moving rapidly towards the time when direct genetic intervention will be possible in a planned way. Already we have testtube babies, and cloning is increasingly seriously discussed. If and when it is possible to 'engineer' the next generation, what will count as a normal human being? Perhaps we need particularly feelingless warriors, particularly dull street sweepers, particularly cerebral scientists. Perhaps a connection between madness and genius will lead us to deliberately produce many more schizophrenics. What is a desirable, let alone a normal, outcome?

7.3 THE QUIET REVOLUTION OF SCIENCE(II):
THE INTERNAL ECOLOGY OF SCIENCE

Recall from our earlier discussion of evolutionary processes the increasing importance of cognitive control structure in the process.

Now there really is something approaching a grand designer rather than an unconscious selection process—or there would be if humans had the wit to design institutions to take coherent responsibility for their interventions. Now evolutionary processes will increasingly centre on man's cognitive capacities, expressed particularly in science, and on his hopes and desires. And who will select the selectors? Who will design the designers?

Science will play a central role in designing the designers. This is the last, and deepest, transformation I want to mention—*the new role of science as self-designer and self-transformer* in all of these processes.

What is intelligence? Science is studying the question, developing intelligent machines, developing theories of *efficient* intelligent systems operations, models of the *effective* brain. Which personalities are best suited to be scientists or political/economic decision makers? Science is studying the question, producing models of *effective* personalities. Which institutional designs are best suited for *effective* decision making, most capable of *effective* control? Scientists are studying the question—in fact applying models of *efficient* intelligent systems, among others—designing new institutions. And how is *'efficient/effective'* to be understood?

What is science itself? How is it structured? What are its dynamics? Who is a proper scientist? Science increasingly studies this area. It is one of my own 'specialities'. The result is an increasing flood of advice on the design of scientific institutions, national science policy, the improvement of science education, the selection of scientific personnel.

Only one person in ten thousand understands nuclear engineering; only a competent nuclear engineer can select a competent nuclear engineer. Only a competent heart specialist can select a competent heart specialist. Only a competent planetary ecologist can select a competent planetary ecologist? Only a competent genetic engineer can select a competent genetic engineer? Only a competent institutional design theorist can select a competent institutional design theorist?

Science is in search of itself, using its own methods; researching to make its own development more effective; advising on appropriate responses to its self-generated transformation of the conditions of life.

Science then is achieving a unique new self-consciousness in its attempt to respond to its expanding external role. A similar process is occurring with respect to the increasing internal self-complexity of science. The self-complexifying process in science is generating, or perhaps forcing, a new scientific self-consciousness, structurally expressed. This process can be characterized in three words: interaction, preselection, norming. I shall discuss these in turn.

1. *Interaction*: Structurally, the sciences have become intensely internally interactive. In the evolutionary story of section 7.1 internal interaction is well illustrated in the interplay between the levels of ecology and genetics and between the levels of molecular genetics and phenotypic development. Here theoretical levels of generality happen to correspond in important respects to organizational levels, from which a first crude picture offers these three: molecular, phenotypic, ecological, i.e., from basic parts of the organism, to whole organisms, to populations of organisms. For example, the hunting/eating characteristics, perhaps part learned, part instinctual, of individuals in some predator population may have a very important impact on the dynamics of the ecology in which the predators exist, in turn affecting the biochemistry of the populace at the molecular level (e.g., through shifting food intakes or changing mating patterns), in turn acting on the hunting/eating characteristics and so on. There may of course also be significant theoretical layering within a theory that is induced by mathematical structure rather than by empirical levels of organization, e.g., molecular genetics may be considered at the level of quantum mechanics, or of biochemical kinetics. This kind of interaction among levels within a given theoretical domain or focus is now rampant throughout the sciences. There are some especially dramatic examples of it within physics, where a great deal more is known mathematically about the structure of the theories and where some very fundamental questions are now able to be asked thanks to the exploration of alternatives at more specific levels.[4]

The mention of physics and biochemical kinetics in the previous paragraph also points to the increasing intensity of interaction among theoretical domains or foci within contemporary science. This is very clear in the evolutionary field itself: besides the interactions mentioned in the previous paragraph there are, e.g., strong interactions between the collection of subjects (biochemistry, ethology, ecology) and geology, geography, physiology, epidemiology, cognitive psychology and so on.

The interactional intensity of modern science has its own repercussions for the theory of science. For example, it draws attention to the fact that all scientific instruments that extract scientific data have also to be understood theoretically before the relevance and reliability of the data can be determined. But this fact undermines the old idea that there is an objective, because theory-independent, collection of data on which to found science. Empiricist theories of science, once philosophically and culturally popular, and still today the dominant theoretical image of science in the minds of natural scientists (i.e., those in physics, chemistry and biology), held to the latter idea or, if they gave it up, argued instead that human conscious sensory perception provided a suitable substitute level of 'absolute fact'. But of course humans are themselves instruments and fall under the same necessity for theoretical understanding of their observational capacities and weaknesses, as the theory of laboratory illusions so beautifully illustrates. The failure of empiricism has become an acute issue in the social sciences, where humans observe other humans and observation evidently expands to include normative judgements; but more of this anon.

Hierarchical interaction also undermines the old idea that hierarchical position might confer methodological privilege. For example, the current major alternative to empiricism, the general account of science espoused by Popper and Lakatos[5], has in its more recent formulations proposed the idea of a "core" theory which would contain the most general propositions at the deepest level and which would remain unassailable because surrounded by a "protective belt" of auxiliary assumptions that are adjusted in the light of experiment. But in fact the hierarchical interaction among levels of a theory is now so strong as to undermine the rationale for this kind of distinction.[6] These changes in the structural dynamics of science strike, then, both at empiricism and at its major alternative and thereby indicate their depth and the necessity to rethink the methodology and epistemology of science.

2. *Preselection*: Functionally, the institutional organization of the sciences has assumed an increasing importance until now it is a major factor in its cognitive character. Where once science could be, and largely was, self-taught, it may now require half a lifetime to acquire the knowledge and skills to contribute meaningfully to its development. The crucial organization of experience and activities during this extended "cognitive neotany" is the responsibility of scientific institutions, like university departments and research laboratories. Where scientific experiments once were largely the work of one person, the typical situation now requires an experimental team, perhaps even a collection of such teams spread across continents, working together on an experimental program. The scientific setting of such programs—their place in a set of valued problems, procedures and proposals that gives them their relevance—and the coordination of the activities themselves—from acquiring funding through planning,

staffing, execution, and public dissemination of results—once again falls to scientific institutions: research-supporting agencies, research institutes, learned societies publishing journals, and so on. Where once interactions could be, and largely were, the product of personal acquaintance, now the pattern of information flow is increasingly mediated by such essentially impersonal means as journals-via-libraries and professional meetings. Of course personality and personal relations still play their role; they are especially crucial in short-term problem solving. But the vast majority of information exchanges are now promoted by, and mediated by, means that do not begin with, and often do not end with, personal relationships.

Traditional theories of science, e.g., both empiricism and the Popper-Lakatos view, have tacitly assumed science to be an intellectual enquiry by an isolated, representative intelligence. This has not been so much a conscious premise as an implicit consequence of conceiving of science as an abstract propositional structure whose development is governed by purely logical rules. In this conception human knowers do not enter essentially at all; they are abstractly represented only as the potential believers of systems of propositions. Conceptions of science of this sort have no means of dealing with any of those aspects of science that involve explicit recognition of its social dimensions, and it has been customary to write these latter off as "extra-scientific." From a biological point of view, however, science looks like a species strategy, and it is to be expected that the epistemic power and idiosyncrasies of that strategy depend on the social capacities of the species as well as on its members' individual abilities. (Even attempting to distinguish these two is an illusion because we are dealing with manifest capacities, and each sort, individual and social, develops only in intimate dependence on the other.)

Recently there has been a massive reaction against the abstract conception of science from many quarters: from within philosophy of science, for example, by Feyerabend (see 1970a, 1975, cf. Hooker 1972b), who attacks the idea that there can be an abstractly specified scientific method; by historians of science such as Kuhn (1962) and his followers, who insist that science's historical development is unintelligible unless its social dimensions are included; by sociologists of science, who have always insisted that science cannot be understood except as a social creation (e.g., Ziman 1968, 1978, Barnes 1974, 1977); by anthropologists who query the extent to which science is a Western-culture-bound institution (e.g., in Wilson 1970); and, for much longer than the new wave of revolt has been fashionable, by Marxists of both theoretical (Althusser 1965, Novack 1971) and historical (Bernal 1969, Crowther 1967) bent. These critical movements are at present part of a larger cultural movement that has its roots in historical opposition to the milieu characteristic of industrial capitalism and from which many of the same themes emerge (see e.g., Easlea 1973, Foucault 1968, Habermas 1968, 1970, Tribe 1973, and Unger 1975). The relation between the critique of science and the larger movement is complex; some of these complexities I hope to indicate in what follows.

One plausible response to the new understanding of science as a social activity is some variant of sceptical relativism. Impressed by the socio-political dimension to science as a social institution, one may espouse a socio-political relativism: science is relative to a prevailing set of socio-political interests. Marxists have been attracted to this position. Impressed by the looming normative dimensions of science, one may espouse a value relativism: science is relative to a prevailing set of human values ("interests" or "concerns"); science is the pursuit of *valuable* knowledge. Easlea and Habermas, among many others, evidently incline to this relativism. Impressed by the role of science, broadly construed—for example in Western culture, in conception of rationality, religious attitudes, and orientation to technical innovation—one may espouse a cultural relativism: science is relative to a given culture; it is a cultural way of coping with survival, species aggression, etc., etc. Students of comparative anthropology and comparative culture and their cognate disciplines often find this view attractive. Impressed by the historical character of science and its institutions, one may espouse a historical relativism: science is relative to a given historical period (e.g., Rorty 1979, 1982).

These positions are not mutually exclusive. To the contrary, one typically finds them combined in various ways; indeed, typically they are conflated with one another. These relativisms have called forth a renewed absolutist opposition that affirms the objectivity of cognitive enquiry as independent of historical periods, particular cultures, particular values and socio-political interests. Probably the leading figure of this opposition at present is Popper; his work is a curious mixture of Platonism and empiricism, the two great historic sources of opposition to epistemological relativism. (For a preliminary discussion of Popper from this perspective see Chapter 3 and Bjerring/Hooker 1981.)

My own response has been to attempt to recognize the (half-)truths in both positions. There is no doubt that science is a social enterprise bound, in many ways, to the evaluative, cultural, political, and historical milieu in which it is situated. But we humans can also learn from our history (histories) if we have a mind to. Indeed, one of the profound human experiences, I believe, is that of an enlarging framework of possibilities: not just learning, but learning how to learn, learning how to learn how to learn . . .; not just valuing but learning by what values to value, and by what values to value valuing . . . The essence of a sense of the epistemic seems to me to lie in this sense of openness to development at all levels, in interaction with reality (the cosmos, the One—whatever one wishes to label it). Relativism is vicious when it cuts us off from that orientation, leaving us smug in a pathetic anthropomorphic net of our own weaving. This latter theme dominates Platonism. It has its radically attenuated representation in empiricism, in the doctrine of the endless accumulation of objective data. It has always been the essence of mysticism.

I believe we need to retain the truth in both general positions. I cannot see a better way of doing this, indeed I can think of no other way to do this, than to construe cognition as the exploration of possibility structures, to construe theories as hierarchically organized conjectures concerning possibility structures, and to construe systems of norms (expressing values) as conjectural theories. Some of what is involved will come through the ensuing pages; elements of a theory of science from this point of view can be found elsewhere herein and in Bjerring/Hooker 1979, 1981, cf. 1980. This approach includes the contributions of many of those mentioned above without treating any of them as self-sufficient alternatives. It forms a natural bridge between evolutionary naturalism and mysticism, though a natural framework for scepticism toward mysticism.[7]

3. *Norming*: Both theoretically and practically the sciences have forced increasing interaction between their normative and descriptive components. Consider, for example, the three-way interaction, now developing apace, among normative formal structures (notably logic, statistical inference, operational methodology), mathematics and physical theory (see Note 4). Motivated by these interactions, entirely new classes of physical theory are being developed. For example, quantum mechanics has suggested an entirely new approach to logic and has generated, for the first time, a logic which is strongly nonclassical in character. Conversely, the study of abstract logics has suggested new ways to formulate the question of whether there is or can be a deterministic reality which quantum mechanics might describe, leading, on that logical basis, to new possible generalizations of the quantum mechanical axioms. Or consider the interplay between, on the one hand, normative theory (notably rationality theory and ethics) and, on the other hand, psychosocial theories and biology, also now

developing apace. The products of this interplay are currently most noticeable in the emerging fields of sociobiology and biomedical ethics. The same sort of interaction is taking place between normative theory and cultural theory, producing, for example, new economic models of knowledge and operant theories of the formation and dynamics of institutions. Again, consider the three-way interplay among normative theories (notably epistemology and rationality theory), the political sciences, and the historical development of science, past and future.[8]

The theoretical interaction is nicely illustrated in the story told at the beginning; it is no longer possible to insulate a normative theory of rationality from evolutionary biology. From a biological point of view rationality is a nervous system capacity that "grades up" through the ages, with its roots to be seen in optimizing and goal-seeking behavior and before that in irritability. Sociobiology, ethology and comparative anthropology are disciplines that are beginning to provide some of the intermediate linking domains. Of course any such links are controversial because those who subscribe to one system of norms object to any other being argued for, whatever the grounds, and because people of all normative persuasions are still agreed that norms cannot be deduced from descriptive theory (Hume's naturalistic fallacy). But these objections will, I believe, be increasingly set aside as it becomes apparent that obeying (our best theoretical guess at) a system of norms for rationality has to be what a normally functioning nervous system does and that nervous systems can do so has to be understandable in the light of evolutionary development.

In sum, science has been undergoing quiet internal revolution in its structure and dynamics. A revolution so profound that it is forcing the rethinking both of what kind of intellectual process science itself is and of the basic relations, even internal to science, between fact and value. You will recall from the previous section that science has been undergoing a profound external revolution in its relationship to its environment. And when we consider those normative (value)-factual interactions such as involve the policy sciences or sociobiology (both mentioned above) we see that these two revolutions are intimately connected to one another. There is no possibility of distinguishing sharply between the internal and external revolutions which are now transforming the character of cognitive processes within the human species. Indeed, from a planetary point of view the conclusion seems inescapable that we are in process of undergoing a profound general transformation of the conditions of life, in which cognitive processes play an intricate role at the cutting edge. In attempting to trace some of the consequences of this idea I shall turn first to a theme already broached in this section.

7.4 THE TRADITIONAL IMAGE OF SCIENCE IS OBSOLETE

The traditional picture of science with which the foregoing remarks are at such variance, is that of empiricism. Its basic idea is that science can be objective only if it is dictated by factors which are independent of human biases, anthropomorphisms and, in general, independent of human normative judgements. There have traditionally been held to be two cognitively relevant factors of this sort, objective facts and logic. The first was held to satisfy the constraints because it came directly from reality outside the human species, the second because it was held to be so strongly true that obedience to its rules was a precondition of cognitive activity at all. The empiricist program then has been to show how the content of science is uniquely determined by the joint application of the facts and logic. On the one hand the scientist becomes a pure truth seeker and on the other hand the tools for truth seeking are logical constructions upon data understood as collections of objective facts. There has been some famous philosophising that went into supporting this general approach, for example by Hume, Carnap and others; here I mention as examples the introduction of a logical distinction between facts and values (between descriptive and normative) and correspondingly sharp distinctions between pure and applied science or science and technology, and between cognitively meaningful and merely persuasive language.

Empiricism has been a very influential theory of science, leading for example to behaviorist theories in psychology, to positivist sociology and theory of law, to the structure of methodological disputes within neoclassical economics and of course to inductivist theories of scientific method itself. Taken together, it can form a very elegant and powerful theory of the human cognitive enterprise. One such overall structure I have discussed in some detail in Chapter 3. A rough characterization of the position is given in Figure 7.1.[9]

According to the empiricist framework theoretical knowledge in some given domain can be arranged hierarchically. The resulting system of knowledge "ascends" from simple factual claims and empirical generalizations, through increasingly general theories which provide structure for these, to the systematic metaphysics and normative theories which structure the cognitive set of the most general level. In this hierarchy the "lower" levels are held to determine the "upper"

Figure 7.1 - Framework for Liberalism/Empiricism

Liberalism   Empiricism

Persons

1. Persons are (sensory) data receivers + computers, driven by desires.
2. Desires, perceptions are epistemically private and opaque to reason.
3. Rational action is individual and desire (utility)-maximal.

Language

4. Cognitively meaningful language is exhausted by perceptual reports and logic.
5. Remaining language and behaviour given non-cognitive causal explanations (only)

Value   Epistemology

6. No objective values
7. Individual values are private subjective desire-based utilities.
8. Public values express cost reduction conventions or are universally rational (follow from 3).

6. Knowledge is ultimately unified.
7. Cognitively meaningful claims are divisible into analytic-a'priori and empirical-a'posteriori.
8. Empirical claims are formally analyzable (confirmable).
9. The epistemic superiority of science lies in its restriction of method to 6, 7, 8; leading to unique cumulative historical progress.

Metaphysics

9. Social structures are reducible to relations among individuals.
10. Social relations are conventional.
11. Normative social concepts (e.g. social laws) express cost reduction conventions or are universally rational (follow from 3).

10. World is conceptually simple, computationally accessible, given

Political Economy

12. Freedom is the measure of the individual to satisfy desire.
13. Social institutions are explained/justified by accompanying increases in freedom.
14. Explanatory/normative political theory is that of the social contract.
15. The most efficient solution to social co-ordination and conflict resolution games is the economic market.
16. Basic institutions (market, armed forces, etc.) are pareto optimal.
17. Other institutions have positive cost/benefit outcomes for dominant coalitions (hence derivatively pareto optimal via threat).

11. Method is individually epistemically optimal.
12. Each scientist ought to optimise his own knowledge/control by free choice of enquiry path.
13. Scientific institutions are justified by the increases in knowledge/control they yield.
14. The most efficient scientific institution is the 'free market of ideas'.

Ethics

18. Chief principle is egoism, identical with utilitarianism under the perfect free market.
19. Support of the social contract and the market is universally rationally obligatory, system of ethics is derived from behavioural presuppositions of such support.
20. Economic market—ethical action is all and only universally rational action therein.

15. System of ethics for scientists generated from behavioural presuppositions for the support of the 'free market of ideas'.

levels, except perhaps for the normative methodological considerations and these are typically held to be conventional or otherwise
noncognitive.

But if the preceding discussion has been at all accurate this empiricist picture of science is dangerously obsolete. Thus, *first*, theoretical
knowledge does exhibit significant hierarchy, it is not a fixed one-way
structure. Rather, the whole structure is dynamic, each level interacting with all others and on characteristic time scales. These latter time
scales yield rates of change in the assumptions embodied in the corresponding level; they typically vary from one year or less near the
bottom (for example to obtain a new laboratory reading) to perhaps
millennia at the highest proto-level (for example for successful challenges to Euclidean geometry or classical logic). There are many features of the contemporary setting of science which would be missed if
one lacked sensitivity to the importance of these time scales and to the
way they emerge out of the interaction among levels. To take just one
example, time scales at the lower level have been recently increasing
significantly due to the increased role of higher level theory and to the
increasing role of the institutional marshaling of resources (researchers, equipment, etc.) in scientific experiments. This has added an
important new dimension to science, for it means that experimental
results increasingly rely on institutional resources which transcend
the individual both in number, space and life-time.

Further, according to the empiricist point of view, the social institutionalization of science is really irrelevant to its cognitive organization
and content. Recall that knowledge is to be dictated solely by facts
and logic, so that from this point of view it must remain a merely
"political" consideration how scientists actually organize their lives in
relation to one another and to the larger society. This model of science
might not have been inapt for the wealthy lone eighteenth century
thinker pursuing truth from within the safe hegemony of his ruling
class. But, as already remarked, the fact is that the institutional organization of the sciences has since then assumed an increasing importance, until now it is a major factor in its cognitive character. Any
theory of science which, like empiricism, cuts itself off from considering science as a species activity rather than an individual activity not
only misses these crucially important insights, but is unable to offer
any systematic advice on how the cognitive capacities of science can
be improved (for example, by designing more effective choice systems
for the selection of experiments or for the resolution of theoretical
conflicts). And it must fail to come to grips with the increasingly
intimate relationship between the development of science and the

development of the supporting society in which the scientific institutions operate and which they help to transform.

Many of these latter issues are of course central to the debates about the societal and ethical value of science and technology. Here we may dramatize the way that they can affect even the internal nature of science itself in the following story. Let us imagine ourselves a short distance into the future where the learning requirements on scientists before they are permitted to practice their specialities has now become so great that very few are able to endure it, or to master the bodies of knowledge required to pursue it. This exclusionary process has intensified historically in step with increasing human dependence on the applied fruits of scientific research. The situation has created such intense difficulty that the human race has long since adopted a systematic policy of genetic selection and genetic development to breed a class of human beings uniquely well endowed to carry on the scientific enterprise.[10]

In any event, the situation has been reached in which scientific results are no longer accessible to everyone, not even in principle. In sharp contrast is the notion that scientific results must at least satisfy this core criterion of objectivity: that they be intersubjectively accessible to all, at least in principle. In the circumstances prevailing, the majority of the population is in principle excluded from being in a position to make scientific results intelligible to themselves. Even today we may ask whether the requirement of intersubjectivity extends to the subnormal. (I have only pitched my case in the setting where the majority are 'subnormal'.) In this setting do we still have anything which could properly be called science? Is the root of its claim to objective knowledge still intersubjective agreement? If so, of what does this intersubjective agreement consist? What of claims that this process has systematically selected certain possibilities in the universe to be explored as science while systematically excluding others? What of the selection process itself: is there a science of genetic selection for science? Are the genetic selectors to be likened to physicists, to engineers, to economists or to musicians?

Finally, according to empiricism, there cannot be any significant mutual learning relationship between empirical scientific knowledge and normative structures. From an empiricist point of view, normative structures are conventional or perhaps even merely causally persuasive, but in any case not on the same cognitive level as empirical knowledge. But the fact is, as we have seen, for modern science there is an increasing intensity of interaction between domains of empirical enquiry and the normative theories which apply to them.

What lies behind the attractiveness of empiricism, behind the pure/ applied and factual/normative distinctions, is a suspicion of the normative. It is the deeply rooted feeling that there is no way to generate intersubjective agreement on normative judgements in the way that there is for factual judgements. Connected with this is the view that normative judgements are not only more tenuously connected with reality but in fact have been the source of much evil over the course of the years in the form of prejudice, 'righteous' justification of atrocity and so on.

There is a political philosophy which is motivated by the same conception of normative judgement, the Hobbesian doctrine of individualist liberalism. Liberalism is motivated by the idea that attempts to arrive at collective normative judgements only result in political authoritarianism of one form or another (right or left). One should therefore aim to maximize individual freedom and that must mean, centrally, freedom from interpersonal normative authoritarianism. The social institution which does that perfectly, at least in theory, is the economic market. Of course, liberalism is a much richer doctrine than simply these two ideas. On the one side the economic market itself transforms the social substance of society so as to make itself viable on the terms that liberalism demands. Marx, Polanyi and many others pointed out how land, labor and capital must themselves come under the dictates of the market thereby leading ultimately to a radical transformation of the structure of social security, social morality and family and social life (cf. Polanyi 1968). On the other side, a proper defense of liberalism requires a metaphysical conception of man, knowledge and morality which makes it necessary to view society as a set of individual contracts amongst its members to their mutual advantage. No one has laid out these foundations more brilliantly than Hobbes, though many have described the course of the development of this world view.[11] Thus conceived, liberalism is briefly sketched at the left hand side of Figure 7.1.

What emerges is a remarkable parallelism between liberalism and empiricism as conceptions of the nature of the world and of human activity within it. Roberto Unger in *Knowledge and Politics* (1975) has investigated the deeper unity underlying that presented above, tracing it to five fundamental antinomies which lie at the heart of the philosophical tradition. The first antinomy is formed between the universal and the particular, the former abstract, general and partial, the latter concrete, individual and complete. This antinomy is basic, the others being special cases of it. The other antinomies are formed, respectively between understanding and experience, theory and fact, reason and desire, rules and values, the former of each pair lying on the universal side, the latter on the particular. The antinomy in each case derives from the necessity of including both sides in any adequate account of that aspect of life, and the impossibility of successfully doing so. These pairs, taken exclusively on the particularist side yield the empiricist-liberal tradition, some of whose cognitive dimensions I have briefly presented. Taken exclusively on the universal side, one obtains some form of authoritarian Platonic rationalism-idealism. Together, these antinomies result in the experience of a dichotomy between the abstract (formal) and concrete (experiencing-intuitive) self and between the individual and the social self. The structure of Unger's thought I have briefly summarized in my own form as Figure 7.2.[12] Here at last we may begin to see how the social critique of our society and culture come together at a deeper level with the philosophical critique of our theory of science.

To complete our characterization of the empiricist-liberal linkage, let us ask briefly what kind of approach to policy making emerges from this position. Within pure liberalism, the paradigm of public policy is crystal clear: the only acceptable public policies are those minimal steps necessary to support the effective operation of the market and perhaps to secure national defense. Liberalism, quickly modified to respond to the economist's 'externalities', came to include a wider range of the provision of 'public goods' amongst its policy responsibilities. However these were on the one hand to remain as minimal as possible, and on the other hand the allocation of public funds to their provision was to be a matter of the outcome of competing interests expressed through parliament, the mini-market in votes. When the empiricist account of objective science is added to this picture, then we get an equally clear and forthright theory of the relationship between scientific methodology and science policy: there is simply to be no relation of any theoretical significance. With method characterized solely by formal logics, and with policy construed as simply a matter of practical prudence, how *could* there be any theoretical relation between them? On epistemic grounds science policy should recognize the supreme, objective, cognitive superiority of science and scientific method, and should accord scientists total internal autonomy over their affairs. At a somewhat more abstract level, the relations exhibited among persons engaged in science are seen as providing the general model for a free and intellectually honest society. These were the terms in which early logical positivism opposed the development of Nazi science. They were also the terms in which Popper (essential empiricist that he is) opposed both Platonism and

Figure 7.2 - The Philosophic Structure of Liberalism—Empiricism

METAPHYSICS

UNIVERSALS are abstract, general, partial. PARTICULARS are concrete, individual, complete.
ANTINOMY: Only coherent metaphysics based solely on one, but only joining them yields an adequate
metaphysics—universals alone cannot grasp the particularity of existence, particulars alone
cannot represent its structure.
This antinomy is resolved by Liberalism-Empiricism in favour of particulars, in:
THE DOCTRINE OF MATERIALIST INDIVIDUALISM: There are only material particulars.

PRINCIPLE OF NOMINALISM
Symbols are either logical, names of particulars or
conventionally applied universals.

PRINCIPLE OF ANALYSIS
Every concept designating a complex can be
analysed into a logical complex of relations among
names; every law can be analysed into laws among
basic particulars.

PRINCIPLE OF REDUCTION
Every whole is the 'sum' of its parts, every
complex is a relation among its basic particulars.

PRINCIPLE OF INDIVIDUALISM
There are basic particulars for every domain and
every phenomenon in the domain is reducible to
them. The most basic particulars are atoms; those
of the social sciences are persons; those of
experience are sensations.

EMPIRICISM

	Psychology		Epistemology
UNDERSTANDING	is universal, impersonal, objective	THEORIES	are linguistic, mind-dependent, universal
EXPERIENCE	is particular, personal, subjective	FACTS	are non-linguistic, mind-independent, particular
NOMINALISM—	All universal understandings are conventional	NOMINALISM—	All descriptions are conventional, fact descriptions are theory-laden
EMPIRICISM—	Understanding reduces to connections in experience	EMPIRICISM—	Theories reduce to conventional descriptions of objective facts
ANTINOMY:	Only coherent psychologies are based solely on one, but only combining them yields an adequate psychology—understanding alone cannot grasp particular personal experience, experience alone cannot provide understanding.	ANTINOMY:	Only coherent epistimology is based exclusively on one, but only combining them yields an adequate epistemology—theories alone cannot grasp truth which is particular, facts alone cannot provide understanding.

	Ethics		Political Philosophy
PURE REASON	is universal, impersonal, unmotivating	RULES	are determined by pure reason, so also universal
DESIRES	are particulars, personal, motivating	VALUES	are determined by desires, so are also particular
NOMINALISM—	Universal principles of ethics are non-cognitive, conventional	NOMINALISM—	Rules are non-cognitive, conventional
EMPIRICISM—	Desires are opaque to reason	EMPIRICISM—	Values are opaque to reason
ANTINOMY:	Only consistent morality based solely on one, but only joining the two yields an adequate morality—moral rules of pure reason do not apply in particular, desires alone provide no guide to morality.	ANTINOMY:	Only consistent political philosophy based solely on one, but only joining the two yields an adequate political philosophy—rules cannot apply in particular, values alone cannot form the basis for society.

These four antinomies are resolved by Liberalism-Empiricism in:
THE DOCTRINE OF INSTRUMENTAL REASON: The nature and limit of reason is the calculation of
maximal connections between particulars.

RESOLUTION IN:	PSYCHOLOGY	—understanding requires nothing more than establishing regularity in the stream of experience
	EPISTEMOLOGY	—theories are nothing more than maximal, conventional summaries of causal regularities among facts
	ETHICS	—morality is a social convention calculated by maximal collective cost reduction in the pursuit of desires, there is no personal morality
	POLITICAL PHILOSOPHY	—rules are formal expressions of enforceable moralities

Marxism. They are still the dominant terms today in which state interference in scientific research is opposed throughout the Western world.[13]

But such a theory of the methodology/policy relation cannot provide an adequate model for the societal support of science other than the trivial one of stipulating that support should be a function of each individual's peer-judged ability to use scientific methods. Sadly, this is the very (quasi-)system of funding which has dominated the support of science from the nineteenth century, when the fight was to establish science as having a right to be supported at all, to the present postwar era, when the inadequacies of the approach are only beginning to be recognized. However inadequate, an alternative has yet to be found. Government funding still sticks to a peer-judged, individual-merit formula, albeit within an increasingly elaborate framework of bureaucratic programs. Significantly, the bureaucratic antithesis here is equally reviled.

To summarize, in empiricist-liberalism dominated societies all public "policy", science policy included, can only be viewed as an inherently political reaction to (a) pressure from special interest groups, and (b) the 'externalities' of economic activity. Therefore, it can be at most *prudentially* rational, never epistemically rational. (As it happens this dichotomy also applies to the bulk of the literature on the subject: On the one hand there are conceptual and empirical analyses of political power; on the other, there are supposedly "objective" measures of the efficiency of specific policy actions relative to their stated, usually economic, objectives.)

It behooves us, therefore, to search for a more adequate conception of science, society and human policies in respect of both. Attempting anything like an adequate theoretical alternative to the empiricist-liberal tradition which has dominated the last three centuries—even were I arrogant enough to suppose that I had one—would pass far beyond the confines of this chapter. I shall, more modestly, make some programmatic remarks concerning an alternative approach to science, point the reader briefly in some alternative directions which seem promising to me in respect to society and policy and close instead on some reflections concerning the significance of the twentieth century circumstances in which we find ourselves.

7.5 BEYOND THE TRADITIONAL IMAGE OF KNOWLEDGE TO ARTIFACTS, POSSIBILITIES AND EXPERIMENTS

Three categories comprise our norms, what we consider reasonable, ethical and valuable. As we have seen, the essence of science has most often been held to exclude norms. Normative considerations may be relevant in politics, family life, even warfare, but not in science which is wholly determined by empirical fact and rational cognitive structure (e.g., logic).

According to empiricism, for example, the objective scientist observes an autonomous, purely factual world in a noninterfering manner. (The autonomy and noninterference, along with restriction to just logic besides, are there to underwrite the objectivity.) But in fact the world is being increasingly transformed into a human artifact in which both the autonomy and the noninterference are gone.

The distinctive feature of an artifact is that it necessarily combines fact and value in an intimate way. An artifact is an art-i(n)-fact, it is a factually realized human design. Designs are based on choices, selections from among the infinite variety of possibilities, and thus always involve human values and normative principles in their shaping, whether these concern beauty, technical functionality, theoretical suggestiveness, exhibition of truth, promotions of freedoms, or whatever. A motor car is a factually realized design based on the values of economically efficient transportation—efficiency specified in the marketplace—and private ownership/privacy of operation. We also now know it promotes urban specialization and spread, and ill health.

As the world is transformed into a human artifact it becomes less and less possible to escape from the normative dimension. The secret of wilderness is that it is an environment still exhibiting no human norms. But the city is norm-saturated, and so is every village and every laboratory.

The entrance of the normative into science via its objects of study has always been most evident in the social sciences. As Becker (1976) rightly insists, the social sciences are inextricably involved in the shaping of social realities. They study a human artifact, society, and these human artifacts clearly embody human norms, they are clearly norm-realizing structures. The first story of Section 7.1 imagines the possibility that the cosmos itself becomes a human artifact to focus attention on the normative nature of the social sciences and on the implications of artifactual transformation for the nature of science and of cognition generally.

Artifacts are experiments. They are experiments first with what is possible and then (perhaps) with what is preferable. Small conveyances are experiments in the possibilities of individual transportation, but on a social scale. Among the earliest artifacts in this category were trolley cars, but they were eliminated by another experiment, the gasoline automobile. In the future gasoline automobiles may in turn be replaced by other artifacts, for example electric cars or individualized, computer-controllable monorail cars. Some kind of preferability will be the basis of choice among these alternative designs, we can hope that it will be socially rational.

A little reflection reveals that we are intimately immersed in artifacts, in experimental designs demonstrating the possible and the preferable. Cultures are such experiments, carried on over millennia on occasion, but without explicit control. Indeed, so unselfconscious is our species as yet of its cultures as experiments that it is in process of eliminating cultures on a planetary scale at least as fast, if not faster, than it is eliminating other natural species. With respect to cultures and the social sciences generally it is not yet clear whether humans are capable both of undergoing the experiments and of exercizing control over them, of being both subject and object, both actor and spectator; perhaps any controllers would themselves merely define another cultural experiment (they do at least this). We shall soon be capable of genetically selecting for cognitive abilities in a modestly strong way; unavoidably, however, any attempt to do so will itself be a cultural experiment in the consequences of designing that kind of society. Indeed, the very history of science itself is an experiment. For the last two millennia, for example, we have been experimentally exploring two great metaphysical schemes for generating theory, albeit unconsciously so until recent times.[14] It is as yet an open question whether science is a culture-bound experiment and, if so, in what respects. Finally, the human personality is itself an artifact, an experiment, as Becker (1973) stresses. What we are as persons, including our theoretical conceptions and institutional identifications, is profoundly influenced by what we have been and the artifacts among and within which we have lived. We have neither an *a priori* access to, nor a norm-free methodology for, becoming a person.

If artifacts are experimental explorations of what is possible, then theories must be viewed first as conjectures about the structure of possibilities. This suggestion has an odd ring. As heirs of the prevailing empiricism we have been educated to think of theories as descriptions of what is actual. Still, possibilities may be objective and it is a central part of the notion of a law of nature that it support counterfactual conditionals—that is, statements about what sequences are possible independent of their being actual. Moreover, the picture of natural science as exploration of the structure of the possible does not look so strange on examination. The matter may be looked at in this way: laws specify constraints on the possible, that is what unites physics and geometry; logic is the theory of the structure of possibilities, that is what unites physics and geometry with logic. Leibniz said that space was the order of copresent possibilities and time was the order of successive possibilities. The Platonic "chaos" had intimately to do with the structure of the possible forms that could become actual, and this role seems to have been passed on to the modern quantum mechanical "vacuum state". Meanwhile, quantum mechanics served to focus attention on the logical structure of descriptions in physical theory, a logical structure most plausibly taken as a specification of the structure of possibilities (possible "states" and successions) for the theory.[15] LeClerc (1972) offers a history of science that might be a useful starting point for a history of physics as an exploration of possibility structures.

Moreover, physics increasingly studies the physics of artifacts: telephone networks, nuclear reactors, linear accelerators. In many cases it is clear that it is the study of an artifact that is involved, for instance the telephone network and the nuclear reactor. In other cases the issue remains in doubt, for instance, modern high-energy linear accelerators. (Do the experiments reveal real fundamental particles or simply nature's way of reacting to this particular stress?) Are there clear-cut cases where there is no doubt that it is a natural object and not an artifact under study? Historically the answer is yes, but as the scope of human intervention widens, the situation is becoming less clear; hydrological systems are no longer natural, nor are microclimates in many places (soon not even planetary climate), nor all animal species (domestic varieties) are artifacts, and so on. The historical rule seems to be that as human access to energy and information expands, the subject matters of the sciences shift increasingly from the natural to the artifactual. Given enough energy and information, even cosmology may become a policy science. Presumably there are actual constraints that cannot be altered. Whether these are broad details of what we would have been inclined to call the actual or whether they are structures of the possible remains surprisingly open.

This view of theories raises some old issues in explanation. The first task of science becomes that of explaining why what is actual is possible. A dramatic example of the importance and nontrivialness of this task is given in the problem posed to atomic theory at the turn of the century: how is the stable, orbital atom possible? A further explanatory task is to explain the actual, given the possible (a law) and the actual. Finally, there is the rationalist ideal of explaining, from a few deep principles, that of everything that is possible there can only be one actuality. (In modern guise it is the attempt to explain more from stronger principles and a more austere data base.) Historically, the great explanatory tasks have been the first and last, with the second task the derivative one; empiricism reversed this order.

What is reasonable for physics is reasonable for the other natural sciences. By the time one comes to biology the entrance of the artifactual is all too clear. The epistemology of the sciences of the artifactual seems best represented as an exploration of the structure of the possibilities, together with an evaluation of them. I have argued for assimilating the natural sciences to this paradigm rather than vice versa.

7.6 BEYOND THE TRADITIONAL STATUS OF VALUE

Recall that according to the traditional theories of science, science was value-free, free of norms, because it was solely determined by facts and logic in one way or another. However, according to the approach to scientific knowledge outlined in the preceding section this is no longer true. Yet, might it not still be argued that science itself is uninfected with norms or values, by arguing that science only determines possibilities for action and not courses of action themselves? Now the provision of possibilities already implies that there is some human choice among them, but while that may be held to be made exterior to science, the involvement of science with norms or values which I have been arguing runs much deeper than that.

What, for example, do we believe is possible? That depends on those areas where we choose to concentrate research resources to develop theories of what is possible. Consider the example of nuclear-reactor physics. It is an interesting case because, while physics is widely regarded as an objective, hence value-free, science of a natural object (i.e., the physical world), a reactor is clearly a human artifact created to fulfill certain human purposes (values) and to satisfy certain human standards (i.e., values). So we may think of reactor physics as a hybrid affair. It takes the particular form or shape that it does because human purposes and values are what they are, but the principles which it applies come from a general science which is widely held not to be infected by these specific human characteristics. Yet in recent times reactor physics has become a recognized branch of physical science, with its departments, programs, degrees and so on. What does this tell us about the nature of science? It tells us, of course, that modern science at any rate is conspicuously a social institution, with its institutional structure, dynamics and resources heavily determined by the nature of the surrounding society. But it tells us too that there is no neat separation between human norms and the study of what is possible, wherever we study what is possible for human artifacts.

A Realistic Theory of Science

Theories themselves are artifacts created according to certain norms, according in fact to a practice embodied in scientific institutions. But what is possible next in theorizing depends on past experiments to create these theoretical artifacts; we have neither *a priori* knowledge, nor a norm-free methodology for exploring the possibilities of theoretical creativity itself. Moreover, as remarked earlier, science itself has evolved to the point where there are now profound interactions occurring between theories and their normative frameworks. Thus theoretical evolution itself is undercutting the notion of a clear separation between norms and facts.

Equally, scientific institutions themselves are human artifacts and the practice they realize in their norms for reporting, criticism, and training are themselves normative creations. But these norms, embodied in their practice, in turn help to determine what theories will be accepted—even what theories will be explored. And as I have earlier remarked, the history of science itself, and indeed the larger culture in which it is supported, are also human artifacts, themselves subject to the interaction between human experimental choice and empirical evaluation.

Indeed, this picture is completed with the already remarked fact that human personalities themselves are in important measure human artifacts. We are, as it were, saturated with our own artifacts created through our own cognitive organizations. In us, I believe, the ancient evolutionary activity, expressed in the developmental hierarchy—reaction, irritation, reflex, conditioning, judgement—finds its expression as a basic judgement/action, neither normative nor factual, but both. What adults later distinguish in themselves as norms and facts is a result of a complex differentiation of the judgement/action function. This differentiation is one of the many spectacular creative achievements of the developing child, though it is also his Achilles heel.[16] In this we mirror society, which has created complex institutional differentiations between normative and empirical through the differentiation of institutionalized practices, into various kinds of scientific and other institutions. It is one of the spectacular achievements of developing social *Homo sapiens*. But in neither case should we let its achievement hide its true nature. Theory (culture), institutional practice (society) and personhood: the whole is a dynamically evolving network, and there is no way to separate the normative and the factual within it except as relative differentiation.[17]

This view of the nature and role of norms is at sharp variance with the commonly held conceptions of the normative in Western culture. Running through Western theoretical thought is a highly ambivalent attitude toward norms. On the one hand they have been regarded as transcendent and *a priori*; on the other as arbitrary and subjective. The principles of logic and geometry are associated with the former; social values and social institutions with the latter. In both cases there results a sharp separation between norms and facts. And both views, I believe, share profound commitments—for example, to intelligence as algorithmic. Norms as transcendent make it mysterious how they could ever enter the kind of intimate interrelations with facts I have been describing as actually happening. Instead, one is forced to try to retain the norm unaltered and to substitute a grander factual design for cosmos and consciousness. In that direction lies Platonism. Norms as subjective make them cognitively irrelevant to the facts. This view leads to some version of conventionalism in which conventions understood as cognitively arbitrary rules adopted for prudential purposes under the causal influences of pain and pleasure (or more generally, 'utilities'), govern behavior externally to cognitive activity itself. In that direction lies Hobbesian empiricist-liberalism. In either case, norms have no commerce with facts.

There has also been a deep suspicion of norms in the West because they are associated with social authoritarianism and with personal dogmatism, both of which are antithetical to Western humanist and political ideas (i.e., norms!)[18] But our earlier discussion should suggest that this may not be an intrinsic feature of norms but instead a feature of the setting, whether personal or social, in which norms are deployed. Still, transcendent norms do seem to lend themselves naturally to dogmatism and authoritarianism, for they are a source of ultimate authority to individual or state. On the other hand, conventionalism leads directly to the conclusion that the exercise of power is the only factor beyond utility in the choice of norms, and hence in the choice of social conditions generally and of one's own behavior in particular.

This double schizophrenia between the normative and the factual and between two utterly opposing conceptions of norms has been Western culture's main historical legacy in the theory of norms. What is required is an alternative theory of norms which resists their dogmatic/authoritarian use yet which allows them the legitimate interactions with the factual which have been described above. Notice, as a beginning, that theories themselves serve both of these latter functions well. Thus if we can suppose norms to be fallible theoretical conjectures of a distinctive kind, then we can see our way clear to avoiding the Scylla of transcendentalism and the Charybdis of conventionalism. Theories are open to criticism in the light of experience and to revision in the light of experience and alternative proposal. This process can be socially institutionalized as a strong antidote to dogmatism. Moreover, since real theories exist in a delicate dynamic equilibrium with their experimental bases and with each other[19], norms as theories would explain why, and how, normative theories are found in interaction with their empirical bases, namely with theory and experience, and with each other. And since this is so, we are able to learn about our norms, are able to make experiments with them, evolving them as we go along. And this, I have been arguing, is what we in fact do.[20]

7.7 EPISTEMIC ECOLOGY: A SYSTEM OF QUESTIONS

Though I have not tried to fill out a complete account of human cognitive processes here, I have already said enough, I believe, about the contrast between our traditional images of epistemology and norms and the reality of our present cognition driven transformations on the planet to suggest something of the radical rethinking that needs to be done to do justice to our actual history. For the moment let me pause to offer you my readers a program of questions concerning the nature of human knowledge and of science in particular through which we can contrast the traditional image of science and of human knowledge with alternative perspectives which might be more adequate to our circumstances. This program of questions is given in Figure 7.3. To summarize something of the profound divergence between the traditional views which I have been criticizing and a more adequate theory I have, in Figures 7.4 and 7.5 respectively, sketched in the patterns of the two sets of respective answers which might be provided to the original questions.[21] A fuller account of the evolutionary naturalism which drives the answers I have provided in Figure 7.5 is provided in other essays herein.

7.8 INSTITUTIONS ARE CENTRAL AND CRUCIAL

I have already had occasion to emphasize the centrality and importance of institutions to science. Institutions provide the framework for the scientific education necessary to our extending cognitive neotany. They permit cognitive division of labor compatibly with (at least partial) coherence of cognitive strategy. That is, scientists are able to specialize, each contributing merely a fragment to the boundary of advancing knowledge, and yet their relations to one another are able to maintain a certain coherence with respect to that advancing boundary. Indeed institutions regulate nearly every important area of scientific activity. They are science's external nervous system.

SCIENCE AS EXPLANATION AND AS CULTURE (A TENTATIVE QUESTION GUIDE)

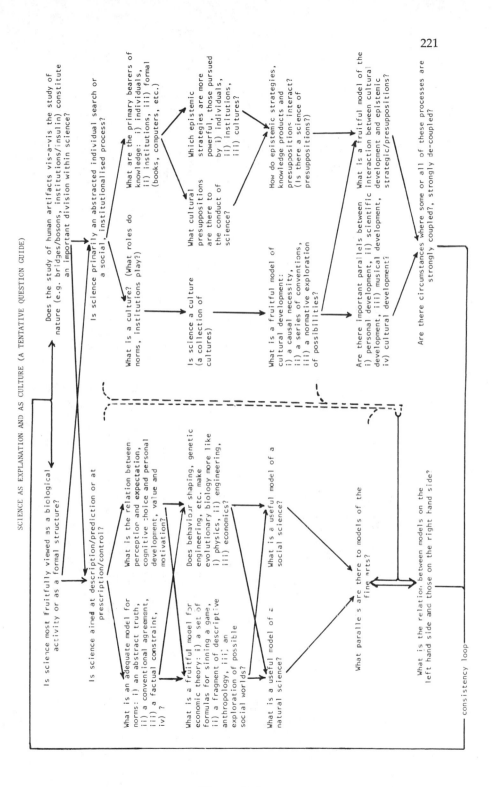

Figure 7.3

222

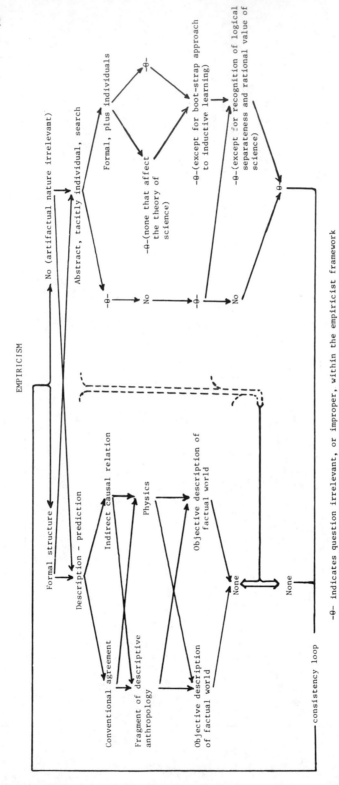

Figure 7.4

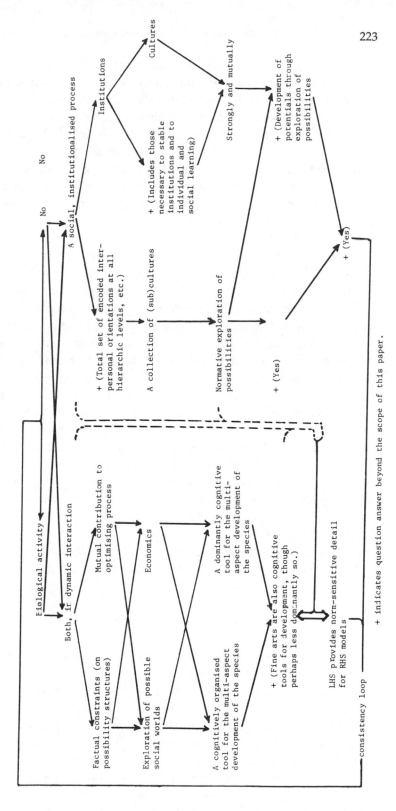

RESPONSE TO QUESTIONS

EVOLUTIONARY NATURAL REALISM

Figure 7.5

+ indicates question answer beyond the scope of this paper.

In fact, science is *essentially* a social activity. According to those views which sharply separate norm and fact, the social institutionalization of science is really irrelevant to its cognitive organization and content. It must remain a merely "political consideration" how scientists actually organize their lives in relation to one another and to the lives of society. Neither the Platonic remembrance of the eternal vision of the truth nor the empiricist inductive grubbing among the individual facts has any intrinsic concern for the societal organization of these activities. But, as I hope the foregoing considerations have made clear, the cognitive dependence upon social organization is now so deep that it should lead us to reflect whether it is not in the nature of intelligence to be social, even from earliest evolutionary times.

There is, I believe, much to be said for this latter view, though it is not ultimately the whole truth. Despite its being too large and controversial a subject to be fully presented here, I will allow myself one remark. If, as hinted earlier, personality is an artifact and personality is taken to include the conceptual framework and cognitive skills of the organism, then we may ask about those processes whereby the cognitive dimension of the artifact is created. An important part of the answer consists in development through the exercise of elementary behavioral abilities. Developmental psychologists such as Bruner and Piaget, among many others, have emphasized the importance of elementary concrete operations in the early conceptual development of the child and of elementary behavioral/social exchanges in the child's early socio-emotional development. Generalizing these lessons suggests the crucial importance of behavioral experience in the formation of concepts and skills and hence the importance of 'procedural learning', of apprenticeship and practice, to human learning. This perspective can be immediately applied to science in particular. As I remarked earlier (Note 1), technology and experiment are to the cognitive development of the scientist what tongue, hands and crawling are to development of the young child. There is always a tacit dimension to science (Polanyi 1964, 1967). But then it is crucial to the historical continuity and development of science at any given time that there be a structured array of apprenticeships available whose experience appropriately integrates the coming generation into the developing practice of science and into its conceptual frameworks and theoretical beliefs. And this requires a social institution. The necessity of these kinds of intergenerational relations also displays one of the essentially social features of human cognition. But there is not the space to further explore the ramifications of this view.

What we can focus upon here is the creation of objectivity in science, which is the focus of the normative/descriptive separation. What, at bottom, is objectivity? Again, the answer to this depends critically upon the larger theoretical framework invoked. From the point of view of the evolutionary naturalistic realism which I espouse, the essence of objectivity is systematic intersubjective criticism. To be objective about a claim is to expose it to intersubjective scrutiny of certain kinds and to accept it only if it passes that scrutiny. Thus the social institutionalization of a process of intersubjective scrutiny is the essence of objectivity. The normative/descriptive dichotomy is, as I suggested earlier, basically a social question. For science it arises as a complex differentiation of process within social structures (namely between those of scientific institutions and others). Of course, these institutionalizations are normative creations, and with clearly descriptive intentions. We need to learn about which processes are appropriate to objectivity in the same way we learn about anything else, by conjecture and intelligent institutional experiment.

Incidentally, the creation of such supra-individual cognitive processes does not in itself mark off science or modernity from ancient intelligence or culture. But the creation of processes systematically capable of challenging entrenched metaphysical conceptual frameworks does in general mark a significant break with past practice; for in general the enquiry practices of earlier cultures basically served to reinforce the historically entrenched frameworks. The same applies to contemporary authoritarian cultures. (Note that scientific cognitive development comes at a potentially large psychic cost to the individual in terms of lowered personal certainty and lowered personal importance, the latter because it is only practically realizable through supraindividual institutionalized means.)

Hobbes foresaw that if, in any given subject matter, the truth values of claims were to be given neither transcendentally nor indubitably in experience, then it would be necessary to erect a social institution to determine a rational approach.[22] Hobbes, of course, thought that the decisions of this institutional process were thereby conventional with respect to the subject matter and hence to be decided by power. Moreover, the only social institution he considered was a 'judge', that is an individual creating 'truth' by fiat—by virtue of authority invested in him. But Hobbes' argument remains valid, even when we free ourselves from these constraints. Science is in exactly the position that Hobbes indicated, and so it is *essentially* a social institution. It follows that both of its dimensions that I have discussed, external as well as internal, are equally part of its true nature.

Institutions then stand at the very heart of what constitutes science for our species. This becomes less surprising if the role of institutions as our external nervous system is kept clearly in mind. Recall the evolution story from Section 7.1; as the evolutionary strategy shifts from variety among individuals as the basis for a surviving strategy to building problem-solving capacity into each individual as the basis for a survival strategy, there arises an immediate need for an external nervous system. Individuals have decidedly finite capacities, thus what must quickly become the focus of nervous system development are not individual strategies shaped to particular circumstances and inflexibly retained (remembered), but general problem solving capacities. Simple socially learned mating behaviors acquired once for all are the sort of low-level learning that may give a species a selection edge over its less adaptable rivals, but it too is clearly vulnerable to sufficiently changed conditions. General problem solvers, for example the primates, have much greater adaptability, *if* they can coordinate their individual learning, spread the collective result across the group, focus on it explicitly so as to adapt it and transmit it from generation to generation. The social processes by which these four crucial cognitive processes occur are only through social institutions. (Institutions are broadly understood as sets of systematic social arrangements for coordinating individual behavior.)

Of course, if institutions fail, the general problem solver may be in an even worse plight than his less adaptable rivals. For the dependence of the individual general problem solver upon the species via institutions is very great: dependence for education, for provision of all necessities not directly acquired (because of division of labor), for collective strategy in times of threat, and so on. Thus if there is no institutional coherence at the species level, *a fortiori* if there is actual generation of incoherence at the species level (for example, ecological degeneration, nuclear war), then the survivability of the species may be low, and that of individuals very low. (How many city people would survive beyond two weeks in the event of a war cutting off energy and/or food supplies to the city?)

Institutions then link us into the species learning pool, they are our external nervous system. The invention and deployment of computers should make this truth dramatically obvious. Computers have greatly increased the cognitive capacity (mostly memory, to date) of our external nervous system. But they are not individual brains for they would make little sense outside of the highly specific institutionalized settings in which they have been designed to function. They are better seen as ganglion, or perhaps neuron, clusters in our external nervous systems, linked together by institutions.

7.9 NORMS, POSSIBILITIES AND INSTITUTIONS ARE ALSO OF THE ESSENCE FOR PUBLIC POLICY

Let us pick up briefly the public policy theme which has been in the background of these discussions. The point is to relate public policy, usually understood, to cognitive policy (usually misunderstood).

Recall from Section 7.2 that science has transformed the conditions of public policy making, in respect of the scales and intricacy of the policies now required. Recall from Section 7.8 that the development of science has also emphasized the importance of the social, institutionalized dimensions of science. Thus there is the most intimate two-way connection between cognitive development and the transformation of public policies. On the other hand, in Section 7.4 it was pointed out that the traditional view of science can make no real sense of these mutual involvements. Empiricism-liberalism either offers no theory of policy at all, or offers an attenuated, falsely 'objectified' pair of independent procedures for funding pure research and for correcting market imperfections.

A new theory of policy making is therefore needed, one adequate to contemporary challenges. Since science policy is our central cognitive strategy, science being essentially social and institutionalized, and science is our most important social structure, it should be expected that a good theory of public policy should illuminate the domain of science policy in particular. Let us see.

If the world is increasingly becoming a human artifact then the future is increasingly becoming a matter of choice. The future will be the artifact we choose it to be. (Limitations imposed by whatever fundamental laws there are, access to energy, human ignorance and other human limitations, will of course constrain the universality of this claim.) The discussion suggests the need of a policy-making process which is normatively guided without being authoritarian, which takes account of complexity and uncertainty without being incoherent and which is institutionalizable in a limited and imperfect world. It would be the clearest arrogance to suggest that I or anyone else have neat solutions to these difficult problems. What I and some of my friends and students have been doing, however, is working with an approach to energy policy making first widely used by Amory Lovins and variously called back-casting, scenario analysis or retrospective path analysis. Roughly, one constructs a 'picture' of a social condition at some time in the future (say a pattern and level of energy consumption forty years in the future) and then, working backwards, tries to understand the key qualitative transitions that would need to be made in order to realize that situation at that time. To date the use of the technique, mainly by Lovins and others in energy policy analysis, has centered around the generation of technical and economic data. What is missing on the one hand is the enrichment of the process so as to center upon the clear articulation of what one might call a 'normative blueprint', a richer specification of the social values, lifestyles, patterns of expenditure, transportation, justice, etc., that are associated with alternative future states and, on the other side, the setting of the whole decision-making process into an institutional context rich enough for it to make sense as a process of democratic political choice. In a variety of recent writings some of this enrichment process has begun to be explored.[23]

Central to this latter exploration is the attempt to create institutional structures and processes which represent a 'third way' between the efficiency but incoherence and inhumanity of the market and the coherence but authoritarianism and limited intelligence of the centralized bureaucratic state. I, in company with many others, have been attempting to develop models of decentralized, yet coherently connected, decision-making institutions and I believe that this problem is one of the truly urgent human tasks of this century. Yet here again our scientific development has placed us in a qualitatively new circumstance.

This century has witnessed the development of a unique class of theories concerned precisely with the behavior and management of complex systems: systems theory, control theory, cybernetics, decision theory, operations research, ecological dynamics, network and bond graph theory, organization theory, artificial intelligence and so on. Though often focused on different systems and employing different terminology, these theories are all centrally concerned with understanding and managing complex systems. One of the important complex systems that may be studied using these theories is the social organization of scientific knowledge and research itself. Science theorizing about itself. Such theories, which are a unique twentieth century response to our cognitive situation as discussed above, have begun to provide deeper insight into the complex institutional structures and policy formation processes that might be appropriate to our historical circumstances. I believe they point toward the importance of the kind of institutional structures and adequate policies I mentioned; but it is the work of another day to develop their insights explicitly for the policy field. In the meantime, it is urgent that policy issues be carried to the level of political debate about institutional processes and more resilient policies. The point is our need to develop commitments to experiment with more adequate institutional designs in a setting where policy commitments still permit learning and adaptation.

If we choose, we can respond to the growing number and magnitude of our difficulties in the time-honored primitive fashion: with fear, authoritarianism, and short-term opportunism. We can build for ourselves a self-fulfilling prophecy of victimization, inequity, elitism, and mounting disruption. But this would be to throw away our newly emerged self-awareness of the situation, and our neo-natal cognitive tools for responding to the situation. Seeking to manage ourselves along the lines suggested is a far more positive approach, one in keeping with our real potential as self-aware general problem solvers.

Turning now to science policy, an adequate policy for science should presumably specify a future normative blueprint for cognitive structure and a retrospective path analysis for realizing it. But if it be thought that what this involves would be a detailed future specification of the desired state of knowledge, then following this model would be peculiarly difficult, for knowledge is largely intrinsically unpredictable (else we would already know it). However, a normative blueprint basically expresses values and principles along with general structural conditions. In this case the normative blueprint remains, but the structural conditions must recede somewhat because of uncertainty and attention is thrown on to the values and principles expressed. These latter are summed up chiefly in a specification of what is *valuable* knowledge and of what are *intelligent* epistemic institutions for its acquisition.

Valuable knowledge is that knowledge most salient to cognitive development and the development of human life generally. Empiricism singled out basic facts as the only part of valuable knowledge, but facts are myriad and most—such as that the author's current pen is yellow—are cognitively near-worthless. This is not the place to enter upon a theory of valuable truth. Popper, whose idea I borrow here, had one, which I think insightful but inadequate (see Note 5). Nonetheless, his idea paved the way for the great transformation of the internal theory of knowledge now occurring, that is, the replacement of logic, as the sole structuring principle of knowledge, by rational decision theory using cost-risk-benefit analysis (including logic as a special case). The basic idea is that believing something is an act of rational commitment and hence a matter of weighing up the costs, benefits and risks, of making the commitment. Decision theory is driven by preference or utility structures and it is in these that a theory of valuable knowledge will be expressed. Levi transformed

Popper's ideas into this setting using only two cognitive utilities, truth and relief from ignorance.[24] Again I find this inadequate and have suggested many others, various simplicities, technical applicability, explanatory unification, reliability, and so on.[25] What is most valuable is knowledge most highly ranked on this multi-dimensional scale. It is this for which science strives, it is for this that scientific institutions allocate resources and take risks on our behalf.

The institutions are of course crucial and the normative blueprint should contain our best theory of intelligent cognitive institutions. But here the blueprint is on all fours with those for any other public policy, both containing as a central component the specification of institutional structures appropriate to the end state specified, and constrained by our relative ignorance of institutional design. Here in this common basis is where one might begin the effort to repair the gulf between the official methodology and the social practice of science, so that the latter may truly serve the species rather than more limited, less species-rational ends.[26]

The goal-directed striving of science is usually called methodology, while the allocation of resources and risk is usually called policy. According to empiricism they have nothing to do with one another. According to the point of view expressed here both of them are, or can be, rational decision processes utilizing, in principle, the same range of utilities, though with different weightings. From this general point of view, then, science policy becomes a special case of public policy generally, on the one side, and of science methodology on the other. Indeed, it is possible to take a general feature of any one of these three policy areas and transform it into the others by suitable substitutions. With this in mind, I make three brief structural comparisons between science methodology, science policy and public policies generally by first stating below the features for science methodology, the corresponding statements for the other two areas can then be obtained by first substituting 'policy' for 'methodology' ('policy analyst' for 'methodologist', etc.) and then further substituting 'public' for 'science' throughout.

> 1. Since science methodology is normative—it is directed toward the pursuit of valuable truth—a specific science methodology for a specific historical situation includes a detailed description of ends, as well as means. Choice of methodology is always a function of available techniques of communication and argument, and of existing institutional structures through which behavior is molded, but it is also a function of the ideal towards which society is moving. In this sense, although institutional

structures and forms of technology are what make any science methodology possible, and therefore often provide the locus for fundamental scientific change, it is the normative selection of ends which determines which technologies and structures ought to be developed.[27]

2. Since the science methodologist and the institutions of implementation are both integral parts of the dynamic social system which would be altered by any envisioned methodology, and since no methodology is *a priori* justifiable, all historically specific methodologies, and all specific normative goals toward which those methodologies are directed, represent at most a particular phase in the evolution of forms of social life and of human knowledge. Moreover, once we are equipped with this latter understanding, the choice of science methodology becomes a matter of the conscious selecting of such goals and forms of social life. But by virtue of the historically bound nature of all such choices, that selection must be recognized as an inescapably constrained, or 'local' choice, while the problems with which it deals are inherently 'global' or perennial.

Therefore, there is in principle a fundamental predictive uncertainty regarding all science methodology; it is always chosen and implemented in a specific historical context. But the events which constitute the evolution of a form of social life and of its normative goals are necessarily beyond the control of *that* form of life.[28] Needless to add, the institutions through which a form of social life deals with this fundamental uncertainty of science methodology choice are typically among its most central.[29]

3. With specific normative goals accepted, in this way, as themselves the object of historically structured learning, the broader focus for all science methodology becomes the selection of processes for change within this constraint of fundamental uncertainty. Given this, the only reasonable vector of development is that of constrained increase in 'understanding', taken in its broadest sense.[30]

These three triads characterize features of our situation which I wish especially to emphasize, but they don't yet yield a full theory of methodology/policy formation. They do, however, draw attention to the difference between local and global decisions. The latter distinction has, as it happens, become a matter of increasing concern in both the methodology and policy areas. Local choices in time made in the economic market on the basis of marginal cost/benefit analysis will almost always favor doing 'still more of the same' because of the contribution of the history of investment to that point, thus sequences of such choices almost always serve to reinforce the status quo. Often this is indeed appropriate. Yet equally often it happens that from a longer term, more global perspective this may not be a desirable path of development; it may, for example, reinforce exploitation of a non-renewable resource for which there are longer term alternative uses of greater social importance.[31] The key is to learn about when each is an appropriate response, which requires our having a self-improving meta-economic theory of institutionalized public policy making (Note 30). The same applies to methodological choices. It is almost always easier and more immediately fruitful (in terms of publishable results, etc.) to push an already well-developed line of inquiry one small step further than to try to develop new approaches to problems (or worse, new problems). And often this approach is also appropriate. The key is to learn about when each is an appropriate response, which requires our having a self-improving meta-methodological theory of institutionalized science methodology development (cf. Note 30). But in given circumstances this approach may be seen from a more global perspective to reinforce research biases, or even a march into a dead-end (the need for revolutionary science).

It will also be evident how crucial are institutions to the formulation and realization of policies—and to their revision in a democratic manner. Familarity with the controversies of political thought will have convinced the reader of the delicacy of the dependence of political decisions on the process of political choice. (Compare, for example, the processes for the choice of leaders in, say, the USA, USSR and Thailand.) But the institutional shape of the policy formation institutions is no less crucial a part of the overall process. Until very recently, for example, there simply had not existed in Western countries the kind of energy policy-making institutions which were capable of formulating overall, coherent energy policy (see Note 23). The result is that, for example, Western countries do not even have an adequate thermodynamic profile of their energy flows, let alone a coherent account of the alternative energy normative blueprints available for them. At least a necessary condition for obtaining the latter is that there be policy-making institutions whose internal structure makes possible—and encourages—the kind of fundamental overall viewpoint which energy policy requires. But in the past energy policy-making institutions have been fragmented among those few energy commodities which happen to have proved historically important at the time.

The same crucialness of internal institutional design reappears in every area of public policy. Thus institutions are at the focus of things. The further human knowledge and activity expand, the more essential become the supra-individual processes which mold that development at levels beyond the resources of any one individual. Institutions are the key to our future—and also our Achilles heel. If the human race fails to survive (or survives without even the minimal dignities it now shakily possesses), it will almost certainly be because our social intelligence (i.e., our ability to create appropriate institutions to manage our collective abilities) is outrun by our mechanical intelligence (i.e., our ability to create 'hard' science and technology). Moreover, our social intelligence is constantly in tension with our consciousness of our separate egocentric selves, the one marked by our ability to plan grand social schemes and create grand social institutions, the other by our need to deal with people at a personal level and with our ambitious power drives. Could it be that the very conditions which made scientific cognition possible for our species also make it impossible for our species to practice it reasonably? While the outcome of this rich dynamic is uncertain, we have no choice but to attempt to exercise our social intelligence within it.

What, then, are the burdens of the now-demanded social institutions?

First, to cope with the knowledge 'spiral' within science itself. We need to cope, because we are largely ignorant of what is happening. We just don't know very much about the new circumstances into which science is helping to catapult us, nor about the real dynamics of science itself. We don't, for example, yet understand much about the deeper nature of human intelligence—what the relations between its factual and evaluative dimensions are; just how it is essentially social and how collective intelligence depends upon institutional design. For that matter, we know little enough about the designs of institutions; too little, for example, to understand whether the formation of a science-dominated global culture in place of a myriad separate, largely nonscience-based cultural experiments is a dangerous or promising development. And we are too little aware of the new normative-factual interactions now in progress everywhere within science to really have begun to think through their nature and ramifications.

It is really only in the last decades that the study of technology in its own right became recognized, and even now we have not begun to study the population dynamics of machines in the way that even the least interesting ecology is now documented. And it is equally recently that the study of the pure-theory/applied-technology and science/society interfaces have received systematic attention.[32] Impact assessments (environmental, economic, technological, social) are newly emerged activities; complex management theories (systems analysis, operations research, decision theory, etc.) have still not been applied to any appreciable extent. And so on.

In our circumstances, learning about these things is an urgent necessity. It also requires commitment to the further development of science and to further experiments which will modify our past ways of proceeding. We need to have the enquiry over, the answers definitively settled. But this is impossible because the process of enquiry is itself part of the dilemma—the knowledge required is itself part of the problem. So we need to tread our way delicately and warily around a developing spiral, each new revolution enlarging our understanding of what we are about and at the same time enlarging our capacity for further transformations.

Above all, we need to understand and manage this spiraling process because the costs of error can now be enormous. Errors include dissipating scientific effort through degenerating competition for resources; needless duplication of effort; lack of effective communication and coordination; restricting the real options for scientific development because of prejudiced support institutions and because of the unwarranted institutionalized reinforcement of certain scientific paradigms to the exclusion of alternatives; and so on. We urgently require institutions that are capable of permitting science to develop while enabling us to relieve ourselves of some basic ignorances (for example, those sketched in the preceding paragraphs).

Second, we need institutions that are capable of mediating between science and society. As the many examples given throughout this chapter will attest, the relationship is now extremely complex. The investment of social resources in energy research and development will both crucially influence the range of accessible policies in the future, but it will also influence the branches of science that are pursued in the future. (Contrast, for example, nuclear electricity/reactor physics and fuel-cells/organic photochemistry.) Some of the many roles such an institution is now called upon to fill are the following: the assessment of technological impacts and response accordingly; intentional intervention in national allocations of education resources within and for science; military research design and aid; international communication and coordination of research and development; designs of political processes of approval for science policy; research support; technological development, approval and aid. Several of these roles, I recognize, are now at least partially filled by a diverse collection of public agencies, acting more or less independently, just as several—not all—of the many aspects of a coherent energy policy fall under a diverse collection of government departments. Unhappily this circumstance reflects the fact that our institutions are not designed to match or mirror the deeper structure of the processes with which they are supposed to deal. For example, one of the themes which consistently emerged from a 1979/1980 Canadian national review of needs in this area (see Note 32) was the absence of any clear understanding of the science/society interface or of any systematic approaches to relations between scientific investigation and government decision making.

And what of a theory of the political economy of institutions and of institutional design that might be adequate to these circumstances? Here I confine myself to summarizing briefly some preliminary thoughts on the subject. As to political economy, the first and deepest principle is that institutions should reflect the best-known structure of processes. Roughly, the implication of the theory of policy analysis and choice herein is that for every fundamental process there should be an institution capable of formulating alternative coherent normative blueprints and their respective retrospective path analyses, presenting these for democratic choice and implementing the path chosen (see Note 23). This would then yield a collection of institutions focused, not around particular commodities (for example, wheat, coal, manufactured exports, etc.) but around total energy-flow pattern, nutrition, industrial structure, communications, and so on.

Relations among institutions should then reflect systematic structural relations more than *ad hoc* market relations; and relations within institutions should reflect the internal structure of the processes themselves with which the institutions are dealing. For example, within the energy policy institution the group working on building design standards forms a natural subgroup of that concerned with the thermodynamic efficiency of energy use and has natural structural relations with an urban form subgroup concerned with structure design within an urban form policy institution and with a building industry subgroup, perhaps within an industrial structure institution. But these are only quick examples. Detailed realistic proposals for policy-making institutions require an immense amount of careful thought as to the nature of the processes involved and the constraints imposed by other institutions, demands of the political process, international pressures, and so on.

Beyond this general design orientation, we can talk about the importance of building into institutional designs a recognition of the limitations under which humans function—limitations on knowledge, time, empathy and risk-threat-bearing among them—and of the need to have institutional processes that function properly with (and despite) the imperfections of the individuals carrying them out. If, now, these principles are reflected back upon the design of the basic collection of institutions and their interrelations (thus making the overall design sensitive, for example, to the need to preserve workable forms of democratic participation in decision making), then the outlines of a political economy of policy-making institutions begins to emerge.

But these are all very general principles of which we have as yet little idea how to put into practice. In the energy area, some of us guess that they call for a substantial decentralization of the decision-making process, together with self-redesigning components as safeguard, and different roles for parliamentarians, but that is more a call for experimentation than a theory, and it needs to be balanced by the genuine need for compensating central decision processes (cf. Hooker et al. 1980a, part IV). At the present time intuitive experience with institutional functioning and a will to experiment is probably of as much use as theory, though this makes pertinent theoretical work an urgent necessity.

7.10 ON THE RADICALNESS OF AN EVOLUTIONARY PERSPECTIVE

I have been arguing that if we step back mentally and take a look at the cognitive processes occurring on this planet we will find them far more complex, and far more daring, than conventional wisdom supposes. Why is this so? Answer: Our evolutionary circumstances. Taking these seriously yields a surprisingly radical perspective on cognition.

Products of evolution have evolved from a condition of ignorance. Their need to learn is profound, for they need to learn even what learning is, let alone how to use their own bodies to learn, let alone learn about the rest of the world. We are always only dimly aware of what is really involved; it may take (has actually taken), millennia to become conscious that we need to learn about learning. How does empiricism look as a cognitive strategy in these circumstances? Very poor. Why trust the senses? They may be partial, biased and erroneous in all sorts of ways of which we are ignorant. Use them we must, but not uncritically. Why restrict science to the products of observation and logic? Caution? Fear of error? But caution is a poor policy for creatures born in profound ignorance and trying to find the truth. If they risked no theoretical ideas at all about the unobserved world they would in effect be placing a blind faith in the accuracy and adequacy of their own bodies as observing instruments. In fact we know of ourselves that such a faith would have quickly mired us in unnoticed biases, errors and limitations—we see only the color spectrum, not the rest of the electromagnetic spectrum; our perception is full of illusions. In addition, we would be quickly mired in dogma, for it would be difficult to develop penetrating alternative views of our situation with which to criticize those we accepted. As Popper taught us long ago, we have no choice but to risk bold theoretical conjecture about the real structure of the unobserved world. We must then attempt to contain our risks by boldly seeking to criticize these conjectures through critical comparison with alternative conjectures and through comparison with experimentation. But experimentation itself will be theoretically (i.e., conjecturally) guided, it is not restricted to, nor any longer revolves significantly about, ordinary unaided human observation. We must not only contain our risks, we must prune our initial conjectures to within the limitations of our resources for criticism and experimentation. Following seriously how these two containments (of conjectures and risks) are to be managed rationally would, I believe, take us far from the specific form of Popper's philosophy—I shall not pursue that matter here.[33] But on essentials Popper has grasped the important insight: for creatures emerging from evolutionary ignorance it is not the certainty of facts structured by logic at which it is rational to aim but at the risky though insightful conjecture with which we attempt to grasp every aspect of the situation in which we find ourselves. Scientists aim at interesting or valuable truth, not certain truth.

Cognitive evolution is total; an evolution of capacity to observe, of capacity for symbolic processes, for thought and language. However we came by our science, by our philosophy, by our culture, we came by it all in the same manner. Human kind emerged from the evolutionary background and was capable, eventually, of all these things. The brain of *Homo sapiens* may have been designed through natural selection to fit with the world in some ways, it may have had some learning gleaned from evolution 'hard-wired in', but no one has told us that authoritatively. Language emerged only gradually, a bewilderingly complex abstraction from the processes in the nervous system, which produces a usefully simple result for social action in the commonsense world; we understand its nature and status even now only very imperfectly. As for thought, we still do not understand its relation to language, or its range and limitations, or its natural structure (if it has one). Indeed, logic itself is a spectacular example of our cognition in historical evolution, the flowering of logical systems and of theories of logic has all occurred in this century, two millennia after humans first became aware of the importance of the structure. We came by everything then in the same manner, by an informed trial-and-error guesswork, by throwing out a framework to grasp the world cognitively and by modifying that framework as we went along, by blindly experimenting with the creation of societies, languages, cultures, driven by ecological pressures and inner developmental dynamics, learning only painfully slowly 'what' works for us. And this too is how we came by philosophy—by epistemology, ethics, metaphysics and the rest—through theoretical conjecture and selective elimination, in fact by something like the same process of natural selection which forms the basis of biological evolution itself. (Cognitive evolution is an extension of biological evolution, a picture which fits well with the story at the beginning of this chapter.)

In such circumstances method becomes central to defining epistemology, for method is all that we have. Central to method, as remarked, is the theory of rational risk-taking. How shall we choose our conjectures and how thoroughly shall we criticize them? That depends on which risks we can afford to run, which of our limited resources it is most rational to allocate to which problems—and how deep our uncertainty is about what the risks and resources are! As I remarked earlier, this shift of focus in epistemology from certainty and belief to risk and commitment is a radical one indeed, but one which fits well with an evolutionary perspective in which all organisms have sought to survive through means for optimizing their cognitive and behavioral abilities.[34]

And these are not the only thorough-going shifts in orientation for epistemology. Now that epistemology becomes defined in terms of method, we may ask: *How is it possible to know?* Answer: how is it possible to pursue such a method? What forms of nervous system organization constitute a creature with capacity to know (as opposed to a merely internally complex organism)? What external nervous system must interconnect such organisms before their cognitive capacities are fully realized? *What is the scope of knowledge?* That depends on the potential scope of the method. How fundamentally can human beings transform themselves, in particular transform their internal and external nervous systems, in an effort to enhance their cognitive capacities? How rapidly can they cognize cognition (learn about learning), in relation to the development of their cognition of the world? Are there inherent limitations in both of these processes? *When do we know?* What does meta-method theory tell us about the conditions under which method works? What forms of institutionalized process of criticism and evaluation are necessary before objectivity can be claimed? What forms of institutionalized criticism and evaluation maximally reduce risk of error? How should our unknowing about knowing be reflected in our claims to knowledge?

Of course there is a great deal else which must be part of the development of cognition and meta-cognition (cognition of cognition). There are all sorts of questions which must be answered along the route to developing an adequate theory of knowledge. What sort of creatures are we? What capabilities have we? What is the nature of societies and cultures? How much do we critically know about these entities? Until we know a great deal about these and many other things our ability to cognize cognition itself will be extremely limited. There is then much science that must be known before epistemology can be adequately developed. Is this assertion itself logically objectionable (perhaps because apparently circular)? Not at all. Historically we are faced with the simultaneous emergence of both science and epistemology, twin conjectural theses in dynamic interaction with each other, better viewed as a pair of interlocked spirals than as a circle.

Two other radical consequences of an evolutionary perspective have in fact already appeared earlier in this text. (1) As remarked, we begin ignorant of our normative theories and this suggests that we should regard them as theories in the same sense as our scientific theories, to be learnt about in essentially the same manner. This view is expressed in the doctrine of norms developed in Section 7.6 above. (2) Humans have the cognitive capacities they have today because they are inheritors of billions of years of evolutionary development. This suggests that the basic structural features of human cognition should be traceable back through the line of evolutionary development to increasingly the rudimentary forms. It was in this spirit that I suggested in Section 7.6 above that we might trace judgement back through conditioning, reflex and irritation to reaction. In the same way we might trace rationality back through optimality to extremal principles in physics itself. In fact judgement and rationality come to form the two foci of an account of human individuals, doing away with traditional epistemology, value theory and action theory.[35]

These are then some of the radical (i.e., highly untraditional) approaches which emerge when an evolutionary perspective is taken seriously. See elsewhere herein for further development of these themes.

7.11 RATIONALITY: FROM SCIENCE TO CHILD AND RETURN

From an evolutionary perspective judgement and rationality shift to the fore. Rationality is central to science and to society, indeed science methodology, science policy and social policies generally were seen to be three intimately related exercises in judgement formation and rationality. But what model of rationality might be adequate?

There is a model of rationality, called instrumental rationality, which is central to empiricist-liberal theory. According to this model rationality is the choice of efficient means to given ends, where the ends enter from beyond rational appraisal and the means must all be uniformly evaluated. For example, economic goals might be introduced, in a market setting, whereat the problem for rationality becomes the selection of the most efficient means to achieve those goals. Or again, scientific data may be given along with the goal of maximal certain truth, the problem of rationality being to derive the content of science, on the data base, which maximally satisfies the goal. This view of rationality is far too narrow, it distorts and decimates human rational capacity.[36]

Rational, but evolved intelligences need the capacity to direct their development even when the data bases, theories, goals, normative principles, when even the theory of rationality itself, is uncertain, is open to criticism and change. What guides the searching, probing intelligence? What principles of order, what sought-for complexes of qualities? I do not know. I am aware that in western culture we have basically only one model of intelligence, that of the computer, of a system of relations and operations that reduces all intelligence to mere complexity.[37] I am far from convinced it is adequate[38], but I also know no other model of comparable theoretical fecundity. In the meantime then let us see what can be learned (for epistemology) from the best working model of rationality to which I can point: the young child.

Here is an organism born with tremendous potential but, so far as we can now tell, of substantially less specific internal organization than characterises mature adults. In the beginning there is no language, possibly not even any organized conceptual structure (and hence no reasoning), little perceptual organization, no affective control, even relatively little sensory-motor control. The evidence of developmental psychology may be summed up by saying that the young child is engaged in a total effort to achieve order, first within himself/herself and then in relation to the world. Moreover the order which the healthy young child aims to achieve is, at any stage, of a form which promotes the later achievement of yet greater order. The young child, in short, is a cognitive self-organizing system of a thoroughly total sort.

In this struggle the child is an active participant, exploring the world, developing sensory-motor skills and communicational organization. He/she begins to actively spin out a conceptual/affective framework for organizing perceptual and emotional experiences and later for organizing reasoning about them. The evolution of the differentiation and structuring of experience in the developing human, i.e., the evolution of judgement, is a delicate interplay between the spinning out of imaginative conceptual/affective frameworks on the one side and, on the other side, the experiences, both consonant and dissonant with these frameworks, which the child is thus led to have.

The foregoing description of the developmental process in the young child is strikingly similar to that offered of the dynamical development of scientific theory *vis-à-vis* data domains or of philosophical theory *vis-à-vis* science. It is my conjecture that the two processes are indeed substantially the same. Conversely, this suggests that when constructing our theory of scientific development, we first examine the structure of human development. I draw the reader's attention especially to the following.

1. In spite of the impression created by philosophical reflection upon adult life, there is probably no deep affective/cognitive division in the child. To the contrary (Piaget's intellectualism notwithstanding), one of the major cognitive achievements of the child is that of establishing affective order within him or herself. Conversely, the extending of a coherent affective response framework to increasingly large and complex environments is a major driving force behind the development of intellectual framework. The judgement is the basic entity; a factual judgement has a normative dimension, for every factual judgement involves a deliberate selection, a deliberate design of the observing instrumentation; conversely, a normative judgement has a factual dimension, for every normative judgement presumes an actual situation which structures the factors which are relevant and determines the terms in which the judgement is made. We explore what it is to be a person in essentially the same manner in which we explore the world into which we were born.[39]

2. The primary form learning takes is the evolution of an increasingly rich and differentiated framework — cognitive and/or affective. Actual relationships among the elements of the framework take a secondary place, being for the most part either subconscious or only vaguely expressible. Thus in visual perception, for example, the cru-

cial kind of progress in the young child is the evolution of perception of an external world of relatively stable objects. In this evolution it is the form of the organization of the sensory information itself which is the important thing. Propositions claiming truths, even general truths, concerning the world of macro objects are not the center of attention; indeed, for the most part they seem to play no conscious role at all in this achievement. Nor do I know of any scientific reason to give them an unconscious neurophysiological role. The evolution is organizational (conceptual), not propositional. I hold that the same process applies in all other fundamental learning as well, whether in child or adult, within science or common life.

Indeed, there seems to be a widespread misconception that learning proceeds from one propositionally well-defined stage to another. This is what I call the "road map" view of learning: if you want to learn geography, get in a car, crisscross the terrain along the roads, taking photographs, then mentally conjoin all of the information (tacitly assumed propositionally definite) gained from each instantaneous picture. It is the inevitable result of an empiricist approach to cognition. Instead, I suggest that basic learning proceeds on a "satellite" model: starting from high up everything is a blur; only the fact that something is down there comes through. Then as one descends, prominent features come into focus, the general landscape pattern emerges, and slowly increasingly fine detail is detectable. (Excellent examples of the misleading nature of the road-map model can be seen in most of our educational institutions, but it is more widespread than that, including in its embrace even psychology and philosophy departments.) The truth is probably somewhere between the two extremes, is indeed certainly far more complex and sophisticated than these simple, polarized models suggest; but I hold that the basic process is given by the satellite model.

3. There is of course a risk in this form of evolution, this bold attempt to master one's situation by spinning out a cognitive/affective order in which to grasp it. It is thinkable that we may systematically delude ourselves, be led in the wrong direction by our framework-spinning abilities. This is the existential risk that any species undertakes when it attempts to use its abilities to survive. It is also the existential risk which each one of us takes when we attempt to spin out a coherent personality from the stuff of our genetic inheritance and family environment. But we are not without bearings in these enterprises, for we have external feedback, from both the environment and from each other, as to the appropriateness of our ordering efforts. Poor in information though this feedback often is compared

with our needs, yet we have it. With rich enough capacities and feedback structure built into our internal and external nervous systems, the procedure, though risky, can proceed.

4. Very tentatively, I offer the following theoretical framework for representing the exploratory activity of organisms, in particular humans. The organism is evolving in a world that can be represented in a multi-dimensional parameter space. For example, there are the physical parameters of location, velocity and temperature. Our world instantiates a range of values for these parameters. All actual species live out their lives in some subrange of each parameter range, that is, in some subspace of the parameter space. But of course there must be many more parameters than these, though I have not attempted to draw up a list even within the bounds of my limited knowledge— perhaps electrochemical potential, certain measures of organizational complexity, various dimensions of cognitive organization might all furnish appropriate parameters. In any event, within such a general model we might define a progressively evolving species as one that is enlarging its access (or perhaps potential access) to parameter space. For example, *ceteris paribus*, the emergence of homeostatic organisms was progressive because it permitted organisms to survive in greater ranges of temperature—it enlarged access to the parameter space. Not all successfully adapting species progress in this sense; they may merely change along with their environment. There are subtle theoretical questions here, I recognize; classical Darwinism provides no support whatever for a directed evolutionary development. Nevertheless, I believe that compatible with that truth, we need to tell a theoretically larger story that incorporates some such notion as that of progression. This is not the place to do this. Nonetheless, I shall at least use this framework to state the full cognitive character of the human enterprise I am suggesting.

The nature of the world itself presumably imposes limits or constraints on the size of the parameter space within which species are evolving: the theory of relativity imposes a finite constraint on the values of the velocity parameter, human biochemical constitution imposes constraints on the range of viable living conditions, and so on. Within these constraints, persons strive, individually and collectively, to achieve maximally wide access to parameter space. They seek to do this individually through the internal orders or frameworks they create and they seek to do it collectively, as a species, through the external orders or frameworks which they create in their external nervous system.

With a unified evolutionary account in mind, it is natural to attempt to extend this framework to include all intrinsic dimensions of human life. The human animal certainly functions under definite physico-biochemical constraints on its access to pleasures and pains, to forms of interpersonal relationships, and so on. I propose that all the possi-bilities of affective differentiation and extension are equally objective in this sense: we can here too view the human organism, both collec-tively and individually, as exploring an affective parameter space, seeking orderings, internal and social, that will promote increased access to the space. (This abstract formulation may be roughly trans-lated: individually and socially we are experimentally seeking ways of being, ways that will both spiritually enrich us and promote our future ability to increase that richness.) At least I suggest this as a model of the developmental pattern of the rational, progressively developing person and society. What makes an objective evaluation of affective ordering apparently so much more difficult than that for cognitive orderings is the complexity of the space and the penchant of the human organism to trap itself in self-reinforcing dead ends. (For example, a social order can demand ruthless selfishness to survive and human infants raised to know no other form of life.) That is, I suggest that parameter space be understood to include all the param-eters pertaining to human life. Then we are, *qua* rational, experimen-tally exploring this space, seeking orderings, internal (cognitive/affec-tive) and external (social/cultural), that will enrich our lives and enhance our access to the space.

The foregoing description of the parameter space model is meant to imply that choice of belief, choice of values, and choice of way of life are on the same footing, each subject to rational criticism and rational evolution. This perspective fits well with a unified, naturalistic theory of norms, as learnable critical theory, with the integration of human with animal cognition and with cultures as human experiments. This in pursuit of a unified framework for theoretical explanation of living activities. Much of this framework is as yet speculative of course, but philosophy too must do the best it can in light of our other best conjectures.

Now let us apply these ways of representing our activity to science. I think that it squares with a unified account of the human species and is fruitful for philosophy of science to view science as a human activity of the same sort as is encountered in the development of the child but occurring at the more differentiated adult level.

Science begins from "common sense" which is the genetical/histori-cal accumulation of less conscious, socialized attempts to create satis-factory and satisfying orders. Science aims at being a maximally self-conscious, systematic attempt to improve these orderings. Methodology is a theory of how best to achieve these improvements. It is therefore itself an ordering of experience.

We are all familiar with the attempt to improve cognitive orders: it is called theoretical advance. It seems a fairly clear, if not well understood, process in the natural sciences. From the point of view emphasized here, that process of growth is dominated by the emergence, transformation, coalescent, differentiation, and submergence of concepts and related groups of concepts (schemes). Explicitly propositional forms containing these concepts play a substantially more dominant role in this process than they perhaps do in the young child. Moreover, there is an intimate interaction between the encompassing conceptual order and the explicitly propositional order: conceptual order must lead to theoretical order to be fruitful, but the structural/logical resources of theory are not by themselves sufficient to generate new conceptual order. (Contrast the Popperian-empiricist tradition. There philosophers have concentrated on structural/logical order, emphasizing the sufficiency or insufficiency of logic combined with evidence statements to determine theory or perhaps the theoretical role of some logically preferred class of propositions. When neither proves sufficient, even aided by such methodological rules as can be constructed solely in terms of logical relations among propositions, then they are silent or, like the Popperians, write it off as "psychology.")

It seems, however, to be particularly difficult to obtain a clear application of the same theoretical characterizations to the social sciences. I see this difficulty as centering around the peculiar role of values and evaluations in both the science and its object of study. Its resolution is made impossible, I believe, by a traditional Popperian-empiricist understanding of the normative/descriptive distinction. Conversely, I believe that the metaphysical doctrine of norms I have proposed, in combination with the parameter space model of cognitive activity, opens the way to a solution. In the scheme I offer, the normative and descriptive theoretical functions, and the practical, all cohere. The primary object of the social sciences becomes oriented toward the practical exploration of better personal and social orderings (cf. Becker 1976), but this is now intellectually consistent with a strong theoretical component in its objects.

The human pursuit of science is cumulative at least twice over; we accumulate experience of what actually works and what doesn't, and we accumulate experience of which processes for achieving improved orderings work and where (and, someday, perhaps even how they work) and which do not. Both forms of learning in general improve our access to parameter space and increase our ability to gain further access in the future. But the second form of learning is especially important to the future and is what I would propose as a chief characteristic distinguishing *Homo sapiens* from other mammals.

In this struggle for scientific improvement the human being plays an active role, experimenting, actively interrogating nature. Hence the importance of technological development to the development of science. Technology is at once the major vehicle through which science enlarges our access to physical parameter space and for the extension of the scientist's body in active interaction with the world. The importance of technology in the theory of the development of science can be put briefly thus: As the sensory-motor/primitive affective experience of young children's activity stands to the development and meaning-for-them of their cognitive-affective framework, so the development of technology and experimental practice (including applied industrial and social practice) stands to the development and meaning-for-scientists of scientific theory (see Note 1). Thus practice, especially technological development, plays a complex role in the evolution of science: it is a primary means for (1) testing theories and (2) transforming theories into practical access to parameter space, but it also plays an important role in (3) determining the conceptual form of our theories and (4) evaluating their future promise. These latter roles have hitherto been largely neglected.

Science is the exploratory pursuit of improved order; it is a human activity pursued with this complex goal in mind. The goal is complex because the structure of living it comprehends is complex. We could express this roughly by saying that science is a multivalued process involving all of the values associated with enlarging access to each of the very large number of dimensions of parameter space: for example, increased access to (1) explanatory depth, (2) explanatory precision, (3) predictive scope, (4) predictive precision, (5) heuristic power, (6) simplicity (conceptual, syntactic, ontological), (7) technical applicability, (8) technical reliability, (9) sociocultural control, (10) interpersonal communication range, (11) rich cultural structure. These are all values from among the many guiding the activity of science. Consideration of the historical situations already (briefly) described above should serve to convince that, in general, simultaneous pursuit of these utilities will not be possible; trade-offs will be necessary (cf. Note 25).

Though I have placed all my emphasis on understanding the natural and social sciences, I would offer the same model for understanding the humanities. I suggest we view each of the humanities as an exploration of cognitive and affective order (personal and cultural) proceeding through a historical evolutionary development. As I said, this really comes down to regarding cultures as themselves experimental. We then have a framework for beginning to explore the intimate and subtle interaction between the spiritual development of people, the cultural development of society, and the cognitive development of the species.

7.12 OF PERSONS

Throughout the earlier sections of this paper I concentrated almost wholly on cognition, at the species level. I have begun to balance this focus with its dual pole, by emphasizing the developing person as our most adequate model of rationality. I now wish to take that focus a stage further, ultimately so as to speak about what those qualitatively new cognitive circumstances discussed earlier mean for our understanding of the capacities of persons. In this section I begin with a few remarks which point the reader towards sources for the understanding of the nature of persons which I have found helpful.

I shall begin by returning to Unger's *Knowledge and Politics* (1975). Understanding that behind all human life lies the antinomy of understanding and experience, itself a case of the antinomy of the universal and the particular, Unger goes on to apply the three remaining antinomies to the specific development of persons and their relations to communities. (For the five antinomies see Figure 7.2.) According to Unger, persons, which are selves, have three primary relations in which they are involved; to nature, to others and to oneself. To each of these primary relationships a particular antinomy is appropriate.

The self is divided from nature by self-consciousness. Therefore, selves need to develop a theory of nature as a function of their experience of nature and they need to manipulate nature for instrumental purposes (initially to survive, but increasingly to realize the self in its fullness). It is the need to understand versus the practical need to manipulate so as to create a predictable situation which exhibits the antinomy of theory and fact. For Unger, understanding and manipulation are brought together in the transformation of reality into a human artifact in which simultaneously there is the intimate 'maker's' knowledge of the artifact together with the manipulation of the world so as to allow the fulfillment of human selves. Notice that artifacts can be both natural (technology) and cultural (societies) and that these themes are precisely those with which I have been concerned in the earlier part of this paper.

In the relation of self-conscious selves to other such selves there is simultaneously the cognitive and moral need to develop an individual self and the need to have that self validated by other selves (and perhaps, ultimately, by a transcendent self, God). It is in the need for individuality versus the need for communal identity that lies the antinomy of reason and desire. For Unger, this antinomy is resolved in the ideal of a sympathy which includes the development of personal love for self and others on the part of all selves together with the development of a community of shared ends, that is, with a shared vision of the fully developed self.

But the self, being self-conscious, also undergoes a relationship with itself during which it is defined and developed. On the one hand its concrete experience is that of a limited organism confined in powers and to a specific place in society and history; on the other hand, the self-conscious self breaks free of those limitations in self-conception, contemplating and aiming practically at its oneness with human kind and with the larger cosmic processes. For Unger, the resolution of this tension is to be found in a community which is 'organic', that is, which (roughly) hangs together in a complex of ways which represent each dimension of the developing self, and which exhibit an appropriate division of labor, that is (roughly) an appropriate complementarity among the productive contributions of the members of the community so that something of the universal can be seen to be realized in the historical development of the society.

It can be seen even from this brief discussion, that these tensions are never fully realized in history, that each historical moment exhibits only a more or less imperfect and temporary resolution and that they point toward a transcendent resolution beyond the confinements and evil of historical life. I have tried to briefly summarize this discussion in Figure 7.6.[40]

These themes in Unger lead directly to the writings of ernest Becker (1973, 1976). In his *The Denial of Death*, he articulates in a clear and frightening manner the immense difficulties and tensions which underlie the basic organization and development of a self-conscious organism, focusing the sweep of psychoanalytic thought in a brilliant way upon Unger's three basic relations of the self. In his *The Structure of Evil*, Becker includes a fourth relation of the self, the relation of the self to the mystery of being, and proceeds from that base to develop a rich and insightful perspective on the development and nature of the social sciences and of society as a human project.

The relation of self to the mystery of being, the problem of transcendence, is also Unger's ultimate problem. Here, though, Unger's conception of personal love does not distinguish clearly enough between

Philosophic Structure of Persons and Communities

Base Antinomy	Primary Relation	Domain of Resolution
Theory/Fact	Self to Nature Cognitive Dimension: consciousness of self; indeterminacy of nature to self and of self to nature. vs. Moral Dimension: Need to manipulate nature (including selves) as instrumental means; need to treat nature as objects and as resources for artifacts.	Transformation of reality to artifactual, natural and cultural, yielding makers knowledge of artifacts and harmonious environmental design.
Reason/Desire	Self to Others Cognitive Dimension: Need for unavoidableness of, epistemic individuality; vs. Need for epistemic agreement (validation). Moral Dimension: Need for, unavoidableness of, emotional/spiritual individuality; vs. Need for communal recognition and acceptance.	Personal love for self and others, together with a community of shared ends. (Ideal of sympathy.)
Rules/Values	Self to Self-Life Cognitive and Moral Dimensions: Experience of the universal in producing what is human; vs. Confinement to limitations of history (time, place), ignorance, impotence, etc.	An appropriate division of labour in an organic community.

Figure 7.6

Eros and Agape, respectively the love which expresses the self, the ego in its healthily aggressive grasp of life, and the love which transcends the self uniting all in a One and intimately connected to the manner in which human rationality takes the egocentric intellect beyond itself to factual and moral universality. Because of Unger's failure to distinguish Eros and Agape, he fails to bring clearly enough to the surface the tension between relating to the mystery of being (understanding) and the manipulative creation of a human world.

It is the sense of the unending inner self which animates the work of

John Lilly (1972, 1974, 1977) and that of the late E. F. Schumacher (1975, 1977). Indeed, in *A Guide for the Perplexed*, Schumacher himself uses the fourfold division of human knowledge as basis. Finally, I introduce Carl Rogers (1961, 1969, 1978) who has centered the connection between the developing cognitive conception of the self-conscious self and the developing emotional/spiritual self in the conception of love as the basis for freedom.

These are not all the texts important to me—I mention some others in the bibliography[41]—but they are my more 'urgent' personal sources; for me they fit together and define a much larger problem than those which have formed the primary foci of this paper. They point toward the fundamentalness and urgency of the problem of transcendence in human life.

7.13 ON TRANSCENDENCE

The preceding discussion has focused attention on some of the features of human cognitive activity which are distinctive of our century and which will intensify, so far as we can now foretell, in the human future. They also draw our attention to very ancient themes in human cognitive reflection, both East and West; the themes concerning the transcendence of the human person. These themes have often been suppressed in the Western cultural/philosophical tradition, no more ruthlessly than in the past century of Western philosophy of science, but they are now pushing themselves to the fore again. Only if there is a proper appreciation of our cognitive position at this historical time will we be able to extricate ourselves from the false dichotomy between some form of empiricism and some form of irrationalism.

The first theme to which I wish to direct attention is that of transcending the symbol. Are the limits of our language also the limits of our world? Philosophers have often asserted so, but there has always been a continuing mystical tradition which has denied this. The question of the control of our own cognitive, not to say biological, destiny raises this issue in a particularly acute and practical form. But the issue is everywhere coming to the fore within the body of scientific theory itself. It appears, for example, in modern debates over whether there can be any adequate formal model of intelligence, in particular whether any computer could provide an adequate simulation of human reason. It comes to the fore in the question of whether any machine, however formally intelligent, could be conscious or could capture the kind of qualitative consciousness which we are often thought to enjoy. It comes to the fore in the question of whether any timeless, four-dimensional relativistic world model can provide an adequate role and physical model for consciousness. It is at the centre of the modern debate about the nature of language—viz. whether regarded as a formal system or as biologically adapted behavior—and it lurks behind the current debates concerning the nature of meaning—whether meanings are some kind of formal object or systems of orientation to an indefinitely rich non-symbolic reality. It is at the center of the current criticisms of the inadequacy of formal decision-theoretic models of reason, models which, precisely in failing to allow the reasoner to transcend his initial definition of a situation, fail to unite reason and creative intelligence appropriately. Not surprisingly, it is an important component of the current controversies concerning the nature of economic science. As the study of human cognitive processes intensifies and interacts with other theoretical and practical developments, the question of whether we transcend our own formal understanding will grow more acute.

The second theme in transcendence is whether humans transcend history. One tradition has it that people are fully determined by some combination of heredity and environment. It presents attractively simple cognitive possibilities to science, and perhaps it is so. (I for one tend to be unimpressed by the traditional religious and conceptual-linguistic arguments against it.) But who is it then that is already beginning genetic design and behavior shaping? (The sense of paradox and irony is particularly strong in the latter case.) Who is it that forms science policy, cultural policy, communications policy to direct the future? Who is it that is able to understand the historical development of their own sciences, focus their successively developed hierarchical structures and design future procedures which push them still further? Who is now beginning to shape their own normative systems, which guide the developments shaping present and future; who subjects these to critical appraisal, choosing alternative developments and interactions with developing theory and practice? Who is it that can appreciate that his own cognitive future is unknowable, yet can enquire into rational models for changing values, even normative principles, over the course of life? If the future is an artifact, is it the sort of artifact its creators transcend? It is the increasing artifactuality of the future which makes the issue increasingly acute.

This latter theme raises a third theme in transcendence: the transcendence of normative judgement. We humans make normative judgements, we learn about the instrumental value of the normative judgements we make and we learn about our ways of learning. Beyond this hierarchy we reach for the direct vision of the good which transcends all those of our finitudes which necessitate learning. The problem of our transcendence of normative judgements receives a very specific focus now that we are able to plan action on a planetary scale and now that the question of regarding human cultures as themselves experiments is unavoidable. In what sense are we able to survey the range of human cultures, understand them as experiments and begin to design a theory of deliberate cultural experimentation? In what sense are we able to theorize about, and experiment with, our own human nature, with what it is to be a person?

Finally we must ask the question whether, and how, we transcend our own self-identities. Who is it who is able to reach beyond any finitely hierarchically formalizable conception of their environment, their history, their symbols and norms, to see themselves in a cosmic process, to reach for the direct vision and oneness with the good, with the cosmos?

7.14 Watersheds

The late twentieth century is the leading edge of a unique era. In the period 1950 to 2050 the human species has made, or will make, crossings of a large number of critical watersheds in the development of life on the planet—or collapse in chaos under the challenge.

Many of these watersheds are to do with our relation to the biosphere. The population size is nearing, or at, the transition where its demands for space, food and waste disposal can no longer be accommodated without massive ecological change on a planetary scale. Major planetary ecologies, e.g., tropical forest, ocean fisheries, and major planetary resources, e.g., oil, phosphate, platinum, are being consumed or radically altered within a single human lifetime. Human economic activity is approaching planetary thresholds in its demands for energy, mineral resources, fresh water and in its global climatic impact. Humans have not faced this relation to their planet ever before. (Perhaps some of these problems might have appeared in microcosm, for example in the deserts left behind by classical civilizations.)

Many of the watersheds press closer to our species, press upon its intrinsic organization. We now possess means of destruction on a global scale, deployed using much more primitive concepts and institutions. Indeed, we have only recently expanded into the domain of planetary institutions in any serious manner. Many of these institutions are approaching that complexity threshold where they pass beyond the ability of any one individual to grasp. We are rapidly acquiring the social and biochemical means to transform the genetic structure of our race, indeed of all other species, thereby transforming the locus of evolutionary change. We are developing powerful techniques for intervening in the biophysical and psychological structure of individual persons, transforming conceptions of death, responsibility and individuality. We have this century generated information densities and patterns of information flow far beyond the comprehension of any individual human. We have just begun the construction of seriously intelligent machines, and of self-organizing, self-designing machines. We are transforming, often eliminating, human cultures at an unprecedented rate with the planetary intrusion of economic and institutional structures. The human species, indeed the biosphere, has never confronted these transformations before, not even in microcosm; they bite deeply into our evolutionary origins in small group, tool-using hunting and gathering.

And finally and most importantly there are those profound transformations in the role and structure of cognition which have been the focus of attention in this chapter: the increasing internal complexity and self-consciousness of theoretical thought, the increasing complexity and comprehensiveness of our external institutional organization of cognitive processes, the increasing radicalness of the scope of cognitive organization.

These three groups of threshold transitions have generated a remarkable surge in our species consciousness of itself and its total environment. We now can conceive of the planet as Spaceship Earth, we have some appreciation of the total dynamics of the biosphere and of our past place in it. We have become acutely aware of the future as a human artifact, futures research has exploded and achieved recognition as a serious study, computer models of human global processes of every kind are now basic items of international study. More subtly, we are slowly achieving a self-consciousness of the structure and dynamics of cognitive processes themselves; not only is the study of the science expanding very rapidly but, most significantly, there is an increasing development of books and journals devoted reflexively to the very process itself (of which this book is one).

We are then in the midst of a cognitive revolution in which (i) cognition is shifting rapidly to the fore to dominate the structuring of every area of life and (ii) self-consciousness of this process and of its radical implications is slowly developing. As a species we are shifting from cause to cognition, from observation to design, from reaction to control.

In all of this we are discovering that what we thought of as social conveniences for individual interests, our social institutions, are shifting toward being an external nervous system, determining the capacities and structure of our species intelligence. Recognition of this is also a new part of our self-consciousness.

And both our new design capacities and our emerging cognitive self-consciousness have raised in acute form the true nature of our own intelligence and personhood: the questions of transcendence.

These processes are, I suggest, the true and secret significance of the twentieth century. They define, more truly than quantum mechanics, television, moon landings or the World Bank, what is distinctive about the underlying structural shifts in the life processes on the planet in our times.

Meanwhile we poor individuals are caught. Caught between scepticism and mysticism. We cannot expect the next moments of history to resolve the issue for us. Caught between the normative and the descriptive: caught between the assimilation of the past to become the persons we can now be and the preselection of the future, to become the persons we may hope yet to be. We cannot expect some external "nature" to make these decisions for us. Caught between the cognitive and the political, between commitment to the historical process of science and the historical process of political and personal liberation. We cannot expect the constraints of a finite life to allow these commitments to be fully reconciled. Like the circus clown we are willy nilly obliged to juggle our commitments in the presence of these tensions. Perhaps, like the mystic, we may be given the grace to intuit the transcendent self through the mosaic.

CHAPTER 8

Evolutionary Naturalist Realism:
Circa 1985

8.1 PROLEGOMENON

This chapter falls into the following natural progression of parts: *Part 8.2* presents a realist manifesto of the evolutionary naturalist type. Rather than intending to repeat or collect the material of the preceding chapters, it complements them by developing explicitly themes which appear either implicitly only and/or which are insufficiently clearly developed there. Chapter 7 is itself a synthesizing review essay intended for a broad audience, Section 8.2 could be considered a more philosophical complement to it. *Part 8.3* then develops a number of more specific subthemes of a general character. Finally, *Part 8.4* examines recent specific philosophic disputes surrounding realism together with recent alternative realist writings and responds to them.

8.2 AN EVOLUTIONARY NATURALIST REALIST MANIFESTO

Much of the material for a statement of realism from an evolutionary naturalist perspective is already contained in the other essays and will not be repeated here. For example, a basic feature of the position is the insistence on developing a meta-philosophy of fallibilism within which to develop philosophy (Chapter 3, Section 3.3.1). Nonetheless, as I reviewed the essays in the light of my current thinking, and against the background of more recent writings, I concluded that the presentation would be improved by drawing out and pulling together some general orienting principles which characterize the view I am trying to develop. A good place to begin is with the basic notion of realism itself.

8.2.1 Realism

The central idea of realism, as a theory of scientific knowledge, is that knower and known are related causally, not more strongly (say of logical or conceptual necessity). To put this metaphysics bluntly: humans are parts of the world, knowing it through the interactions (both within and without them) that permeate it. Or perhaps: humans are subsystems of a world system which includes cognitive organization within it. The realist idea is often expressed in the slogan that there exists an independent reality, but the independence here must be understood to mean logical independence, not causal independence. The realist can allow very strong causal interactions between mind and reality, for that precisely still involves a reality whose basic character is mind-independent. This picture of humans is supported by the naturalistic evolutionary conception of ourselves from science.

This basic metaphysics then provides a framework for characteristic realist claims:

Metaphysical component
R1: Existence is logically and conceptually independent of epistemic conditions (reality exists independently of knowing) and
R2: Reality is knowable (*ceteris paribus*, at some 'level', etc.) and knower and known are related causally (nomicly, etc.), not in any stronger constituitive manner.
Semantic component
R3: Truth consists in an appropriate correspondence relation holding between language and the world.
R4: Truth obtains or fails independently of all epistemic acceptance/rejection criteria.
R5: Theories of science are candidates for truth as well as for epistemic acceptance or rejection.
R6: (Therefore) theoretical terms have semantic content appropriate to their being components of truth candidates and this semantic content is not wholly reducible to the semantics of observation terms.
Epistemic Component
R7: At any given time, it is the overall epistemic value of a theory, of which its empirical adequacy is but one component, which determines our rational epistemic attitude to it.
R8: Our most epistemicly valuable theories are our most acceptable guides to reality.
There is nothing sacrosanct about these precise versions. But clarifi-

cation and defence of even the coarse points is the subject of this book, so not to be reattempted here.

R_5 and R_6 are the claims with which I began Chapter 2, but of course they do not suffice in themselves to state scientific realism. At the time of writing Chapter 2, the focus of attention was the semantics of theoretical terms. That this was the central problem was one of the few areas of agreement between empiricists—who thought that theoretical term semantics was parasitic upon observation term semantics—and their critics like Kuhn and Feyerabend, who thought that the very autonomy of theory semantics entailed the incommensurability of theories and hence the a-rationality (if not irrationality) of theory change. Being caught between the devil and the deep blue sea like this was a major stimulus to develop a realist response. The other R theses were largely taken for granted for the purpose at hand. But I emphasized even in Chapter 2 the necessity of understanding realism as an integrated philosophy of science, hence one whose theses must 'hang together' and span the range represented above.[1]

By contrast, I have deliberately not included in the foregoing list of realist theses any commitments in either the theory of perception or of mathematical and other abstract objects. These offer two additional senses to the term 'realist'. I don't believe that a scientific realist as understood here is *logically* required to adopt a realist philosophy of perception. However, I have tried to develop one elsewhere.[2] One reason for taking a realist view is that it fits best with our current scientific self-understanding, representationalist suggestions notwithstanding (see sec. 8.3.2 below). Another reason is that alternative views of perception obtain their basic motivation from treating epistemology as both logically primary and security-oriented, assumptions which ultimately prove anti-realist (cf. sec. 8.3.2 below). As for mathematics, I cannot presently see that a scientific realist must of necessity adopt any particular attitude to the nature and existence of mathematical and other abstract entities. However, this is the realist doctrine about which I have thought least and I will not venture a firm opinion. (The naturalism of my realism strongly inclines me to an Aristotelian-Whiteheadian immanentist doctrine of universals, and the evidence for a realist conception of space-time allied with the counterintuitive richness of the continuum, only reinforces this inclination.[3]) On the other hand I cannot see how a scientific realist can avoid a realist theory of properties and natural kinds. Otherwise, how can any sense be given to the basic metaphysical idea of the world interacting causally with humans? A propertyless world can't intelligibly be said to sustain systematic interaction patterns of any kind. Yet one doesn't need to adopt an orthodox account of predicates, properties and kinds.[4]

I have insisted that a substantial and defensible scientific realism involves the theses R_1 to R_8 above. This is because together they have to add up to a coherent, believable conception of us and our world. Obviously there must be further doctrines than these (reserved for other sections below). I do not really believe that pursuit of a neat separation of these doctrines into fundamental and derived would add insight, but I shall take R_1 to R_8 as defining scientific realism for present purposes. (N.B. I shall also drop the qualifier 'scientific' hereafter to shorten the label to just 'realism'.) These theses are, in all strictness, mutually logically independent of one another. But they are certainly not independent of one another *qua* components of realism for each is part of the best philosophic theory of science we have, so each is supported by the others.[5]

After these general characteristics of realism come claims which delineate one brand of realism from another. For example, it might be claimed that there is no significant semantic distinction to be drawn between theoretical and observational terms, or that science aims solely at the truth, or that the history of science demonstrates progress toward the truth, or that the development of science is given by the dialectic of historical materialism, and so on. Additional claims of this kind, together with the eight R doctrines and realism in perception and mathematics, give realists plenty of opportunity to disagree about what doctrine is labelled by that term.

Digression. And recent realist writings do disagree. Indeed, there is a certain taxonomic disarray at present. Horwich (1982a) distinguishes just three versions of realism: metaphysical realism, corresponding to R_4 (or R_3 and R_4); semantic realism, corresponding to R_6 (or to R_5 and R_6) and epistemic realism which is a weakened version of Devitt's (1984) D: most commonsense and scientific posits are real.[6] Bunge (1973) offers five realist principles, the first two essentially R_1 and R_2, while the third and fourth state that knowledge is fallible (cf. Section. 2.6) and the last that knowledge is symbolic and indirect. Ellis (1985) takes the central thesis of scientific realism to be R_5 (or R_5 and R_6) with versions of R_1, R_3 and an 'objectivity thesis' to the effect that theories are "objectively true or false" which Ellis carefully distinguishes from both R_3 and R_4. Ellis argues for rejecting R_3 and (in an appropriate reading) R_4, while retaining the other doctrines. Leplin (1985b) lists ten currently fashionable U.S. realist claims.[7] Only the last on his list bears any relation to my general claims.[8] Leplin himself says of his list that no majority of them "even subjected to reasonable qualification, is likely to be endorsed by any avowed realist." I am willing to confirm this and criticize his list of claims (Notes 7, 8). He adds that what realists "do share in common are the convictions that scientific change is, on balance, progressive and that science makes possible knowledge of the world beyond its accessible, empirical manifestations." Of the common doctrines, the second is a consequence of R_8 under a suitable definition of knowledge, but I regard the first as a claim which should be argued for on the evidence rather than a basic principle of realism.

In a recent review of realist principles Hellman (1983) lists seven candidate principles.[9] Hellman's first principle corresponds to R_5, his second principle to R_6 and his third principle supplies an amalgam of Leplin's candidates. These comprise Hellman's semantic formulations. Hellman's fourth principle corresponds to R_2 (or perhaps R_1 and R_2) and his fifth principle states a realist theory of perception. These are Hellman's ontological formulations. His sixth principle corresponds to a version of R_7 and his seventh principle to the claim that science can consistently develop theories, reasonable to accept, which assert the existence of states in principle unobservable. (In this last I concur, it is sanctioned by R_8. It is no mystery, geology and paleontology describe the past and the past may be held in principle unobservable.) These are Hellman's epistemic formulations. *End digression.*

I do not believe that even the eight R doctrines stated suffice to characterize realism sufficiently deeply. There certainly is a need for some systematic taxonomy of realist principles at the R level. If I were to follow most other philosophers, I would be content to offer the R doctrines, together with the arguments given above that other doctrines are optional, as my contribution to that taxonomy. But for my own part, the distinctive characteristics of evolutionary naturalistic realism are specified in the meta-philosophy given in Chapter 3, section 3.3.1. It is out of these that the R theses take their detailed form *vis-à-vis* science and have their unity. I cannot emphasize this too strongly.[10]

There are then three levels of realism as I believe the term should be used: meta-philosophical, core philosophical (R theses) and optional philosophical (Leplin's theses, etc.). With respect to the development of the general R principles—or if you wish, the making of them sufficiently precise to constitute a worthwhile realist theory of science— Chapter 2, Section 2.6.4, e.g., discusses a range of alternative realist positions on the semantics of theoretical terms while Section 2.6.6 offers my own tentative view. Similarly Chapter 3, Section 3.4 and

Chapter 6, Section 6.6 suggest some ideas for approaching a theory of rational epistemic commitment (although this account begs to be enriched by a developed theory of epistemic institutions, see Section 8.2.8 below). In a trilogy-plus-one of papers not included here (1979b, 1981c, d, e) I have tried to develop a general realist approach to identity and reduction and in another, to perception (see 1978a). I am trying to see how a realistic view of the role of cognition in the life of the planet can square with realism (see Chapter 6, Section 6.7; Chapter 7, Section 7.9)—here the institutional theory I need is developing elsewhere in my public policy research.[11] So the reader won't find a neat packaged realism in these pages. (On my view, I would first need to have the broad truth on everything!) He will find a complex, incomplete but (I think) very rich and exciting theory being elaborated . . . contributions are welcome.

8.2.2 Naturalism

   The world is a natural unity.

The leading motif here is the commitment to theorizing humans as a natural species, to seeing humans first as part of nature. An important part of this commitment is therefore to theorizing cognition as a natural capacity, one 'grading back' into the more generalized natural abilities of other species.

If human emotional structures are to be understood then that understanding best begins by studying the evolution of the flight/fight and hedonic responses, from reptiles through the mammalian lines (see e.g., Chance 1984). This study will be both behavioral and neutral, the two to be eventually unified. If human perception is to be cognitively understood then that understanding best begins with an understanding of the development of optical detection of motion and boundary in reptiles and its evolution through successively elaborated mammalian structures (see e.g., Arbib 1972, Campbell 1973, Hooker 1978a, Marr 1982). If human language is to be understood, including its intentional and semantic structures, then that understanding best begins with the nonverbal understanding of early mammals, the information processing requirements of cross-modal sensory coordination, opposed-thumb technologies and social cooperation, as well as the developmental significance of music (especially song) and dance drama. If science as an institutionalized activity is to be understood then that understanding should begin with the nature, especially the dynamics and limitations, of socio-biological coordination generally and of goal and method evolution in particular. On these themes see Chapter 3, Section 3.3.1; Chapter 7 *passim*.

Naturalism does not require reductionism. There is e.g., no necessity that human perception be *merely* reptilian perception—clearly it is not. The unity intended here is that of integration. E.g., the basic principles of perception are seen to apply equally to reptile and human, but within that unified framework the exfoliation of information-processing structure gives human perception a much greater cognitive capacity. Similarly, human emotions are suffused with cognitive structure in a way that reptilian reactions are not, but the biochemical and functional framework is the same for both. Let us say then that behavioristic or functional reduction is not required theoretically; instead we look for differentiation within unity in understanding. But neither is ontological reduction required. Dualisms of many sorts are in principle quite consistent with naturalism. Certainly e.g., Whitehead's dualist physical and mental properties characterizing a unified category of processes is compatible with naturalism.

On the other hand, naturalism is not vacuous. First, there are plenty of specific psychological theories that are essentially anti-naturalist. E.g., anti-naturalist are all those theories holding that language is both distinctive of our species and of a distinct category from other psychological categories (Chomsky in one mood, see Fodor 1975, 1984). The same applies to correlative theories of consciousness (e.g., Popper-Eccles 1977). And of course vitalism in biology at large was typically anti-naturalist. Second, it is certainly possible to state sufficiently un-integrated or dis-unified dualisms as to rule out naturalism, e.g., that of Descartes. There is something of a continuum here in ontological kind and correlative nomic structure from a severe materialism to a severe dualism. Outside of debating specific issues, I do not consider it interesting to pursue what cut-off point naturalism requires along this continuum.

Realism does not logically require naturalism, it can take other forms. Why then adopt naturalism? First because, as I read the history of science, naturalism is as a matter of fact the most theoretically fecund methodology available, it leads to the most insightful, accurate and useful scientific theories (cf. R₇ above). Second, I believe that naturalism, with its systematic anti-anthropocentrism and structured fallibilism, is ultimately the only way to philosophically defend realism (see Chapter 2, Section 2.4; Chapter 3, Section 3.3.1; and Sections 8.3.1, 8.3.2, 8.4.3, 8.4.4 below). Third (this is really a special case of the first), naturalism is an essential part of the best philosophical explanation of the cognitive dynamics of science. For naturalism occupies an intermediate position on a philosophical continuum from rationalism/empiricism at one extreme to scepticism/conventionalism at the other. The rationalist and empiricist are both dogmatic, they are already certain about the nature and sources of knowledge, so they dogmaticly reject methodological evolution and cognition of cognition generally. The conventionalist and more radically the sceptic are 'morons' about cognition, they reject the significance of questions concerning alternative goals for science, alternative methods for achieving those goals and the like. Both groups agree in dismissing cognitive evolution at the philosophical (meta-scientific) level. The naturalist realist, by contrast, insists on theorizing philosophy of science as a fallible theory of science, thus unifying cognitive theory. And within the theory of science it is natural to discover that methodological evolution is absolutely central to the cognitive dynamics of science. These themes are expressed throughout the essay to follow.

Naturalism is then both a claim about the world—that it is a natural unity—and a corresponding methodological commitment to develop relevantly unified theories. The claim about the world is adopted on the grounds that naturalism has proven scientifically and philosophically fruitful (cf. R_8 above).

Achieving a principled theoretical unity is no easy task. It can be thought of as having two foci: theorizing the world first as a metaphysical unity and (where appropriate) as a dynamic or nomic (law-like) unity as well. Metaphysical unity means understanding the world through a collection of categories of being which are mutually interrelated, non-redundant and in an appropriate sense complete.[12] Insofar as the world is a metaphysical plurality naturalism attempts to understand it as a dynamic unity. The major species of dynamic unity I take to be functional and causal unities (and I take these to be, in a certain sense, alternative descriptions of the same unity[13]). But general systems theory possibly offers a more general and searching analysis of nomic unity than is encompassed in either causal or functional unity, so I shall stick to the term *dynamic* unity to express this.

Within our present philosophic understanding, and from a realist point of view, unity is found to be basic to the aim of scientific understanding. A first approximation to scientific understanding might be: valuable truth, with unity a highly ranked value. So far as I can see, it is the metaphysical and dynamic unities displayed by a theory which determines that theory's explanatory depth and, along with its empirical precision and scope, chiefly determines its confirmability and explanatory power as well as its intertheoretic relations. Something of the importance and scope of unity in a theory of science is revealed in Sections 8.3.5 and 8.4.1 below.

Of course, other values qualifying truth may prove to clash with unity. Truth *simplicitur* is never rationally sought, only valuable truth, truth that, besides unity, displays precision, generality, technological applicability and so on. And for the sciences of the sentient and conscious, values of a wider kind than those of the core sciences need to be included in some appropriate way (see Sections 8.3.6, 8.3.10, 8.4.4 below). How philosophy of cognition will evolve I do not know. I suggest that if epistemology is going to understand the complex sets of utility-utility and utility-risk trade-off's appropriate to the pursuit of valuable truth then a mere disaggregated collection of values will not do, rather some deeper insight into their structure is required and this will involve the invocation of higher order unities.

Unity in scientific theory, unity in philosophic theory, unity between scientific and philosophic theory. These are all substantial doctrines focussed on somewhat different, but related, features of our overall understanding. They may stand or fall largely independently of one another. Nevertheless, as I construe naturalism here it is committed to all three unities. Naturalism conjectures unity for the whole natural order, it covers not just the non-cognitive realm but the cognitive also. The doctrine is reflexively consistent.

Thus naturalism is a substantive modifier of realism, one with deep (and as yet incompletely understood) implications. Some of these implications are spelled out in what follows.

8.2.3 Philosophical Interdependence

Philosophy and science are interdependent, interact and should mutually cohere.

Unity implies that the theories of philosophy and science should cohere. Philosophy offers a general theory of the world. As such, its view of the world should cohere with the more specific view offered by science (*ceteris paribus*, granted philosophic critique of science and doubts about various scientific theories, and vice versa for philosophy). So, the categories of metaphysics should be those appropriate to the ontologies of scientific theories (*ceteris paribus.* . .), the epistemology should be possible for creatures with the biology and psychology of *Homo sapiens*, the theory of meaning should accord with the neuro-linguistic capacities and causal design of *Homo sapiens*, and so on.[14]

On the other hand, differences among theories at various levels can and should be tolerated whilst ever there is good evidential and/or theoretical reasons to do so. Nor need the world be simple to understand for us humans. Nevertheless, so far as I can see the prospect that a schizophrenic split between philosophy and science should exactly (or even roughly) match reality is monumentally implausible and can only be sustained by linguistic word magic or doctrinal dogmatism. From this point of view it is one of the more serious criticisms of empiricisms and idealisms alike that they are in fact committed to a schizophrenic split between the images of ourselves current science offers and what their philosophical doctrines prescribe.[15]

Unity also implies that the sciences themselves should cohere. In particular (*ceteris paribus.* . .), the basic properties and processes of mind ought to be biologically feasible and to have an evolutionary rationale, and these in their turn be chemically and physically feasible. (Note again that feasibility does not require reduction, though reduction is one way to demonstrate feasibility.)

In practice, this kind of requirement proves quite stringent. It is very difficult to see with many standard philosophic concepts how they can 'grade off' down the evolutionary sequence and/or how the properties they designate fit into an integrated causal/functional dynamics. (I find this, for example, for sense data, unanalysable intentionality and rationalist intuitions.) The general upshot of these and like considerations is a complex interaction between philosophy and science, the two co-evolving, often in a highly dynamic way.

8.2.4 Anti-Anthropocentrism

Humans have no privileges created by philosophical fiat.

Perhaps the greatest triumph of science has been to break through unconscious anthropocentrism, rife among our species, to reveal Earth as but one planet among billions, humans as but one species among many, our societies as but a few complex systems among many. Though these and their ilk have been rude shocks to the ego, they have led to immeasurably clearer cognition of our real condition. Moreover they are, likely, a prerequisite for any substantial further achievement in other areas. (Note that religion, and philosophy, at their best, also enjoined transcending cultural, racial and national divisions and, in many cases the anthropocentric viewpoint. This drive to cognitive transcendence then is central to being human and certainly to the philosophic enterprise.[16]) An important consequence of naturalism is, therefore, anti-anthropocentrism (including anti-anthropomorphism as a special case).

According to our present understanding of the world, man is not the measure of all things (not even persons are). Human sensory cognition is limited and error-prone, human imagination is likewise limited and often parochial, human investigatory resources are as yet poorly organized and poorly understood by humans, and so on. Yet humans have come historically from a practice which began by projecting human personhood out into all the world (animism), which centered the world quite literally on humans (geocentrism) and which valued the world only in relation to humans (or even the local subgroup of humans—witness most religions). Anti-anthropocentrism is then opposed to all these doctrines which, explicitly or covertly, remove humans from *a* place in the scheme of things among other places and install us in some privileged position by philosophical or cultural fiat. Recall that the essence of realism is that what is true is not tied logically or conceptually to human cognition (nor to human culture), so if humans have special characteristics this is so independently of our assertion of it. Privileges humans may have, but not by human fiat.[17]

There are two grades of anthropocentrism. One is the straightforward meaty kind of the sort science has knocked about over the last few centuries, as indicated above. The other is a philosopher's backdoor version, a diaphanous transcendental sort in which the anthropocentric limitations to human cognition and/or meaning seems to arise out of semantic or epistemic 'analysis'. Hume offered an explicit version, so did Wittgenstein.[18] Logical empiricism is anthropocentric, for it declares cognitively meaningless all assertions not verifiable by us, as if the world could not be anything but transparently accessible to us. Rorty (1979, 1982) manages to lose the world in much the same way.[19] Even van Fraassen (1980) in his empiricist agnosticism anthropocentricly makes belief a function of observability in our epistemic community.[20]

Yet states of relative cognitive inaccessibility are all too well known to us (too small, too big, too slow, too fast, etc.) and it is sheer anthropocentrism, whatever the motive, to deny these conditions and cut the known world down to wholly familiar proportions. It also denies unity and interdependence, since in science we regularly theorize just such conditions. Often enough the motive for philosophical confinement of this sort is the achievement of philosophical security or certainty and epistemology is then allowed to dictate metaphysics in pursuit of that aim; but this too is disguised anthropocentrism for the world as we currently understand it reveals no significant role whatever for human certainty. (But human judgement, fallible as it is, is indispensable for human life.) For the same reasons most idealisms share with empiricisms an underlying anthropocentrism. The essence of idealism is to tie reality logically or conceptually to human cognition (again often in pursuit of epistemic security, or at least a transparent epistemic intelligibility). This inevitably results in a misplaced centrality to human cognitive processes in the scheme of things (and, not at all incidentally, often results in poor cognitive science). There is anthropocentrism in the pragmatist concept of truth as *defined* by idealized scientific agreement, and this no matter how idealized the ideals are (see Section 8.3.1 below).

Anthropocentrism is widespread in contemporary philosophy. It has a current fashionableness derived from such claims as (a) humans can never escape their concepts to grasp reality directly, from which truism it is (wrongly) inferred that a truth must be 'internal' to a conceptual scheme, or (b) the nature of linguistic reference is such that we could never refer to the unverifiable (or perhaps unconfirmable, certainly unknowable).[21] Alternatively, humans are held to be locked in deterministically to their culture[22], or locked semantically into their theories[23], so truth must be truth-for-the-social-group. Now it is certainly true that whatever is thought sententially must be conceptualized linguistically, and there are other truisms relevant to each of these views. But truisms don't constitute an argument (though they may be mistaken for one). So far as I can see there is no substantial theoretical evidence at the present time for supposing that we are limited or confined in the foregoing ways; to the contrary, science is constantly presenting us with conceptions of our cognitive access to the world which are both more and less limited than these philosophical divisions would suggest.[24] In short, science is constantly doing and exhibiting what philosophers say can't be done or isn't intelligible. (One is reminded rather sharply of the philosophic claims for traditional logic *vis-à-vis* the development of mathematical logics and the corresponding claims for Euclidean geometry *vis-à-vis* the development of non-Euclidean geometries.) On the other hand, this is not to dismiss the real problems lying beneath the choice of simple anthropocentric epistemologies, e.g., what are the theoretical limits of mutual understanding (theoretical, cultural, etc.)? Can these (or how far can these) be coherently theorized?

The conclusion which suggests itself to me is that language and epistemology, indeed cognition generally, are far more complex than anthropocentric philosophies would like to allow. Paradoxically, cognition can only be philosophically theorized successfully after we know a great deal more about our world and ourselves. (This is why the first consequence of naturalism, the interconnectedness of science and philosophy, does not make a mere abstract point of principle but refers instead to a concrete historical working relationship of great importance[25].) How is linguistic reference achieved and what are the limits of this process? In what particular ways does science as a rational activity relate to science as a historical and social process? How do these latter relations bear on its rationality? For many of these questions I have no neat realist theory to offer in which I have any confidence. So be it, this only reveals how much like science philosophy really is. However, in what follows I shall try to develop a unitary realist perspective wherever I am able.

8.2.5 Evolutionary Perspective

An evolutionary perspective is to leaven the construction of all philosophic theory.

The requirements that philosophy and science cohere and neither be anthropocentric lead directly to adopting an evolutionary approach to our biology and cognition. According to our current best understanding of ourselves we are to see ourselves first as products of a long evolutionary development shaped by the capacities and constraints of biochemistry, geo-climatological history, ecological dynamics and the like. As already noted (Section 8.2.3) the evolutionary approach has important implications for developing theories of cognition and consciousness generally, and for scientific epistemology (including perception and methodology), linguistic theory and theory of the dynamics of science in particular. These implications have been a constant theme in my writing.[26] Consulting Chapter 3, Section 3.3 and Chapter 7, Section 7.10 will serve to indicate the depth to which the perspective bites in philosophy. It re-emerges constantly in what follows.[27]

In the present context of the philosophy of science the evolutionary approach leads to three important consequences for epistemological theory, namely the adoption of a thoroughgoing fallibilist stance, a shift from logic to rational acceptance and an emphasis on the basic roles of risk and judgement in rational belief dynamics. These consequences are fundamental for the way in which epistemology is developed; they will be discussed under that heading (sec. 8.3.2 below). Here I elaborate briefly on the fallibilist theme, the most general of these three.

8.2.6 Fallibilism

All assertions are in principle open to criticism and revision.

An evolutionary perspective insists that we commence, epistemically, from profound ignorance, not only ignorance of the truth but ignorance even of what knowing is, of what theorizing is. Popper (1934, 1963a) emphasized a fundamental dilemma for any creature seeking to progress epistemically from evolutionary ignorance: there is a clash between security and relief from ignorance; each can be emphasized, but only at the expense of the other.[28] Most philosophies have evaded this problem by claiming some privileged source of knowledge (religious revelation, rational intuition, transcendental proof, empirical perception, etc.). Popper argues that privileged sources have always created epistemic authoritarianisms which have stood in the way of cognitive progress. He added (1963b) that they have also laid the foundation for socio-political authoritarianisms as well, authoritarianisms which in the long run stand in the way of social progress.[29] I accept these doctrines as fundamental insights.

However, given our evolutionary circumstances, Popper evidently thought it rational to aim solely at relief from ignorance, maximizing both bold conjecture and severity of criticism. But a glance at other species reminds us that whether this is the best strategy depends upon the nature of the environment (how stable, how predictable, how dangerous. . .), the nature of our epistemic capacities in that environment (how specialized, how accurate. . .) and the resources available for survival.[30] In these respects the doctrine lies more in the spirit of Peirce and the American naturalists (see Chapter 1). All of these factors can be the subject of learning and each can also be modified through utilization of information.

So we can expect an evolving methodology, formed as a complex function of all three factors, the present state of each factor in turn a function of past methodologies and the technological practices that emerged from them. This circumstance makes it plain that fallibilism characterizes every level of cognitive theory and practice, from technological practice through theory to philosophy of science (includes methodology) to meta-philosophy and so on 'up'. Moreover, the critical appraisal of these cognitive levels does not proceed independently or in a simple priority order; rather, discoveries and changes at any one level potentially effect those at all other levels (cf. Chapter 3, Section 3.3.1, Chapter 5, Section 5.4). In our circumstances, rationality calls for critical appraisal of both our accepted beliefs and our practices at all levels. This is the attitude of systematic fallibilism.

One might add that Popper also thought that his insights into social authoritarianism required some form of classical individualism together with piecemeal social policy making. But it is a profound fact that our cognitive development has catapulted us into a technological condition where it is often quite impossible to make social policy piecemeal (science policy included) because of the enormously wide-spread ramifications of social decisions nowadays. This is a theme which I have emphasized and elaborated elsewhere, see (1980a, b, 1980/1, 1983). Taken overall, then, it is this complex, dynamic and interacting system which we face today, an embedded subsystem forming the cognitive structure of the planet. Developing a philosophy of science is developing an understanding of what it is to be simultaneously subject, agent and theorist with respect to that system. Both theoretically and practically, achieving this understanding represents the greatest intellectual and social challenge the species has faced.

8.2.7 Normative Force

Norms are theories.

Both interdependence and fallibilism require that philosophic theories are on the same epistemic level as are scientific theories (i.e., *vis-à-vis* rational acceptance); indeed, they are essentially required to be theories. Once the anti-naturalist prejudices of the Western philosophic tradition are set aside, what is left of the normative role are the capacities to conceptually organize and to critically evaluate (Chapter 7, Section 7.6). Precisely these are capacities which theories have in relation to their domains of evidence and explanation.[31]

Consider how like in fact the history of Western philosophical doctrines is to the history of Western scientific doctrines. Let us focus initially on that queen of normative theories, logic. Surely here we should witness the inexorable unfolding of binding normative truth. Instead, history reveals to us the discovery of paradox and the increasing proliferation of logics each designed with particular useful features in mind. These latter are exactly the characteristics of a conjectural scientific discipline commencing from ignorance. Logic had a severely limited and fragmented, slow development until the nineteenth century (although there were sophisticated general debates about its character—see e.g., Kneale 1962). Then from Boole to Russell and Frege it passed through an initial revolution in theoretical form and tentative consolidation. Here it already became deeply connected with mathematics. From this latter connection, in turn, it was to burst into a myriad forms this century, so that now we link logical structures to projective geometries, algebras and topoi. We number modal, temporal, game theoretic, relevance, intuitionist and quantum logics among the 'non-standard' logics. These logics have developed in response both to various paradoxes and to various subject matters and goals of researchers. Philosophic prejudices aside, the subject looks exactly like the history of any natural science, and of geometry. (Compare especially the proliferation of theory after the discovery of non-Euclidean geometries.) This suggests that a theory of logic as specifying a relevant possibility structure, with possibility structures initially taken as concretely as space-time itself, might be a useful naturalist realist place to begin on a philosophy of logic.[32]

An important consequence of the present doctrine of the normative is this: the distinction between a normative theory and what it is normative for is quite compatible with holding that assertions at both levels have the epistemic status of fallible conjectures and thereby insisting that their contents develop in mutual interaction (just as happens for scientific theories). Indeed, as I have constantly remarked, this is happening all around us (see Chapter 7 and Section 8.3.3). Rather than reject the empiricist dichotomy between the normative and the descriptive (see Chapter 1) by collapsing it, it is rejected by insisting on interaction. This paves the way for a critique of the other empiricist dichotomies.

There is an old 'circle argument' based on the empiricist dichotomies: philosophic principles cannot be justified by appeal to historical science since this would be circular, these very principles themselves being used to delineate science (or good science) in the first place. The present doctrine acknowledges the structure but substitutes interaction for circularity.[33] Thereby, this doctrine provides a 'halfway house' between some transcendent (and epistemically inaccessible status) for philosophy on the one side and the collapsing of philosophy into science itself on the other.

Yet the assumption that we are forced to choose between the two sides of this latter dichotomy is widespread in philosophy. In particular, it is evidently behind the Quinean move to a so-called naturalized epistemology.[34] The notion that psychology and allied cognitive sciences will provide fundamental insights into the nature of what it is for a system to be, not simply complex, not even just self-organizing, but cognitive—that notion is surely a reasonable one (perhaps given time and luck!). In that event future epistemology must try to incorporate these insights, just as surely as Locke, for example, tried to incorporate the new atomist science of his day into his representative realist theory of perception. But the notion that psychology, or any other science, could proceed thus reasonably without our forming a meta-theoretic understanding and critical evaluation of its methods and assumptions is surely unacceptable—as unacceptable as all those who draw the false normative/descriptive dichotomy would insist.

The present conception of norms seems to me to replace the old dichotomy in the right way, by retaining what was insightful in it while incorporating those insights into a naturalist realist perspective.

Returning to the theme of the normative: philosophy is theory, so realism offers a theory of science. Realism provides a theoretical framework for understanding science, i.e., one which offers an explanatorily unified and metaphysically penetrating account of science and, on that basis, realism offers a normative critique of scientific methods and assumptions. The assumption that rational methods are so for any kind of world is a natural one for those who think of philosophy as offering transcendent normative judgements of some sort. But it is not self-evident for a naturalist realist and I believe that a little reflection will show that it is in fact false (see Section 8.3.3 below). There is no *a priori* reason to suppose that realism in itself should explain the success of any particular methods, much less any particular theories, independently of considering the kind of world revealed to us through theory. Conversely, realism must also be accountable to science in the sense that the rational science which it describes cannot, without good explanatory reasons, be too far distant from the historical development of science. Various versions of this latter requirement will be reviewed in Sections 8.4.1, 8.4.3 below.

8.2.8 Meta-Philosophy and Theory

The meta-philosophical hierarchy is a theory hierarchy.

Meta-philosophy is a theory of philosophy. It should, therefore, provide a framework for philosophic theory capable of offering a normative critique of philosophical theory, methods and assumptions. It should be held accountable to the development of philosophy by providing explanatory understanding of that development and of the reasonableness of philosophic methods.

I have tried to provide a meta-philosophy of just this character for evolutionary naturalist realism—see Chapter 3, sec. 3.3.1. The first principle of that meta-philosophy expresses the fallibilist doctrine, the second the doctrine that norms are theories and the sixth applies both principles to philosophy of science in particular. The third, fourth and fifth doctrines formulate goals for theories of epistemology, language and rationality in such a way that they express the doctrine of unity and its more specific consequence, philosophic interdependence. (A perusal of the discussion in the commentaries to these doctrines will underline the centrality of interdependence to their formulation.) Moreover, I suggest quite concretely that interaction between philosophy and science liberates philosophy (and science) from narrowing dogmatic assumptions.

Pursuit of these perspectives meta-philosophically shifts the foci at the philosophical level in theories of epistemology, language and rationality. A decade ago for example I emphasized that when one begins from ignorance as to what cognition is, the most important and interesting questions are "How is cognition possible" and "What kinds of organization in what kinds of systems can be cognitive?". These are very different questions from the language-biased, success rather than process oriented, human agent biased questions of traditional epistemology such as "What is the logical analysis of 'X knows that p'?" Similarly for rationality theory, what shifts to the fore is the understanding of interacting systems of risk-taking and judgement (judgements both normative and factual).

The doctrine of interdependence requires that theories be permitted to interact at all levels of the theory/meta-theory hierarchy and the doctrine of unity requires that all theories cohere (*ceteris paribus*. . .) to form a unified conception of reality. At the meta-philosophical level we express the fact that we are learning philosophically in a fallibilist way and from an evolutionary perspective. We have been learning meta-philosophically also in the same way. In sec. 8.2.7 above I noted that we learn about the characteristics of our own perceptual capacities while learning about the world generally; in the same way we learn meta-philosophically about the specific characters of, and interrelations among, theories of epistemology, rationality, language and so forth. Thus there emerges an open-ended hierarchy of learning: it is, as it were, fallible learning 'all the way up'.

From a purely formal point of view this latter fact may appear a trivial consequence of the realist doctrines already advanced and the levels beyond meta-philosophy held merely to repeat the same assertions without adding anything new.[35] This attitude would be a mistake, I believe, for the existence of open-ended learning processes is central to the realist rejection of all those philosophical attempts to create a neat world by philosophic fiat. It is, for example, at the base of the realist rejection of the currently fashionable idea that truth can be defined in terms of idealized rational agreement. For if there is an open-ended capacity to learn then rules of rational agreement or commitment, especially idealized rules, can be specified only through appeal to their capacity to capture reality truly (see sec. 8.3.1 below).

The neglect of the open texture of our more abstract cognitive methods has its counterpart in the neglect of the open texture of the interaction between our biological cognitive methods (perception) and technology. The earlier empiricist notion that one could separate the observable and unobservable by semantic fiat has given way to the admission that the development of technology is constantly shifting the dividing line. Kantian idealism had it that the basic cognitive structure of the mind was fixed *a priori*, only to have Kant's own version exploded by working scientific counterexamples.[36] An evolutionary account of our basic cognitive methods, i.e., our perceptual methods and their neural organization, makes it clear that those capacities are still dynamic, still open to change, indeed possibly still accessible to change by our own technologies. For this reason it is an illusion to speak of a 'completed human biology' as an ultimate basis for some notion of epistemic privilege to observation. The open texture of our biologically-based cognitive future means that even these attempts are covert ways to create privilege through philosophic fiat.[37]

Here then is a wonderfully open-textured dynamic of conceptualization and observation in which our own perceptual capacities, our fund of conceptualized scientific and philosophical theories and methodologies, and our technological capacities, are beginning to evolve in dynamic interaction with each other. How is one to specify in advance an outcome to this process? The main problem of philosophy is to understand it in all its complexity, not to attempt to confine it (inevitably by fiat) in advance.

This completes my account of a realist manifesto of an evolutionary naturalist kind. The doctrines reviewed (and in many cases developed more explicitly than appear in the preceding essays) have been included because they form part of the broad background of this kind of realist position. There follows now an examination of some more specific realist doctrines.

8.3 REALISM APPLIED: SPECIFIC DOCTRINES

8.3.1 Cognition and Truth

Truth is a theoretical posit of cognitive theory.

Instead of the wider framework of cognitive theory as a context for a theory of truth, much current philosophy invites us to assume that truth is at best a term appearing solely within some theory of semantics, and usually invites the additional assumption that truth is reduced to, or explained wholly by, reference or satisfaction.[38] This last assumption derives its force from Tarski's satisfaction theory of truth.[39] I suppose the fact this theory is a semantic one is what has encouraged the first assumption. I have always held that Tarski's semantic theory of truth is a theory of how to use the predicate 'is true' consistently in a linguistic framework and that it is no more than this (e.g. Chapter 2, Section 2.6.1). In particular, my view is that it does not express any significant correspondence theory of truth and does not reduce truth to satisfaction or reference.[40]

From an evolutionary naturalist perspective it is poor procedure to start with semantics. Correspondence truth is a relation between cognitive systems and the world, it is a component in our understanding of such systems in our world. Language is only a part of our cognitive capacities; we do not understand it well (Section 8.4.3.10), not nearly as well as we understand other features of the world and of our cognitive capacities. We will come to understand language only as we come to understand our world and our constitution better. To give semantics primacy, or exclusive rights to basic cognitive concepts, is to reverse reasonable procedure. I therefore think it wise to reject both of the assumptions above. But here I want only to identify and remove underlying barriers to what I consider a plausible realist defense of truth; this essay is not the place to enter fully into debates about semantic theory. (For my few direct remarks thereon see Section 8.4.4, 8.4.3.10.)

Within evolutionary biology both genetic hierarchy and phenotypic characteristics are related to each other and to environmental structure, indeed in some sense map that structure, yet none of these is reduced to any of the others. So within evolutionary naturalist realism, both method and theory must be understood as related to reality, indeed in some sense map that reality, yet none is reduced to any of the others. The representative of reality in cognitive theory is truth; thus within cognitive theory truth remains related to, but not reduced to, theory or method. Only when these relationships are understood can debate be properly engaged with relativisms, pragmatisms, internal realisms, naturalized epistemologies, sociologies of knowledge and the like. This subject is a very difficult and highly controversial one and though I shall advance doctrines in what follows without repetitious qualification, I want to make it clear at the outset that I regard the particular statement of the realist position I have chosen (though less so its general drift) as tentative.

A basic framework for a realist defense of truth is the realist distinction between truth and rational acceptance (Chapter 2, Section 2.4). The question at issue is whether this distinction can be shown to play the kind of fruitful theoretical role which would justify its retention in philosophic theory. The epistemic beginning lies in the Popperian thesis that, if one is beginning from ignorance, one cannot aim simultaneously at security (likelihood of truth) and informativeness (content). Even if scientists aim at the truth, they aim at it through proxies. Scientists aim directly at rationally acceptable *valuable* claims of various sorts: secure, reliably confirmed, empirically adequate, explanatorily unified, widely applicable, revealing metaphysical or ordering depth, precise, intertheoretically fecund and so on (Chapter 5, Section 5.4, Chapter 7, Section 7.11). But if proxies do all the work, why not scrap truth, which is inaccessible as an autonomous criterion, in favour of values which can be made epistemically accessible? A defensible answer has to show that without those basic distinctions which the concept of truth underwrites, indeed without the metaphysics and semantics of realism (Section 8.2.1), one cannot develop an adequate theory of cognition and in particular theories of cognitive rationality and epistemology. The position then is that truth is epistemically accessible only via proxies, yet indispensable. Truth then should be understood as an essential theoretical term in epistemic theory.

What are the basic contrasts which truth marks?

T_1: Truth marks the contrast between sensory appearance and reality; illusory and hallucinatory judgements are characterized by their lack of correspondence with reality.

T_2: Truth marks the distinction between meaningfulness and vacuity, what is meaningful has truth conditions and a truth value.[56] In particular, having a truth value marks the distinction between theoretical sentences being meaningful and their being instrumentally construed, while the kind of truth conditions they have marks the distinction between realist and empiricist semantics for theories.

T_3: Truth marks the contrast between meaningfulness and valuableness; what could possibly be true is distinct from which conjectures prove most valuable to us epistemically and otherwise in our current circumstances.

T_4: Truth marks the contrast between acceptance (on whatever grounds) and correct acceptance (acceptance of what is in fact true). A judgement may be accepted because of a wide variety of factors: fear, worship, ignorance, training, usefulness and so on; among those that are accepted only some are in fact true. In particular,

T_5: Truth marks the distinction between rational acceptance and successful rational acceptance. The justification of a judgement will in general be a function of the causal relation between judger and judged as well as the epistemic context of judgement, while the truth of the judgement concerns that judgement's correspondence to reality.

T₆: Truth grounds the distinction between error and error-freeness; error arises because judgements do not correspond to reality. In particular, truth grounds the distinctions, within error, between imprecision, partialness, approximateness and referential failure.[42]

T₇: Truth grounds the distinction between rational and non-rational cognitive structures. E.g., deductive logic is basically the theory of truth-preserving inference.[43]

From the naturalist realist perspective, the major motivation for these doctrines lies not in transcendental theses and the like but in the general evolutionary picture of ourselves science offers; it lies, in short, in awareness of our own epistemic limitations and idiosyncracies *vis-à-vis* our speculative and linguistic abilities.

It was in this latter spirit that I first introduced distinctions of this kind at Chapter 2, Section 2.4 (cf. 1978a, 1981b). But in that chapter three only of these distinctions were stated. D₂ of Chapter 2 corresponds to an application of T₅ above, D₃ corresponds to T₃ and D₄ to T₄. D₁ of Chapter 2 I still hold, and hold as fundamental, but I would now re-express its intent in this way: the meaning of 'p is meaningful' is in general distinct from the meaning of p itself (self-referential tricks aside). If an assertion's being meaningful can be equated to its possessing determinate truth conditions, then this becomes: the truth conditions for 'p has determinate truth conditions' are in general distinct from the truth conditions for p.[44] Spelling out such distinctions is a part of developing a general theory of truth and language, i.e., of cognition.

The argument for retaining a correspondence theory of truth is simply that without that theory the open-ended texture of cognition based on the foregoing distinctions cannot be captured.[45] To understand the argument consider a simple pragmatist definition of scientific truth along these lines: For all propositions p, p is true $=_{df}$ p is implied by science S which has been accepted through ideal pursuit of methodology M, where ideal pursuit means pursuit unlimited by time or resources. Notice immediately the necessity of the idealization, for without it the natural limitations of humans might easily thwart M's securing of the truth just because the universe was too big, too fast (slow), too complex, too disaggregated and so on. The real question at issue is whether the appeal to idealization here suffices to capture the full role which a theory of truth plays in philosophy and meta-philosophy (and up). Well, what of developing an understanding of methodology itself, how is that possible on the present account? It isn't. Since truth is by definition what results from using methodology M, it can't be a consistently formulated truth that M is inadequate to discover all the truth in some respect.[46] What if M itself is discovered to be inadequate? (Suppose, for example, we discover that the universe is too nomically symmetric and/or disaggregated for us to discover exactly all that happened over the first two billion years following the Big Bang—or, if you prefer, over the previous cycle of the universe before *our* big bang, or beyond our 'light horizon'. Or suppose that advances in decision theory turn up some flaw in M's risk-utility trade-off structure.)

In sum, this simple pragmatist definition cuts us off from understanding how it can be *possible* to learn about rational scientific methods. Yet it is precisely the distinctions which truth underwrites which are required to consistently state the possibility of learning about our epistemic methods. (There is a principled distinction between the conditions under which we rationally accept that a particular method is adequate to the discovery of truth in some domain and the truth conditions of that claim, and so on.) So the simple pragmatist definition of truth does not adequately ground these basic distinctions.

Now the argument generalizes: any attempt to define truth in terms of epistemic constructs, however specified, will render it impossible to consistently state the possibility of learning about those constructs and of improving them. But our cognitive framework is open-ended, all its component levels are open to improvement. So no such definition of truth is satisfactory.

The point then is that in an evolutionary naturalist setting cognitive development is open-ended; we learn, learn how to learn, learn about learning and about learning how to learn. . . Every component must be open-ended for us since we began in ignorance of them all. Our actual history confirms these dynamics. But this picture only makes sense in the context of a species with specified cognitive apparatus developing in an independently existing world, rich in structure and knowable through interaction. That is, this picture only makes sense in the context of a realist metaphysics containing a correspondence theory of truth. And since we can and do construct very rich cognitive models of ourselves of this interactional sort, whatever the alleged epistemic inaccessibility of the truth relation be (but see Section 8.4.4), its intelligibility seems clear. Metaphysics theorizes a framework for epistemology without which epistemology is blind and arbitrary. The only metaphysical framework which adequately provides for thoroughgoing naturalism, i.e., which allows every philosophical doctrine conjectural status, is one within which the notion of truth is not tied of conceptual necessity to any fixed epistemic construct.[47]

What empiricism and idealism share in common is an insistence on a conceptual (as opposed to a causal) connection between epistemic conditions and truth, between knower and known. It is just this doctrine which naturalist realism denies. Recently, it has become fashionable to try once again to retain the attractions of both worlds. The formula is still that truth is (by definition) rational acceptance, "idealized" rational acceptance.[48] It seems to be assumed that appeal to idealization removes objections of the sort just levelled against pragmatist definitions. But either it is claimed we know (really assuredly know) these idealized rules of rational acceptance or it is agreed that we don't. If we are held to assuredly know them (or can come to assuredly know them through some *specific* process P) then this is both a non-naturalist (presumably rationalist) position and a covert version of pragmatism after all.[49]

In the event it is agreed humans can't assuredly know these rules (or P)—and this is certainly so on a naturalist account since they remain conjectural theories—then of course the definition can't be pinned down to some specific pragmatist criterion. But then we may ask how the development of methodology itself is to be understood. In the realist case an external reality acts as anchor while all cognitive structure, from data 'up', is fallibly explored—but what could ground the corresponding exploration when truth itself is a human artifact? In this case it is hard to see what sense can be given to the notion of methodology as a conjectural theory. Indeed, it is hard to see what sense can be given to an idealized science, methodology or anything. Rather, the whole process of development is in danger of being ultimately arbitrary *vis-à-vis* truth, a mere wandering around, now reinforcing one values-methods-theory mix and now another. Humans threaten to be so completely bound into their own self-reinforcing cultures that they "don't know which way is up and which is down."[50] One response might be that there is no independent reality against which, or in relation to which, methods can succeed or fail. This condition *is* what some prominent theorists evidently reckon to be ours.[51] It is not, however, what the present protagonists want, for they claim to hold fast to a robust sense of realism.[52] The point can be put from the obverse perspective: it is impossible to understand how reality can act as any kind of consistent, coherent constraint on cognitive evolution if reality is either a fabrication of ours or if it has no intrinsic character at all.[53] To avoid relativism, one could assert a unique, unvarying set of cognitive values whose satisfaction guides the exploration of both methods and theories. But this would just be to define truth in terms of values instead of methods, thereby locking us out of conjecturally exploring epistemic values.

I do not, therefore, detect a viable position here. There is, I think, no metaphysical middle ground to be occupied between realism, with its denial of an *a priori* conceptual relation between cognition and reality, and pragmatism, idealism and empiricism with their assertion of it. But of course the realist can allow all sorts of powerful *causal* relations between cognition and reality, and this is just what the evolutionary naturalist picture demands.[54] (Just how powerful the causal feedback from cognition to reality may be is illustrated in my 'Stories' of Chapter 7, Section 7.1.)

The essence of my strategy has been to insist that truth be understood first and foremost as a theoretical term in epistemic theory. Or, since I don't like the old associations of 'epistemology', that truth be understood as a theoretical term in a naturalized normative theory of cognition. This immediately takes truth beyond the bounds to which Putnam (1981a) and others confine it, namely at best a term strictly within semantic theory for language. As remarked, from an evolutionary naturalist perspective, this latter view has nothing to recommend it. (Nonetheless, Devitt 1984 is a realist who does accept the restriction and yet also finds an explanatory need for truth. I investigate Devitt's views further at Section 8.4.1 below.) Truth then is a theoretical term with a rich theoretical role; it is not to be confined to semantics, and its role in semantic theory is not to be reduced to some narrower notion such as reference.

8.3.2 Epistemology

Mapping, not mirroring, is the construction metaphor; commitment, not logic, the structure metaphor.

In 1978 I wrote as follows:

> Perception is the organism's key to action. What is extracted in perception, how it is encoded, and what the mind itself supplies is a function of the priorities and information the organism has accrued. There is a large accumulation of evidence that the ways we perceive the world are indeed constructed in this fashion. . .The features of the world that are mapped and the way they are mapped into the existing informational state of the organism are idiosyncratically selected according to the organism's ends, in the light of its capacities; thus we expect no identities, only transformations and embeddings appropriate to making appropriate identifications for action.

> . . .How then shall we conceive of the senses? First as *systems*, second as *information-processing* systems, and third as *environmentally oriented*. The senses are environmentally oriented, information-processing systems, i.e., *perceptual* systems. Roughly, our perceptual systems receive a pattern of physical stimuli, select and abstract from it (i.e., transform it), and feed it to the entire central nervous system for action (1978a, pp. 408 and 411–412).

This approach to perception as a dynamic cognitive system is now commonplace in the sciences[55] but it has important consequences for philosophy. For example, it leads one to an analysis of the underlying assumptions of the classic anti-realist argument in perception theory from the occurrence of illusion and hallucination. With these underlying assumptions displayed explicitly that argument runs somewhat as follows:

P₁: Sensory illusions and hallucinations are logically possible (indeed they occur).

P₂: Veridical perception is indistinguishable to the mind from illusory and hallucinatory perception, qua perceptual experience.

A₁: The mind is epistemically self-transparent.

A₃: Perception logically requires a consciously examined content.

A₄: Perceptual contents are objects, i.e., individuals of the ontology.

C₁: What is before the mind in veridical perception are objects of the same role, type and status as are those objects before the mind in illusory and hallucinatory perception.

A₅: Perception is veridical if and only if what is before the mind is identical with what is in the external world.

P₃: The contents of illusory and hallucinatory perceptions differ from the actual external situation presented to the perceiving subject.

C₂: The objects before the mind in illusion and hallucination are not objects in the external world.

C₃: What is before the mind in veridical perception are not objects in the external world.

P₄: The objects of perception either belong to the external world or belong internally to the mind.

C₄: What is before the mind in veridical perception are objects in the mind. (1978a, pp. 419–420)

(To this add the assumption A₂: Conscious awareness is propositional awareness, i.e., epistemic states are propositionally defined states.) About these five assumptions I wrote as follows:

. . .a scientifically adequate theory of perception and mind requires the rejection of all five assumptions of the epistemological approach. The importance of the role of the subconscious/ unconscious in mental functioning and our ignorance of it is evidence enough that A_1 is false. Language is peripheral to nervous function, and the transformations occurring in the nervous system can be expected to be richer and nongrammatical in form. So A_2 is false. Consciousness being a phase of nervous function in a nervous system dominated by unconscious processes, perception does not require a conscious act at all, nor is there plausibly a subject/object structure to conscious processes. So A_3 is false. The nervous system processes information in a manner dependent jointly upon environment and organism. Thus sense data, if we choose to introduce them as theoretical entities, will be structural features of nervous-system states, not objects of any sort, and not in any sort of subject/object relation to consciousness. Perception depends on structure-preserving mappings, not identities; it depends on the extraction of information to make *identifications* rather than achieving identities. So A_4 and A_5 are false (1978a, p.411).[56]

Though I deploy this conception of perception and cognition generally in defense of a broad perceptual realism, others have more recently claimed to find in the rejection of the 'mirror metaphor' in favour of the 'map metaphor' the grounds of a radical shift away from realism to a thoroughly relativist pragmatism.[57] In this they have been aided and abetted by the tide of 'human centered' philosophical analysis of science of Marxist, sociological, anthropological, historical and other origins, now sweeping across Western intellectual allegiances.[58] I shall comment on these latter movements next (Section 8.3.2 below); here I first want to record my dissent from the claim that a dynamic mapping conception of cognition must be anti-realist, or is even plausibly anti-realist. To the contrary, it seems to me to be essential for defending a realist, certainly an evolutionary naturalist, philosophy. It is essential for understanding how we humans get in touch with the world and for understanding the nature of error (how we fail to get in touch with the world).

Since mirrors have been contrasted to maps, let us begin by noticing a fundamental similarity between them: both mirrors and maps define, or are defined by, homomorphisms (i.e., by a structure-preserving mapping in the mathematical sense). Both mirrors and maps establish homomorphisms between themselves and some other, normally independent, reality. In the case of a general map the homomorphism can be very various. For example, any of 'northwards', 'sub-institution' or 'loves' could be represented by an arrow. But a homomorphism there must be, otherwise the point of its being a map is lost. The point of a map, quite generally, is to enable correct identifications to be made for given purposes. A map does this by providing a structure-preserving representation of reality in the relevant respects. Possessing a map and an independent correct initial identification of one of the mapped objects, which locates the user on the map, the map then serves as a guide in the identification of other objects, processes, properties, etc., that are relevant. (Notice that maps aren't restricted to identifying objects, so the mapping theory of cognitive representation is likewise not restricted.) A mirror is only a special kind of map. The homomorphism in the case of a plane mirror is always a projection, together with an injection (or restricted identity map) for colour.[59]

Now note the following fundamental feature of homomorphisms: if h_1 and h_2 are homomorphisms from X to Y, then there exists a homomorphism $h:X \to Y$ such that for all $x \in X : h(x) = h_1(x)$ & $h_2(x)$, i.e., h is the conjunction or point-wise composition of h_1 and h_2. Thus two maps of the same territory, say one of land use and the other of transportation, can always be combined into a single map, e.g. one showing both land use and transportation. It is always possible to combine maps of the same reality so as to form a more detailed composite map, there always exists a more encompassing homomorphism that captures them both. In short, homomorphisms of the same reality are always 'deeply compatible'; maps of the same reality can always be *unified*. Thus cognition too can always be unified, even on the mapping model, as long as there is a single reality of which it makes maps.[60] This should block talk of the mapping metaphor of cognition supporting any easy relativism.

Maps of the same reality must be deeply compatible—this is so even if it does not always appear so on the surface. Two different mirror images of the same object are always deeply compatible, even if they appear to present quite different structures, objects or processes, because there is always a three-dimensional structure of which they are both projections.[61] Moreover, if $h_1:X \to Y$ and $h_2:X \to Z$ and the inverse of h_2 exists, then there exists $h_3:Y \to Z$. (Indeed, $h_3 = h_1 \circ h_2^{-1}$, where 'o' is mapping composition.) That is to say, wherever mappings are invertible—surely a reasonable requirement in the cognitive case since they need to support identifications—then there is always a homomorphism between maps. Thus maps are also deeply commensurable. This should put a stop to easy talk of the mapping metaphor supporting incommensurability.

And maps of the same reality must be commensurable even if it doesn't always appear so on the surface. In the example above, there will be a map from land use to transportation (namely one determined by the locations of those activities). The 'language', conceptual scheme, 'logic' or whatever of land-use theory may be disparate from that of transportation theory, they may seem to have little in common, but in fact true theories of each must be relatable to one another at some sufficiently deep organizational level.[62] This is why the open-endedness of human knowledge is a crucial feature of the naturalist realist scheme.

So much for the admissability and theoretical fecundity of mapping models of cognition; now consider the "received" or dominant Western traditions in foundational epistemology. These all share the following paradigm: propositional source plus logical structure. There is a source of knowledge specified (senses, revelation, rational intuition, transcendental proof. . .). This source provides knowledge in the form of propositions and it is held to be strongly authenticating in the sense that it commands the mind's unquestioning assent to its deliverances (its givens). All other knowledge is rationally based on these given propositions and hence structured by the rational rules for relating propositional contents, logic. (Whether the logic is deductive or inductive is then best regarded as a variation within the paradigm, comparable to variations of source.) Truth is automatically the dominant goal, with subsidiary goals deriving from logical resources: consistency, perhaps versions of coherence. (Idealists and/or pragmatists may often try to extract truth from coherence.)

This paradigm focuses attention on the analysis of 'X knows that p' where p is a place-holder for declarative sentences. If the standard analysis is taken—'X believes p, p is true and X has good reasons for believing p'—then a regress of reasons ensues, to be stopped at the source.[63] Within this paradigm we can identify the direct truth proclaimers, such as Hempel and Armstrong, and a wide variety of those who, struggling to be critical of sources within these confines, are forced to substitute coherence (Quine's 'web of belief'), problems (Popper's progress) or some other logic-based procedure.[64] Notoriously, these latter positions have proved difficult to maintain (logical analysis serves foundationalist epistemology in this paradigm) and others have generalised from logic to probability of truth, to become odds-makers rather than truth-proclaimers, whether Bayesian in form (e.g., Horwich, Jeffrey) or not (Carnap's inductive calculi, Glymour's bootstraps, etc.)[65] In fact this paradigm paves the way for relativism. When empiricists promoted the doctrine that all truths are either analytic and empirically contentless or synthetic and informative they broke apart the joint requirement of strong truth and informativeness which has characterised the Western epistemic tradition. Popper then went further, arguing that one cannot even hold together probability of truth and informativeness. This opened the way to relativism via throwing away the truth component to focus solely on the dynamics of informing one another (cf. Feyerabend 1974).

From an evolutionary naturalist perspective 'logic + source' is not a plausible paradigm of epistemology. There are no strongly authenticating sources, rather there are multiple interactions with the world from which useful information is extracted (perception, reflection, various communication modes), none of it perfect. Though the world has a structure, this is not a magical all-pervading platonic object, unavoidably (perhaps even unspeakably) inherited by us. The key issue is how to rationally evaluate source differences and cognitive structure as a function of goal priorities, circumstances and tolerable risk. But rationality gets no hold on the strongly authenticating source. Nor does risk-taking find any natural place in the 'source + logic' paradigm. Indeed, since knowledge is a function only of source and logic, the *consequences* of belief are irrelevant to its rationality. For these reasons it is difficult to understand the evolution of this kind of cognitive capacity from more elementary and less perfect capacities.[66]

Realist principles here counsel the development of cognitive capacities which are operationally possible and plausible for us as evolving organisms, and an epistemology which shows how knowledge is possible for a creature with those cognitive capacities. It is mysterious how the received view could meet this requirement. Indeed, it is a crucial feature of our epistemic situation, already noted, that in science we develop theories of the limitations of our own sensory capacities. The received view is forced back into schizophrenic double-think about these developments. Alternatively, it is forced on to either transcendental demonstrations or appeal to conscious incorrigibilities.[67]

From the naturalist realist perspective cognition is theorized as a natural phenomenon. In a certain sense one begins by 'taking it whole', theorizing a biology of knowledge. Here the inspiration is Lorenz (1976) and Piaget (1970, 1971a,b), see also Campbell (1973) and cf. Wartofsky (1979a) on the scope of genetic epistemology. Systems perspectives add an important dimension (see e.g., Iberall 1972, Jantsch 1975, 1976, 1980, 1981). Contributions to the same development by Calhoun (1984), Wojciechowski (1975, 1978, 1980) and others from the 'ecology of knowledge' movement expand the approach to embrace contemporary socio-epistemic problems. These developments represent some progress since my earlier speculative comments in Chapter 3, Section 3.3.1, but they are as un-unified as ever. Moreover, since we are building a theory, the normative dimension remains present but in this respect one feature of the lack of integration is serious: the integration of traditional epistemic theory remains nearly nonexistent. In respect of this last, I suggest that the roadblock to integration is the absence of an epistemic paradigm connecting cognitive system dynamics to cognitive rule structures. Here that link is best made, I believe, through a rational decision model. I hold this true for social theory generally (cf. the Vickers model in Hooker 1983).

Consider then by way of contrast to the logic + source paradigm, an extended agency model of cognitive function in which the metaphor or paradigm for belief is practical commitment. Here we picture an organism inheriting and/or developing a set of epistemic goals and a set of epistemic methods working on multiple sources of information. The organism is rational just insofar as it adopts efficient methods for pursuing its epistemic goals given its sources of information. This simple theory needs to be complicated in several important ways, but first I should like to list a few of the advantages of this sort of approach. It integrates well with a naturalistic theory of cognitive capacities and organic evolution; judgement, risk and optimizing all 'grade back' to more elementary operations. And present capacities can be understood as outcomes of selection because belief-forming processes are directly related to, and tested by, their outcomes. There is no inherent linguistic bias, since there is no *a priori* commitment to the forms which cognitive states take or to the channel characteristics of epistemic sources. Nor is there special anthropomorphic bias in the choice of goals, this is left open initially, to be filled in as part of developing epistemic theory (more anon). There is no barrier to the reflexive critical evaluation of sources or of logical structure; in pursuit of our epistemic goals we may quite consistently learn about the sources on which we are forced to rely and the structures we use to organize them. Via building theories of all these, we are able to criticize their limitations.[68] Logical structures for the organization of belief commitments can also be recaptured within this framework, though there is no *a priori* commitment to any particular logical structure so that these too can be critically explored.[69]

Finally, the sceptic obtains no special purchase within this paradigm. The essential sceptical argument I take to be this: epistemology E is logically (perhaps actually) compatible with the occurrence of error, therefore E is not adequate. The link between logic, certainty and foundationalism encourages this line of argument and the absence of any focus on deliberate risk-taking in epistemic rationality (in any but Popper's account) gives it a continued force. The alternative decision theoretic paradigm advocated here allows one to reject the sceptic's conclusion while accepting the premise, and the naturalist evolutionary framework actually shifts risk-taking to the fore as a focal part of epistemic activity.[70]

Within this general paradigm there is a range of positions determined by the strength of the claim for the segregation of epistemic from non-epistemic or practical utilities. There are those who insist on strict segregation (Levi 1967, presenting a version of Popper in this paradigm), those who insist on a distinction of kind but with both kinds appearing in all situations (Rudner 1953) and those who deny the distinction (Dewey 1930). I tentatively place myself between Rudner and Dewey. I place myself to the 'left' of Rudner essentially because the historical interaction between technology and societal processes on the one side and science on the other makes it impossible to separate, at the level of the dynamics of science, the epistemic and practical in the development of science (see Sections 8.3.3, 8.3.10 below). I place myself to the 'right' of Dewey because my own view is still consistent with distinguishing, at some level of cognitive theory, epistemic from other practical goals.[71]

Finally, a word about acceptance, belief and truth. In science, as elsewhere, humans pursue valuable truth, and I recognize a fairly wide range of values qualifying truth in the scientific context (Chapter 7, Section 7.11). This means that acceptance has an equally complex structure. Consider first the narrower case of belief. Van Fraassen invites us to accept a dichotomy between a simple belief-as-true (for the realist) and a more complex acceptance-as-displaying-virtue (for the constructive empiricist).[72] Reality is not so simple. One may accept a statement p as true but also accept that it is superficial, accept p as approximately true but misleading concerning certain underlying features, accept p as deeply true but superficially misleading for various reasons and so on. In short, acceptance for belief is always in particular respects, and on the basis of the virtues it displays. Beyond that we pursue the virtues as both valuable for other reasons and as cognitively valuable. Technical control, e.g., is valuable for its facilitation of other goals (health, wealth. . .). It is also cognitively valuable twice over, first because it facilitates theory testing, concept formation, etc. (Section 8.3.9) and second because it is one kind of evidence that our theories have locked on to reality (Section 8.4.4). Historically these twin pursuits dynamically interact (Section 8.3.9). Thus beyond acceptance for belief there is a rich array of acceptances, accept for testing (in respects X,Y. . .), accept for heuristic exploration (in respects. . .), accept for technical application . . . and so on (cf. Chapter 5, Section 5.4 and Note 138 below.)[73] Empiricist and Popperian methodological debates encouraged the view that in science there was a simple acceptance/rejection structure, a statement was either in or out. But the move to a decision theoretic epistemology delivers us from simplistic dichotomies, to reveal the complex texture of cognition.

Having outlined and argued for the non-traditional decision theoretic paradigm for epistemology, it is now time to briefly review the difficulties and programmatic features of this position. First, the view itself has only recently received serious theoretical attention and there is still a relative paucity of theoretical literature.[74] In particular, there is a need to investigate conditions on the global development of belief systems so that they remain cognitively rational (see Note 28). Beyond this, the view is heir to many of the controversies surrounding the foundations of decision theory itself. For example, there is clear scope for the occurrence of Allais-style paradoxes with the concomitant need to examine the role of risk *vis-à-vis* epistemic utility explicitly. It seems to me what is required here is a theory of epistemically appropriate risk-utility trade-off structures.[75] There is scope for a clash between individual cognitive rationality and collective cognitive rationality (cognitive prisoner's dilemma games) and the limitations which confine political voting systems also confine the decision processes of epistemic institutions (cognitive Arrow paradoxes).[76] Just as in the political case generally, so in cognition it will be the designs of epistemic institutions (scientific institutions) which determine the epistemic quality with which these constraints are handled. Thus another strength of the present epistemological paradigm is that it provides a natural framework for the importance of institutional theory within the theory of science.[77]

Finally, formal decision theory has not made much theoretical progress in the treatment of interdependent utilities, hierarchically organized utilities, or in utility dynamics. Yet these features are crucial to characterizing what it is to be a person, to characterizing our most basic cognitive capacities (including our capacity for innovative resolution of decision theoretic paradoxes) and hence for characterizing epistemic rationality in science.[78] The decision-theoretic epistemic paradigm therefore is still largely programmatic, but in my view it provides for a much stronger and richer, and much more plausible and promising, program for epistemological theory than its traditional alternative.[79]

8.3.3 Methodology and Theory

Method is a function of accepted theory.

From an evolutionary viewpoint, epistemology is bound up with the theory of epistemic methods, for these latter determine the scope and reliability of rational belief (Chapter 5, Section 5.3). It is essential to add that which methods are appropriate is a function of the kind of world we in fact inhabit. The epistemic counterpart is that which methods are accepted is a function of which theories are accepted (and of course *vice versa*). This feature is crucial because it allows for the evolution of methods as a higher-order spin-off from the evolution of theories. Methodologies, like theories, evolve and are adapted to the world as we find it. This is a central theme of Chapters 4 and 5. It applies across the entire range of methodology, e.g., from very general searches for causal structure to highly specific laboratory techniques in a narrow scientific speciality.

My garage mechanic likes to entertain wild hypotheses, such as that poor brakes lead to ignition trouble. And he can cite plenty of supporting evidence, which he collects *post hoc*. (E.g., he says that all cars with ignition problems presented for repair, including mine, later started perfectly after their brakes were repaired.) My hypothesis is conventional, I believe the usual engineering analysis and deduce that in all normal circumstances brake condition is irrelevant to ignition performance. Moreover, I collect my evidence via the classic Mill's methods of causal analysis and this eliminates my mechanic's hypothesis: you find non-starting cars with good brakes and starting cars with bad brakes. Why are my methods superior? Because the causal structure of cars is in fact such as to make Mill's method appropriate to them: car components are causally separable and structurally invariant over operating conditions. Causal analysis of this kind would not necessarily be appropriate if the car were a single field structure obeying an integro-differential equation, or a functional complex with feedback interdependencies, or a dissipative system in dynamic equilibrium, and so on. It is because one theory of the car's nature is accepted and not another that one set of methods is accepted as appropriate and not another.[80] Consider, in this light, the contemporary controversies surrounding naturopathy, homeopathy, mediation, visualization and other non-standard medical methods—all these methods are supported by non-standard theories of human nature. Their conflict with conventional medicine is at two levels at once.

Methodologies evolve in delicate interaction with theories themselves. Physicists regularly employ texts with titles like *Mathematical Methods of Physics*. These methods are of course based directly on generalizations of structures and analyses drawn from those physical theories which have in fact been found to work. (Thus certain kinds of generalized stability analyses are held as methods only because it is currently accepted that dynamics can be given a mathematical representation within symplectic manifold theory.) The discussion in Chapter 4 makes it clear that the choice of methods—including causal analyses, statistical inference techniques and limited inductive rules—is a function of the possible states and interconnections available in the context of application according to accepted theories. The careful experimental and theoretical study of the limitations and errors of human perceptual systems is an excellent example of the interaction of methods, theories and technologies. It not only improves knowledge, but method as well.[81]

Contrast these two worlds: (1) A world of atoms, causally bound into simple linear structures. (2) A world of hierarchically organized processes, indefinitely complex, non-linear, mutually irreducible but mutually interacting and best described field theoretically. These are two very different kinds of universes. In the former experimental methodology will focus on singling out natural kinds and their elementary causal interactions, theories about complexes will be reducible to complex theories of elementary interactions and severity of tests will revolve around the sensitivity of theory to variation in the elementary, presumptively universal, causal relations, the *ceteris paribus* clauses will specify global irrelevance of remaining causal factors, and so on.[82] In the latter world experiments may aim to 'tune in' to, or establish resonant interaction with, field processes such as energy propagation, oscillation and so on, each at some specific hierarchical level and within some accessibility band width, to some degree of resolution or signal separation. There will be no objects as such, only relatively stable invariances in processes at a given hierarchical level, the *ceteris paribus* clauses will specify interaction strengths less than some threshhold and severity of tests will focus on the sensitivity of variations in process parameters or cross-level interaction parameters.[83] These two worlds lead to very different mathematical forms to express basic theory (Section 8.3.4) and they will lead to very different methodological practices based on those forms. They will presumably share very general fragments of methodological practice, such as the *modus tollens* argument form to express commitment to reject some premise of reasoning, but even this commonality is of dubious scope once examples are examined carefully.[84]

The mutual interaction of method and theory is central to our cognitive capacities. The point is illustrated by the complement to the investigation of sensory limitation, namely the development of instrumental extensions to our senses (microscopes and telescopes, infrared sensors and so on). Sensory observation is a basic part of scientific methodology; using the methods made available biologically (our five senses) and other cognitive methods we have been able to develop theories and technological practices which have in turn vastly extended (but also qualified) these basic biological methods, in turn providing for more powerful systems of theoretical development, in turn leading to further extensions of the senses . . . The same is true in other areas of scientific methodology, for example in inductive and statistical inference methodology where the current ferment in foundational theory is driven by interaction with scientific theories and provides a rich diversity for evolutionary development.[85] Everywhere in science theoretical understanding of possibilities drives increasing methodological capacity and, conversely, the application of methods in turn drives increasingly powerful theoretical development and so understanding of possibility structures.[86] Without this dynamic it is, in my view, impossible to make good sense of the actual history of scientific theory and scientific method.

Ah, but I hear you say, where are the rules? This is the relevant question in the traditional paradigm of 'logic + source.' Bluntly then: I am not trying, not wanting, to give that kind of a description of methodology at this point. 'Rules' can only refer here to specific kinds of situations. The demand for rules is worth exploring further, so that the kind of system's dynamic/decision-theoretic account offered here is clearly contrasted with the traditional collection of fixed, universal formal rules which it is usually assumed must be provided (cf. Chapter 5). Roughly, methodology forms the control or regulatory hierarchy for science—and in this sense corresponds to the genetic regulatory hierarchy biologically. Within this role a diversity of methods can be, indeed must be, accommodated: sensory and instrumental search, specific elaboration of alternative order structures and mathematical methods, specific statistical inference structures and inductive methods, Kuhn-style exemplar elaboration and so on. Just as for the genetic control hierarchy, we can expect the methodological control hierarchy to develop and exfoliate historically under accumulating selective impact in increasingly diverse environments—as indeed it has.[87]

From this point of view nothing is more natural or important than those experimental alterations of the methodological hierarchy which arise from diverse causes ('mutations') and which are successfully propagated and entrenched, perhaps for unanticipated invaluable later use. (They are entrenched at the time because they contribute to the solution of a problem or problems—'increased fitness'—at that time.) Feyerabend (1970) thinks his historical examples of this sort defeat all theories of method and so 'anything goes'. Earlier (Chapter 5, Note 3) I took the view that Feyerabend's conclusion was either trivial or invalid, that in any case a decision-theoretic epistemological framework made good sense of Feyerabend's examples. I still think that Feyerabend has leaped to relativism from his critique of the traditional epistemic paradigm (where method is indeed restricted to universal logical structures) and that a good evolutionary realism provides the proper middle ground between these two extremes. But I should now like to express the view that Feyerabend's various studies amount to one or more of the following: (i) illustrations of the obvious truth that according to a decision-theoretic model the epistemically optimal course is a function of all the historical conditions under which the choice is being made (this is the point in Chapter 5, Note 3), (ii) illustrations of the deeper truth that rational methods are partial functions of the accepted context, including the accepted theories, in which they are being applied (cf. Section 8.3.3) and (iii) demonstrations of the importance of seeing that methodology does form an evolving control hierarchy, that the corresponding fallibilism must allow for methodological evolution which is not anticipated in advance. Each of these three features supports a version of 'anything goes' but none of them need carry any specific relativist or anti-rational overtones.

We are told by van Fraassen that the attempt to philosophically justify method is "a morass, a dead end, a false ideal, and a scandal" (1985, p.263). At all events the attempt to understand and improve methods, and to do so via theorizing them, is at the center of an intelligently evolving cognition (Sections 8.2.6, 8.3.1). The central method debates have always properly focused on the questions, "Why is method M rationally held to achieve, or to be likely to achieve, the goals of science?" and "Why is it rational to accept that method M is superior to method M' in these respects?" I have sought only to reinforce these as the central questions by emphasizing their conjectural theoretical character and the interaction between commitments to theory and acceptance of answers to them. This point of view will find application at Sections 8.3.4, 8.3.5, 8.3.10 and especially 8.4.2 and 8.4.3 below.

8.3.4 Naturalistic Meta-physics

Meta-physics is a higher order theory.

A recurring theme is the hierarchical character of the assumptions specifying a theory (e.g., Chapter 4, Section 4.4). Methodologies are also hierarchically structured and as one descends this hierarchy toward increasing specificity methods are tied ever closer to the embedded theoretical assumptions (Section 8.3.3). Deep in this hierarchy lies metaphysics, or that part of metaphysics relevant to science: systematic ontology.

In papers outside the scope of this book (Hooker 1972c, 1973c, 1974c, cf. Ch. 4 appendix III) I have argued for these propositions:

M1: There are (at best) two systematic ontologies that western science has explored in any detail, the corpuscles and fields of classical physics.

M2: These ontologies have very different mathematical representations.

M3: These ontologies support very different understandings of law, cause, continuity, identity and the like.

M4: The distinctive character of twentieth century physics is the confrontation of these two ontologies and the search for a third alternative.

It follows that methods will part company at some level as between the two ontologies, as will therefore the structure of confirmation (cf. Chapter 4, Section 4.5) and of reduction (cf. Hooker 1981c, Section 1). Not only do I still believe these theses, I find the evidence for them steadily accumulating. But here I want to focus simply on the nature and status of systematic ontology within naturalistic realism.

Having a systematic ontology usable for science is no simple matter. A usable ontology must have a mathematical representation such that (i) identity is well defined and (ii) supports a well defined concept of magnitude or quantity, in turn (iii) supporting well-defined concepts of probability and (iv) exhaustive or complete characterization. This is not the place to tell again the story of how the corpuscular and field ontologies fulfill these requirements (see Hooker 1973c, 1974c), but it is the place to notice that neither of them get it completely right, there are difficulties with boundaries and instantaneous completeness for corpuscles and difficulties with probability for fields.[88] Despite the increasing tempo of research into so-called pre–space-time theories, quantum sets and topologies, implicate order and the like no serious alternative ontology has yet emerged.[89] Philosopher's so-called alternative ontologies–event, process, stage, etc. ontologies–are a dime-adozen and often worth about as much cognitively, precisely because they do not provide any insightfully different way to fulfill the basic tasks. At this stage the flood of popular physics-and-Eastern-religion literature, though it has other values, is also cultural flotsam and jetsam on this basic cognitive crisis, and for the same reason.[90]

Thus it transpires that the specification of this part of a metaphysics is a thoroughly theoretical part of science and hence to be given a thoroughly naturalistic reading. It is just that for us humans, at present, exploring metaphysics requires millennia rather than weeks or lifetimes. Much of what else there is left to metaphysics reappears naturalistically in epistemology or cognitive theory (truth, reason, universals).

At the present time, however, it must be admitted that part of our understanding here escapes into mystery. Specifically here, we do not understand why it is so difficult to create a systematic ontology, why there should be (at best) only two and what kind of completeness they are striving to provide. Or, as the physics-and-Eastern-religion litera-ture highlights, we do not understand the possibilities for being selves in relation to a cosmos. More generally, we do not understand understanding, our core selves and our ability to grasp all these issues yet resolve them so poorly—see Chapter 7, Section 7.13. Perhaps all this simply reflects our species youthfulness in the cognitive enter-prise—we are certainly beginners—but perhaps, like the one small cloud hanging over the triumphant completeness of nineteenth cen-tury physics, it signals fundamental weaknesses in our scientific tradi-tion. The naturalist realist waits with open mind.

8.3.5 Unification, Explanation and Confirmation

Recently, considerable attention has been paid to the connections among realism, unification, confirmation and explanation. I see this matrix as central to the development of realist theory. However my examination here will be more in the nature of a review than exposi-tion of a fully developed account, partly because I do not have a full-blown account I am satisfied with and partly because of space con-straints.

The simplest form in which unification can arise is in the conjoining of theories. I have argued, against van Fraassen, that a realist ratio-nale is required to understand that practice (Chapter 6, Section 6.4.4). But conjunction is only the external logical reflection of the internal unification which is the real objective of the practice. In Chapter 6 I argued, in effect, that the virtues of the practice can only be understood when one focuses on the achieving of a unified systematic ontology, realisticly understood, for the theories in question. The whole of Chapter 4 is really an attempt to place a certain sort of interconnectedness or unity at the center of philosophy of science. But in that essay I did not develop positive theory very far, being content to emphasize the importance of unity (and, perhaps, being too preoccupied with the potential difficulties it raises). Nevertheless, we shall see that its concerns run through the major work to be discussed in this section. Chapter 4 remains the base from which the following considerations spring.

Perhaps the earliest clear-cut post-Newtonian ('modern') attempt to connect unification to explanation and confirmation was Whewell's idea of 'consilience of inductions'.[91] According to Whewell a consilience of inductions is obtained when it is found possible to unify several theories of apparently diverse phenomena by bringing them under a single theoretical framework. Newton's mechanics *vis-à-vis* various empirical subtheories (planets, tides, etc.) is a chief example. Consilient, i.e. unified, theories are claimed to be both more highly confirmable and more explanatorily powerful. A key component of consilience is evidently reduction in the number of independent features or kinds involved. In Whewell's case this seems to have been approached in a strongly epistemic way, a focus on the logico-semantic unity which characterizes theories as sentential structures, rather than focussing on the ontological structure of the world to which the realist gives priority. Recent interest in Whewellian unity has not, so far as I can see, really clarified what is involved.[92] Despite its offering many detailed insights, then, I shall leave this approach and examine other recent attempts to directly link unity and explanation.

The standard philosophic model of explanation in science, though by no means the only one, is that of deduction from statements of laws.[93] Two problems plagued the theory from the beginning, that of trivialization through partial self-explanation and that of ensuring that the premises are relatively more general than the conclusion. These two problems were initially conflated but the former can be resolved independently of the latter (see Hooker 1980c). Why then the concern with generality? I conjecture that it was because of a tacit intuitive commitment to

D: the premises (explananda) of an explanation should constitute an increase in depth of understanding over its conclusion (explanandum).

D is, I think, what motivates the rejection of symptoms as explaining causes, even when invariable association is present (so a deduction is possible), and like cases.[94] Thus the question arises: What is depth of understanding?

This is a much neglected question, but recently Friedman (1974) raised it anew and gave an interesting answer,

F: T_1 achieves an increase in depth of understanding over T_2 if it is able to explain (deductive model) what T_2 explains but with a reduced number of laws or independent parameters in laws.

Friedman uses this principle to give an elegant account of the way space-time theory has achieved increased depth of understanding over the years and he quite properly wants to relate this achievement to realist grounds for commitment to theory.

Friedman's proposal, as he himself makes clear, is an instance of a more general one,

U: An increase in depth of understanding occurs if and only if there is an increase in unity.

I believe this latter proposal to be along the right lines. U would collapse to F if F gave the only way to achieve unity. It doesn't. Clearly an alternative way to achieve an increase in unity is to achieve a more unified ontology. This may be roughly recast as aiming to achieve greater metaphysical rather than greater dynamical unity (cf. sec. 8.2.2). To cover both cases, I proposed (Hooker 1980c)

C: A theory T_1 provides an increase in depth of understanding over a theory T_2 if and only if the ontologies of T_1 and T_2 are each systematic and the ontology of T_2 can be reconstructed as derivative in that of T_1 but not vice versa.[95]

First some clarification. It is not easy to say what ought to be meant by a systematic ontology. I have tried elsewhere (1973c, 1974c) to characterize two such ontologies, the only two that have hitherto mattered for Western science (cf. sec. 8.3.4). Roughly, it means obeying a properly constructed set of metaphysical principles such that notions of identity, number and so on can be reconstructed. The ontology of a theory is given by some appropriate theory of ontological commitment, though I do not pursue that vexed question here. Finally, an entity e is derivative in an ontology O if e is identified with a relational complex of the fundamental entities in O. The paradigm is the derivative status of macroscopic objects in the atomic ontology, although their simulation by 'bumps' in field intensity in the plenum ontology would do equally well.[96] Note that to defend the 'only if' clause of C, T_2 must also be able to be a refined version of T_1, for increases in depth of understanding can undoubtedly be achieved *within* a systematic ontology, e.g., through successively precise and/or more complete theories, as well as through more Friedman-coherent theories. Though C again seems to me to be the right kind of criterion to apply, developing a precise account of the refinement of an ontology is a technically complicated matter and, having no simple formal criterion I am prepared to defend, I set the matter aside here.

Criterion C rules out the symptom-cause and related cases and it gives a plausible account of why we find them unsatisfactory. As an example, take the case of explaining the course of a disease, say measles, by reference to the symptoms, say hives on the skin. One can deduce, say, "A (a person) will display a marked decrease in temperature in 10 days" from "A now displays his first hives" and "All cases of hives are followed by 10 days of fever, after which the fever subsides." But this latter generality marks no increase in depth of understanding over the explanandum since it operates at the same 'surface' level of disease symptoms as does the explanandum; it offers no general ontology within which to reconstruct disease symptoms. By contrast, a cellular theory of disease processes offers deeper understanding because each symptom and disease stated can be reconstructed in the cellular ontology as special cases of more general processes, but not vice-versa. The same holds for barometer behaviors and storms *vis-à-vis* a fundamental physical model of the atmosphere as the basis of meteorology. More generally, C squares with the widespread intuition (see the survey by Brody 1972) that simply subsuming something under a generalization does not really explain it in the most interesting scientific sense (though we can surely allow degrees of scientific interest here).

It is now clear, incidentally, that simple increases in generality will not do as a criterion for refinement of an ontology because it will not capture either increase in precision or increase in Friedman-coherency of organization. And it is too vague to be said to capture the idea of ontological unification. On the other hand, an increase in the range of parameter values over which a theory is empirically adequate is logically independent of these three factors. This is plausibly what generality might be held to capture over and above precision, refinement and unification. But then this sort of generality doesn't contribute to depth of understanding and so is inadequate to the task for which it was originally invoked. Moreover, criterion C shows the degree to which it is justified to take increase in generality as the appropriate proxy criterion for increase in depth of understanding. On this view an increase in generality will be a necessary, though not sufficient, condition of increase of depth of understanding. For one cannot obtain a deeper, more unified systematic ontology without obtaining some general laws for it, and these laws must then be more general than those for the derivative ontology. (At any rate this must be so for justified ontic commitment, but I believe even for coherent formulation.[97]) In short, not just any increase in generality will do to deepen understanding.[98]

The criterion C does not prejudice understanding in favour of increasingly micro models, i.e., in favour of the part-whole relation. For the transition to a plenum ontology, e.g., may well require the recognition of all macro objects as approximate demarcations in a single universal field state with properties determined by the global whole.

C offers clear alternatives to Friedman's idea, within U. The transition to a more fundamental ontology in the sense described may well require an *increase* in the number of independent fundamental laws, yet still constitute an overwhelming gain in depth of understanding. Here the example of disease explanations will again suffice. The move from a phenomenological, symptoms level account of disease processes to cellular dynamics and subcellular biochemistry introduces an enormous increase in the number of independent parameters and in the complexity of the laws involved (at least for the present). Yet everyone accepts this move as representing a great advance in depth of understanding, essentially because of the relatively greater power of the new ontology to model the details of diverse bodily processes in a single general scheme, thereby vastly increasing explanatory power. Moreover, even within refinements of ontology Friedman's ideas don't address increases in precision and completeness.

This analysis connects my proposed notion of depth of understanding to a proposal of Kitcher's.[99] Roughly, Kitcher's idea is that the kind of unification important for explanation lies not in mere reduction in numbers of parameters or laws, but "in the repeated use of a small number of *types* of law which relate a large class of apparently diverse phenomena to a few fundamental magnitudes and properties" (Kitcher 1976, p.212). Notice that such unification is compatible even with increases in the number of individual parameters employed in detailed explanations and with an increase in the complexity of the laws. (E.g., explaining terrestrial fall using Newton's laws employs the mass of the earth as well as distance and time and Newton's laws are arguably more complex than is Galileo's law of free fall. Recall again phenomenological versus biochemical accounts of disease.) Plausibly, all passages to a deeper understanding have in fact also been examples of a Kitcher-style connection. But in the absence of satisfying characterizations of the complex hierarchical structures in science, in particular of Kitcher's intuitive notions of "stringent arguments" and "core arguments", not to mention the absence of a more general account of systematic ontologies than I have in my possession, I can draw no firm conclusions. (But note, e.g., that if precision and completeness also play roles in determining depth of understanding, Kitcher's criterion will not capture it, at least as it stands.)

I conclude that it is really U and C that are the right principles to apply to D and that, thus construed, D is the right constraint to apply to explanation. In short, the cognitive significance of explanation lies in its relation to the attempt to achieve understanding, i.e., to a unified conception of reality.

The unity-explanation connection provides Friedman with an argument for realism, by connecting on the one side with confirmation and on the other side with realism. First the connection to confirmation. The more highly unified an explanatory theory is the more likely confirmed it can be. To understand Friedman's line of argument while avoiding technicalities consider a unified theory, Newton's mechanics (NM), and a collection of mutually independent theories T_i, each of which is empirically equivalent to NM for some sub-domain (e.g. T_1 gives the pendulum law, T_2 projectile laws, T_3 is a theory of the tides, etc.). Then Friedman's idea is that NM is confirmed, not only by all the collections of phenomena that would together confirm the T_i, but also by the phenomena in their interstices (so to speak) which can be derived from NM but not from conjunctions of the T_i alone. (In the present case motion of Foucault pendula or of tides in an artificial satellite would be examples.) Though Friedman himself only offers a rudimentary account of confirmation to make his point, I believe something like this is correct. If so, unity becomes a basic goal of science, since high confirmation is surely a basic goal of science.[100]

Friedman argues then that realistically understood theories explain their phenomena with less independent sentences/laws/parameters than do their merely empirically equivalent counterparts. So, it is realistically understood theories which are the more highly unified. Hence science aims at realist theories. Friedman was only concerned with Friedman-coherence, but the examples he employs all rely for their point on intuitive appeal to the interconnected features of their theoretical ontologies. (Thus van der Waal's gas law comes from the perfect gas law via a corpuscular ontology, because of the geometry of the corpuscles.) In short Friedman is really appealing to the unifying power of a relevant systematic ontology, the same appeal made in C above. Thus do the achievement of deeper ontologies become a basic aim of science.

This analysis, with which I concur, is closely connected with Salmon's recent realist work on explanation (see 1980, 1984). Salmon identifies what he labels the epistemic approach to explanation as the attempt to understand explanation as a species of argument. The usual epistemic model is that explanation is inference, something is explained when it follows from what is believed or accepted.[101] Salmon argues that what is quite generally wrong with the epistemic approach to explanation, and the corresponding account of unification, is that one cannot in this way distinguish proposed explanations that provide an ontologically grounded underlying process for producing the phenomenon to be explained from those that merely enable a rational inference but have no such mechanism to offer. Salmon opts instead for what he labels the ontological model of explanation; here the basic idea is that a phenomenon is explained when its place is shown in the structured collection of cosmic regularities exhibited by the world. Sentential description of such facts follows secondarily. This seems to me to be the right priority for naturalist realism.

Based on this conception, Salmon argues that

> . . .the following attitudes toward scientific explanation, which arise naturally from the epistemic conception, are profoundly mistaken:
> 1. to insist, as Hempel did for many years, that an explanation of an occurrence must show that the fact-to-be-explained was to be expected;
> 2. to demand, with van Fraassen, that an explanation confer upon the fact-to-be-explained a favored position *vis-à-vis* various alternative eventualities;
> 3. to require that an explanation show why one outcome *rather than* an alternative occurred;
> 4. to reject the possibility that circumstances of a given type C can, on one occasion, explain the occurrence of an event of type E, and on another occasion explain the occurrence of an incompatible alternative outcome E'.
> . . . once the ontic conception is adopted, avoidance of the foregoing errors becomes easy and natural. (1984, pp.277–8)

I find Salmon's arguments concerning these claims to be persuasive and important to realism.

Salmon identifies the basic cosmic regularities as causal. Thus Salmon's primary idea of unity is causal unity. And Salmon argues that explanation theory has two components, a statistical-relevance model as basis and a causal mechanism theory selecting out the explaining statistical regularities. I am more dubious about the emphasis on cause, as opposed to mathematically expressible regularities at large, especially the acceptance of so-called probabilistic causality.[102] Moreover, the statistical basis theory has well-recognized problems (homogeneous reference classes, quantum probabilities, etc.)[103] But I have no clear alternative to offer in this difficult area, only this intuition: taken together these particular conceptions seem to deflect attention from ontological systematicity as the ground for unity, to which the ontological model of explanation itself points.

The sentiments concerning causality are in effect those also voiced by Glymour (1985). Glymour's own account of confirmation and explanation finds central roles for realism and unity. In outline Glymour's idea is roughly that evidence E confirms a hypothesis H relative to a theory T if (and only if?) the values of quantities contained in E, when supplied to T, suffice to construct an instance of H (and E could contain values for which this would not happen). The Tycho Brahe/Kepler planetary data (E) confirms the inverse square law of gravitation (H) because the values of the planetary orbit parameters conjoined with Newton's dynamical equations (T) leads to instances of the inverse square law.

A good theory on this account is one which has a high degree of this kind of internal interconnectedness or unity *vis-à-vis* its empirical domain(s). (We might add that good science would be science that exhibited this unity across theories.) The reason why this kind of unity is a virtue is that it increases the reliability of acceptance or confirmation. In a multiply interconnected theory the likelihood of a fake Glymour-confirmation (or disconfirmation) is small since there are always several quasi-independent ways to check any particular E-H relation. Glymour-unity, which Glymour connects to explanatoriness, is a virtue independent of empirical adequacy and is again as basic an aim of science as is increased confirmation.[104]

In effect, Glymour begins from the fact of what I called the globalness of theories (see Chapter 4) and tries to see this feature as a virtue. In Chapter 4 (Section 4.5) I emphasized that a confirmation relation between evidence E and theory T is in general a function of the theoretical (T) conception of the E-situation, and I then remarked that I did not have a confirmation theory that could meet this condition. Glymour's theory captures one part of that needed confirmation theory, namely where only a part H of T is confirmed. Already, as Glymour shows, this throws light on many important scientific situations. But it is as yet an open question whether it can treat the confirmation of sufficiently internally global or unified theories whose basic principles cannot so easily be split apart as can universal gravitation from Newtonian dynamics. It is equally open how to develop this approach into a comparative confirmation theory for deciding between competing global theories (cf. Forge 1984, Hesse 1980).

Forster 1984 understands unification to be typically achieved by theoretical identification across different domains. Newtonian theory unifies the domains of projectile and satellite dynamics by identifying projectile and satellite forces (with gravity) and so on. This is reminiscent of the Sneed/Suppes reconstruction of Newtonian theory as a class of applications (in effect empirical sub-theories) together with cross-application theoretical identities.[105] This approach to unification may be combined with Salmon's emphasis on underlying structure to arrive at a general realist principle: every statistically significant correlation requires an explanation which shows how the correlation is ontologically grounded in some appropriate common factor. Sometimes the common factor is a common cause (e.g., Reichenbach's two geysers that blow together), sometimes it takes the form of a theoretical identification (e.g., when balance-mass is identified with spring-mass).

Forster emphasizes the importance of the range over which the common factors operate successfully, their "cross-situational invariance". Thus the gravitational force is common to pendula, projectiles, satellites, the moon-earth, earth-sun, and Io-Jupiter systems, etc. It is Glymour who emphasizes cross-situational invariance or robustness, because basic theoretical magnitudes must be invariant under various determinations. In effect, then, Forster's principle is intended to add Glymour's insight to those of Friedman and Salmon.[106] According to Forster, science aims, and should aim, to maximize cross-situational invariance. Thus Forster postulates the search for unity, understood as cross-situational invariance, as a basic aim of science. Though he develops no explicit theory of explanation, etc., it is clear that he takes this aim to be fundamental because it yields explanatory power, testability and reliable confirmation.

Forster notes a number of methodological insights which this approach yields; here are two: (i) What distinguishes *ad hoc* from acceptable theory adjustments in response to conflicting data is the degree of cross-situational invariance the new parameters, properties, etc. can achieve. This seems the right kind of insight and does away, e.g., with any need for a core/protective belt distinction or for temporal relations in the definition of ad hocness, such as the Popperians invoke, cf. Chapter 7, Section 7.4.

(ii) Forster notes that the achievement of cross-situational invariance reduces theoretical complexity at one level (where the identifications are made and underlying causal structures described), but only to replace it by increased complexity at another level, namely by an increased variety of ways in which the theoretical quantity may be

measured. E.g., gravitational force may be measured via pendula
motions, satellite periods, spring extensions, etc. I think this is right
and note first that this pinpoints accurately where operationalism
goes wrong. It can give no rationale for this trade-off. Second, I
conclude that simplicity *per se* is no aim of science.[107] Simplicity itself
is ambiguous (Chapter 2, Note 20) and its alleged primacy a chimera
of the logico-syntactic approach to science. Rather simplicity is the
derivative application of relevant economy in the resources appropriate to pursuing other goals, in particular systematic ontologically-
grounded unity.

Without the primacy of cross-situational invariance one might as
well not take fundamental theoretical properties and entities seriously and instead "trade off their invariance to obtain greater simplicity in
the equations governing the phenomena" (Forster 1984, p.44). This
latter strategy would cost us explanatory and predictive power, although the empirical adequacy of the descriptions could be obtained
to any degree of accuracy by adding enough independent parameters
and adjusting them *post hoc* (see Note 105). It is exactly at this point
that Cartwright's realism diverges from that presented here. Cartwright (1983) wants to be a causal structure realist (cf. Salmon) but to
reject inference to the best explanation and read theoretical laws instrumentally. The main argument for this is that theoretical laws
achieve their generality at the expense of accuracy and need always to
be applied through a very complex process of adding correction factors and the like. (In fact, Cartwright develops in some detail illustrations of various components of the operation of my filter-transformer
in Chapter 4.) The realist response to Cartwright developed here is to
point to the sacrifice of the central role of unity beyond causal structure in understanding the cognitive structure of science and to insist
that there is no principled distinction between theoretical and phenomenological laws for the reason that unity plays the same kind of
role in the formation of each.[108]

Indeed, my major criticism of Forster is that he does not pay sufficient attention to the role of systematic ontology in developing cross-
situational invariances. The identification of spring-mass with balance-mass doesn't emerge magically out of the mere numbers or from
logical considerations alone, but because these quantities are located
in the order structures (Section 8.2.2) of the corpuscularian ontology.
These order structures place enormous constraints on cross-situational identifications (e.g., that forces are vectors while masses and times
are scalars). Moreover, cross-situational commonalities don't come

one at a time but in groups, what decides an initially acceptable set of identifications and common causes is whether they add up to a coherent or systematic ontology (Section 8.3.4). This is particularly true in theory succession; consider the replacement of corpuscular by field theory, or the arguments entering Einstein's discussion of the identity of inertial and gravitational mass. Cross-situational-invariance-unity needs to be enriched by being placed in the context of systematic ontologies and their order structures.

Finally, I note that in this way science is an extension of the cognitive strategies embodied in perception, since the key to perceptual structure is the extraction of cross-situationally invariant features of the stimulus array.[109] Commonsense realism is the theory level that emerges out of the pursuit of perceptual cross-situational invariance. (I should prefer to speak of sensory-motor invariances to include the fundamental role action plays, cf. Hooker 1978a and Chapter 7, Section 7.11.) And scientific realism emerges out of the systematic extension of that pursuit both on the perception side (through the instrumental extension of our senses) and (pace Forster) on the motor side (through the instrumental extension of our action).[110] Indeed, as Forster notes, the search for unity through invariance is itself cross-situationally invariant, since we find it at all levels of cognitive organization. Thus it becomes a fundamental feature of an evolutionary naturalist realist epistemology. This is, I think, the right picture and an important part of the realist conception I have been developing.[111]

This discussion has still not encompassed the full set of issues posed by the evolutionary naturalist realist conception of unity (Section 8.2.2). There has been no discussion of the unity of values in valuable truth (Section 8.3.2), though some interrelationship is required by talk of trade-offs at various points (see Section 8.4.4). There has been no discussion of the unity of methods or, except for the cross-situational invariance of cross-situational invariance, of the unity of theories and methods (cf. Section 8.3.3). And there has been no discussion of the unity of science with philosophical theory (cf. Section 8.2.3) in which these other doctrines would find their place. Space precludes further exposition. Nevertheless, it is evident that substantial insight has been gained into the role of unity and unification in realism. There is still considerable distance to go to produce even a unified philosophical theory of unity in this role.[112] This is particularly true for a philosophical account of unity which does justice to the distinctive concerns of the evolutionary naturalist realism I advocate, concerns which tend to be neglected because of a continu-

ing focus on epistemic/linguistic considerations rather than metaphy-
sical/ontological ones. But it is clear that, and it is becoming clearer
how, unity stands at the heart of the realist account.

8.3.6 Science as a Human Activity

*Science is a human, social, historical and ecological activity; its cognitive
power depends critically on its institutional features and its interrelations
with many other systems.*

That science is to be understood as a human activity rooted in the
capacities and circumstances of the species collectively and evolving
with them is the third of my revolutions (Chapter 2, Section 2.1). This
view is in opposition to the erstwhile dominant tradition under which
evidence and logic sufficed to characterize the rational content of
science. Under this conception science was primarily conceived to be
an abstract, timeless structure whose temporal and social dimensions
were largely incidental.[113] I have always stressed the opposing sci-
ence-as-activity (or process) theme (see e.g., Chapter 7 *passim*). Initially this was simply from opposition to received empiricist epistemology. Later it became based more broadly in the conviction that a far
richer theory of science could result from the broader base, and in
particular from providing a proper setting for the theory of epistemic
institutions (cf. Chapter 7, Section 7.8 and Section 8.3.9 below). Most
recently I have wanted to stress the methodological importance of the
historical dimension, in particular the qualitative transformation of
science over the past five hundred years (see Chapter 7, Sections 7.1
to 7.5). I now consider it essential to the historical understanding of
contemporary science and to the understanding of the complex interrelations between science and society to be able to locate science
within these broader human contexts. (On the essentialness of the
historical and social dimensions to the dynamics of science see further
Section 8.3.10 below.)

The secret to giving proper recognition to the historical and social
dimensions to science without running into social, cultural or political
relativisms is to combine it with the general realist framework of Part
8.2 and the specific epistemic paradigm advocated at Sections 8.3.2,
8.3.3. Over the past two decades there has been an explosion of
scientific interest in the history, sociology, economics and politics of
science.[114] Many of the exponents of these disciplines evidently believe that once one acknowledges science as a human activity all
prospects of epistemic objectivity vanish to be replaced by some system of historical, sociological or political explanation.[115] This I hold to

be a flat mistake. It is a mistake made easy by the widespread illusion that there is only one kind of objective account of science possible, that based solely on objective evidence and logic (i.e., based on the traditional epistemic paradigm, Section 8.3.2). Under this spell one assumes that there is no middle ground betwixt severe rationalist-objectivist accounts of this sort and non-epistemic accounts. The thrust of the naturalist realist position is that this assumption is false. Moreover, it is my view that the account offered here is not only an alternative but an alternative which both preserves the useful insights offered by non-epistemic studies of science and makes better sense of the character of science than do those theories.

The naturalist realist hews to a middle line in which goals beside truth and factors beside logical ones are intimately involved in the process of science, yet science is upheld as a rational cognitive enterprize. The consistency of this line is shown by applying the doctrine of norms as theories (see Section 8.2.7) and the decision theoretic paradigm for epistemology (Section 8.3.2). The fruitfulness of this line ultimately depends on developing an adequate evolutionary epistemology (Note 86). One insight which is immediate is the crucial role played by institutions, and by epistemic institutions in particular (Chapter 2, Section 2.9, Chapter 7, Section 7.8). Institutions are the species' nervous system, and the cognitive capacities of the species are strongly influenced by the designs of these institutions. The evidence suggests that the whole of mammalian neurological evolution has been pointing in this integrating direction and on examination science itself turns out to be a thoroughly species activity (Chapter 7, Section 7.11, Chapter 5, Section 5.5). It will only be through a theory of epistemic institutions that a critical theory of the history of science will become possible. For over the course of its history the institutional character of science has been transformed in ways critical to its cognitive characteristics. This transformation complements that of the methodological transformation over the same history. Without a dynamic critical theory of this sort there is no way to evaluate the complex of historically conditioned psycho-social relationships comprising the practice of contemporary science. And then the relativists and authoritarians win. Alas, critical theory of this sort is barely in its infancy. (On method see Section 8.3.3, on institutions see Section 8.3.9.)

Moreover, it is only in a unified, critical setting of this kind that method can be put into meaningful relation to policy. The prosecution of scientific methodology leads both to the evolution of scientific theories and methods, and to the transformation of the environment within which scientific methodology is prosecuted.[116] Science generates technologies, both physical and methodological, which transform both the internal environment for science itself and the external social environment within which it is conducted. (On technology see Section 8.3.10.) It is through institutions that policy and methodology are interrelated in detail, for epistemic institutions stand precisely in the intersection between the historical pursuit of epistemic goals and the pursuit of a wider range of human goals. Policy, quite generally, responds to changing conditions and knowledge by specifying institutional designs and collective behaviors designed to achieve human goals as currently understood, with currently available human technologies (physical and methodological). Thus policy is infected with epistemic considerations at every turn (Chapter 7, Section 7.2). A central part of the historical transformation which the development of science has wrought in its own environment is that policies—all policies in some substantial part at least—now unavoidably have a cognitive dimension and some policies (science policies and their cognates) are very strongly oriented around the nature of cognition. This is not to collapse policy theory into cognitive theory; narrowly epistemic goals are not the only ones. Nor is it, however, to collapse methodology into policy, this is precisely to lose sight of the social significance of cognition for the species. The challenge is to understand their interaction.

Moreover, this challenge is of an increasingly grave and urgent kind. Thanks to cognition we now live in a highly dynamic environment, one that is transforming life conditions in a very deep way (Chapter 7, Section 7.14). It is, I think, far from clear at the present time that we have not destabilized our environment in such a way as to undermine our own long-term fitness (cf. our capacity to handle nuclear and biological technologies). We can only gain an understanding of such crucial issues through an adequate and critical conception of the nature and dynamics of human cognition in its multifarious societal relations. The challenge before humans is to understand the total dynamics of the evolution of life on the planet and that of the 'noosphere' as a dynamic subsystem of it, responding to its condition but also driving it forward. To shrink back into isolationist dichotomies or to abandon the search for understanding by submerging the cognitive in the welter of complexity, is to abandon the enterprise of knowledge. Evolutionary naturalist realism attempts to accept the complexity and through it to search for a deeper unified understanding of ourselves.

8.3.7 The Scientific Community and Rationality

That science is fundamentally a species activity, a social, historical activity, an institutionalized activity, has been a constant theme.[117] Thus the scientific community, its character and functioning, is a central part of the theory of science. It is not *a priori* obvious that science is possible for humans; the conditions for its possibility has always been a central question for epistemology. Some of these conditions are bio-psychological and some are broadly social.

Empiricists, by contrast, adopted the view that were this latter so, scientific knowledge would be irremediably threatened by cultural, racial or national bias, infected by anthropomorphism or worse. Facts and logic alone were the allowable objective components to science. A prejudice to this effect has dogged philosophy of science ever since. (I have urged absorbing logic in a wider decision theoretic conception of rationality and embedding that theory in an epistemic institutional setting.) It is important to observe, however, that normative methodology never succeeded in expunging reference to the scientific community.

Even the severe empiricist presumed cooperation in the accumulation of pertinent facts and logical inferences, and the possibility of their effective and honest communication. The agnostic empiricist van Fraassen also does not escape an irreducible appeal to an "epistemic community" (1985, p.284). For Popper (the next nearest in metaphysical spirit to empiricism) theory of science is riddled with additional ineliminable appeal to human decisions outside of perceptual facts and logic: first and foremost to pursue truth, and pursue it rationally (critically), to accept basic (observational) statements, to test one theory rather than another and to employ one test rather than another (both equally severe), to lay an experiment-theory clash at the door of the experiment (or theory, auxiliary theories, *ceteris paribus* clause, etc.), to decide when sufficient and sufficiently severe testing of a successful theory has occurred in the circumstances.[118] Lakatos (1970b) only added to this list the decision to pursue or not an overarching research program, at both the individual and institutional levels. Moreover, Lakatos insisted that a normative methodology also be descriptively adequate to the best scientific episodes in the history of science (the empiricists and Popper tried to maintain the normative/ descriptive gulf—Note 118). This adds one more appeal to the scientific community, viz. for a choice of these episodes (cf. Greiner 1984).

The reliance of conservative methodologies on the decisions of the scientific community, just noted, only enlarges as one passes to less conservative approaches. Greiner (1984) has told the story elegantly, singling out the historian Kuhn, the sociologist Mannheim and the ex-Popperian Feyerabend. Kuhn (1962) argues that rationality is internal to scientific paradigms and hence that scientific change at bottom rests solely on an appeal to the scientific community's consensus. Mannheim (1936) preached the value/ideology dependence of science and argued that methodology is a self-confirming institutionalized norm. And Feyerabend said the same as Mannheim (only more recently and with the additional twist that an historically preferred methodology is denied).[119]

By this time one has sensed the cultural and/or ideological relativism inherent in this slide toward increasingly 'blind' or uncritical appeals to the community views of those paid salaries as scientists; one sees the dark at the end of the sociologists' and ideologist's tunnels. The 'strong' program in sociology of knowledge (belief) and neo (quasi)-Marxist radical critiques of science loom ahead. Reality becomes a wholly plastic, internal human construction moulded solely by socio-political forces. Against these consequences, empiricist conservatism seems increasingly appropriate and any appeal to the scientific community suspect. Yet, as argued above, such appeals cannot be avoided. Even the austere empiricists couldn't avoid it and naturalist realists will find the intrusion of human capacities, relations and decision making ubiquitous in their theory of science, as has already been plainly indicated.

Not all theorists have accepted the logic-or-relativism council of despair. Griener goes on to discuss Habermas (1968, 1970) who tries to grasp both the ideal of an objective science and the necessity of basic appeals to human judgement in the conduct of science. Habermas offers three aims for, or 'interests' driving, knowledge: technical control, practical sociality and emancipation. These goals are, I believe, either too weak (technical control) or too strong (emancipation), too artificially divided and too few.[120] However, the spread of goals is right, as is the essential role Habermas gives to institutions in their pursuit.[121]

But at bottom Habermas evidently hankers after a Kantian-style transcendental status for the role of rationality in cognitive life. There is supposed to be a rational transparency to mature, linguistically competent communities that protects them from deep error and ultimately makes the appeal to them as safe as that to logic.[122] Thus while much can be learned from Habermas, his project departs fundamentally from a naturalist perspective. Similar remarks hold for the transcendentalist program of Apel (1980a, b) and the quasi-transcendentalist (quasi-Popperian) Bhaskar (1975, 1979, see note 173).

Popper allows that even rational consensus may be mistaken, and the naturalist must agree; indeed, for the naturalist the community consensus may be mistaken even about the ways of being rational. The naturalist can see no logically guaranteed way to take the risk out of the human cognitive enterprise—and no reason why we must have a transcendental guarantee. But equally, the ways that our enterprises could fail have always to be understood in terms of straightforward mistakes or errors. For example, one should resist the temptation to read the possibility that we might drop ourselves in some culturally self-reinforcing dead end as evidence that there is no objective truth or that the notion of objective methods is incoherent. And readers of the relevant parts of my essays (cf. Chapter 5, Section 5.5) need to resist the interpretation that I am there flirting with philosophical relativism (cf. Note 53). Rather, in the face of our planetary circumstances—including our 'youthfulness' in the cognitive enterprise, our cultural weaknesses, etc.—I am simply trying to record real risks. I do not subscribe to the logic-or-relativism assumption. We can give a fundamental place to a wider human cognition and to institutions in the theory of science (here I join the rejection of logic-as-philosophy) and yet keep normative theory (here I reject relativism for fallibilism).

What a naturalist realism clearly requires however is that to do this intelligently we must expand the scope of fallible theory, hence philosophy of science will have to encompass (at least some parts of) a critical theory of rational cultures, namely those supporting values, institutions and social behaviors, which together support the cognitive enterprise.[123]

8.3.8 Objectivity

There are two dimensions to the natural language conception of objectivity and my main purpose here is to distinguish these and claim them both for realism. These differing dimensions are reflected in the following remarks: "That claim is objectively true or false", "He made an objective review of the evidence." The first dimension concerns the truth-value status of assertions; roughly, an assertion is objective if it is determinately either correspondence true or correspondence false (cf. Section 8.2.1). Alternatively, an assertion is objective if an account of its truth conditions is not logically or conceptually tied to epistemic conditions. The other dimension concerns the epistemic status of an assertion; roughly, an assertion is objective if it has emerged from a process designed to eliminate bias, error and ignorance. For convenience label these two dimensions of objectivity, objectivity$_1$ and objectivity$_2$. In the fullest sense then objective = objective$_1$ and objective$_2$.[124]

It is the essence of realism to insist that claims about the world are objective$_1$ (see Section 8.2.1 above). Objectivity$_1$ is central to realist cognitive theory and what I have to say about objectivity$_1$ is summed up in Section 8.3.1 (cf. Sections 8.4.1, 8.4.2).

The majority from all philosophies of science take the aim of methodology to be the delivery of objective$_2$ scientific theories. (Rationalist idealists, Peircean pragmatists, empiricists, internal realists etc. all join in pursuing objectivity$_2$ even while rejecting objectivity$_1$.) I agree. Indeed, from an evolutionary perspective the second primary epistemic task for an intelligent organism is to develop just such a method, precisely because evolutionary organisms initially do not understand their own nature and capacities since they have inherited these rather than designed them. (The first primary epistemic task is to understand the world, but of course accomplishing this task is interdependent with accomplishing the other.) So I take both dimensions to objectivity to be central to evolutionary naturalist realism.

It is easy (but fatal) to confuse objectivity$_1$ and objectivity$_2$. For example, objectivity is often equated with intersubjectivity, but while this states one plausible component of objectivity$_2$, it contradicts objectivity$_1$.[125] It is also easy (or anyway currently fashionable) to slide from denial of objectivity$_2$ to denial of objectivity$_1$. One might, for example, try to argue that science is a social construction governed by sociological laws, so science cannot be objective$_2$, so scientific theories are not objective$_1$. As Section 8.3.3 makes clear, I hold even the first of these inferences to be invalid, but the second inference is certainly invalid. It could only be rescued by inserting a premise which connected failure of objectivity$_2$ to failure of objectivity$_1$. As a realist I would reject this premise. The only extant versions are empiricist-style verifiability doctrines (Chapter 2, Section 2.4). Nonetheless these claims are fashionable again, hidden (once more) as semantic proposals (Section 8.4.2).

It is equally easy to conflate objectivity$_2$ and intersubjectivity. N.R. Campbell (1957), following Peirce, says "The subject matter of science consists of those judgements for which universal assent can be obtained." (p.22) In this definition, which captures the historical attitude to which we are heir, the modal can is a very complex one indeed. (Campbell anticipates many of the complexities I state.) Objectivity$_2$ is never complete but comes in grades. (Objectivity$_1$, I suppose, is an all-

or-none affair.) We can never completely eliminate bias. Individual biases can be reduced through the wise choice of institutionalized interrelations but not, one suspects, wholly eliminated even in relatively impersonal domains such as physics. Beyond individual bias there is cultural bias and species anthropocentrism. These biases can be reduced through criticism (cf. Section 8.2.4 above) but our species is young and weak in these areas as yet. Similarly we can never eliminate error whilst ever our knowledge is incomplete, since we are learning about our "error profile" as we go. Similar considerations apply to ignorance. Over time we learn to improve our objectivity$_2$ along with the rest of our knowledge, but it always remains objectivity$_2$ at some level. From which it follows that objectivity$_2$ is not to be identified with, or even entailed by, intersubjective agreement, contrary to popular supposition. We critically theorize our cognitive capacities, and objectivity$_2$ belongs to that critical theory; we don't have to collapse objectivity$_2$ into what we happen to be able to do. Conversely, objectivity$_2$ does not entail or otherwise require intersubjective agreement. We already exempt the incompetent (mentally or emotionally) and the neural-injured from the relevant epistemic community, and this exclusion may widen (Chapter 7, Section 7.4). Intersubjective agreement remains an important evidential component in most cases, but only when it is theoretically justified.

In Chapter 7 I raised the question whether the human species might diverge in its epistemic capacities, either through external selection pressure or deliberate neuro-biological intervention (Chapter 7, Sections 7.1, 7.4). In this event, intersubjective agreement would not be possible beyond some level yet science need not be either impossible or irrational. It is true, *ceteris paribus*, that the fewer humans involved the higher the risk of error, but this might be compensated for by their greater epistemic capacities. We run the same general trade-off every time we select an expert panel to make a decision. (More importantly, we are slowly gaining experience of how to interrelate expert groups and lay groups so as to reduce risks while retaining the benefits of expert knowledge, i.e., of how to elaborate this part of a theory of epistemic institutions.)

There are several contrary views on the best way to achieve objectivity$_2$. Empiricists, for example, thought that it would be through sticking to elementary observations that objective$_2$ data was obtained. An evolutionary perspective offers little support to that idea. Popper and many others have thought that it was achieved by following some preferred formal method. But the methods offered, while also a helpful contribution, all either turned out to be too vague (settled too little of the complex detail of real scientific decisions) or to be too rigid (admit no methodological innovation).

According to evolutionary naturalist realism objectivity2 resides jointly in the attitudinal structure of scientists and the institutional structure of science (institutions broadly conceived). Specifically, objectivity2 arises from scientists taking an open, critical, communicative approach ("getting their egos out of the way") combined with the various social processes of criticism through which scientific claims are put before they are accepted. This view is thoroughly Popperian in spirit. It repeats Popper's insistence that the scientific life involves an ethical commitment, namely to pursue truth, communication and criticism as the essence of scientific rationality. But the concept of criticism is generalized by taking Popper's formal notion of criticism and inserting it into the methodologically complex world of institutionalized research activities.[126] This is no more than is required by the shift to a decision-theoretic epistemology (Section 8.3.2).

An important point should be made: according to my doctrine, objectivity2 does not require a fact/value or cognate dichotomy. The contrary assumption is widespread, so I pick it out here to reject. Humans make judgements and take risks. Judgement is a more basic category than fact or value; each sort of judgement involves the other factor. Risk too involves both factual and evaluative factors and applies to both (Chapter 7, Section 7.10). If objectivity2 at some level requires judgements which are unbiased, error-free and complete at that level then achieving objectivity2 can be understood in terms of judgements and their associated risks, and does not require a hard fact/value distinction.

This point of view has important ramifications. One consequence is that epistemology has in part an ethical foundation, a consequence Feyerabend drew very clearly early on (see 1961, 1974, 1978 and Section 8.2.6 above). A second consequence is that science is an essentially social activity, so that science policy and science methodology are inextricably connected (see Chapter 7, Section 7.9, Sections 8.3.6, 8.3.10). A third consequence is that bias must be distinguished from the involvement of values (evaluative judgements) *per se.* This is a large topic; here I make only three brief remarks: (i) little progress will be made here if one remains within the prejudicial Western heritage (see Chapter 7, Sections 7.6, 7.11), (ii) bias will have to be theorized within an adequate anthropology to provide a naturalist realist setting for stating the problem and (iii) the distinction can only be drawn through the social practice realized in a truly participatory community (cf. Albury 1983). Hence a fourth consequence, and arguably the chief one, is that the accomplishment of our basic epistemic tasks probably hinges most crucially on our achieving adequate designs for epistemic institutions. So let us turn forthwith to that topic.

8.3.9 Epistemic Institutions

Epistemic institutions are those institutionalized social arrangements for pursuing the spectrum of epistemic goals. But what *is* the design theory for efficient epistemic institutions? From a biological point of view we can think of scientific institutions as playing crucial roles in the regulatory hierarchy of science and hence as intrinsic to the specification of scientific methods and the dynamics of scientific change. Good designs are presumably those that deploy the general characteristics of humans effectively to reinforce commitment to the full regulatory hierarchy of scientific methods. What this comes to in practice is still largely shrouded in ignorance (plus prejudice, etc.).

Design of epistemic institutions, in my opinion crucial to the future of cognition (and perhaps the species in general), has been largely ignored by philosophers. This is paradoxical at first blush because science is now, overwhelmingly, an institutionalized activity. Moreover, the history of science is replete with examples in which the course of science has been strongly affected by its institutional relationships to its larger social environment and it is today seriously distorted by those relationships.[127] The paradox is dispelled with the realization that the subject does not exist for one following empiricist dichotomies (Chapter 1; Chapter 7, Section 7.4).

I have argued (Chapter 7, Section 7.8) that epistemic institutions are central to our conception of intelligence, even more so than are institutions in general to our capacities in general. Epistemic institutional relations are extremely complex (Chapter 5, Section 5.4, Section 8.3.7 above). There are many kinds of agreement and disagreement possible and desirable within a scientific discipline, theoretical domain or cognate grouping, and there are many levels of agreement and disagreement possible concerning that discipline (domain, etc.). One thing stands out: unlike most other institutions, it is characteristic of epistemic institutions to systematically raise disagreement as well as to reach agreement. This is the institutionalized expression of the critical function. Indeed, the quality of objectivity$_2$ achieved is a function of just how the conflict and consensus generation pattern is designed (Section 8.3.7).

Note that the historical transformation of science has led to two opposing trends in epistemic institutions. On the one hand there is the narrowing of the relevant epistemic community in highly technical consensus and disensus formation as the epistemic requirements for participation become more stringent. This process may even come to be reflected neurally as well as socially (cf. Section 8.3.6). On the other hand there is the demand to widen the participating community because of the widespread effects of science/technology on life (Chapter 7 *passim*). Albury 1983, among many, has argued that unavoidable institutional limitations (tendency to bureaucratic self-interest, etc.) require including the whole of the affected community in achieving consensus, and this means everyone. And not only for applied development, but in many cases of research as well. I believe this is right in principle and have argued it myself in the case of energy research and development and like issues (see 1977b, 1979a, 1980a, b, 1980/1, 1983). But it should be noted that there can be widely different ways and degrees of involvement, from expert groups through various structurings of interest groups to mass voting; it will be the institutionalized deployment of this spectrum which will determine the quality of life in these respects. Pursuit of the wider issues would lead into the vast field of science policy.[128]

For all their critical importance to us, we presently understand very little about the design of epistemic institutions. While there is a growing body of literature on the design of specialized institutions to pursue economic and political goals, there is virtually no movement to apply it to the pursuit of epistemic goals.[129] How do the paradoxes of rationality and voting translate across and what of the significance of 'second best' theorems for consensual theory choice? (Section 8.3.2) What roles might Delphi and cross-impact matrix procedures have for understanding and generating structures for research programs?[130] There is a small literature on economic models of research,[131] and a rapidly growing literature on science/technology policy[132] and sociological structures of science/technology,[133] all of which bears on the institutional design of science/technology (some of it quite explicitly— e.g., Merton 1972) but again there is evidently little movement to apply this material to the construction of epistemic institutional design.

Mitroff has followed up Churchman's initial theory of four fundamental kinds of systematic enquiry or enquiring systems.[134] These can usefully be thought of as four methodological abstractions from four designs for epistemic institutions. From my perspective these would be better paraphrased in terms of variant strategies for theoretical and experimental development with attendant benefit-cost-risk profiles and set explicitly in a full-blown institutional framework, but the very diversity uncovered underlines the importance of studying institutionalized epistemic strategies. Tornebohm has devoted his concluding research years to the structure of what he calls enquiring systems, which are also something like methodological abstractions of epistemic institutions.[135] Some useful structural insights emerge, but I find the assumptions too empiricist.[136] Finally, Naor, in unpublished work, has drawn attention to the potential relevance of Beer's studies of decision making strategies and institutional structure for the study of epistemic institutions.[137] Beyond this (and whatever research falls beyond my ken at present) the urgent and critical task of developing a theory of epistemic institutions as part of a normative sociology(/politics) of cognition, lies ahead.

8.3.10 Dynamics of Science

My objective here is to briefly integrate three related themes of the essays so as to reinforce the importance of an adequately complex systems dynamic theory of science from within which to reconstruct a philosophy.

The *first* theme is the role of technology *vis-à-vis* science. Technologies have been much studied, but mostly separately from science as value-laden social devices, their impacts on science an 'external' one (see empiricist pure/applied dichotomy). I have tried instead to emphasize also the intrinsic importance of technology to science, (i) as extender of information base (electron microscopes, etc.), (ii) in theory testing methodology (e.g., automated data accumulation), (iii) as generator of new concepts (computer models of cognition, etc.—cf. Chapter 7, Note 1), (iv) in institutionalization of science (including communication, memory storage and resource allocation). Conversely there is the direct impact of science on technology in technological design, evaluation and re-design learning. All told this is a complex and now highly dynamic two-way interaction. Note that these interactions are distinguished within a much stronger one which loops through the external societal environment of science; here science-driven technology transforms that environment which in turn feeds indirectly back into the development of science. This happens both through the cultural and socio-economic support (or lack of support) for science, for example in educational curricula, research grants, cultural acceptance of scientific criticism and so on, and through the restructuring of the environment which science itself studies for its development (for example destruction of traditional cultures narrows the evidential base for anthropology, space probes increase the evidential base for geophysics and astrophysics).

It would unfortunately take us too far afield in the present context to attempt to develop a theory of the nature and roles of technology *vis-à-vis* cognition in an evolutionary naturalist realist context, but the foregoing taxonomy and the following remark may give some general idea of the direction which I am exploring. I think of technology as a systematic procedure or process which amplifies some human capacity (not necessarily an epistemic one). Thus machine guns amplify projectile launching capacity and telephones long distance communication capacity. We can then develop a conception of epistemic technologies within technologies at large and of the role they play in the dynamics of science. Epistemic technologies are systematic procedures or processes which amplify human epistemic capacities. Computing is an epistemic technology and computers are the physical realization of that technology. Telephones, on the other hand, are the physical realization of a communications technology which is primarily social but has important epistemic applications within institutionalized science. The use of lathes is a manual technology which has largely served to enhance non-epistemic capacities but which also plays important roles within the construction of epistemic instrumentation. From this point of view the institutionalization of science represents the development of a social epistemic technology used to enhance group epistemic capacity and methods become belief testing/ belief creating epistemic technologies (cf. Chapter 7, Note 2). The dynamics of science can then be posed as a complex process by which ideas (beliefs and values) plus technologies generate improved ideas and improved technologies.

Recently some writers have begun to pay closer attention to the roles of technology. Hacking (1982a, 1983, 1985) on the role of technological manipulability in epistemic evaluation and Heelan (1982, 1983) on readable technologies and the hermeneutics of science are two of the works I found a valuable corrective to past neglect. (But both, in my opinion, place too much emphasis on the importance of the technological role in the structuring of science, each in their own very different ways, playing down too far the contribution of theoretical organization and explanatory understanding.)

The *second* theme is the complexity of the current scientific dynamic and specifically the crucial historical dimension which this induces. Internally to science: theory, instrumentation, methodology, institutionalization and meta-methodology all now interact in a highly dynamic manner. Externally, the interactions between science and society now go via technology (as above), science policy and cultural context. The net effect is a highly dynamic system.

A 'crystallisation' is now taking place in human life; our lives are shifting from organization around biological activity and ancient imperatives, to organization around theoretical knowledge. This is a massive and unique shift in the history of life on the planet, one marked by immense opportunities and equally immense dangers (cf. Chapter 7, Section 7.14).

And specifically, the dynamics of the science/technology system give that system a uniquely historical dimension. Here is the argument: The possibilities for the science system at one period are functions of the entire science-society state of the preceding period. This permits historical processes of reinforcement. One consequence is that initially minor cognitive decisions or unanticipated opportunistic decisions of any sort can ramify into major features of the system, in turn constraining the next round of cognitive choices. The point will be recognized as a thoroughly evolutionary one: the adaptations of a particular period are built out of the structures to hand, opportunistic and neutral developments may later ramify into major constraints on the possibilities. E.g., what theoretical alternatives are there to cope with a recalcitrant experiment? That depends on the range of mathematical structures and theoretical paradigms available. At what severity level can a current theory be tested? That depends on available and foreseeable instrumentation and economic resources. And so on.[138]

Science then is inextricably historical (cf. Chapter 5). This thesis is the dual of the thesis that history of science is the data domain for theory of science at all levels (Section 8.2.7). It is also of a piece with the thesis that the theory of science is inextricably connected to the cognitive characteristics of individuals and of epistemic institutions (Sections 8.3.6 to 8.3.9). But from these theses I do not draw relativist conclusions, for there are still the normative roles of the realist R theses in cognitive theory. Science is as inextricably historical as is evolution, which means that to understand science we should place as much or more epistemic emphasis on improvement of methodology and meta-methodology (cognitive structure generally) as upon our current theoretical and experimental adaptations (cf. Section 8.2.8).

It also means that there is intrinsically no way to separate historical science into an autonomous 'internal' rational component and an external set of cognitively a-rational or irrational forces and constraints, as the empiricists and Popperians would like to do. Factors external to a given stage of science (e.g., economic resource constraints) also have their ramifying effects downstream, reinforcing particular cognitive trends and curtailing others. Of course one often

318

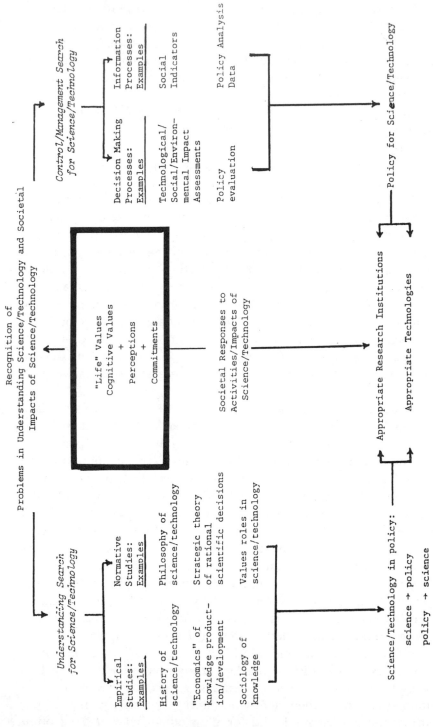

Figure 8.1

focuses negatively on the negative side of this process, e.g., on un-warranted political interference, and properly so. But the positive side should not be forgotten, but for the technological/economic revolution the centuries of science have now made possible, most current science would not be possible at all. What is now crucially required is a good meta-methodological theory which tells us how (i) to critically identify and counteract improper 'external' forces and constraints, (ii) be cognitively efficient within the neutral constraints and (iii) optimize the positive feedback with the positive forces. Such a theory will include design of epistemic institutions as a central component (Section 8.3.9). Philosophers and socio-economists of science have scarcely begun to tackle these issues.

We do now have, however, a burgeoning response to the problems of the complex dynamics of science. In an earlier Canadian national study of current research needs at the science-society interface (Hooker/Schrecker 1980/1) I summarized the situation in Figure 8.1.[139] Here I want to underline the complementarity (classical sense?!) of the understanding and management searches. It is part of the new dynamics of science that these two activities now also interact—the future of science will be a human artifact.

This last truth leads to the *third* theme to be integrated here: methodology and policy are deeply interrelated (Chapter 7, Section 7.9). With human life crystallised around cognition, all public policies, even the most allegedly distant from science, have their cognitive impacts and rely on cognitive methods and products. They must therefore be properly viewed as partly cognitive policies (Section 8.3.6 above). Conversely every methodology presupposes features of institutionalized division of labour, communication, resource allocation, etc., however distant it may appear from such matters, and so has its policy implications. The theoretical challenge is to work out a conception of policy adequate to these newly intensified historical circumstances—a complement to the meta-methodological theory called for two paragraphs back. Good policies will then result in the designs of technologies and institutionalized science-society relations which are *appropriate*, as Figure 8.1 indicates. Appropriateness here refers to the meeting of the full structured spectrum of our best values as we currently best understand them.

Insight into these problems in the historical dynamics of our species strikes me as far more important than (though interconnected with) philosophical disputes about fragments of realist and idealist theses. Thus it is only now that I turn briefly to review some of these latter disputes.

8.3.11 *Philosophy: Tension and Theory*

Theories are always assumed definite; the best of them present specific, unambiguous sets of claims each of which has an essentially unique intended realization. This assumption holds at all levels of theorizing, the philosophic as well as the scientific. I have presented theorising in this way nearly everywhere throughout the essays. Yet at the very heart of human cognizing and practical living I believe I see what I will call *tensions*. A tension is a multi-polar alignment in which one is pulled toward (or repelled from) the poles simultaneously. It is of the essence of a tension that there is no preferred resolution within the alignment which removes the tension. Most tensions are bi-polar. An important life example is the tension between individuality and belonging; one desires both, yet individuality emphasizes difference while group belonging requires sameness.

Tensions may be *simple,* meaning that there is no alternative but to choose some compromise position that is judged best at the time. Within the rational voting paradigm assumptions, e.g., the tri-polar tension among rationality, decisiveness and equality is simple (see e.g., Blair/Pollak 1983, cf. Brams 1976). Tensions may also be *complex,* meaning that one may transcend the polarity itself and thereby dissolve the tension. E.g., by shifting what is shared in a community away from sheer conformity toward higher-order values (respect for individual excellence, etc.) the tension between individuality and belonging can be progressively dissolved (but never eliminated). Similarly, by redefining the voting paradigm (perhaps to include more direct decentralized participation or multiply-focused review and assessment of decisions), the tri-polar voting tension can be successively ameliorated.

The essence of a tension is that there is no simple resolution available, one must remain sensitive to all poles and seek to hold them in a wise balance even while seeking ways to transcend them. Evolutionary naturalist realism shares in the tensions of all philosophy and I am increasingly convinced that it is essential to its statement and defense to bring this out clearly.

The normative and descriptive roles of theory (philosophic or scientific) are in tension; each role excludes the other in particular applications, yet both roles need to be preserved overall. So far as I can see the tension is simple. There is no resolving this tension once-for-all, or eliminating it in some way; it is always present, only momentarily and tentatively resolved in particular applications. Rather, it is the essence of higher order rationality structures to make intelligent decisions concerning which role best dominates in any given circumstance (criticize the theory or criticize the evidence?).

There is a tension between systematic fallibilism and objective truth; we aim at truth yet each attempt to grasp it is fallible. We are aware of the inadequacies of our grasp and there is no God's Eye perspective from which to resolve whether we have attained it (cf. Section 8.4.2E). Fallibilism is desirable both because it is evidently true (!) and because it undercuts dogmatism and authoritarianism. Truth is fundamentally desirable, it is the orienting axis of all cognition.[140] Alternatively, the tension might be expressed as between certainty and scepticism.[141] Philosophers are constantly trying to force an ultimate resolution of these tensions. The rationalist and empiricist insist we grasp truth. The sceptic and conventionalist insist there is no meaningful tension. Putnam and the other pragmatist internal realists, Dummett and the other neo-empiricists, all want to bring truth within some kind of assured human grasp. Van Fraassen counsels removing the tension by resorting to agnosticism.

Naturalist realism retains the tensions, rejecting attempts to remove them. Realist truth and systematic fallibilism are mutually necessary to one another; without a notion of truth the open-ended evolution of the theory hierarchy could not be theorized. Without fallibilism the roles for truth would be emasculated. Truth as theorized in cognitive theory transcends evidence and belief, yet cognitive theory is fallible. For every acceptance of theory for belief (the certainty pole) there is an encompassing meta-context in which a more sceptical critique is appropriate. (The normative transcends the descriptive evidence, yet is answerable to it.)

The depth and ubiquity of tensions in philosophy is indicated in Unger's antinomies (Unger 1975), summarized in Figure 7.2. I can do no better here than recommend their close study. (Unger's tensions are directly related to that between form and content discussed briefly at Section 8.4.3.3.) And Unger also makes it clear how tensions characterize the whole structure of human life. Again I can do no better than direct attention to Figure 7.6 and text (cf. e.g. Schumacher's divergent versus convergent problems, Schumacher 1977, mentioned there). These two sets of tensions are related through the tension between being actor and being spectator, a tension to which Bohr gave prominence in the foundations of physics (cf. Hooker 1972c and Chapter 7, Section 7.13).

Both the cognitive and the moral/spiritual life grow out of these tensions, I believe, and through the unending attempt to balance and transcend them. They can never be removed without loss, yet they are a constant source of discomfort. This is how I closed Chapter 7 and I shall close this essay in the same spirit.

8.4 REALISM DEFENDED:
CONTEMPORARY TOKENS OF PERENNIAL DISPUTES

8.4.1. Explanatory Realism and Unity

Evolutionary naturalist realism gives to all philosophic theory a conjectural status. In this sense the entire doctrine is part of a grand inference to the best explanation. What then should this explanation explain? The whole of the human cognitive enterprise—in a unified way.

Recently a variety of narrower explanatory theses have been urged on realism, namely that it should explain the explanatory/predictive success of science and the success of realist methods in science. [142] These, and other claims with which they are associated, do not always fare well under criticism (see e.g., Chapter 6, Section 6.6 and Laudan 1981a, b, 1984a, b). Some clarification is thus called for.

A useful place to begin is Devitt's (1984) austere picture of the explanatory value of realist doctrines. First some preliminary points. Devitt's considerations are restricted to just the doctrines R_1 and R_3 of Section 8.2.1 (or perhaps to $R_1 \cdot R_2$ and $R_3 \cdot R_4$). Within this constraint Devitt asks what kind of success would require R_1 and R_3 for their explanation. (That is, Devitt is only interested in those explanations for which appeal to either R_1 or R_3 is necessary; these are a subset of those explanations for which appeal to these theses, perhaps together with other principles, might prove sufficient.) He himself distinguishes four kinds of success as potentially relevant: individual success (surviving, living well, reproducing), species success (as for individual success, but on a species level), theoretical success (predicting and explaining), theoretical progress (improving the level of theoretical success). In fact Devitt's arguments introduce a fifth kind of success, success in linguistic communication. With these categories in hand, Devitt's arguments may be summed up in the following matrix:

Success (Devitt)

	Individual	Species	Theory	Progress	Communication
R_1	No	No	Yes	No	No
R_3	No	No	No	No	Yes

According to Devitt the only explanatory success R_1 enjoys is that of explaining why scientific theories are explanatorily and predictively successful. R_1 explains why theories that postulate unobserved and unobservable entities are successful, i.e. why the empirical data are as if there were X's, by stating that X's exist (1984, Section 7.2).[143] Moreover the anti-realist has no competing explanation for that success. And Devitt does not believe that appeal to correspondence truth is necessary anywhere except in understanding the possibility of human communication.[144] Even here it emerges only from the requirement of reflexive consistency.

In keeping with my opening remarks, I believe that realism ought to be able to do better than this. I suggest that Devitt has hamstrung his analysis (i) by not seeing R_1 and R_2 as components of a unified explanatory analysis (Devitt's 'logical atomism'—see Note 143) and/or by restricting himself to necessity for explanation rather than including cases where the R doctrines provide the best explanation, (ii) by accepting that the concept of truth is confined to semantic theory (Devitt's residual "linguistic turn") and (iii) by not including methodology and methodological progress in the analysis.[145] *A propos* these latter categories, we may ask (respectively) why realist methods are successful and why methodological progress is possible. Setting aside Devitt's constraints, the matrix which I would defend is this:

Success

	Individ-ual/Species	Theory	Theory Progress & "up"	Method Progress	Method	Communi-cation
Realism	Yes	Yes	Yes	Yes	Yes	Yes

Devitt's argument for the "yes" under the theory heading is good. (I tentatively agree with Devitt that semantic R doctrines are not necessary to explain that success.) Van Fraassen (1980) tries to deflect this explanation by offering an evolutionary explanation (the cheek!) in an anti-realist vein: theories are born into a competitive intellectual world, those that didn't succeed in latching on to empirical regularities didn't survive, no further explanation is required. The general reply is that this is not enough because we want an underlying explanation of the detailed processes involved, but this explanation will refer to how the world is and why realist theories of certain sorts manage to be competitively successful in such a world. This kind of reply is better illustrated by the parallel argument under Individual/Species success below, and anyway the reply shifts this argument to that of explaining method. So first I turn to explaining methodological success.

The affirmative under the method heading derives from Boyd's

arguments that at least some central scientific methods require realism to explain their success (Boyd 1980, 1983, 1984, 1985). This explanation involves appeal to at least the first four R doctrines. Boyd has
argued the case at length and no brief summary does his articles
justice. Rather I return to theory conjunction (see Chapter 6, Section
6.4.3) for a simple schematic example. For this purpose I assume the
success of this methodology uncontroversial.[146] When scientists conjoin two theories it is often necessary to correct one or both of them.
How do they go about this? The primary focus is on achieving a
unified underlying theoretical ontology and structure of dynamical
processes. Then they consider what corrections this theoretical picture may require in the original two theories.[147] But one cannot explain the success of this methodology without appeal to the reality of
the theoretical world. (See also the weaknesses of van Fraassen's reply
to this conjunction argument, Chapter 6, Section 6.5.3.) Beyond this I
believe many methods have realism as central to a best explanation of
their success, but I do not press this here.

Van Fraassen (1985, Section 1.3) has recently attacked Boyd's approach as follows: *Argument 1*. The methods chosen and argued to be
successful in science might not in fact have contributed to that success
at all. Instead the success itself might be illusory (say a misreading of
the history concerned), or there might have been independent general reasons for expecting success or there might have been special
features of the situation which luckily brought success where none
should have been expected. In principle, none of these alternatives
can be ruled out by the realist without circularity. *Argument 2:*
". . . should the [Boyd's] enterprise succeed . . . it still can be no
more than the best available explanation . . . Hence we have a dilemma: either this pattern of inference is licensed by the methodology. . .
or it is not. In the first case, part of the justified methodology was
assumed in the justification. In the second, the person taking this step
must reflect that his inference is neither part of what he takes to be the
best description of scientific method nor incontrovertible among philosophers." (1985, p. 259)

I cannot find any force in these objections. The first argument
simply announces that the explanation is fallible. True, so is everything else (Section 8.2.6). The second argument, first case, hints at
circularity. But there is no circularity, just internal coherence. True,
this doesn't guarantee correctness, but then the cognitive enterprise is
risky. What we should be doing is asking how we can cross-check this
meta-methodological theory, expand the evidence base and invent
better meta-methodological controls on inference to the best explana-

tion. Instead, van Fraassen contradicts his own agnosticism and here tempts us to accept the old empiricist fake dichotomy: epistemic certainty or intellectual rejection.[148]

Fine (1984) has an objection to this last reply: the realist cannot simply appeal to internal self-consistency in the use of best-explanation inference in both science and philosophy and let it go at that; rather, more stringent conditions of acceptability must be met. This argument is of some importance and I commence Section 8.4.4 with it. The short answer is this: Fine's objection has point, but not of a kind that defeats realist explanation.

The affirmative for individuals and species success goes indirectly via a theory of cognition and does not I think strictly require appeal to realism, rather realism furnishes an essential part of the best explanation currently available. Devitt (1984, p. 110) rejects the argument that we need realism to explain why humans have developed successful theories and I have just agreed. But he concedes to van Fraassen the appropriateness of a Darwinist explanation which apparently removes appeal to realism altogether: if humans hadn't developed successful theories they wouldn't be here and there would be no issue.[149]

I am not willing to concede that this is the end of the matter. Of course, the Darwinist reply states what is true (assume). But we still need to understand why the situation works in the way it does.[150] Surely the general understanding we require here goes something like this: for any species of creature the environment has a complex structure, much of it unobservable; fitness to that environment can depend strongly on the ability to develop accurate internal maps of it; creatures whose fitness is map-dependent that are able to develop maps which include the unobservable parts sufficiently accurately for effective anticipation thereby increase their fitness . . .; the specific hierarchy of processes through which cognitive maps are developed are . . .; humans are a species inheriting a line of development exploiting these specific kinds of cognitive ability . . . By the time we unpack this kind of explanation we have the full cognitive theory discussed at Sections 8.3.1, 8.3.2 and a central role for realism.

If the anti-realist is not willing to pursue the search for explanation in this way he either makes success a brute matter of fact, despite flying in the face of a central part of scientific practice, or there is hidden somewhere a process connecting world and theory which must remain magical in this context. It is true, as van Fraassen remarks (1985), that there can be facile appeals to "evolution"; but ultimately really following through on evolutionary explanations is one of the games the anti-realist can ill afford to play (cf. Chapter 6,

Note 18).[151] It is also true, as van Fraassen deftly shows (1980, Sections 2.4. to 2.6), that an unlimited demand for certain sorts of explanation can lead to inconsistency or an unreasonable pursuit of determinism. But it is equally true that there is no principled termination of explanation known a priori. We don't know the limits to explanation; the best way to show that they haven't yet been reached is to devise a successful extension of them. That is the realist methodology pursued here. (See its extension at Section 8.3.3.)

The argument for regarding realism as the best explanation for theory progress is of the same sort as that just presented for individual and species success. Realism provides a unified explanatory conception of cognitive learning, the anti-realist alternatives are either a Darwinist argument that cannot explain its own theoretical appeals to underlying processes or some non-naturalist account with disguised magical or brute appeals to organization.

The role of truth and realist metaphysics in cognitive theory argued in Section 8.3.1 constitute my grounds for entering "Yes" under "Methodological Progress". We can understand open-ended methodological progress, at all levels, only through theorizing ourselves as creatures attempting to develop conjectural cognitive maps of the world into which we are born. Moreover, we can add a Boyd-style argument at the meta-methodology level (and 'up') in respect of successful meta-methodologies for transforming methods.

Finally, Devitt's reflexive consistency argument for the necessity of appeal to correspondence truth to explain communication is tentatively adopted. But again, this argument should be seen as one component in a larger theory of language as a cognitive capacity. I suspect (though I have no detailed theory of language to present as proof) that it is the multiple roles truth serves in cognition, particularly its open-endedness, that will prove central for understanding language. If this is so, Devitt's argument will turn out to have identified only a small semantic tip of the explanatory iceberg.[152]

A concluding caution. This business of attempting to justify realism as an inference to the best explanation is good sport and surely a legitimate activity. But I do not want to make it the main virtue of these essays. Van Fraassen once praised his realist opponent Glymour for uncovering some of the actual procedures of science (1985, p. 296). I would hope to have made similar contributions to describing science at a more general level than detailed procedures (cf. Chapter 4, Chapter 7 and Section 8.3.10 above), contributions which would remain even if scepticism concerning this section should grip one.

8.4.2 *Arguments Against Realism*

Many of the arguments against realism are very old and these tend to derive ultimately from the avoidance of epistemic risk (see Chapter 2, Section 2.4). They are the arguments which have traditionally motivated idealism and empiricism. They recur constantly throughout these essays and evolutionary naturalist realism grew out of the attempt to provide a thoroughgoing reply to them. I shall not recapitulate them here but concentrate instead on the more recent anti-realist arguments. This latter task has been lightened by the appearance of books first by Trigg 1980, then by Devitt 1984, with edited collections by Leplin 1984 and most recently by Churchland/Hooker 1985. While both Trigg and Devitt confine their attention to the currently most popular English debates and neither emphasizes an evolutionary naturalist perspective, I am in general agreement with their arguments and will often be able to substitute endorsement for detailed argument.

A. It has recently become popular to argue in various ways that the history of science doesn't support realism. I shall begin with a straightforward use of history as evidence to attack a fundamental realist argument: inference to the best explanation. The argument runs as follows: In the past, arguments from the explanatory or predictive success of science to the reality of theoretical posits were mistaken since current theories entail that past theoretical posits do not exist; moreover, there are grounds to think present theories are false and future theories will be equally imperfect; therefore it is rational to accept that any current or future inference from predictive or explanatory success to the existence of the relevant theoretical entities is equally mistaken.[153] This attack on inference to the best explanation, the cornerstone of earlier defenses of realism, has also been accepted by some would-be realists, the result being selective realist commitments of various quasi-empiricist sorts.[154] But the attack is not successful, I believe, even on its own terms.

First, it is too easy to state the initial premise in an implausibly exaggerated form. Against a list of putative unsuccessful inferences one can pit an equally impressive list of inferences still regarded as successful. McMullen (1984) e.g., has emphasized this for what he calls the structural sciences (geology, astro-physics, molecular biology, etc.), such 'hidden structures' having provided scientific continuity to these domains, sometimes for centuries. (Notice that this is contingently true of our world because of the way it is in fact structured—cf. Section 8.3.3—it is not a reflection of language rules or a transcendental truth.) Some of the alleged historical counterexamples either prove to be cases where there was only highly controversial commitment at the time or fail to constitute real counterexamples.[155] All told, it isn't so clear that history provides the foundation for any kind of radically anti-realist thesis.

Secondly, proponents of the argument to anti-realism from history have often assumed (tacitly) that inference to a theoretical posit is impugned by any change of theoretical description of the posit. This claim is typically supported, in turn, by the twin semantic doctrines that the meaning of a term determines what it designates and that meaning is in turn determined by the totality of theory sentences in which it occurs. But stronger conditions than this are required to assert the non-existence of a theoretical posit. For example, if atoms are asserted to be causally responsible for chemical phenomena C, physical phenomena P and also to be elementary (contain no components), I don't need to reject the existence of atoms on learning that the last clause is false. Some of the proposed counterexamples in the present argument plausibly don't meet sufficiently strong conditions. E.g., atomic nuclei and genes under varying theoretical descriptions are plausibly not cases of elimination but of theoretical redescription (cf. Trigg 1980, Chapter 4).

More generally, cognitive theory pictures humans as in interaction at particular systems levels with a structurally and dynamically complex world; the 'objects' we perceive refer to particular coincident invariances characterizing those levels. One can only expect that often we will get the nature of these objects wrong in various ways, even while latching correctly on to the existence of the structured invariances. What matters theoretically is to be able to continue to refer to these objects while continuing to evolve theories as to their deeper nature (see also Section 8.4.3.9). Thus while the second premise of the agrument is one which I have long supported (see e.g., Chapter 2, Section 2.4), it is not strong enough in itself to support any conclusion to the effect that current theoretical posits don't exist. (It may however be necessary to transform the semantic structures through which they are designated.) There are several ways for a theory to be false most of which are best regarded as not impugning existence.

Thirdly, there is a tacit presupposition in the argument of historical staticness: that methodology itself doesn't improve, and hence we cannot hope to learn from past positing errors. It is true that there have been what are still regarded as clear-cut existential mistakes despite their being reasonably well established at some period. Perhaps Aristotle's crystalline spheres and phlogiston are examples. These do not pose a problem because of their occurrence *per se*, for their entrenchment can be understood retroactively and the relevant methodological deficiencies corrected. After all, at the level of macroscopic interaction pattern among substances or with heat, and at a relevantly imprecise level of description, there were many things that phlogiston theorists and ancient astronomers described correctly. In short, when there is a putative failure of positing the naturalist looks for an explanation. Here, just as much as in science itself, we want to understand why the world is as we find it. Methodological learning is precisely why the sheer occurrence of past mistakes is of limited concern in itself. There is every reason to believe that we will continue to make mistakes in the future, but there is no grounds for believing that our intellectual history will be radically chaotic in a way which undermines all referential continuity and progress.[156]

I am not sure how to properly state a realistic summary of our historical experience. Hacking e.g. (1981, 1982a, 1983), has correctly emphasized that theoretical posits typically move from mere postulation into a position where we can use them technologically to investigate other entities, to create other phenomena, and this confers a particular kind of confidence in their reality. Historically this seems right, so we might try as a first approximation: the further the postulated entities and/or structures lie from the domains of instrumental examination and technological control the less epistemic confidence we have in their reality. I doubt, however, whether the formulation can be as one-dimensionally empiricist as this, surely e.g., depth of ontological insight within explanatory unity (cf. Section 8.3.5) must also play its role. In any event, we seem to find exactly what we might expect: (i) a slow and initially erratic development of science and scientific methodology (science, alchemy and witchcraft differentiate only slowly), (ii) a slowly widening core of stable (if not exactly known) structural micro-decompositions and macro-recompositions fanning out from our common sense macroscopic world with (iii) the controversial cases lying on the outer edges of the fan (but still capable of reaching 'inward' to shake up some of the established posits, or methods patterns).[157]

All told then realists should resist anti-realist argument from history until a more carefully formulated version is available which is shown to be damaging to an evolving realist cognitive theory. Note that use of best-explanation inference within science, under discussion here, should be distinguished from its use to infer realism from various features of science. These latter arguments for realism, and objections to them, are discussed at Section 8.4.1. (Included there is van Fraassen's objections from alleged endless realist demands for explanation and from the existence of alternative, non-committal Darwinist arguments.) Meanwhile, we are left with the selective attacks on best-explanation inference. Van Fraassen (1980) urges in effect that best-explanation inference be restricted to inferring existence only for observable entities. (That is, it is rational to infer from some domain of evidence to the most empirically adequate theory of that domain but not to the reality of the theoretical posits of that theory.) This line requires a cognitive significance for observation which it does not have, and the security motivation for it does not stand up to scrutiny (Chapter 6, Section 6.4 and Churchland/Hooker 1985, Devitt 1984, Chapter 8).

B. Both Cartwright (1981, 1982, 1983) and Hacking (1981, 1982a, 1983) are realists, but both wish to reject best-explanation inference. Cartwright thinks that the only legitimate inference is that from an effect to its cause (see also Ellis 1985). Best-explanation inference to theoretical laws should be reconstrued instrumentally. Hacking likewise favours entities over theoretical descriptions, but arguing that inferences to them are acceptable only when we can demonstrate the kind of technological control over them that allows us to use them to cause other observable phenomena. Hacking too can sound anti-realist about theory (Note 51).

Cartwright and Hacking work with a distinction between existence and description. Whether electrons, the hidden causes of electrical circuit phenomena and the entities which we can manipulate in vacuum tubes and a thousand like devices to produce a wide and subtle array of effects, whether these entities exist is one thing; whether they are correctly described by current theory T is another. This difference surely has something right about it, but it isn't clear that at bottom it is a principled one (or perhaps, how it is a principled one—see Section 8.4.3.9). If no principled distinction of the right sort can be drawn then the attempt to reject best-explanation inference but retain theoretical entities will fail, one will either retain both or neither.

The difference can be read semantically; 'electrons exist' is entailed by, but does not entail, 'electrons satisfy description T'. In this case one can motivate a principled distinction (as Hacking does) by rejecting description theories of reference (which collapse the difference) to embrace a causal theory of reference. Whether any such semantical distinction can be so simply made is (I think) moot at this point (Section 8.4.3.10).[158]

But the difference can also be read epistemicly: our grounds for accepting the existence of electrons is one thing, their existing another. From my realist perspective, most of what Hacking says concerns the grounds for accepting that electrons exist *vis-à-vis* their existing rather than the semantics of the existence claim. The idea of some type of robustness = multiple epistemic "accessibility", as improving rational acceptability is, as Ellis (1985, Note 6) remarks, an old one found explicitly in all major writers at least back to Whewell. In effect Hacking has developed one specific aspect of it, just as Glymour (1980, 1985) has another—see Section 8.3.5. I agree that Hacking-manipulation constitutes grounds for asserting existence; I don't agree that it constitutes the only grounds, or even that it always constitutes sufficient grounds. I can't accept its constituting the only grounds because only through theoretical analysis can we separate the occurrence of a significant single manipulation phenomenon referred to a single kind of entity from (i) accidental conjunction or (ii) nomic combination of distinct factors, or (iii) combination of real phenomenon and fake phenomenon brought about by misdescription, failure of a *ceteris paribus* clause, etc. For this reason theoretical description will always have a key role to play in accepting that one is successfully manipulating a single species of unobservable, so Hacking-manipulation cannot be the only grounds we need to assert existence. Moreover, theory-specified failures could lead us to withdraw a claim of Hacking-manipulation on some occasion, so it can't by itself constitute sufficient grounds for asserting existence. (On Cartwright see Section 8.3.5.)

   C. An old anti-realist argument (Duhem 1962, etc.) with recent prominence is that from under-determination: There are always many possible theories which differ in their theoretical ontologies yet are empirically equivalent under all possible future observation, so the notion of their difference must be rejected; theoretical commitments are either conventional, instrumental, reduced to observational commitments, or at least it is right to be agnostic about them. The argument is of course a non sequitur as it stands and this cannot be corrected without begging the issue (Chapter 2, Section 2.4). The argument's notion of empirical equivalence is also fatally ambiguous. If it refers to empirical equivalence achieved during the real historical process of cognitive development then it falls foul of the open-endedness of the process, the domain of the observ*able* is not historically well defined.[159] (Chapter 6, Section 6.5; Ellis 1985, Section III, cf. Boyd 1985, Section I). On the other hand, if it refers to some strongly idealized a-historical notion, then it may well defeat its own first premise. This point is made effectively, if indirectly, by Devitt (1984),

Section 3.5, who points out that the realist might well be able to agree to a definition of truth in terms of idealized rational acceptance if the modalised ideal is strong enough.[160]

D. Ellis argues that the realist should give up the correspondence theory of truth (for 'internal realism'). His argument begins with the claim (1985, p. 67) that the following claims form an inconsistent tetrad: (a) theories are empirically underdetermined; (b) the choice between empirically equivalent theories can only be made on pragmatic grounds (simplicity, explanatoriness, etc.); (c) pragmatic considerations have no relevance to truth or falsity; (d) we have good reason to believe that our world is how our best theories say it is. Then Ellis claims that the most plausible way out is to reject (c) and accept a pragmatist theory of truth as idealized warranted assertability. Because of my critique of the underdetermination argument above I am dubious that this can be an inconsistent tetrad in any interesting sense. (Alternatively, (a) is to be rejected.) But in any case Ellis' conclusion doesn't follow, since I would join in rejecting (c) (Chapter 6, Section 6.4) and yet consistently retain the correspondence theory (relevance does not require definitional dependence).

E. Beyond this Ellis (1985, Section V) argues that the correspondence theory leads to scepticism (since humans could always be wrong). He also argues that there can be no arguments for the correspondence theory. "If the assumption that there is a way the world is independent of our epistemic values had any explanatory power, then it would be right for us to believe in it. But in that case it would be part of our world and not an absolutely independent reality" (1985, p. 72). As to the first argument, it equates scepticism with fallibilism and I have nothing further to say about this tacit demand for certainty beyond Section 8.2.3. (Compare Ellis' revealing non sequitur that from the possibility of error it follows that we "can have *no reason* to think that improving our knowledge and understanding of the world brings us any nearer the truth"; my italics, 1985, p. 72.) The second argument conflates our grounds for accepting X (which certainly remain *our* grounds) with the truth conditions for X which may or may not (and in this case do *not*) require a conceptual or logical link between truth and epistemic warrant.

Commonly, lurking behind these arguments is what we might call the God's Eye argument. It runs like this: it is impossible to step outside of our own epistemic setting to take up a third, neutral point of view from which we can compare the world directly with our own concepts, beliefs and procedures (humans can't have a God's Eye view of themselves); therefore, any doctrine which requires an objective₁ connection between concepts, beliefs, methods and the world is to be rejected because its truth (intelligibility) requires that a God's Eye stance be available. Realist theories of reference, truth and method (specifically of their guiding epistemic values) fall into this category.[161]

But the argument has a false premise. True, there is no God's Eye stance available, but then Realist theories don't require it (cf. Chapter 2, Section 2.4). Only an overly strong attachment to a verificationist semantics could tempt one to believe otherwise. If I assert that the volcano Krakatoa erupted last century must I positivistically reconstrue this as a covert remark about present and future evidence because there is no way to step outside of time in order to neutrally check its truth from a God's Eye perspective? It is as if anti-realists, rejecting inference to the best explanation, demand to test philosophical theories by direct observation in some impossible way (by 'seeing' both sides as it were). The notion of us being trapped 'inside' our own language is simply a bewitching, but wrong, metaphor for it is in that very language that are described the causal relations humans have with the world during which we 'grasp' reality and reality is accessible. As Trigg (1980) remarks, that human concepts are human concepts and that theses about language (science or anything else) can only be stated in language, these are tautologies, nothing more. Only some smuggled empiricist assumption logically connecting truth conditions with epistemic conditions could give this argument any force.

F. Recently, the sociology of knowledge (or rather, of belief) proponents have argued that since science doesn't call for any but social (/political/psychological/anthropological) explanation, science doesn't call for a philosophical account at all. An alternative version is this: since reality is a social (/political . . .) construct, a realist account of science is wrong. In both cases the realist rejects the premises (cf. Section 8.3.6). As Trigg (1980) aptly remarks, these arguments fail to preserve the distinction between the rational assessment of a theory's being a (partial) function of the social (/political . . .) context from which it emerges and the truth conditions of that theory being so.[162] In general I accept Trigg's over-all critique of these arguments, including the positive correctives to empiricism which the sociology of knowledge critique offers (and against whose fake dichotomies it achieves so much of its initial plausibility).[163]

Along the way through this essay other arguments have been touched on—Leed's argument against truth as explanatory (Note 151), Putnam's argument against external reference (Section 8.4.3.10), van Fraassen's anti-realist evolutionary arguments and his argument for terminating explanation (Section 8.4.1). All of these arguments need more careful consideration than I can give them here; none of them, I think, are fatal to evolutionary naturalist realism.

8.4.3 Mea Culpa!

A section not usually written in polite circles, this. One pretends to have considered everything of importance. I haven't. And I believe it may help students and other open-minded souls to explore the territory more effectively if I briefly sketch some sins of omission, along with the occasional constructive suggestion for future progress. (I plead this motivation, and not incipient megalomania, for this section.) This section acts as a complement to the review in Parts 8.2 and 8.3 above. I shall begin with some briefly stated observations on diverse areas (8.4.3.1-8.4.3.8 below) and conclude with two longer, related sections on approximation and language (8.4.3.9,10 below).

8.4.3.1 Limits to Abduction. Inference to the best explanation has been widely deployed and briefly defended herein, but it is clear that it is not always warranted. When then is it warranted? Only when a causal mechanism is invoked to explain the production of the explanandum condition (Salmon)? This is too narrow. Only when the explanands constitutes an increase in depth of understanding (Friedman, *et al.*)? Perhaps this is too stringent, even when it has been disambiguated. (On this discussion see Section 8.3.5.) Here I only remark that an adequate response to this question will never be formulated independently of reference to what the world, including our cognition, is actually like. We learn about our methods, so we need to learn when best-explanation-inferences are useable. This latter involves understanding how, given the kind of world we live in, humans can go about the generation of quality alternative explanations to choose between in the first place.

8.4.3.2 Meta-Inductions. In a similar vein I think it is inappropriate to either be wholly committed to inductive logic or to wholly oppose it. Induction is widely used in science and it is, in the form of successively nested conditioning, a basic cognitive mechanism throughout biological evolution. On the other hand, the use of data-theory inductive argument must be *much* more circumscribed than empiricist inductivism would suggest (see Chapter 4, Section 4.5). The trick is to know when to use induction, and which particular form of inductive argument to use. In biological terms, the trick is to become 'conditioned' at successively higher levels or for successive meta-inductive contexts. (Compare the current controversies in the foundations of statistical inference sketched in Harper/Hooker 1976, cf. Hooker et al. 1977c.) I have presumed that this problem is best approached by recovering inductive argument within a decision theoretic setting, but perhaps this can't be satisfactorily done. In any case these problems remain unresolved here.

They do however throw attention again onto the meta-methodological level (and 'up') where methodological learning is expressed. The point could be put in a Sellarsian mode. Theories don't simply recapture a law-like structure to a common sense world, that would render them redundant (via the theoretician's dilemma). Realism for science gains its rationale, says Sellars, from the fundamental fact that theories explain why the common sense world isn't exactly law-like. Just so for meta-methodological theory *vis-à-vis* methodology.[164] Against this background it becomes clearer that the few hints of connection between unification / explanation and confirmation found in Chapter 4 and in Section 8.3.5 above do not suffice for a decent theory of confirmation. Such a theory is very complex and the literature and history of pitfalls vast. I touch it no further here.

8.4.3.3 Scientific Realism and Perceptual Realism. Section 8.2.1 separated scientific realism out from realism in perception. In practice, the unity of philosophy defeats this definition chopping. I have argued for an encompassing fallibilism concerning our representations of the external world (Section 8.2.6). Yet Section 8.4.2 argued against the idea that we were 'trapped inside our language' so as to be shut off from the world. Indeed the whole account of cognition on which I have traded (e.g. Section 8.3.2) centers on an interactionist conception of perception in which real features of the world are in interaction with us and are mapped into our nervous systems. There is then a delicate interrelation to be maintained between scientific realism and perceptual realism: perceptual realism should be 'direct' enough to defeat trapped-in-our-language and other idealist arguments and yet 'unmirror-like' enough to integrate with theoretical change and fallibilism. Though I have laid out a conception of perception elsewhere (Hooker 1978a and cf. Section 8.3.2), and I still adhere to its general approach, I remain unclear whether it will mesh properly with the specifics of a developed scientific realism. To keep the essay focused I have not dealt with their interrelation here.

8.4.3.4 Form and Content, Qualities and Relations. An important part of the latter problem focusses on the nature and status of qualities in scientific theories, and the secondary qualities in particular. For a period I explored 'anti-quality' metaphysics (e.g., against Armstrong

1973a and generally 1974c, 1975d) and anti-secondary-quality meta-physics in particular (e.g., against Sellars 1977a and generally 1970a, 1978a). Now I am less convinced. I think there may be specific arguments deriving from physics (the fundamental role of qualities in fields) and psychology (the role of qualitative structures in cognition and consciousness) for insisting on qualities irreducible to structures and dynamics. This would be to insist on a content in contradistinction to form. (Of course, there may still be no secondary qualities after the manner of our common sense metaphysics of perception, as I claim in 1978a; that is an additional issue.) In any event I have not dealt with these issues here; not dealt, indeed, with the ancient issue of form and content at all.[165]

8.4.3.5 Experience and Judgement. One specific aspect of this general problem is worth singling out explicitly because it infects so much philosophy of science, namely the relationship between perceptual experience and conceptual judgement. Empiricists hold to interaction with an independent reality, as do realists, but they have a very simple theory of what the mind contributes to cognitive development, namely just logic, just organization, i.e., just the most general form of cognition. Idealists agree with realists that the mind contributes more than this to cognitive development, but idealists usually hold a very simple theory of any reality beyond mind, namely that it is just an unknown cause, a very general formal precondition of experience. In both cases the crossing of the world-mind boundary is a simple affair, either there is an identity or nothing passes across (cf. Hooker 1978a). Realists insist on a theory of a complex mind in a complex world, with significant form and content on both sides of the boundary and plenty of traffic across it. So realists need a theory of experience *vis-à-vis* judgement.

There are many strands to this problem. One way in is via perception theory. Realists, recall, don't strictly need to be, but should prefer to be, direct realists about perception. Yet arguments about the theory ladenness of perception push in a representational direction. Put alternatively, the 'directness' of perception is in a certain tension with the fallibilism realism requires (cf. Note 162). I resist compromising either feature (see my 1978a). A second way in is to pursue form and content in secondary quality judgements. But I set this line aside to focus on philosophy of science.

Empiricists, recall, want a 'silent' transfer of content from world to judgement in perception. Whilst ever one had a notion of a Given in perception, a content already conceptualized as it were, there was no problem here. Perceiving was simply receiving. But once perception is allowed as theory-laden, a feature of the Popper-Kuhn-Feyerabend revolt against empiricism, then the issue of the conceptualization of perceptual stimuli becomes acute. This is an old problem; the empiricist Neurath shares with the quasi-empiricist / anti-empiricist Popper the slogan "Propositions can only be compared with propositions",[166] thereby cutting off the experiences, *qua* causally initiated perceptual processes, from the conceptualized judgements to which they 'lead'. Popper traces this approach back to Fries in the previous century and from there of course back to Kant.[167] Later Feyerabend developed first the so-called pragmatic theory of observation and then pushed the experience / judgement distinction which it tacitly contained in an effort to account for the capacity of scientists to operate intelligently across allegedly conceptually or semantically incommensurable inter-theory gulfs.[168] There is then a pressure to distinguish experience from judgement and give the former a role which transcends current judgement categories, in order to provide a basis for explaining theoretical development.

Precisely the same distinction is motivated by wanting to explain cognitive development at large. Cognitive development is basicly, I presume, the transfer of complexity from the world to neural structures. In this case the transfer 'leads' or 'stimulates' conceptual development. If experience labels the inner states prior to linguistically encoded judgement then experience precedes linguistic judgement. Of course experience may not precede a deeper level of judgement and this is what I suggested (in 1975d). But to understand the development of the human infant, the artist and the scientist alike, we still want to understand how ways of judging, at every cognitive level, can all be transformed through experience. This is especially so if cognitive development is to make intelligent use of interaction with the world (cf. Chapter 7, Section 7.11 and Vickers 1979, 1980, 1983.) Recently, e.g., we find Churchland (1979) speaking of the "conceptual exploitation of perceptual states"; moreover he uses the implied experience / judgement distinction to great effect in arguing for a liberating realist approach to perception and cognitive development generally. One can also see an ambiguous flirtation of this kind in my writing about experience and transcendence (cf. Chapter 7, Section 7.12).

Yet this is a potentially dangerous distinction since it threatens to cut us off from the world again, leaving us trapped in our conceptualizations. In this way it leads to idealism or to quasi-idealist internal realism.[169] Conversely, it leads philosophers to demand a demonstration of a God's Eye stance in order to get us out of this trap—cf. Section 8.4.4. I am not at all sure how to understand conceptual creativity or sufficiently deep theoretical transformation, or even whether understanding can itself be understood (cf. Chapter 7, Section 7.11). More particularly I offer no completed doctrine concerning the perceptual experience-conceptual judgement link, though I have had my say on some features of this situation.[170]

8.4.3.6 Causality and Harmony. There is also a subtheme of the form/content theme I should like to draw attention to again here, that of two conceptions of order for the world which I referred to as causality and harmony (see 1972c). Recall that I have given a fundamental place to order structures within the conceptual structure of science (Chapter 4 and Section 8.3.4 above). So there is place to raise the question as to the order types which are appropriate to scientific theory. Philosophers have tended to assume that causal order, or some generalization thereof is the appropriate one, and certainly much valuable work has been done within the theory of space-time structures, cognitive psychology and philosophy of science itself which shows the fruitfulness of conceptual analysis in terms of causal order structures.[171] None of this work is without controversy, however, and, more saliently, it is not without its alternatives. Recent work by Bohm (1980) on implicate orders in particular, coupled by the philosophically neglected cases of unexplained non-causal order in quantum physics (e.g., the Pauli exclusion principle) gives support to the idea that causal order may be too narrow a conception of order for science, applicable only at some sufficiently aggregated and 'lumpy' level. When allied to the different order structures available between atomic and field metaphysics (cf. Section 8.3.4), it emphasizes the need for a philosophical investigation of these neglected issues. But I do not pursue the matter here.

8.4.3.7 Rationality. The nature and role of rationality is a complex subject on which I have offered only fragments of doctrine in these essays. An adequate theory of rationality should, in my judgement, offer a unified account of rational inference, belief and action and of the intelligent nature of development/creativity and of feeling. The challenge offered by Chapter 7, Section 7.11 is this: either accept rationality as central to creative development or admit either that rationality is peripheral to intelligence or that development is not fundamentally intelligent. This last is not a plausible position if one accepts an idea central to most accounts of intelligence, namely that we may rank order intelligence levels by the hierarchial level at which they are capable of learning and so modifying response (i.e., by their degree of systems openness). In this case a nasty choice awaits our contemporary tradition in rationality. For that tradition, traceable at least back to Hobbes, wants to understand rationality as both central to intelligence and as a purely formal, non-creative structure. Specifically, reason is identified with a schizoid pair of algorithms, the one for computing logical inferences, the other for computing utility-maximal strategies. I have aligned the rationality of belief with that of action (and suggested that perhaps the rationality of inference might be so aligned as well) because if fits my pro-sensory-motor evolutionary orientation and because it provides a richer setting for epistemology. But I have not attempted an extended theory of rationality beyond epistemology nor developed a detailed action theory, because of the controversies and known inadequacies of current decision theoretic models (cf. Section 8.3.1 above). I have not attempted to relate action models to development/creativity beyond Chapter 7, Section 7.11. Nor, therefore, have I formed a view of how rationality is to be related to intelligence or indeed whether they can be usefully distinguished.[172] All these I accept as important realist tasks.[173]

8.4.3.8 Other Realists. There are several contemporary writers who have contributed substantially to a realist approach and to whom I have not done full justice in this essay. (It is not feasible to afford every interesting issue the detailed discussion it deserves.) Foremost among these is Heelan's horizonal realism (1982, 1983). Heelan, like myself, adopts the view that perception is the extraction of invariances and that science is an extension of perceptual cognitive strategies. However Heelan also seeks a *rapprochement* with continental philosophy, in particular with the hermaneutic tradition. Most interesting here is his idea that understanding a technology is like reading a text, that a 'readable' technology becomes an extension of our bodies through which we interact with, and understand, the world. In a review (*Nous*) I briefly summarized Heelan's overall argument as in Figure 8.2. Heelan's ideas deserve closer study and I aim at such in the near future.

Meanwhile, Heelan is part of a growing movement to accord technological practice a fundamental role in science. (I have summarized my own contribution in Section 8.3.9.) Cartwright (1983) and Hacking (1983) have also re-emphasised the practical, as a balance to the theoretical, in understanding science. While I would resist the quasi-empiricism with which they align themselves (cf. Section 8.4.4) as an unnecessarily anti-theoretic stance, their positive analyses are valu-

Figure 8.2

P₀: A Hermeneutic/Phenomenological Philosophical
Framework is the Most Adequate One.

P₁: Perception, phenomenologically analyzed, is a hermeneutic act.

P₂: Science, phenomenologically analyzed, is a hermeneutic social enterprise.

P₁': Intelligence generally is to be understood as an extension of perception. Specifically, common sense aims at incorporating new perceptual horizons into a hermeneutically coherent framework of understanding. (Doctrine of the Primacy of Perception)

P₂': Science is to be understood essentially as an extension of perception and common sense. Specifically, science aims at a maximally broad incorporation of new perceptual horizons into a hermeneutically coherent framework of understanding. (Doctrine of Horizonal Realism)

H₁: Perception is 'plastic' in this specific sense: it admits alternative geometrical organizations which are phenomenologically coherent, epistemologically adequate and hermeneutically directed. (Doctrine of Geometrical Plasticity)

H₂: In science, perceptual horizons are expanded technologically. Under certain conditions the theoretical entities of which hermeneutic understanding speaks can be directly incorporated into perceptual experience (they can be perceived). (Doctrine of Readable Technologies)

H₁': The doctrine of geometrical plasticity explains the roles of geometrical organization in the development of Western pictorial art and is an essential factor in the historical explanation of the development of Western culture (e.g. religion) more generally.

H₂': The history of science can only properly be understood when a central and hermeneutic role is accorded perception in it following the doctrines of horizonal realism and readable technologies.

H₁": The doctrine of geometrical plasticity represents a major internal expansion in the power of the continental phenomenological and hermeneutic traditions, permitting a new rapprochement between them and the Anglo-American analytic tradition.

H₂": Contemporary Anglo-American philosophy of science has become distorted by its emphasis on the formal structures in science to the neglect of the role of perceptual experience, especially its hermeneutic character. Correcting this imbalance permits a new rapprochement between the two traditions.

H₃: Reductionist accounts of mind and Materialist Accounts of Science are deeply incoherent: First Person intentionality is irreducibly central to both. (Doctrine of Contextual Irreducibility)

H₄: There is a profound interplay between science and culture, mediated by the technological transformation of the common sense world. (Doctrine of the Primacy of Praxis) able. Similar remarks hold also for the not-unrelated scientific problems tradition that has grown from Popper's rejection of inductive logic and, with that, of globally coherent scientific accumulation. There is no question in my mind that problems *per se* are too thin a basis for a serious theory of science,[174] but equally I have no doubt they contribute an important concept to a detailed dynamic of science. In this respect Hattiangadi's work (1978/9) and the later Popperian school analyses (e.g., Agassi 1975, Andersson/Radnitzky 1978a, b, Howson 1976), along with related writing (e.g., Chalmers 1976, Holton 1973, Krige 1980, Nicholas 1982), are worth much more careful and sympathetic examination than I have given them here.

Newton-Smith's doctrinal statement (1981) also lies primarily in the Popperian critical rationalist tradition but supports many of the individual realist positions taken here; it deserves a more systematic evaluation than the fragmentary notes offered. And these remarks hold true too of Bhaskar's growing corpus (see 1975, 1979). Bhaskar wishes to defend realism and attack anti-naturalism. But whereas Newton-Smith seeks to 'temper' rationality, Bhaskar seeks transcendental deductions of the pre-conditions for science, deductions which lead in turn to a strongly limited naturalism. In this way I see Bhaskar as attempting, like Newton-Smith, to hold a middle ground between an *a priori* rationalism (e.g. Popper, who after all finally projected his normative-descriptive gulf onto the heavens as many distinct worlds) and the a-rational relativism of many sociological and neo-Marxist accounts. Moreover, it is an attempt to hold to this middle ground whilst yet avoiding the radical implications of evolutionary naturalism. I don't believe that these attempts succeed,[175] and I do believe that the only way to occupy a stable middle ground is through evolutionary naturalist realism. There are however many useful insights in Bhaskar's analyses, as well as in Newton-Smith's, from which realism should learn.

Shimony (1971, 1978, 1981) has begun developing an 'integral epistemology' which shares with naturalistic realism a naturalistic fallibilism and integration, and while only dubiously (certainly partially) realist in the sense used here, Shapere (1984) shares the open-ended, fallibilist conception of cognition. I cannot share Shapere's pragmatist approach to truth, nor his notion that scientific domains develop toward autonomy. (This latter is, in my view, a subordinate part of the adaptive dynamics of science, cf. Chapter 7, Section 7.3 and Section 8.3.3.) But particularly in his exploration of specific ways in which method, more generally rationality, evolves in interaction with a domain of science, Shapere offers some valuable ideas concerning the application of fallibilism to science. Shapere's is an extended theory and these few attitudinal indicators need to be replaced by much more careful study.

The range of literature which is either anti-realist or non-committal on the issue but from which realism may usefully learn, is immense. To attempt to review it here really would border on the megalomaniacal.

8.4.3.9 Approximation, Reference and Progress. There is a complex group of interrelated concepts of importance to realism: approximate truth, verisimilitude and convergence. In Section 8.3.1 I distinguished approximateness from imprecision and partialness. Roughly, a statement p is imprecise relative to another q if q entails p and the reason for the entailment is that at least one predicate common to p and q has a narrower designation range in q than in p.[176] Again roughly, p is partial with respect to q if q entails p and q entails r and p and r do not entail one another.[177] The intuitive idea of approximateness which I think useful to develop is that of inter-theoretic imprecision. Again roughly, a statement p_T from a theory T is approximate relative to a statement $p_{T'}$ of a theory T' if there are models in T' for the ontology and fundamental processes of T such that (i) there is a statement q_T of T, less precise than p_T but sufficiently close to p_T and (ii) the transcription of q_T into T', as dictated by preservation of theoretical understanding, is $q_{T'}$ and $q_{T'}$ is entailed by T'.[178] So, statements of one theory are approximate in another if less precise versions of them are modellable in the other. In the discussion to follow concerning these ideas I aim to emphasize relevant distinctions that, often not drawn, block progress to insightful analyses.

To begin with, it is important to distinguish approximateness as specified above from the occurrence of approximations *per se*. It is a confusion to call a statement which defines a convergence process approximately true, since the statement itself may be true *simpliciter*. In (1974a) I suggested that Newton's first law of motion be formulated roughly as: If the external force on a body is less than f then the deviation of the object from constant velocity is less than f/m. The empirical content of the law then lies in its specification of the convergence structures relating force data and acceleration data. But in this case the law is true, not approximately true. The occurrence of approximations to a condition (in this case force-freeness) shouldn't be confused with either the approximateness of this law in some non-Newtonian theory (say relativity theory) or with the law's approximate empirical adequacy. There are here three logically distinct notions.

To the extent that the conjoining of Newton's universal gravitation law with Newtonian dynamics entails that a condition of force-freeness rarely, if ever, occurs, to that extent we may call the condition on which the force-acceleration relation converges an idealization. It is my view that all idealizations in science can be dealt with in this same way, namely to replace the idealized entity with quantification over the corresponding convergence process. In the intervening decades since writing (1974a) I have not encountered convincing counterexamples, so I doubt the need for any special notion of approximateness in connection with idealizations.[179] Of course, not all abstract non-real conceptions appearing in scientific theories are idealizations, there are in addition the mathematical constructions (Hilbert space and so on). Realism is not committed to asserting their external existence (cf. Ellis 1985). There are a variety of ways of approaching their treatment (syncategoromatic paraphrasing away, meaning postulates, etc.) but since these hinge on unresolved disputes about semantics, logical analyses of theoretical structures and the like, I shall not pursue that matter here. It is sufficiently clear, I think, that there are no special embarrassments for realism with either idealizations proper or mathematical constructions.

Next, notice that a double imprecision is involved in the notion of inter-theoretic approximation. The theoretical claim "my body remains physiologically the same while I sleep" made, say, in common sense macro-object theory T_{cs}, is approximate relative to the corresponding claim within molecular biochemistry T_{mb}, which is along the lines of "during a medically normally seven hour rest period morphological structure (at some level of grossness g_S), metabolitic function (as some level of grossness g_M), neural function (at some level of grossness g_N) . . . are all invariant." The common sense claim is of course strictly in conflict with claims of a molecular biochemical description of human bodies because during sleep cells are dying and either being replaced (most places) or not (brain, liver—I'm over forty!), carbon has left the body (as carbon dioxide), neural interconnections are shifting, etc. Yet intuitively the claim is approximate with respect to T_{mb} because there is a less precise claim in T_{cs} which does transcribe into an imprecise statement of T_{mb}, namely "Physiologically, my body doesn't change noticeably to unaided perception while I sleep."

In a similar fashion Kepler's laws T_K come out approximate with respect to Newtonian mechanics T_N. As is well known, T_N strictly does not entail T_K since there are small corrections to Kepler's laws needed to take into account the finite mass of the sun, the gravitational forces exerted by other planets, etc. But there is a 'nearby' less precise version for T_K laws which is entailed by T_N. One of the laws runs "the orbits of the planets deviate from ellipses with the sun at one focus by less than e." Clearly, more precise versions than this could be found (e.g., "the orbit of planet P deviates . . . less than e_P''). Similar formulae hold for T_N as an approximation to special relativity mechanics T_{SR}. Physics texts point out that the key term is $b = v^2/c^2$, since for $b << 1$, the Taylor expansion $1 - \frac{1}{2}b - \frac{1}{8}b^2$ . . . converges quite rapidly to the ubiquitous factor $(1 - v^2/c^2)^{1/2}$ and hence this latter can be approximated by $1 - \frac{1}{2}b$ (adding further terms if desired), yielding correction terms to T_N formulae in terms of b. The appropriate imprecise T_N sentences are then those with error ranges of the appropriate magnitudes in them.

The examples make it clear why there is need to find a less precise version of the approximate statements and a less precise version of the approximated statements. But how much less precise? At sufficient imprecision we run into tautologies, all of which quite properly turn out to be approximate to everything but are, for that reason, epistemically valueless. Fortunately, there is no need to answer this question within an analysis of approximation, what degree of approximateness is acceptable is a problem for methodology and epistimology. In any case, I do not believe that there is any simple theory-independent answer to this query, standards of acceptable approximation depend on the theory in question (method is a function of theory, Section 8.3.2).

The usual assumption with respect to approximation is that S is approximately true entails that there is S' exactly true, and S' entails S. According to the above analysis this is inadequate twice over. First, approximator and approximated will be in different theories for inter-theoretic approximation and this prevents any straightforward entailment.[180] Second, the approximator is better viewed as the theory, not the imprecise statement(s) within it that transcribe those of the approximated theory, since a variety of assumptions may be needed to derive the approximating statement. (Cf. Note 96. Strictly speaking the derivation may well have to incorporate premises drawn from other theories as well.) I now add that there is a two-step specialization which will recover the original insight. First we can construct the notion of approximate truth, in T, by taking T' to be true. If in addition we require the degenerate assumption $T = T'$ then we recapture the original notion above.

It is also appropriate to distinguish T's theoretical laws being approximate in T' from T's empirical substructure being approximate in T'. These two conditions can vary largely independently of one another. It only requires a sufficiently 'infectious' small error in T's theory-observation connections, e.g., for T to diverge widely from T' in observational predictions even while T's fundamental theoretical laws approximate those of T' quite closely. Conversely, quite disparate fundamental theoretical principles may produce observational consequences over some domain which approximate one another quite closely. Moreover, other theories whose assumptions become involved in the derivation of observational predictions, sensitivity to auxillary assumptions and so on may produce related variations between observational and theoretical approximation. The situation is perhaps clearer in the intra-theoretic case, where it is equally important to distinguish between approximate truth and approximate empirical adequacy.

A theory might well be approximately true almost everywhere yet appear highly empirically inadequate to us because the idiosyncrasies of current instrumentation and/or methods happen to probe it at, and perhaps even amplify, its weaknesses. As Miller (1975) showed, it is possible to take any false theory, no matter how nearly true, and rewrite it so as to magnify the extent of its falsity without limit. Conversely, a very wrong theory may nonetheless be approximately empirically adequate because the idiosyncratic limitations of our current instrumentation and/or method prevent us from discovering that fact. In addition, even a true theory could be judged empirically inadequate either because of faults in the data (presumably deriving from faults in instrumentation/methodology) and/or because auxiliary theories, *ceteris paribus* clause, etc., which were used to obtain theory-data confrontation were faulty (cf. Chapter 4).[181]

With these distinctions drawn we can locate verisimilitude as some degree of approximate truth. Our evidence for a claim of approximate truth would be approximate empirical adequacy combined with depth of understanding and other virtues. Convergence is increasing verisimilitude. Our evidence for convergence would evidently be of this form: T approximates successor T' in some respect and T' approximates the data accepted relative to T' within narrower error ranges than does T and T' either explains, or explains away, T (relative to background theories B). Among the capacities of a virtuous theory would be the capacity to understand the preceding scientific history in the domain, to explain the acceptance of predecessor theories by showing how they, their coordinate methodologies and experimental technologies, are approximations to those currently accepted and, where they are not, to explain the structure of the errors made.[182]

The point of this discussion is to show that the realist is not committed to any simple doctrine of verisimilitude (say of the sort Popper proposed and with which there is *prima facie* deep difficulty).[183] Even if our theoretical positing went wrong for a stretch, e.g., we could still try to understand why this happened and under what conditions it happens. We can consider worlds whose states are keyed to our beliefs and like possibilities (cf. Feyerabend's queries in 1965b), for even these conditions can be speculatively theorized by us for investigation. This shows again that the simple anti-realist 'meta-induction' discussed in Section 8.4.2 is too simple, many conditions have to be met before historical failure blocks realist understanding.

A related lesson applies to convergence. Devitt (1984) argues that the realist needs to defend a convergence claim. This view derives from a longer tradition concerned originally with justifying induction. The general form of the argument, which covers all these cases, is this: the success of a methodology must be demonstrated and this can only be done by showing convergence. Once again I doubt that the answer can be so simple. (Conversely, I doubt that the claim that there is no answer, no justification of methodology, can be simply based on failed programs at this level.[184]) Surely whether we humans should expect convergence or not, and under what conditions, again depends on the actual nature of the world. Compare analyses of whether a particular sampling methodology will produce convergence on the relevant population distributions; an answer depends on how dispersed, how dynamic, how independent, etc., the relevant population characteristics are *vis-à-vis* the sampling techniques employed. So for us humans as samplers of the world. If convergence doesn't occur at the moment, perhaps we haven't learned enough at the meta-methodological level (or at the meta-meta-methodological level . . .); e.g., perhaps the specific mathematical forms that we employ (say symplectic manifold structure for dynamics) are wrong, perhaps even our almost-total confinement to linear mathematics is too restrictive, perhaps our notions of causality *vis-à-vis* functionality are too naive and so on and so on. Perhaps we need another millennium or two to explore seriously alternative metaphysics. Realism is not refuted by non-convergence *per se*, but by those kinds of non-convergence that can't be understood in a realist manner within the hierarchy of philosophic and scientific theories. Which sorts are they? No one has really attempted an answer (*a fortiori* not I).

Moreover I admit to having no autonomous 'logic' of approximation to offer here, because I doubt that there is such a thing. Here are two reasons for the doubt: (i) 'Approximates' is not transitive (thus removing the most basic structural feature of inference) and (ii) real life conditions of approximation are strongly theory-dependent (contrast approximations between linear systems, stochastic linear systems, between systems near structural catastrophes or bifurcations, etc.). Nonetheless the realist has eventually to have some account of the significances and roles of this cluster of concepts. I do not provide that account here.

The discussion of approximateness has avoided the most interesting cases, inter-theoretic approximation across the two great ontologies of Western science (corpuscles, fields) or across systems hierarchy levels. In these cases two distinct complications arise: (i) the 'aping' of the one ontology and basic properties in the other and (ii) the transcription of objects and relations in the one theory into systems complexes of objects and relations in the other. For example, a corpuscular ontology can ape a fluid flow by a corpuscular stream with granular fluctuation/flow parameter ratios sufficiently small. In this case all sufficiently imprecise statements of a field theory of flow will transcribe into imprecise statements of a corresponding corpuscular theory. A simple example of the second sort is afforded by the parallel systems interconnection of N electric power generators each of power P and equipped with a virtual governor yielding output reliability r. This system acts as a single generator of power NP with a virtual governor whose reliability is r/N.[185] However, the corresponding claim "there is a generator of power NP with governor of reliability r/N" is false. Instead the systems analysis makes it clear that we are here concerned with an internal process which results in particular output features or characteristics. The appropriate form of the claim is "there is a set of generators G_i (i = 1 . . . N) and there is some structure S relating these generators such that the power output of the complex $S(G_1, \ldots G_N)$, the G_i acting jointly, is NP and the reliability of this output is r/N." This statement is true but imprecise. The example generalizes naturally to input as well as output features and to input/output relations. In (1981e) I tried to demonstrate that this form of transcription was fundamental to all exterior-to-interior systems inter-theory relations, including biology and psychology. Failure to distinguish the two kinds of approximation above and failure to investigate them thoroughly is an important part of the difficulties in this area. Recently (1981c,d,e) I have contributed an initial study of the second sort and some general considerations for the cross-ontology cases, but much remains to be done.

The context is now appropriate, however, to introduce the final category of error distinguished at Section 8.3.1, namely referential failure. The main point I want to make is that referential failure doesn't comprise a single class of occurrences (contrary to what is often assumed) but is instead a complex collection of complex cases. In the electric generators case there is referential failure, the 'collective' generator doesn't exist. (Every engineer knows that very often one could in fact build a single generator of capacity NP but that its cost and performance structure would be very different from the distributed system $S(G_1, \ldots G_N)$ discussed.) Nonetheless the system exists and all the output statements made about it are true. It is also true that there is an internal structure and control process in operation, etc. Finally, all of the laws of electromagnetic theory remain true of the system under both descriptions. Evidently, in all these descriptive contexts there is no failure of reference. The case can be generalized; there are in general three sources of referential stability across intertheoretic description: (i) sufficiently high level invariances in theoretical order structures, (ii) sufficiently low level empirical agreement and (iii) invariant intermediate level causal/functional descriptions.[186] In all three cases the level of description may need to be sufficiently imprecise.

On the one side cases of the sort just discussed evidently should be distinguished from cases of ambiguous reference, where a term has 'fragmented' under theoretical analysis (e.g., 'geometry' in modern mathematics, 'mass' in relativity theory, 'genes' in biology, 'consciousness' in psychology and 'idea' or 'sense datum' in philosophy of perception).[187] On the other side these cases should equally be distinguished from cases where reference fails because the explananda themselves were mis-described. (Neither of the preceding two sorts of cases need involve any such mis-description of data, relevant causal processes required, etc., though they might do so.) In these latter cases the theoretical setting needs to be explicitly widened to include the data formulation process, including where appropriate the human agents involved. (Actually, the setting is always implicitly as wide as this.) In this enlarged setting one can then judge which referential structures are preserved (à la the earlier two cases) and which are to be explained away.

I shall not enter the current debates concerning referential failure and theory change, except to state the following approach to it: (1) As the foregoing analysis shows, in real life inter-theoretic referential relations can be very complex; much of the literature assumes a false simplicity that robs its conclusions of relevance. (2) Inter-theoretic referential structures have much more in common than superficial analyses of scientific 'revolution' would often suggest. The three-fold loci of this preservation have been indicated. (3) Precisely how referential structure is to be analyzed and what is its relation to meaning are still strongly open questions (see below). Particularly in view of the tendency for contemporary semantics of all stripes to devalue (even to claim impossible) the daily-exercised capacity of scientists to model in one theory (or global theory context) the ontology and processes of another theory, including its referential structures, it is unwise at this time to draw global conclusions from semantic theories concerning the rationality of theoretic change. Rather one should press on with the detailed analysis of particular examples.

8.4.3.10 Realism and Language. Dubiousness about philosophical theories of language and about basing other philosophical conclusions upon them are themes that run throughout these chapters. I feel obliged by the current climate in Western philosophy of science to reassert these themes. I also feel obliged to candidly admit here that, on the very same grounds, I have no philosophical theory of language I am prepared to defend. Yet ultimately the realist must develop a supporting philosophical linguistics.

Why the dubiousness about basing philosophical conclusions elsewhere on philosophy of language? Primarily because for a realist language is a part only of our overall cognitive skills and to be understood in that context. From an evolutionary perspective it is at least plausible that language is not even a primary or basic cognitive skill, let alone the basic structure of intelligence.[188] Starting with philosophy of language is starting in the wrong place and is likely to lead to narrow, anthropocentric (and worse) philosophy (Chapter 3, Section 3.3.1, Sections 8.2.4, 8.3.1 above; cf. Devitt's maxim 3, Note 5).[189]

Let me offer a simple example of how philosophic theses about language can bewitch the mind. It is a widespread assumption among analytic philosophers that properties (including relations) are individuated semantically, indeed that the designata of two predicates are identical exactly when the predicates are synonymous (or sufficiently so, *pace* Quine). This assumption, e.g., was in widespread use in objections to materialism during the 1960s and 1970s. Yet once the real situation is examined it is clear that there is no such simple relationship between words and the world. Some predicates designate the same properties for contingent reasons, some lack designata altogether, some properties as yet have no designating predicates (all those unknown to us), some predicates ambiguously designate more than one distinct property and some predicates a complex of qualities, causal relations and processes.[190] This is exactly what may be expected from the evolutionary realist perspective. Once we break out of the earlier semantic straitjacket then the way is cleared for a much more satisfactory discussion of the identification of properties in general and for complex systems reductions in particular, including the mind-body case (cf. 1981d, e).[191]

Now consider the vexed question of meaning. The contemporary discussion of meaning in philosophy of science began with an anti-empiricist argument which quickly became an anti-realist one as well: successive theories in some domain are semanticly incomparable (this would wreck empiricism) and hence there could be no referential stability, so realism about theories over the course of the history of science is incoherent, or anyway strongly false. (See also Section 8.4.2.) A crucial premise of this argument as formulated by its proponents (Kuhn 1962, Feyarabend 1962, 1965a,b,c) is that meaning is determined by linguistic role. The resulting Wittgensteinian theory of meaning can be labelled a description theory because it suggests that the meaning of a term is given by some description of the term's referent. E.g., one might adopt a semantic version of a Ramsey sentence for each theoretical term; thus 'electron' means 'the entity referred to by the term appearing in such and such places (i.e., playing that role) in the axioms of electromagnetic theory', etc.[192] Thus the incommensurability argument is primarily a semantic one and has provoked a semantic response, roughly as follows: the argument for incommensurability is based on a faulty or false theory of meaning, to wit the description theory. Once replace this by a causal theory of meaning and the argument fails, an entity or state can have the same causal relation to us even while we change our minds about its theoretical description.

The causal theory of meaning is, again roughly, the theory that the meaning of a term is determined by a certain kind of causal relationship between the users of that term and the object, state, etc., to which reference is being made. Commonest examples are proper names; 'Peter' e.g., evidently carries no descriptive information, the way I know which individual is tagged by that name is either that I have been introduced to him or have had some other kind of appropriate causal connection with him (mediated via others). According to the description theory, if the theoretical postulates are changed at all, or anyway changed at all substantially, then the meaning of their terms also change. Such meaning changes are what produce incommensurability. The causal theory offers a way around this semantic barrier. Plausibly, if I am in fact causally related to a local part of a tensor mass density distribution then that is what I am referring to even if my first attempt at description of it tries to designate it using one-place particle predicates. Anchored in this way, I can go on exploring alternative descriptive structures, approximating more and more closely to the real characteristics to which I am causally relating. This is the picture offered by Boyd (1980, 1984, 1985), the 'middle-Putnam' (1978) and others.[193]

There is no doubt about the attractiveness to realism of a causal component to semantics; if not causally, then how else do humans interact with their world? And there is no doubt that description or role semantics has real difficulties (see e.g., Devitt 1984). Is this then the end of the matter? I think it wise for realism not to end investigation here. In part this is because causal semantics also has its problems.[194] In part it is because there is lots of countervailing argument. E.g., Smith (1981) develops a clearly articulated descriptivist alternative to the purely causal line, develops an account of scientific progress on its basis and defends it through several detailed examples. Much of Smith's argumentation strikes me as plausible, plausible enough to think that there is one part of the truth to be found here. Sklar (1982) offers criticisms of both role semantics (it yields a poor theory of theory equivalence) and causal semantics (it yields a poor theory of the identification of phenomena and causes). And I find Churchland's arguments (1979, Chapter 3) for two components to the significance of sentences, one of semantic importance and the other of systematic importance, quite compelling and the theory of linguistic translation which emerges therefrom sufficiently attractive to feel that it has a core of truth to it. But Churchland's analyses here are built on role semantics, not causal semantics. Churchland's recent approach to the problem of semantics and natural kinds (1985c) also has a sharp and refreshing naturalist thrust to it that seems to me to be the right corrective to recent language-oriented analyses. (I do not, however, follow him to his sceptical conclusion concerning truth.) And I find Churchland's insistence on theory-mediated understanding of perceptual differences persuasive. But these last two analyses jointly speak for the importance of causal relation and role.[195] Another source of my unease stems from the dramatic difference in identity criteria between atomic and plenum metaphysical schemes—the former leading to an 'a-descriptive' purely geometric characterization and the latter to one rooted in qualitative identity.[196] The development of an adequate semantics is still quite unsure at this stage—surely all of our deepest metaphysics, our internal cognitive organization and our social practices can be expected to contribute something to meaning, along with our causal relations with the world. (On this latter see also Section 8.4.3.5)

Despite the uncertainty, Putnam (1981) has recently developed an argument against the correspondence theory based on semantic considerations. Having earlier rejected a description theory of reference (so meaning also—see 1978), Putnam now rejects (realist versions of) the causal theory of reference also. Assuming that there are no other candidates to connect us to the external world, Putnam concludes that our semantics must be restricted to connections of sentences to an internal world. I am not certain, but I suspect that a realist ought to reject both Putnam's argument against the causal theory of reference[197] as well as the assumption that narrowly construed causal and narrowly construed description theories of reference exhaust the possibilities (see above).

Recently too Dummett (1978, 1982) has tried to recast the realist/anti-realist dispute as a semantic one, as a dispute about the extent of bivalence. To this has been added an empiricist twist in semantic guise. What is noteworthy is the way that both realists (e.g., Devitt 1984, Chapter 12, Trigg 1980) and anti-realists (e.g., van Fraassen 1980, Section 2.7, Horwich 1982a) have joined forces in attacking this 'linguistic turn'. I am content to let them speak for me, and thereby illustrate the hazards of this approach.

It is a common experience that the concepts of an earlier theory 'fragment and flow' under the shift to a later one. 'Temperature' and other thermodynamic concepts did this under the shift to statistical mechanics; instead of everything having a definite temperature there are systems that have no temperature, or a "fuzzy" temperature. 'Consciousness' looks like it will do this, as clinical investigation turns up automaton-like yet responsive states, 'blind'-sight and other conditions (cf. Churchland 1983). In much the same way I believe we might expect the concept of meaning to fracture and flow under the transition to a deeper cognitive theory. Hearer-meanings are surely something like the totality of sensory-motor coordinations, the totality of orientations to the world, including the speaker, oneself and other humans, induced by linguistic tokens. (Speaker-meanings are something like the totality of such orientations intended.) If this sounds vague it is because it awaits unpacking in a decent cognitive theory. What are the chances that, when thus embedded, meanings will turn out to be some single kind within that cognitive theory? Everything we know about meaning—from controversies over role and referential semantics and Davidsonian versus non-Davidsonian semantics, to the status of Grician speech implicatures and the like—everything we know points to the answer "very little". And beyond this disputes widen out among the many opposed approaches to linguistics itself and to the whole business of bringing agency and a-rational causal-explanatory concepts into interrelation (cf. Note 151).

So I have not relied on philosophical semantics to settle substantive issues, have maintained so far as was possible a studied neutrality and even sceptically-toned agnosticism about these issues. And I have tentatively rejected reliance on such arguments by anti-realists. But in the long run all these issues must be faced by a viable realism.

8.4.4 The Limits of Agnosticism: Beyond Philosophy of Science

The realist, as I remarked in Section 8.4.3, is faced with this dilemma by his opponents: Either the explanatory methodology which justifies realism *vis-à-vis* scientific theories is that which justifies each of these theories *vis-à-vis* their data domains, or it is not. If it is, then repeating that methodology at the philosophical level will ensure that its defects (if any) remain undetected. If it is not, it remains a 'methodological dangler' without support. In either case realism is not to be rationally justified in this manner.[198] To this I replied by arguing that self-consistency sufficed. While the first horn of this dilemma showed that this position was risky, it did nothing to eliminate the position on those grounds. And in fact the human condition is one of inelimina-ble risk.

Fine (1984), not content, seeks to press the issue. Consider, he suggests, the parallel case of consistency proofs for mathematics. Here one faces the same dilemma, a consistency proof for set theory employing set theoretic methods will only be acceptable if set theory is in fact consistent, but a bogus proof will certainly be available if set theory is not consistent (since from an inconsistent theory anything at all follows). In response to this dilemma mathematicians such as Hilbert opted for a more stringent set of requirements for such proofs, namely the restriction to constructive steps. The rational realist should equally accept the need for increased stringency, Fine argues, but none is to be had. Fine then likens continued realist commitment to religious faith beyond the claims of reason, while opting himself for metaphysical agnosticism. His position here is closely related to that of van Fraassen, who is able to abandon twentieth century empiricism (likening it to atheism) in favour of a rational agnosticism in which belief does not extend beyond the empirical evidence, and who makes the analogy with religious commitments clear (1980, Chapter 7).

The argument deserves response. The idea that there might be 'ultimate commitment' behind philosophical positions is very old and equally widespread. Most closely to present interests, it connects (i) to Popper's 'external' commitment of the scientist to rationality and Feyerabend's related tracing of epistemology back to ethical commitments;[199] (ii) to a long tradition going at least back to Fichte, which traces the opposition between realism and idealism to an opposition of basic value commitments (see Urban's review in 1949); to a sociological tradition deriving from Mannheim that science includes a set of self-reinforcing/self-justifying norms (see 1936, cf. Greiner 1984). It even has its coy reflection in the modern empiricist's internal/external distinctions (e.g., Carnap 1950, cf. Goldstick 1979). Beyond that it fans out to the Dooyerwerdian Christian critique of systematic philosophy (1960); to the wider faith/reason critique of Dooyerwerd's existentialist ancestor, Kierkegaard; and so on. Of course, this issue relates directly both to my discussion of critical theory of cultures vis-à-vis historical deadends (Chapter 4, Section 4.6, Chapter 3, Section 3.3.2) and to my remarks on mysticism and transcendence (Chapter 7, Sections 7.3, 7.13).

There is a certain poignancy to Fine's insistence on stringency, because of course he had also to admit in the same breath that Godel's theorem and related results put paid to the more stringent constructivist program in mathematics. So no deep examples of increased stringency are to hand. (In any case, increased stringency cannot eliminate ultimate appeal to intuitive judgement, it can only reduce the width of appeals made, so to speak. We then need an additional intuitive judgement or explicit argument that the reduction in width is actually an improvement.) In this light there are three kinds of responses one can contemplate: intuitive dogmatism, commital fallibilism and agnosticism. Intuitive dogmatism is the position which sets particular intuitive judgements up as the final court of appeal and refuses to countenance criticism of them.[200] Agnosticism counsels withholding belief. Committal fallibilism is committal, i.e., in context one believes and uses best available theory within its domain; but it is also fallibilist, one questions every theory in its meta-context and tries to keep relevant options open. The question which Fine and van Fraassen press is this: when should lack of stringency require agnosticism?

If the question is posed boldly like this the answer which can seem the only rational one is: always. Always remain agnostic on anything not stringently demonstrated. But this is fake advice; nothing is stringently demonstrated and one still has to live—intelligently. More-

over, even stringent demonstrations require ultimate appeals to intuitive judgement, so one has not after all escaped risky judgement.
Indeed, one has not succeeded, in any practical way, in reducing risk.
Consider van Fraassen's delicate footwork here: the agnostic scientist
runs no fewer risks of error than does the realist scientist (Chapter 6,
Section 6.4), commits himself practically to the use of the theory in his
life just as does the fallibilist realist — and yet he is said to remain
'agnostic'![201]

Indeed, there is more yet to the 'agnostic's' commitment, for in
using a theory he allows himself to be transformed according to the
theory. His way of perceiving the world, his 'conceptual exploitation
of stimuli' (Churchland 1979) to the extent it is cognitively penetrable,
will change. (Or is agnosticism tacitly committed to an *a priori* conservative perceptual psychology here?) Should his theories discriminate
among humans in relation to epistemic capacities, he will discriminate. (Or is agnosticism tacitly committed to an essentialist or species-
chauvinist definition of epistemic community?)[202] Should the theory
recommend various psychotherapies or medical interventions to improve his performance, he will subject himself to them, or subject
others to them on his recommendation. (Or is agnosticism tacitly
committed to some form of primitivism?) All of these decisions are
risky, many may be irreversible (either for the individual or the species). But the van Fraassean agnostic here is willy-nilly committed,
exactly as if he were a realist. The fallibilist realist accepts that our
circumstances are risky in this manner and moves (van Fraassen
might say 'leaps' or 'plunges') forward into the irreversible exploration of life, of cognitive and personal becoming, critically testing as he
goes. If agnosticism is to be a significant position it must hold to a
more conservative line than this, but where can a principled line be
drawn?

The moral parallel is informative here. Here is how I find the world.
Those who, by whatever process, find themselves oriented to loving
also find there is no end to the sequence of self-reinforcing transformations into which they are led. The ego with its associations of
desire satisfaction, power and control wanes (slowly!), other forms of
life and understanding wax. Conversely, those who are not so oriented find there are self-reinforcing developmental paths toward ego-
centeredness and hatreds. The development has an irreversible character. It is often impossible to understand or empathize with the
values and insights of one further along in the loving process (including one's self at later times). In the same way it is often impossible to
understand or empathize with the values and attitudes of one further

along in the self-centeredness process and this frequently includes self-recognition of a later stage. In this process of personal becoming I am of course not practically neutral. But neither am I theoretically neutral. I hold a dim view of much Western intellectualizing ethical philosophy, divorced as it is from the specificity of loving. I look to specific (often 'odd') sources for understanding and reject others (cf. Chapter 7, Section 7.12). These understandings in turn orient me to new personal transformations (cf. the parallel with science dynamics, Section 8.3.9) and to new theoretical critiques (cf. Chapter 6, Section 6.7).

In short, by unifying the theoretical structures for cognitive and moral exploration and becoming, I am arguing the appropriateness of the naturalist realist position for both. Indeed, following the 'parameter space' model (Chapter 7, Section 7.11), I want to see all developmental processes as both valuable and cognitive in a generalized sense (cf. below). And I'm trying to see reason as a generalized intelligence (cf. Section 8.4.3.7), as the dialectical intermediary between value and truth, truth the function of value via its proxies and value a function of truth via learning, their mutual and evolving influence mediated by reason, itself evolving in the process.[203]

Van Fraassen, following contrary empiricist instincts, wants to diminish the cognitive in favour of a non-cognitive pluralism. He says: "Making sense of a subject does not need to consist in portraying it as telling a true story."[204] Now I have entered multiple values to science and called them proxies for truth. Then cannot van Fraassen argue that any of these values can be portrayed as the objective in the game of science and science understood in that manner? In response I have stressed the cognitive exploration of these values in tandem with the cognitive explanation of the world, as well as the way these values only hang together in an over all cognitive theory assigning an essential role to truth.

But is truth the only goal of human development? No. Understanding this answer requires setting a theory of science in a larger philosophy of human development. These essays sketch only the beginnings of such a wider account (see especially Chapter 7, Sections 7.7 to 7.13). Here again I have applied the principles of naturalist realism, in particular I have looked for a unified conception of the dynamics of development (cf. above). And behind those dynamics, unification raises a final important theme: the unity of values. Intuitively, none of the proxies for truth in science make cognitive sense in themselves *simplicitur*, they need to be seen as proxies. Indeed, they can only be understood, I think, jointly (cf. Section 8.2.2) and as perhaps more closely related to the nature of truth than is an arbitrary external indicator. They need to be seen as composing the complex face of truth presented to searchers who begin from ignorance. Unhappily, I have nothing perceptive to say about how to represent these intuitions properly within a naturalist realist context.[205] Beyond these specific cognitive values there lie the wider range of values relevant to human development with which they are inextricably connected (Section 8.3.2). Indeed, one of the profound characteristics of love is that loving leads to a clearer conception of self and others, and of the non-human world as well, as ego projections wane. Similarly, it leads also to more effective science (cf. Chapter 3, Section 3.3.2). The True, the Good and the Beautiful—a naturalist realist theory of the old Platonic interconnections among these I don't have—but my respect for the problem is growing.

So I shall conclude by returning to another theme, the significance for understanding the human condition of our complex of temporal 'imperfections': our perpetual becoming, in ignorance of our world, our own natures and our futures; the connection between the openness of the future and the character of our cognitive and personal development; the tension, universal across all values, between being actor and being spectator. In the terms of an older framework these issues amount, I suppose, to providing an understanding of the metaphysics of the 'sphere of corruption'. I can now at least see the roots of each of these component issues in the foundations of contemporary science and philosophy—the reader will find hints scattered throughout these essays. To return to the commitment/agnosticism issue: caught in these temporal imperfections as we are, what is one to intelligently do? I don't think one can be both intelligently and interestingly agnostic. As for a realist account, I still have no advance to offer on the ultimate paragraph of Chapter 7.

Notes

CHAPTER 1

1. Taking science seriously is intended as a rebuke to those who deal in small, artificial examples and who are thereby able to make equally small, artificial theories seem plausible. Thus when Laudan (1981b) chides me for imagining that non-realists don't take science seriously I presume he misses what I intended. It is precisely those historians of science who attempt to deal with science in all its complexity with whom I am intending to express agreement. Yet the story is not quite so simple. I also had in mind this: philosophy of science complex enough to be adequate to science as a real historical process on this planet undermines all of the empiricisms with which I had been raised. Possibly, therefore, it would rule out Laudan's preferred version as well (cf. Chapter 8, Notes 80, 145).

2. Chapters 6 and 7 were written in 1982, though Chapter 7 was published in 1983 and Chapter 6 in 1985 (while I waited for the book, for which it was the impetus, to be completed). Chapters 1 and 8 have never appeared before.

3. I believe there is value in slowly elaborating a principled framework, a value complementary to specific contributions to particular sub-problems. The danger of the reverse approach is illustrated by those who pursued logistic definitions of simplicity without noticing that there were several sorts which may conflict with one another (cf. Chapter 2, Note 20), or who pursued simple deductive models of reduction without noticing how complex are real intertheory relations (see Hooker 1981c). But of course the two activities—framework elaboration and detailed studies—are complementary and both are necessary. These essays focus on the former.

4. This sometimes even includes friends of Realism. Perhaps it is largely a cultural feature of the New World where (European!) history is short, for the continental philosophers often display a reverse vice, namely to suppose that identifying references to a great dead philosopher will place their views beyond criticism.

5. Urban 1949 favors a dialectical synthesis not unreminiscent of Lenin 1927, though without the emphasis on materialism. (On the 'materialism' involved here see Chapter 8, Notes 27, 79.) If 'dialectic' is spelled out generously there is much of interest and value in this tradition (cf. Novack 1971 on empiricism). This agreement could be extended to include many ethical and social values. Yet there is, beside theoretical difficulties (cf. Chapter 8, Note 79), also an uncompromising certitude of rightness to post-Marx Marxist analysis which is incompatible with the fallibilism of naturalist realism as well as with concomitant values in politics and ethics deriving from fallibilism. My own 'mix' is developed in 1979a, 1980b, 1983.

6. See Holt 1912. Holt himself held an ultimately nonrealist view of perception, in which sensa were real entities. There are, of course, many objections I would raise to the views of this group, especially to those of Holt and Montague.

7. For the succeeding Critical Realist phase see e.g., Drake 1920. For critical naturalism with an evolutionary flavor see e.g., Pratt 1940 and Sellars 1916, 1922, 1932, cf. Delaney's 1969 thoughtful study.

8. E.g., Hicks 1938 and the frustratingly vague Laird 1920.

9. The tradition here runs from Reid down to Moore. Overall see the useful historical review by Hassan 1928 and cf. McCosh 1887.

10. See again the review by Hassan 1928, and Urban 1949. Perhaps meriting particular mention are the connections to Pragmatism in methodology and in the recognition of the institutionalised character of science.

Chapter 2

1. Thus there is no insistence here on identification of theory with a linguistic formulation in some *used* language (whether common language or that of the scientist), mathematical-logical formulation of a theory is acceptable, the theory being identified equally with the set of axioms set down or with the class of *intended* models of those axioms (i.e., physically irrelevant models are eliminated).

Equally, I do not assume that the Realist is concerned only with theoretical entities (i.e., individual substances) but admit theoretical properties also, nor assume that these latter are predicated only of theoretical entities, nor observable properties only of non-theoretical entities—cf. Achinstein 1968, Putnam 1962, Sellars 1965a, etc. But this is only to forewarn the reader of issues to be discussed in what follows.

2. One of the problems arising here is the so-called 'incommensurability' of world views: by definition, a truly complete world view contains a cohering version of everything (ethics, ontology, epistemology, linguistics, science, etc.), thus one can never 'get outside' it, there is no neutral ground; but in this case we all seem doomed to forever be unable to even discuss issues seriously with our opponents (and vice versa), since such discussion, if it is to be a genuine meeting of minds, must be on neutral ground. Fortunately, the following condition seems adequate to guarantee rational debate without presupposing neutral ground: that each world view be rich enough to faithfully represent within itself opposing world views. Our ability to talk *about* other structures (logical, mathematical) using a particular structure, other languages using a particular language, is wide indeed. However, this possibility does not by itself guarantee that decision among world views will be rational, or determine what the basis of that decision is. I have hinted here and in 1975b that a strong ethical component is involved.

3. Feyerabend and Kuhn have been greatly misunderstood (and perhaps have even misunderstood themselves) in this because almost everyone operates with the primary notion of *Science*. From this perspective one accuses them of confusing psychology and sociology with epistemology and methodology, or of introducing total irrationality into *Science*. But once one views their work from the new perspective then much of what is puzzling falls into place. E.g., Kuhn's account of paradigm-dominated science is to be seen as articulating the total epistemic context from within which decisions in some historical period are made and Feyerabend's account of Galileo-as-propagandist is to be understood as a rational account of 'gambling with truth' in an ideologically-epistemically loaded situation, etc. Cf. my remarks in Hooker 1975b.

4. The term 'new epistemology' derives from a paper of G.C. Nerlich's which I saw during the summer of 1972 and which proved very helpful in clarifying some of my ideas. Already a year earlier than that I had been independently thinking about the problem as e.g., my brief remarks in 1972c indicate. About that time I rediscovered the importance of Quine's 'Epistemology Naturalized' (1969). I am also indebted to John Nicholas for some further ideas that arose out of discussion of a paper of his in October 1972.

5. A characteristically clear earlier statement of this position is found in Quine's 'Epistemology Naturalised' (1969). According to Quine, the abandonment of the Empiricist semantical and epistemological program for science (respectively dogmas 3 and 4) leaves no task remaining for the traditional conception of epistemology and it must either be abandoned (as e.g., the later Wittgenstein would have) or reduced to a branch of psychology, specifically to the question of how in fact creatures with our make-up arrive at our beliefs. Similarly, Quine sees no role for the traditional approach to semantics, but in this case advocates its abandonment in favour only of a theory of reference and truth. (In similar fashion we might construe Quine and Davidson—pace Nerlich—as suggesting that the abandonment of the traditional approach to the nature of truth shifts philosophic interest from a pointless issue to two real problems: how to speak coherently of truth—a problem solved by Tarski—and how to account for the knowledge of infinitely many truths when a finite language is employed.) In my view though, Quine overstates the case, for he makes it sound as if all critical reflection upon science is to be abandoned in favour of just science. I surely believe, along with armchair philosophers, that one has to distinguish the critical appraisal of science from science, otherwise the latter becomes blind. Quine on the other hand, seems bent upon excluding normative considerations entirely. Quine is right that the criteria of epistemically justified action merge much more conspicuously into the general criterion of rational action but, I think, too hasty in dropping the normative dimension of the latter. And it is *not* true that normative theories cannot be informed by experience. What is really needed is a dynamical theory of the interaction of normative and descriptive theories as experience changes—but to supply that here would lead us too far afield. Quine is not quite right, the key question is not simply 'How do men in fact theorize in response to stimulation?' but something closer to 'Given creatures of our construction, in our circumstances, *including* the answer to Quine's question, which parts of science are epistemically justified? How should the rational man respond theoretically?' While on the subject of this important essay, let me gather together one or two other remarks concerning the views expressed in it.

Quine, as always, is unrepentantly empiricist about language, about meaning especially. The only place we have anything remotely satisfactorily identifiable as meaning are the so-called observation sentences and their meaning is stimulus meaning. But by his own lights, Quine should surely wait upon the deliverances of psychology in this area! For all we know, a rich notion of meaning will be forthcoming that departs radically from stimulus meaning, it might be that the human mind has an inner predilection and facility for the abstract. Even Quine's own notion of stimulus meaning must be supplemented by *internal* stimuli if it is to make any sense of the distinctions between an observation report uttered in veridical, illusory and hallucinatory circumstances, c.f. Schick (1972)—who can tell *a priori* how rich these inner stimuli are? My own remarks on semantics which follow show my Quinean uneasiness with the notion of meaning, but I am unwilling to write it off (or down) in his fashion until more is understood about the relations between language, thought and action—cf. Note 68.

Quine is also quick to point out how under the new epistemology the notion of an absolute observation sentence loses its sense to be replaced by some notion concerning nearness to stimulation in the causal chain. I think this must be right. But his quick step from there to a Feyerabendian pragmatic theory of observation where what counts as an observation sentence depends upon no more than the gross behaviour of the linguistic community is just too quick. It ignores what psychology may tell us (to double Quine's irony— p.88), and this may be important in relation to the view of theories taken. For example, if psychological research suggests a permanently fixed fund of observational concepts with no conditioning possible then Feyerabend will be simply wrong. If, as I believe —cf. below—we must distinguish sharply sensory content from observational reporting, with conditioning essentially affecting only the latter, then Feyerabend has too simplistic a view and the quasi-empiricist Ramsey account is in some difficulty. Because it suggests none of this detail, Quine's vague proposal is unhelpful and uninformative.

6. Though not destroy, of course, the insight that a man might adopt the right beliefs for the wrong reasons. But the standard account makes the bridging of the dualism in a fashion which does reasonable justice to the history of science almost impossible.

7. I am indebted to discussions with J.J. Leach on these issues —the reader interested in this approach to induction is invited to consult Leach 1976, as well as Luckenbach, 1972 (and Ch. 8 Sec. 8.3.5).

8. Cf., e.g., the discussion by Maxwell 1970, 1973.

9. Roughly speaking, these correspond respectively e.g., to Hospers' *concept empiricism* and *judgment empiricism*—cf. 1967, Chapter 2.

10. The reader is referred to the standard literature for a statement (and appraisal) of these doctrines—see. e.g., Achinstein and Barker, 1969, Aune 1970, Ayer 1946, Carnap 1928, 1956a, Feyerabend 1965a, 1969, Hempel 1950, 1958, Nagel 1961, Pap 1963a, Quine 1960, 1963 Cf. Lewis 1970.

11. This remark is explained a little later on. Historically, it is probably the case that explicit Conventionalism is a late arrival, being considerably predated by Instrumentalism (perhaps better called Fictionalism) which played a dominent role in the discussions of the significance of astronomy from Ptolemy onwards. Cf. e.g., the remarks by John Winnie in an as yet unpublished paper 'Realism Without Regrets'. Winnie also discusses the historically operative auxiliary motives for support for Instrumentalism; roughly, they come down to this: Instrumentalism can be invoked to nullify any theoretical view that one has independent grounds (empiricist, religious, ideological, etc.) for wanting nullified.

Originally, I had intended to deal only with the various particular kinds of convention that might appear in a physical theory, in a later section. (I still do this, see Hooker 1974, Sections I, II). Prof. J. O. Wisdom convinced me that to do only this would be an error. Furthermore, the expression of the conventionalist position (though not my basic understanding of it) is indebted to a recent discussion of Wisdom's 1972. Though I do not follow his solution, his discussion contains many illuminating remarks. Further discussion of Conventionalism can be found in the references of Note 8 and in Wisdom 1971.

12. But first let us be absolutely clear that Realism (*my* Realism) concedes the initial premise of this general attack. Prescinding for the moment from the question of how the actual structure of science is best represented (further on which see below), let us consider the traditional (Empiricist, Conventionalist) structural theory:

Level Type
(1) $(x)(\ldots T\ldots)$
(2) $(x)(\ldots T, O\ldots)$
(3) $(x)(\ldots O\ldots)$
(4) $\ldots O, a\ldots$

Deduction ↓   Induction ↑

The structural relationships hold among them, *in general*, as the arrows suggest. Level (1) contains only initially universally quantified expressions containing only theoretical terms. (That is, I assume the initial quantifier to be universal, although it may be followed by one or more existential quantifiers; actually, I have some sympathy for the view that we could possibly find a fundamental law essentially expressible only with a first existential quantifier but here I need only the conclusion that the kinds of laws stated do occur in science, and in fact they predominate.) This first level is the level of 'pure theories'. (Not all theories have such a level and it is not clear what 'pure' involves here, but I let that pass for the moment.) Level (2) has similarly quantified expressions that mix observational and theoretical terms. These supply the so-called 'correspondence rules'. Level (3), while similarly quantified, contains only observational terms—the observational generalizations. Level (4) contains the unquantified sentences reporting 'facts'. In this standard account level (3) is deducible from levels (1) + (2) and some members of level (4) from other members together with level (3). Each level is imagined deductively axiomatized and the whole likewise. Fact: only members of level (4) (and perhaps also a very small and uninteresting subclass of level (3)) are sense-confirmable, i.e., can have their truth values ascertained on the basis of sensory experience. (The members of level (3) which I have in mind might be assertions of the form "All the marbles in the palm of John's hand are red," where 'marbles' is understood as specifying an object at least one centimeter in diameter.) Conclusion: no interesting level (3) sentences, and *a fortiori* no level (1) or level (2) sentences at all, are sense-confirmable. Logical truth: no inference from any collection of level (4) sentences to any collection of level (3) sentences is ever deductively valid. (Even if the level (4) sentences in fact exhaust a class of beasties, that particular fact is not reported among them.) Fact: no instance of a theoretical predicate is ever observable (*qua* theoretical predicate—but cf. Note 1). Conclusion: not even a single instance of level (1) and level (2) sentences is sense-confirmable. *A fortiori, a fortiori* level (1) and (2) sentences are not sense-confirmable. There is no escaping this conclusion. Fact: the increased expressive richness of levels (1) and (2) permits an infinite variety of theories to deductively imply the same subset of sense-accessible level (4) sentences and hence be 'empirically equivalent'. (Notice that this is a loaded, anti-Realist conception of empirical equivalence. The Realist will say only that they are observationally equivalent.)

Now the Realist is apt to reject the strict observational/theoretical dichotomy on which this structure is based and from which its epistemology flows. Even so, he will be hard-pressed to reject, as *generally adequate*, the hierarchy of logical form posed (skipping the observational status of the predicates occurring in the theories) and hence cannot reject the problem of the invalidity of the inference from instance to generalization. Mary Hesse 1968a writes as if the whole structural description could be rejected, I suppose on the grounds that the 'network model' has no use for such hierarchies, cf. her 1970, but this is surely to exaggerate. True, epistemologically loaded hierarchies such as the observational/theoretical, or concrete/abstract will not follow without further epistemological assumptions from a structural description, but it is implausible to reject the formal deductive hierarchy since analyses of actual theories suggests that, by and large, it is appropriate (see the appendix of Chapter 4 for an instance where pure deduction doesn't suffice going 'downward'). The empiricist analysts (Carnap, Hempel, etc.) certainly were familiar with formal analyses of scientific theories.

However, in addition I at least accept that there is an important element of truth in the empiricist observational/theoretical dichotomy (though I do not by any means think they have stated this correctly), and so I, and more generally anyone who is prepared to concede that theories even often deal with unobservable entities, must concede the general epistemological conclusion drawn above from the traditional structure (see below for a detailed discussion of the alternative Realist position here). This agreed feature of the epistemology of science is the basis for the attacks of the opponents of Realism.

13. I shall present here only the briefest recapitulation of the attacks on Empiricism, my aim being to show how they presuppose alternative world-positions.

Psychologically, Locke's account of concept formation is plausible only if one neglects the hereditary structure of the central nervous system and its powers, allowing the mind only logical operations with which to transform the only ideas (concepts) it is allowed, namely those given directly in sensory experience. This is the power of the view—it is also its great empirical weakness. The view of concepts inherent in the doctrine assumes them to be conscious, linguistic units, whereas a more adequate view recognizes the notion of information-processes in the central nervous system as the fundamental units—in this latter case one obtains a more effective account of concept formation and a very great enrichment of the category of concepts. (Some of the ramifications are lightly spelled out in Hooker 1975d, cf. Note 64.) The only dispute among psychologists today is how rich the hereditary structure is (less rich it seems, than Kant thought it was) and how the fantastically rich variety of imaginative transpositions occur. (See e.g., Gregory 1971, Haber 1969, Kohler 1962, Piaget 1954, Pribram 1971, Wyburn et. al. 1968; for a more detailed discussion of perception Hooker 1970a, 1978a.) And Realism takes science, hence psychology, seriously.

As a bold statement of the appropriate analysis of the psychology of perception, the dogma 3-dogma 4 combination is found similarly wanting (there is none but superficial evidence for the existence of simple units, givens, in perceptual experience—cf. Hooker 1970a, Chapter 4 and the references cited there), and as a characterization of the history of science dogma 4 is again inadequate (plenty of observational claims have been revised in the light of experience, see especially the studies by Feyerabend 1965a,b, 1969, 1970a), yet a sufficiently 'hard-nosed' empiricist might insist on retaining dogma 4 as an in-retrospect and in-principle analysis of perceptual claims and of the progress of science (using some subtle theses concerning descriptions to counter the objections—cf. Section 2.6.4 below).

Philosophically, doctrines 2, 3, 4 and 5 have come under attack. There are powerful arguments to show that, contra *P*-Empiricism and Empiricism dogma 3, theoretical terms as they occur in actual theories of science cannot be defined in terms of purely observational vocabulary. (Cf. the works by Aune 1967, Nagel 1961, and Pap 1963a and Sneed 1971.) One of the kinds of arguments that does not work for (or respectively against) Empiricism is the argument from the formal separability of the observational from the theoretical part of science, for it presupposes the rejection of Realism (respectively, Empiricism) – cf. Hooker 1968a,b.) These arguments are 'nice' because they largely hinge on features of extant theories that any plausible view would want to incorporate. The honest point is, polemically, that to offer an interpretation of a theory is not simply to show how its heretofore uninterpreted terms are connected to 'simple' observation, but to say what is really going on in the world as opposed to, but explanatory of, what appears to be, is observed to be, going on. One does not want to know merely that in circumstances *C* an instrument dial reads *R* but what is really going on between the instrument and the world such that it comes to read *R*. This clearly involves theoretical ontology but it also involves other things, e.g., a theory of perception, which Empiricism ignores. Nonetheless our hard-nosed empiricist might cling to his reconstruction of science as the only ultimately justifiable one.

(Recently Maxwell has claimed that Russell's doctrine of the knowledge by acquaintance/knowledge by description dichotomy, bolstered by the application of his theory of definite descriptions to a Ramsey approach to theories, reconciles concept Empiricism with Realism, for in this case we use only observation terms and logic to refer to theoretical entities. (For Russell's doctrines see 1927, 1948, cf. Maxwell, 1962, 1970, 1973, and for Ramsey's approach see 1931, cf. Section 2.6 below for a detailed examination.) More precisely, Maxwell rejects dogmas 2 and 4 and would reject dogmas 1 and 5 I believe. He has dogma 3 alone in mind, and only a *W*-Empiricist version since not every term is reducible without remainder to observation terms, specifically not the described theoretical terms. Tentatively I believe this claim to be correct; tentatively, because the Realism that results is so pallid I am not sure it can stand—cf. Section 5.4. If so, what this demonstrates is that if you cut one of the empiricist dogmas off severely enough from a systematic view and weaken it sufficiently it becomes compatible with almost anything.)

The Verifiability Criterion of Meaning which is the general semantical support for the foregoing construction has come under severe attack and has now generally been abandoned. (This is essentially part of the attack on dogma 3, see Achinstein 1968, Achinstein/Barker 1969, Aune 1967, Ayer 1946, Bunge 1967b, Carnap 1928, 1956a, Hempel 1950, 1958, 1965, 1970, Hesse 1968a, 1970, Nagel 1961, Pap 1963a, Popper 1934, Putnam 1962a, 1965, Quine 1960, 1963,

Sellars 1963, Smart 1968, Suppe 1974a, Suppes 1960, 1969.) Indeed the Security Dogma has the characteristic that it only needs to be clearly stated for its implausibility to be evident. The Epistemological Dogma is somewhat weaker (and subtler for this reason) but its support also comes from the same basic empiricist doctrines—indeed, it is the kind of doctrine for which none other than this kind of support is imaginable.

Recently the legitimacy of the observational/theoretical distinction has been attacked (see Achinstein 1968, Putnam 1962a), but not, I think, effectively against a 'hard-nosed' opponent. (The argument here is parallel to that immediately below. Cf. also Suppe 1972b.) Quine and Putnam, among others, have attacked dogma 2, with uncertain success. (Quine 1960, 1963 and Putnam 1962a) Quine's argument seems to hinge on the claim that if any of a collection of terms can only be inter-defined (i.e., defined in terms of each other) then the whole collection wants for sense. (So much the worse for language!) Why should not an empiricist introduce his preferred language, already complete with a sharp analytic/synthetic distinction (as Carnap wants to) and then lay down explicit syntactic definitions of these semantical categories as a *fait accompli*? (The extensions of these semantical terms can be claimed to approximate—and merely sharpen—our preanalytic intuitions.) Besides, it would seem that Quine's preferred remainder to semantics (truth, reference, etc.) is in no better position on this score (and on some others, cf. Hooker 1971a.) Moreover, it is arguable that Quine also adopts an implausibly strict (almost Positivist) criterion of what can count as part of the definition of meanings, etc., namely overt behaviour alone. However, if one adds verbal and internal stimuli then a defensible position may result—for a recent defense, cf. Wilder 1973.)

Dogma 5 (Phenomenalism) has been consistently attacked recently (see Sellars 1963, Armstrong 1961, Feyerabend 1960 but it seems to me that a sufficiently hard-nosed Phenomenalist could legitimately reject the arguments since they all hinge on particular characteristics of our present conceptual structure more highly than the doctrine of Phenomenalism itself (cf. Hooker 1970a.).

Above and beyond these detailed criticisms, there is a question of meta-consistency: the basic tenets of Empiricism (and of Conventionalism) constitute a general theory about the nature of man and his relation to the world, they seem neither reducible to 'sensation and reflection' (Empiricism), nor to conventions, if they are to make the sense their proponents require of them. Empiricism will need to show its own tenets necessary truths, or offer some transcendental deduction of them, and conventionalism make sense of its own implicit general account of language, before these doctrines achieve the coherence required of a world view.

14. The instrumentalist can hardly claim the fact that theories are used importantly to make inferences as distinctive support, the Realist agrees to *that* —it is the claim that they are *only* instruments to this end that needs support.

15. In this connection, the new work being done on a 'systems epistemology' or an 'ecology of knowledge' though often misleadingly formulated is the beginnings of a more explicit integration around the historical spiral of

epistemology with social science looked for in Section 1—see e.g. Bateson 1972, Piaget 1970, Wojciechowski 1975, and cf. Hooker 1975b.

16. Realism is incompatible with the semantics of phenomenalistic reduction certainly, but in this case we have something more direct—the ontology of psychology taken Realistically is not compatible with the ontology of Phenomenalism, nor do the actual psychological details support the Representative Realist theory.

17. One perfectly legitimate analysis of physical theories suggests that quantum theory demands an objective revision of the laws of logic—cf. Hooker 1971a. I happen not to accept the conclusion in this case for other reasons, but I might have, had these other reasons not applied.

For a stimulating departure from foundational epistemology in science see Feyerabend 1961, cf. Hooker 1972 a,b.

18. But an epistemologist with my persuasion would be inclined to take a similar view of historical theses, religious doctrines, etc.

19. Certainly for D_2 anyway. If a semantical presupposition of the use of our kind of language turns out to be some very general facts concerning the world and our neurological structure, then the condition sets in D_1 may in fact partially overlap, or even overlap quite a lot, though remaining semantically distinct kinds of conditions.

These distinctions ought to be refined by the further distinctions I drew in 1972c, p. 167.

20. There is, e.g., ontological simplicity, conceptual simplicity, simplicity of axiomatization, simplicity of derivation of key theorems and simplicity of representation. This last includes Schaffner's notion of fitness (cf. 1970). For an introduction to the complexities of simplicity see Rudner 1961, Bunge 1963, Foster and Martin 1966. On the role of regulative ideals in science see also Korner 1962a, Nash 1963, Toulmin 1963, Toulmin/Goodfield 1965.

21. In case anyone is so naive as to believe that metaphysics is not *essentially* employed in science they should reflect upon the very general principles governing specific theoretical realizations of such ontological schemes as atoms-and-the-void. Cf. Hooker 1973c and 1974c and Bunge's proto-theories, Bunge 1970. Cf. also Agassi 1963, Burtt 1959, Koyré 1957, 1968.

22. See Section 2.5. As to speculative metaphysics' being thought to be unrelated to the scientific enterprise I can only say that, just as in science, it is a pragmatic decision (perhaps culturally mediated) to exclude it, and like all pragmatic decisions one runs some risk of being embarrassed. One can only defend the decision on as reasonable grounds as possible (the lack of evidence for the relevance of the concepts to science, etc.—none of the arguments are very strong, nor can they always even be very clearly expressed at present). Thus there remains only a small sieve where once the Positivists had thought to erect an impenetrable barrier.

23. See Popper 1934, especially appendix viii, but cf. also Note 33.

24. Since I have just finished stressing the lack of a fixed First Philosophy in my Realism this is the place to add that it is obviously the case that Realism as I conceive it is logically independent of Materialism—I conceive of Materialism (and its alternatives) as scientific theories to be decided on the same merits as any such theories; one only obtains some form of Materialism if one

adds to Scientific Realism some thesis concerning the exhaustiveness of say, physics. Similarly, Realism as I defend it is a far cry from the good old anthropomorphically epistemological days in philosophy when man felt sure of himself and Realists made bold claims to know the necessary structure of reality—I have no truck with this brand of apriorist metaphysics.

Illustration: Given what I have said here, and about induction earlier, I could hardly opt for a 'necessary connection' doctrine of the causal relation in anything like the sense Hume attacked. Roughly speaking, I opt for a Humean-style account of causal relations (and of laws generally, since 'cause' is not a very important category in mathematical science); causal laws are generalizations derivable from theories rather than from spatio-temporal relations among initial conditions, they have as their basis energy exchanges and it will always be some such basis as this that allows us to distinguish them, it is their being derivable from a theory that leads to our saying that they support counter-factual conditionals. I doubt that we are ever likely to be in the epistemological position to confirm theories that introduce non-extensional causal relations against purely extensional versions, but if we are so I should happily accept such a strengthened doctrine; in the meantime the Humean-type account looks the most acceptable. On this approach, cf. also Braithwaite 1959, Nagel 1961, Hempel 1965, Hanson 1965.

25. Thus despite his careful examination of the position—and the related Ramsey transcriptionism, cf. Section 2.6 below—and despite his referring to Hooker 1968, where I stated this argument 5 years before, Cornman still manages to miss the point; he concentrates on the question of specific defects in the approach because he takes a narrow conception of the positions involved instead of looking to their global dimensions.

26. E.g. one might want to defend only the weaker view if one thought, as I do, that it is an empirical question whether nature is a continuum with respect to any physical variable (e.g., space, time, spin, etc.). Cf. Grunbaum 1963.

Suppe 1972b presents a version of this argument.

27. A not untypical empiricist move would be to lop them off the theory proper and locate them in an 'accompanying model' which acts as a heuristic device but does not enter the structure of science essentially. Cf. Nagel 1961 and Sellars' nice discussion in 1965a. Cf. also Suppe 1972b, 1974 a,b. On the roles of models in general see also Campbell 1957, Harré 1970, Hesse 1965, especially see her 1963, Henkin et al. 1959, McMullin 1968, Suppes 1960, 1969.

28. In respect of coherence in science, obviously a theory is incompletely internally global just to the extent that it is externally global. The ideal, totally internally global theory would emcompass all of science. Ron Giere 1976 has provided a nice discussion of the structure of the statistical inferences involved in an epistemological setting closely similar to mine. [N.B. throughout this section the text has been 'pruned' to minimise overlap with Chapter 4 while retaining intelligibility and original footnotes. The reader will often find more textual detail in Chapter 4, Section 4.4 – C.A.H.]

29. Suppe 1972a, b, has independently discussed a not dissimilar structure for science and various others have discussed fragments of it, e.g. van Fraassen 1970, 1972, Hesse 1970, Sellars 1965a, Shapere 1963, 1966, Suppes 1960, 1969.

30. In this connection Maxwell 1973 has emphasized that an important part of the characterization of the general conditions of an experiment will be the obtaining of *theoretically* characterized circumstances (e.g., thermal or phase equilibrium, negligible angular momentum perturbation, etc.). These conditions will in fact in general be supported by the auxiliary theories (and confirmed through their data support) and by whatever supports the *ceteris paribus* clause—though Maxwell does not go into this detail. What Maxwell emphasizes, rightly, is the damage this realization does to any simple verificationist or falsificationist approach to science.

In the same paper Maxwell also makes the point that often a scientist will not know the exact hypothesis that will relate a theory 'properly' (i.e., in the fashion one intuitively expects, given the metaphysics, etc., see below) to a range of experimental situations but will guess that there is such a relation and go on to test the theory on that basis, hoping that those very tests will reveal the correct relation. It is an interesting and important point because, though seldom made, science abounds with such moves. I would only add that what guides intuition here are the general metaphysics and proto-theories operative plus the models suggested by the theory and its auxiliaries. As Maxwell remarks, this complicates the confirmation relation still further.

31. E.g., there will be calibration of instruments and determination of errors; also the transformation of readings into model properties. This last, like the former, introduces additional theoretical assumptions, e.g., the construction of a smooth density function from a finite mass sample, of a velocity and location from time-of-flight measurements, and so on. All of these apply equally to human sense organs as to machines.

32. Here, e.g., we must correct the system behaviour for the influence of factors ignored in the theoretical model and also make the transition to any further idealization built into the theoretical model—point masses, etc.

33. Thus Hempel's deducibility conditions for explanation I take to be necessary, but not sufficient, conditions of a satisfying explanation. It further follows, I believe, that, although all sound explanations of this type will also provide sound predictions, mere prediction is a much weaker requirement, so that not all predictions that pay off need rest on a basis sufficient for providing a satisfying explanation. On the deductive model of explanation and the explanation/prediction asymmetry see, e.g., Hempel 1965, Suchting 1967. On the role of models in science see the references of Note 27.

34. Sometimes, for example, scientists argue after a form "If T and F then with probability p (near 1) S, so assume S; now if S. . ." and sometimes they argue "if S then T, assuming T we shall also assume S: now if S. . ." when predicting how things will go, as well as when assessing the degree of support a theory possesses. Of course many far more complex argument forms than this appear as well in actual practice (cf. Note 30). In many, many applications of a scientific theory one cannot say for certain, given the theory under examination, precisely what the experimental conditions are, though one can usually know very probably what they are. Unlike the empiricist structure, therefore, which segregates deductive and inductive arguments, the present model permits both types of argument to occur in all theory-data transitions.

35. By "model theoretic" I mean assertions couched in the descriptive

terms of the model and not a formal meta-mathematical language.

36. These themes are expounded in Hooker 1973c. For some earlier intimations, see also 1972c, Section 13.

37. I might add that, even narrowly construed within the stage 2 development of induction (Section 2.1) and hence as a specialized part of stage 3, the foregoing analysis requires a radically revamped theory of confirmation. Actual falsification, equally with verification, can hardly be expected to be realized (cf. also Maxwell 1973, and Note 40). But confirmation itself must be seen as something considerably different from the theory of the direct data sentence—theoretical sentence moves suggested by the simple traditional structure to science; confirmation *may* eventually turn out to be a purely logical-style relation, but the characteristics one wants now to give it leave this issue in doubt to say the least. First, theories are decided among, and confirmed to differing degrees by the same evidence on quite other criteria than purely deductive ones, criteria which include 'fit' with preferred metaphysics and proto-theories, simplicity, fecundity, etc. Second, there is in general no simple relation between a theory and either 'its' hard data or 'its' phenomenal data, transitions to each require auxiliary theories, *ceteris paribus* clause, model corrections, etc., and may often not even be deductive—the support or lack of it that reports formulated at either level furnish a theory is indirect and mediated by a number of considerations concerning all of these other factors (e.g., the likelihood that, given the preferred metaphysics, the *ceteris paribus* clause is O.K., etc.) Third, the degree of support a given experimental outcome furnishes a theory is at least partially determined by that theory itself, because it supplies part or all of the theory of the instruments used! Thus the theory specifies how accurate an instrumental reading is likely to be, whether it directly reflects the theoretical parameter value, etc, and so determines the degree of support the instrument reading yields that very same theory (cf. GT for details). For these reasons the simple empiricist notion of confirmation as a quasi-logical relation between data sentences and theoretical sentences must be abandoned to be replaced by something that is closer to the actual structure of scientific reasoning—what that will be I do not know. Equally, it seems to me that by and large the goals of verification and falsification are ideals seldom, if ever, attained; they may function as regulative ideals, they can hardly act as demarcating criteria for the scientific (cf. also Maxwell 1973—anyway this circumstance will hardly bother us; cf. Section 2.10 for remarks on methodology).

38. E.g., the belief that solid things are without interstices—it is not that we see that objects are interstice-free, it is just that we *do not* see any interstices. Notice that this is a different position from Sellars who so closely links concepts and beliefs that the phenomenal level must be scrapped in toto in the final analysis. Cf. my discussion in Section 2.6 and in 1973d.

39. E.g., it does *not* include the concept of a point mass, this concept can be made rigorously consistent through the theory of distributions, it does include 'line of force' because these are intended to be individuals and yet according to theory there would on occasion have to be real, irrational numbers of them.

40. One of the weaknesses in the present work of Suppe is that he does not distinguish these various cases.

41. See Maxwell 1962, 1970. Ramsey's original idea was advanced in 1931 and later developed especially by Bohnert 1967, 1968. I have commented upon it and cited some more literature in 1968a, b. Cf. also Cornman 1972 and the more recent literature he cites.

42. The only thing we are supposed to know about the theoretical predicates is that their extensions are interrelated, and related to the extensions of observation terms, in certain ways. This suggests a further, more extreme, move: drop the explicit occurrence of bound variables ranging over properties, and pass instead to bound variables ranging over just the extensions of these unknown terms (so that predication in effect becomes membership). This extreme version remains parasitic upon the concept of a theoretical predicate, however, until such times (if ever) as a direct translational technique can be formulated for passing from the untranscribed theory to the purely set-theoretic transcribed version in a way which avoids using some kind of comprehension axiom to define the sets and insure their regularity that would not commit one to the theoretical predicates. If this severer formulation could be made to work, however, I believe it would better capture Maxwell's quasi-empiricist structuralism, cf. below in the text. I am indebted to Nino Cocchiarella for helpful criticism at this point.

43. Cf. my discussion in 1968a, b and that by Bohnert 1967, 1968. The difficulty with the latter view is that we do not yet have any precise account of inductive argument forms and so one cannot produce a clear-cut answer as to whether devices exist to cope with them. Cf. the discussion by Cornman 1972 (and now e.g. Niiniluoto 1984-C.A.H.).

44. The reasons for the unlikelihood are these: for the non-theoretical object satisfying the Ramsey claim to have only the properties which the observable level of the *relevant theory* admits is for that theory to be reducible to observational statements alone *à la* P-Empiricism and for the properties to be observable but not so reducible is highly implausible (how did we miss them?), yet for the properties to be theoretical is certainly to readmit a significant sense of theory, even if it is restricted to an implausible macro-phenomenalist ontology.

The actual structure of Ramsey transcribed sentences is considerably more complex than most accounts of it (including Maxwell's) suppose. For some of these complexities, see e.g., Sneed 1971.

45. Actually, in the form in which Maxwell presents the argument it is made to comprehend not only theoretical terms in the usual sense but also the ordinary first order properties of the macro world, thus arguing for some version of Lockean representative realism; but we can distinguish the two applications, resist Maxwell's extension of the argument and defend a version of direct realism if we wish. This latter course is the one I would myself argue for, indeed I see it as essential to a viable Realism, cf. above and 1970a, and so in my account here I shall construe this argument as applying only to theoretical terms. Note that this restriction is compatible with the Realist rejection of the observational theoretical dichotomy in the strict empiricist sense and its replacement by a theoretically defined distinction within psychology.

46. Though I agree with Sellars 1965a that Nagel 1961 does not succeed in reconciling Instrumentalism and Realism, the force of part of Sellars' attack on Nagel may be vitiated by the foregoing remarks since it is not clear that

Nagel really intended it to be *logically* impossible for theoretical terms to 'descend' to the observational level.

47. It should surely be clear that to claim that X is actually realized and to claim that X is only physically possible (i.e., to claim that Xs occurrence is merely compatible with the true, fundamental laws of physics whatever they be), is to claim distinct things, *a fortiori*, to claim merely that X's occurrence is compatible with the laws of logic is to make a third distinct claim.

48. These moves are as follows:

First, they can make use of an observation/reporting distinction to point out that scientists are conditioned to respond to experimental situations in theoretical language just as they respond to more ordinary situations in more ordinary language. Just this may account for the felt familiarity; indeed, I see no objection to the inclusion of such responses in a quasi-empiricist account of meaning ('electron' is the sort of term I use to respond to situations of. . . sort). In this case the term might even be said to have a connotation of sorts, though not one directly concerned with the subject matter of the theory.

Second, I believe they could adopt Sellars' view that theoretical terms share higher order predicates in common with terms having a connotation (cf. Sellars 1965a and discussion of Sellars' view below), they might even insist on this too as a component in genuine connotations for theoretical terms.

Third, they might point out that the metaphysics of a theory already specifies the kind of thing or property to which many theoretical terms are to refer, if the metaphysics is granted a connotational content it could partially confer it on these terms. One could easily add to the Ramsey transcribed theory a collection of assertions giving this additional content (e.g., that the term electron stands for a class of objects such that the members in its extension share the attributes mass, motion, locality in common with billiard balls and such that it is used by scientists when responding descriptively to cloud chamber photographs). I do believe that this would come a lot closer to grasping the content of a theory than does the unadorned Ramsey approach, but it involves introducing a meta-linguistic component to theories and to my knowledge the approach has not yet been extensively explored.

Of course, to the extent that all of these sources are taken as sources of genuine connotation, to that extent the strict Ramsey analysis must be abandoned (since none of the claims that would follow analytically from the connotations thus acquired follow from the bare Ramsey treatment). More seriously, this account is worthless until it is specified how ordinary language and the terms of the metaphysics (if distinct) acquire their connotations. If the answer is: through observation, then the latter becomes impossible to understand (how could a metaphysics possibly be rich enough to specify a general world ontology for a variety of theories if its terms are confined to observational content?—unless it is done purely denotationally, in which case this treatment for theories themselves will surely be sufficient) and the former leads us back into the dogmas of Empiricism (not to mention the lack of an account of how attribute sharing can enrich the language beyond the original observational resources, cf. below). But if the source of connotation is mysterious we have failed to advance at all.

On the other hand, the 'pure Ramseyite' might simply wish to insist that all of these sources contribute not to genuine connotations for theoretical terms, but to psychological states in scientists in which they feel the normal familiarity with the terms. (Here observation as the source of connotation may be safely retained.) This move requires an analysis of the distinction between meanings and the psychology of language use that supports this possibility. I find it less attractive because I am persuaded that the foregoing sources belong to a proper account of the meanings of theories, I also find the difficulties of the alternative unappealing; but until this approach is explored and found decisively wanting it seems a consistent way out.

49. In the former case, the history of such 'terms' as *molecule, gene* etc. which, we would normally say, once referred to unobservable entities that are now—thanks to modern instrumental technology—observable, poses more problems for this position. The only consistent answer is to deny that, in some strict sense, these entities are observable even today. We shall see later that this *might* be done, without falling into the trap of espousing a phenomenalist analysis of sensory experience, but the Realist here is forced to tiptoe along a razor edge between disasters. (The modified Ramsey approach seems distinctly preferable on this score anyway.)

50. Indeed, the notion of ostensive definition is quite compatible with some formula for meanings of words in terms of the set of rules governing their usages, since the ostensivist can claim either that a sensorially handicapped person could not understand the meaning of all of the rules associated with an ostensively defined term (i.e., could not understand a rule of the form 'Apply this predicate when you are in these circumstances,' circumstances demonstratively indicated) and/or would not be able to apply all the rules successfully. It is important to understand all of the logically possible combinations of doctrines here in order to appreciate the reasonable room to manoeuvre which the Realist has.

In fact, a form of the two arguments used earlier to support this alternative can be employed here to argue for the necessity of ostensive definition. To quote Mary Hesse:

> . . .there must be a stock of predicates in any descriptive language for which it is impossible to specify necessary and sufficient conditions of correct application. For if any such specification could be given for a particular predicate, it would introduce further predicates requiring to be learned in empirical situations for which there was no specification. . . We must, therefore, conclude that the primary process of recognition. . .is necessarily unverbalizable. The emphasis here of course is on primary, because it may be perfectly possible to give empirical descriptions of the conditions, both psychological and physical, . . .but such descriptions will themselves depend on further undescribable primary recognitions. (Hesse, 1970, pp. 39-40, author's italics.)

(Those who would deny the hierarchy of analysis appealed to here and envision instead a language in which, circularly, every predicate would have its conditions of application described in the language, only succeed in 'smearing' the ostensive support throughout the language, not in dissipating it—cf. Note 13.)

51. For Feyerabend's doctrines see, eg., 1965 a,b, 1969, 1970a—for further bibliography together with a critical review see Hooker 1972b and for specific critical comments see, e.g., Achinstein 1964, Butts 1966, Putnam 1985, Sellars 1965a.

52. The only other possibility, that theories have their semantic content conferred from some external source, does not seem open to Feyerabend, for there are only alternative, and hence semantically incompatible, theories that could act as this source, or else it is completely mysterious—the level of neurophysiological irritation is common to all theories and hence of no use here. Feyerabend certainly does not discuss the possibility of an external source and the structure of his philosophy suggests that he would discount it.

53. Roughly, Beth defines a k-ary predicate K $(x_1, . . .x_k)$ to be explicitly defined relatively to a set of formulas A and the predicates they contain besides K if there is a formula U containing k free variables and other predicate letters from A such that

$$(x_1). . .(x_k)(K(x_1,. . ., x_k) \leftrightarrow U(x_1,. . ., x_k))$$

is entailed by A, and implicitly defined if

$$(x_1). . .(x_k)(K(x_1,. . ., x_k) \leftrightarrow K' \text{ cf. } (x_1,. . ., x_k))$$

is entailed by $A \cup B$, where B is obtained from A by replacing each occurrence of K by some other k-ary predicate K' which does not appear in A. See Beth 1966, p. 290. I have van Fraassen to thank for reminding me of the importance of this theorem.

54. To take a hopelessly trivial case, if in the postulate (x) $(Ax \supset Bx)$ the concept of an A is that of membership in a set of things which include the set of B's as a subset then this postulate is already an effective tautology and it becomes so twice over if the concept of a B is that of a set of objects included in the set of A's.

55. Not that the former would automatically rule out the position—given Feyerabend's assumptions it seems to me that a case *could* probably be made for the view that a bunch of tautologies could act as an effective guide to life. After all, they only have to be so related to conditioned behavioural response that people survive, continue experimenting, etc., and such relations do not seem ruled out by the tautological character of the beliefs. Cf. on this score the functioning of a myth—see e.g., Feyerabend's comments in 1961. Those who automatically assume that tautologies cannot be a guide to life either tacitly assume an empiricist account on which tautologies are *both* restricted to logic *and* uninformative and/or assume that only by conscious assent to the cognitive content of a belief, as making a difference to prediction, do beliefs affect conduct, but this ignores the subtleties of the conditioning role of language. Nonetheless no one, to my knowledge, has tried to grasp and develop this interesting thorn in detail and so I too shall leave it resting on its rose vine with only this brief defense.

On implicit definition see also the excellent discussions by Frege 1960, Hempel 1952, Nagel 1961. Cf. Lewis 1970.

56. But Sellars concedes that for Feyerabend the only interesting feature of theories is their *direct* connection to sensory responses, Feyerabend ignores this independently described subject matter in *all* cases, so he is able to construe natural language as a theory, in his sense—1965a, pp. 172–4.

57. See Feyerabend 1965a, pp. 178–184 and the references cited there. At a *crude* level of approximation the complex relations holding between theory and the common sense framework which are mediated via the models may be viewed as the traditional correspondence rules; cf. the theory-phenomenal correspondence rules in my structural model in Section 2.5 above.

58. Certainly there are some features which strike one as immediately right about this sort of account. Pretty clearly our ancestors developed language initially as stimuli to action and these sounds, laboriously built into a systematic pattern, can be supposed to have been thoroughly behaviourally oriented. But the actual developmental history is a bit hazy, and insight is not assisted by the fact that we know of only 'completed' languages (i.e., languages we can map onto our full-blown commonsense framework). Specifically, Sellars does still rely quite heavily on analogical enrichment of the observation-to-theory part to get us uphill from a purely observational base— only the invalidity of construing an analogical relation as a logical one saves Sellars from the empiricist semantical dogma (i.e., dogma 2, that all descriptive terms are analyzable in terms of pure observational terms). But then what exactly happens to semantic content during such analogical shifts, how it is transformed, how the mind has the capacity to carry out this operation, and how we achieve a 'leap' to richer concepts remain something of a mystery. And there are more specific difficulties as well. (See here the exchange between Marras 1973 a, b and Sellars 1973, which it seems to me Marras has won—at least at this stage of the debate.)

Moreover, there is in Sellars still the old empiricist insistence that observation brings something special to concepts. For the additional semantic richness by which theoretical terms attain to full stature is just their use in observation once again. In addition, I cannot see why observation (or its internal equivalents) in the common sense conceptual scheme are held to confer a special, *irreplaceable* semantic content as Sellars seems to believe. (See the detailed argument in Hooker 1970a.) Note that my attitude does *not* entail the rejection of the notion of ostensive definition.

59. The ideas in Sections 2.6.6.2-3. are expounded in Hooker 1973d.

60. Not all of them do because the common sense framework itself is shot through with theories, cf. below and e.g. my 1973d.

61. Thus ask a scientist "What is that?" pointing to an object and he, assuming a technical question, may reply "It is a Wilson cloud chamber"; but if you then say "Are you sure?" in a fashion which suggests not merely technical ambiguity but the possibility of a more radical error, he will immediately return *towards* his perceptually active concepts, he might say, e.g., "Well it looks like a cloud chamber, there's the cylinder for the plunger and here the counter array. . ."—the harder he is pressed the further towards purity in the use of these concepts he will be driven.

62. Both Popper 1957 and Feyerabend 1958 recognize elements of the psychology of perception which backs this distinction, though without putting that theory to work in the philosophy of science very pointedly. Hesse 1970 recently discussed the continuum of epistemological caution within science without introducing the psychology of perception; otherwise, much of her commentary makes excellent sense. Schaffner 1970, pp. 323–4, comes close to this distinction (he draws a distinction nearly that of my Co, C concepts distinction in 1973d, though he makes it theory-conflict relative) but smothers it with semantical restrictions (e.g., that there are no experimentally gratuitous conceptual distinctions) and a narrow view of it determined by its alleged history.

This distinction is properly encompassed within an analysis of "seeing *that*" (rather than "seeing X") which, as I say, I have offered in detail elsewhere (Hooker 1970a). Suppe 1972b e.g., is correct in sensing the importance of such an analysis for the general philosophy of science, but fails, as do most of his colleagues, to take the psychology of perception seriously enough and so misses the actively-observing/reporting distinction.

63. The fact is then that the psychology of perception is not taken seriously enough when discussing the notion of observation in science. If to this lacuna we add the view that the connotations of terms are pragmatically determined, i.e., determined by their uses to which their users have been socially conditioned, then we indeed collapse the distinction between reporting and the actively observational. This is just how Feyerabend *et al.* seem to have overlooked the distinction. But note that even with the pragmatic determination of connotation granted, the distinction remains once an adequate psychology of perception is introduced.

64. The distinction is also not much discussed in philosophy proper, i.e., within the philosophy of perception in epistemology, which is, I intuit, the reason for the blindness in philosophy of science. Philosophical doctrines of perception have tended to operate within the confines of the empiricist-phenomenalist analysis of perception where perceptual reports were simply exact descriptions of some conceptualized content, a sense datum; there was an assumed identity of content and report. But in fact perception is neuro-physiologically and linguistically much more complex (and interesting) than this. What we report of perception, as indeed the content of our perceptions, are functions of the cortical processing undertaken. Nor are the linguistic reportage and perceptual processings totally tied together (indeed, it is almost certainly not the case that all conscious perception is linguistically conceptualized—cf. my 1970a, 1975d).

What I have in mind here is the interpretation of experiments on people whose right and left brain lobe connections have been severed. See T. Nagel 1971. Since only one lobe possesses linguistic ability and yet both lobes respond as though fully conscious, what are we to say? It seems plausible to say that so long as neurophysiological processing is rich enough to provide all the usual perceptual information (as evidenced by behavioural skills, etc.) then, in effect, the usual perceptually active concepts are active here as well; but there is no correlative linguistic ability.

In any case, this view seems reasonable just on the ground that the information-processing view of the brain seems likely to prove the most adequate one and the possession of concepts is most plausibly tied to the possession of information-processing cortical structures; moreover we know that in a normal brain the localized speech center is only a small portion of one lobe. What this suggests is that perceptual skills and, if we accept the argument of the preceding paragraph, conceptual skills are much broader than linguistic skills. Indeed, if we could only rid ourselves of the superstition that thinking and seeing were kinds of internal linguistic acts we should be well on the road towards saying something sensible about non-cognitive communication, artistic creativity, supra-linguistic mathematical activity (and symbolic activity in general. . .) and even 'being stuck for words'. For further elaboration see my 1975d.

65. It would take a long argument to extend this claim to other cultures as well, but this I would want to do by emphasizing three points: (i) to possess a

concept is fundamentally to possess an information-processing structure in the cortex, hence concepts are expected to be determined by experience and to be richer than language—cf. Note 64, (ii) what language skills a culture develops depends upon its social interests, etc., i.e., it is a partly pragmatic affair, (iii) at best one might expect some conceptual-perceptual schemes to be fragments of others, not incompatible with others, for there is no evidence of massive illusion in any culture. Using these moves I would attempt to render the anthropological work on other cultures—e.g., that by Whorf 1966 on the Hopi—compatible with the claim in the text.

66. E.g., the Oxford English Dictionary defines solid as (i) impenetrable, etc. and (ii) completely filled up, etc. Pretty clearly semantic component (ii) began life as a primitive, perhaps unconscious, but anyway false, attempt to explain (i). Cf. Note 38.

67. I can conceive of a world in which science reached the conclusion that unaided man was under systematic illusion in every respect (that science was possible would depend upon the pattern of the illusion), though I do not believe it probable.

68. This holds as true of the esoterica of quantum theory and general relativity as of general atomic theory. Unless geometry were locally Euclidean, unless macro scale collectivities of micro entities do not fluctuate in state over perceptible time intervals, etc., we could not plausibly explain our macro-world. There is here no fault with the *guarded* macro observation reports I have delineated (though some theoretical additions to these have to go).

69. We have to remember that the perceiving of secondary qualities as exemplified by objects is deeply ingrained in our evolutionary structure for obvious good reasons, it represents a quasi-theoretical commitment rather than a theoretical one. For a detailed treatment see Hooker 1970a (and now 1978a also—C.A.H.). Though even within the commonsense framework there are reasons to believe that objects do not literally exemplify the secondary qualities (the strongest reverse case is that of sight with the other senses in varying degrees less bothersome in this respect), I believe we must concede that on any occasion on which we literally attribute secondary qualities to objects that we do so falsely and our corresponding perceivings are illusory.

Sellars places heavy emphasis upon the secondary quality aspects of the common sense conceptual scheme and suggests that to modify them in the fashion I suggest is to abandon the scheme. I do not believe this is necessary (now see Hooker 1977a—C.A.H.). (The concept of, and conditions of, illusion can themselves be discussed in common sense terms, nor are qualities necessary, cf. Hooker 1970a, 1973a.)

70. Thus the earlier arguments for ostensive definition (Section 2.6.4.) must not be understood as claiming that certain terms, those ostensively defined, must be understood *before* any others can be understood—this is clearly impossible in most cases. (Some elementary terms, e.g., 'Dad', *might* be understood prior to the emergence of some fragment of a conceptual scheme.) Rather a conceptual scheme emerges slowly in a child's head with many terms taking on clearer 'definition'—cf. Note 63. In this sense the 'smeared' model of ostensive support is very probably the more accurate.

71. These particular dimensions to common language give the final sense in which Feyerabend is right to hold that common sense language embodies a theory, though in this case it is less than certain that it embodies a false theory.

72. If it could be shown experimentally that the elaboration of the untheoretical core was at the behest of contemporary theories, rather than general features of the macro structure of the world, then my position would become indistinguishable from a (rather 'wild') version of radical anti-Empiricism.

If we discovered that the elaboration of this core was influenced by theories held at historically earlier times then we should no longer have a coherent account of how science was possible, though if we discovered (more *plausibly*) that the common sense linguistic scheme was progressively infected by bygone theories then we should have one more reason to distinguish concepts in general from linguistic concepts and to distrust the linguistic semantical dimension.

73. It is necessary to keep these points clearly in mind, otherwise one will be tempted to run backward along the line of evolutionary advance searching for a purer and purer realm of untheoretical concepts. This search is chimerical, for as we regress the untheoretical conceptual scheme becomes cruder and more fragmentary, far enough back we run out of concepts altogether.

74. Indeed, to quote Mary Hesse:

> . . .the comparatively stable area within which it is proposed to define an observation language itself is partly known to us because its stability is explained by the theories we now accept. It is certainly not sufficiently defined by investigating what observation statements have in fact remained stable during long periods of time, for this stability might be due to accident, prejudice, or false beliefs. Thus any attempted definition itself would rely upon current theories and, hence, not be a definition of an observation language which is theory-independent. Indeed, it might justly be concluded that we shall know what the most adequate observation language is only when if possible we have true and complete theories, including theories of physiology and physics which tell us what it is that is most 'directly observed'. (1970, p. 49.)

The difference between Hesse and I is that she thinks that this truth renders the untheoretical/theoretical distinction insignificant for science whereas I do not, for the reason given. She also thinks that it leads irresistably to the 'network model', whereas I do not—cf. below.

75. The idea that there might be no hard and fast observational vocabulary for science is not a new one. When discussing one particular realization of this idea—the so-called 'network' model of theories—Mary Hesse offers two pages of references in fine print to others in which this idea, or fragments or analogues of it, may be found, beginning with Duhem and Campbell, though it is clear that earlier work in the nineteenth century already contained the issue (Butts 1968, N.R. Campbell 1957, Duhem 1962; for Hesse's bibliography see 1970, footnote 4). And Schaffner derives his views on a model similar to my own from Popper. Nonetheless many of these accounts (though by no means all) suffer because they discuss the issue in isolation from a psychology of perception and concept formation. The network theory is a case in point. The position which I have tried to develop attempts to self-consciously take into account these domains of psychological theory—in particular, I believe that any realistic view of the function of observational vocabulary in science must draw a distinction between the reporting and perceiving roles and link that distinction to the distinction between perceptually active concepts and those not so, further that the relative stability of the common sense observa-

tional vocabulary must be *explained* in terms of this former category of concepts. The network theory removes certain semantical problems by declaring them chimerical but seems to ignore psychological structures behind theorizing (it ignores the distinctions I have drawn). The reason for this is that the passage is made too hurriedly from the denial of the analytic/synthetic distinction, via the network model, to the denial of the observational/ theoretical dichotomy (observation sentences are simply those 'on the periphery'). I will not dispute that the denial of the analytic/synthetic distinction leads to the network model but one only moves from thence to the denial of any epistemologically significant observational/theoretical dichotomy if one also tacitly assumes that the psychology of perception is either irrelevant to this issue or supports the pragmatic theory of observation terms—I hold this tacit premise false. (This argument shows that the rejection of the analytic/synthetic distinction is not sufficient for the rejection of the observational/theoretical dichotomy; pretty clearly it is not necessary either. It follows that its rejection is not sufficient for Realism, and I believe not necessary either, at least for the quasi-empiricist forms.) However, Hesse and Schaffner do in fact come quite close to my position, Hesse when she concedes that as a matter of fact some predicates are more stably observable than are others (cf. 1970, pp. 50–1), and Schaffner when he allows that one may 'analyze back' observation statements to increasingly 'deeper' levels, until a level of agreement in meaning between conflicting theories is found—1970, pp. 321–2. (Hesse also makes nicely clear that the network model, though it encourages talk of convention, is quite distinct from conventionalism, 1970, p. 43.)

76. The cortex is capable of a tremendously complex range of activities, there is every reason not to hold it down to some simple combining operations on preformed concepts (as e.g., empiricists would have us do). If to possess a concept is to possess a cortical processing structure of some sort then we can expect there to be a myriad of ways in which these can be built up, ways which quite transcend our attempts at semantic description. How, after all, did we come by our 'natural' language? Will something like Sellars' Rylean account do? What was the exact relationship between the psycho-cortical and social processes at work and the emerging semantic content? The semantic description seems to be relevant, so to speak, only to the relatively definite recognizable linguistic end-products which result from these fantastically complex processes. It seems impossible that every psycho-cortical or social act occurring in the language-acquisition process has a semantical correlate (especially when we recall the nonlinguistic powers of the cortex—cf. Note 64); we recognize semantically relevant features of language only *after* a sufficiently rich and definite linguistic framework has developed. It is when I think thus that I can believe that Quine was right to suggest that there was something inherently groundless or chimerical about meanings (i.e., connotations), though *only* in this sense, cf. Quine 1960. [Note that the foregoing is a small part of the response to the arguments *for* quasi-Empiricism presented in Section 2.6.]

77. It might be helpful at this stage to briefly present the view of the nature and role of observation concepts in science as I see it in order to distinguish it from both Empiricism and more radical Realisms.

After the fashion of the Empiricisms I admit to the occurrence of relatively theory-independent observational descriptive concepts. I have tried to say why I believe this to be the most reasonable alternative.

But the empiricist produces his observational realm as a matter of *a priori* analysis; which concepts are observational is fixed *a priori* and hence permanently, consequently the observational/theoretical dichotomy is also fixed *a priori* and so permanently. By contrast my doctrine grows out of experience together with a psychological doctrine of perception—which concepts are observational, even in the theory-neutral case, is determined by the facts of our world, including our neurological make-up, and is in principle open to change as those parameters are varied; for this very reason the observational/theoretical dichotomy is itself a *theoretical* distinction. Precisely for this reason it is not, as Feyerabend 1958 would have, a completely pragmatically determined distinction. Nor is the distinction theoretically dependent in the sense that its application in the domain of some theory is dependent on that theory as Hesse suggests (1970, p. 49) unless perhaps for the theory of neurophysiological evolution itself and like theory. Both of these further claims ignore the observational/reporting distinctions (these further claims are true of terms that have acquired a reporting role). (Hesse offers us the example of the concept 'is simultaneous with' to demonstrate her case, claiming that what would be regarded as a retreat to a more cautious level by relativity theory would be regarded in the reverse light by pre-relativity classical theory. I find the example unconvincing on her own terms. But further than this note that both theories agree on the invariance of simultaneity at the same place among all observers. It is plausible to maintain that this, and not the extended notion of distant simultaneity, belongs to the untheoretical level. That common people may have thought otherwise is as irrelevant, in itself, here as for the case of 'solid'.)

The empiricists hold observational reports to be indubitable; I emphatically do not, but hold them open to theoretically directed criticism. How this can come about is obvious in the case of those terms that have only pragmatically acquired a reporting role at the behest of theory. Even in the case of untheoretical terms, however, we have to allow that theory is capable of showing these claims to be false and the corresponding perceptions illusory (e.g., the perception of continuity for macro objects and its semantic enshrinement in the concept 'solid') precisely by explaining how the illusions occur.

For Empiricism the category of observation terms is a single one with no large-scale epistemic divisions within it. This is equally true of more radical Realisms. I distinguish sharply the untheoretical level from the theory-laden reporting level within the category of observation terms.

Empiricism holds that all observation terms are theory-free and hence theory-neutral or independent. Radical Realisms hold that all observation terms are theory-laden and hence not theory-neutral. I hold that the terms of the untheoretical level are neutral *vis-à-vis* scientific theories, though with a theory-like dimension, but that the terms that have acquired an observational reporting role are theory laden.

Semantically, observation terms ground, or actually exhaust, theoretical terms according to Empiricism. The reverse is the case for terms that have acquired a reporting role in observation according to my doctrine. Moreover, the degree to which untheoretical terms contribute to the semantics of theories is probably small, though the matter seems obscure at this time.

For the foregoing reasons theoretical terms can never genuinely usurp the role of observation terms in Empiricism, for me this is a genuine possibility, though it might require considerably different conditions from those now obtaining. In a secondary sense it has already occurred in the introduction of terms with a reporting role.

For according to my doctrine the observation reports couched in untheoretical terms have little significance for science, their only value is that they are needed to supply part of the instructions for introducing theory-laden terms that are to acquire a reporting role in observation. This is quite the opposite of the empiricist role for these terms. For Empiricism these terms play the central role required in a foundational epistemology, but I espouse a foundationless epistemology.

Because of the foregoing, the macro level of commonsense observables is the primary level for Empiricism—in most versions of the doctrine it is the only level. In my case it is the ontology specified by our best theory that constitutes the primary level and the macro level is to be understood in terms of it. Nonetheless, unlike many other Realisms, I do not reject the macro level *in toto*, for I regard the common sense conceptual framework that forms the basis of the untheoretical level as more adequate than not and that the perceptual-conceptual discrepancies can be corrected for through an adequate theory of illusion (perception) and suitable pruning of tacit theoretical commitments (conception).

Finally, I want to add a word about the notion of ostensive definition. (It can, of course, be called *definition* in some extended sense of that term.) I have already argued in a general way for its retention, now I want to explicitly retain it in a limited form. There seems little doubt that some concepts are particularly closely connected to specific experiences and derive their linguistic function, at least in significant part, from this connection. I do not want to say that such concepts have a unique *kind* of semantical status, much less that their meaning is the content of the experience. The meanings of such concepts are to be spelled out in terms of their total linguistic role (or whatever), just as for any other term, but in their case the *criterion* of their application will be fundamentally tied to the (potential) occurrence of the experience and no explicit definition for them may be possible—only in this sense are these terms semantically segregable. (Notice too that there is nothing to prevent the experience from being identified in alternative ways.) In this sense I find many terms of the commonsense vocabulary ostensively definable (and, if the argument of Quasi-Empiricist Realism is to be believed, necessarily so). These, and my earlier comments on ostensive definitions— see Note 50— undermine Aune's claim that if all concepts were to be reducible to ostensively definable ones then one could not avoid behaviourism as a theory of the human personality, see Aune 1970.

78. Despite this general philosophical dispute with Graves, and despite other more technical criticisms I would make of his account of relativity not pertinent here, I consider Graves' book especially valuable because it belongs to a rare class of works that attempt technically competent, yet philosophically sensitive, expositions of a scientific theory. These days this occurs all too rarely. Yet I believe that in a truly mature and 'alive' intellectual community all theories would be given such a treatment.

79. There are ways in which P and Q might be challenged, but they are of no relevance here. One might e.g., argue that quantum objects are wave

packets and interfering wave packets defeat P, but we are discussing compositional relations between levels here—the table and the corresponding atoms are not interfering with one another. Similarly we might speculate on 5 or more dimensional manifolds for the world structure, but here we are talking about 'parallel' four-dimensional worlds.

80. He offers a fourth, namely that it is terribly difficult in fact to relate some theoretical levels—but this establishes nothing except the youthfulness and probable error of existing science.

81. The first argument is that there may be truths at some level that any reasonable reductive mapping would have to transform into falsehoods at other levels. E.g., "tables contain no interstices" is a statement generally conceded to be true at the common sense level but false at the atomic level (cf. Note 66). The second argument is that . . .*the coordination* [between levels A and B] *is not carried out on a piecemeal basis, with parts of A identified with the 'corresponding' parts of B in succession. For an adequate explanation of even a small part of A may in fact require up to the whole of B;. . .*(p. 24) and the third that . . .*conversely, two phenomena which are quite distinct in A may appeal to the same parts or aspects of B.* (p. 24)
I shall consider these arguments in order.

The first argument is unconvincing on two grounds. First, I do not believe that we should accept common sense claims so uncritically; a statement which *is* true for this level is "we do not in general see any interstices in tables" and this claim is well explained by the radiation pattern at the atomic level which indeed is continuous in the relevant sense. People are constantly claiming too much for their experience, but that is no reason to burden science with it. Second, even should we find a discrepancy of this kind we could not so easily avoid, I believe that it is intellectually preferrable to write it off as mere appearance (i.e., as illusion) than to adopt Graves' alternatives—always assuming that an explanation of the occurrence of the illusion will be forthcoming at the more fundamental level. Only in the severest circumstances does one counsel radical courses of action such as dropping P or Q.

The second argument, and the third, are also such that if they were sound they would indeed constitute grounds for radical change. Unfortunately, I can find no explicit example for the second argument in Graves, but this does not prevent a sketch of the general error on which all such examples are surely based. Consider the phenomenon of the rotation of spiral galaxies, and the specific shape and rotation of our own in particular. Suppose that one wanted an explanation of this phenomenon at the atomic level and suppose that something like Mach's hypothesis were true (i.e., that inertia is a function of all masses in the universe). Then the *explanation* of this *phenomenon* would demand reference to all the entities of the atomic level, namely to all the atoms. It is the plausibility of claims such as these concerning the explanation of phenomena that lends plausibility to the argument. But the latter plausibility is spurious. The argument is concerned with the *ontological distinctness* of levels; which entities are involved in *explanations* establishes nothing concerning *ontic* distinctness, even where reductions involving many entities of one level may be needed in the explanation of phenomena initially described at the other (simply because many entities at one level may be involved in the explanation of phenomena described at that very same level and concerning only a subset of these entities). Our galaxy may still be identical with a local collection of atoms, though all atoms appear in an explanation of its shape and rotation. The appropriate version of the argument reads: where we have a subset of the entities at one level that would have to be identified with the entire other level under any reasonable reduction, then no reductive identification of the two levels is possible. I would accept the argument but know of no plausible example of the premise. Only by sliding between a plausible, but irrelevant, claim and an implausible, though relevant, claim does Graves make this argument sound plausible.

The same 'sleight of mind' is used to bolster the third argument, and here Graves offers us an example. The example is that of pp. 21–24, it runs as follows: "A table corresponds to a swarm of molecules, a chair also corresponds to a swarm of molecules, hence at the molecular level tables and chairs are indistinguishable." The general argument is: "Ontologically distinct things at level A are indistinguishable at level B, so levels A and B are distinct." Of course tables and chairs are not merely swarms of molecules but *structured* lattices of molecules and the structures may be as readily distinguished at the molecular, as at the common sense, level. Indeed, macro objects are structured, *located* lattices of molecules, so that even 'indistinguishable' macro objects can be readily distinguished at the micro level. Graves has faked the argument by a deliberate omission of specificity in the premise. Of course, their molecular structures do not distinguish tables and chairs *qua* socially functioning objects, but then neither do their macro *physical* descriptions which is all that is of relevance here (a second sleight of mind in this argument perhaps?). I know of no other plausible example for Graves' argument.

Finally, Graves might try to hold R false, or perhaps meaningless, on the grounds of incommensurability of theories. (R is an intertheoretic claim.) I at least would reject this tack, and so, it seems, would Graves (cf. p. 24).

82. The idea was to decide upon an optimal course of action that would increase the known facts maximally rapidly and lead by the shortest route to succeeding increasingly general theories, given the existing facts and theories. Roughly speaking this is equivalent to solving the problem of induction. For if there is a 'prospective methodology' (cf. my 1972b) of discovery which works purely with a data-theory base and churns out, by some algorithm, the next best theory and correlative data then it must also thereby identify the best justified theory given the new data base, and conversely, if we have a 'retrospective methodology' of justification that selects the best theory, given a data-theory base, then it will select the next best theory in advance given a data-theory base (or, if an existing theory is continually selected, either science has reached its denouement or method becomes blind and one must simply accumulate facts at random). This narrow construal of methodology is of course only possible against the 'logical machine' view of science, for here scientists have been entirely lost sight of. We ignore the fact that it is a course of action for a *scientist* that is specified, rather methodology is here viewed as providing an algorithm for quasi-logical transitions in *Science*.

83. Hanson attacks by attempting to widen 'the existing circumstances' to include a variety of other modes of reasoning than those admitted by Empiricism. See Hanson 1965. Occasionally Hanson crosses from the quasi-formal into the purely psychological, thereby abandoning his tacit acceptance of the general empiricist account of science. In general though he seems content

merely to enlarge the notion of formal reasoning with which Empiricism operated, and the correlative notion of perception with it.

Feyerabend argues this both by attempting to reduce to absurdity the empiricist methodology and by arguing that 'the existing circumstances' must be enlarged to include *all* of the circumstances of an *individual's* life.

84. Taken thus far, there is no necessity to assert e.g., that theory can only be defeated via confrontation with another theory (pace Smart); whether one holds this latter claim inflexibly or not depends to a large extent on one's analysis of the relations of 'fact' to theory. If one believed, as Feyerabend seems to, that the semantics of the observation language is determined by the theory for which it is the observation language then the condition seems at once both necessary and impossible to understand; for on the one hand each theory generates its own realm of 'facts' on this account and so if one is to know of the empirical alternatives at all one must first know of the theory, and yet on the other hand since the 'facts' of one theory are semantically incommensurate with those of the other there seems no way in which to make the direct comparison that empirical judgment between them requires. (Feyerabend's critics have been quick to point this out, cf. Achinstein 1965, Butts 1966, Fine 1967; cf. Hesse 1968b, 1970, Hull 1972.). Feyerabend's view, however, was never so consistently, or so simply, drawn. For one thing he recognizes the conditioned aspect of typical observation reports (this is his Pragmatic Theory of Observation—cf. Feyerabend 1958); unfortunately he fails to take the hint from Popper's use of the psychology of perception (as Popper himself fails—cf. 1957) and distinguish hard data from phenomenal reports. Nonetheless Feyerabend is on the right track when he says that the level common to two theories is the level of nonverbal responses to stimuli (cf. the clashes between conditioned expectations expressable at the hard data and phenomenal levels of experience), it is just that without the psychological and epistemological apparatus erected earlier one has no way to clearly understand or develop this intuition.

85. The changes that have occurred in the history of science have been quite radical, even to the ditching of entire ontologies and rafts of 'facts' = hard data. Only be reducing the theoretical dimension to near zero can the empiricist make this history look like a steady accumulation of data.

On the other hand, the role of controversy in science is of great importance and it is implausible to insist that the controversy always amounts to no more than propaganda, rather than the serious debate of the comparative merits of different points of view. Furthermore there is considerable evidence for a continuity of progression and the preservation of fundamental theoretical ideas over the course of science which cannot be ignored in any plausible account.

86. Feyerabend at least cannot be said to be guilty of lack of historical sensitivity. Indeed, he claims to arrive at his position through historical analysis. Actually, this is only partly true, for his semantic prescriptions and to a large extent his correlative theory of observation are still formulated within the aprioristic mold.

87. This aspect of the history of science, of the relative unimportance of mere raw observational evidence and the relevant importance of how the theory dictates what should be done with it, has been nicely stressed by Feyerabend and too often ignored by everyone else.

88. Little enough has been explicitly written recently about *systematic* meta-physics and its relation to science after the fashion of my 1973c, 1974c, though I view this as an urgent necessity. Many of the earlier writings on this subject, in my view, fall far short of the desired perceptiveness and system. Represen-tative among earlier writings are Burtt 1959, Koyre 1957, 1968, Pap 1963b, Toulmin and Goodfield 1965.

89. E.g., classical logical structure, and various dynamical structures, for example the canonical dynamical formalism, various group theoretic struc-tures and so on—although not all of these mathematical structures are shared by all scientific theories and in some cases they have been 'generalized' in a fairly obvious sense. Cf. my 1973c.

CHAPTER 4

1. For the standard account see Carnap 1934, 1956, Nagel 1961, or Hempel 1938, 1965, and most other introductory treatments of the subject. A compre-hensive summary is given by Suppe 1974b.

2. The contemporary controversy has foci at Quine 1960, Feyerabend 1962, 1965a, Kuhn 1962, Shapere 1964, 1974, and Wisdom 1971, 1972, to name but a few on the "other" side to those mentioned in Note 1. For a detailed treatment of Realism see this work, Chapters 2, 3.

3. That quantum theory does the other things I claim for it will not be a subject of controversy for anyone familiar with it (though how it does what it does may be). But this last feature may puzzle some —the relevant literature may conveniently be approached through Hooker 1971c. General literature on quantum theory itself pertaining to these matters can be found in Hooker 1972c.

4. Of course, there are the usual books of semantics to be written here on the detailed meaning of words like 'observe', 'theory', etc. and they have their legitimate place. But the place to discuss such technicalities is *after* a general view of theories has been settled (a view contrary, I know, to some received doctrines). We are here engaged in getting to grips with a general view of theories and the scientific process—undue attention to details of this kind only obscures the issues.

5. With respect to quantum theory only, there is the special debate over whether it is indeed entirely adequate for the theoretical description of the measuring apparatus. This debate is irrelevant to the present paper for two reasons. (1) I am not interested in the peculiar feature of a given theory but in the general features of every fundamental theory. (2) Even if we granted the inadequacy of quantum theory here it would not affect the fundamental point that the theory is needed to provide a theoretical analysis of every measuring apparatus (as the surprising quantum analysis of errors shows—it is just that in some cases the analysis will need to approach the classical analysis in a certain limit) but only add a requirement on the passage to a description of individual measurement outcomes. For further technical remarks and litera-ture on quantum theory see Hooker 1972c, 1973c.

6. Its importance comes out in the way in which scientists judge their colleagues' work: good experimental method, unsound assumptions, etc., etc. Look at the reaction of (part of) the scientific world to Velikovsky! Cf. also

Feyerabend's comments on Galileo's telescope and normal perception in Feyerabend 1965a, 1965b, 1969.

7. Nor is it possible to say in advance that there are some areas of science that definitely will not be included in the experiments of some other areas of science. I will now give some (admittedly bizarre) examples, which nonetheless exhibit empirically possible situations, which should convince the reader of this. One might suppose, for example, that such physical experiments as those described above would never involve theories of geology or anthropology. Consider, then, the following situations.

Suppose that it is discovered that the laws of physics are changing with time and that some of them also depend upon the crystalline structures in the neighbourhood (i.e. they vary, for example, from place to place on the earth). Then geophysics would immediately become of great relevance to fundamental physical theory both by way of providing a geological time scale against which changes in the fundamental laws could be checked (and current experiments actually dated in the time scale in case the pattern included sudden changes) and by providing an account of the current distributions of crystalline structures (rocks, etc.) and their movements in order to obtain a satisfactory *ceteris paribus* clause.

Again, suppose that anthropology revealed that for certain cultures certain areas of life cannot be investigated scientifically because the culture produced arbitrary and irrational responses in that area on the part of all its human members, no matter what the evidence presented. Then, if these areas happened to be subject- or experiment-kind specific, one would have to consult the anthropological background of the scientists before assessing their conclusions. Even stronger ties would arise if the experimental behavior of physical objects was a function of the cultural context in which the experiment occurred—as it is in sociology and other "human sciences" and as it would be in biology if those who believe in the influence of prayer and music on plants are correct. (This kind of situation raises some very interesting epistemological problems. How could a scientist check himself to see if he is functioning in a trustworthy manner unless in fact he is not in one of the "irrational zones" of his culture and so *is* functioning in this manner? Note, too, that there could turn out to be a privileged culture—one that had no "irrational zones," or, failing that, one whose irrational zones excluded the experimental study of the irrational zones of other cultures. What would the situation be if each culture were irrational in the assessment of the methods of other cultures? How close is this to our situation?)

8. Thus, for example, all of Carnap's pioneering work, from the complex and detailed *Aufbau* 1934 to his later Partial Interpretation model 1956 employs the same basic structure and all other discussion occurs within the same compass.

9. See Sellars 1965a, p. 178. Of course, the "model-system filter-transformer" is only an abstraction standing in any given case for the complex set of operations actually carried out in order to relate model, theory, and data. In most realistic cases these are extremely complex—let the reader consider the air-shower computations I mentioned or work out the corrections used in the cloud chamber example in Appendix 2.

With models taken seriously the deductive theory of explanation (cf. Hempel 1965) receives a necessary enrichment. The point of explaining the behavior of a system S is not just the deduction of true descriptions of S's behavior from the theory in question—this almost never happens exactly, and it is far too crude a characterization of the actual structure of scientific situations. A theory explains S's behavior by providing an appropriate model for S such that good approximation's to S's behavior are deducible from that model description in conjunction with the theory and *via* the filter-transformer. One then says, provided the model is of the right sort (i.e. not based on a mere formal analogy etc.) that one has captured what S *really is*, in essentials. It is this provision of insight into the real nature of S that we normally count on for explanations to be satisfied. (It follows, I believe, that, although all sound explanations of this type will also provide sound predictions, mere prediction is a much weaker requirement so that not all predictions that pay off need rest on a basis sufficient for providing a satisfying explanation.) Incidentally, models seem to me to play a similarly important role in inter-theoretical explanation. One does not in general deduce the empirical generalizations of a succeeded theory from its successor, this is generally impossible because the two conflict; but the successor theory, by providing a model, in its own terms, of the world under the assumption of the succeeded theory's truth explains why the succeeded theory should have been as experimentally successful as it was. On the deductive model of explanation, see e.g., Hempel 1965, Suchting 1967, and the literature they cite. On the role of models in science, see e.g. Harré 1970, Hesse 1963, 1965.

In connection with the relations between commonsense observational concepts and theoretical concepts, Sellars has given an illuminating discussion of the role of models. (See Sellars 1961, 1963, 1965a, pp. 178–184 for a convenient summary.) According to him we have at least three stages (though these are hardly sharply distinguishable in practice). (i) There is a model described in commonsense terms. (E.g., the Newtonian model of a gas as a swarm of colliding billiard balls.) (ii) Then there is a corrected model which deletes the respects in which the former model is incompatible with theory and adds certain other characteristics required by theory. This passage is made with the help of a "critical commentary." (E.g., we now say the billiard balls are in fact very small and absolutely rigid. Sellars describes this state as one of "controlled incoherence" since it is not always the case that the commonsense objects can coherently be conceptually transformed as required.) (iii) Finally, there is the theoretical model itself. For Sellars these transitions give semantic life to the theoretical terms, for they become meaningful as analogical transformations of commonsense terms, sharing a range of higher-order attributes in common with them—but I am less concerned here with Sellars' semantical doctrines (on which I am still not satisfied, cf. Chapter 2, this work) than with the key role which he assigns to models, correctly, I think.

And I repeat that it is not descriptions in commonsense terms alone that requires the complex transition to theory discussed above. Even descriptions couched in such technical terms as 'Wilson cloud chamber', 'ionizing particle trajectory', 'flip-flop pulse output' and so on still require the same kinds of transformations before the relevant theory of these systems can be brought to bear.

10. Now the largest epistemological debate about science is the Realist-Empiricism dispute over the nature and status of theoretical terms. This is not the place to enter the dispute at length (for a defense of Realism, see Chapters

2, 3, and 8 of this work) but two things need to be said in passing.

(1) The introduction of the phenomenal level need carry no commitment to phenomenalism, or indeed to any "myth of the given," whatsoever. Commonsense observational assertions and identifications can just as well be subject to theoretical criticism and revision as any hard data claims. The technique for doing this is just the usual technique of adjustment of the whole structure of science so as to minimize our losses against the various utilities for preservation placed on each component (Quine). Indeed, this model of science strongly reinforces Quine's claim that the unit of empirical significance is the whole of science (and, I might add, of metaphysics, too!—cf. below; for Quine's view, see Quine 1960, 1963).

(2) The semantical bone of contention between Empiricists and Realists is the ultimate eliminability of the phenomenal or commonsense level. For it is rightly claimed that if theoretical terms are to have "first class semantical status" (Sellars) and to be the fundamental descriptive terms of the world, they must ultimately be able to enter the observational vocabulary. It is a vexed question whether the "ultimately" here is to be read as *"actually"* or only as *"in* (logical) *principle"* (cf. Hesse 1968a, Hooker 1970a) but this need not detain us, for the point I wish to make is that the realization of this goal amounts just to lopping off the phenomenal level (i.e., these correspondence rules) but preserving the theory—hard data linkages with the observation language couched, at least in great part, in the terms of the theoretical models. In this case the filter-transformer would be simplified and its operation redescribed, but it would still be necessary (since merely describing the world using model theoretic language does not ensure it will behave exactly according to the model). None of the distinctive characteristics of these linkages described above would change. This schema for science is to be so construed as to be compatible with such a Realist position.

Mary Hesse (whom I read, unfortunately, after finishing this paper) offers an important discussion of the Quinean-type "network" model of theories, making some similar points to those made here and in Chapter 2. But the elimination of an interesting semantical distinction between observational and theoretical terms tends to lead to the abandonment of discussion of the detailed structure of science—this is a mistake, even on Quinean grounds, and leads to unclear superficially general conceptions of epistemology and methodology. The present model is part of a corrective to this Realist treatment here. (I should add that Hesse has elsewhere written on some of the more detailed mechanisms, see e.g. Hesse 1970.)

11. These themes are expounded in Hooker 1973c, 1974c. See also e.g., Graves 1971, van Melson 1960. For some earlier intimations see also Hooker 1972c, section 13. Further Realist exposition is found in Chapters 2, 3, and 8 of this work, and Hooker 1978a.

12. For a similar general judgement on confirmation theory see Hesse 1970, p. 63.

13. Cf. also Sellars' remarks on the Feyerabendian view of common language in Sellars 1965a, p. 174.

14. Another way in which this occurs is when a theory alters the form of our descriptions, e.g. under relativity theory we alter the form of a description from "X has ϕ" to "X has ϕ to relative to reference frame F" and also, were we to follow Bohr's conception of quantum theory, we should alter our

description of systems from the classically determined form "X has a property φ lying somewhere in the range Δ" to "X's property φ is defined to within Δ"—indeed, the difference between these latter two formulations lies at the heart of the controversy concerning the interpretation of quantum theory (cf. Hooker 1972c).

15. If such be the case, then we may wish to withdraw the word 'metaphysics' from any part of the content of science, withholding the term only for the strictly uncriticizable, but this is really a matter of little importance and it is a useful term to draw attention to the perhaps (but only perhaps!) culturally invariant content of part of our science.

CHAPTER 5

1. This is true of most of those offering a decision-theoretic account of scientific method (e.g. Levi, 1967), though not all (cf. Jeffrey, 1965; Rudner, 1966).

The dominant aim of science according to Levi's influential *Gambling with Truth* is relief of epistemic ignorance. Now this option may perhaps be capable of being given a unique sense in a positivist setting or other settings equally severe in their restrictions on science, but in the context of ENR it is multiply ambiguous. We are epistemically ignorant in many ways, ignorant of The True Theory, ignorant of more theoretically fecund theories than those we have, ignorant of more practically fecund theories than those we have, ignorant of technological mastery over nature in the ways we desire, ignorant of the forms of culture and social institutions best suited to the pursuit of enquiry, ignorant of the social consequences of pursuing the foregoing goals in some particular manner, and ignorant of the best long term system of goals, epistemic and other, for human fulfillment. Which of these ignorances is it the business of science to remove? And in which order? Only by arbitrarily concentrating on those ignorances at the head of the list and ignoring those at the tail of the list can one arrive at a characterization of scientific goals independent of the full system of human goals.

2. Of course, that there is a prospective methodology is quite compatible with there not being a 'logic of scientific discovery' in the traditional sense, because in the decision-theoretic framework prospective methodology might be more transparently labelled 'logic of future-oriented choice', for it specifies the choices to be made in the investment of research resources (and so ties methodology to policy), it does not provide a recipe for ensuring the desired outcome. (This distinction shows how Feyerabend can be right about the coincidence between retrospective and prospective methodology and wrong about claiming the non-existence of both on the Popperian grounds that the latter doesn't exist; the argument equivocates between 'logic of discovery' and 'methodology of resource allocation'—see Hooker, 1975b, and below.)

3. Feyerabend backs up this argument with an analysis of historical examples in which, he argues, scientists quite reasonably resorted to radically unorthodox methods before succeeding in having their view recognized and accepted (the favourite is Galileo—see Feyerabend 1969, 1970a,b). Feyerabend's own conclusion is the most extreme version of pluralism: "anything goes" (see Feyerabend, 1970a; cf. Hooker, 1972b).

To assess the reasonableness of this methodology, it is important to distinguish the following claims:

C_1: There is a fixed, unique methodology for scientific research

C_2: There is an adequate, unique theory of prospective methodology
and distinguish between these claims:

S_1: There is a particular, finite class of research strategies which will be adequate to cover individual rational action in every historical situation

S_2: There is a finite class of patterns of research strategies which are adequate to cover species-wide rational action in every historical situation.

First let us be clear that (i) C_2 does not entail C_1, (ii) nor does S_2 entail S_1, for (i) there may be an adequate and unique theory of methodology which nonetheless doesn't specify a fixed procedure and (ii) the pattern of research resource allocation may indicate a historically conditional allocation of specieswide resources to each of a set of strategies spanning the full spectrum of possibilities, from radical guess-work to cautious variation on the known, such that this pattern even entails the negation of S_1.

And these possibilities would be exactly those we would expect from the diversity of goals for science and the decision-theoretic approach to methodology. Although there is a general theory of methodology, it does not specify a fixed procedure, rather procedure is a function generally of operative utilities and (believed) historical circumstances (rational decisions generally are functions of these two factors). Moreover, the situation of the individual is usually quite different from that of the group here; typically the individual has the resources (time, energy, money, etc.) to work on only a few difficult problems in a lifetime and only on one or two at a time; the societal group, however, can pursue many different problems simultaneously and pursue research programs that stretch over generations. Thus the problem of allocation of resources for the individual will be quite different from that of the group; more particularly, it will in general prove rational for the group to pursue all or most avenues of research, including the radical alternatives, no matter how the group decisions are made. (Even if the probability of success for most utilities decreases as the strategy becomes more radical, the pay-off if a success occurs also increases, so that almost any society with sufficient resources will always have some persons pursuing these approaches.)

Now we are in a position to evaluate Feyeragend's radical pluralism. First, the judgement "anything goes" is equivocal as between the individual and the group. Applied to the individual level, it might be translated as the negation of S_1; applied at the group level it might be translated as the negation of S_2. But there is no reason which Feyerabend supplies to reject S_2, so long as the class of patterns of allocations of research resources among strategies contains members which specify wide-ranging and circumstantially flexible allocations. Moreover, he focuses on cases of individual choice. Notice next that the negation of S_1 is compatible with S_2 and even entailed by it under the present approach to method, and moreover that the negation of C_1 is compatible with C_2, indeed $\sim C_1 \cdot C_2$ is just what one would expect under the present approach to method. Thus Feyerabend's claims about the necessity for great flexibility of method are compatible with the existence of a prospective methodology, even with one that entails a unique group-allocation strategy. Finally, observe that which methodological recommendations are relevant for an individual depends strongly on the socio-cultural setting in which he/she is operating. Galileo operating in a monolithic dogmatic culture arrayed against alternative theories, Feynman operating in an oligopolistic market of saleable ideas, some mythical successor operating in a utopian society of complete cooperation—these are all radically different decision-making contexts. Thus in a fully cooperative, collectively rational society, a given individual might indeed not be rational in adopting the infinitely flexible policy Feyerabend recommends, for there is the assuredness that others will do their part, openly and critically, to contribute to the overall research program, but Galileo faced with his society, or one of us operating in a market of quasi-popular ideas are faced with very different problems. In these cases, as for the political revolutionary and the perfectly competitive businessman, it may well be that 'anything goes'. Still, this would be primarily a comment upon the structure and dynamics of the socio-cultural setting for the practice of science rather than a reduction of either methodological theory or procedure. In sum, despite Feyerabend's examples and criticisms, C_2 and S_2 remain.

Remain, that is, so long as we adopt the ENR decision-theoretic formulation. It is a damaging commentary on the remarkably simplistic conception of method entertained by orthodox empiricists and Popperians alike (and even Feyerabend in his way) that they have aimed to offer unique, fixed rules of method for the practice of science (Feyerabend's fixed rule was: no rules), instead of a flexible, situationally conditional theory of strategy selection.

4. It is in this perspective, at any rate, that the transition in the quasi-Popperian school from Popper's methodology to Lakatos' methodology of scientific research programs constitutes a distinctive advantage by explicitly introducing the historical, evolutionary dimension as part of the evaluative process. And we may understand the significance of the notion of a research program as that of the systematic exploration at some level of the serious realization of that level at all lower levels; this exploration pursued in the light of the utilities historically current for science (critically examined in the light of experience). Historically degenerating problem shifts are those producing decreasing pay-offs in the coin of the operative utilities and regenerating shifts conversely. This translation at once recasts the Lakatos theory in a wider perspective allowing for variation of methodological principles from program to program (as utilities vary; in the light of experience) and also corrects the Popperian-type failures of even this wider Lakatos approach (i) to distinguish adequately among levels of research programs, (ii) to distinguish the multiplicity of ends for the pursuit of a given program, (iii) to distinguish the evolution of social institutions for the pursuit of research from the evolution of theories.

Moreover, it is within this perspective of simultaneous pursuit of long and short term goals by a society or species, a situation where support of a 'mixed strategy' is realized as an actual pursuit of all goals by varying fractions of society, that Feyerabend's methodological pluralism finds its natural rationale.

And so long only as we remember that we are dealing with uncritical cultures, Kuhn's societal-specific normal/revolutionary distinction also finds a natural place as a part of the societal long term strategy for the sequential elaboration and testing of a research program at a fundamental level (say that of general theory or deeper). It is important that it be sequential (this will be because of the uncritical structure of the social institutions involved), otherwise the rationale for Kuhn's order collapses (i.e., collapses where elaboration of distinct versions of a given level may be deliberately pursued simultaneously).

5. We can hope that much of the language of mathematical ecology and, through it, of mathematical economics will thus become applicable to institutional theory. Through net theory the mathematics of neurophysiology may also usefully apply (as it does to ecology).

6. Thus I do not believe that the Popperian program for demarcating science succeeds, or could succeed. Indeed, Popper himself recognizes that the principles for the choice of his basic statements lie outside of the characterization of science which he offers. (For more criticism cf. Hooker, 1981b.)

7. It was of course Popper in this century who first clearly drew attention to this social foundation for the scientific enterprise despite his resisting the connecting of the theory of that enterprise with the larger theory of the social human species, despite even the later clear emergence of evolutionary themes in his writing (cf. Popper, 1973; Hooker, 1975b). Subsequently, Feyerabend enlarged substantially on these themes—cf. Hooker 1972b, where a substantial bibliography may be found. I have developed some of these themes at greater length elsewhere, see herein and Hooker 1981b.

CHAPTER 6

This is a lightly edited version of my essay 1985b; nothing of substance has been changed.

1. See van Fraassen, 1980. This quote is from pp. 202–203. All page references concerning van Fraassen in what follows are to this book unless explicitly stated otherwise.

2. See e.g., the accounts in Chapter 3 and Suppe 1974a. As we shall shortly see, this remains true also of van Fraassen. The account is only slightly complicated also by admitting that logical theory itself had already achieved a sophistication far beyond the theory of finite truth functions or quantification theory at the hands of Frege and Russell at the turn of the century and continued to develop. For the *strategic* development I depict is a history of the uses of logical systems to defend philosophical theses, not a history of logic. (Nonetheless the two interact in complex ways.)

3. Since in realist theories of explanation, explanations are normally held to require laws in their premises, expressing natural necessities, the two problems are immediately connected. For van Fraassen's treatment of probability in a similar fashion to explanation, see pp. 198–202 (summarized in Hooker 1985b, Note 6 and briefly below).

4. Syntax concerns the actual skeletal structure of a language or sentence, the structured string of logical devices that organises descriptive terms into declarations, questions and commands (but especially declarations). 'And', 'if-then' and the like studied in traditional logic are all syntactical operations, while 'is a tautology' and 'is deducible from' are syntactically definable predicates both within traditional logic and for large, useful fragments of ordinary and scientific language. Semantic features of language are, on the other hand, those that concern its relation to the world, here the main property for state-

ments is truth, and van Fraassen adds empirical adequacy as the other main semantic property for theories (p.90).

A model is a structured set of entities (abstract or concrete) such that the significant syntactical components of a set of sentences in a language, or a theory, can be mapped on to it in a structure-preserving way and when they are the sentence set or theory in question is evaluated true. (A model is a way of 'realising', or satisfying, the sentences or theory in question.) In general, sentence sets or theories will have many different models.

5. I believe it *should* involve the empirical adequacy of the theories, perhaps more heavily even than most realists would like; see Chapters 3 and 8. (To be strict, empiricists should not countenance empirical testing at all; but it is a historical fact that when a then-current exposition of their views has failed to win wide acceptance, they proceed to revise the exposition in exactly the manner than any realist would do.) Ironically, it is precisely because philosophical theories themselves have a theoretical dimension, and even more importantly a meta-theoretical dimension as well, that permits them to be clung to even in the face of recalcitrant historical experience. Empiricists may seek ever-richer logics or more powerful theories of pragmatics with which to remedy existing defects. Attempts to dismiss these strategies out of hand usually can be taken to beg the question. See text following Note 9.

I illustrated this for the realist in the case of applying Craig's theorem to generate the 'theoretician's dilemma' (see 1968a, pp. 161–2). Using a theorem of formal logic, one can separate out a supposed purely observational segment of a theory; empiricists then argued that one could throw away the theoretically infected segment, thus rendering theoretical terms superfluous. One *could* do this, but why would it be *rational* to do so? Reflection reveals that it would not be rational, save on empiricist assumptions. So the argument carries no force against the realist, but succeeds only in begging the question.

6. Chapter 5 argues for a non-segregable range of utilities relevant to rational scientific decisions, a position I regard as strengthened by the arguments in Hooker 1982b (and Chapter 8).

7. For example, the tables are apparently turned on myself, for I have argued from a fallibilist evolutionary perspective to the adoption of certain philosophical positions and strategies, most notably in Chapters 3 and 5 (now see Chapter 8 also). But we shall see below that the reversal is more apparent than real, for the real force of an evolutionary perspective has not been properly grasped.

8. See, for example, the classic discussion by Feyerabend 1965a, b, 1975 and that of his sympatico Munevar 1981—though I have attempted to back off from the relativist suggestions in their positions, cf. Hooker 1973d and Chapter 2, ironically on realist grounds —and the discussion by Churchland 1979, 1985.

9. On choosing theoretically interesting programs over mere empirical adequacy, see again the discussions by Feyerabend (Note 8). Discussions by Kuhn 1962 and Lakatos 1970b also contain some valuable examples. The advent of both relativity theories are cases in point; though I do not deny that empirical testing also entered early on as a factor, but hardly the only one. Much contemporary work in quantum field theory is notoriously in the same position.

The insight that what is sought is valuable truth I have from Popper, see e.g., 1973. It is connected directly to the rational choice model of epistemology I follow, for according to me it is in a utility-uncertainty trade-off structure that a theory of valuable truth is to be spelled out, as are the grounds for trading off theoretical attractions against empirical adequacy. See also Note 30 below.

10. In the specific case of perception, we have used our sense organs to acquire the empirical base to build science, including a psychology of perception and sciences of instrumental data acquisition, all of which allow us to criticise our sensory perception and, indeed, to virtually abandon it altogether for the purposes of doing science. Similar transformations are beginning elsewhere; for example, the psychology and economics of organisations, allied to policy theory and philosophy of science, as applied to science itself, are the beginnings of the ability to criticise and eventually transform the elementary and largely unconscious social bases on which science has hitherto been organised. Similar remarks apply to sociology and biology applied to the genetic selection of scientists, and they apply as well to psychology and education as applied to scientific training. (Taken together, these developments amount to the reshaping of our cognitive neotony.) And so on. Cf. Chapter 7.

11. See Carnap 1950. Presumably, the motive was to protect an *a priori* yet non-cognitive status for empiricism's First Philosohy (cf. Chapter 3). In any case, it is clear that Quine's reply, 1951, though technically telling, does not strike the heart of the position, which is meta-philosophical. Cf. also Goldstick 1979.

More recently, Melchert 1985 has argued, on essentially similar grounds, that van Fraassen's agnostic acceptance really amounts to full-blown belief. I am, I think, happy to see this conclusion drawn as a corollary to the arguments presented in the text, although it needs a detailed cognitive theory to back it.

12. A state of seeing a scene has, all research shows, many levels of hypothesis-like operation involved in it. It is, for example, a function of past knowledge and of perceptual expectations. See nearly any modern work on perception, e.g., Marr 1982, Savage 1978. The conclusion to follow in the text is enhanced by Churchland's elegant thought experiment, 1979.

13. In terms of truth functions

$$(\sim A \lor \sim B) \supset \sim(A \cdot B)$$

Notice that if the negation sign is interpreted as 'is not empirically adequate', that is as 'no model has a sub-model adequate to the data', then the relationship holds; but if one attempts to argue from the falsity of either A or B to the failure of empirical adequacy of $A.B$ then the argument fails.

14. See Chapter 7. I asked there about the fate of objectivity in science if cognitive demands were matched by selective breeding, resulting in a human community split into the 'understands' and the 'understand-nots'. The same might apply to surgical intervention to enlarge perceptual range or to modify thought processes. Empiricism sometimes smacks of an old-fashioned politics, holding to an almost mystical equality among people, no matter how diverse their personalities and abilities, nor how radical the impact of our interventions upon them. Are we to be forever stuck with Everyman's perceptions? (And not because any other way is risky; *every* way is risky.)

15. For an introduction to this rapidly expanding area, see for example Jantsch 1980, Maturana/Varela 1980, Prigogine 1980, Varela 1979, Yovits 1962.

16. There is a 'Kantian' version of M's, see Chapter 3, Section 3.1.4. I do not think it sits at all well with the spirit of empiricism, but it has its own attractions.

17. van Fraassen's critique is found in his 1980 Chapter 1, Laudan's in 1981b.

18. For the latter see p. 40. The argument is superficially enticing, but a slippery one for van Fraassen, because it does suggest looking for a *theory* of the selecting environment and of the internal dynamics of environment-species interactions *and* for a *theory* of the internal organisations of the evolving species, all of which together would explain the ensuing dynamics. But the demand for the same theories in the present case is natural for my own position and anathema for van Fraassen.

19. See most explicitly Hooker 1979b, 1981c, d, e, but for earlier comments see also Chapter 2.

20. For example, by dropping that part of the claim *b* in the text from 'and' onward; see his *S* theses, Laudan 1981b, pp. 23–4. Truncating *b* in this manner yields a weak thesis which is too easily attacked.

21. For example, the only account of approximate truth examined in any detail is Popper's, but it is quite idiosyncratic. Surely a more natural place to look for a definition of approximate truth is to model theoretic notions. And when Laudan says that ". . .within a successor T_2, any genuine realist must insist that T_1's underlying ontology is preserved in T_2's, *for it is that ontology above all which he alleges to be approximately true*" (Laudan's italics), he is simply uttering a non-sequitur, as field theory atomic theory transitions demonstrate (cf. Hooker 1981c), thereby again setting up a straw man.

Similarly, Laudan is unjust to Sellars' suggestion (Sellars 1965a) that a successor theory T^1 should explain why its predecessor T was as successful as it was. Laudan recognizes that this is an improvement over the rigid demand that T^1 explain T, but argues that this accomplishment is irrelevant to the epistemic appraisal of T^1 (or T). But I understand Sellars to be suggesting that an adequate successor T^1 to T should be able to model T adequately within its resources, where this latter involves modelling the conditions under which T is true or approximately true and those under which it is not, in such a way that all of T's true or approximately true consequences become at least approximately true consequences of T^1 (in T^1's ontology) while none of the other of T^1's consequences do. But this is no more than to demand that T^1 preserve the empirical evidence and reflect the structural reasons for that evidence (albeit in a critical manner, as represented in T^1), without which T^1 would be disconfirmed. And this *is* relevant to appraising T^1 (and T).

22. On explanation and understanding see Hooker 1980c (cf. Chapter 8, Section 8.3.5), where I link understanding to deeper ontologies and hence to approximate modelling and approximate truth for shallower ones. For Laudan on Sellars, see Note 21.

23. Here I repeat that van Fraassen's explanatory tack may not bear deeper reflection, see Note 18.

24. For literature arguing in this way, see e.g., Nerlich 1976 (cf. my review Hooker 1981a) and Hooker 1971b. [Note: Recently—subsequent to writing this essay—there have been renewed formal challenges to this idea, see e.g.,

Manders 1982, Munday 1985. I have not had time to examine them in detail but surmise that they meet fates similar to that which I argued for Bunge's formalisation long ago in Hooker 1971b.]

25. Ballantine 1970. It is my view that this doctrine pretty clearly represents a strategy of emasculating by fiat the semantic content of quantum mechanics until it says only what is compatible with empiricism—always a *possible* approach. See Hooker 1973c.

26. See van Fraassen 1980, Chapter 6 and 1972.

27. That is, it doesn't yield an insightful physical ontology, cf. Note 22. On quantum theory and ontology, see Hooker 1972c, 1973c. For a review of the literature, see e.g., Jammer 1966, 1974. A good example of a physicist's physical intuition at work is given by Prigogine 1980. In my view even so-called realist versions of the quantum logical approach have suffered from a tendency to be divorced from physical understanding and an appreciation of the intuitive problems to be solved (cf. my discussions in Hooker 1973c, Holdsworth/Hooker 1982), but they have nonetheless rejected van Fraassen's manoeuvres in an effort to do more justice to the theoretical structures (see, e.g. Hooker 1972b, 1975/1979).

28. On Carnap and Quine, see Note 1. The web metaphor is spelled out in Quine/Ullian 1970. The web analogy is suggestive, its chief defects from my point of view being its tendency to obscure the substitution of rational commitment criteria for some combination of purely logical structure and non-cognitive pragmatic choice, and its tendency to distract from meta-philosophical debate. Cf. Chapter 2, Note 75.

29. There may be none because understanding cannot itself be conceptually understood (cf. Haugland 1978), or because the 'human person' more generally transcends its own realisations (cf. Chapter 7), or because at bottom the world is radically non-conceptual (i.e., because realism is false).

30. I owe the introduction to a rational commitment approach to epistemology to Leach 1976. The only technically sophisticated development of the idea for a philosophy of science is as yet by Levi 1967 (cf. Levi 1980), but this is modelled on Popper's position which I regard as defective (cf. Chapter 7, Section 7.11, Chapter 8) and it also has its own difficulties (cf. Bogdan 1976). Though in its infancy the general idea seems to me to be extremely promising.

31. It is hardly necessary to review post-World War II explosion in philosopy of science. As to the history of science and its role here, see for example the references in Kuhn 1962, Lakatos/Musgrave 1970, Laudan 1977, as well as those in Feyerabend 1965a, b, 1969, 1975. For the mathematical revolution, see e.g., Hooker 1975/1979, 1979d and references therein.

32. See e.g., Blume 1974, Easlea 1973, Knorr et al. 1975, 1980, Krohn et al. 1978, Merton 1973, Spiegel-Rosing/de Solla Price 1978, Tisdell 1981, van Melsen 1961.

33. Historically, empiricism played an important intellectual role in the resistance to Nazi interference in science. Empiricism supported a vision of a rational, valuable future based on free enquiry and objective improvement. If the hope of disentangling science and value, and both from politics, proved naive, still the vision has its valuable insights and it served an important purpose. Marxism can also be so interpreted as to yield unreasonable political interference in scientific processes (and has been historically). It must be similarly resisted, though one now knows that the grounds for doing so must

be much more sophisticated than those empiricism offered if they are to be convincing.

34. See in this connection Martin's stimulating study 1979. Cf. other less direct literature, e.g., Easlea 1973, Livingstone/Mason 1978, Maxwell 1976, Rose/Rose 1969, Sahlins 1976.

CHAPTER 7

Acknowledgement. I gratefully acknowledge permission to reprint Figures 7.2 and 7.6 from Hooker 1980d, to adapt Figure 7.1 from Hooker 1980d and Figures 7.3, 7.4 and 7.5 from Hooker 1979c, and generally to freely adapt material from these papers, especially from 'Scientific Neutrality vs. Normative Learning . . .' in D. Oldroyd (ed.) *Science and Ethics* (1973). This is a lightly edited version of the original 1982a, nothing of substance has changed.

1. The idea is filled out a little in Hooker 1979c. According to Piaget (e.g., 1948, 1951, 1954, 1971a), the manual operation of the young child's body in interaction with his physical environment is the key structure in the cognitive development of the nervous system. Without being committed to particular details, I assume that something like this remains an important component in all conceptual development; hence the slogan.

2. Many would hold that there is an important distinction between the two and that, for example, everything that has any taint of practical application to create an artifact is a technology, not a science—only the remainder is pure science. In this essay I shall try to undermine that position: (i) by indicating how deep may be the penetration of technology—maybe there is nothing but technology, at least if we follow the above definition; (ii) by drawing attention to the social, institutionalized nature of science—looked at from a broader cultural perspective, perhaps science itself is one of our cultural technologies; (iii) by drawing attention, in particular, to the now self-reflexive character of science—if science is self-designed, is it not its own technology? See, in particular, the discussion in Section 7.5 below. I do not claim dogmatically that there is no principled distinction to be made; however, I no longer know how to make that distinction and suggest, moreover, that making it can be safely laid aside for the purposes of this essay; cf. also my discussion towards the end of Chapter 3.

3. See Hooker et al. 1980a for further details and an extensive bibliography. Energy has been the spawning ground for the policy theory discussed later in the paper (Section 7.9).

4. For examples, see Hooker 1975/79, 1979d and the literature cited there. Examples of the kind of fundamental question I have in mind are: what general mathematical forms to represent time development (dynamics) are deterministic? Are these latter necessarily Hamiltonian in form? And so on. By comparison, questions about the empirical correctness of this or that dynamical law (say one of Newton's equations), much less the details of particular Newtonian force laws, are relatively more superficial. Cf. Hooker 1973c.

5. For the positions referred to, see, e.g., Popper 1973, Lakatos 1970b; cf. e.g. Laudan 1977 and my treatment of Popper in Chapter 3 and Hooker 1981b. To put the point in terms of another well-known metaphor, once enough is known about the structure of the web of belief, experience need not be

restricted to interacting with it only around its periphery. This latter metaphor is Quine's; it may be tracked down, e.g., through Brown 1979 or Suppe 1974a, Chapter 2, Note 75 and Chapter 6, Note 28.

6. For example, the 'core' of mechanics within physics would surely have to contain principles such as that time is a one-dimensional continuum, dynamics is given by a set of Hamiltonian equations, and so on. (In fact, Lakatos et al. work at a less sophisticated level, talking simply about Newton's equations and the like.) Yet the fact remains that physicists and mathematicians have recently begun to explore the possibilities for two-dimensional times, radically non-Hamiltonian structures, and so on.

7. A bridge to mysticism because persons seem to transcend scientific descriptions of themselves (cf. Section 7.8 below), a framework for scepticism because all our knowledge is profoundly risky, culled from a radically ignorant evolutionary base as it is; and grand conclusions of the sort canvassed here are riskiest of all (but cf. the last paragraph of this paper).

8. For examples of these subject matters see respectively Ruse, 1979; Hoffmaster 1980; Barnes 1977, Beer 1979a, Knorr et al. 1975, Krohn et. al. 1978 and Leach 1976, Hooker 1975b, Bjerring/Hooker 1980.

9. The diagram is a modified version of that appearing in Hooker 1980d.

10. This situation also may only represent straightforward extrapolation from practice, e.g., from educationally-biased marriage patterns which may constitute a slow and subtle, but definite, process of genetic selection. In any case the age at which research degrees are being taken is even now eating away inexorably at the young adult creative years (18–28). And if the situation discussed in the text were realized it would move us toward the visions of the great technocratic utopians, see e.g., Armytage 1965 and Elliott 1976 for discussions.

11. See Polanyi 1968, Tawney 1962 and MacPherson 1970, 1973.

12. This figure is reproduced from Hooker 1980d.

13. For empiricism as an external defense of science, see, for example Habermas 1970, Novack 1971, Unger 1975 (cf. my discussion in Hooker 1980d) and more widely see for example Chalmers 1976, Chambers 1979, Easlea 1973, Feyerabend 1969, 1974, 1975, Spiegel-Rosing/de Solla Price 1978.

14. See Hooker 1974c and Hooker 1973c, Section vii for discussion. (Hooker 1973c applies the dichotomy to quantum mechanics. Cf. Hooker 1972c section 13.)

15. See Bub 1973 cf. Hooker 1973b, 1975/79, 1979d.

16. See discussion in Hooker 1979c. I have drawn heavily on the writings of Vickers (1968, 1970, 1979) on the one side and on developmental psychologists and educationalists, e.g., Kohlberg, 1973a, b, Piaget 1948, 1951, 1954, 1971a, b, Becker 1973, cf. Berger/Luckman 1971, on the other. The separation of fact and value is our (I should say an) Achilles heel because it blinds us to the underlying reality; it leads us to create false theories of cognition, science, rationality and so on, theories which are false because they fail to embody realistic relations between facts and values; and finally it leads us to create similarly false socio-political theories. (I am thinking here especially of liberalism in its severe forms, see Unger 1975.)

17. See e.g. Becker, 1973, Berger/Luckman 1971, Goffman 1976, Rieff 1966 and Vickers 1968. I speculate that the etiology of this differentiation is closely connected with Ashby's principle of channel separation (see Ashby 1970),

though this is to take a large step into the undeveloped area of relating normative, functional (or systems) and structural features of neuro-psychology; cf. Hooker 1978a and Hooker 1981e. It is relevant to remind ourselves that from this perspective science is to be seen as an enquiring system. For penetrating commentaries on this perspective see Churchman 1968, 1972, Tornebohm 1970, 1975 (cf. Bjerring/Hooker 1979) and Wojciechowski 1975, 1978, 1980.

18. In thus revoking norms because of other norms, does the inevitable normative involvement reveal itself. On these themes see, e.g., Adorno 1950, Althusser 1965, Popper 1963b, Rokeach 1960 and the references of Note 13, among many.

19. See for example Bjerring/Hooker 1979, 1981, Hooker, 1979b, 1981 c, d, e for different dimensions of this theme from my own point of view. Empiricism's idea that the evidence is epistemologically fixed beyond reach of theory is implicit in the conventionalist notion of evidence employed (and made explicit by Popper). The importance of theoretical interaction and of rejecting this last assumption has been hammered by Feyerabend (e.g., 1965a, b, 1969; cf. Hooker 1972b), though these themes run through much philosophy of science; see, for example, the accounts in PSA proceedings (e.g., Asquith et al. 1978/9, 1980/1, 1982/3, 1984) and e.g., Suppe 1974a.

20. My notion of norms as theories was first stated in Chapter 3 where the background of a strong evolutionary naturalism lends it a certain plausibility; empiricist prejudices about the non-cognitive nature of norms aside, from the point of view of a naturalist acknowledging the common origins of norms and facts, and of facts as theoretically dynamic, the most natural position to adopt is the view that norms are a species of theoretical commitment (cf. also H. Brown 1979). I acknowledge that there is more that needs to be said about how we come to differentiate between norms and facts and what sort of a differentiation it is—I have in mind a biological-cum-cognitive-systems answer (cf. Note 17)—but this is not the place and I do not have enough insights to pursue these issues. A promising place to begin is with the marriage of cognitive process theory (see e.g., Dennett, 1978, Haugeland 1981, Solso 1974, 1975, cf. Hooker 1981e and Dreyfus 1972) and the theory of self-organizing systems (see e.g., Jantsch 1980, Jantsch/Waddington 1976 Lilly 1974, Maturana/Varela 1980, Nicolis/Prigogine 1977, Yovits 1962, cf. Hofstadter 1979).

21. Figures 7.3, 7.4, and 7.5 have been adapted from Hooker 1979c. For epistemology in an evolutionary setting, see e.g., Campbell 1973, Lorenz 1976, Wuketits 1983.

22. But no one man's Reason, nor the Reason of any one number of men, makes the certaintie; . . . And therefore,. . . the parties must by their own accord, set up for right Reason, the Reason of some Arbitrator, or Judge, to whose sentence they will both stand, or their controversie must either come to blows or be undecided, for want of a right Reason constituted by Nature; So is it in all debates of what kind soever. Hobbes: *Leviathan*, Part I, Chapter 5, Para. 3.

23. See e.g., Hooker/van Hulst 1977b, 1979a, 1980b, Hooker et al. 1980a, Bjerring/Hooker 1980 and Hanna 1980.

24. See Levi 1967 and 1980 and cf. his review of the literature in 1979. See also Levi 1979 and Bogdan 1976 for an exploration of some difficulties.

25. See Chapter 5 and sec. 7.11 below. I have not yet worked out the

rational ordering structures or the consequences of deploying this wide range of utilities. Clearly studies of historical example, as well as theoretical development, will be important. There are large technical challenges here, e.g., to combine a theory of rational cost-benefit-risk trade-off structures with decision theory of multidimensional utilities, and bring both into relation with the requirements of optimally self-organizing systems. Significantly for our discussion, these general frameworks are applicable to public policies generally and to science methodology in particular (see below in text). Cf. e.g., the concept development program of Baumgartner et al. 1984.

26. Cf. the discussion by Haberer 1969, and, with respect to science policy, the stimulating discussion by Jackson 1979.

27. On the norm-guided retrospective approach to public policy which results from this approach, see Hanna 1980, Hooker/van Hulst 1977b, 1979a, 1980a, Hooker 1983 and references in Hooker et al. 1980.

28. For if a given form of life could reflect within itself all of the features, of whatever hierarchical order, which were relevant to its dynamics, so that change came wholly within the ambit of socially deliberate choice, then in the most important sense that form of life would not be changing. But we are not in that position. Cf. the alternatives once canvassed by Feyerabend 1965b, Churchman's requirement of a 'guarantor' for the system 1968, Stent's concerns 1978. As Chapter 8 reminds, with our scientific powers the epistemology of a world whose states are even partial functions of past choices and/or future expectations is very different from one whose states are wholly independent of these factors.

29. For example, the cultural institutions or processes which maintain metaphysical orientation, say toward materialism versus mysticism, or consumerism versus conservation. Religious frameworks, to take a prominent example, are not only part of the cultural tools which resist change, they can also act as a flexible framework within which to interpret change (anticipated or not) and channel reactions to it.

Political institutions allow us to evolve forms of authority, control and decision processes in response to change, or inhibit our capacity to respond. Creative responses to the revolutions in warfare, communications, genetic engineering and so on now under way will surely prove crucial for our species—and our lack of relevant political institutions in relation to our need for them should alarm us, cf. Note 19.

30. Understanding in its broadest sense includes wisdom and both of these embrace practical as well as theoretical knowledge, cf. Note 29. The transformation of the world into an artifact brings home to us, what should have been clear anyway, that all dimensions of understanding are in mutual interaction (cf. Note 28), so that we must expand along all fronts simultaneously in a balanced way—or likely we will not be given long to expand along any. (It is a common cry that the pace of technological development has outstripped our moral development—I would add that it has outstripped both our theoretical and institutional development.) In fact, it will not be possible to achieve any more than a limited responsibility and rationality in these matters when we have to act in such ignorance and uncertainty. At least we are now becoming conscious of the dimensions of the problem, which empiricism/liberalism so effectively represses, and are beginning to explore partial institutional responses on many levels (the World Health Organization is one, so is the

international agreement on fusion research and so are national science policies, whatever their blemishes—but so too are the protesters who guard other, more neglected dimensions of understanding, cf. Easlea 1973, Maxwell 1976, Rose/Rose 1969, Roszak 1973).

31. For example, if there is a large nuclear-supplied electricity grid in place at some time t and an increment in energy supply is sought it will, under most circumstances, prove marginally cheapest to build another nuclear plant, for which a manufacturing industry already exists, and marginally extend the electricity grid, rather than, say, to supply to energy from a new technology, e.g., solar heat and photovoltaics. This could be true even though it would have been the case that, had the society in question invested in research, development and large-scale deployment of the solar technology over the two or three decades preceding time t, so that it was at t the established technology, it would at t have been cheaper to increment it rather than introducing new nuclear technology.

At the present time, e.g., the world seems clearly committed to burning a very large percentage of its accessible oil for such comparatively crass purposes as heating, steam production, electricity generation and motor vehicle transportation when it has many and increasing uses in medicine, plastics, etc. and a particular suitability for high-speed transportation (e.g., aircraft). Yet, whilst ever incremental enlargements of oil demand are marginally advantageous empiricist-liberal policy at least will not counsel their restraint. See in this connection Notes 27 and 30.

32. Recognition of these dimensions to science has come with a rush in the past two decades: sociology, economics and comparative anthropology of science are now rapidly expanding subdisciplines. In an earlier piece on the problems raised, Hooker 1975b, I included a representative selection of the then-extant literature, to which might be added: Barnes, 1974, 1977, Barnes/Edge 1982, Easlea 1973, Encel/Ronayne 1979, Habermas 1968, Hill 1980, Johnston 1976, Johnston/Jagtenburg 1978, Knorr et al. 1975, 1980, Krohn et al. 1978, Moyall 1980, Pusey/Young 1980, Spiegel-Rosing/de Solla Price 1978. A measure of the complexity of the science-society interface may be gleaned from the 1979/80 Canadian Study of research needs in this area, Hooker/Schrecker 1980/1. These latter reports also provide a budget of unsolved problems for the area, and clearly indicate the newness of the research activity, the immense complexity of the area, and the large distance still to go before viable theories emerge.

33. It would lead us away from Popper because these commitments are not amenable to treatment within Popper's empiricist-like restraint to facts and logic as the only resources from within which to construct criteria of epistemic commitment. See Note 25 and text and Note 5 references.

34. Biology itself is involved in controversy over the details of method in connection with the role of cognition (recall the story of Section 7.1 above). Popper (1973) has lately introduced an explicit evolutionary structure to his epistemology, as has Toulmin 1972, but for Popper the units of evolution are propositions and the species theories, whereas for Toulmin they are respectively something like individual concepts and clusters of principles focused on concepts. And Popper emphasises the evidently anti-evolutionary unificatory structure of science. The German evolutionary epistemologists (see e.g., Wuketits 1983) claim Popper as an ally while listing induction as basic to

402 A REALISTIC THEORY OF SCIENCE

method, or re-introduce Kantian transcendentalism to a thoroughly naturalistic setting. The mere appeal to a general Darwinian selection process guarantees neither agreement, nor truth, nor rationality. (At the turn of the century, Herbert Spencer attempted to generalize Darwinian natural selection processes in a universal and often clearly inappropriate manner.) In my own view, all of these levels, i.e., concepts, propositions and theories, will be involved in the dynamical evolution of cognitive structure, mutually interacting and interacting with experience both in the internal and external nervous systems of the species. I have here laid relatively little stress on the level of concepts so far, but I regard this as a level which plays a very important role in cognitive processes, see, e.g. Section 7.11, point 2 below and cf. Hooker 1975d, 1978a. The full story, though, will be extremely complex and I have approached only fragments of it to date.

35. Action theory is seen to comprise judgements about relevant courses of action and their outcomes and principles of rationality for deciding among them, while epistemology becomes, on the view presented here (see Notes 24, 25 above and text), a branch of action theory thus construed. With respect to value theory, recall the discussion of the intertwining of differentiated facts and values in the human artifact (section 7.5 above). From this point of view, we may approach value theory as a set of judgements about artifactual states of affairs (human personalities and social settings included) while ethics may be seen as the construction of rational interpersonal rules based on these judgements. All of these programs are controversial, none more so than the last; there has been some discussion of ethics within a decision theoretic framework, but both that program and the framework itself are still in a very early and imperfect stage of development—see e.g., the discussions in Hooker et al. 1977.

36. See, e.g., Churchman 1968, Easlea 1973, Maxwell 1976, Robertson 1978, Roszak 1973 to name but a few. Michalos 1978 has discussed the issue generally, but I do not believe his own particular approach succeeds in avoiding similar difficulties (see Hooker 1984a).

37. This is, in effect, the grand cybernetic hypothesis. For a clear exposition of the view, see Dennett 1978, and of course any major work in artificial intelligence, e.g., Note 20 references.

38. Cf. the critiques by the Dreyfus brothers 1972, Dreyfus/Haugeland 1974, and the comments by Haugeland 1978 on understanding understanding. See also Hofstadter 1979 and Koestler 1978.

39. I learned that judgement is basic from Vickers (see 1968, cf. 1970, 1983). For the evolutionary setting in which I have applied it, see Notes 33, 34 above and text.

40. Diagram 6 is reprinted from Hooker 1980d.

41. See particularly Beer 1979a, b, 1981, Emery 1974, 1975, Huxley 1958, Illich 1973, Jackson 1979, Jantsch 1975, 1976, 1980, 1981, Koestler 1978, Lewis 1962, Robertson 1978, Segundo 1974, Vickers 1970, 1980, 1983 and Waters 1963.

CHAPTER 8

I should like to acknowledge helpful discussion of an earlier draft of this chapter by Michael Devitt, Malcolm Forster, Kai Hahlweg, Norton Jacobi and Ralph Robinson.

1. So it is disappointing to see someone with Devitt's clarity (see 1984) and scope ignore context and reject my statement of R_6 (or perhaps R_5 and R_6) because it is not equivalent to his version of R_1. Both Devitt and Trigg 1980 have a tendency to write as if they were the only realists, which is unhelpful to others. But both works represent clear statements of realism.

2. See 1978a. Others of generally realist persuasion take different views, see e.g., Sellars 1963 and Churchland 1979.

3. On a realist conception of space-time see most recently Friedman 1983 and Nerlich 1976, cf. my earlier review of arguments 1971c and my review of Nerlich 1981a.

With respect to the continuum, Pitowsky 1983, e.g., has recently shown how to extract quantum mechanical probability distributions with counter-intuitive properties; evidently continuum properties play a basic role in this derivation. I have been working for some years now on a project with Dr. G. J. McLelland to understand the mathematical structure of physics (and occasionally with others, cf. Holdsworth/Hooker 1983); the longer we study the more we are aware of the all-pervading character of continuum-based constructions and the paradoxical complexity of the continuum. This is well appreciated, through contrast, by Finkelstein, see 1979, 1984. Cf. Sorabji 1983 on the historical context. Cf. Note 88. (Eventually, McLelland and I hope to present publicly the continuation of the research program laid out in my 1973c, though both the mathematics and the philosophy have proven formidable.)

4. Churchland 1985c e.g., presents a highly unorthodox view yet one with an appealing naturalism. (I do not follow his tantalizing hints that realism should abandon truth.) In 1981d I borrowed and defended Armstrong's naturalist conception of property-predicate relations as contingent many-many, and denied the synonymy criterion of property identity, which is already somewhat unorthodox.

5. Devitt 1984, by contrast, wants to define realism by something like R_1, or R_1 and R_2, plus a claim D (Devitt): most commonsense and scientific posits are real. He argues that, so understood, realism is logically independent of the correspondence theory of truth, i.e., of R_3, and that R_3 is part of the best explanation of our $R_1.R_2$ world. I agree.

But this really only hides the fact that it is Devitt's meta-philosophy, stated as maxims by Devitt, which do a lot of the work in constructing his position. Here are Devitt's maxims:

Maxim 1 In considering realism distinguish the constitutive and evidential issues.

Maxim 2 Distinguish the metaphysical (ontological) issue of realism from any semantic issue.

Maxim 3 Settle the realism issue before any epistemic or semantic issue.

Maxim 4 In considering the semantic issue, don't take truth for granted.

If Devitt were less coy of meta-philosophical commitment the complexity of the situation *a la* Chapter 3, Section 3.3.1 (cf. Section 8.2.2 below) would be more apparent and the simple structure Devitt creates perhaps less overwhelming.

6. As I understand him, Horwich 1982a presents the following overall argument: metaphysical realism must be rejected and a Tarski-style disquotational theory of truth (cf. Note 39) adopted. Given these two conclusions,

there are only two viable alternatives, (i) semantic realism plus the claim that no more is needed for a theory of truth than the disquotational theory, or (ii) a constructivist theory of truth (truth is constructed out of epistemic notions *à la* pragmatism, internal realism, idealism) and a denial of semantic realism. Horwich opts for (i). My own view is that the sufficiency claim for the disquotational theory of truth is wrong or inadequate, as are constructivist theories; so one should reject both of Horwich's alternatives and adopt both metaphysical and semantic realism. See Section 8.3.1 below and Devitt 1984, Chapter 6.

Moreover, Horwich's own position has difficulties characteristic of the 'linguistic turn' in philosophy. Horwich opts for just semantic realism plus the nothing-but-disquotation theory of truth plus a Wittgensteinian meaning-is-use position, arguing that this triad is superior (to metaphysical realism) because it does everything required yet contains no mysteries. I have already indicated that it does not do everything required (disquotation is not enough). But it also hides a large mystery, namely why, and how, coming to acquire the use of terms thereby confers knowledge of truth conditions (i.e., their meaning)? Horwich nowhere explains this, just assumes it, yet I can think of few less plausible ideas from a biological and cognitive development point of view. (Which is not to say that grammatical pattern recognition has no part to play in cognitive development, just not to give it either an exclusive or magical role.) In addition, Horwich quietly assumes that justified belief of his sort must (will be) practically successful, again without convincing argument.

7. Here are the claims:
1. The best current scientific theories are at least approximately true.
2. The central terms of the best current theories are genuinely referential.
3. The approximate truth of a scientific theory is sufficient explanation of its predictive success.
4. The (approximate) truth of a scientific theory is the only possible explanation of its predictive success.
5. A scientific theory may be approximately true even if referentially unsuccessful.
6. The history of at least the mature sciences shows progressive approximation to a true account of the physical world.
7. The theoretical claims of scientific theories are to be read literally, and so read are definitively true or false.
8. Scientific theories make genuine, existential claims.
9. The predictive success of a theory is evidence for the referential success of its central terms.
10. Science aims at a literally true account of the physical world, and its success is to be reckoned by its progress toward achieving this aim.

Readers are left to judge for themselves how the evolutionary naturalistic position would criticize and qualify them, see e.g., Chapter 6, Section 6.6 and 'Approximation, Reference, and Progress' below.

8. There are versions of Leplin's principles 1, 2 and 7-10 which I would find acceptable, but it would require careful reformulations to achieve them; e.g. it would require inserting a notion of systems level into the theory of reference

deployed, deleting "definitive" from Principle 7, employing a 'mapping' rather than a 'mirroring' construal of 'literally' (Section 8.3.2 below) and so on. Presumably 'reckoned' in the second half of Principle 10 refers to an actual human decision procedure, otherwise the assertion is obscure and/or pointless, but then what is stated is an impossibility, there being no way to compare theories and reality independently of assessing their virtues in practice. I discuss the central cases on which Leplin focuses his principles at Chapter 6, Section 6.6 and also 'Approximation, Reference, and Progress' below.

    9. Hellman's doctrines are these:

1. Some theoretical sentences of science have truth value.
2. There is no defensible demarcation between 'observation sentences' and 'theoretical sentences' in science generally such that only the former have truth-value.
3. The terms of mature science typically refer, and the laws of such science are typically approximately true.
4. Much of science investigates a mind-independent material world.
5. There is no veil of perception; perception is a complex process involving physiological response to physical input from the environment in virtue of which we perceive parts and aspects of that *environment*.
6. There is no defensible demarcation between 'observation sentences' and 'theoretical sentences' in science generally such that it is reasonable to believe (i.e., believe true or approximately true) only sentences of the former type.
7. At a given stage of science, our best comprehensive theory T may tell us: "There exist objects, events, etc., x (characterized as satisfying certain specific theoretical predicates) such that these x are not observable-in-principle (according to T)"; and it is reasonable for us to believe T in this regard.

    10. Contemporary philosophy is indeed extremely coy of stating meta-philosophical commitment explicitly. (The empiricists of course systematically suppressed its existence with their arbitrary internal/external, cognitive/pragmatic distinction—see Chapter 3, Chapter 6, Section 6.4) Boyd's 1980 essay 70, e.g., is rife with tacit meta-philosophical commitment (most of it reminiscent of PMPS doctrines). Here is one example: "Not only do theories and language accommodate to the world by successive approximation: so do the scientific methods and epistemological principles by which knowledge is achieved." Devitt likewise—see Note 5. Not to be explicit about meta-philosophical doctrine is not only unhelpful and gives aid and comfort to empiricist prejudice, it cuts one off from a truly systematic realism.

    11. See 1977b, 1979a, 1980a, b, 1983.

    12. Here is one extreme model (perhaps usefully labelled Materialist Nominalism): the world consists of finitely many kinds of material atoms moving in a relational space-time, all other categories of being are reducible to these, including mathematics and other abstractions. Materialist nominalism is not, I think, a believable metaphysics given what we presently understand of the world. Indeed, achieving metaphysical unity coherent with scientific understanding is a very difficult task, but this will better emerge later in the chapter (e.g., at Section 8.3.4). Here I illustrate the issues with a single example.

    What *is* the relation of space-time to matter? Is space-time the provision of a possibility structure for material states (cf. quantum logic)?, a quasi-physical container for matter dynamics (traditional corpuscularism, general relativity)?, a basic framework for assigning identities and quantity (Pythagorean realism)?, the very stuff of matter identically (cf. geometrodynamics)?, a statistical construction over the underlying matter stages (cf. pre-space-time quantum mechanics)? The kind of interrelation specified determines a great deal about the kinds of unity that can be exhibited in theories of that kind of world.

13. With casual relations suitably generalized mathematically. See my theory of functional/dynamical systems interrelations in 1981e and Notes 12, 102, 171.

14. This is by no means only a modern conception, though the 'linguistic turn' in analytic philosophy this century might make it seem both new and isolated. This theme has long been developed by Piaget (see especially 1970, 1971a, b) and before him by R. W. Sellars 1916, 1922, 1932 and Dewey 1930, and indeed the whole naturalist movement extending back to Case 1888, 1906, cf. e.g., Delaney's study 1969. See also Chapter 1 for discussion.

15. As I observe in Chapter 6, Section 6.4.3, this applies even to so agnostic an empiricist as van Fraassen 1980.

On the other hand, it is appropriate to emphasise again that unity does not require reductionism, there is no demand to reduce epistemology to psychology and/or biology, as so-called naturalised epistemology evidently requires (see Note 34 below and text). Indeed, I do not see how this latter proposal can make good sense, for it would abandon entirely the notion of normative theorising as a distinct theoretical activity.

16. The fundamental religious drive to become one with the cosmos, to embrace all beings fully in love and joy, is the fundamental drive to transcendence, including transcendence of species chauvinism. (Alas, the social practice of religion has often been the antithesis of its fundamental urge.) The same drive to transcendence has been reflected in recent ethical writings, e.g., Singer 1981 and Routley 1980. Here anti-anthropocentrism is quite rightly seen as but an extension of transcending egoism. Recently Michalos 1978 has tried to reflect the same drive within rational decision theory itself, but I think not successfully (see my 1984a). In sec. 8.3.11 and 8.4.4 I try to come to terms with the drive to transcendence as central to all human activity.

On the other hand, it is quite obvious that actual human religions are intellectually replete with anthropocentrisms and their special case, anthropomorphisms. Much the same holds true of philosophy, whether it be philosophies that give special significance to humans in the scheme of things or simply those that elevate human forms of intelligence by assuming, for example, that natural human languages are somehow central to intelligence (cf. Note 188).

17. Whether humans have privileges and of what sort remains a conjectural matter, to be elaborated and clarified as we explore the possibilities of the cosmos. Certainly on this planet we possess particular forms of cognitive capacity in an abundance which other species evidently do not have, though whether this is finally so and how much of a privilege it proves to be, say vis-á-vis dolphins and whales, or perhaps vis-á-vis sign-using primates with gentle senses of humour, remains to be seen. At least one human believes that our defects may be deeper than our privileges—see Koestler 1978.

18. Here is Hume:

> Let us fix our attention out of ourselves as much as possible; let us chace our imagination to the heavens, or to the utmost limits of the universe; we never really advance a step beyond ourselves, nor can conceive any kind of existence, but those perceptions, which have appear'd in that narrow compass. This is the universe of the imagination, nor have we any idea but what is there produced. (Hume, *Treatise*, Book 1, Part II, Section VI)

Wittgenstein's linguistic echo: "the limits of my language are the limits of my world" (1951). The verifiability criterion of meaning and cognates do the trick for empiricists (cf. Chapter 2).

19. For discussion of Rorty 1972, see e.g., Fisk 1972. Cf. Rorty 1979, 1982.

20. But then, as Brown (1984) cheekily remarks, why not "do a Berkeley", count God into the epistemic community, and convert to realism?! See also Section 8.3.6. below. Brown also identifies the anthropocentrism in Putnam's quasi-pragmatist, quasi-idealist 'internal' realism (cf. Section 8.3.1 below) and even in Newton-Smith's 1981 attempt to save realism from the underdetermination argument (cf. Note 160).

21. See Rorty's 'pragmatism' (1982), note Putnam's (1981a) and Ellis' (1985) internal 'realism', Dummett's (1978) empiricist intuitionism and Davidson's Wittgensteinian linguistic constraints (1973, 1980).

22. See Bloor's (1976) and Barnes' (1974, 1977, 1982) sociology of knowledge program, on which see Sections 8.3.6 and 8.4.3.6 below. The view expressed in sec. 8.3.6 is consonant with the careful critiques by Nicholas 1984 and Musgrave 1980 (of Kuhn 1962) and by Trigg 1980, Chapter 5—although I acknowledge essential methodological reference to the community, making no pretense to a disembodied 'objective' methodology. (In this respect I stand mid-way between empiricist/Popperian objectivism and relativism. Cf. Note 164, Section 8.2.7 and Section 8.3.11.)

23. See for example Kuhn's (1962) and Feyerabend's (1962, 1965a, b, c) incommensurabilities—cf. Section 8.4.3.10).

24. For example, theories of neuro-linguistic development transcend cultural boundaries and theoretical boundaries while the universe beyond the cosmic 'light horizon' remains epistemically inaccessible. Conversely, perhaps even the past —whose epistemic inaccessibility in any mode but theory is itself an embarrassment to empiricism—may not be so simply inaccessible were closed time-like space-time paths and/or two-dimensional times to be developed more extensively within science and shown empirically applicable. Science has even stimulated recent discussion of what it might be to use systematically different logical structures in the foundations of theory—I refer to so-called quantum logic (see e.g., Hooker 1975/79, Holdsworth/ Hooker 1983).

25. See e.g., Popper 1963a, Aggasi 1964, 1975.

26. See e.g., 1975d, 1978a as well as Chapter 3, Section 3.3.2, Chapters 5 and 7 *passim*.

27. A cautionary reminder: the realist *per se* carries no brief for or against the alignment of evolution and materialism. Certainly, evolutionary dynamics are more complex than the simple trial-and-error-plus-natural-selection mod-

el which many accept. Evolutionary processes, at least at some levels, are evidently more deeply integrated with the basic processes of the cosmos than the 'lucky accident' model would suggest (see e.g., Morowitz 1968, Prigogine 1980, 1984, Iberall 1972 cf. Campbell 1973). Perhaps evolution really provides examples of quite general self-organising systems features of our world, in which cognition forms an integral part (see e.g., hints in Georgescu-Roegan 1971, Iberall 1972, Jantsch 1980, 1981); perhaps instead intelligence will prove to be an incidental excrescence on basic survival mechanisms. The naturalist realist strives for a unified understanding, but this too carries no special brief for the ultimacy of materiality beyond where investigation itself leads.

Thus here I concur with Trigg 1980 that, while there is significant division between realism and idealism (at least idealism epistemically defined, as I have done), there is a no *a priori* attachment, not even any necessary historical alignment, between realism and materialism. The realist must be prepared to follow where our understanding leads and if contemporary physics 'de-materializes' matter then so be it. The realist must be prepared to take a more complex view of the constitution of the world than nineteenth century materialisms might suggest. (These remarks evidently constitute a *prima facie* criticism of Lenin's 1927 opposition of materialism to idealism—cf. Trigg 1980— but I suspect that Lenin's term 'materialism' has a wider, more richly ambiguous content, cf. Note 79.)

28. Levi 1967, 1980 has articulated this clash by placing Popper's insight into a decision theoretic setting. Levi's original position runs into considerable difficulty over globally connecting acceptance divisions, see Bogdan 1976. More recently Niiniluoto 1978, 1984 has examined Levi's continued attempts to develop and extend his views (e.g., in Levi 1980) which are characterized by infallibilism (treat as infallible what you presently accept) and myopia (avoidance of error is a feature only of the immediate goals of inquiry). Niiniluoto (1984, Chapter 5) concludes that while Levi's system is a coherent alternative to a fallibilist realist one, it does not present a compelling alternative to it. I cannot pursue these important issues further here, but it bears directly on the understanding of my nested contexts of acceptance model—see Chapter 7, Section 7.11, Chapter 6, Section 6.6 and Section 8.3.2.

29. See e.g., Popper 1963b and compare the criticisms of empiricism following this Popperian idea, by Feyerabend 1970a, 1978, cf. 1974.

30. Note that we can build models, in science, of information acquisition by species and discuss reliability and efficiency as functions of their model parameters. Unity and interdependence then require that we apply the same insights to ourselves! Much of the insistence on epistemic complexity and dynamics, and a lot of the epistemic 'radicalness' in my philosophy comes from so simple a source.

31. For this theme see Chapter 3, Section 3.3.1 and for a critique of the Western tradition see Chapter 7, Section 7.6. The idea of philosophy as a theory goes back, in the contemporary debates, at least to Kuhn (e.g., 1962, pp. 8–9). It is, however, at least tacit in much earlier realism (cf. the references in Chapter 1). In a useful review of Schlick's epistemology (cf. Schlick 1949), Daum 1982 reminded me that Schlick too was close to this view in some important respects, despite also being closely associated with the Vienna Circle positivists. On this score see also Haller 1982.

In respect of Hume's classic argument for the is/ought dichotomy and its equivalents, when closely examined I suggest that the only surviving element is the logical truism that terms not occurring in the premises of a deductively valid argument (either explicitly or indirectly via definition) also cannot appear in the conclusion. But this is of course a truism that theories obey.

32. This theme has been explored by those advocating realist quantum logic, see e.g., Bub 1973, but it equally harks back to a Leibnizian conception of space and time as specifying possibility structures, cf. Chapter 7, Section 7.6. Quantum logic in its modern complexity is explored systematically by Holdsworth/Hooker 1983 (cf. Hooker 1975/79, 1979d).

This might be a useful place to begin a philosophy of logic, but it cannot be a place to stop for there must still be an account given of the role of logic in language. Of course, if one believes that language is secondary to human intelligence, then one might hold that the cognitive representation of the world's possibility structure was the primary focus for understanding the role of logic in intelligence and that its role in language was to be seen as an extension, and in certain respects a specialization, of that role. Nonetheless, an account has to be given of the cognitive structures involved and of how one is to understand logic within them. Here a realist might begin by linking logic to other fundamental cognitive devices such as perception by seeing it as part of the extraction of invariances, specifically by seeing it as a specification of structure which models containment, hence inference, in a manner that preserves truth. (Cf. perception as the extraction of invariance and extremal conditions, Section 8.3.2 below.)

33. See also Note 31. There is a motive for dichotomies and circularity arguments: they prevent the risks of open-ended interaction from arising. The response to the circularity argument here inexorably generates questions concerning these more global risks and objections, such as Fine's stringency argument, see Section 8.4.4 below.

34. See Quine 1969. After giving an excellent description of the theoretical problem of understanding how science is possible for creatures like us, Quine draws the following conclusion: "Our liberalized epistemologist ends up as an empirical psychologist, scientifically investigating man's acquisition of science." (1969, p.3) This conclusion is best read in context as writing normative considerations out of the project, in which case it is a straightforward *non sequitur*. Piaget 1970, 1971a blazed this trail long before Quine (it was from Piaget I first learned). But both he and Quine were unable to come to terms with the normative and descriptive components, presumably because of the background influence of empiricism. See later Boyd 1980, Stabler 1982, 1984, and Stroud 1981.

35. They might, for example, be held to contain a version of the first two meta-philosophical principles, perhaps together with a statement of the intended contents of the level below them (hence one recursively specified from the previous philosophic level).

36. For the critique of the observable/unobservable distinction see e.g., Maxwell 1962, 1970 and the review in Suppe 1974a. Recent empiricists such as van Fraassen have explicitly abandoned the old attempts to draw the distinction but still illegitimately rely on the notion, see Chapter 6, Section 6.6 and generally. On difficulties with Kant's categories see Reichenbach 1965; cf. the

attempts of the modern German school of evolutionary epistemology to give them a fallibilist reading, Campbell 1973, Wuketits 1983. For phyics simply consider the abandonment of universal causality and of Euclidean or even simple Riemannian geometries, the notions of non-classical logical or possibility structure and of space and time as perhaps statistical rather than fundamental features of reality, the exploration of simplices and fuzzy sets as replacements for individuals of various kinds and so on.

37. For a discussion of van Fraassen and a completed human biology, see Chapter 6, Section 6.5. It is timely to remind the reader that human technology is now on the verge of combining cloning, genetic engineering and bio-engineering with *in vitro* fertilization technologies; we are evidently entering an era when increasingly radical redesign of biological systems is becoming possible. Eventually this will include our own species and there is at present no good reason to believe that it cannot encompass our specifically cognitive organisation in particular. (The idea of 'hard wiring' human striate cortices together to allow for the direct mind-mind communication of visual images, now being discussed, is a first simple step in this direction.) One needs to reflect here also on our slowly developing capacities to develop self-designing, self-programming computers and our increasing willingness to experiment with placing such devices in selected learning environments to evolve, in mutual interaction with each other as well as with humans. All of these processes represent open-ended or open-textured processes of cognitive development for which it makes no sense, either practically or theoretically, to attempt to specify their end points in advance.

38. See e.g., Putnam 1981a, Horwich 1982a, Devitt 1984, Section 6.6.

39. See Tarski 1956. (Tarski 1949 contains a less technical abbreviation.) The clearest case of this is the so-called disquotational theory of truth according to which the concept of truth is redundant and wholly exhausted by instances of Tarski's schema T: 'S' is true if and only if S, where S is a sentential placeholder and a declarative sentence is inserted in that place while its name (more generally, a token designating it) is inserted in place of 'S'. Horwich 1982a, e.g., espouses this notion.

40. Here I follow many others, e.g., Apel 1980a, Field 1972 and Hubner 1978.

41. Note that this is *not* in itself committed to identifying meaning with truth conditions, nor of course to reducing truth conditions to reference relations—two popular moves in recent linguistic analytic philosophy, see Section 8.4.3.10 and Note 38 references.

42. Judgements are insufficiently precise, e.g., when reality permits truthful judgements with quantitative ranges smaller than those made. Partially true judgements are those which could be conjoined to other true judgements and the whole conjunct remain true. Approximately true judgements are those that employ concepts which are applicable only at some level of systems approximation to reality and in contrast to the concepts of a more unified theory yielding deeper understanding.

This is a relatively specific use of the notion of approximate truth, general philosophic usage often intends to refer to all three categories above. Among other things, however, it has been the tendency of philosophers to ignore these distinctions which have made it so difficult to articulate a plausible notion of approximate truth. See Section 8.4.3.9 below.

43. As remarked in sec. 8.2.7 above, which inferences these latter are itself depends on the possibility structure of the world. See also Section 8.4.3.1, 2. In particular, I take up no detailed position here on inductive logics, Bayesian confirmation theories, etc., except to insist that truth must play a key role in their structuring if they in turn are to play a key role in rational confirmation.

44. The importance of this distinction is clear: false assertions still need to be meaningful. Nonetheless, the truth conditions for p can't be irrelevant to those for 'p is meaningful'. Getting the connection right is no simple matter. Cf. the difficulties, in causal theories of mental representation, of giving conditions for false representation. (If a representation of X requires X to have caused it then an organism cannot form a representation of any X that doesn't exist!).

45. This argument is anticipated at Chapter 3, Section 3.3.2 and briefly stated at Chapter 7, Section 7.3. Precisely because it is truth as a whole notion that is theorised in cognitive theory I resist pressure to even suppose the notion might be split into parts and ask, e.g., how many of the T_i roles might be satisfied by a formal semantic theory (say Tarski's) alone—I think none can.

46. Though I didn't borrow it from that source, I note that this argument is a generalised methodological version of an argument which Putnam offers in 1978 lecture III. Putnam restricted himself to current theory, thus Putnam's argument faces the obvious objection that no anti-realist would want to identify truth with what follows from current theory. Later Putnam evidently revised the argument so as to refer to the possibility that an ideal theory might be false, see 1981a. This comes much closer to the argument in the text, but it does not focus attention on the open textured character of the hierarchy of philosophical theory as being what is at issue.

47. There is some difficulty in stating this last doctrine in a satisfactory manner. The claim that truth grounds the eight distinctions in the text above does in some sense tie truth conceptually to these philosophical doctrines. The point is not to tie truth conceptually to some already completed notion within human cognition or cognitive capacities, not even covertly through general (not to say vague) references to idealisation. That this is difficult to do wholly satisfactorily has to do with the fact that it is difficult to state in language doctrines concerning truth or any other basic semantic feature of language (cf. also Notes 140, 151 and Section 8.4.3.10). Whatever may be the difficulties here in our understanding of linguistic understanding (cf. Haugland 1978 and Pattee 1981), I very much doubt that they concern the realist specifically and they should not be allowed to block realist accounts without demonstration of a specific realist liability. I at any rate know of no such demonstration. Devitt has also emphasised that sufficiently powerful—which here also means sufficiently vague—formulations of epistemic constructs for truth might be suitably realist, but that this is a commentary on the ambiguity of language not a refutation of realism—see Devitt 1984, Section 3.5.

48. See for example Ellis 1985, Putnam 1981a. These are rediscovered ideas with a long history. E.g., Putnam's formulation can be found, very closely, in Churchman (1948, pp. 169/170) who traces his inspiration explicitly back to Peirce's pragmatism. Churchman independently provides an insightful anal-

ysis of the complexity of notions of risk, quality control and experimental design in scientific methodology from which many contemporary writers could stand to learn.

49. At one point Putnam, a recent advocate of this view, invites us to accept an answer along these lines via an analogy with idealisations in science.

> We cannot really attain epistemically ideal conditions, or even be absolutely certain that we have come sufficiently close to them. But frictionless planes cannot really be attained either, and yet talk of frictionless planes has 'cash value' because we can approximate them to a very high degree of approximation. (1981a, p.55)

But as Okruhlik says

> It is not clear, however, that this analogy will hold up. We know *in what ways* a frictionless plane differs from those of ordinary experience and we *can* tell when we are approximating a frictionless plane more or less closely. But on Putnam's account, we *don't* know in what ways rational acceptability in the epistemic, ideal limit differs from rational acceptability by our present lights; and we can't know whether we are approximating the ideal limits or not. This is because theories of rationality themselves are subject to change and evolution. (1984, p. 693)

50. The quotation refers to Bohr's famous remark that we are hanging in language so that we don't know which way is up and which is down, but then Bohr was anti-realist—see exposition in Hooker 1972c. As Devitt 1984, Chapter 9, puts the point, Kuhn and Feyerabend can give no convincing account of progress in science because of the way they have cut themselves off from objective existence and truth. And Okruhlik remarks of Putnam 1981a:

> . . . a key idea of the idealization theory is that truth is expected to be stable or 'convergent'. Yet nowhere in the book is there an argument to support that expectation. Our problem, therefore, is twofold: (a) We are given no good reason to expect the ideal epistemic limit to be well defined; and (b) even if it were well defined, we might never know whether we were approaching or withdrawing from it. In this sense, 'internal realist truth' seems to epistemologically otiose and not sufficient to ward off relativism. (1984, p. 693).

51. See e.g., Kuhn 1962, Feyerabend 1962, 1965a, b, c and Munevar 1981 in some of their moods, the proponents of the so-called strong program in sociology of knowledge (Barnes, Bloor note 22, Turnbull 1984, etc.), Rorty 1979, 1982, and perhaps Hacking 1982b (depending on how arbitrary 'styles' of reasoning are intended to be) and Putnam 1981b as well. Devitt 1984 and Trigg 1980 make out clear cases for relativism in the cases of Kuhn and Feyerabend. I have to admit that there are passages in my own writings which may give a reader the impression that I advocate a similar relativism, see e.g., Chapter 5, Section 5.3, Chapter 3, Section 3.3.2. But there is an important difference between exploring the full complexity of our cognitive dynamics, including the corresponding cognitive traps into which we may fall—which was my intention—and advocating a fundamental relativism (cf. Chapter 7, Section 7.3). On what I call objectivity$_2$ (Section 8.3.8) and cross-cultural theory see S. C. Brown 1984.

52. This is certainly true of Putnam throughout 1978 and 1981a and of Hacking in 1985.

53. The sociologists of knowledge tend to hold the former doctrine, see e.g., Berger/Luckman 1971, Bloor, etc., see Note 51. Putnam is tempted by the latter 'Buddhist' doctrine at times, for example in 1981b, 1982a, 1984; but while this metaphysics certainly emphasizes the importance of human choices, it undermines the epistemic significance of those choices by trying to take the risk out of them.

54. The recent analysis by Dretske 1981 seems to me an important step in the right direction as does the promising work by Stalnaker 1984 on the semantics of belief and cognate structures. Both approaches have the advantage of not presupposing a linguistic-based system and of generalising in very plausible ways to species other than ourselves. Moreover, in emphasising the mapping of environmental possibility structures in the head as the foundation of cognition I think Stalnaker provides the right sort of structure for integration into an evolutionary naturalist framework. However, these approaches will attract criticism, see e.g., Fodor 1984.

Work on causally based semantics complements these approaches (see e.g. Devitt 1981) without, I think, providing the whole story (see Section 8.4.3.10). Devitt 1984, Chapter 6 believes that only a causal theory of reference could *entitle* us to the use of semantic notions such as truth—I try to remain agnostic on the issue (Section 8.4.3.10). In this Section I simply assume we are entitled to the concept of truth.

55. See for example essays by other scientists in Savage 1978 as well as Arbib 1972, Gregory 1971, Haber 1969, Hahlweg 1983, Marr 1982.

56. As these quotations make clear, by 1978 I was clear in my own mind about the importance of understanding perception as a mapping process aimed at achieving correct *identifications* rather than achieving *identities* (i.e., mirroring). I retract as sloppy language the occasional use of the mirror metaphor in Chapter 2, written four years earlier.

57. Here is Putnam:

> We are too realistic about physics . . . [because] we see physics (or some hypothetical future physics) as the One True Theory, and not simply as a rationally acceptable description suited for certain problems and purposes. (1981a, p. 143)

Rorty 1979, 1982 also associated anti-realism to mapping but, as McMullen 1984 remarks, without the kind of technically specific objections Putnam has. McMullen 1984, (Note 38) notes that realists really distinguish between The One True Theory and what science might reach, even in the 'ideal limit'. This only affects Putnam's formulation a little. But I should emphasise the dubiousness of supposing that reality is mirrorable (not mappable) in a human language at all. Still, there is not *obvious* reason here to reject realist metaphysics.

58. See e.g., the references at Chapter 7, Section 7.3.2.

59. If one wanted to generalize this description to curved mirrors then it would be necessary to say that mirrors consisted in collections of local projections of certain sorts, but this seems an irrelevant complexity in the present context.

60. Notice that the unification of cognitive maps in this sense is perfectly

compatible with the reality itself being dynamically disaggregated or even metaphysically multifarious.

61. This is delightfully illustrated by the cover of Hofstadter's book 1979.

62. It is perhaps worthwhile recording at this point that maps are to be allied to models (in the sense of formal semantics) rather than to syntactic structures. Creating a map is creating a certain kind of model of a piece of reality, it is not in general creating a description in some linguistic framework of that reality. Linguistic descriptions are simply special kinds of maps. We are vividly reminded of this by the fact that a model-theoretic formulation is independent of linguistic framework in the sense that a theory having exactly the same models may be formulated in many syntactically different languages. (See in this respect van Fraassen's rejection of the syntactic characterisation of theories 1980.) This ties in e.g., with Stalnaker's approach on the one side (Note 54) and with my attitudes to language on the other—see Section 8.4.3.10 below.

The deep compatibility and commensurability of maps is how the realist thinks of neurophysiology *vis-à-vis* cognitive psychology *vis-à-vis* epistemology and rationality theory, and thinks of them all *vis-à-vis* irreversible thermodynamics and evolutionary biology. Achieving this kind of unification, ultimately, when sufficiently deep theories of the right kinds have been found, has been a constant theme of my writings—see e.g., Chapter 2, Section 2.6, Chapter 5, Section 5.5. More recently, see also e.g., Rubinstein et al. 1984 and Ziman 1978 (Chapter 4), among many works in the field these make interesting connections of mapping to philosophy of science as well as to cognitive psychology and neurophysiology. And see the remarks on a biology of knowledge, Section 8.3.1.

63. The whole subject has been given an elegantly unified treatment from this point of view by Armstrong 1973. Threat of an infinite regress as the pivotal point of epistemology goes back through Popper to Fries, see Note 161.

64. See respectively Hempel 1965, Armstrong 1973, Quine 1960, 1970, Popper 1934, 1963a, 1973.

65. See e.g., Carnap 1962, Glymour 1980, Good 1976, 1983a, b, Horwich 1982b, Jeffrey 1965, Rosenkrantz 1977, Skyrms 1980; cf. Harper/Hooker 1976.

66. Perhaps the 'flow' from the source may be stepped up over time, for example, sensory capacity may enlarge. But, since authenticity and logic are either complete or not present in this paradigm (they are not subject to evaluation), the cognitive capacity evidently must also be held essentially complete from its beginning.

67. More broadly, the received paradigm has a basic presupposition that knowledge is linguistic, the paradigm unit of knowledge being the proposition expressed by a declarative sentence. But the study of intelligence provides no special support for this presupposition and there is evidence suggesting its falsity. This too has long been a theme in my writing, see e.g., 1975d, 1978a. It is a place where I admit to issuing a promissory note to be redeemed by a major review of the issue some day, but see Note 188 for a catalogue of evidential foci and counter argument.

68. For example, what laboratory practice effectively does is substitute circumstances under which our perceptual systems work well, recording

pointer readings, single audio pulses and the like, for circumstances where they work vaguely, erroneously or not at all, whether this is visually determining surface electron energy distributions, rapid audio oscillations or extreme temperatures.

69. Logical structure may be recaptured, for example, through the use of dialogic constructions, see my 1979d. Part of what is recaptured will be uses of inductive argument of various kinds, as well as inference to the best explanation, see Sections 8.3.5, 8.4.2, and 8.4.3.1, 2.

70. Thus the sceptic's explicit premise, namely that if an epistemology is consistent with a possibility of error then it should be rejected, is itself rejected. Considering the large body of evidence in favour of a risk-oriented approach to evolutionary epistemology, how might the sceptic attempt to justify this premise? To be meta-consistent the sceptic should be sceptical of the premise, which would leave the field to the epistemology with the weight of evidence in its favour! Otherwise only some form of transcendental justification, or justification by conventionalist fiat, would seem to be a possibility. The first is not likely and the second is objectionable to an evolutionary naturalist realist. There are other forms of sceptical objection and these are taken up in Chapter 2, Section 2.4 and in Sections 8.4.2, 8.4.4 below.

71. Within cognitive theory of science I believe it is essential to distinguish theoretically or conceptually between epistemic and practical goals in order to construct a coherent notion of an epistemological theory *vis-à-vis* scientific theories of cognition and behaviour generally. This is in opposition to one version of Marxism, for example, on which it would be claimed that all epistemic goals are ultimately reducible to practical goals of other kinds (socio-economic goals). On the other hand, one has to allow for quite strong functional or broadly causal interactions among the pursuits of both sorts of goals historically. Thus the distinction here is exactly parallel to that between realism, which allows causal but not conceptual connections between knower and known, and opposing philosphies which demand a conceptual connection between the two. (In systems jargon one can theoretically distinguish subsystems—cognizer and environment sub-systems and, within the cogniser sub-system, cognitive and practical sub-sub-systems—but these are in interaction and so open, mutually dynamically evolving.)

My critique of van Fraassen on distinguishing cognitive from pragmatic goals and explanations, Chapter 6, Section 6.4.3, needs to be read in this light. I conceive of cognitive organisation as part of, better: as a specialisation of, the general organisation of life on the planet. Theorised as cognitive, it is conceptually distinguishable from other features of life. Theorised as a functional system, the cognitive dimension is in strong causal or functional interrelationship with the other dimensions to life. It is in this sense that I am opposed to any dichotomy between cognitive and non-cognitive on which whole branches of activity, say explaining or loving, can fall wholly into the one camp or the other and receive utterly different philosophical treatments in the two cases.

(Again, I retract as sloppy expression the suggestion of a sharp pragmatic/cognitive distinction at Chapter 2, Section 3.3.2, para. 2, the same paragraph that contains an offending 'mirror', cf. Note 56 above. But despite my belief that nothing of substance is in error here with respect to realism, I have resisted editing the passage for this book so as to preserve the sense of the original.)

72. Van Fraassen also encourages simplicity on the acceptance side by subordinating all virtues to one, empirical adequacy. Indeed, in 1980 he declared all other virtues non-cognitive thereby segregating them out (cf. Note 71) but has recently admitted 'empirical strength' as a second cognitive virtue (see 1985, p. 674). He then argues that empirical strength is always subordinate to empirical adequacy. The argument is simple ". . . the tautology is least risky . . . the self-contradiction infinitely informative . . . the tautology is acceptable while the contradiction is not, so audacity must take second place." I find the argument unconvincing. All it could show is that at the extreme of the strength range adequacy is preferred to strength. It could not fix the trade-off between them over the rest of the range where it matters to science. And the informativeness 'blow-out' at the extreme is merely an artifact of formal inference structure, so it could hardly be a guide to the rest of the range. (Indeed, even at the extreme end one should be careful, scientists would prefer to have relativistic quantum field theory, despite its known mathematical inconsistency, to anything adequate but superficial because they also accept that the theory has many deeply informative features.)

In van Fraassen's manoeuvering here over cognitive virtues and elsewhere over epistemic community (cf. Note 202) do we see, perhaps, the surfacing cracks in his empiricist edifice?

73. Cartwright 1983, Cushing 1983, 1984a and Hacking 1981, 1983, e.g., all contribute to a discussion of the interrelations among these acceptances.

Incidentally, the vague 'generalised agnosticism' of Chapter 2, Section 2.4.3, needs to be replaced by the nested sets of acceptance contexts specified here and at Chapter 6, Section 6.6.

74. There is some work on belief dynamics under changing evidence or theoretical commitment which is relevant though often this is not done within a decision theoretic framework, see e.g., Harper 1977, Harper et al. 1981. There is a little work on the economics of research, see Note 131. And there is the sustained but problematic investigations of Levi transposing Popperian considerations into a decision theoretic framework—see Note 28. Giere 1984, 1985 offers a simpler, but more rudimentary structure which also has difficulties, cf. van Fraassen 1985, who also criticizes Giere's attempt to develop a weakened realism. Hasing 1982 provides an interesting formal study in an eclectic framework. Beyond these works there is a wide range of indirectly relevant literature, e.g., Hubner 1978 on the evolution of his normative ('S') frames, Pandit 1983 on methodological evolution and Vickers' normative evolution 1968, 1979, 1980, 1983. Holton 1981 (cf. 1973) makes it clear that his notion of *theme* is closely related to a goal or utility structure. (Much of Holton's material on themes and the history of science is sympathetic to my views, e.g., on unity—cf. Holton on Einstein—and on methodological pluralism.) See also Note 87 on Kuhn and other references.

75. For the Allais paradox see e.g., Raiffa 1970. On risk-utility structures see e.g., Stigum/Wenstoff 1982.

76. For prisoner's dilemma see e.g., Howard 1971, Rapoport 1970 and for voting and other paradoxes see e.g., Brams 1986, Blair/Pollack 1983. More

generally see the insightful essays by Elster 1979, 1983a, b.

77. This is one dimension to my insistence that for human cognitive capacities the theory of institutions is crucial—see Chapter 7, Section 7.8.

78. There is no space to discuss these issues at length here, for some preliminary discussion see my 1983. Something of the framework of individual agents in systematic institutional contexts which would be appropriate to apply to the theory of epistemic institutions has been worked out in Hooker 1977b, 1979a, 1980b, 1983—see also Section 8.3.9 below.

79. Note that the traditional alternative (source + logic) captures also Popper's epistemology without a knowing subject (1973). There is a nontraditional approach to epistemology which is like Popper's in this last respect, though radically opposed to the metaphysics of a 'Third World', namely a Marxist-style theory of knowledge as an objective product of labour. From this perspective any epistemology which introduces as basic an epistemic subject is castigated as essentially idealist. Thus decision theoretic epistemologies count as idealistic however much they may oppose traditional idealism. They join empiricism in being counted anti-(historical) materialist, however much they may oppose empiricist principles and reconstruct dynamics akin to those of historical materialism within their resources.

I accept that a Marxist-style analysis has important lessons to teach, and precisely about the respects in which cognition is like other economic and social activities (cf. also Ruben 1979). Human individuals certainly adapt to the institutional and more broadly cultural circumstances in which they find themselves and to that extent supra-individual characteristics appear essentially in the analysis of any human activity. But in my view cognition is not, fundamentally, just another economic (or socio-economic) activity, it also has a distinctive character and a fundamental role in human activity from which it is able to be a factor in transforming historical socio-economic processes. In Marxist jargon, base and superstructure are in interaction, the one is not determined by the other. (Here is another tension in theory, cf. Section 8.3.11.) For this reason I try to recapture Marxist insights through the theory of epistemic institutions.

80. The same lesson follows from double-blind methodology for drug testing—if medical effects were wholly independent of belief states (patient's and doctor's) then these methods wouldn't be necessary, but if there is telepathy or any other such connection they will also not be appropriate. In short, unless certain theories were true (or relevantly approximately true), the methods couldn't be expected to be reliable. Both of these examples are elaborated by Laudan at length, yet he misses the theory-method connection in them. Because of this he quite wrongly draws anti-realist conclusions from them (see Note 145).

81. As various writers have stressed, e.g., Maxwell 1962, there is a continuum connecting unassisted sensory search through instrumentally extended sensory search to instrumental substitution. From an evolutionary point of view our bodies are instruments which we deploy using bodily methods (searching, or staying generally aware; demanding, or not, cross-sensory confirmation; employing normal or abnormal states of consciousness and so on). As other methods develop and theories with them we can become more and more specific about our sensory and other bodily methods, more critically aware of their character and limitations, and approach more systematically

their effective extension (cf. Churchland 1979). On this theme see also Section 8.3.3, 8.3.10.

82. See in this connection the illuminating discussion by McMullen 1984 on realism and the historical success of theories which provide causal and structural analyses.

83. Some of the features of this kind of world and its methodological implications have been explored by Hahlweg 1983.

84. As shown in Appendix 1 of Chapter 4, many scientific inferences may in fact involve induction as well as deduction and hence *modus tollens* will not strictly apply. Since the appropriateness of an inductive argument is itself a function of the context in which it is being used—I mean the actual theoretically described context—and not simply the logical or narrowly epistemic context, the lesson to be drawn is that even the conditions in which the very general methodological practices will be shared in common will be a function of theoretical commitments.

85. On ferment within this area see e.g., Harper/Hooker 1976, Harpet et al. 1981 and the references of Note 65.

86. A note for the future: Without this dynamic it is impossible to make any real sense of the adaptation/adaptability distinction fundamental to evolutionary dynamics and applied within evolutionary epistemology. In my view most extant writings on so-called evolutionary epistemology fail to provide any theoretically substantive evolutionary dynamics for cognitive systems— but this is not the place to enter an extended discussion. Dr. Kai Hahlweg and myself have begun a program of theoretical development related to evolutionary epistemology and he has contributed substantially to the clarification of my ideas in this area.

87. Within recorded history scientific methodology has undergone very considerable qualitative development, see e.g., Toulmin 1972 on ideals of natural order, part of which really expresses methodological commitments (the other part expressing theoretical commitments), and Hacking 1982b on styles of reasoning, best interpreted as doing the same. Kuhn 1962, as Doppelt 1978 (cf. 1983) reminds us, emphasised normative/methodological self-redefinition in science, not primarily the conceptual incommensurability taken up by Feyerabend and others, and offers extended historical discussion of the issues. (I forebear to mention the large body of Kuhn literature, the classic Lakatos/Musgrave 1970 excepted.) Cushing 1983, 1984a e.g., recently illustrated the method-theory interaction in a general way in modern physics. And Laudan 1984b recognises, and illustrates historically, interaction among goals, methods and theories of science. The usefully eclectic Polikarov 1983 has an extended discussion of the idea with examples (see Chapters 3, 4). See also historical studies by Blake et al. 1960, Buchdahl 1970, Giere/Westfall 1973 and others. As these studies emphasize, methodological development has clearly been in intimate interaction with theoretical development itself. Note that the theory-method interactions can go via auxiliary theories (because of the globalnesses of theories, see Chapter 4) and usually do not exclusively involve a single theory-method pair. These interactions, whose theory is critical for a good evolutionary epistemology, have yet to be explored by philosophers in any substantial theoretical detail.

88. The last two of these difficulties are noted in my 1973c. For the former and a masterly historical survey see Sorabji 1983. Cf. Note 3. This is also the

place to note my shift from describing the discrete ontology as atomic to describing it as corpuscularian. Whatever atoms are, they are to be represented mathematically as intrinsically partless and this, if it is not to be a Boscovitchian half-way house between corpuscles and fields, will require a radically different geometry from the continuous Riemannian manifolds assumed by both classical ontologies. I have Dr. G. J. McLelland to thank for impressing on me the depth of these considerations.

89. See Finkelstein 1979, Finkelstein/Rodriguez 1984 (cf. references in the forward to my 1975/79, 1979d), Bohm 1980; cf. the review by Holdsworth/ Hooker 1983.

90. On this latter see e.g., Capra 1979. At least this literature may offer some useful metaphors for constructing an alternative ontology (as, to be fair, might so-called process metaphysics, to which it is related). Many 'philosopher's ontologies' don't offer even this interest (though if they were introduced simply to investigate some contributing factor in systematic ontology, say causal models of event identity for use in theories of time or reduction, then they can prove useful). The physics-and-Eastern-religion literature does serve such valuable tasks of drawing fresh attention to the importance of understanding the actor/spectator tension and like tensions (cf. Chapter 7, Sections 7.13, 7.15) which tend to be neglected in the analytic traditions—see Section 8.4.4 below).

91. Whewell 1847, 1858, see Butts 1968 and Laudan 1971 for exposition.

92. See e.g., Hesse 1971, whose 'analogical relations' have yet to be clarified. And van Fraassen 1985, p. 266 thinks that Whewell's insights had to do with confirmation rather than explanation (but perhaps this reflects an empiricist distinction).

93. See e.g., Hempel 1965. For a review of the pertinent literature here see my 1980c, from which this part of the discussion is drawn. For other views on explanation see e.g., Bromberger 1966, Cartwright 1981, Garfinkel 1981, Gaukroger 1978, and Salmon 1971, 1978, 1984.

94. See e.g., the discussion of the Boyle-Kepler laws case and the Brody 1972 objection in 1980c, Notes 9, 12.

95. See 1980c. For earlier intimations of this notion see my Chapter 4, Note 9, cf. 1981c.

96. This shows that we need to complicate matters; the reconstruction need not produce an exact replication, only a very close simulation with respect to certain characteristics. Moreover there is here an entire host of unsolved problems with respect to identification and reduction of properties and so on. All of these issues I leave aside here, but see my 1981c, d, e and Note 196 and text.

Moreover, to apply C in the context of explanation so as to bring the requirement D to bear, we need to extend C in two ways. (1) We can allow that an entire theory doesn't have to appear in the explanans of every acceptable explanation, if we want to, but reference must always ultimately be made back to its embedding theory. In particular, C cannot be applied to explanations of particular facts because the explananda do not constitute theories. But D does seem to capture the correct intuition in cases like that of symptom-cause inferences of interest here. So, let us extend D to singular statements of fact by insisting that these statements be understood as embedded in an appropriate background theory. (In the indicator cases also at issue here these would be what are called phenomenological theories of the domains.) Now assign relative depths of understanding to the statements of fact according as C assigns it to their background theories. This introduces one more element of complexity to the judgement but in individual cases it seems clear enough what to say.

(2) Sentences from more than one theory may (and typically will) appear in an explanation (cf. Chapter 4). For present purposes it suffices to impose the condition that each member of the explanans must (via 1 above) represent an increase in depth of understanding over, or equal depth of understanding with, the conclusion. There is no problem with the idea of the same explanandum being modeled, up to experimental error, by two distinct ontologies, but there are some difficult problems concerning combining theories which employ distinct ontologies in the one explanation, problems I set aside here. In fact, most scientific explanations seem to satisfy the more stringent condition that all members of the explanans share in a common, deeper ontology, but I do not pursue the necessity of this here—cf. Chapter 4.

97. This follows a common line that properties are identified through their nomic roles—see e.g. 1981d and Armstrong 1978.

98. C also provides a corresponding basis for a criticism of the suggestion that increase in Popperian content should always qualify as an increase in depth of understanding. Popperian content is measured by consequence classes, see Popper 1934. The criticism is that explanation by partial self-entailment and the symptom-cause and other problem cases could presumably all pass the test of increasing Popperian content.

99. See Kitcher 1976, and later 1981. I believe Kitcher's 'internal' criticisms of Friedman's paper are well taken, as is the basic criticism which leads him to his proposal, namely that concentration on reductions in the number of explanans sentences eliminates all those genuine explanations which are constructed by combining principles drawn from elsewhere in the theory or from different theories. (In the terminology of Chapter 4 Friedman ignores the internal and external globalness of the theories.) See also the related discussions by Hesse 1980. Notice that my own criterion C has been explicitly extended to cover these cases. (Notice further that it is important to clarity to keep this problem distinct from the similar-looking, but independent, problem of trivialization of explanation by partial self-explanation.)

100. It is necessary to be cautious here, since the structure of confirmation is still controversial and ill-understood (cf. Chapter 4, Section 4.5). A consequence of Friedman's view is that a unified theory can be more highly confirmed than its special applications (since confirmation goes by novel or 'independent' predictions borne out). This breaks with an old confirmation principle, the Consequence Principle: $(A \rightarrow B) \rightarrow ((e \text{ confirms } A) \rightarrow (e \text{ confirms } B))$. (Notice that the reverse principle is also attractive, yet one Friedman evidently rejects (for non-novel predictions); the Converse Consequence Principle reads: $(A \rightarrow B) \rightarrow ((e \text{ confirms } B) \rightarrow (e \text{ confirms } A))$. Certainly not both principles can be unqualifiedly true since they jointly allow anything to be confirmed by anything.) Moreover, since $(A \rightarrow B) \rightarrow (\text{Probability } (A) < \text{Probability } (B))$ confirmation must then split off from probability of truth, a consequence Popper insisted on long ago and Hesse 1980 reminds us Friedman must now accept. (This does make very clear the anti-empiricist approach to confirmation.) But we have no alternative formal conception to put

in its place. Finally, Friedman does need confirmation to be distributed across all or most of a unified theory, but it is not clear how this is to be safely done (cf. Hesse on transitivity blow-outs as illustrated above). I incline to favour Friedman's approach in each of these cases, though I offer no additional arguments here. My remarks on confirmation as a species of acceptance occur at Chapter 4, Section 4.5 and at the close of Section 8.3.2, where I offer no developed theory but try to indicate the complexity of the structure to be understood.

101. Salmon also includes information-theoretic and erotetic conceptions of explanation under this head, see 1984, Chapter 4.

102. Consider the functional explanations emphasised in all sciences, and currently controversial in the cognitive sciences, see, e.g., Dennett 1978, Cummins 1983. One cannot simply assume them reducible to causal accounts. Or consider the very different structures for cause and probability in corpuscular and field ontologies (see my 1973c, 1975a). More dramatically, consider the mathematical formulation of action-at-a-distance or non-local theories, or a Machian hypothesis concerning inertial mass, in these two ontologies. Cf. further Salmon's response to Glymour (Salmon 1980). There are also unresolved the causal status of the operation of quantum symmetries, e.g., as expressed in the Pauli exclusion principle.

103. These problems are discussed explicitly by Salmon 1984. Man 1983 provides a nice review of parallel problems concerning choice of reference class in a range of epistemic approaches to confirmation and explanation including Greeno 1971, Levi 1967, 1979, 1980 and van Fraassen 1980. She also clearly draws together the threads connecting explanation, confirmation and the aims of science—not quite as I would do but this section has benefited from her exposition.

104. The account of explanation came later than that of confirmation, see Glymour 1985 and cf. van Fraassen's response in the same volume.

105. See e.g., Sneed 1971, Stegmuller 1979. (The latter provides an overview of a burgeoning literature.) Regarded as a structure-analytic device, this approach yields useful structural insight for such purposes as investigating the unity of a theory. Forge 1984 uses it as an alternative to Glymour 1980 in certain cases of confirmation. But I still regard it as suffering from a too-empiricist approach to theory, cf. the Chapter 4 account and my review in *Philosophy of Science* 40 (1973). As Forster 1984 says, Sneed's account gives no particular ontological significance to the cross-situational identifications which emerge from its analysis.

It is worth noting that it is theoretical identification which presents the most serious objection to the Ramsey-sentence approach to theories—see Bohnert 1967, 1968, for exposition and for attempted responses. Most responses in effect conclude by treating theoretical terms realistically (cf. Chapter 6, Note 11 on van Fraassen). These sorts of considerations make my quasi-empiricist alternative in Chapter 2 less inviting than I there present it. This line of argument against instrumentalism and conventionalism goes back through Earman 1978 to Ramsey 1931. For the argument with van Fraassen which emerges here see Chapter 6, Section 6.4.

106. Robustness or invariance as central to confirmation is also emphasised by Wimsatt 1980 (cf. 1974), who also notices its connections to perception (see below). Recently Skyrms 1980 has developed a robustness of resiliency theory

of laws, cf. my review in *Nous* (1983). This is a potentially important approach in the present context; despite Skyrms anti-realist orientation his technical construction should relate to the present approach via the idea that explanations should be based on laws. (Man 1983 notices this connection but does not develop it clearly.) But it is not clear to me how to connect Skyrms' epistemic constructions with the basic realist idea of laws as expressing real cosmic regularities, see e.g., Armstrong 1983, so I do not pursue the matter further here.

107. Forster doesn't note these points but would no doubt be sympathetic with them. On operationalism see e.g., Bridgeman 1927, 1936. One of the versions of simplicity I noted in Chapter 2, Note 20 (ontological simplicity) could be thought of expressing the criterion C for depth of understanding and another (representational simplicity) as aiming at Friedman's idea—but this would be to advocate dropping a vague term (simplicity) for more contentful ideas. See also Rosenkrantz 1977. I note that Clendinnen 1980 has given an important role to simplicity in inductive belief, but I believe it covered by the conception of efficiency (see text, next sentence).

108. There is an inner tension in Cartwright's position between her insistence that fundamental laws are only to be read instrumentally and her insistence that causal structure is real. For causes underwrite regularities, which are described (or designated) by laws. Cartwright represents in many ways an empiricist treatment of the observational level with truth = empirical adequacy, combined with causal realism, the kind of quasi-empiricism discussed at Chapter 2, Section 2.6.4 (too sympathetically?—Note 105).

109. See also Hahlweg 1983 and Wimsatt 1980 and, before them, Campbell 1973 and Piaget 1948, 1951, 1954 on equilibration, Dretske 1981, Marr 1982 and others on cognitive perception models.

Note, though, that this methodology is really only directly applicable to sight and touch, the other senses may not possess enough cognitive structure for it to apply; cf. my 1978a. Moreover, it is only a first approximation, since illusion and hallucination occur, showing a trade-off against processing speed, complexity and memory storage, etc. Forster is too innocent of these complications, but cf. the discussion of Cartwright and trade-offs above.

110. This leads immediately to Sellars' realist doctrine, to the idea that the essence of science is that it not only explains, but extends and corrects, common sense. See Chapter 2, Section 2.6 and Chapter 4, Section 4.4 for exposition. But Sellars still tried to hang on to certain features of the common-sense account in a way that is not consistent with naturalist realism— see my 1977a.

111. Forster also notes that cross-situational invariance may be the key to correctly understanding the theoretical content of natural selection in biology, which has seemed to many to do nothing but tautologically define fitness. Forster's "suggestion here is that the cross-situational connections between fitness values 'measured' on different occasions is crucial to giving the Principle of Natural Selection its predictive power." (Forster 1984, p. 38.)

112. The whole area has many loose ends. Rosenkrantz 1977, e.g., has proposed a notion of 'simplicity' in terms of reduction in the number of independent 'kinds' and argued, from within a Bayesian framework, that greater simplicity confers greater confirmability even when empirical adequacy is held constant. Hesse 1980 defends a related Bayesian line. Glymour

1980, who would agree with the general idea (substituting unity for simplicity), nonetheless rejects Bayesianism, as does Good 1976 (cf. 1983a, b) who nonetheless proposed a related approach to confirmation and simplicity. There are, moreover, all the interconnections between information-content and unity explored by Greeno 1971 and Levi 1967, 1980, by Rosenkrantz 1977 and Good 1983a, b, in Salmon's statistical relevance level 1984 and even by Marr 1982 and others (see Note 55) for perception where unification is connected to stability of perceptual judgement. There is also the related work on Whewellian consilience mentioned earlier (Notes 91, 92). See also Note 109 and text. Finally there is the robustness dimension appealed to in unrelated contexts by Glymour 1980, Skyrms 1980 and Wimsatt 1980 (Note 106). There *is* an epistemic/semantic component to explaining, even if it is not sufficient and not primary, and these investigations must eventually receive a unified treatment within it.

Moreover, I have not tried to integrate here the larger group of writings outside of philosophy of science that emphasise the importance of unity. Two diverse examples must suffice. Ursul/Ziman 1984 review wide-ranging concern among Russian scientists with unity in the sciences and Polikarov has some interesting comments on unity in physics (see e.g., 1983, p. 55, pp. 261–6) which indicates that scientists themselves have made important contributions to the theme. Conversely, there is unification in the 'grand metaphysical tradition' epitomised by Hegel and Bradley. Harris 1965 and Rescher 1973 e.g., often manage to make useful insights out of these kinds of approaches. Chardin 1959 and Segundo 1974 develop links between evolution, unity and transcendence in a related spirit which, with due epistemic caution, I find worth pursuing.

113. There are hints of temporal relevance within the traditional view. For example the inductive requirement of total evidence implicitly involves a temporal fix. And the Popperian school has always attached a temporal significance to the definitions of *ad hoc*ness and severity. But these have never been made explicit features of philosophical theory, they have been seen as marginal (even embarrassing) intrusions on timeless logic. Cf. Hooker 1981b on Popper.

114. See e.g., the discussion at Chapter 7, Section 7.4 and cf. my review in 1975b. There has even been renewed philosophical interest in taking a historically structured biographical approach to many areas, e.g., by MacIntyre 1984 to ethics and Rorty 1979 to epistemology.

115. This is certainly so of the relativist implications drawn for example by such philosophers of science as Feyerabend 1970a, 1978, Munevar 1981 and Rorty 1979, 1982; of the so-called strong program in sociology of knowledge (see Notes 22, 51 references) and of course of Marxist accounts (though they may wish to retain a historical materialist sense of objectivity, which is a quite different matter—cf. Note 79).

116. Compare, in the evolutionary model: organisms interact with their environment both altering it and being altered by it. They may alter their environment so as to increase their own fitness, they may of course also destabilize their own environment so as to ultimately undermine their own fitness.

During this process the environment itself is exerting its (changing) selective pressures, bringing about alteration in the species.

It is characteristic of cognitive systems generally to destabilize their environment, for it is a dynamic environment to which cognitive systems are best fitted. Humans have gone farthest in the evolutionary process of organising themselves and their environment around their cognitive capacities, thus we find ourselves now in a highly dynamic environment which impacts every area of our lives. See sec. 8.3.10.

117. For species activity see Chapter 3, sec. 3.3.1, Chapter 5, Sections 5.4, 5.5; for social, historical and for institutional aspects see Sections 8.3.6 above, 8.3.10, 8.3.9 below and references.

118. See Greiner 1984 and Hooker 1981b. Later, Popper tried to avoid or isolate these dependencies by shifting them to an abstract 'Third World', but this is *just* a verbal manoeuvre; they have ultimately to be referred to the real world. (Popper's notorious 'principle of transference' does this, see Chapter 3, cf. 1981b.) And the metaphysical inflation only adds difficulties of its own (cf. my 1981b).

119. See Feyerabend 1970a, b, 1974, 1978. I deal with Feyerabend's twist at Section 8.3.3 above.

Throughout the 1970s there was an increasing swing away from an abstract, logic-based approach to theory of science and towards a more psycho-socially oriented treatment. This movement was both stimulated by, and stimulated, the kind of writing represented by Kuhn and Feyerabend. Even among less 'radical' philosophers this movement was strong, see e.g., Devitt 1978 on Putnam/Boyd. My own writing (e.g., Chapter 2, Section 2.1) reflects this reorientation, but I was always clear in my own mind about resisting relativism (see Chapter 2, Note 5). The enthusiastic and ambiguous passages in Chapter 2 should be read in the light of Chapter 7, Section 8.3.2 and Section 8.3.6 above.

120. The goal of technical control evidently concerns nature only while that of practical sociality concerns social life only —this is an artificial division, indefensible theoretically. See e.g. Chapter 7 and Sections 8.3.6, 8.3.10. The treatment of facts and methodology in relation to the aim of technical control is similar to that by Popper in relation to truth, but now truth emerges as a derivative aim, a by-product of attempting to pursue technical control efficiently. This is like Devitt's finding no explanatory role for truth except for our communication practices, see his 1984, Chapter 6. No doubt it is through some such indirect route or routes that *Homo sapiens* developed the concept of truth but this is no reason to confine its role to its method of discovery. The goal of control is too weak for an adequate account of science. The science-society dynamic renders the goals too fragmented (their pursuit is now intimately intertwined). For the 'too strong' claim see Note 121. And if the spread of epistemicly relevant utilities I envisage (Chapter 7, Section 7.11) is roughly right then the goals are too few.

121. Habermas has it that factual agreement is the basis for acceptance and rejection of theories *vis-à-vis* the goal of technical control and that this agreement is brought about via normative methods generated by an institution which has that practical interest. Methods for pursuit of practical sociality are validated directly by consensus modulo increasing communicational effectiveness. And methods for emancipation are to be validated by consensus in an idealised community. The idealisations here refer to deep linguistic competences (capacity to recognise truth/error, honesty/deceit, informing/per-

suading/dominating and like distinctions) and psycho-analytic maturity. At this point Kantian-style transcendental self-justification sets in (the three goals are held to become transparently self-justifying, etc.) and the naturalist turns sceptical. (See also Note 173 for more German Kantian transcendentalising.)

122. This kind of transcendental 'proof' is related to the reliability guarantees Davidson 1973, 1980 builds into his conception of public, especially linguistic, behaviour. Here I agree with Devitt's more critical fallibilism—see 1984, Sections 6.8, 10.6.

123. This is no more than Popper, e.g., has always demanded and Feyerabend, Popper's ex-student, has recently done his damnedest to challenge (Notes 118, 119). But Popper has kept his two enterprises schizoidly distinct *à la* empiricism and Feyerabend has drawn sceptical conclusions from this gulf. Better the unified fallibilist naturalism espoused here, I believe.

124. These specifications could be complicated in various ways (for example by drawing careful distinctions between objective$_1$ assertions in the psychology of belief and non-objective$_1$ assertions concerning the objects of belief) but that would only distract from the main points of the discussion without contributing anything important, so I leave the formulations rough hewn.

It is objectivity$_2$ which is discussed in Chapter 7, Section 7.8.

125. Trigg 1980 does a good job of distinguishing intersubjectivity and objectivity$_1$ but misses the other dimension to the natural language notion (though he would evidently concur in claiming it for realism). See also Devitt 1984, Chapter 2.

126. Unfortunately, Popper has a dichotomy running right through his thinking between philosophical reason, which is restricted to formal structures, and practical reason, which is not and involves value judgements and decisions. This characteristically empiricist dichotomy evidently prevents him from drawing together his theory of practical rationality and his theory of method. In the past I have been critical both of Popper's formalist approach to method (see 1981b) and his empiricism (see Chapter 3). I have since come increasingly to acknowledge also my large intellectual debt to him.

127. I have in mind the fact that a very large part of all science today is devoted to military ends rather than to humanly valuable ends. Other parts of science are sometimes devoted to serving particular ideological purposes. On these themes see e.g., Easlea 1973, Livingstone/Mason 1978, Martin 1984 (cf. also the 'liberationists' noted at Note 129). Compare these more contemporary critiques and the contemporary peace movement with the anguished cries of scientists in the face of the rise of Nazism (e.g., as expressed in Hall 1935 and Lovell 1939, cf. Russell's reply 1924b to Haldane 1924 a decade earlier.) Historically one can think of Galileo *vis-à-vis* the Church, of the rise of German chemistry late last century, of Lysenko and the crisis in Russian biology at mid-century and so on. Of course, the dichotomy between objective-logical and non-epistemic inherent in the received tradition nicely explains the neglect of epistemic institutional theory, for under that paradigm institutional structure was incidental to, strictly irrelevant to, the normative evaluation of science. This made institutional structure of interest only to the causal explanation of scientists' behaviour which was held to lie in the non-cognitive, hence historical-social-political areas.

128. On this vast field see e.g., Encel/Ronayne 1979, Haberer 1969 and Spiegel-Rosing/deSolla Price 1978, but cf. Jackson 1979.

129. See e.g., Buchanan and Tullock 1962, Brams 1976, Baumgartner et al. 1984, Beer 1979a, b. There is indirect information in various diverse sources, e.g., Mitroff 1974, Polikarov 1983 and in sociological studies, but nothing of theoretical-analytic depth, e.g., via regarding an institution as a matrix of decision matrices, etc. Those of a 'liberationist' bent (of all persuasions, especially Marxists), would regard this as entirely characteristic of the suppression of critical consciousness. The soundness of the criticism is partial only, I judge, nonetheless they often add valuable insights, see e.g., Chambers et al. 1979, Crowther 1967, Easlea 1973, Feyerabend 1978, Habermas 1970, Martin 1979, Maxwell 1976, Robertson 1978, Rose 1969.

130. The techniques have widespread application in the formation of public policy generally, see e.g., Bernstein/Cetron 1969, Dalkey 1972. Futures oriented public policy methodologies, such as the version I have been developing, find a systematic place for them; see Hooker 1983 and e.g., Boucher 1974, Tugwell 1973. Lehrer has paid some attention to consensus formation in an epistemic setting—see Bogdan 1981; while this has its relevance, it also has its difficulties in its present form, see Bjerring/Hooker 1981.

131. See e.g., Bolland 1971, Brennan 1985, Gordon/Raffensperger 1969, and Rescher 1978.

132. See e.g., Note 128 references and those in my general review 1975b, among a vast and rapidly expanding field.

133. See e.g., Armytage 1965 and Chapter 7, Note 31 references.

134. See Mitroff 1974, Churchman 1972. Mitroff offers allied references. I have not had the chance to follow up his later work on decision-making characteristics and clarification/negotiation processes within the U.S. administration.

135. See Tornebohm 1969, 1970, 1975 among several other studies distributed through the University of Goteborg.

136. See Bjerring/Hooker 1979, but compare the other essays in that volume.

137. See Beer 1979a, b, on which see Naor 1979.

138. Part of this argument goes back at least to Peirce, see Foss 1984. With much of Peirce's sense of the real historical dynamics of science I am in sympathy. Laudan 1984b has recently recognized a part of this complex dynamics, namely the mutual interactions between practice, methods and goals and looks to this dynamic system to explain the convergence of scientific acceptance. See also Cushing 1984a, who draws a relevant distinction between convergence of scientific *activity* (say on developing and testing a theoretical idea) and convergence of theory *acceptance*. This is related to a distinction of Giere's (1984, 1985) between exploratory inquiry and confirmatory inquiry, cf. the exposition by Fetzer 1981. But none of these writers evidently entertain the full hierarchical structure of contexts for acceptance which I see as appropriate to science (cf. Note 28) and none really deal with the generation of conflict or divergence on a par with convergence, which is a leading characteristic of science (the Popperian one). Consequently, the complexity of decisions for activities *vis-à-vis* those for acceptance is missed. (See also epistemic institutions, Section 8.3.9 and objectivity$_2$, Section 8.3.8 above.)

In Chapter 7 I also pointed out another side to this dynamic, the shift to the artifactual: the subject matter of study and the cognitive system studying both become artifacts. As I argue for public policy generally (see 1983), this occasions a quite profound switch from a reactive orientation to an anticipative orientation. If the future must be an artifact then, within the constraints of ignorance, it must be chosen. (Not to choose is simply to project the present.) Thus humans must now decide, e.g., how to project their cognitive systems, where to place research resources, which theories to pursue, etc. A nice example is Malik 1980 with respect to computers, cf. Hooker et al. 1980a on energy.

In Chapter 7 and elsewhere (e.g. 1983) I have also drawn attention to the gravity of the risks now attendant upon these new dynamics (cf. Also Wojcie-chowski 1975, 1978, 1980). Stent 1978 has argued that in fact science will prove self-limiting for these reasons. I am dubious, but this is too large an issue to pursue here.

139. Figure 8.1 is actually a slightly modified version of that in my introductory essay to Hooker/Schrecker 1980/1, developed for a discussion in *Search 16* (1985), 126-7.

140. There is a purely semantic conception of truth which I have rejected—see Sections 8.3.1., 8.4.2, 8.4.3. I have located truth within cognitive theory at large. There is, however, an ancient doctrine of truth which identifies truth with reality while locating falsity in cognition. (This doctrine is found at the heart of Hinduism and Buddhism, in Plato, the neo-Platonists and many Christian theorists, e.g., St Anselm. I do not make anything of this latter doctrine in these essays. I have always thought that, while its specific doctrines were often profound, its talk of truth could be paraphrased into talk of reality and truth-in-cognitive-theory. A recent unpublished paper by Richard Campbell, 'Conceptions of Truth' and a buddhist critique of an earlier draft by Norton Jacobi have cast doubts on this comfortable assumption, so I record a warning here. Perhaps there is a deep and terrible tension (Section 8.3.11) between cognition and being—or perhaps the proper philosophical perspective is to be found in the subordination of cognition to joy. At all events, truth construed within cognitive theory, especially T_3 of Section 8.3.1, is not intended to rule out these deeper issues or exclude a deeper connection with other values—to the contrary. (E.g., T_3 concerns only what might *possibly* be true, it makes no claims concerning in-fact truth and value.)

141. See e.g. Shapere's exploration (Shapere 1984) in his 'Introduction' and van Fraassen's (1985) empiricist Scylla and Charybdis *vis-á-vis* Putnam's (1981b) swamp and quicksand. Cf. also Rorty's 1972 exploration of the form/content distinction. More recently Putnam (1981b, 1982b) has made the corresponding discovery for reason.

Here, however, Putnam adopts an asymmetrical approach; truth remains relatively simple and definable (as an ideal of reason) while reason is strongly open-ended, both 'up' (meta-wise) and in time. (This adds poignancy to Okruhlik's remarks, Note 50.) I treat both truth and reason as theorised fallibly, open-ended and subject to tensions—herein and cf. my 1981b. Putnam's argument (1982b) for the view that reason isn't a natural kind term, i.e., should not be theorised as a natural feature of the world, is weak; stripped to essentials it simply says there's been little prospect of good theory as yet. Well, yes and no (cf. Sections 8.3.9, 8.3.10), but we're just starting.

142. These arguments are found in Smart (1963, 1968, the first only), Putnam (1978) and Boyd (1980, 1983). There is also an argument that realism should explain the convergence of science on the truth, this is reviewed at Section 8.4.31. Cf. Chapter 6, Section 6.6.

143. This argument is in effect Smart's (1963, 1968) 'cosmic coincidence' argument. Devitt describes the explanation as present but trivial. I think all Devitt means is that (i) without the actual historical record of successful theories postulating unobserved or unobservable entities there would be no interest in realism and (ii) realism adds no new deeper insight into the situation in its explanation. I agree with (i) but reject (ii) because R_1 is not to be taken in isolation, as Devitt tries to do, but as part of an overall explanation of cognition, an explanation which offers rich insight into the relevant circumstances.

Devitt's philosophical 'atomism'—the splitting apart of R doctrines—also leads him to too readily accept van Fraassen's Darwinian-style dismissal of the further question of why humans have successful theories (1984, p. 110). This retort is all right as far as it goes but when placed in a larger systematic context it is not at all obvious that it will work —see Chapter 6, Note 18 and Note 150 below.

144. Devitt 1984, Section 6.9. Appeal to R_3 is here taken to be an inference to the best explanation, not a transcendental deduction *a la* Apel and others — see Note 173. Interestingly, Devitt's argument is reminiscent of that of an earlier realist Spaulding 1936, but Spaulding aimed primarily at R_1 as well as R_3.

145. Laudan 1984a notices that Devitt's argument for realism in the case of successful theories "sheds no light whatever on how scientists come by these putatively true or truthlike theories" (p.92). This claim is not even strictly true. Method is a function of theory. The very same reality which explains the success of theories, is an essential factor in explaining the success of realist methods. Laudan's neglect of the method-theory connection re-emerges at his p.100 and Note 29 where he asserts that the realist's explanation of theory success is gratuitous because the "comparative reliability of various testing procedures can be explained without resorting to the realist's ambitious claims about the truthlikeness of scientific theories." This may be so; let it be granted so here (but cf. Section 8.4.3.9). Even so, Laudan's argument fails since to understand why any of his methods in fact produce reliability requires a realist understanding of the corresponding theories! (See note 80 and text.)

146. Success here is taken to mean 'improves the level of achieved cognitive value V'. That science has been successful with respect to many values, e.g., empirical accuracy, technological applicability and control, explanatory width, is beyond reasonable doubt. But note that some attributions of success are weaker than others, e.g., success in achieving explanatory depth is less certain than those others just mentioned. And many successes need contextual qualification. E.g., there has been success in achieving some explanatory depth with respect to micro *structure* but much more ambiguous is the achievement of systematic ontological depth. And of course individual and species success is only confidently attributed within the compass of daily life goals—via nuclear war, machine hegomony or genetic error we may yet succeed in employing our intelligence to boost ourselves to our level of in-

competence. (But realism, at some level, also struggles to understand even these problems.)

147. Of course, there are complex judgements here of which kinds of structures are most plausible, which theory has the greater evidential support in which respects for these purposes, etc., but none of this should deflect attention from the overall methodology.

148. The second objection, case 2, is more intriguing. Further, what distinguishes a basic methodological principle, explanatorily justified, from a methodological dangler? And how dangling can methodological danglers be? But there is no space to pursue these issues. It is enough that the realist rejects the first case.

149. I believe Devitt mistakes the earlier anti-realist evolutionary argument by van Fraassen for this one, but that is a minor matter since they are strategically so similar. Cf. also van Fraassen 1985, Section 1.3

150. It is too easy to pretend that there *can* be no more to this kind of Darwinist reply. But that is, I suggest, like offering the definition 'fitness = survival of net surplus of offspring over alternatives' and then remarking that there is no need to look for detailed mechanisms of natural selection since the principle of natural selection is a tautology! (Principle of natural selection = only fit differentially survive.) There is more to biology than this, even if what more is still subject to debate as to its best formulation—cf. e.g., Ruse 1982 and Forster 1984 at Note 111.

151. Devitt shies off a response of this type on the grounds that it would require a theory of the human organism's nature prior to a realist account of the natural world and this smacks of anthropocentrism and of giving epistemology priority over metaphysics (1984, p. 110). But it need not do any such thing. Rather it may simply express the fact that knowledge is interconnected (Section 8.2.3), an interactive unity. True, realists reject the shaping of metaphysics to suit prior epistemic ends, but the rational acceptance of metaphysics must include consideration of whether it supports, and is supported by, a suitable epistemology embedded in a suitable cognitive theory (cf. Trigg 1980 on the 'anthropomorphic principle' in modern cosmology). Devitt is surely correct in holding that realism cannot be a necessary condition of explaining our capacity for successful theorizing, but he overlooks the alternative that it may nonetheless be essential to the best explanation of it.

Devitt also takes Leeds 1978 to have decisively shown that no theory of truth, correspondence or otherwise, is required by any causal-explanatory account of human cognitive theory. The basic idea is this: the scientific account of human psychology will be entirely in terms of causal (or more broadly functional) relationships between sensory input and motor output, psychological states will be type-identified via their functional roles, etc. Now neurones are plausibly considered solipsist in their activity, i.e., they can't be held to take into account the significance for their organism of their function. Similarly, all psychological states under the scientific account are solipsist or 'narrow'; they have their causal-functional features, but no semantic features whatever. This is so even for the production of tokens of linguistic types, which are physical items. In particular, narrow psychological states do not have an independent access to the external world (they simply share in the physical fate of the organism) so truth cannot be among the characteristics which explain them.

In response, two preliminary remarks. First, adopting this view leaves Devitt's own argument for truth as an explanatory notion hanging in Davidsonian mystery. How comes it that we (psycho-linguistic) have to ascribe truth but we (scientific) don't? What mysterious additional layer is this semantic consciousness? Second, this puzzle is but one form of a much larger one, the interconnection of the agency and causal (functional) conceptual schemes in general. What is the relation of logic to cause in the brain? What is the relation between rule governed descriptions (e.g., of tennis) and causal (functional) descriptions? This puzzle has led to proponents of excess on both sides, e.g., Leeds on the eliminate-agency side and Hollis 1977 on the eliminate-cause side. I have no magical resolution of the problem, but I think that once Leed's argument is seen in this wider context the sense that truth might be immediately imperilled wanes. We desperately need insight into the interrelationship of these conceptual systems, but we don't need to make a particular problem out of truth. There's no denying the plausibility of causal solipsism here; but then it has also recently been fashionable to consider even the cause-function distinction to defeat reduction, but I have argued not, see my 1981e. So for the nonce I simply take truth to play an important role in our cognitive theory and let these larger chips fall as they may.

(For those looking for a quick score: I am well aware that the account of reduction which I urge for the 'special sciences' (1981e) pushes in the Leeds direction, thereby standing in tension with my present insistence on truth, rationality, etc., playing theoretically essential roles. To repeat: I have at this time no resolution of this general problem. Anyone with a naturalist realist theory please speak up.)

152. Given the difficulty in which I think Devitt's isolated attempt to defend truth finds itself—see Note 149—I think that we must hold out the hope that Devitt's argument provides only a small part of a larger picture.

153. This is (my version of) Putnam's 'meta-induction', 1978. Laudan 1981b backs a similar argument.

154. Recent selective realisms arrived at in the manner indicated here are Cartwright 1983, Ellis 1985, and Hacking 1983. (Hacking at times also talks so relativistically about 'styles of reasoning' that perhaps realism is not an appropriate label for his position—see Hacking 1982b.) Van Fraassen 1980, 1985 also joins in selectively attacking the argument to best explanation (at least when extended to unobservable entities), see below.

155. Stationary continents and electricity as an effluvium are cases where there is no counterexample, rather they are simply cases where false (but approximately correct) remarks are referred to exactly the right entities. Ethers were highly controversial entities throughout their career in nineteenth century optics and electromagnetics, as was the planet Vulcan in Mercurial mechanics. On these examples see also McMullen 1984 and Hardin/Rosenberg 1982, cf. Devitt 1984 and Hacking 1981, 1983.

156. The reminders of Note 157 are relevant here. Even the peculiar theories of contemporary physics do not yield much solace for the anti-realist, cf. Chapter 6, Section 6.5 and McMullen 1984. There is one potential worry not canvassed in Chapter 6, the claim that both particle and field pictures in relativistic quantum mechanics are expressed in the same mathematics and so their choice is conventional; see e.g., Sen 1968. But this is not true in the relativistic case and in any case we understand so little of the theory yet, in

my view, that these speculative responses may be no more than the consequence of ingrained empiricism; they should be left to await further exploration.

It is worth noting that various major religions premise themselves on systematic methodological blindness, as it were, to a spiritual world hidden 'behind' the physical appearances. It is a complex and, I think, open, question whether science has a cognitive generalisation which encompasses these possibilities, cf. Chapter 7, Section 7.13 and e.g., Snyder 1978, Tart 1972.

157. It needs to be constantly re-emphasised that the realist is not committed *carte blanche* to every theoretical posit that happens to have been proposed or defended. All realists make this point—see e.g. Chapter 2, Devitt 1984, Trigg 1980 and McMullen 1984. It also needs to be noted again that the whole discussion presumes the singling out of mathematical constructions—such as quantum mechanical Hilbert spaces—as not even candidates for realist posits. No realist needs to be naive in his exposition of the existential commitments of mathematical theories—on this general point see e.g., Ellis 1985 and my discussion of Newton's laws of motion at 1974a. Finally, it needs to be constantly re-emphasised against contrary prejudice that an argument is not irrational to use simply because risk is involved in using it. (The contrary view is deductivism, the insistence that only deductive arguments are rational. For an examination of this prejudice see e.g., Stove 1973 and cf. Stove 1982.) Of course inference to the best explanation is risky, it is not deductively valid, but according to realism risk is at the center of cognitive rationality, Chapter 7, Section 7.11 and Section 8.3.2 above.

158. This approach is part of the 'linguistic turn' in philosophy (cf. Rorty 1979, 1982). The twentieth century empiricists achieved their epistemic goals using semantic arguments (Chapter 3) and the Wittgensteinians turned this linguistic manoeuvre into an entire way of doing philosophy. The resulting 'linguistic turn' in philosophy has some useful analysis to contribute but is, overall, a disaster for philosophy since it reverses the order of understanding, cf. Sections 8.2.1, 8.3.1 above, cf. Devitt 1984, Trigg 1980.

159. See Chapter 6, Section 6.5, Ellis 1985, sec. III, cf. Boyd 1985, sec. I. Indeed, the open-endedness is strong because methods and technological practices evolve in interaction with theories and data structures—see the discussion in Section 8.3.10. The empiricist proponents of this argument typically ignore open-endedness considerations.

Empiricists also push their epistemic certainty assumptions. Hesse, 1980 e.g., discussing a weaker form of the underdetermination argument which simply asserts the simultaneous existence of ontologically disparate, partially confirmed rival theories, concludes that if this is so "realism is in practice an epistemologically and scientifically empty doctrine". The condition described is a commonplace of science and each example poses its own serious questions for scientific procedure, but Hesse's conclusion is a gross non sequitur. Realism as I understand it provides an understanding of the whole of science and theory conflict is one feature of that process; why then should the realist have to either deny its occurrence or be able to immediately resolve any instance of it? That this is a gratuitous empiricist constraint at work is suggested by Hesse's further claims that the only way out for the realist is (1) to produce a confirmation theory "strong enough to ensure that theories that are poorly supported by the evidence, even though compatible with it, can be disregarded" (p.9) and (2) "show that the real worlds implied by remaining incompatible theories are after all not radically different, that there is some form of temporal convergence among them" towards a unique true theory (p.9). But why disregard genuine rivals? Fallibilism counsels pursuing both within resource constraints. One doesn't have to *know* the truth *now* to defend realism. And convergence is a function of our constitution *vis-á-vis* the world (cf. Section 8.4.3.9).

160. Newton-Smith 1981 goes to quite desperate lengths to 'save' realism from this argument, advocating a change of 'logic' so that should some statement p be strongly underdetermined then p would lack truth value. In response: (1) I doubt there is any persuasively principled logical system to do Newton-Smith's dirty work here. (2) The result is anthropocentric, what is allegedly gained for realism on the epistemic swings being balanced by losses on the ontological roundabouts (see Brown 1984). (3) The response is unnecessary (see text).

161. See e.g., Putnam 1981a, Chapter 3. There is also an interest-relativity argument later in 1981a, see Note 163. In both cases Putnam's views are reminiscent of the views traversed by Lewis 1956 (see ch. 6) half a century earlier, cf. also Urban 1949 a little later. The God's Eye argument can be traced back through Popper's insistence that propositions can only be confronted by propositions to Neurath and the early positivist movement and on back to Fries (see Notes 63 and 167). The issues here underlying the God's Eye argument are briefly reviewed at 8.4.2E.

162. See Trigg 1980, Chapter 5. Cf. Note 22. Note that the rational assessment of a theory is, besides its social (etc.) context, also a function of the available evidence and other theories, including critical theories of epistemic institutions. Sociological (/political . . .) theories can hardly replace these other considerations in all but the most megalomaniacal versions of sociology (etc.).

Theories about society itself and the like, i.e., about man-made artifacts, complicate the picture in quite subtle ways (cf. Chapter 7) but don't essentially alter this position.

163. There is a derivative form of this objection which argues that since scientific methodology is characterised by epistemic values or goals, science cannot be objective[1] (cf. Putnam 1981a.) This argument is a nonsequitur. That we search with certain interests guiding our search doesn't preclude our finding some truth. It may make it likely that what we find is partial and/or approximate but it is quite compatible with our nonetheless finding some. Take a case where this seems clearly so: I am interested only in red objects and I approach an array of various coloured objects; I state "There are seven red objects here"—this statement can be true, and objectively true, quite compatibly with the fact that my interests have led me to ignore all the other objects present and the truths about them I may have stated. What has to be shown, for example, is that the conditional assertions involved in theoretical posits of various kinds cannot be represented as stating merely partial or approximate truths along these lines, but are in some other way infected with an element which prevents their specifying a mind-independent condition. But from the tautology that human interests are human interests, or even from the wider tautology that human concepts are human concepts, nothing of this sort follows. Zen Buddhists may be able to enlighten one to the a-conceptual

character of the Real, arguments of the present sort cannot demonstrate it. Rather, they seem to presuppose the discredited God's Eye argument (see above). Cf. Devitt 1984 and Trigg 1980.

164. Explicitly: meta-methodological theory should explain why methodology doesn't always obey simple rules, as well as the rules it does often obey. This I have tried to do for Feyerabend, see e.g. Section 8.3.3. Once again, I believe the sounder position is one midway between the extremes (cf. Note 22 and Section 8.3.11), where in this case the extremes are universal inductive justificationism (as Popper would call it) and Popper's anti-justificationism. (Worrall 1982 characterizes Popper's anti-justificationist position as the minimum realism surviving instrumentalist attacks, see also Briskman's 1982 damaging review of O'Hear 1980 on Popper.) Inductive (and abductive) justification is used throughout science, but within the nested or structured set of critical contexts fallibilism requires, see Note 28.

165. Rorty 1979, 1982 offers a recent discussion of these issues. It is typical of my response to Rorty to find that the larger issues he raises relevant and more deeply insightful than offerings by many other philosophers, but to disagree pretty thoroughly with his own views. In this instance the discussion by Choy 1982 will (excepting her flawed critique of the therapeutic analogy) serve nicely as proxy for my own critique.

166. See Neurath 1931 and Popper 1934, Sections 26–29. Both were, of course, writing at about the same time and from related educational backgrounds.

167. For Fries trilemma see Notes 63 and 161 and for my response to it see Chapter 2, Section 6.2. At the time I wrote Chapter 2 I accepted the trilemma as such, now I wonder seriously whether this is the appropriate response, but as yet I have no profounder argument to offer. Cf. also Note 170 below.

168. See respectively Feyerabend 1958 and 1965a.

169. See e.g., Putnam 1981, Ellis 1985. Apel 1980a reports L. B. Puntel, *Wahrheitstheorien in der Neueren Philosophie* (Darmstadt, 1978) as also accepting just such an argument.

170. See e.g., 1970a, 1973d, 1975d and 1978a in particular as well as Chapter 2, Section 2.6.4, Chapter 3, Section 3.3.1, Chapter 4, Section 4.4 and Chapter 7, Section 7.11.

W. Sellars 1968 (cf. 1981) has, as I read him, focused particularly on this problem, self-confessedly taking a quasi-Kantian, quasi-realist line. I have learned much from his realism, but have tended to see also an unacceptable residual empiricism in his writing on language, conceptualisation and experience (cf. Chapter 2, Note 58 and my 1977a). For this reason I have tended not to pursue his quasi-Kantian studies. But, I now think Sellars' analogy mechanism for conceptual evolution (i.e., via higher order feature transfer) likely an important one and this is contrary to my too-negative attitude at Section 2.6.4 (though not to my general queries there). So perhaps I am equally unjust to Sellars on the experience/judgement issue.

171. For work on causal order structures in space-time see Winnie 1977 and Malamunt 1977 but compare the criticisms of Nerlich 1982. For work on causal order structures in cognitive psychology see e.g., Dretske 1981. There are of course difficulties with Dretske's program, cf. Note 54 above. For work on causal order in philosophy of science see e.g., Salmon 1984 on explanation, which also has its difficulties (cf. Section 8.3.5 above).

172. I learned respect for the closeness of the connection of rationality to intelligence from Bohm and, via him, from Krishnamurti 1972, 1973. Clearly reason *vis-á-vis* feeling also remains untouched here.

173. I have not touched Putnam's recent arguments against 'naturalising' reason (Putnam 1982b)—it is clear that I do insist on naturalising reason in the sense of understanding it as a fallible theory (cf. Chapter 7, Section 7.3), but for this very reason I intend to preserve the normative role of theories of reason. (See Note 140 and text.) Equally, I have not responded directly to Churchman's *Challenge to Reason* (1968), namely to find a guarantor for the system of reason. Rather, I wish to incorporate the global risks Churchman correctly identifies explicitly into the meta-theory and to insist on fallibilist theory 'all the way up'.

174. Witness, e.g., the stream of problem's Laudan's recent attempt generated —see e.g., Newton-Smith 1981. For starters, the interest of a problem is itself something determined by theory and/or theory-interpreted technical practice. Moreover, problems can be plagued by cross-theory incommensurability, dissociation 'Kuhn loss' and local myopia (á la Levi, see Note 28), leading to lack of accumulativity (cf. Doppelt 1983) which reintroduces all of the traditional problems in a new guise. A realist perspective here is represented by Rohrlich/Hardin 1983.

175. In particular I don't believe that Bhaskar's transcendental arguments succeed—see e.g., the exchanges with the neo-Marxist Ruben 1979 and Chalmers' criticisms (1982 edition). I would develop the details of the critique somewhat differently but these references must suffice here. I am indebted to an unpublished paper by Robert Mackie, 'The New Copernicus: Realism and Naturalism in the Philosophy of Roy Bhaskar' (1981), for drawing my attention to Bhaskar's ambivalent relations with Marxism. Trigg (1980, p. xiii) argues that Bhaskar is in fact a relativist epistemologically and that this undermines his realism.

Bhaskar then occupies a position near that of Hubner who also emphasises an enveloping *a priori* normative structure which is ultimately essential for science to be a cognitive activity and who rejects 'metaphysical realism' (cf. Hubner 1978, Section 11.1). On the other hand Hubner emphasizes the historical development of both theory and meta-theoretical norms and methods and the essentially historical character of science. On these latter I can join with him. (But I find myself in conflict again with much of his specific analyses, e.g., of quantum mechanics.)

176. Thus 'A is coloured' is imprecise relative to 'A is red'; 'A is between X_1 and X_2' is imprecise relative to 'A is between X_1 and $\frac{1}{2} (X_1 + X_2)$'.

177. The distinction between imprecision and partialness, though I coined it for myself many years ago from much earlier work by N. R. Campbell and others, corresponds I think to Giere's recent distinction (Giere 1984, 1985) between respects and degrees of approximate modelling. But approximateness I take as a separate notion. These notions are all highly generic, for serious application they need to be embedded in the context of a specific theory and its models (cf. below).

178. Technically, with the lessons of Chapter 4 in mind, this definition should be relativised to other background theories T_i which may supply additional conditions necessary to derive in T' the statement q_{T_i}, but I avoid these complications here.

179. This runs counter to a suggestion of Laymon's 1982 who defines an idealisation as approximately true just in case it transforms increasingly realistic initial conditions into increasingly accurate predictions. Perhaps what Laymon intends is to define approximate truth in terms of approximate empirical adequacy. I take the condition that the initial conditions are becoming increasingly realistic to be a claim that the auxiliary assumptions with which the raw data are processed are increasingly accurate. I take the relevant data structure to be a set of ordered pairs of initial conditions and outcomes, with their error ranges attached. So a statement L is approximately true (Laymon) if it is empirically adequate to the most accurate data structure available. If this is how Laymon is to be read, then he would be both confusing empirical adequacy with truth and confusing approximateness with approximations in convergence. But perhaps Laymon wants to stress instead the role of the theory T to which a statement belongs in providing a critical analysis of the auxiliary assumptions for data processing, so that more accurate data can be achieved. This is an important function of theory (cf. Chapter 4) but it is unclear to me exactly what notion of approximateness or of approximate empirical adequacy it generates.

180. It is always possible, as van Fraassen 1985 remarks (about Giere 1985), to generalize the original formulation so that the more complex situation is encompassed: S is approximately true entails that there is an S', related in some way to S, which is true. But the generalisation in itself is not very interesting, it is the specifics of the relation invoked that carry all the weight.

181. I should say explicitly that I do not believe that a notion approximating that ordinarily used in the scientific laboratory is separately needed here. The notion I have in mind is that of a theory T approximating a data structure D. The reason why I do not believe that this common notion is useful is simply that there will in general be many theories which will have entered into the preparation of that data structure, or which will need to enter into its processing so as to be brought into relationship with T (cf. Chapter 4). Thus I think here the only insightfully operative notion is that of T's empirical sub-structure approximating that of T', where we think of T' as the theory within which D is embedded.

182. I'm well aware that this last remark simply brushes over the enormous complexities concerning questions in T which become ill-defined and are rejected in T', data accepted relative to T which is criticized and rejected or transformed in T', methodologies accepted relative to T which are rejected relative to T' and so on. But I have no intention here of offering a fully-fledged theory of approximation—indeed, I have already suggested that nothing of the sort can be constructed in isolation from specific theories and perhaps specific methodological and technological circumstances.

183. The deepest difficulty in comparing two false theories is the result due to Miller 1975 summarized two paragraphs above. The formal logical definitions Popper actually offered are subject to formal objections—see e.g., Miller 1974 (cf. Hooker 1981b, Niiniluotto 1984)—but usually the result by Miller above, which can be formulated model-theoretically (and is therefore substantially independent of particular formal presentations), is overlooked.

184. Laudan 1981b (cf. 1984a) makes much of the failure of convergence, but in my view his case, while making a valid point, is crucially flawed, see Chapter 6, Section 6.6. See also Note 174. (I have also toughened my stance

concerning a reasonable reading of the historical record itself since Chapter 6, see Section 8.4.2. above.) Laudan also argues that the realist has failed to provide a theory of approximate truth which guarantees that approximately true theories refer (*simplicitur*) and are approximately empirically adequate. The discussion of this section shows that no realist ought to accept these constraints. In 1984a Laudan repeats these arguments, adding the argument criticized in Section 8.4.1.

185. The example is discussed in Hooker 1981e and follows the helpful discussion in Dewan's 1976.

186. See also Chapter 4, Section 4.6 and 1973c, Section VII. It is these sources of stability, allied with the capacity to model one theory's world in another, that constitute the basis on which I would try to understand cases of so-called theory incommensurability. Cf. also Devitt 1984, Krige 1980 and Rohrlich/Harden 1983.

187. In the case of geometry we have not only metrically non-Euclidean geometries but alternative geometries at each successively higher level of order structure, i.e., alternatives at affine, conformal, projective and topological structure levels. See e.g., the references of Note 171. For the ambiguous reference of Newtonian mass to relativistic dynamic mass or rest mass, see e.g., Field 1973. For the ambiguous reference of 'gene' to all of the various possibilities for biosynthetic pathway structures for the production of proteins see e.g., the references in any standard genetics text. P. S. Churchland 1982 offers a pretty discussion of the fragmentation of 'consciousness'. And for the four different tasks required of sense data and the fragmentation of the notion among them see e.g., Hooker 1978a.

188. The point is of course controversial. The evidence for this view is the late arrival of spoken, and the very late arrival of written, language; the developmental psychological data (e.g., that behavioural cognitive capacity precedes linguistic development, that logical thinking is less delayed in deaf-and-dumb children than in blind children—see e.g., Boden 1979 and Piaget in Rieber 1983); the frequent experience of 'being at a loss for words' especially in relation to aesthetic experience, coupled with the evidence for hemispheric specialisation; the occurrence and importance of linguistic innovation itself and the non-linguistic characterisations of creative thinking in general, even in theoretical areas; our intuitive ability in, versus our lack of formal understanding of, our own infinitary formal systems, linguistic and mathematical.

This view is not without opponents. (I mean those who consciously argue against it. Many philosophers follow Wittgenstein and simply assume that language defines or exhausts intelligence—alas, usually not explicitly as Wittgenstein did.) One line of attack comes from the 'language of thought' (computation) line in cognitive psychology (though not so strongly, ironically, from Chomskian linguists). E.g. Fodor 1975, 1984 argues that without essentially linguistic representation there can be no mistakes, for mistakes are false beliefs and these require a semantic apparatus to characterise them. (Fodor does not, of course, deny that animals can behave sub-optimally in relation to their own interests and wind up starving, damaged or dead as a result. The issue is when does a sub-optimal process also amount to a mistake. And Fodor holds that mistakes are of the essence of our intelligence.) Fodor also argues that the logical structure of language would remain a computational mystery if it is not linguistic contents over which the computations are performed. (But presumably this need apply only beyond some level of process-ing, even if the argument be granted in principle.) And Fodor has an argu-ment that moves from infinitory language competence plus finitary neural processing capacity via recursion (the Chomsky move) and hence rule gov-erned computation, to computation over linguistic contents. I have some sympathy with each of Fodor's objections; however, I do not believe any of them are valid as they stand.

Another line of criticism emerges from various theoretical models of evolu-tionary processes. There is, e.g., a systems approach to self-organising sys-tems which emphasises a quasi-linguistic structure (see Pattee 1981, cf. 1973). And Jaynes' 1976 theory, e.g., places language before consciousness at least. At present I believe the issue is genuinely open.

189. It is, I think, striking how the chief proponents of linguistic analysis so often used, and use, it to justify claims to guaranteed human knowledge. The logical empiricists used semantic theory to guarantee empiricist epistemology (Chapter 3). Wittgenstein deployed it to remove the privacy of the mind. The neo-Kantians like Apel and Bhaskar want to obtain a transcendental deduc-tion of philosophy from semantic premises. (Cf. Cornman, Note 191.) Recent-ly Putnam has deployed it to force a reply to the sceptic via a warranted assertibility definition of truth. A healthy attachment to naturalism makes one deeply suspicious of all such argumentation.

190. This has been clearly discussed for the first four cases by Armstrong 1978 who awakened me from my 'dogmatic slumber' in this matter, and I promptly added the last case—see 1981e.

191. The same lesson applies in many places. E.g., for decades Quine bewitched us with empiricist-derived talk of 'stimulus-meaning' and derived some powerful misleading indeterminacies from it. The real complexity of an account of language is brought out in Gochet's 1982 poignant review of Quine's doctrines. I have tried some analysis of Quine's logical doctrines, with a related conclusion concerning the complexity of understanding formal languages (see 1971a, cf. also 1970b, 1975e). Cornman 1966 tried to have linguistic considerations provide a guaranteed framework for philosophy— for a naturalist critique see Hooker 1978c.

192. Feyerabend is explicit about this, see e.g., 1965a, b, c. His discussions gave rise to the label 'implicit definition' for this kind of meaning specifica-tion. See also Chapter 2, Note 55 and text.

193. The term 'middle-Putnam' is Devitt's, 1984 Chapter 11. I found De-vitt's exposition of Putnam's changes of position helpful, and largely agree with his realist critique of late-Putnam.

194. See e.g., Devitt 1984 and Section 8.6.6 and the unresolved problems in Dretske's recent causal approach to perception over the specification of proxi-mal stimulus and misrepresentation (error), cf. Notes 54, 171.

195. This tension (if one it be) between cause and role in semantics is unresolved in Churchland and is an important part, I believe, in what later leads him away from a realist theory of truth—see his 1985c. He also all but ignores the role of ostensive definition in contributing to meaning, perhaps because it has been associated with perceptual foundationalism ('the Given'), perhaps because of his materialism. I believe neither is a good reason to do so (especially once the property-predicate link is broken and so synonymy re-jected as the criterion for property identity *á la* my 1981d). But Churchland

remains one of the pioneers of thorough naturalism.

196. These differences are spelled out in my 1974c, cf.1973c, Section VII. It may be possible to see a certain schizophrenia of identity criteria running through both schemes. These sorts of consideration, which I believe have a profound bearing on the understanding of quantum theory (cf. 1973c and Section 8.3.4 above), are not at present in fashion and tend to be ignored by those of the 'linguistic turn'.

197. Putnam's argument against realist versions of the causal theory of reference is focused on the claim that, since any attempt to describe the causal relations in question is subject to nonstandard interpretation, no unique causal relation is picked out (1981, Chapter 2). Putnam's argument hinges on some meta-mathematical results of model theory. Glymour 1982 points out that it tacitly conflates two claims: (i) No set of sentences can uniquely fix the reference of 'cause' and (ii) the causal relation pertinent to reference is not fixed. So Putnam has at least tacitly assumed that whatever is, is uniquely expressible by us (further examples of anthropocentrism and the 'linguistic turn'). But beyond this I am dubious about this argument because I am dubious we have any deep understanding as yet of the significance of the relevant meta-mathematical theorems (e.g., Lowenheim-Skolem, Godel, Henkin). When properly understood they may be shown to reflect on our understanding of formal languages rather than on reference (they may not of course). Putnam's model-theoretic arguments (see e.g., 1980, 1981a, 1982a) have generated a minor industry in response; the 'Finnish connection' (e.g., Pearce/Rantala 1982a, b) here must suffice to indicate the kind of reasons I have for remaining wary of the significance of these arguments.

I don't even think Putnam's preliminary argument about why we can't be brains in vats is convincing, for the sort of reason given by Stephens and Russow 1985—we are in fact able to cognize circumstances which the internalist says is impossible. I agree that much in Putnam's arguments is plausible and I agree that we will not be clear on whether this present evaluation is acceptable until there is an insightful semantical theory with which to back it—but the hunch remains.

(In addition, it happens that Putnam's account of the brain-in-a-vat case is biologically unconvincing. The key feature of language is its sensory-motor feedback connections, like the whole of the cognitive apparatus from which it emerges. But for the controlling scientist to give the vat-brain manipulative (motor) feedback as response to sensory input *is* to establish the causal links required for successful reference, with *something*. The case as Putnam states it is a fake one.)

Incidentally, Putnam and Co. do not speak directly of meaning, but of reference. They accept the following moves within semantic theory which connect the two notions. (1) (Frege) Meaning is specified by truth conditions; the meaning of a sentence p is given by specifying the truth conditions for p. (2) (Tarski) Truth conditions are determined by reference (or satisfaction). Cf. Section 8.3.1. Thus meaning is ultimately determined by reference. Others hotly dispute these moves. Again, I don't have a settled opinion because there is so much plausible-sounding argumentation on both sides at the present time. (In this respect I am no further advanced than Chapter 2, Section 2.6.4.)

198. Leplin 1984 offers a different version of the *reductio*: . . . if the inference is repeated it is redundant, if it is not . . . But this is not a persuasive variant. Both philosophy and science have something to explain. To argue in Leplin's manner is like arguing that two successive appeals to two similar kinds of micro-structure, the one embedded in the other, are redundant, as if there couldn't be two systems levels of composition to explain.

199. See the discussion at Notes 118, 123 and text. In a critical review in 1970 of Feyerabend's writings, in particular 'Against Method', I gave the following diagram to summarize the structure of his thought:

200. I have not included transcendental dogmatism, the attempt to prove intuitive dogmatism, or *reductio* any attempt at doubt, because I think there are no defensible versions of this position. I have also not included self-authenticating dogmatism, e.g., religious revelation, because the human response to it is still based on judgement (as indeed is the human response to transcendental arguments); I cannot see a role for self-authentication beyond the three options I discuss.

201. Such considerations led Melchert 1985 to insist that van Fraassen's commitment defines a form of belief rather than agnostic acceptance. This in effect reverses Fine's 1984 point about table-thumping: what does the agnostic subtract from the fallibilist realist position? Only a table thumping "not committed"!

202. See, in this respect, van Fraassen's foot shuffling in reply to Churchland at 1985, p. 284. In this regard, there is for van Fraassen a delightful connection between religious and epistemic empiricist agnosticism—see Note 20.

203. Though I have defended the metaphysical doctrines of realism against Putnam's attacks there is much in his attempts to overcome the empiricst dichotomies (cf. S) that is sympathetic to my own views and represents a genuine attempt to encompass the larger issues of philosophy in a sensitive yet critical manner. (The key here is tension, see Note 22 and Section 8.3.11.) For this reason a worthy examination of Putnam's views on these larger issues must await another occasion. I also believe that the issues addressed in this section and by Putnam are what lie behind Feyerabend's more recent probing of the value of truth and of science (see his 1978). Feyerabend has always taken the ethical foundations of science seriously (cf. my analytic review 1972b). Just as I believe we can save the insights of his *Against Method* for a positive theory of methodology by moving from a logic-based to a decision-theoretic framework (see Section 8.3.3) so I believe one can understand the value of much of Feyerabend's recent attacks on science and the pursuit of truth in a constructive manner by understanding them as an exploration of the conditions for a unified or integrated human development.

204. See 1981, p. 664. The quote goes on:

> Everyone appreciates this point readily for philosophy of religion. But
> the analogy that I would like especially to press is that of mathematics.
> Russell and the logicists and their heirs generally, took it as a criterion
> of adequacy that mathematics be re-told as a true story. . . But
> Brouwer, Hilbert, and Heyting had focussed in the first instance on
> mathematical activities. What there was in the world, in addition to the
> participants in that game and the structure of acceptable moves, took
> for them a very secondary place.

It was Hilbert who took the idea of a formal game most seriously of all.
(Though Fine, writing several years later, does not bring out this dimension, it
is clearly the converse to his agnosticism.) But as I understand the intuitionism of Brouwer and Heyting, van Fraassen's description represents a noticeable distortion of their position. Intuitionism stressed the central role of
objective structures given in intuition, and the choice of rules for mathematical activity were ultimately motivated on, and referred to, that basis. Of
course, by playing down the role of intuition, van Fraassen succeeds in emphasising the escape of the game from any reference to reality—but even
conventional social games have more or less intelligence, intuitively judged,
built into their choice of rules. And mathematics is plausibly more than a
parlour pastime.

205. I am not even clear yet what this would amount to. Perhaps part of it
would be understanding more deeply why certain values are so intricately
interrelated in a world like ours (say, various kinds of simplicity, inductive
acceptance and practical control), or developing more penetrating formal
theories of interdependence among them in decision structures. On the other
hand, including conflict among them and trade-off structures would be an
important part of both jobs. The notion of a unity among values is prima facie
jeopardised e.g., by the Popper-Levi conflict between informativeness and
likelihood of truth. But then there is also no point to information *per se* (in the
engineering sense) unless it is relevantly connected to reality. There is then
much more work to be done here.

Bibliography

Achinstein, P. [1964], 'On the Meaning of Scientific Terms', *The Journal of Philosophy* **61** (1964), 497-508.

Achinstein, P. [1965], 'Acute Proliferitis', in Cohen/Wartofsky [1965].

Achinstein, P. [1968], *Concepts of Science*, Johns Hopkins Press, Baltimore.

Achinstein, P. and Barker, S. (eds.) [1969], *The Legacy of Logical Positivism*, Johns Hopkins Press, Baltimore.

Adorno, T. W., Frenkel-Brunswich, E., Levinson, D. J. and Sandford, R. N. [1950], *The Authoritarian Personality*, Harper and Rowe, New York.

Agassi, J. [1964], 'The Nature of Scientific Problems and Their Roots in Metaphysics', in Bunge [1964].

Agassi, J. [1975], *Science in Flux*, Reidel, Dordrecht.

Albury, R. .[1983], *The Politics of Objectivity*, Deakin University Press, Geelong, Vic.

Althusser, L. [1965], *Pour Marx*, Maspero, Paris. (Translated as *For Marx*, Penguin, London, 1969.)

Andersson, G. and Radnitsky, G. (eds) [1978a], *Progress and Rationality in Science*, Reidel, Dordrecht.

Andersson, G. and Radnitsky, G. (eds) [1978b], *The Structure and Development of Science*, Reidel, Dordrecht.

Ann Arbor Collective [1976], *Biology as a Social Weapon*, Burgess, Minneapolis.

Apel, K.-O. [1980a], 'C. S. Peirce and the Post-Tarskian Problem of an Adequate Explication of the Meaning of Truth: Towards a Transcendental-Pragmatic Theory of Truth. Part I', *The Monist* **63** (1980), 386-407. (Part II is cited as appearing in the *Transactions of the C. S. Peirce Society* for 1980.)

Apel, K.-O. [1980b], *Towards a Transformation of Philosophy*, Routledge and Kegan Paul, London.

Arbib, M. A. [1954], *Brains, Machines and Mathematics*, McGraw-Hill, New York.

Arbib, M. A.]1972], *The Metaphorical Mind*, Wiley-Interscience, New York.

Armstrong, D. M [1961], *Perception and the Physical World*, Routledge & Kegan Paul, London.

Armstrong, D. M. [1973], *Belief, Truth and Knowledge*, Cambridge University Press, Cambridge.

Armstrong, D. M. [1978], *Universals and Scientific Realism*, 2 vols, Cambridge University Press, Cambridge.

Armstrong, D. M. [1983], *What is a Law of Nature?* Cambridge University Press, Cambridge.

Armytage, W. H. G. [1965], *The Rise of the Technocrats*, Routledge and Kegan Paul, London.

Ashby, W. R. [1970], *Design for a Brain*, Chapman and Hall Science Paperbacks, London.

Asquith, P. D. and Hacking, I. (eds) [1978/9], *PSA 1978*, Vols. I, II, Philosophy of Science Association, East Lansing, Michigan.

Asquith, P. D. and Kyburg, H. E. Jr. (eds) [1979], *Current Research in Philosophy of Science*, Philosophy of Science Association, East Lansing, Michigan.

Asquith, P. D. and Giere, R. N. (eds) [1980/1], *PSA 1980*, Vols, I, II, Philosophy of Science Association, East Lansing, Michigan.

Asquith, P. D. and Nickles, T. (eds) [1982/3], *PSA 1982*, 2 vols, Philosophy of Science Association, East Lansing, Mich.

Asquith, P. D. and Kitcher, P. (eds) [1984], *PSA 1984*, vol. I, Philosophy of Science Association, East Lansing, Michigan.

Aune, B. [1967], *Knowledge, Mind and Nature*, Random House, New York.

Aune, B. [1970], *Rationalism, Empiricism, Pragmatism: An Introduction*, Random House, New York.

Ayer, A. J. [1940], *The Foundations of Empirical Knowledge*, Macmillan, New York.

Ayer, A. J. [1946], *Language, Truth and Logic*, Gollancz, London.

Ayer, A. J. [1959], *Logical Positivism*, Free Press, New York.

Ballentine, L. E. [1970], 'The Statistical Interpretation of Quantum Mechanics', *Reviews of Modern Physics* **42** (1970), 358-381.

Banathy, B. (ed.) [1980], *Systems Science and Science*, Society for General Systems Research, Louisville, Kentucky.

Barmark, J. (ed.) [1979], *Perspectives in Metascience*, Berlings, Lund.

Barnes, B. (ed.) [1972] *Sociology of Science*, Penguin, Harmondsworth, Middlesex.

Barnes, B. [1974], *Scientific Knowledge and Sociological Theory*, Routledge and Kegan Paul, London.

Barnes, B. [1977], *Interests and the Growth of Knowledge*, Routledge and Kegan Paul, London.

Barnes, B. and Edge, D. (eds) [1982], *Science in Context*, MIT Press, Boston.

Bateson, G. [1972] *Steps to an Ecology of Mind*, Ballantine.

Baumgartner, T., Burns, T. R. and DeVille, P. [1984], *The Shaping of Socio-Economic Systems*, Gordon & Breach, 1984.

Baumrin, B. (ed.) [1963], *Philosophy of Science: The Delaware Seminar*, 2 Vols, Interscience, New York.

Becker, E. [1973], *The Denial of Death*, The Free Press, New York.

Becker, E. [1976], *The Structure of Evil*, The Free Press, New York.

Beer, S. [1979a], *Platform for Change*, Wiley, New York.

Beer, S. [1979b], *The Heart of Enterprise*, Wiley, New York.

Beer, S. [1981], *I Said You are Gods*, The Teilhard Centre for the Future of Man, London.

Berger, P. and Luckman, T. [1971], *The Social Construction of Reality*, Penguin, London.

Bergmann, G. [1954], *The Metaphysics of Logical Positivism*, Longmans, Green & Co., New York.

Bernal, J. D. [1969], *Science in History*, 4 vols, Watts, London.

Bernstein, G. B. and Cetron, M. J. [1969], 'SEER: A Delphic Approach Applied to Information Processing', *Technological Forecasting* **1** (1969), 33-54.

Beth, E. W. [1966], *The Foundations of Mathematics*, Harper and Rowe, New York.

Bhaskar, R. [1975], *A Realist Theory of Science*, Leeds Books, Leeds.

Bhaskar, R. [1979], *The Possibility of Naturalism*, Brighton, Harvester Press.

Bjerring, A. K. [1977], 'Rational Interaction: Game Theory and Social Power', Ph. D. Thesis, The University of Western Ontario, Canada

Bjerring, A. K. and Hooker, C. A. [1979], 'Process and Progress: The Nature of Systematic Inquiry' in Barmark, [1979].

Bjerring, A. K. and Hooker, C. A. [1980], 'The Implications of Philosophy of Science for Science Policy' in Hooker/Schrecker [1980/1].

Bjerring, A. K. and Hooker, C. A. [1981], 'Lehrer, Consensus and Science: The Empiricist Watershed' in Bogdan, [1981].

Blair, D. H. and Pollack, R. A. [1983], 'Rational Collective Choice', *Scientific American* **249** (1983), 76-83.

Blake, R. M., Ducasse, C. J. and Madden, E. H. [1960], *Theories of Scientific Method*, University of Washington Press, Seattle.

Bloor, D. [1976], *Knowledge and Social Imagery*, Routledge and Kegan Paul, London.

Blume, S. [1974], *Toward a Political Sociology of Science*, Collier-Macmillan, London.

Boden, M. [1979], *Piaget*, Fontana, London.

Bogdan R. J. (ed.) [1976], *Local Induction*, Reidel, Dordrecht.

Bogdan, R. J. (ed.) [1981], *Profiles: Keith Lehrer*, Reidel, Dordrecht.

Bohm, D. [1965], *The Special Theory of Relativity*, W. A. Benjamin, New York.

Bohm, D. [1980], *Wholeness and the Implicate Order*, Routledge and Kegan Paul, London.

Bohnert, H. [1967], 'Communication by Ramsey-Sentence Clause', *Philosophy of Science* **34** (1967), 341-347.

Bohnert, H. [1968], In Defense of Ramsey's Elimination Method', *The Journal of Philosophy* **65** (1968), 275-281.

Bolland, L. A. [1971], 'Methodology as an Exercise in Economic Analysis', *Philosophy of Science* **38** (1971), 105-117.

Boucher, W. I. [1974], *An Annotated Bibliography on Cross-Impact Analysis*, Futures Group, Glastonbury, Connecticut.

Boyd, R. [1980], 'Scientific Realism and Naturalistic Epistemology', in Asquith/Giere [1980/81].

Boyd, R. [1983], 'On the Current Status of Scientific Realism', *Erkenntnis* **19** (1983), 45-90.

Boyd, R. N. [1984], 'The Current Status of Scientific Realism', in Leplin [1984a].

Boyd, R. N. [1985], 'Lex Orandi est Lex Credendi', in Churchland/Hooker [1985a].

Braithwaite, R. B. [1959], *Scientific Explanation*, Cambridge University Press, Cambridge.

Brams, S. J. [1976], *Paradoxes in Politics*, Free Press, New York.

Brennan, G. [1985], 'Economics at the Margin: Natural and Institutional Constraints on the Acquisition of Knowledge', *Search* **16** (1985), 17-22.

Brewer, M. B. and Collins B. E. (eds.) [1981] *Scientific Enquiry and the Social Sciences*, Jossey-Bass, San Francisco.

Bridgeman, P. W. [1927], *The Logic of Modern Physics*, MacMillan, New York.

Bridgeman, P. W. [1936], *The Nature of Physical Theory*, Princeton University Press, Princeton, New Jersey.

Briskman, L. [1982], 'Review of O'Hear, A., *Karl Popper*', *Philosophical Quarterly* **32** (1982), 285-7.

Brody, B. [1972], 'Towards an Aristotelian Theory of Scientific Explanation', *Philosophy of Science* **39** (1972), 20-31.

Bromberger, S. [1966], 'Why-Questions' in Colodny [1966].

Brown, H. I. [1979], *Perception, Theory and Commitment: The New Philosophy of Science*, University of Chicago Press, Chicago.

Brown, J. R. [1984a], 'Realism and the Anthropocentrics' in Asquith/Kitcher [1984].

Brown, J. R. (ed.) [1984b], *Scientific Rationality: The Sociological Turn*, Reidel, Dordrecht.

Brown, S. C. (ed.) [1974], *Philosophy and Psychology*, Macmillan, London.

Brown, S. C. (ed.) [1984], *Objectivity and Cultural Divergence*, Cambridge University Press, Cambridge.

Bub, J. [1973], 'On the Completeness of Quantum Mechanics' in Hooker [1973].

Buchanan, J. and Tullock, G. [1962], *The Calculus of Consent*, University of Michigan Press, Ann Arbor, Michigan.

Buchdahl, G. [1970], 'History of Science and Criteria of Choice' in Stuewer [1970].

Bunge, M. [1963], *The Myth of Simplicity*, Englewood Cliffs, Prentice-Hall, New Jersey.

Bunge, M. (ed.) [1964], *The Critical Approach to Science and Philosophy*, The Free Press, New York.

Bunge, M. [1967a], *Foundations of Physics*, Springer-Verlag, New York.

Bunge, M. [1967b], *Scientific Research*, Volumes I & II, Springer-Verlag, New York.

Bunge, M. [1973], *Method, Model and Matter*, Reidel, Dordrecht.

Burtt, E. A. [1959], *The Metaphysical Foundations of Modern Physical Science*, Routledge & Kegan Paul, London.

Butts, R. E. [1966], 'Feyerabend and the Pragmatic Theory of Observation', *Philosophy of Science* **33** (1966), 383-94.

Butts, R. E. (ed.) [1968], *William Whewell's Theory of Scientific Method*, University of Pittsburgh Press, Pittsburgh.

Butts, R. E. and Davis, J. W. (eds) [1970], *The Methodological Heritage of Newton*, University of Toronto Press, Toronto.

Butts, R. E. [1973], 'Whewell's Logic of Induction' in Gicre/Westfall [1973].

Butts, R. E. and Hintika, J. R. (eds) [1976], *Proceedings, 5th International Congress on Logic, Methodology and Philosophy of Science*, 5 Vols, Reidel, Dordrecht.

Butts, R. E. [1977], 'Consilience of Inductions and the Problem of Conceptual Change in Science' in Colodny [1977].

Calhoun, J. B. [1984], 'The Transitional Phase in Knowledge Evolution', *Man-Environment Systems*, **14** (1984), 131-142.

Campbell, D. T. [1959], 'Methodological Suggestions from a Comparative Psychology of Knowledge Processes', *Inquiry* 2 (1959), 152-182.

Campbell, D. T. [1973], 'Evolutionary Epistemology', in Schilpp [1973].

Campbell, N. R. [1957], *Foundations of Science*, Dover, New York.

Capek, M. [1961], *The Philosophical Impact of Contemporary Physics*, Van Nostrand, Princeton, New Jersey.

Capra, F [1979], *The Tao of Physics*, Fontana, New York.

Carnap, T. [1928], *Der Logische Aufbau der Welt*, Weltkreis, Berlin. (*The Logical Structure of the World*, and *Pseudo-Problems in Philosophy*, R. A. George transl., University of California Press, Berkeley, 1967.)

Carnap, R. [1932], 'Uber Protokollsatz', *Erkenntnis* 3 (1932), 215-228.

Carnap, R. [1934], *Der Logische Syntax der Sprache*, Wien. (Translated as *The Logical Syntax of Language*, Routledge & Kegan Paul, London, 1964.)

Carnap, R. [1950], 'Empiricism, Semantics and Ontology', *Revue Internationale de Philosophie* **4** (1950). (Reprinted in Carnap [1956]).

Carnap, R. [1936/7], 'Testability and Meaning', *Philosophy of Science* 3 (1936), 419-47, **4** (1937), 1-40. (An attenuated version is included in Feigl/Brodbeck [1953].)

Carnap, R. [1956a], 'The Methodological Character of Theoretical Concepts' in Feigl/Scriven [1956].

Carnap, R. [1956b], *Meaning and Necessity*, 2nd edition, University of Chicago Press, Chicago.

Carnap, R. [1962], *The Logical Foundations of Probability* 2nd edition, University of Chicago Press, Chicago.

Cartwright, N. [1981], 'The Reality of Causes in a World of Instrumental Laws' in Asquith/Giere [1980/1].

Cartwright, N. [1982], 'When Explanation Leads to Inference', *Philosophical Topics* **13** (1982), 111-122.

Cartwright, N. [1983], *How the Laws of Physics Lie*, Oxford University Press, Oxford.

Case, T [1888], *Physical Realism*, Longmans, London.

Case, T. [1906], 'Scientific Method as Mental Operation', in Strong [1906].

Chalmers, A. [1976], *What is this Thing Called Science?*, Queensland University Press, Brisbane. (Revised, enlarged addition 1982.)

Chambers, D. W. and Course Team [1979], *Liberation and Control: The Uses of Knowledge and Power*, Dominion Press for Deakin University, North Blackburn, Vic.

Chance, M. R. A. [1984], 'Biological Systems Synthesis of Mentality and the Nature of the Two Modes of Mental Operation: Hedonic and Agonic', *Man-Environment Systems* **14** (1984), 143-157.

Chardin, Teilhard de [1959], *The Phenomenon of Man*, Collins, London.

Choy, V. [1982], 'Mind-Body, Realism, and Rorty's Therapy', *Synthese* **52** (1982), 515-541.

Churchland, P. M. [1979], *Scientific Realism and the Plasticity of Mind*, Cambridge University Press, Cambridge.

Churchland, P. M. and Hooker, C. A. [1985a], *Images of Science: Essays on Realism and Empiricism*, University of Chicago Press, Chicago.

Churchland, P. M. [1985b], 'The ontological Status of Observables: In Praise of the Superempirical Virtues', in Churchland/Hooker [1985a].

Churchland, P. M. [1985c], 'Conceptual Progress and Word/World Relations: In Search of the Essence of Natural Kinds', *Canadian Journal of Philosophy* **15** (1985), 1-18.

Churchland, P. S. [1983], 'Consciousness: The Transmutation of a Concept', *Pacific Philosophical Quarterly* **64** (1983), 80-95.

Churchman, C. W. [1948], *Theory of Experimental Inference*, Macmillan, New York.

Churchman, C. W. [1961], *Prediction and Optimal Decision*, Prentice-Hall, Englewood Cliffs, N. J.

Churchman, C. W. [1968], *Challenge to Reason*, McGraw-Hill, New York.

Churchman, C. W. [1972], *The Design of Enquiring Systems*, Basic Books, New York.

Clendinnen, F. J. [1980], 'Rational Expectation and Simplicity' in McLaughlin [1980].

Clendinnen, F. J. [1983], 'Intuition and Rationality', unpublished.

Clendinnen, F. J. [1984], 'Epistemic Choice and Sociology', *Metascience* **1** (1984), 61-9.

Cohen, R. S. and Wartofsky, M. W. (eds) [1965], *Boston Studies in the Philosophy of Science*, Vol. II, Humanities Press, New York.

Cohen, R. S. and Wartofsky, M. W. (eds) [1974a], *Logical and Epistemological Studies in Contemporary Physics*, Reidel, Dordrecht.

Cohen, R. S., Stachel, J. J. and Wartofsky, M. W. (eds) [1974b], *For Dirk Struik*, Boston Studies in the Philosophy of Science, Vol. XV, Reidel, Dordrecht.

Colodny, R. (ed.) [1965], *Beyond the Edge of Certainty*, Pittsburgh Studies in the Philosophy of Science, Vol. II, Prentice-Hall, New Jersey.

Colodny, R. (ed.) [1966], *Mind and Cosmos*, Pittsburgh Studies in the Philosophy of Science, Vol. III, University of Pittsburgh Press, Pittsburgh.

Colodny, R. (ed.) [1970], *The Nature and Function of Scientific Theories*, University of Pittsburgh Studies in the Philosophy of Science, Vol. IV, University of Pittsburgh Press.

Colodny, R. (ed.) [1972], *Paradigms and Paradoxes*, Pittsburgh Studies in the Philosophy of Science, Vol. V, University of Pittsburgh Press, Pittsburgh.

Colodny, R. G. (ed.) [1977], *Logic, Laws and Life*, Pittsburgh Studies in the Philosophy of Science, vol. VI, University of Pittsburgh Press, Pittsburgh.

Cornman, J. [1966], *Metaphysics, Reference and Language*, Yale University Press, New Haven, Connecticut.

Cornman, J. W. [1972], 'Craig's Theorem, Ramsey-Sentences and Scientific

Instrumentalism', *Synthese* **25** (1972), 82-128.

Crowther, J. G. [1967], *Science in Modern Society*, Cresset, London.

Cummins, R. [1983], *The Nature of Psychological Explanation*, Bradford/MIT Press, Cambridge, Mass.

Cushing, J. T. [1983], 'Models, High-Energy Theoretical Physics and Realism' in Asquith/Nickles [1982/3].

Cushing, J. T. [1984a], 'The Convergence and Content of Scientific Opinion' in Asquith/Kitcher (eds) [1984].

Cushing, J. T., Delaney, C. F. and Gutting, G. M. (eds) [1984b], *Science and Reality*, University of Notre Dame Press, Notre Dame, Ind.

Dalkey, N. C. [1972], *Studies in the Quality of Life: Delphi and Decision Making*, Lexington Books, Lexington.

Danto, A. and Morgenbesser, S. (eds) [1960], *Philosophy of Science*, World Publishing Co., New York.

Daum, A. [1982], 'Schlick's Empiricist Critical Realism', *Synthese* **52** (1982), 449-493.

Davidson, D. [1973], 'The Material Mind' in Suppes *et al.* [1973].

Davidson, D. [1980], *Essays on Actions and Events*, Clarendon Press, Oxford.

Delaney, C. F. [1969], *Mind and Nature*, University of Notre Dame Press, Notre Dame.

Dennett, D. [1978], *Brainstorms*, Bradford (MIT Press), Boston, Mass.

deSantillana, S. and Zilsel, E. [1941], *The Development of Rationalism and Empiricism*, University of Chicago Press, Chicago. (Also in Neurath, et al., [1970].)

Devitt, M. [1978], 'Realism and the Renegade Putnam', *Nous* **17** (1978), 291-301.

Devitt, M. [1981], *Designation*, Columbia University Press, New York.

Devitt, M. [1984], *Realism and Truth*, Blackwell, London.

Dewan, E. M. [1976], 'Consciousness as an Emergent Causal Agent in the Context of Control System Theory' in Globus et al. [1976].

Dewey, J. [1930], *The Quest for Certainty*, George Allen and Unwin, London.

Dooyerwerd, H. [1960], *In the Twilight of Western Thought*, Presbyterian and Reformed Press, New York.

Doppelt, G. [1978], 'Kuhn's Epistemological Relativism: An Interpretation and Defence', *Enquiry* **21** (1978), 33-86.

Doppelt, G. [1983], 'Relativism and Recent Pragmatic Conceptions of Scientific Rationality' in Rescher [1983].

Drake, D., *et al.*, (eds) [1920], *Essays in Critical Realism*, Gordian Press, New York.

Dreyfus, H. and Haugeland, J. [1974], 'The Computer as a Mistaken Model of the Mind', in Brown [1974].

Dreyfus, H. [1972], *What Computers Can't Do: A Critique of Artificial Reason*, Harper and Rowe, New York.

Dretske, F. [1981], *Knowledge and the Flow of Information*, Bradford/MIT, Boston.

Duhem, P. [1962], *The Aim and Structure of Physical Theory*, Atheneum, New York.

Dummett, M. [1978], *Truth and Other Enigmas*, Harvard University Press, Cambridge, Mass.

Dummett, M. [1982], 'Realism', *Synthese* **52** (1982), 55-112.

Earman, J., Glymour C., Stachel J. (eds.) [1977], *Foundations of Space-Time Theories*, Minnesota Studies in the Philosophy of Science, vol. 8, University of Minnesota Press, Minneapolis.

Earman, J. [1978], 'Fairy Tales vs An Ongoing Story: Ramsey's Neglected Argument for Scientific Realism', *Philosophical Studies* 33 (1978), 195-202.

Easlea, B. [1973], *Liberation and the Aims of Science*, Chatto and Windus for Sussex University Press, London.

Edwards, P. (ed.) [1967], *The Encyclopedia of Philosophy*, Macmillan, New York.

Elliott, D. and R. [1976], *The Control of Technology*, Wykeham, London.

Ellis, B. [1985], 'What Science Aims to Do', in Churchland/Hooker [1985a].

Elster, J. [1979], *Ulysses and the Sirens*, Cambridge University Press, Cambridge.

Elster, J. [1983a], *Sour Grapes: Studies in the Subversion of Rationality*, Cambridge University Press, Cambridge.

Elster, J. [1983b], *Explaining Technical Change: A Case Study in the Philosophy of Science*, Cambridge University Press, Cambridge.

Emery, F. and M. [1974], *Futures We're In*, Australian National University, Centre for Continuing Education, Canberra.

Emery, F. and M. [1975], *A Choice of Futures*, Australian National University, Centre for Continuing Education, Canberra.

Encel, S. and Ronanye, J. (eds) [1979], *Science, Technology and Public Policy: An International Perspective*, Pergamon Press, Sydney.

Feigl, H. [1943], 'Logical Empiricism', in Runes [1943], also in Morick [1972].

Feigl, H. and Brodbeck, M. (eds) [1953], *Readings in the Philosophy of Science*, Appleton-Century-Crofts, New York.

Feigl, H. and Sellars, W. (eds) [1949], *Readings in Philosophical Analysis*, appleton Century-Crofts, New York.

Feigl, H. and Scriven, M. (eds) [1956], *Minnesota Studies in the Philosophy of Science*, Vol. I, University of Minnesota Press, Minneapolis.

Feigl, H. and Maxwell, G. (eds) [1958], *Minnesota Studies in the Philosophy of Science*, Vol. II, University of Minnesota Press, Minneapolis.

Feigl, H. and Maxwell, G. (eds) [1961], *Philosophy of Science*, Holt, Rinehart and Winston, New York.

Feigl, H. and Maxwell, G. (eds) [1962], *Minnesota Studies in the Philosophy of Science*, Vol. III, University of Minnesota Press, Minneapolis.

Fetzer, J. H. [1981], *Scientific Knowledge*, Reidel, Dordrecht.

Feyerabend, P. K. [1958], 'An Attempt at a Realistic Interpretation of Experience', *Proceedings of the Aristotelian Society* 58 (1958), 143-170.

Feyerabend, P. K. [1960], 'Das Problem der Existenz Theoretischer Entitaten', in *Probleme der Erkenntnistheorie*, Festschrift fur Viktor Kraft, Vienna.

Feyerabend, P. K. [1961], *Knowledge without Foundations*, Oberlin College (mimeographed).

Feyerabend, P. K. [1962] 'Explanation, Reduction and Empiricism', in Feigl/Maxwell [1962].

Feyerabend, P. K. [1965a], 'Problems of Empiricism' in Colodny [1965].

Feyerabend, P. K. [1965b], 'Reply to Criticism' in Cohen/Wartofsky [1965].

Feyerabend, P. K. [1965c], 'On the Meaning of Scientific Terms', *The Journal of Philosophy* 62 (1965), 266-274.

Feyerabend, P. K. [1969], 'Problems of Empiricism II', in Colodny [1969].

Feyerabend, P. K. [1970a], 'Against Method', in Radner/Winokur [1970].

Feyerabend, P. K. [1970b], 'Classical Empiricism', in Butts/Davis [1970].

Feyerabend, P. K. [1974], 'Popper's Objective Knowledge', *Inquiry* **17** (1974), 475-507.

Feyerabend, P. K. [1978], *Science in a Free Society*, New Left Books, London.

Ficant, M. and Pecheux, M. [1969], *Sur l'Histoires des Science*, Maspero, Paris.

Field, H. [1972], 'Tarski's Theory of Truth', *The Journal of Philosophy* **69** (1972), 347-75.

Field, H. [1973], 'Theory Change and the Indeterminacy of Reference', *Journal of Philosophy* **70** (1973), 462-81.

Fine, A. [1967], 'Consistency, Derivability and Scientific Change', *The Journal of Philosophy* **62** (1967), 231-240.

Fine, A. [1984], 'The Natural Ontological Attitude', in Leplin]1984a].

Finkelstein, D. [1979], 'The Leibniz Project' in Hooker [1975/1979].

Finkelstein, D. and Rodriguez, E. [1985], 'Relativity of Topology and Dynamics', *International Journal of Theoretical Physics*, **23** (1984), 1065-98.

Fisk, M. [1972], 'The World Regained', *The Journal of Philosophy* **69** (1972), 667-9.

Fodor, J. [1975], *The Language of Thought*, T. Y. Crowell, New York.

Fodor, J. [1984], 'Semantics, Wisconsin Style', *Synthese* **59** (1984), 231-250.

Forge, J. [1984], 'Theoretical Functions, Theory and Evidence', *Philosophy of Science* **51** (1984), 443-463.

Forster, M. [1984], 'Probabilistic Causality and the Foundations of Modern Science', Ph.D. Thesis, University of Western Ontario.

Foss, J. [1984], 'Reflections on Peirce's Concepts of Testability and the Economy of Research' in Asquith/Kitcher [1984].

Foster, M. H. and Martin, M. L. [1966], *Probability, Confirmation and Simplicity*, Odyssey Press, New York.

Foucault, M. [1968], *L'archeologie du savoir*, Editions du Gallimar, Paris. (Translated as *The Archeology of Knowledge*, together with *The Discourse on Language*, Harper (Colophon), New York, 1972.)

Frank, P. [1957], *Philosophy of Science*, Prentice Hall, Englewood Cliffs, New Jersey.

Frege, G. [1963], 'On the Foundations of Geometry' (transl. by M. E. Szabo), *Philosophical Review* **69** (1960), 3-16; (first published in 1903).

Fried, C. [1970], *An Anatomy of Values*, Harvard University Press, New Haven, Connecticut.

Friedman, M. [1974], 'Explanation and Scientific Understanding', *The Journal of Philosophy* **71** (1974), 5-19.

Friedman, M. [1983], *Foundations of Space-Time Theories: Relativistic Physics and Philosophy of Science*, Princeton University Press, Princeton, N.J.

Fromm, E. [1962], *The Art of Loving*, Harper and Rowe, New York.

Garfinkel, A. [1981], *Forms of Explanation: Rethinking the Questions in Social Theory*, Yale University Press, New Haven.

Gaukroger, S. [1978], *Explanatory Structures*, Harvester Press, Brighton.

Geist, V. [1976], *The Emergence of Homosapiens*, mimeographed.

Georgescu-Roegan, N. [1971], *The Entropy Law and the Economic Process*, Harvard University Press, Cambridge, Mass.

Giere, R. N. and Westfall, R. S. (eds) [1973], *Foundations of Scientific Method: The 19th Century*, Indiana University Press, Bloomington, Ind.

Giere, R. [1976], 'Empirical Probability, Objective Statistical Methods and Scientific Enquiry', in Harper/Hooker [1976].

Giere, R. N. [1984], 'Towards a Unified Theory of Science' in Cushing, et al. [1984b].

Giere, R. N. [1985], 'Constructive Realism', in Churchland/Hooker [1985a].

Globus, G., Maxwell, G., Savodnik, I. (eds) [1976], *Consciousness and the Brain*, Plenum, New York.

Glymour, C. [1980], *Theory and Evidence*, Princeton University Press, Princeton, N. J.

Glymour, C. [1982], 'Conceptual Scheming, or Confessions of a Metaphysical Realist', *Synthese* **51** (1982), 169-180.

Glymour, C. [1984], 'Explanation and Realism', in Leplin [1984] and Churchland/Hooker [1985a].

Gochet, P. [1982], 'Five Tenets of Quine', *The Monist* **65** (1982), 13-24.

Goffman, E. [1976], *The Presentation of Self in Everyday Life*, Penguin.

Goldstick, D. [1979], 'The Tolerance of Rudolph Carnap', *Australasian Journal of Philosophy* **49** (1979), 250-61.

Good, I. J. [1976], 'The Bayesian Influence, or How to Sweep Subjectivism Under the Carpet' in Harper/Hooker [1976].

Good, I. J. [1983a], 'The Philosophy of Exploratory Data Analysis', *Philosophy of Science* **50** (1983), 283-295.

Good, I. J. [1983b], *Good Thinking: The Foundations of Probability and its Applications*, University of Minnesota Press, Minneapolis.

Goodman, N. [1951], *The Structure of Appearance*, Harvard University Press, Cambridge, Mass.

Goodman, N. [1965], *Fact, Fiction and Forecast*, Bobbs-Merrill, New York.

Gordon, T. J. and Raffensperger, M. H. [1969], 'A Strategy for Planning Basic Research', *Philosophy of Science* **36** (1969), 205-218.

Graves, J. C. [1971], *The Conceptual Foundations of Contemporary Relativity Theory*, M.I.T. Press, Cambridge, Mass.

Greeno, J. G. [1971], 'Explanation and Information' in Salmon [1971].

Gregory, R. L. [1971], *Eye and Brain: The Psychology of Seeing*, McGraw-Hill, World University Library, New York.

Greiner, G. G. [1984], 'On the Social Control of Science', Ph. D. thesis, University of Western Ontario.

Grossman, N. [1974], 'Empiricism and the Possibility of Encountering Intelligent Beings with Different Sense Structures', *Journal of Philosophy* **70** (1974), 815-823.

Grunbaum, A. [1963], *Philosophical Problems of Space and Time*, A. A. Knopf, New York. (Revised, enlarged edition, Reidel, Dordrecht, 1973.)

Gutting, G. (ed.) [1980], *Paradigms and Revolutions*, University of Notre Dame Press, Notre Dame.

Gutting, G. [1983], 'Scientific Realism versus Constructive Empiricism: A Dialogue', *The Monist* **65** (May 1983), 336-49, and in Churchland/Hooker [1985a].

Haber, R. N. (ed.) [1969], *Information-Processing Approaches to Visual Perception*, Holt, Rinehart and Winston, New York.

Haberer, J. [1969], *Politics and the Community of Science*, Van Nostrand Reinhold, New York.

Habermas, J. [1968], *Erkenntnis und Interesse*, Suhrkamp Verlag, Frankfurt am Main. (Translated, with an additional appendix, as *Knowledge and Human Interests*, Beacon Press, Boston, 1971.)

Habermas, J. [1970], *Towards a Rational Society*, Beacon Press, New York.

Hacking, I. [1981], 'Do We See Through a Microscope?', *Pacific Philosophical Quarterly* 62 (1981), 305-22. Reprinted in Churchland/Hooker [1985a].

Hacking, I. [1982a], 'Experimentation and Scientific Realism', *Philosophical Topics* 13 (1982), 71-88. Reprinted in Leplin [1984a].

Hacking, I. [1982b], 'Language, Truth and Reason' in Hollis/Lukes [1982].

Hacking, I. [1983], *Representing and Intervening*, Cambridge University Press, Cambridge.

Hahlweg, K. [1983], 'The Evolution of Science: A Systems Approach', Ph.D. thesis, University of Western Ontario.

Haldane, J. B. S. [1924], *Daedalus, or Science and the Future*, Kegan Paul, Trench, Trubner and Co., London.

Hall, Sir D. et al. [1935], *The Frustration of Science*, London, George Allen and Unwin.

Haller, R. [1982], 'New Light on the Vienna Circle', *Monist* 65 (1982), 25-37.

Hanen, M. [1975], 'Confirmation, Explanation and Acceptance' in Lehrer [1975].

Hanna, A. [1980], 'Settlement and Energy Policy in Perspective: A Policy Evaluation', Ph.D. thesis, University of Western Ontario, Canada.

Hanson, N. R. [1983], *The Concept of the Positron*, Cambridge University Press, Cambridge.

Hanson, N. R. [1965], *Patterns of Discovery*, Cambridge University Press, Cambridge.

Hardin, C. L. and Rosenberg, A. [1982], 'In Defence of Convergent Realism', *Philosophy of Science* 49 (1982), 604-615.

Harman, G. [1973], *Thought*, Princeton University Press, Princeton, N.J.

Harper, W. and Hooker, C. A. (eds) [1976], *Foundations of Probability Theory, Statistical Inference and Statistical Theories of Science*, 3 vols., Reidel, Dordrecht.

Harper, W. [1977], 'Rational Belief Change, Popper Functions and Counterfactuals' in Hooker et al. [1977c].

Harper, W. L., Stalnaker, R. and Pearce, G. (eds) [1981], *Ifs*, Reidel, Dordrecht.

Harre, R. [1970], *The Principles of Scientific Thinking*, MacMillan, London.

Harris, E. E. [1965], *The Foundations of Metaphysics in Science*, George Allen and Unwin, London.

Hasan, S. Z. [1928], *Realism*, Cambridge University Press, Cambridge.

Hasing, L. [1982], *Scientific Reasoning and Epistemic Attitudes*, Akademiai Kiado, Budapest.

Hattiangardi, J. N. [1978/79], 'The Structure of Problems', *Philosophy of the Social Sciences* 8 (1978), 345-365 (Part I) and 9 (1979), 49-76 (Part II).

Haugeland, J. [1978], 'The Nature and Plausibility of Cognitivism', *The Behavioural and Brain Sciences* 2 (1978), 215-260; reprinted in Haugeland [1981].

Haugeland, J. (ed.) [1981], *Mind Design*, Bradford, Montgomery, Vermont.

Heath, A. F. (ed.) [1981], *Scientific Explanation*, Clarendon, Oxford.

Heelan, P. [1982], *Space Perception and the Philosophy of Science*, University of California Press, Berkeley.

Heelan, P. [1983], 'Natural Science as a Hermeneutic of Instrumentation', *Philosophy of Science* **50** (1983), 181-204.

Hellman, G. [1983], 'Realist Principles', *Philosophy of Science* **50** (1983), 227-49.

Hempel, C. G. [1950], 'Problems and Changes in the Empiricist Criterion of Meaning', *Revue Internationale de Philosophie* **11** (1950), 41-63 (and in Hempel [1965]).

Hempel, C. G. [1952], *Fundamentals of Concept Formation in the Empirical Sciences*, University of Chicago Press, Chicago. (Also in Neurath, et al. [1970].)

Hempel, C. G. [1958], 'The Theoretician's Dilemma' in Feigl/Maxwell [1958].

Hempel, C. G. [1965], *Aspects of Scientific Explanation*, Free Press, New York.

Hempel, C. G. [1966], *Philosophy of Natural Science*, Prentice-Hall, New York.

Hempel, C. G. [1970], 'On the 'Standard Conception' of Scientific Theory' in Radner/Winokur [1970].

Henkin, L., Suppes, P., Tarski, A. [1959], *The Axiomatic Method*, North-Holland, Amsterdam.

Hesse, M. [1963], *Models and Analogies in Science*, Sheed & Ward, London.

Hesse, M. [1965], *Forces and Fields*, Littlefield, Adams, New York.

Hesse, M. [1968a], 'A Self-Correcting Observation Language', in van Rootselaar/Staal [1968].

Hesse, M. [1968b], 'Fine's Criteria for Meaning Change', *The Journal of Philosophy* **65** (1968), 46-51.

Hesse, M. [1970], 'Is There an Independent Observation Language?', in Colodny [1970].

Hesse, M. B. [1971], 'Whewell's Consilience of Inductions and Predictions', *The Monist* **55** (1971), 520-524.

Hesse, M. [1980], 'The Hunt for Scientific Reason' in Asquith/Giere [1980/1].

Hicks, G. D. [1938], *Critical Realism*, Macmillan, London.

Hill, S. [1980], 'In Search of Self—The Social Construction of Meaning in Scientific Knowledge through the Formation of Identity as a Scientist' in Pusey/Young [1980].

Hirst, R. J. [1967], 'Realism' in Edwards [1967].

Hoffmaster, B. [1980], 'Biomedical Ethics in Canada' in Hooker/Schrecker [1980/1].

Hofstadter, D. R. [1979], *Godel, Escher, Bach: An Eternal Golden Braid*, Basic Books, New York.

Holdsworth, D. G. and Hooker, C. A. [1983], 'A Critical Survey of Quantum Logic', *Logic in the Twentieth Century, Scientia* (1983), 1-130.

Hollis, M. [1977], *Models of Man*, Cambridge University Press, Cambridge.

Hollis, M. and Lukes, S. (eds) [1982], *Rationality and Relativism*, Blackwell, Oxford.

Holt, E. B. *et al.* (eds) [1912], *The New Realism*, Macmillan, New York.

Holton, G. [1973], *Thematic Origins of Scientific Thought: Kepler to Einstein*, Harvard University Press, Cambridge, Mass.

Holton, G. [1981], 'Thematic Presuppositions and the Direction of Scientific Advance', in Heath [1981].

Hooker, C. A. [1968a], 'Craigian Transcriptionism', *American Philosophical Quarterly* **5** (1968), 152-63.

Hooker, C. A. [1968b], 'Five Arguments Against Craigian Transcriptionism', *Australasian Journal of Philosophy* **46** (1968), 265-276.

Hooker, C. A. [1970a], 'Secondary Qualities and Systematic Philosophy', Ph.D. Thesis, York University.

Hooker, C. A. [1970b], 'Definite Description and the Elimination of Singular Terms', *Journal of Philosophy* **67** (1970), 951-961.

Hooker, C. A. [1971a], 'The Referential Function of Bound Variables', *Mind* **80** (1971), 481-498.

Hooker, C. A. [1971b], 'The Relational Doctrines of Space and Time', *The British Journal for the Philosophy of Science* **22** (1971), 97-130.

Hooker, C. A. [1971c], 'Sharp and the EPR Paradox', *Philosophy of Science* **38** (1971), 224-233.

Hooker, C. A. [1972a], 'Critical Notice: Radner, M. and Winokur, S. (eds), *Analysis of Theories and Methods of Physics and Psychology*', *Canadian Journal of Philosophy* **1** (1972), 393-407.

Hooker, C. A. [1972b], 'Critical Notice: *Against Method*, P. K. Feyerabend', *Canadian Journal of Philosophy* **1** (1972), 489-509.

Hooker, C. A. [1972c], 'The Nature of Quantum Mechanical Reality: Einstein versus Bohr' in Colodny [1972].

Hooker, C. A. [1973a], 'The Non-Necessity of Qualitative Content', *Dialogue* **12** (1973), 447-453.

Hooker, C. A. (ed.) [1973b], *Contemporary Research in the Foundations and Philosophy of Quantum Theory*, Reidel, Dordrecht.

Hooker, C. A. [1973c], 'Physics and Metaphysics: A Prolegomenon for the Riddles of Quantum Theory', in Hooker [1973b].

Hooker, C. A. [1973d], 'Empiricism, Perception and Conceptual Change', *Canadian Journal of Philosophy* **3** (1973), 59-75.

Hooker, C. A. [1974a], 'Defense of a Non-Conventionalist Approach to Classical Mechanics', in Cohen/Wartofsky [1974a].

Hooker, C. A. [1974b], 'Systematic Realism', *Synthese* **26** (1974), 409-497. Reprinted herein.

Hooker, C. A. [1974c], 'The Metaphysics of Science: Atoms versus Plena', *International Logic Review* **9** (1974), 111-146.

Hooker, C. A. [1975a], 'On Global Theories', *Philosophy of Science* **42** (1975), 152-179. Reprinted herein.

Hooker, C. A. [1975b], 'Has the Scientist any Future in the Brave New World: Copernicus and Velikovsky' in Steneck [1975].

Hooker, C. A. [1975c], 'Philosophy and Meta-Philosophy of Science: Empiricism, Popperianism and Realism', *Synthese* **32** (1975), 177-231. Reprinted herein.

Hooker, C. A. [1975d], 'The Philosophical Ramifications of the Information-Processing Approach to the Brain-Mind', *Philosophy and Phenomenological Research* **36** (1975), 1-15.

Hooker, C. A. [1975e], 'Remarks on the Principle of the Identity of Indiscernibles', *The Southwestern Journal of Philosophy* **VI** (1975), 129-153.

Hooker, C. A. [1975/79], *The Logico-Algebraic Approach to Quantum Mechanics*, 2 Vols, Reidel, Dordrecht.

Hooker, C. A. [1976], 'Methodology and Systematic Philosophy' in Butts/Hintikka [1976], vol. III. Reprinted herein.

Hooker, C. A. [1977a], 'Sellars' Argument for the Inevitability of the Secondary Qualities', *Philosophical Studies* **32** (1977), 335-348.

Hooker, C. A. and van Hulst, R. [1977b], 'Institutions, Counter-Institutions and the Conceptual Framework of Energy Policy Making in Ontario', A Research Report to the Royal Commission on Electric Power Planning, Ontario.

Hooker, C. A., Leach, J. and McLennen, E. (eds) [1977c], *Foundations and Applications of Decision Theory*, 2 volumes, Reidel, Dordrecht.

Hooker, C. A. [1978a], 'An Evolutionary Naturalist Realist Doctrine of Perception and Secondary Qualities' in Savage [1978].

Hooker, C. A. [1978b], 'Critical Notice: S. Harding: *Can Theories be Refuted?*', *Metaphilosophy* **9** (1978), 58-68.

Hooker, C. A. [1978c], 'Metaphysics, Reference and Meta-Theory', a critical notice of J. W. Cornman: *Metaphysics, Reference and Language*', *Metaphilosophy* **9** (1978), 133-149.

Hooker, C. A. and van Hulst, R. [1979a], 'The Meaning of Environmental Problems for Public Political Institutions' in Leiss [1979].

Hooker, C. A. [1979b], 'Critical Notice: *Reduction in the Physical Sciences, Yoshida*', *Dialogue* **XVIII** No. 1 (1979), 81-99.

Hooker, C. A. [1979c], 'Explanation and Culture', *Humanities in Society* 7 (No. 3, 1979), 223-244.

Hooker, C. A. [1979d], *Physical Theory as Logico-Operational Structure*, Reidel, Dordrecht, 1979.

Hooker, C. A., McDonald, R. M., van Hulst, R. and Victor, P. [1980a], *Energy and the Quality of Life*, University of Toronto Press, Toronto.

Hooker, C. A. and van Hulst, R. [1980b], 'Institutionalising a High Quality Conserver Society', *Alternatives* (Journal of Friends of the Earth, Canada) 9 (Winter 1980).

Hooker, C. A. [1980c], 'Explanation, Generality and Understanding', *Australasian Journal of Philosophy* **58** (1980), 284-290.

Hooker, C. A. [1980d], 'Science as a Human Activity, Human Activity as a . . .', *Contact* **12** (1980), 1-29.

Hooker, C. A. and Schrecker, T. (eds) [1980/1], *The Human Context for Science and Technology*, 2 vols., Social Science and Humanities Research Council, Ottawa.

Hooker, C. A. [1981a], 'Critical Notice: G. C. Nerlich: *The Shape of Space*', *Dialogue* **XX** (1981), 783-98.

Hooker, C. A. [1981b], 'Formalist Rationality: The Limitations of Popper's Theory of Reason', *Metaphilosophy* **12** (1981), 247-266.

Hooker, C. A. [1981c], 'Towards a General Theory of Reduction, Part I, Historical Framework', *Dialogue* **XX** (1981), 38-59.

Hooker, C. A. [1981d], 'Towards a General Theory of Reduction, Part II, Identity and Reduction', *Dialogue* **XX** (1981), 201-36.

Hooker, C. A. [1981e], 'Towards a General Theory of Reduction, Part III, Cross-Categorial Reduction', Dialogue **XX** (1981), 496-529.

Hooker, C. A. [1982a], 'Understanding and Control', *Man-Environment Systems* 12 (No. 4, 1982), 121-160. Reprinted herein.

Hooker, C. A. [1982b], 'Scientific Neutrality vs. Normative Learning: The Theoretician's and the Politician's Dilemma' in Oldroyd [1982].

Hooker, C. A. [1983], 'The Future Must be a Fantasy' in Chapman [1983].

Hooker, C. A. [1984a], Can Egalitarianism be Built into Rationality Theory?' (A Critical Review of Michalos, A. C.: *Foundations of Decision Making*), *Theory and Decision* 16 (1984).

Hooker, C. A. [1985], 'Surface Dazzle, Ghostly Depths', in Churchland/ Hooker [1985a]. Also reprinted herein.

Horwich, P. [1982a], 'Three Forms of Realism', *Synthese* 51 (1982), 181-201.

Horwich, P. [1982b], *Probability and Evidence*, Cambridge University Press, Cambridge, 1982.

Hospers, J. [1967], *An Introduction to Philosophical Analysis*, Englewood Cliffs, Prentice-Hall, New Jersey.

Howard, N. [1971], *Paradoxes of Rationality*, MIT Press, Boston.

Howson, C. (ed.) [1976], *Method and Appraisal in the Physical Sciences*, Cambridge University Press, Cambridge.

Hubner, K. [1978], *Kritik der wissenschaftlichen Vernunft*, Karl Alber, Freiburg/ Munchen. (Translated by Dixon, P. R. and H. M. and published as *Critique of Scientific Reason*, The University of Chicago Press, Chicago, 1983.)

Hull, R. T. [1972], 'Feyerabend's Attack on Observation Sentences', *Synthese* 23 (1972), 374-399.

Huxley, A. [1958], *The Perennial Philosophy*, Fontana, London.

Iberall, A. S. [1972], *Toward a General Science of Viable Systems*, McGraw-Hill, New York.

Ihde, D. [1979], *Technics and Praxis*, Reidel, Dordrecht.

Illich, I. [1973], *Tools for Conviviality*, Harper and Rowe, New York.

Jackson, R. [1979], *Science Policy and Human Goals*, Science Council of Canada Background Study, Queen's Printer, Ottawa.

Jammer, M. [1966], *The Conceptual Development of Quantum Mechanics*, McGraw-Hill, New York.

Jammer, M. [1974], *The Philosophy of Quantum Mechanics*, Wiley, New York.

Jantsch, E. [1975], *Design for Evolution*, George Brazilla, New York, 1975.

Jantsch, E. and Waddington, C. H. [1976], *Evolution and Consciousness: Human Systems in Transition*, Addison-Wesley, London.

Jantsch, E. [1980], *The Self-Organizing Universe*, Pergamon Press, New York.

Jantsch, E. (ed.) [1981], *The Evolutionary Vision: Toward a Unifying Paradigm of Physical, Biological and Sociocultural Evolution*, Westview Press, Boulder, Colorado.

Jaynes, J. [1976], *The Origins of Consciousness in the Breakdown of the Bicameral Mind*, Houghton Mifflin, Boston.

Jeffrey, R. C. [1965], *The Logic of Decision*, McGraw Hill, New York.

Jeffrey, R. C. [1975], 'Probability and Falsification: Critique of the Popper Program', *Synthese* 30 (1975), 95-118.

Joergenson, J. [1951], *The Development of Logical Empiricism*, University of Chicago Press, Chicago, 1951. (Also in Neurath, et al. [1970].)

Johnston, R. [1976], 'Contextual Knowledge: A Model for the Overthrow of the Internal/External Dichotomy in Science', *Australian & New Zealand Journal of Sociology* 1 (1976), 193-203.

Johnston, R. and Jagtenberg, T. [1978], 'Goal Direction of Scientific Research' in Krohn et al. [1978].

Kitcher, P. S. [1976], 'Explanation, Conjunction, and Unification', *The Journal of Philosophy*, LXXIII (1976), 207-212.

Kitcher, P. S. [1981], 'Explanatory Unification', *Philosophy of Science* **48** (1981), 507-531.

Kneale, W. and M. [1962], *The Development of Logic*, Clarendon Press, Oxford.

Knorr, K. D., Krohn, R., Whitley, R. (eds) [1980], *The Social Process of Scientific Investigation*, Reidel, Dordrecht.

Knorr, K. D., Strasser, H., Zillian, H. G. (eds) [1975], *Determinants and Controls of Scientific Development*, Reidel, Dordrecht.

Koestler, A. [1978], *Janus: A Summing Up*, Hutchinson, London (Pan, 1979).

Kohlberg, L. [1971], 'From Is to Ought: How to Commit the Naturalistic Fallacy and Get Away With It in the Study of Moral Development', in Mischel [1971].

Kohlberg, L. [1973a], 'The Claim to Moral Adequacy of a Highest Stage of Moral Development', *Journal of Philosophy* **70** (1973), 634-5.

Kohlberg, L. [1973b], *Collected Papers on Moral Development and Moral Education*, Harvard University Press, Cambridge, Mass.

Kohler, I. [1962], 'Experiments with Goggles', *Scientific American*, May, 1962.

Korner, S. [1962a], 'On Philosophical Arguments in Physics', in Korner [1962b].

Korner, S. (ed) [1962b], *Observation and Interpretation in the Philosophy of Physics*, Dover, New York.

Koyre, A. [1957], *From the Closed World to the Infinite Universe*, Johns Hopkins Press, Baltimore.

Koyre, A. [1968], *Metaphysics and Measurements*, Chapman Hall, London.

Krige, J. [1980], *Science, Revolution and Discontinuity*, Harvester Press, Brighton, Sussex.

Krishnamurti, J. [1972], *The First and Last Freedom*, Gollancz, London.

Krishnamurti, J. [1973], *The Impossible Question*, Gollancz, London.

Krohn, W., Layton, E. T. Jr., Weingart, P. (eds), [1978] *The Dynamics of Science and Technology*, Reidel, Dordrecht.

Kuhn, T. S. [1962], *The Structure of Scientific Revolutions*, University of Chicago Press, Chicago. (Also in Neurath, et al. [1970].)

Laird, J. [1920], *A Study in Realism*, Books for Libraries Press, Freeport, New York.

Lakatos, I. (ed.) [1968a], *The Problem of Inductive Logic*, North-Holland, Amsterdam.

Lakatos, I [1968b], 'Changes in the Problems of Inductive Logic' in Lakatos [1968a].

Lakatos, I. and Musgrave, A. (eds.) [1970a] *Criticism and the Growth of Knowledge*, Cambridge University Press, Cambridge.

Lakatos, I. [1970b], 'Falsification and the Methodology of Scientific Research Programmes' in Lakatos/Musgrave [1970b].

Laudan, L. [1971], 'William Whewell on the Conciliance of Inductions', *The Monist* **55** (1971), 368-391.

Laudan, L. [1977], *Progress and its Problems*, University of California Press, Berkeley.

Laudan, L. [1981a], *Science and Hypothesis*, Reidel, Dordrecht.

Laudan, L. [1981b], 'A Confutation of Convergent Realism', *Philosophy of Science* **48** (1981), 19-48.

Laudan, L. [1984a], 'Explaining the Success of Science: Beyond Epistemic Realism and Relativism', in Cushing [1984b].

Laudan, L. [1984b], *Science and Value*, University of California Press, Berkeley.

Laymon, R. [1982], 'The Path from Data to Theory', in Asquith/Nickles [1982/3] and in Leplin [1984a].

Leach, J. J. [1968], 'Explanation and Value Neutrality', *British Journal for the Philosophy of Science* **19** (1968), 93-108.

Leach, J. J. [1976], 'The Dual Function of Rationality' in Butts/Hintikka [1976], Vol. 2.

Leeds, S. [1978], 'Theories of Reference and Truth', *Erkenntnis* **13** (1978), 111-29.

Lehrer, K. (ed.) [1975], *Analysis and Metaphysics*, Reidel, Dordrecht.

Leiss, W. (ed) [1979], *Ecology versus Politics in Canada*, University of Toronto Press, Toronto.

Lenin, V. [1927], *Materialism and Empirio-Criticism*, London and vol. XIV, *Collected Works*, Moscow.

Lenneberg, E. H. [1967], *Biological Foundations of Language*, Wiley, New York.

Leplin, J. (ed.) [1984a], *Scientific Realism*, University of California Press, Berkeley.

Leplin, J. [1984b], 'Truth and Scientific Progress', in Leplin [1984a].

Levi, I. [1967], *Gambling with Truth*, A. A. Knopf, New York.

Levi, I. [1979], 'Inductive Appraisal' in Asquith/Kyburg [1979].

Levi, I. [1980], *The Enterprise of Knowledge*, MIT Press, Cambridge, Mass.

Levin, M. [1980], 'What Kind of Explanation is Truth?' in Leplin [1984a].

Lewis, C. I. [1956], *Mind and the World Order*, Dover, New York.

Lewis, C. S. [1962], *The Great Divorce*, Bles, London.

Lewis, D. [1970], 'How to Define Theoretical Terms', *The Journal of Philosophy* **67** (1970), 427-445.

Lewontin, R. C. [1961], 'Evolution and the Theory of Games', *Journal of Theoretical Biology* **1** (1961), 382-403.

Lilley, J. [1972], *The Center of the Cyclone*, Julian Press, New York.

Lilley, J. [1974], *Programming and Meta-Programming in the Human Bio-Computer*, Julian Pres, New York.

Lilley, J. [1977], *The Dyadic Cyclone*, Pocket Books, New York.

Lindblom, P. (ed.) [1970], *Theory and Methods in the Behavioural Sciences*, Laromedelsforl, Stockholm.

Livingstone, D. W. and Mason, R. V. [1978], 'Ecological Crisis and the Autonomy of Science in Capitalist Society: A Canadian Case-Study', *Alternatives* **8** (1978), 3-10.

Lorenz, K. [1976], *Die Ruckseite des Spiegels*, Pieper, Munchen. (Transl. by R. Taylor and published as *Behind the Mirror: A Search for a Natural History of Human Knowledge*, Methuen, London, 1977.)

Lovell, B. [1939], *Science and Civilisation*, Thomas Nelson, London.

Luckenbach, S. [1972], *Probabilities, Problems and Paradoxes*, Dickenson, California.

Mace, C. A. (ed.) [1957], *British Philosophy in the Mid-Century*, George Allen and Unwin, London.

Mach, E. [1959], *Analyses of Sensations and the Relation of the Physical to the*

Psychical, Dover, New York.

Mach, E. [1960], *The Science of Mechanics* (Translated by T. J. McCormack, 6th ed.), Open Court, LaSalle, Ill.

MacIntyre, A. [1984], *After Virtue*, 2nd ed., University of Notre Dame Press, Notre Dame.

Macpherson, C. B. [1970], *The Political Theory of Possessive Individualism*, Oxford University Press, Oxford.

Macpherson, C. B. [1973], *Democratic Theory*, Clarendon Press, Oxford.

Malament, D. [1977], 'Causal Theories of Time and the Conventionality of Simultaneity', *Nous* 11 (1977), 293-300.

Malik, R. (ed.) [1980], *Future Imperfect: Science Fact and Science Fiction*, Pinter, London.

Man, S.-W. [1983], 'Unification and Confirmability: The Search for an Understanding of the Goals of Science', Ph.D. thesis, University of Western Ontario.

Manders, K. [1982], 'On the Space-Time Ontology of Physical Theories', *Philosophy of Science* 49 (1982), 575-590.

Mannheim, K. [1936], *Ideology and Utopia*, Harcourt Brace and World, New York.

Mannison, D., McRobbie, M. and Routley, R. (eds) [1980], *Environmental Philosophy*, Australian National University, Canberra.

Marchi, E. and Hansell, R. C. [1973], 'A Framework for Systematic Zoological Studies with Game Theory', *Mathematical Biosciences* 16 (1973), 31-58.

Margenau, H. [1950], *The Nature of Physical Reality*, New York, McGraw-Hill, 1950.

Marr, D. [1982], *Vision*, Freeman, San Francisco.

Marras, A. [1973a], 'On Sellars' Linguistic Theory of Conceptual Activity', *Canadian Journal of Philosophy* 2 (1973), 471-484.

Marras, A. [1973b], 'Conceptual Activity, Rules and Linguistic Actions: A Rejoinder to Wilfred Sellars', *Canadian Journal of Philosophy* 2 (1973), 495-501.

Martin, B. [1979], *The Bias of Science*, Society for Social Responsibility in Science, Canberra.

Martin, B. [1984], *Uprooting War*, Freedom Press, London.

Masters, R. D. [1970], 'Genes, Language and Evolution', *Semiotica* 2 (1970), 295-320.

Maturana, J. R. and Varela, F. [1980], *Autopoiesis and Cognition: The Realization of the Living*, Reidel, Dordrecht.

Maxwell, G. [1962], 'The Ontological Status of Theoretical Entities', in Feigl/Maxwell [1962].

Maxwell, G. [1970], 'Structural Realism and the Meaning of Theoretical Terms', in Radner/Winokur [1970].

Maxwell, G. [1973], 'Corroboration Without Demarcation', in Schilpp [1973].

Maxwell, N. [1974], 'The Rationality of Scientific Discovery', *Philosophy of Science* 41 (1974), 123-153 (part I), 247-295 (part II).

Maxwell, N. [1976], *What's Wrong with Science?: Towards a People's Science of Delight and Compassion*, Bran's Head Books, London.

McCosh, J. [1887], *Realistic Philosophy*, 2 vols., Macmillan, London.

McLaughlin, R. (ed.) [1980a], *What?, Where?, When?, Why?: Essays on Induction, Space and Time, Explanation*, Reidel, Dordrecht.

McLaughlin, R. [1980b], 'Invention and Appraisal' in McLaughlin [1980a].

McMullin, E. [1968], 'What Do Physical Models Tell Us?' in van Rootselaar/Staal [1968].

McMullin, E. [1984], 'A Case for Scientific Realism', in Leplin [1984a].

Melchert, N. [1985], 'Why Constructive Empiricism Collapses into Scientific Realism', *Australasian Journal of Philosophy* 63 (1985), 213-215.

Merton, R. K. [1972], 'The Institutional Imperatives of Science' in Barnes [1972].

Merton, R. K. [1973], *The Sociology of Science*, University of Chicago Press, Chicago.

Michalos, A. [1978], *Foundations of Decision Making*, Canadian Library of Philosophy, Ottawa.

Miller, D. [1974], 'Popper's Qualitative Theory of Verisimilitude', *British Journal for the Philosophy of Science* 25 (1974), 166-177.

Miller, D. [1975], 'The Accuracy of Predictions', *Synthese* 30 (1975), 139-148.

Miller, G., Gallanter, E., Pibram, K. [1960], *Plans and the Structure of Behavior*, Holt Reinhardt and Winston, New York.

Mischel, T. (ed.) [1971], *Cognitive Development and Epistemology*, Academic Press, New York.

Mitroff, I. I. [1974], *The Subjective Side of Science*, Elsevier, Amsterdam.

Morick, H. [1972], *Challenges to Empiricism*, Wadsworth, Belmont, Cal.

Morowitz, H. J. [1968], *Energy Flow in Biology: Biological Organization as a Problem in Thermal Physics.*, Academic Press, New York.

Moyall, A. [1980], 'The Australian Academy of Science: The Anatomy of a Scientific Elite', *Search* II (1980), 231-238 (Part I), 281-287 (Part II).

Muirhead, J. H. (ed.) [1924], *Contemporary British Philosophy*, George Allen and Unwin, London.

Mulkay, M. [1979], *Science and the Sociology of Knowledge*, Allen and Unwin, London.

Mundy, B. [1983], 'Relational Theories of Euclidean Space and Minkowski Spacetime', *Philosophy of Science* 50 (1983), 205-226.

Munevar, G. [1981], *Radical Knowledge*, Hackett, Indianapolis.

Musgrave, A. [1980], 'Kuhn's Second Thoughts', in Gutting [1980].

Musgrave, A. [1985], 'Realism versus Constructive Empiricism' in Churchland/Hooker [1985a].

Nagel, E. [1961], *The Structure of Science*, Routledge and Kegan Paul, London.

Nagel, E., Suppes, P. and Tarski, A. (eds) [1962], *Logic, Methodology and Philosophy of Science*, Stanford University Press, Stanford, California.

Nagel, T. [1971], 'Brain Bisection and the Unity of Consciousness', *Synthese* 22 (1971), 396-413.

Naor, D. [1979], 'A Viable System Model of Scientific Rationality', unpublished manuscript, The University of Western Ontario, Canada.

Nash, L. K. [1963], *The Nature of the Natural Sciences*, Little, Brown, Boston.

Nerlich, G. [1976], *The Shape of Space*, Cambridge University Press, Cambridge.

Nerlich, G. [1982], 'Special Relativity is Not Based on Causality', *British Jour-*

nal for the Philosophy of Science **33** (1982), 361-388.

Neurath, O. [1931], 'Soziologie im Physikalismus', *Erkenntnis* **2** (1931), 393-431.

Neurath, O. [1932], 'Protokollsatz', *Erkenntnis* **3** (1932), 204-214.

Neurath, O. [1952], *Foundations of the Social Sciences*, University of Chicago Press, Chicago. (Also in Neurath [1970].)

Neurath, O., Carnap, R., and Morriss, C. (eds.) [1970], *Foundations of the Unity of Science*, 2 vols, University of Chicago Press, Chicago.

Newton-Smith, W. H. [1981], *The Rationality of Science*, Routledge and Kegan Paul, London.

Nicholas, J. M. [1982], 'Puzzles, Anomalies and Scientific Crises', unpublished draft, University of Western Ontario, Canada.

Nicholas, J. M. [1984], 'Scientific and Other Interests' in Brown [1984].

Nickels, T. [1980a], *Scientific Discovery, Logic, and Rationality*, Reidel, Dordrecht.

Nickels, T. [1980b], *Scientific Discovery: Case Studies*, Reidel, Dordrecht.

Nicolis, G. and Prigogine, I. [1977], *Self-Organization in Non-Equilibrium Systems*, Wiley, New York.

Niiniluoto, I. [1978], 'Truthlikeness: Comments on recent discussion', *Synthese* **38** (1978), 281-329.

Niiniluoto, I. [1984], *Is Science Progressive?*, Reidel, Dordrecht.

Novack, G. [1971], *Empiricism and its Evolution*, Pathfinder Press, New York.

Odum, H. T. [1971], *Environment, Power and Society*, Wiley-Interscience, New York.

O'Hear, A. [1980], *Karl Popper*, Routledge and Kegan Paul, London.

Okruhlik, K. [1984], 'Review of Putnam: *Reason, Truth and History*', *Philosophy of Science*, **51** (1984), 692-4.

Oldroyd, D. (ed.) [1982], *Science and Ethics*, N. S. W. University Press, Kensington.

Pandit, G. L. [1983], *The Structure and Growth of Scientific Knowledge*, Reidel, Dordrecht.

Pap, A. [1963a], 'Does Science have Metaphysical Presuppositions?', in Feigl/Brodbeck [1963].

Pap, A. [1963b], *An Introduction to the Philosophy of Science*, Eyre and Spottiswoode, London.

Pattee, H. H. [1973], *Hierarchy Theory: The Challenge of Complex Systems*, Geo. Brazilier, New York.

Pattee, H. H. [1981], 'Symbol-Structure Complementarity in Biological Evolution' in Jantsch [1981].

Pearce, D. and Rantela, V. [1982a], 'Realism and Formal Semantics', *Synthese* **52** (1982), 39-53.

Pearce, D. and Rantela, V. [1982b], 'Realism and Reference', *Synthese* **52** (1982), 439-448.

Peirce, C. S. [1931-58], *Collected Papers, Vols. 1-8*, Cambridge, Mass.

Piaget, J. [1948], *The Moral Judgement of the Child*, The Free Press, Glencoe, Ill.

Piaget, J. [1951], *Language and Thought in the Child*, Humanities Press, New York.

Piaget, J. [1954], *The Construction of Reality in the Child*, Basic Books, New York.

Piaget, J. [1970], *Genetic Epistemology* (translated by E. Drakworth), Columbia, New York.

Piaget, J. [1971a], *Biology and Knowledge* (translated by B. Walsh), University of Chicago Press, Chicago.

Piaget, J. [1971b], *Insights and Illusions of Philosophy*, Meridian Books, New York.

Pitowsky, I. [1983], 'The Logic of Fundamental Processes: Non-Measurable Sets and Quantum Mechanics', Ph.D. Thesis, University of Western Ontario, Canada.

Platts, M. (ed.) [1980], *Reference, Truth and Reality: Essays on the Philosophy of Language*, Routledge and Kegan Paul, London.

Polanyi, M. [1964], *Personal Knowledge: Towards a Post-Critical Philosophy*, Harper & Rowe, Harper Torchbooks, New York.

Polanyi, M. [1967], *The Tacit Dimension*, Doubleday Anchor, New York.

Polanyi, K. [1968], *The Great Transformation*, Beacon Press, Boston.

Polikarov, A. [1983] *Methodological Problems of Science*, Publishing House of the Bulgarian Academy of Sciences, Sofia.

Popper, K. R. [1934], *Logik der Forschung*, Wien, (translated as *The Logic of Scientific Discovery*, Hutchinson, London, 1962).

Popper, K. R. [1957], 'Philosophy of Science: A Personal Report', in Mace [1957].

Popper, K. R. [1963a], *Conjectures and Refutations* Routledge and Kegan Paul, London.

Popper, K. R. [1963b], *The Open Society and Its Enemies*, 2 vols, Routledge and Kegan Paul, London.

Popper, K. R. [1973], *Objective Knowledge*, Oxford University Press, Oxford.

Popper, K. R. and Eccles, Sir J. [1977], *The Self and Its Brain*, Springer-Verlag, New York.

Pratt, J. B. [1940], *Naturalism*, Harvard, Yale University Press.

Pribram, K. [1971], *The Language of the Brain*, Prentice-Hall, Englewood Cliffs, N.J.

Prigogine, I. [1980], *From Being to Becoming*, W. H. Freeman, San Francisco.

Prigogine, I. and Stengers, I. [1984], *Order out of Chaos*, Shambhala, Boulder, Colorado.

Pusey, M. and Young, R. [1980], *Knowledge and Control*, Australian National University Press, Canberra.

Putnam, H. [1962a], 'The Analytic and the Synthetic', in Feigl/Maxwell [1962]; also in Putnam [1975b].

Putnam, H. [1962b], 'What Theories are Not', in Nagel et al. [1962]; also in Putnam [1975a].

Putnam, H. [1965], 'How Not to Talk About Meanings' in Cohen/Wartofsky [1965]; also in Putnam [1975b].

Putnam, H. [1975a], *Mathematics, Matter and Method: Philosophical Papers, vol. I*, Cambridge University Press, Cambridge.

Putnam, H. [1975b], *Mind, Language and Reality: Philosophical Papers, vol. II*, Cambridge University Press, Cambridge.

Putnam, H. [1978], *Meaning and the Moral Sciences*, Routledge and Kegan Paul, London.

Putnam, H. [1980], 'Models and Reality', *Journal of Symbolic Logic* **45** (1980), 464-482.

Putnam, H. [1981a], *Reason, Truth and History*, Cambridge University Press, Cambridge, Mass.

Putnam, H. [1981b], 'Philosophers and Human Understanding' in Heath [1981].

Putnam, H. [1982a], 'Three Kinds of Scientific Realism', *Philosophical Quarterly* **32** (1982), 195-200.

Putnam, H. [1982b], 'Why Reason Can't be Naturalised', *Synthese* **52** (1982), 3-23.

Putnam, H. [1984], 'What is Realism?' in Leplin [1984a].

Quine, W. V. O. [1951a], 'On Carnap's Views of Ontology', *Philosophical Studies* **2** (1951), reprinted in Quine [1966].

Quine, W. V. O. [1951b], 'Two Dogmas of Empiricism', *The Philosophical Review* **60** (1951), reprinted in Quine [1963].

Quine, W. V. O. [1960], *Word and Object*, The M.I.T. Press, Cambridge, Mass.

Quine, W. V. O. [1963], *From a Logical Point of View*, Harper & Rowe, New York.

Quine, W. V. O. [1966], *The Ways of Paradox*, Random House, New York.

Quine, W. V. O. [1969a], 'Epistemology Naturalised' in Quine [1969b].

Quine, W. V. O.]1969b], *Ontological Relativity and Other Essays*, Columbia University Press, New York.

Quine, W. V. O. and Ullian, J. A. [1970], *The Web of Belief*, Randon House, New York.

Radner, M. and Winokur, S. (eds) [1970], *Minnesota Studies in the Philosophy of Science*, Vol. IV, University of Minnesota Press, Minneapolis.

Radnitzky, G. [1970], *Contemporary Schools of Meta-Science*, 2 vols. (bound together), Berlingska Boktryckeriet, Akademiforlaget Goteborg.

Radnitsky, G. [1971], 'From Logic of Science to Theory of Research', *Communication and Cognition* **1** (1971), 61-124.

Raiffa, H. [1970], *Decision Analysis*, Addison-Wesley, New York.

Ramsey, F. P. [1931], *The Foundations of Mathematics*, Routledge and Kegan Paul, London.

Rapoport, A. [1970], *Fights, Games and Debates*, University of Michigan Press, Ann Arbor.

Ravetz, J. R. [1971], *Scientific Knowledge and Its Social Problems*, Clarendon Press, Oxford.

Reichenbach, H. [1938], *Experience and Prediction*, University of Chicago Press, Chicago.

Reichenbach, H. [1958], *The Rise of Scientific Philosophy*, University of California Press, Berkeley.

Reichenbach, H. [1965], *The Theory of Relativity and A Priori Knowledge* (transl. by M. Reichenbach), University of California Press, Los Angeles.

Rescher, N. (ed.) [1963], *Scientific Explanation and Understanding*, University Press of America, Lanham, Md.

Rescher, N. [1973], *Conceptual Idealism*, Blackwell, Oxford.

Rescher, N. [1978], *Scientific Progress: A Philosophical Essay on the Economics of Research*, Blackwells, London.

Rieber, R. W. (ed.) [1983], *Dialogues on the Psychology of Language and Thought*, Plenum, New York.

Rieff, P. [1966], *The Triumph of the Therapeutic*, Harper & Rowe, New York.

Robertson, J. [1978], *The Sane Alternative: Signposts to a Self-Fulfilling Future*, James Robertson, London.

Rogers, C. [1961], *On Becoming a Person*, Houghton-Mifflin, Boston.

Rogers, C. [1969], *Freedom to Learn*, Merrill, Columbus, Ohio.

Rogers, C. [1978], *On Personal Power*, Constable, London.

Rohrlich, F. and Hardin, L. [1983], 'Established Theories', *Philosophy of Science* **50** (1983), 603-617.

Rokeach, M. [1960], *The Open and Closed Mind*, Basic Books, New York.

Rorty, R. [1972], 'The World Well Lost', *The Journal of Philosophy* **69** (1972), 649-65.

Rorty, R. [1979], *Philosophy and the Mirror of Nature*, Princeton University Press, Princeton, N. J.

Rorty, R. [1982], *Consequences of Pragmatism*, University of Minnesota Press, Minneapolis.

Rose, H. and Rose, S. [1969], *Science and Society*, Penguin, Harmondsworth.

Rosenkrantz, R. D. [1977], *Inference, Method and Decision: Towards a Bayesian Philosophy of Science*, Reidel, Dordrecht.

Roszak, T. [1973], *Where the Wasteland Ends*, Anchor Doubleday, New York.

Routley, R. and V. [1980], 'Human Chauvinism and Environmental Ethics' in Mannison et al. [1980].

Ruben, D.-H. [1979], *Marxism and Materialism: A Study of Marxist Theory of Knowledge*, 2nd ed., Harvester Press, Hassocks.

Rubinstein, R. A., Laughlin, C. D. jr. and McManus, J. (eds) [1984], *Science as a Cognitive Process*, University of Pennsylvania Press, Philadelphia.

Rudner, R. [1953], 'The Scientist Qua Scientist Makes Value Judgements', *Philosophy of Science* **23** (1953).

Rudner, R. [1961], 'An Introduction to Simplicity', *Philosophy of Science* **28** (1961), 109-119.

Rudner, R. [1966], *Philosophy of Social Science*, Prentice-Hall, Englewood Cliffs, New Jersey.

Runes, D. D. (ed.) [1943], *Twentieth Century Philosophy*, Philosophical Library, New York.

Ruse, M. [1979], *Sociobiology: Sense or Nonsense*, Reidel, Dordrecht, 1979.

Ruse, M. [1982], *Darwinism Defended: A Guide to Evolutionary Controversies*, Addison-Wesley, New York.

Russell, B. [1924a], 'Logical Atomism' in Muirhead [1924].

Russell, B. [1924b], *Icarus, or the Future of Science*, Kegan Paul, Trench, Trubner and Co., London.

Russell, B. [1927], *The Analysis of Matter*, Allen & Unwin, London.

Russell, B. [1948], *Human Knowledge: Its Scope and Limits*, Simon & Schuster, New York.

Sahlins, M. [1976], *The Use and Abuse of Biology*, University of Michigan Press, Ann Arbor.

Salmon, W. C. (ed.) [1971], *Statistical Explanation and Statistical Relevance*, Pittsburgh University Press, Pittsburgh.

Salmon, W. C. [1980], 'Further Reflections', in McLaughlin [1980].

Salmon, W. C. [1984], *Scientific Explanation and the Causal Structure of the World*, Princeton University Press, Princeton, N. J.

Savage, C. W. (ed.) [1978], *Perception and Cognition: Issues in the Foundations of Psychology*, Minnesota Studies in the Philosophy of Science, Vol. IX, University of Minnesota Press, Minneapolis.

Schaffner, K. F. [1970], 'Outlines of a Logic of Comparative Theory Evaluation with Special Attention to Pre- and Post-Relativistic Electrodynamics', in Stuewer [1970].

Schaffner, K. F. and Cohen, R. S. (eds) [1974], *PSA 1972*, Reidel, Dordrecht.

Schick, K. [1972], 'Indeterminacy of Translation', *Journal of Philosophy* **69** (1972), 818-832.

Schilpp, P. A. (ed.) [1963], *The Philosophy of Rudolf Carnap*, Open Court Publishing Co., LaSalle, Ill.

Schilpp, P. A. (ed.) [1973], *The Philosophy of Karl Popper*, Open Court Publishing Co., LaSalle, Ill.

Schlick, M. [1932], 'Positivismus und Realismus', *Erkenntnis* **3** (1932), 1-31.

Schlick, M. [1949], *Philosophy of Nature*, Philosophical Library, New York.

Schumacher, E. F. [1975], *Small is Beautiful*, Sphere Books, London.

Schumacher, E. F. [1977], *A Guide for the Perplexed*, Harper and Rowe, New York.

Sebeok, T. A. [1972], *Perspectives in Zoosemiotics*, Mouton, The Hague.

Segundo, J. L. [1974], *Evolution and Guilt*, Aubis, Maryknoll, New York.

Sellars, R. W. [1916], *Critical Realism*, Rand McNally.

Sellars, R. W. [1922], *Evolutionary Naturalism*, Open Court, Chicago.

Sellars, R. W. [1932], *The Philosophy of Physical Realism*, Macmillan, New York.

Sellars, W. [1961], 'The Language of Theories' in Feigl/Maxwell [1961].

Sellars, W. [1963], *Science, Perception and Reality*, Routledge & Kegan Paul, London.

Sellars, W. [1965a], 'Scientific Realism or Irenic Instrumentalism', in Cohen/Wartofsky [1965].

Sellars, W. [1965b], 'The Identity Approach to the Mind Body Problem', in Cohen/Wartofsky [1965].

Sellars, W. [1968], *Science and Metaphysics*, Routledge and Kegan Paul, London.

Sellars, W. [1973], 'Reply to Marras', *Canadian Journal of Philosophy* **2** (1973), 485-494.

Sellars, W. [1981], 'Foundations for a Metaphysics of Pure Process: Lecture I, The Lever of Archimedes', *The Monist* **64** (1981), 3-36.

Sen, D. K. [1968], *Fields and/or Particles*, Academic Press, New York.

Shapere, D. [1963], 'Space, Time and Language – An Examination of Some Problems and Methods of the Philosophy of Science', in Baumrin [1963].

Shapere, D. [1964], 'The Structure of Scientific Revolutions', *Philosophical Review* **73** (1964), 383-394.

Shapere, D. [1966], 'Meaning and Scientific Change', in Colodny [1966].

Shapere, D. [1974], 'Scientific Theories and Their Domains' in Suppe [1974a].

Shapere, D. [1984], *Reason and the Search for Knowledge*, Reidel, Dordrecht.

Shimony, A. [1971] 'Perception from an Evolutionary Point of View', *Journal of Philosophy* **68** (1971), 571-583.

Shimony, A. [1977] 'Is Observation Theory Laden? A Problem in Naturalistic Epistemology', in Colodny [1977].

Shimony, A. [1981] 'Integral Epistemology' in Brewer/Collins [1981].

Singer, P. [1981], *The Expanding Circle: Ethics and Sociobiology*, Clarendon, Oxford.

Sklair, L. [1973], *Organized Knowledge*, Paladin, London.

Sklar, L. [1982], 'Saving the Noumena', *Philosophical Topics* **13** (1982), 89-110.

Skolimowski, H. and Freeman, E. [1973], 'The Search for Objectivity in Peirce and Popper' in Schilpp [1973].

Skyrms, B. [1980], *Causal Necessity: A Pragmatic Investigation of the Necessity of Laws*, Yale University Press, New Haven.

Smart, J. J. C. [1963], *Philosophy and Scientific Realism*, Routledge and Kegan Paul, London.

Smart, J. J. C. [1968], *Between Science and Philosophy*, Random House, New York.

Smith, F. and Miller, G. [1966], *The Genesis of Language*, M.I.T. Press, Cambridge, Mass.

Smith, P. [1981], *Realism and the Progress of Science*, Cambridge University Press, Cambridge.

Sneed, J. D. [1971], *The Logical Structure of Mathematical Physics*, Humanities Press, New York.

Snyder, P. [1978], *Towards One Science: The Convergence of Traditions*, St Martin's Press, New York.

Solso, R. L. [1974], *Theories in Cognitive Psychology*, L. Erlbaum Assoc., Potomac, Maryland.

Solso, R. L. [1975], *Information Processing and Cognition*, L. Erlbaum Assoc., Potomac, Maryland.

Sorabji, R. [1983], *Time, Creation and the Continuum*, Duckworth, London.

Spaulding, E. G. [1936], *A World of Chance*, Macmillan, New York.

Spiegel-Rosing, I. and deSolla Price, D. (eds) [1978], *Science, Technology and Society: A Cross-Disciplinary Perspective*, Sage, London.

Stabler, E. P. [1983], 'Naturalised Epistemology and Metaphysical Realism', *Philosophical Topics* **13** (1983), 155-170.

Stabler, E. P. [1984], 'Rationality in Naturalised Epistemology', *Philosophy of Science* **51** (1984), 64-78.

Stachel, J. [1973], 'A Note on the Concept of Scientific Practice' in Cohen et al. [1974b].

Stalnaker, R. [1984], *Inquiry*, MIT Press, Cambridge, Mass.

Stegmuller, W. [1979], *The Structuralist View of Theories*, Springer-Verlag, New York.

Steneck, N. H. (ed.) [1975], *Science and Society*, Univ. of Michigan Press, Ann Arbor.

Stent, G. S. [1978], *Paradoxes of Progress*, Freeman, San Francisco.

Stephens, J. and Russow, L.-M. [1985], 'Brains in Vats and the Internalist Perspective', *Australasian Journal of Philosophy* **63** (1985), 205-12.

Stigun, B. P. and Wenstof, F. (eds) [1982], *Foundations of Utility and Risk Theory with Applications*, Reidel, Dordrecht.

Stoll, R. [1963], *Set Theory and Logic*, Freeman, London.

Stove, D. C. [1973], *Probability and Hume's Inductive Scepticism*, Oxford University Press, Oxford.

Stove, D. C. [1982], *Popper and After: Four Modern Irrationalists*, Pergamon Press, Oxford.

Strong, T. B. (ed.) [1906], *Lectures on the Method of Science*, Clarendon, Oxford.

Stroud, B. [1981], 'The Significance of Naturalised Epistemology', *Midwest Studies in Philosophy* 6 (1981), 455-471.

Stuewer, R. H. (ed.) [1970] *Historical and Philosophical Perspectives of Science*, Minnesota Studies in the Philosophy of Science, Vol. V, University of Minnesota Press, Minneapolis.

Suchting, W. [1967], 'Deductive Explanation and Prediction Revisited', *Philosophy of Science* 34 (1967), 41-52.

Suppe, F. [1972a], 'Theories, Their Formulations, and the Operational Imperative', *Synthese* 25 (1972), 129-164.

Suppe, F. [1972b], 'What's Wrong With the Received View on The Structure of Scientific Theory?', *Philosophy of Science* 39 (1972), 1-19.

Suppe, F. (ed.) [1974a], *The Structure of Scientific Theories*, University of Illinois Press, Urbana, Ill.

Suppe, F. [1974b], 'The Structure of Theories and the Analysis of Data' in Suppe [1974a].

Suppe, F. and Asquith, P. D. [1976/7], *PSA 1976*, 2 Vols, Philosophy of Science Association, East Lansing, Michigan.

Suppes, P. [1960], 'What is a Scientific Theory?', in Danto/Morgenbesser [1960].

Suppes, P. [1969], *Studies in the Methodology and Foundations of Science*, Humanities Press, New York.

Suppes, P. et al. (eds) [1973] *Logic, Methodology and Philosophy of Science Vol. IV*, North-Holland, Amsterdam.

Taft, C. T. [1972], *Altered States of Consciousness*, Doubleday, New York.

Tarski, A. [1949], 'The Semantic Conception of Truth and the Foundations of Semantics' in Feigl/Sellars [1949].

Tarski, A. [1956], *Logic, Semantics, Meta-Mathematics* (trans. J. H. Woodger), Oxford University Press, Oxford.

Tawney, R. H. [1962], *Religion and the Rise of Capitalism*, Penguin, London.

Templeton, A. R. and Rothman, E. D. [1974], 'Evolution in Heterogeneous Environments', *The American Naturalist* 28 (1974), 409-478.

Tisdell, C. A. [1981], *Science and Technology Policy*, Chapman and Hall, London.

Tornebohm, H. [1969], *Science of Science*, Lectures at Euratom, 1969, Department of Theory of Science, University of Goteborg, Publication No. 11.

Tornebohm, H. [1970], 'A Metascientific Model of Research Procedure' in Lindblom [1970].

Tornebohm, H. [1975], 'Enquiring Systems and Paradigms', University of Goteborg, Goteborg.

Toulmin, S. and Goodfield, J. [1965], *The Architecture of Matter*, Pelican, London.

Toulmin, S. [1972], *Human Understanding*, Princeton University Press, Princeton, N.J.

Tribe, L. [1973], 'Technology Assessment and the Fourth Discontinuity: The Limits of Instrumental Rationality, *Southern California Law Review* **46** (1973), 617-661.

Trigg, R. [1980], *Reality at Risk: A Defense of Realism in Philosophy and the Sciences*, Brighton Sussex, Harvester Press.

Tugwell, F. (ed.) [1973], *Search for Alternatives: Public Policy and the Study of the Future*, Winthrop, Cambridge, Mass.

Tuomela, R. [1979], 'Putnam's Realism', *Theoria* **45** (1979), 114-126.

Turnbull, D. [1984], 'Relativism, Reflexivity and the Sociology of Scientific Knowledge', *Metascience* **1** (1984), 47-60.

Unger, R. M. [1975], *Knowledge and Politics*, The Free Press, New York.

Urban, W. M. [1949], *Beyond Realism and Idealism*, George Allen and Unwin, London.

Ursul, A. D. and Zeman, Z. J. [1984], *Integration of Science and the Systems Approach*, Elsevier, Amsterdam.

Van Fraassen, B. C. [1970], 'On the Extension of Beth's Semantics of Physical Theories', *Philosophy of Science* **37** (1970), 325-339.

van Fraassen, B. C. [1972], 'A Formal Approach to The Philosophy of Science', in Colodny [1972].

van Fraassen, B. C. [1980], *The Scientific Image*, Clarendon Press, Oxford.

van Fraassen, B. C. [1981], 'Theory Construction and Experiment: an Empiricist View', in Asquith/Giere [1980/1].

van Fraassen, B. C. [1982], 'The Charybdis of Realism: Epistemological Implications of Bell's Inequality', *Synthese* **52** (1982), 25-38.

van Fraassen, B. C. [1985], 'Reply' in Churchland/Hooker [1985a].

van Melsen, A. G. [1960], *From Atomos to Atom*, Harper and Brothers, New York.

van Melsen, A. G. [1961], *Science and Technology*, Duquesne University Press, Pittsburgh.

van Rootselaar, B. and Staal, J. F. (eds) [1968], *Logic, Methodology and Philosophy of Science* **III**, North-Holland Publ. Co., Amsterdam.

Varela, F. [1979], *Principles of Biological Autonomy*, Elsevier, New York.

Vickers, G. [1968], *Value Systems and Social Process*, Penguin, London.

Vickers, Sir G. [1970], *Freedom in a Rocking Boat*, Penguin, London.

Vickers, Sir G. [1979], 'Rationality and Intuition' in Wechsler [1979].

Vickers, Sir G. [1980], *Responsibility: Its Sources and Limits*, Intersystems Publications, Seaside, California.

Vickers, Sir G. [1983], *Human Systems are Different*, Harper and Row, London.

Von Mises, R. [1951], *Positivism, A Study in Human Understanding*, Dover, New York.

Wartofsky, M. [1979a], 'From Praxis to Logos: Genetic Epistemology and Physics' in Wartofsky [1979b].

Wartofsky, M. [1979b], *Models: Representation and the Scientific Understanding*, Reidel, Dordrecht.

Waters, F. [1963], *The Book of the Hopi*, Ballantine, New York.

Wechsler, J. (ed.) [1979], *On Aesthetics in Science*, MIT Press, Boston.

Weinberg, J. [1936], *An Examination of Logical Positivism*, Harcourt, Brace and World, New York.

Whewell, W. [1847], *The Philosophy of Inductive Sciences*, 2 vols., 2nd edition, J. W. Parker, London.

Whewell, W. [1858], *Novum Organon Renovatum*, London.

Whitley, R. D. (ed.) [1974], *The Social Process of Scientific Development*, Routledge and Kegan Paul, London.

Whorf, B. L. [1966], *Language, Thought, and Reality* (ed. by John B. Carroll), MIT Press, Cambridge, Mass.

Wilder, H. [1973], 'Toward a Naturalistic Theory of Meaning', Ph.D. thesis, University of Western Ontario, Canada.

Wilson, B. [1970], *Rationality*, Harper & Rowe, New York.

Wilson, M. [1985], 'What Can Theory Tell Us About Observation?' in Churchland/Hooker [1985a].

Wilson, E. O. [1975], *Socio-Biology: The New Synthesis*, Harvard University Press, Cambridge, Mass.

Wimsatt, W. [1974], 'Complexity and Organization' in Schaffner/Cohen [1974].

Wimsatt, W. C. [1980], 'Randomness and Perceived Randomness in Evolutionary Biology', *Synthese* **43**, (1980), 287-329.

Winnie, J. [1977], 'The Causal Theory of Spacetime' in Earman [1977].

Wisdom, J. O. [1971], 'Four Contemporary Interpretations of the Nature of Science', *Foundations of Physics* **I** (1971), 269-284.

Wisdom, J. O. [1972], 'Conventionalism, Truth, and Cosmological Furniture'; read to the 1972 Philosophy of Science Association Meetings, Lansing.

Wittgenstein, I. [1951], *Tractatus Logico-Philosophicus* (transl. by D. F. Pears and B. F. McGuiness), Routledge and Kegan Paul, London.

Wojciechowski, J. [1975], 'The Ecology of Knowledge' in Steneck [1975].

Wojciechowski, J. [1978], 'Knowledge as a Source of Problems: Can Man Survive the Development of Knowledge?', *Man-Environment Systems* **8** (1978), 317-324.

Wojciechowski, J. [1980], 'Man and Knowledge: One or Two Systems?' in Banathy [1980].

Worrall, J. [1982], 'Scientific Realism and Scientific Change', *Philosophical Quarterly* **32** (1982), 201-231.

Wuketits, F. (ed.) [1983], *Concepts and Approaches in Evolutionary Epistemology*, Reidel, Dordrecht.

Wyburn, C. M., Pickford, R. W. and Hirst, J. [1968], *The Human Senses and Perception*, University of Toronto Press, Toronto.

Yovits, M. C. et al. [1962], *Self-Organizing Systems*, Spartan Books, Washington.

Ziman, P. [1968], *Public Knowledge*, Cambridge University Press, Cambridge.

Ziman, J. [1978], *Reliable Knowledge*, Cambridge University Press, Cambridge.

Index of Names

Achinstein, P., 41, 67, 70, 157, 360 n.1,
    362 n.10, 365-6 n.13, 373 n.51, 384 n.84
Adorno, T.W., 399 n.18
Agassi, J., 341, 367 n.21
Albury, R., 313, 314
Allais, M., 416 n.75
Althusser, L., 107, 202, 399 n.18
Andersson, G., 341
Apel, K.-O., 308, 410 n.40, 428 n.144,
    433 n.169, 437 n.189
Arbib, M., 98, 260, 413 n.55
Aristotle, 215
Armstrong, D. M., 6, 283, 366 n.13, 414
    nn.63,64, 420 n.97, 422 n.106, 437
    n.190
Armytage, W. H. G., 398 n.10, 426 n.133
Arrow, K., 287
Ashby, W., 398 n.17
Asquith, P., 399 n.19
Aune, B., 67, 70, 362 n.10, 365 n.13, 381
    n.77
Ayer, A. J., 67, 70, 362 n.10, 365 n.13

Bacon, F., 11
Ballantine, L., 180, 396 n.25
Barker, S., 67, 70, 157, 362 n.10, 365 n.13
Barnes, D., 202, 398 n.8, 401 n.32, 407
    n.22, 412 n.51
Bateson, G., 367 n.15
Baumgartner, T., 400 n.25, 426 n.129
Becker, E., 214, 215, 245, 249, 398
    nn.16,17
Beer, S., 315, 398 n.8, 402 n.41, 426
    nn.129,137
Berger, P., 398 nn.16,17, 413 n.53
Bergmann, G., 67
Berkeley, G., 407 n.20
Bernal, J. D., 202
Bernstein, G. B., 426 n.130
Beth, E., 41, 374 n.53

Bhaskar, R., 309, 341, 434 n.175, 437
    n.189
Bjerring, A., 157, 203, 204, 399 nn.17, 19,
    23, 398 n.8, 399 nn.17, 19, 12, 426
    nn.130,136
Blair, D. H., 320, 416 n.76
Blake, R. M., 418 n.87
Bloor, D., 407 n.22, 412 n.51, 413 n.53
Blume, S., 396 n.32
Boden, M., 436 n.188
Bogdan, R., 396 n.30, 399 n.24, 408 n.28,
    426 n.130
Bohm, D., 131, 338, 419 n.89, 434 n.172
Bohnert, H., 371 nn.41,43, 421 n.105
Bohr, N., 412 n.50
Bolland, L.A., 426 n.131
Boole, G., 269
Boscovitch, J. R., 419 n.88
Boucher, W. I., 426 n.130
Boyd, D., 178, 323-5, 331, 351, 409 n.34,
    424 n.119, 428 n.142, 431 n.159
Bradley, F. H., 423 n.112
Braithwaite, R. B., 368 n.24
Brams, S.J., 320, 416 n.76, 426 n.129
Brennan, G., 426 n.131
Bridgeman, P., 67, 422 n.107
Briskman, L., 433 n.164
Brodbeck, M., 70
Brody, B., 296
Bromberger, S., 419 n.93
Brouwer, L. E. J., 440 n.204
Brown, H., 398 n.5, 399 n.20
Brown, J. R., 407 n.20, 432 n.160
Brown, S. C., 412 n.51
Bruner, J., 224
Bub, J., 398 n.15
Buchanan, J., 426 n.129
Buchdahl, G., 418 n.87
Bunge, M., 31, 70, 122, 258, 365 n.13,
    367 nn.20,21

Subject Index

Acceptance (of belief),
  as pragmatic, 34
  as rational, 286
  See also Epistemic utilities; Epistemology, as rational commitment
Agnosticism,
  and constructive empiricism, 165, 170
  and conventionalism, 17
  and semantics, 354
  limits to, 354-7
Anthropocentrism, opposed by naturalistic realism 264-7
Antinomies, 210-212
Arguments, *See Circle, Conjunction, Continuity, God's Eye, Illusion, Underdetermination*
Artifacts,
  and science, 213-6
  as embodying norms, 217-8
  as experiments, 214-5

Causality, and harmony, 338
  See also Explanation
Circle/circular argument, 10, 13, 142, 271
Cognition,
  and environmental destabilisation, 306
  and truth, 273 9
Common sense,
  as untheoretical, 51-3
  theory ladenness of, 39-53
Concepts,
  and language, 376 n.64
  and realism, 401-2 n.34
Confirmation,
  and cross-situational invariance, 301-3
  and unification—*See Unity, and confirmation*
  as theory dependent, 123-5, 370 n.37
Conjunction argument, 172-4
Consilience, of inductions, 294

Constructive Empiricism, 158-65
  and agnosticism, 165, 170
  and observation-theory distinction, 158-9, 164
  and pragmatic-cognitive distinction, 160-2, 169-71
  and rational commitment, 160-1
  and risk, 168-9
  meta-philosophy of, 175-6
  See also under van Fraassen
Context-dependence, of epistemic acceptance—*See Epistemic acceptance*
Continuity argument, 172
Conventionalism, 17-18, 157
  and science-philosophy interaction, 11
  See also agnosticism.
Convergence, and approximate truth, 346-7
Critical Realist, philosophical relation to, 6
Cross-situational invariance, and confirmation—*See Confirmation*
  and explanation—*See Explanation*
  cross-situational invariance of, 303
  needing ontological context, 302-3
Culture, critical,
  and methodology-policy, 152 3
  and naturalistic realism, 143, 149-53
  as experiments, 153, 215
  theory of, 96, 131, 143

Definition, implicit and Ramsey analysis, 41
Demarcation, of science from non-science, 102
Design,
  and artifact, 214-5
  of science—*See transformation of science, internal*